Executing Data Quality Projects

Second Edition

Executing Data Quality Projects

Ten Steps to Quality Data and Trusted Information™

Danette McGilvray

ACADEMIC PRESS

An imprint of Elsevier

ELSEVIER

Academic Press is an imprint of Elsevier
125 London Wall, London EC2Y 5AS, United Kingdom
525 B Street, Suite 1650, San Diego, CA 92101, United States
50 Hampshire Street, 5th Floor, Cambridge, MA 02139, United States
The Boulevard, Langford Lane, Kidlington, Oxford OX5 1GB, United Kingdom

Notices
Knowledge and best practice in this field are constantly changing. As new research and experience broaden our understanding, changes in research methods, professional practices, or medical treatment may become necessary.

Practitioners and researchers must always rely on their own experience and knowledge in evaluating and using any information, methods, compounds, or experiments described herein. In using such information or methods they should be mindful of their own safety and the safety of others, including parties for whom they have a professional responsibility.

To the fullest extent of the law, neither the Publisher nor the authors, contributors, or editors, assume any liability for any injury and/or damage to persons or property as a matter of products liability, negligence or otherwise, or from any use or operation of any methods, products, instructions, or ideas contained in the material herein.

Library of Congress Cataloging-in-Publication Data
A catalog record for this book is available from the Library of Congress

British Library Cataloguing-in-Publication Data
A catalogue record for this book is available from the British Library

ISBN 978-0-12-818015-0

For information on all Academic Press publications
visit our website at https://www.elsevier.com/books-and-journals

Publisher: Mara Conner
Acquisitions Editor: Chris Katsaropoulos
Editorial Project Manager: Andrae Akeh
Production Project Manager: Omer Mukthar
Cover Designer: Miles Hitchen

Typeset by SPi Global, India

In Praise Of

Great books do not sit on your shelf, pristine and beautiful, without so much as a crease in them. The best books occupy precious desk space, dog-eared and highlighted. By this standard, Danette McGilvray's book, *Executing Data Quality Projects: Ten Steps to Quality Data and Trusted Information™*, will be absolutely ravaged, and never more than arms-length away. The power of the content and techniques she has brought into one volume is a testament to the book itself: by applying the principles covered inside, the author has assembled a collection of knowledge and tools to help readers at every point in their data quality journey. This is not a book you will read once and put on a shelf -- this will be a faithful companion guiding you daily.

Anthony J. Algmin, Founder, Algmin Data Leadership

Within my field of expertise, computer security, I hadn't had much exposure to the concept of "Data Quality." Now that I've been introduced to it, however, I am convinced that data quality is essential to computer security and that security professionals will never successfully defend systems until they incorporate it into their practice. To get started, I recommend reading McGilvray's book *Executing Data Quality Projects: Ten Steps to Quality Data and Trusted Information™*. I literally tell people that this book changed my (professional) life. Not only did it do a great job of teaching core data quality concepts in a way that even a newbie like myself could understand, digest, and apply, but the Ten Steps themselves, the real meat of the book, are amazingly actionable. The overwhelming emphasis on practicality and contextualization creates a framework that can be used in almost every possible environment to improve an organization's data quality.

Seth James Nielson, PhD, Founder and Chief Scientist,
Crimson Vista, Inc.

There is nothing better than learning from a practitioner.

An architect can consider a design, draw a blue print and write a book about how wonderful their buildings meet human needs. But they may never hit a nail with a hammer.

But when someone writes, not only from what they *know* but what they have *done*, now you have something. The second edition of Danette's data quality book fits that description.

Not only did Danette write a great book on data quality in 2008, she learned more, made changes, evolved, and then decided to do it again. The second edition is just as important and excellent as the first. It is required reading for a data practitioner and needs to be on your book shelf – and put to use.

John Ladley, Data Thought Leader and Practitioner, Consultant and Mentor for Business and Data Leaders

I've known the Ten Steps and Danette for 10 years. Through the decade, many data practitioners in China apply the method to real data quality and data governance projects and programs. By doing so, the organizations benefit from higher data quality. The Ten Steps Process itself has evolved and I believe more data, more people and more organizations will get more value from the deep thought and experience embedded in this book. The legacy of this book to the data community cannot be overstated.

Chen Liu, CEO of DGWorkshop (御数坊)

If we don't recognize that we are living in a knowledge economy in which data has significant value, it's time we did. Yet, further research by the University of South Australia and Experience Matters on three continents shows irrefutably that data is not managed well. Amongst many other findings, its value and benefits aren't measured. Boards and executives don't understand why information assets are important and, unlike financial assets, nobody is held truly accountable for their management. *Executing Data Quality Projects: Ten Steps to Quality Data and Trusted Information™* is a knowledgeable and pragmatic guide to managing data well. I highly recommend it for anyone who wants to make money out of their data and / or improve their service delivery. And that will be the vast majority of people reading this.

James Price, Managing Director, Experience Matters

When Danette said that she was working on a second edition of *Executing Data Quality Projects: Ten Steps to Quality Data and Trusted Information™*, my first thought was, "Why? The first edition was so good and the process is sound." But I am pleased to say that the second edition is even better. In the second edition, McGilvray has clarified and updated the process steps and supporting templates and incorporated valuable examples and case studies (The Ten Steps in Action), while accounting for the evolution of technology and data production over the past decade. The presentation is clear and crisp. People who are new to data quality management should read this book cover to cover. Experienced practitioners should have it on their desks at all times for reference.

Laura Sebastian-Coleman, Author, *Measuring Data Quality for Ongoing Improvement*

I have consistently used this book in my courses for years and I recommend this book to all of my students in the Information Quality Graduate Program at the University of Arkansas at Little Rock. *Executing Data Quality Projects: Ten Steps to Quality Data and Trusted Information™* is an excellent guide for navigating the journey toward organizational data excellence. Danette McGilvray delivers an outstanding job in making a difficult topic easy. The concepts in this book are easy to understand. Her Ten Steps process and recommendations for how to apply these steps to a variety of projects are easy to follow. The techniques she showcases are easy to implement. In summary, this book is for anyone trying to find well written, practical, and effective advice for making their data great.

Dr. Elizabeth Pierce, Chair, Information Science,
UA Little Rock

If you are looking for a practical data quality book, updated with the latest developments worldwide, this is the one. For beginners or those experienced in data quality, this book will help you in different phases of your project, putting you in the best position to succeed.

Ana Margarida Galvão, working more than 20 years
in the financial services industry, with over a decade focusing
on data quality

The University of Arkansas at Little Rock Information Quality Graduate Program has been using the first edition of *Executing Data Quality Projects* as the textbook for our course on project and change management since 2012, and it has proved to be a tremendous resource for our students. Comprehensive and detailed, yet full of practical advice and helpful templates, it has become a "must have" book for information quality practitioners around the world. The new edition is even richer and deeper. While keeping the original foundation, it brings in new content to address the changes and emerging trends in data management and technology since the first edition. I am excited to introduce our students to the new edition.

Dr. John R. Talburt, Acxiom Chair of Information Quality,
University of Arkansas at Little Rock, and Lead Consultant for
Data Governance and Data Strategy, Noetic Partners

Since Danette wrote the first edition of this book, the volume of data in all organizations has grown enormously. If, at this time, your organization is not investing resources into ensuring high-quality data, and managing this data as a valuable asset, you are heading for trouble. The Ten Steps methodology outlined in this book has proven an invaluable guide for both experienced data practitioners as well as those who are embarking on their own data quality journey. Furthermore, if you need to convince your executive team of the benefits of investing in high-quality data, this book is an invaluable place to start.

Peter Eales, CEO MRO Insyte, and project leader
of ISO 8000-110 edition 2

Whether you are a data quality professional, IT leader, data analyst, or just someone trying to solve a complex problem, Danette's Ten Steps approach is the perfect guide to help you through the process. *Executing Data Quality Projects: Ten Steps to Quality Data and Trusted Information*™ can be used as a textbook, an informational read, or my preference as a "shop manual." The updated 2nd edition helps readers navigate through modern and less structured database problems.

Andy Nash, Data Quality Professional

Danette McGilvray's Ten Steps to Quality Data took our data quality initiative from theoretical to possible. The techniques taught by Danette provided concrete and practical methods to deliver on our data quality initiative through our Data Governance Council. Showing the return on investment for a data quality initiative was always one of the most challenging endeavors for this effort. Ten Steps to Quality Data helped cultivate those ROI ideas that ultimately led to a successful and sustainable implementation.

Brett Medalen, Principal Architect, Navient

As a data-driven organization, Seattle Public Utilities continually seeks to leverage best in class methodologies to manage our data. Danette McGilvray's Ten Steps to Quality Data and Trusted Information™ is one such methodology. Robust, extensible and transparent, Danette's methodology can be applied quickly and effectively to data quality issues as they surface. Perhaps more importantly, in this second edition, Danette illustrates how the methodology can be leveraged in the software /system development lifecycle (SDLC). Doing so leads to pro-actively managed data quality that raises the usability of an organization's data, lowers the risk of poor decisions and outcomes and reduces costs of data management across large organizations.

Duncan Munro, Utility Asset Information Program Manager,
Seattle Public Utilities

The name of the book is remarkable in the extent to which it covers what the book is about. What is less clear from the name, however is the quality of the book's content.

Ms. McGilvray writes very well, and her organization is ideal for conveying a great deal of information. As she puts it, "There is just enough structure to show you how to proceed, but enough flexibility so that you can also incorporate your own knowledge, tools, and techniques."

In addition to extensive descriptions of data quality "key" concepts, the heart of the book contains instructions and guidance to carry out each of the Ten Steps, followed by how to structure your project, and other techniques and tools.

It is with great pleasure that I endorse this book.

David C. Hay, Data Modeler emeritus, Essential Strategies
International

Tasked with designing data quality metrics for my organisation and faced with a blank piece of paper, I turned to the 2nd edition of Danette McGilvray's book *Executing Data Quality Projects*. Within a short space of time I was able to utilise the information on metrics to kickstart my project – with so much more practical advice available in the 2nd edition, I would thoroughly recommend it as an upgrade to those who already have the 1st edition.

Julie Daltrey, Senior Data Architect,
Intellectual Property Office, UK.

McGilvray has come up with a pragmatic approach to improving data quality. This book will increase your skills, arm you with useful tools when facing data management challenges, and widen your perspectives regarding the challenges of ensuring quality data. And there are indeed challenges as everyone works with data in their daily lives and data are created everywhere by almost any kind of technology. This book will help you know where to start, who to involve or persuade, and what actions to take.

Håkan Edvinsson, author, trainer and practitioner in data governance and business data design, the inventor of the Diplomatic Data Governance approach.

The second edition of Danette McGilvray's book, *Executing Data Quality Projects: Ten Steps to Quality Data and Trusted Information*™, is timely and a must-read for every person and organization focusing on being data-centric. In the 13 years since her first edition arrived on the scene, data quality has become the driving force required to demonstrate a return on most, if not all, data-oriented projects and programs. From data analytics and data science, to data governance, to metadata management, to the improvement of interoperability, data quality is the primary factor used to determine success or failure. Danette's straight-forward approach, and the practical tools and processes that she shares throughout the book, are immediately applicable to everyone's information landscape and will quicken the pace toward achieving your organization's goals. I highly recommend this book.

Robert S. Seiner – KIK Consulting & Educational Services (KIKconsulting.com) and The Data Administration Newsletter (TDAN.com)

Danette has provided a solid methodology with easy to follow action steps that can be used today and in the future for trusted data that supports business goals and objectives. This second edition is a must have reference and guide as the importance of data quality continues to grow with enhancements in data technologies and the explosion of data.

Mary Levins, President Sierra Creek Consulting LLC

I was highly impressed with Danette's Ten Steps to Quality Data and Trusted Information™, especially as I began a data quality project to develop an ontology-driven data quality framework for biobanking research and capture clinical trial data for cancer research. The book teaches data practitioners ten simple, timely, and powerful steps to improve overall quality standards of data across the enterprise. I can see many data leaders leveraging the steps to deliver clean and trusted data across the enterprise, especially while meeting business outcomes covering insights and analytics, regulatory compliance, data literacy, and digital transformation.

Kash Mehdi - Data Governance Domain Expert, Informatica | Ph.D. Candidate Information Science, University of Arkansas at Little Rock in collaboration with MIT

For the past 10 years Danette McGilvray has been the pre-eminent international expert in data quality and its improvement. Her vast experience in both teaching and consulting is evident in this book.

Michael Scofield, M.B.A. Professor

As a researcher in the field of Data and Information Management and Governance, as one of the authors of The Leader's Data Manifesto and as strong supporter of industry/academia collaboration, I am honoured to endorse this book by Danette McGilvray. In the digital world we live in, there is an increasing need to raise awareness about the importance of data and information. An understanding of data and information quality is more relevant and critical now than ever before. As Danette suggests: "Teaching tomorrow's leaders to be data-aware is a good place to start". In fact, all our students need to learn why we have to manage data and information as vital assets, how to improve their quality and the resulting benefits to organisations in all industries. What strikes me most about this book is the way it can be used to bring the real world into the classroom - the templates, detailed examples, and practical advice to enhance data and information quality will be very useful for students in their future careers. I will certainly recommend this book for our Masters of IT and MBA students studying courses related to Data and Information Management, Privacy, Governance and Quality.

I strongly support Danette in her mission: "Let's continue to add data and information to the conversation…"

Associate Professor Nina Evans, Professorial lead: UniSA STEM, University of South Australia

This book is dedicated to:

Jeff

For your love and support—I am a better person because of you

Mom

For always believing in me—I am glad you are here to see this book finished

Dad and Jason

Hope you are both looking down and smiling

Tiffani, Tom, Aidric, Michaela, Zora, Christie, Colby, Chancey

More love than you can know

My dear friends and extensive extended family

You know who you are—I am lucky to have all of you in my life

All the readers

In the hopes you will use what is in this book to make the world a better place

Now voyager go thou forth to seek and find.
Walt Whitman, *Leaves of Grass*

Contents

Acknowledgments

"Gratitude attitude." "It takes a village." "Couldn't have done it without you!" Somehow these well-worn phrases do not feel like clichés - not when thinking of the many people who made this book possible.

Thanks to the clients who made use of this methodology as part of my services and solutions, others who applied the methodology after attending one of my courses, students who learned about it through other educational institutions, or those who picked up the first edition book on their own and put it to work. Many are mentioned in the pages that follow and I am ever grateful for their contributions. Equal thanks to those I could name, those who had to remain anonymous, and those who did equally good things but could not be included due to space or time constraints. The Ten Steps improved with each experience and readers of this second edition will benefit from your willingness to share.

At the risk of missing someone, I will, nevertheless, call out a few people who should be recognized.

Tom Redman, John Ladley, James Price, Laura Sebastian-Coleman, Gwen Thomas, David Plotkin, Michael Scofield: My go-to people when I need to get inspired, talk through an idea, get honest feedback, or have a "quick" question. Everyone needs people like this. I have learned from all of them and much of that is reflected in this book.

Anthony Algmin, Masha Bykin, Peter Eales, David Hay, Mary Levins, Chen Liu, Dan Myers, Andy Nash, Daragh O Brien, Katherine O'Keefe, Dr. John Talburt: Who unselfishly shared their time and expertise on specific subjects. This second edition is much better because of it.

Michele Koch and Barbara Deemer: For their support over the years and for writing the foreword. I am fortunate to have worked with people like them and their teams.

Carlos Barbieri, Maria Espona, Walid el Abed, Ana Margarida Galvão, Jennifer Gibson, Brett Medalen, Kash Mehdi, Duncan Munro, Seth Nielson, Graeme Simsion, and Sarah Haynie: Whose encouraging words motivated me just when I needed it (and they probably never knew). And thanks, Carlos, for always asking about my mother.

Larry P. English: The information and data quality world lost a leading light and great thinker this past year. He started me on the path to data quality and what I learned from him continues to influence my work.

My colleagues at Elsevier: Chris Katsaropoulos, Senior Acquisitions Editor, who encouraged this second edition; Andrae Akeh, Senior Editorial Project Manager, who spent the most hours with me over many months, provided sound advice, and stayed steady through the ups and downs of creating a book; Miles Hitchens, Senior Designer, who patiently worked with me as he developed the interior design and updated the book cover (which I love) for the second edition; Omer Mukthar, Production Project Manager, the liaison between me and the production team, for his prompt answers to my questions. Thanks to those at Elsevier who I never met, but who spent many hours, using their expertise, getting this book to a finished product.

Laura Sebastian-Coleman: Gets a second shout out, because I was lucky enough to have her as my copyeditor, making use of both her copyediting skills and subject matter expertise. Not only was she one of my go-to people, but I was fortunate she was my listening ear throughout the long process of writing this book.

Connie Brand and Julie Daltrey: For their hours of reviewing and helpful feedback.

Miriam Valere: Who kept Granite Falls going while I wrote this book, made sure I didn't miss anything important, and did her own share of checking and reviewing.

Rick Thomas and his team at ProTechnical: Who kept my systems going and continue to provide the best IT support I could ask for.

Jeff: My husband, best friend, and cheerleader. My life has been happier and more fun than I could ever have imagined because of him. His support and encouragement throughout the long process of writing this second edition was another example, in a long line of examples, where I could not have done it without him. As we always say, "We are a great team!"

The second edition would not exist without the first, so I have included the acknowledgments from the first edition below in its entirety. To all – thank you, thank you, and thank you!

Acknowledgments (from First Edition, 2008)

I now have a better appreciation for the long lists of people who authors' acknowledge. Writing a book is definitely not a one-person effort and this book is no exception.

To Judy Kincaid, who unknowingly started me on the path of information quality. Many years ago she called me into her office and asked me to work with Larry English, who was to come to Hewlett-Packard to consult on information quality. She felt that by working with him the knowledge we gained would not leave the company when he was no longer there. Her words were, "It will be full time this week and then taper off after that." Thanks to Judy that assignment turned the course of my career and more than fifteen years later I'm still working on information quality full time!

I owe a debt of gratitude to Larry English who provided my initial education in information quality, mentored me through my first project, and brings visibility to this important topic.

Special thanks to Mehmet Orun, Wonna Mark, Sonja Bock, Rachel Haverstick, and Mary Nelson for their feedback, time, and expertise when I was creating the first fully written version of my methodology. Their knowledge, probing questions, thoughtful comments, and insight shaped that version and provided the foundation for this book. Without their efforts this book would not have been possible.

Thanks to those who reviewed the original proposal, or the detailed manuscript, or spent time discussing and providing input for specific sections of the book—David Hay, Mehmet Orun, Eva Smith, Gwen Thomas, Michael Scofield, Anne Marie Smith, Lwanga Yonke, Larissa Moss, Tom Redman, Susan Goubeaux, Andres Perez, Jack Olson, Ron Ross, David Plotkin, Beth Hatcher, Mary Levins, Dee Dee Lozier—and to those who chose to remain anonymous. Your honest comments for improvement and encouragement regarding what worked have made this a much better book.

Thanks to those over the years who have put into practice or supported the ideas presented here as sponsors, project managers, team members, and practitioners in various organizations. Unfortunately, there is not room to name you all individually, but thanks to you the knowledge gained and practices evolved from those experiences are being used to help others on their information quality journey.

To those who have attended my workshops and courses—thanks for your participation and willingness to share ideas, lessons learned, and successes. Your enthusiastic feedback and response provided motivation for me to write this book.

To the many leaders in this and related fields who have taken the time to write or teach so that I and others can learn. One look at the bibliography shows the extent of my appreciation to those who have made that effort; I have certainly been the beneficiary of their work. Special thanks to Tom Redman, David Loshin, Larissa Moss, Graeme Simsion, Peter Aiken, David Hay, Martin Eppler, Richard Wang, John Zachman, Michael Brackett, John Ladley, Len Silverston, and Larry English.

In addition, my thanks to those who lead professional associations, provide the venues for me to teach or publish, or offer behind-the-scenes advice and support. Although I cannot name all the individuals involved, I would like to recognize Tony Shaw and all those at Wilshire Conferences, all those at TDWI, Jeremy Hall and all those at IRM UK, those involved with IAIDQ and DAMA International, Mary Jo Nott, Robert S. Seiner, Larissa Moss, Sharon Adams, Roger Brothers, John Hill, Ken Rhodes, and Harry Zoccoli.

To my colleagues at Morgan Kaufmann, my appreciation for their excellent work—particularly Nate McFadden for his guidance and insight, and Denise Penrose, Mary James, Marilyn E. Rash, Dianne Wood, Jodie Allen, and the production team who finished making this book a reality.

To the teachers in the Logan City School District and Utah State University, where I received the education that created opportunities that have led me where I am today.

To Keith and Myrtle Munk. I was fortunate to have parents who stressed education, encouraged my activities, and always believed in me—even when I did not believe in myself. I am lucky to be part of a large extended family and a network of friends who provide fun, laughter, and lots of loving support—the reasons for working hard and what makes life worthwhile.

To my daughter, Tiffani Taggart, and my late son, Jason Taggart—they were the motivation for me to keep going even when times were tough.

The most special appreciation goes to my husband, Jeff McGilvray, for his unwavering love, encouragement, and support. None of this could have happened without you.

Foreword

Our enterprise Data Governance journey started in 2006. Periodically, over the course of the next couple of years, we would ask our Data Governance Council members how we could quantify the business value for the data quality issues that we had resolved. They would all intrinsically understand that we had saved the company money through either increased revenue, decreased operating costs and/or decreased risk but no one could come up with a way to consistently measure and report that business benefit. We didn't have the experience, techniques, or the skillset to make the leap as so many others still do not. This went on for a couple of years until we could get funding for developing a formalized, enterprise Data Quality Program under our Data Governance Program. As part of this effort, we wanted to show business value for improving the state of our data quality and we were looking for a practical approach to attacking and resolving our data quality issues. This led us to Danette McGilvray and her *Ten Steps to Quality Data and Trusted Information* methodology.

We engaged Danette in 2009 as we formally embarked on an enterprise Data Quality Program. Prior to 2009, our approach to data quality was more of a grass roots effort with no formal training or methodology to move from reactive to proactive measures. Danette worked with us to design and establish our Data Quality Program and to teach us her Ten Steps methodology. She helped us define the structure and content of our data quality services and how we could leverage her methodology to determine metrics for the program. Additionally, Danette taught us simple, yet effective, techniques to determine business value for the work we were doing to improve the quality of our data. We chose the Ten Steps Methodology since it was easy to use and was customizable for our organizational culture.

By adopting the *Ten Steps to Quality Data and Trusted Information* methodology outlined in this book, we were able to quantify our data quality efforts and show business value to our senior management and everyone participating in our enterprise Data Governance program. It was invaluable to us as we strove to become more mature in this space and to adopt a structure that would allow us to work through data quality issues in a measured and consistent manner. Danette provides helpful tips and best practices to identify data quality dimensions, business impact techniques, data quality categories and roles and responsibilities, just to name a few.

Danette's step-by-step instructions coupled with her explanation of basic concepts associated with information quality can propel you to successfully demonstrate business value as it did for us. As a result, our program has won several industry awards over the years. This book and Danette's approach contributed to that success. We hope that will be true for you and your organization as well.

Over a decade later our data quality work continues to bring value to our organization. During this time the business benefits we have achieved have funded other corporate initiatives and helped us to increase revenue and decrease cost and complexity. Most importantly, it has given us confidence in our data and increased our data literacy across the organization.

We remain grateful to Danette for working with us, sharing her expertise and experience, and for teaching us her *Ten Steps to Quality Data and Trusted Information* methodology, all while becoming good friends.

– Barbara Deemer, Chief Data Steward and Managing Director of Corporate Finance, Navient

– Michele Koch, Data Governance Program Director and Senior Director of Enterprise Data Intelligence, Navient

In loving memory of Barb Deemer, who was a wonderful colleague and friend.
Her positive attitude, generosity, and loving spirit inspired everyone she came in touch with.
She will be deeply missed. (April 2021) – Michele and Danette

Introduction

Your organization's best opportunities for organic growth lie in data. Data offers enormous untapped potential to create competitive advantage, new wealth and jobs; improve health care; keep us all safer; and otherwise improve the human condition.

—The Leader's Data Manifesto, dataleaders.org

The Reason for This Book

My life is a data quality problem. I didn't know it at first. I'm minding my own business and wham! A data quality issue smacks me in the face. It has happened again and again. The interesting thing is that *your* life, as an individual, is a data quality problem, too. Your corporation is a data quality problem. Your government agency is a data quality problem. Your educational institution is a data quality problem. *Any* organization is practically a living, breathing data quality problem. It's just that most of them haven't put a name to it yet. All organizations depend on data and information to provide their products and services – *without exception*. And the quality of that data and information, in most cases, is not up to the task.

Look at your own life. As a consumer, patient, or citizen how many times have you been overcharged on an invoice, had health care records that were wrong, or been called to jury duty multiple times in a year (instead of once) because your name was duplicated in the government records? How many times have you tried to access information over the phone, but could not because the identifying data on your account was wrong, or an automated payment did not go through because the data was wrong? Or your spouse's medical information mysteriously changed between the physician's office and the hospital on the day of surgery? All these things have happened to me.

Look at your organization. The right-quality information helps inventory managers keep the supply chain lean, CEOs make long-term plans for growth based on dependable performance measures, and social services identify high-risk youth who need their help. Right-quality information instills trust in voters that election results are accurate and helps government officials determine where to place scarce resources during a pandemic. Whether for market research, patent applications, manufacturing improvement metrics, taking sales orders, receiving payments, or analyzing test results, information is as essential to the functioning of an organization, and a society, as it is to providing a competitive edge.

Information quality contributes to that edge by delivering the right information, at the right time, in the right place, to the right people. Neither human beings nor machines can make effective decisions with flawed, incomplete, or misleading data. They must have data and information they can trust to be correct and current if they are to do the work that provides products and services and satisfies the organization's customers.

It is not unusual to find that information quality issues prevent organizations from realizing the full benefit of their investments in fulfilling strategies and goals, addressing issues, or taking advantage of opportunities. The business therefore does not receive the expected improvements to customer satisfaction, products, services, operations, decision-making, and business intelligence processes.

The good news is that we know how to deal with the data and information quality issues that get in the way of what the organization is trying to achieve. We have a methodology called Ten Steps to Quality Data and Trusted Information™, the subject of this book.

The remainder of this *Introduction* summarizes what is in the book, along with its intended audiences and how they can use it. I then explain why a second edition was needed and my goals for you. After encouragement to get started, the structure of the book is outlined.

What Is in This Book

This book describes the Ten Steps methodology, a structured yet flexible approach for creating, assessing, improving, sustaining, and managing data and information quality within any organization. The methodology is comprised of three main areas:

- **Key concepts**. Fundamental ideas that are crucial for the reader to understand in order to do data quality work well and are integral components of the methodology (Chapter 3)

Executing Data Quality Projects. https://doi.org/10.1016/B978-0-12-818015-0.09996-5

- **Structuring your project.** Guidance for organizing your work, not to replace other well-known project management practices, but to apply these principles to data quality projects (Chapter 5)
- **The Ten Steps Process.** Instructions for putting the key concepts into action through the Ten Steps Process - the actual Ten Steps for which the overall methodology is named (Chapter 4)

Other chapters contain supporting material to help apply the Ten Steps. More information about each chapter and its contents can be found in the section *Structure of This Book* at the end of this *Introduction*.

The book's format is designed for finding what you need quickly and easily. It can be read front to back, but is equally valuable when looking for steps or techniques to address a specific question or concern. Use the book as a reference guide, returning to it when new data quality situations or projects arise.

Projects as the Vehicle for Data Quality Work

This book uses projects as the vehicle for data quality work through which the methodology is applied. But don't use the word "project" too narrowly. Generally, a project is a unit of work that is a one-time effort to address specific business needs. The duration is determined by the complexity of the desired results.

In this book, the word project is used broadly to mean any structured effort that makes use of the Ten Steps methodology to address business needs. Three general types of projects are discussed:

- **Focused data quality improvement projects.** When the project is tasked to take care of a specific data quality problem that is impacting the business. For example, improving data used in supply chain management or data used in analytics and business intelligence. A variation on this is to use the Ten Steps to create an organization's own data quality improvement methodology.
- **Data quality activities in other projects.** When the project has a broader purpose, yet data is an important component of the project, and the quality of the data is addressed within the larger project plan. For example, when building new applications and migrating data from legacy systems or untangling data due to organizational breakups. A variation on this is using the Ten Steps to enrich the organization's standard solution/software/system development life cycle (SDLC), whether Agile, sequential, etc. The Ten Steps methodology also complements other improvement methodologies such as Six Sigma, which eliminates defects in any process, or Lean, which works to maximize customer value while minimizing waste.
- **Ad hoc use of data quality steps, techniques, or activities in the course of daily work.** When any portion of the Ten Steps is used to address a short-term need. For example, a key business process has halted, and data is suspected to be part of the issue. Techniques from the Ten Steps can be employed to uncover root causes so the issue can be addressed and the process restored. This use of the Ten Steps is not normally considered a "project" in the traditional sense, but it fits into the expanded definition of project as used in this book.

A data quality project can apply the full Ten Steps Process or selected steps and techniques. Project teams can be small or large, consisting of one person, a few or many people. In highly complex projects, multiple teams can apply the methodology, as needed, while coordinating to meet overall requirements. A project can take a few weeks to more than a year. No two data quality projects are the same, but the flexible nature of the Ten Steps means the methodology can be applied to all.

"In Between" and "Just Enough"

It is helpful to understand how this book relates to other resources in the data management and information quality space. Some resources thoroughly cover data quality concepts or discuss methodologies at a high level or the "what" of data management. Others provide deep detail on a few aspects of data quality work, such as a book which focuses strictly on how to deal with duplicate records. I have learned from them and am grateful they are available. The Ten Steps approach is in between high-level concepts and very detailed aspects of one piece of the data quality pie. It is, I believe, complementary to most of them.

My "Just Enough Principle" was another guide for what I included. The "Just Enough Principle" states "Spend just enough time and effort to optimize results." The book includes just enough description of underlying concepts to help you understand the components necessary for information quality. Knowledge of these concepts helps you apply the Ten Steps to the many situations where they will help. The Ten Steps Process provides just enough step-by-step instructions, examples, and templates to enable you to understand what needs to be done and why. There is just enough structure to show you how to proceed, but enough flexibility so that you can also incorporate your own knowledge, tools, and techniques. If you need more detailed information on some aspect of the Ten Steps, other resources, such as those mentioned throughout the book and in the bibliography, can be used to augment your work.

You will have to apply this principle when using the Ten Steps. Just enough is not about being sloppy or cutting corners. It takes good critical thinking skills to avoid one extreme of diving too far into unnecessary detail (analysis paralysis) and the other where you jump headlong into solutions before knowing what problem you are trying to solve, which causes chaos and unnecessary rework. Your ability to know what is just enough will increase with experience.

The Art and Science of Data Quality

The Ten Steps methodology can be considered the *science* of data quality—knowledge of data quality principles within the discipline of data management. Selecting which steps, activities, or techniques are needed and applying them effectively are part of the *art* of data quality. The Ten Steps methodology can be used in any situation where the quality of data and information affect high priority business needs—the strategies, goals, issues, and opportunities that must be addressed to satisfy customers and provide products and services. The Ten Steps Process was designed to be flexible. It is iterative so you can keep moving forward, yet you can revisit previous steps if more detail is needed at a later time. Guidelines are given to help decide what is relevant and what level of detail is needed at any point. But only you know your situation. Even with the step-by-step instructions, how you absorb those instructions and advice, your judgment in selecting what to do and when, and your ability to apply them in various situations and projects are all part of the *art* of data quality. Your skill will increase the more you use the Ten Steps.

Intended Audiences and How to Use This Book

This book will help anyone responsible for or who cares about the quality of data and information in their organization. However, individuals in different roles will find different aspects of the methodology useful. Using a proven approach such as the Ten Steps gives all a jumpstart so the bulk of their efforts are spent applying the methodology to fit their particular needs, not reinventing the basics.

Individual Contributors and Practitioners

Who—Members of a data quality project team or staff who do the hands-on work of managing the quality of data as part of their daily responsibilities.

Sample job titles—Data analysts, data quality analysts, data stewards, business analysts, subject-matter experts, developers, programmers, business process modelers, data modelers and designers, database administrators. Data scientists who have found themselves in a position of dealing with poor-quality data before they can start the "real" job for which they were hired.

How to use—Become familiar with The Ten Steps methodology by scanning the table of contents, reading each of the Step Summary Tables in *Chapter 4*, and skimming the book from beginning to end. This orients you to what is available and where to find it in the book.

As the project proceeds or in the course of your daily responsibilities, come back to particular sections or steps for detail when the time is right. Use the Ten Steps to:

- Understand, prioritize, and select the critical business needs and data quality issues to address in your project and the most important information which supports them
- Show others why data quality is important to their business needs and concerns
- Learn how to speak the language of business, not only the language of data
- Gain support from your manager, project manager, team members, and other resources for what needs to be done
- Apply the Ten Steps to your organization's high priority situations, concerns, and needs by:
  - Determining how to do the hands-on work, and
  - Actually doing it
- Show value to and help your manager, project manager, and team members

Note: There are other individual contributors who can benefit from this book. They do not consider their jobs to be "data" jobs. However, they use data and, in the course of their daily work, they impact data by creating, updating, and deleting it. For example, a buyer who uses data to make decisions about which supplies to purchase and creates data when generating a purchase requisition.

These users of data (also known as information consumers, information customers, or knowledge workers) have felt the pain of poor data quality in carrying out their standard responsibilities. Users of data who are enlightened as to how data quality impacts their organization can bring issues to light and help gain support to address those issues. They can provide help to a data quality project, either as a core team member or as an extended team member who is consulted and provides input when their expertise is needed. To help this audience use this book, see suggestions under the management section below.

Management

Who—Managers of teams or individuals who:

- Are on a data quality project team
- Are doing data quality work as part of daily responsibilities
- Use data and also create, update, delete data in the course of their daily work and standard responsibilities. These users may or may not be aware of the impact they have on data quality.

In addition, those who are accountable for business processes, such as supply chain management, or who lead data-driven initiatives will benefit from knowing that such a resource exists to help their teams.

Sample job titles—Managers, program managers, project managers, supervisors, team leads, business process owners, functional area managers, application owners.

Managers also include those with matrixed management responsibilities. Some managers are responsible for the work of team members who do not report directly to them based on the organizational chart. These managers evaluate team members and are themselves evaluated on the performance of the team. For example, enterprise data stewards who lead teams responsible for specified data subject areas across an organization and have a vested interest in the quality of the data.

How to use—Read this *Introduction* and *Chapters 1-3* for why data quality is critical, important concepts relating to data quality, and an overview of the Ten Steps Process.

You do NOT need to read all of *Chapter 4*, which contains the details to implement the Ten Steps Process. However, it is useful to get a feel for what is involved. You can quickly familiarize yourself with the Ten Steps process by reading the Step Summary Table that is found at the beginning of each of the Ten Steps. It provides a short overview of each specific step. Read each of them in order – only ten tables in total. You will see the relationships between the steps by the flow of the inputs, outputs, and checkpoint questions, along with what should be accomplished and why, and ideas for increasing success by addressing the people and project management aspects of a data quality project. Learn just enough about the Ten Steps to:

- Know why data quality is important to your organization as a whole and your business unit/department/team in particular
- Use that knowledge to gain support from whoever is needed – from executives, upper management and those who prioritize resources, people needed to carry out the work and their managers, etc.
- Understand at a high level what data quality work entails and how it will be accomplished
- Assign appropriate resources – money, people, time, tools, etc.
- Determine the skills and knowledge needed to carry out the work, who is available to work on the project, and how to close any gaps (e.g., we have people available but they don't have the skills and knowledge – provide training and coaching; or we have people with skills and knowledge but they are not available – shift assignments)
- Anticipate and prevent roadblocks to the data quality work

- Remove roadblocks if they arise
- Support your individual contributors and team members

Boards, Executives, and Senior Management

This book is NOT geared for these high-level roles, though some might get value from this *Introduction* and parts of *Chapters 1, 2, and 3*. They are mentioned here because people in these roles make decisions about funding, if data quality work is given priority, and whether those efforts will be supported. They set the tone and attitude which affects whether others will participate in what it takes to have high quality data - or not. It is imperative that people in these positions understand how poor-quality data affects their organizations in ways such as decreased revenue, increased risk and costs, and others that are harder to quantify yet are equally impactful.

Managers and individual contributors often have to gain support for data quality work from board members, executives, and other senior managers. They can use what is in this book to help do just that. I guarantee that once executives truly understand what high-quality data can do for their organization, they will want the work to be finished yesterday! They will benefit from knowing that resources exist, such as this book (along with training and consulting if desired), to give their teams the ability to start quickly and help them work effectively and efficiently.

All Audiences

Never do data quality work for the sake of data quality itself. Only spend time, effort, and resources on projects that address your organization's most important business needs associated with customers, products, services, strategies, goals, issues, and opportunities. Make use of the many different ways to use the Ten Steps to boost and enhance your efforts. The best results come from a cooperative effort between the right people representing the roles listed above.

Why a Second Edition

I originally wrote *Executing Data Quality Projects* because I saw what a difference the Ten Steps methodology made to the effectiveness of projects and the benefits that come from a focus on data quality. I wanted to share it so others could make use of what worked. My claim that the Ten Steps Process is flexible, applies to a myriad of situations where data is a component, and applies to all kinds of organizations has proven to be true. In addition, I learned that the methodology applies no matter the country, language, or culture. It has been exciting to see how others have taken the Ten Steps, and applied the methodology in creative and useful ways to help their organizations. Some of those uses, from various countries and types of organizations, are shared in this second edition in a new type of callout box called Ten Steps in Action, which you will see sprinkled throughout.

I continue to stress that data quality work must be tied into an organization's business needs – for its customers, products, services, strategies, goals, issues, and opportunities. The high-level Ten Step Process itself has stayed the same, with only minor changes to three of the titles for clarification. The structure of the Framework for Information Quality remains the same. I added two new data quality dimensions and three new business impact techniques to address areas worthy of

attention. The importance of communicating, managing the project, and engaging with people throughout is further emphasized.

Every chapter, step, and technique have been updated based on experience gained since the first edition. While this book focuses on projects, I have always known that projects are not the only way to address data quality. Therefore, I included my Data in Action Triangle so readers can put the projects into context with other ways data quality work gets done.

Since the first edition, our world has continued to change, as will be discussed in *Chapter 1: Data Quality and the Data-Dependent World*, and at the same time much has stayed the same. The Ten Steps methodology has stood the test of time and what is in this book still applies. Data quality is even more relevant today than it was when the first edition was released. I wanted to ensure that what we know about managing data quality – why we do it, how to do it, and the benefits to our organizations – doesn't get lost in the shuffle of the excitement, or fear, generated from changes to our world. An overarching motivation for me is the hope that another generation, or more, can learn from what is offered here and apply it for good.

My Goals for You

I wrote this book because I have seen what a difference using this approach can make to the effectiveness of your data quality work. I have seen the benefits from high-quality data to customers, products, services, and what is important to your organization. I hope you will:

Make a difference! Start where the need is greatest and take action on what is most important to your organization. Identify critical business needs. Find the most important data and information that support those needs. Use the Ten Steps to gain support, educate others, and practically apply to your current situation. Bring value to your customers, suppliers, employees, business partners, and your organization. It has been exciting for me to see the many ways people have put the Ten Steps to good use.

Learn, think, and apply! Learn something new, be reminded of things you knew but had forgotten, put a name to something you have already been doing, get confirmation on the direction you are going, or see familiar things from a different perspective. Be able to think in such a way that you can actually put to use what is in the Ten Steps and apply to the many different situations you will face, where a focus on data quality can provide solutions and address critical business needs.

Increase your skills! Understand that the more you use the Ten Steps, the easier the methodology will be to use and the better you will make good choices as to which steps and activities are most applicable to any given situation. Learn from your experience. Your ability to help your organization will increase.

Build on other's knowledge! See that even if you are the first person who is attempting to deal with data quality problems in your organization, you are not alone. There is a strong foundation of concepts, tools, and methods related to managing data quality. Many data professionals have been working on this subject over many years. I am grateful for what I have learned from them and several are named within this book. You will see recent techniques in addition to techniques invented years ago that are still applicable today. You will hear from those who have successfully applied the Ten Steps in a variety of organizations from countries around the world. Again, use the many references in the chapters and bibliography for additional help.

Share with others! Share the Ten Steps with others so they too can get the benefits from its use.

Get Started!

Any time I thought data quality wasn't the most important thing I should be doing, another problem grabbed me by the shoulders, looked into my eyes, and said "Don't forget data quality!" So here I am, over 25 years since starting a career in data quality and 12 years after writing the first edition of this book, still helping others wrestle their data quality goblins.

I am writing this second edition more convinced than ever that many of the ills in our world could be solved or minimized by taking care of the information and data quality aspects underlying those problems. The issues we face can seem urgent and overwhelming. Yet there is hope and this book is here to help! If your organization is troubled by data and information quality issues and doesn't know where to start, you can say, "Don't worry – we have the Ten Steps!" Get going and provide value. You've got this!

Structure of This Book

This book includes numerous templates, detailed examples, and practical advice for executing every step. At the same time, readers are advised how to select relevant steps and apply them in different ways to best address the many situations they will face. The layout allows for quick reference with an easy-to-use format highlighting key concepts and definitions, important checkpoints, communication activities, best practices, and warnings. The experience of actual clients and users of the Ten Steps are highlighted in callout boxes called Ten Steps in Action.

Main Sections

Chapter 1: Data Quality and the Data-Dependent World—Highlights topics in our world today, shows how they are dependent on data and information, and why data quality is more relevant and critical now than ever before.

Chapter 2: Data Quality in Action—Provides an overview of the Ten Steps methodology and introduces the Data in Action Triangle, which shows how data quality is put into practice through programs, projects, and operational processes.

Chapter 3: Key Concepts—Discusses the philosophy and fundamental concepts that are integral components of the methodology and on which the Ten Steps Process is built. The concepts must be understood to successfully apply the instructions provided in *Chapter 4*.

Chapter 4: The Ten Steps Process—Provides the process flow, instructions, advice, examples, and templates for completing information and data quality improvement projects. This is the longest chapter as it contains the full Ten Steps Process with concrete instructions, examples, templates, best practices, and warnings.

Chapter 5: Structuring Your Project—Describes general types of data quality projects, provides help in setting up a data quality project, and gives advice about creating a project plan, timing, and assembling a team.

Chapter 6: Other Techniques and Tools—Outlines techniques that can be applied in various ways in several places throughout the methodology. It also contains a section on tools for managing data quality. This approach is not specific to, nor does it require, any particular data quality software (e.g., data profiling or cleansing tools), but the methodology can be used to help implement these tools more effectively if they are available to you.

Chapter 7: A Few Final Words—A summary of the other chapters and words of encouragement.

Appendix: Quick References—Consolidates key materials that were presented throughout the book into an easy-to-read reference format. Keep close at hand to provide an at-a-glance reference while doing your work.

List of Figures, Tables, and Templates—Lists the titles and page numbers of visuals, information formatted as tables, and templates which you can use as a starting point for the data quality activity described. Once you are familiar with the Ten Steps, use this section to quickly find a favorite example.

Glossary—An alphabetical list of terms discussed in the book together with their meanings.

Bibliography—The list of books, articles, websites, and other resources used during the writing of the book. Use to further your data quality work and deepen your knowledge and skills.

Companion Website

A companion website can be found at www.gfalls.com with pdf downloads of the items in the Quick References and many of the templates shown in the book.

Conventions

Italicized Text—*Italicized* text is used to indicate references to chapters, steps, substeps, figures, tables, templates and important words or concepts in the book (e.g., See *Step 1 – Define Business Needs and Approach*, Go to *Step 4.6 – Risk Analysis*, Reference the *Framework for Information Quality* in *Chapter 3: Key Concepts*.)

Callout Boxes—*Table I.1* shows the types of callout boxes, along with their symbols and descriptions, that you will see throughout the book. Within a callout box, the specific topic (such as the word being defined) will be **bolded**.

The Ten Steps Process Format

In *Chapter 4: The Ten Steps Process*, each of the Ten Steps contains the following elements and sections:

- **You Are Here Figure**. Each step (1–10) begins with the "You Are Here" figure, a graphic of the Ten Steps Process which indicates where you are within the overall process and which step will be discussed.
- **Step Summary Table**. Each of the Ten Steps contains a Step Summary Table, which orients you to that step. It provides a short overview of that specific step and a reference to the main objectives, purpose, inputs, tools and techniques, outputs, communication suggestions, and checkpoint questions for each of the Ten Steps. See *Table I.2 – Step Summary Table Explained* for further

Table I.1 Callout Boxes, Descriptions, and Icons

Symbol	Type of Callout Box	Description
	Definition	Explains key words or phrases
	Key Concept	Describes significant, essential, and/or important ideas
	Best Practice	Recommendations, based on experience, to most effectively implement the Ten Steps
	Ten Steps in Action	Actual examples and case studies of how the Ten Steps methodology has been practically applied
	Quote to Remember	Memorable statements
	Warning	Cautions and things to watch out for
	Communicate, Manage, and Engage	Suggestions for working effectively with people and managing the project
	Checkpoint	Guidelines, in the form of questions, to help determine completion of each step and readiness to move on to the next step

Table I.2 Step Summary Table Explained

Section	Description
Objective	**What am I trying to achieve?** Goal or intended results of the step
Purpose	**Why should I do it?** Why the activities in this step are important
Inputs	**What do I need to perform this step?** Information needed to execute the step, including inputs from other steps
Techniques and Tools	**What can help me complete this step?** Techniques, tools, and practices to help accomplish the goals of the step or facilitate the process
Outputs	**What is produced as a result of this step?** Results from completing the step, with most steps containing sample output and/or templates
Communicate, Manage, and Engage	**How can I address the human element and project management aspects of this effort?** Suggestions for working effectively with people and managing the project during the step
Checkpoint	**How can I tell if I am finished or ready to move to the next step?** Guidelines to determine completeness of the step and readiness to continue to the next step

details about the sections in the Step Summary Tables. (Hint: to quickly familiarize yourself with the overall Ten Steps Process, read each of the Step Summary Tables in order. You will see the relationships between the steps by the flow of the inputs, outputs, and checkpoint questions, along with what should be accomplished and why, and ideas for increasing your success by addressing the people and project management aspects of your project.)

- **Business Benefit and Context**. This section contains background helpful for understanding the step and benefits from completing the step.

- **Approach**. This section contains step-by-step instructions for completing the step.
- **Sample Output and Templates**. This section contains examples and forms that can be used to guide your work and develop your own project outputs.

Note: Some of the Ten Steps contain substeps with their own detailed instructions. The substeps are also presented using the same format of Business Benefit and Context, Approach, and Sample Output and Templates described above.

Chapter 1

Data Quality and the Data-Dependent World

We recognize that people get fizzy about big data, blockchain, cyber security, data science, digital disruption and the rest, but the incontrovertible truth is that none of these nice, shiny ideas can work effectively without high-quality data.

— James Price, Managing Director, Experience Matters

Executing Data Quality Projects. https://doi.org/10.1016/B978-0-12-818015-0.00021-9

Data, Data Everywhere

Data, data, data. Follow the data. We need data! I am writing this book during the worldwide coronavirus pandemic. Never before has data figured so prominently in the international conversation. Information first shared with the public came in the form of reports by geographic location showing the number of people tested, positivity rates, patients hospitalized, and deaths. As more was learned, data showed that simple measures (wearing a mask, social/physical distancing, washing hands, and limiting the size of crowds) helped slow the spread of COVID-19. Data was required to conduct contact tracing. Around the world, pharmaceutical companies went to work developing a vaccine. Testing the vaccine, determining whether to move it forward, getting it approved – all required data – the representation of everything that happened throughout the process.

As I update this chapter in December 2020, the first vaccines are about to be given to high-priority populations around the world. These efforts depend on data, at every step. During shipping, the vaccines must be kept cold. Some require subzero temperatures. Which locations have the capability to store the vaccines at the needed temperatures? What is happening throughout the "cold chain" as the vaccine moves from the manufacturers to the administration sites such as hospitals and pharmacies? How many doses will be sent to each location? Some vaccines require a second dose. Who needs to receive a second dose and when? Who has not returned for the second dose? How can they be contacted? How many doses are on hand at each location? How many more must be sent and when? Who has had an adverse reaction? What is that reaction? The success of vaccination efforts depends on high-quality data being created, collected, shared, and well-managed every step of the way so effective actions can be taken in response.

Two questions must be answered "yes" for data to be used effectively:

- **Is the data of high quality?** That is, is it an accurate representation of what happened in the real world, is it available when needed, is it secure from unauthorized access and manipulation, etc.?
- **Do we trust the data?** That is, do we have confidence in the data and information, and do we believe it is of high quality?

Sadly, trust was lacking in the data about the COVID-19. Lack of trust turned the health pandemic into an infodemic. Legitimate sources of data were overshadowed by those deliberately shouting dis-information (false information that is deliberately created to mislead, harm or manipulate a person, social group, organization or country), as well as those inadvertently sharing mis-information (information that is false, but not created or shared with the intention of causing harm). People did not believe data about the severity of the virus, the number of cases, or the death rate. Many refused to wear masks or take other simple actions within their control to help slow the spread of the virus. Legitimate discussions and disagreements about how to act on the facts are to be expected. However, rejection of the facts contributed to the number of deaths and devastating economic impacts of the pandemic.

Now that a vaccine is here, officials realize that having a high-quality vaccine is not enough. The public must have confidence in the vaccine. And so, communications, marketing campaigns, and public service announcements aimed at building that critical trust are starting to appear. Leaders are stepping forward to share their willingness to take the vaccine when it is their turn. In the same way, data professionals must communicate and engage with people to address the human elements of their data work. Executives and managers must support this aspect of the data work and do their part. High-quality data and trust in that data must come together. Of course, politics and other motivations influence how data and information are used and communicated. But as data professionals, we have the responsibility to provide the highest-quality data possible and encourage confidence in it. That is the foundation. Leaders also have the responsibility to be honest about how the information is used.

Data quality and trust *must* go hand in hand, which is why both are addressed by the Ten Steps methodology covered in this book. The Ten Steps methodology is a structured yet flexible approach for creating, improving, sustaining, and managing data and information quality within any organization. The first nine steps in the Ten Steps Process relate to ensuring high-quality data. The tenth step is about communicating, managing, and engaging with people. This is where trust comes in. While implementing any component of *Steps 1-9*, individuals and teams must build trust and confidence as they interact with people. For data quality work to be successful, *Step 10* must be successful.

The pandemic has demonstrated how intricately data and information are woven into society, our organizations, and our personal lives. Even with these clear examples, do we really understand the implications of living in a data-dependent world?

Note that I said data-*dependent*, not data-*driven*. What is the difference? Data-driven refers to *specific and deliberate* efforts an organization makes to improve business efficiency or to gain competitive advantage through its data. I *do* support businesses being data-driven and deliberately using data. Managing data quality is essential for all data-driven organizations.

Data-dependent goes further. Societies, families, individuals, and organizations of all types (for-profit, non-profit, government, education, healthcare, medicine, science, research, social services, etc.) all depend on information to succeed – *whether they consciously recognize it or not*. All are data-dependent, whether they deliberately manage their data and information to make better use of them – or not. The law of gravity works on both the scientist who understands the principle and the schoolchild who is blissfully unaware there is a reason she is not floating off into space.

As individuals, we make decisions based on data and information, every day, throughout the day. I look at my smartphone to access my calendar, get a phone number, text a car to pick me up, or see stock prices. A text notifies me that a prescription is due to be refilled. Can I trust election results? What is the air quality today? What is our household income vs. expenses? Will the children attend school in person or online? Data and information are integral to all.

Even though my definition of data-dependent broadly covers all uses of data, this book focuses on what *people within organizations* can do to manage the quality of data and information on which their organizations' success depends. Employees, volunteers, and contractors all make decisions and take action based on information. Some use data to complete transactions. Others use reports to adjust marketing strategies and assign sales territories. Many decisions are automated, based on data and algorithms to automate activities. Parts are routinely ordered when inventory levels are low, with no human intervention. Product prices are calculated based on the type of customer and corresponding discounts. From the multinational corporation using sophisticated technology to a small shopkeeper using a notebook, all depend on correct information about accounts, buying preferences, and inventory to take care of customers, collect money owed, and order supplies.

Organizations who are consciously trying to be data-driven can use what this book has to offer. Even if no formal data-driven initiatives are in place, individuals who are dissatisfied with the data they use to accomplish their daily work can take advantage of the Ten Steps methodology. Because they recognize their organization is data-dependent, they can work on data quality themselves and bring others along.

Being data-dependent is not new. What is new? More data, more kinds of data, more data being created, more automation, less visibility to the inner workings of how the data flows and is being used, information moving faster and faster around the globe. The excitement of new technology overshadows the data it creates or uses. The environments that create, update, and store data and make it available for use are more and more complex and opaque. The stakes are high. How many decisions are made every minute by your organization's employees, business partners, and machines? What kinds of actions come out of those decisions? How does the data's quality, or lack of quality, impact what they are doing?

If I give you high-quality data and information, I cannot guarantee you will make good decisions and act appropriately and effectively. That is based on factors such as your professional skills, knowledge, and experience. Politics, fears, and personal values also come into play. However, I *can* guarantee if you have bad (i.e., incorrect or wrong) data and information, that any decisions and resulting actions will at a minimum be less effective and in many cases the outcomes could be disastrous.

We MUST have data and information to survive. And the better the quality of the data, the better we can make decisions and take effective actions for the sake of our societies, families, ourselves as individuals, and our organizations. Many of you reading this will nod your head in agreement and repeat the adage, "Garbage in, garbage out" that has been casually thrown about for decades. But what does that phrase really mean in practical terms? Is your organization doing the work necessary to ensure the data and information on which it depends are trustworthy and of high quality?

The good news is that we know how to improve and prevent data quality problems. The rest of this chapter highlights examples of why information and data quality are so important in today's data-dependent world, and what the Ten Steps methodology can do to enable action and improvement.

Trends and the Need for High-Quality Data

Dr. Walid el Abed, founder and CEO of Global Data Excellence, once described the need to solve problems driven by two tsunamis:

the rules and regulations tsunami and the data tsunami. To these, I add the technology tsunami.

Legal and Regulatory Tsunami

GDPR, DPA, HIPAA, CCPA, APPI – organizations must comply with an alphabet soup of legal and regulatory requirements specific to data protection, security, privacy, and the ability to share data. They must also prove compliance with a variety of other regulations. How is that compliance shown? Through data.

Every country has its own legal and regulatory requirements. Many affect organizations outside the physical boundaries of those countries. Laws continue to be put in place, increasing the pressure to keep up with the changes. Organizations must establish procedures and show evidence of compliance. An essential part of managing data quality involves knowing and complying with requirements that apply to your data.

Sadly, many organizations see these regulations only as a burden. The threat of bad publicity and high fines, along with the risk of a CEO going to jail motivate the minimum level of compliance. What a missed opportunity! How much better to jump in with enthusiasm because you understand that compliance can improve processes, decrease risk, and increase opportunities to keep customers happy. By improving the quality of your data, all are within reach.

Technology and Data Tsunami

What amazing things we can do because of technology: a machine tracks a sleeping patient's breathing and sends the information to a physician, sensors help farmers monitor crop yields and predict growth patterns, a biochip transponder is inserted under the skin of an animal for identification (removing the need for ear tags or brands), a washing machine is started from a smartphone, an app shows who is ringing your doorbell, a smart building automatically adjusts the temperature, a wearable device monitors your health, data from in-car navigation is used to predict equipment malfunction and design safer roads, and smart cities filled with sensors help to understand and control the environment. The devices that give the ability to accomplish these examples are part of the IoT – the Internet of Things. Some are commonplace and others have yet to reach their potential, but the overall set is growing every day.

Technology creates, changes, and uses data to accomplish its purposes. Data is integral to digital transformation, the use of digital technologies to solve problems and the resulting cultural changes. The following topics illustrate the close relationship between more recent technological innovations and data.

Internet of Things (IoT)

IoT is a system of connected interrelated "things" with sensors and unique identifiers (UIDs) which can transfer data over the internet without requiring human-to-human or human-to-computer interaction. These things can be computing devices, machines, objects, animals or people. IoT is a sensor network of billions of smart devices that connect people, systems, and other applications to collect and share data and to communicate and interact with each other.

IoT has many advantages such as the ability to access information from anywhere at any time on any device. At the same time, it is challenging to collect and manage the massive amount of data generated by the devices. There is also a high potential that hackers can break in and steal information. The need for high-quality data is fundamental to receiving the benefits from any "thing" that is part of IoT.

5G

In telecommunications, 5G is the fifth-generation technology standard for cellular networks meant to replace 4G networks which provide connectivity to most current cellphones. 5G increases download speeds through greater bandwidth speeds and lowered latency (the period or time delay between data as it travels from one node to another or the delay between stimulus/instruction and response). Increased bandwidth means 5G can be used not only for cellphones but as a general internet service provider for laptops and desktop computers. Simply said, 5G moves data faster. Moving good data faster is good. But moving low-quality data faster simply accelerates impacts to risk, costs, and revenue.

Big Data

To illustrate the close relationship between data and the technology which manages it, consider Big Data, a term first used in its modern context by Roger Mougalas in 2005 (Dontha, 2017). Increasingly large amounts of data were being generated from computers, smart phones, and devices connected through the Internet of Things. This sparked the development of non-relational systems (NoSQL – for Not only SQL) to handle the volumes of data (big data) that could not be adequately handled by traditional relational systems. A data lake has become somewhat synonymous with big data technologies and a data warehouse with relational databases. As experience has already shown, many of the data lakes have turned into data swamps – once again, a data quality problem.

Big data was first described using three "V's" by Doug Laney: volume (huge scale of data); velocity (the frequency and speed of data generated, produced, created, refreshed, and processed); and variety (different forms and types of data, both structured and unstructured). George Firican (2017) outlined additional V's to describe big data: variability (inconsistent data); veracity (concerns over trustworthiness of the data or knowing the reliability of the data source); vulnerability (security concerns); volatility (rate of data decay); visualization (challenges to visually depicting large amounts of data); and value (insights coming from analysis of the data).

The challenges from these V's put pressure on the quality of the data. We are looking for valuable insights from big data that will help our organizations be more competitive, make more money, protect the environment, ensure a safe society, and find answers to social ills. Data quality could not be more important.

Some are already talking about the Post Big Data Era, where the challenges come from lots of computing capacity, lots of data, and the need to learn and reason quickly and reliably with lots of data. Enter Artificial Intelligence and Machine Learning.

Artificial Intelligence and Machine Learning

PwC forecasts that Artificial Intelligence (AI) technologies will add US$15.7 trillion to the global economy by 2030. Their broad definition of AI is "a collective term for computer systems that can sense their environment, think, learn, and take action in response to what they're sensing and their objectives" (2020). Machine Learning (ML) is a discipline within AI which uses sophisticated algorithms to help computer software get better at making decisions.

For more on AI, ML, and related topics, see Thamm, Gramlich, and Borek, *The Ultimate Data and AI Guide* (2020).

ML and AI are behind image recognition, such as the ability to recognize the difference between a plant and a weed, that is being built into a prototype weeding robot being developed by a firm near Salisbury, in southwest Britain. ML and AI are used to develop insights from associations between products that people buy, and, using that, to increase sales. Banks use their algorithms to prevent fraud. Speech recognition, medical diagnosis, and predictions are only a few of its other applications. Yet there is a downside. In June 2020, a man was wrongfully arrested based on a false hit produced by facial recognition technology, the first-known documented example in the US of this happening (Allyn, 2020).

Donald Soulsby, Principal, Metawright, Inc., shared a cartoon that has been around for many years (artist unknown). The boss turns to four programmers and says, "I'll go and find out what the customer wants and the rest of you start coding!" Donald updated it to an alien robot boss saying to four alien robot programmers, "I'll go and find out what the customer wants and the rest of you start algorithming!!" He labeled it "Plus c'est la même chose," meaning the more things change, the more they stay the same. Let's not repeat the mistakes of the past.

Achieving the promise and potential of AI and ML, while minimizing the risks, can only be done with high-quality data as part of the mixture. As Tom Redman (2018) points out, "Poor data quality is enemy number one to the widespread, profitable use of machine learning." He goes on to explain that the problem shows up first in the historical data used to train the predictive model and second in the new data use by that model to make future decisions.

Tom Redman and Theresa Kushner developed a "Data Quality and Machine Learning Readiness Test," designed to help organizations understand the most important issues around the subject, baseline where they are, and determine which issues to address in the short term (Redman & Kushner, 2019). The readiness test can be found at dataleaders.org.

Let's not miss the promise and potential of technology and the many ways it can improve our organizations, personal lives, and societies because we did not address data quality – this is something we know how to do.

 Quote to Remember

"AI is a misnomer because it isn't really intelligent. It cannot intrinsically differentiate between fact and fiction, good and bad, right and wrong. All it can do is consume massive amounts of data and look for patterns that fulfill its programming mandates. If the data is incorrect, or is interpreted incorrectly, the pattern will be skewed and the results will be faulty.

In this light, the real intelligence behind artificial intelligence lies where it always has: the human brain. Only through proper oversight in the collection and preparation of data will AI be able to deliver the greatest benefit to digital services and operations.

The smarter we are about data, the smarter our machines will become in the quest to achieve greater productivity."

– Arthur Cole, "The Crucial Link Between AI and Good Data Management"
(2018)

Data and Information – Assets to Be Managed

What can we do to ensure the quality of the data on which our world depends? One of the first steps is to recognize that data and information are vital assets to be managed as intentionally as other assets. As assets, data and information have value and are used by an organization to make profits. As resources, data and information are essential to performing business processes and achieving organizational objectives. Historically, organizations understand that people and money are assets with value and must be managed to be successful. Information, however, is often seen only as a byproduct of technology, with lip service paid to the data while actions focus only on technology. Let's do some comparisons.

Managing Information vs. Managing Money

Every organization manages its money, often through a dedicated Finance department, with roles such as chief financial officers, controllers, accountants, and bookkeepers. Each role helps to manage financial assets, and no one would consider running their company without them. But when it comes to information, how many people know those with specialized skills to manage data quality even exist?

Everyone knows finance-related roles must be budgeted for and people hired. No one expects the person who supports the financial software to set the chart of accounts. So why should an organization resist the idea of hiring professionals whose expertise is centered on data? Most people know accountants are necessary and understand generally what they do. In the same way, I hope that in my lifetime most people will generally know what data professionals do and no organization would think of running the enterprise without their specialized expertise.

Managing Information vs. Managing People

Every organization has to manage its people. The Human Resources department oversees this process, but many roles are involved. When managers hire people and offer contracts, they must stay within the parameters of the job classes, job roles, titles and compensation guidelines set by the central Human Resources department. Everyone understands that a line manager does not have the authority to negotiate benefits packages on behalf of the whole company. Yet when it comes to information, how often do managers create their own databases or purchase external data without considering what company-wide information resources already exist to fill their needs? Is that wise management of information assets? Similarly, every person who creates data, updates data, deletes data, or uses data in the course of their job (just about everyone) affects the data. Yet how many of them understand the impact they have on this important asset called information? Are we really managing our data and information assets if people do not understand how they affect them?

Management Systems for Data and Information

Similarities between managing human and financial resources and information resources are clear. In the details, people are managed differently than money and differently than data and information. An appropriate management system is required to get the most value from a particular resource or asset type. Management system refers to how an organization manages the many interrelated parts of its business such as processes, roles, how people interact with each other, strategy, culture, and "how things get done."

We also need what Tom Redman (2008) calls a management system for data. Data and information *quality* management is an essential component of data management.

Managers and executives must lead the way by investing in data quality – to ensure data is properly managed, with enough money, time, and the right number of skilled people involved. Individual contributors can help others to understand the value of information assets and do their part to manage them appropriately.

The Leader's Data Manifesto

A document called "The Leader's Data Manifesto" (coauthored by myself, John Ladley, James Price, Tom Redman, Kelle O'Neal, and Nina Evans) provides another way to talk about data and information as vital business assets and encourages the change needed to manage them as such. See *Figure 1.1*.

Figure 1.2 highlights the three main sections of the Manifesto: 1) Data's promise, 2) Current state of most organizations with regards to data, and 3) Calls to action for three audiences: boards and senior leadership, anyone who needs data to do their job, and data professionals. The third column in the figure offers questions to start conversations about managing data and information assets.

Note that it is NOT called The Data Leader's Manifesto. It is The Leader's Data Manifesto and is meant for *all* leaders, not just for data professionals and others who manage data. See dataleaders. org to download a copy of the Manifesto, which, at the time of writing, is available in 14 languages. Show your support for these ideas by signing the Manifesto and putting it to work in your organization. Use it as a focal point for discussions. Share it with others. Get at least one other person to sign it. Offer to translate it into another language. Make use of other free resources on the site.

The more everyone in the world generally, and your organization specifically, understands the importance of managing information and data assets, the more time can be spent actually managing the data – and the less time spent convincing others it should be done. The Leader's Data Manifesto is offered to help you start gaining support for managing data assets, which will also move the data quality work forward.

What You Can Do

For all the attention to and money spent on technology, there is a lack of the same money and attention paid to ensuring there are qualified people to manage the data and information. What can be done? Anyone in any organization can do the following to help:

- Act on the calls to action in The Leader's Data Manifesto just mentioned
- Add data and information to the conversation
- Increase data literacy in the workplace
- Include data (quality) management in learning institutions

Add Data and Information to the Conversation

Almost every conversation about the best ways to execute strategy, create opportunity, meet goals, avoid issues, and please customers through high-quality products and services includes the usual triad of people, processes, and technology. What is missing? Data and information!

THE LEADER'S DATA MANIFESTO

 YOUR ORGANIZATION'S BEST OPPORTUNITIES FOR **ORGANIC GROWTH** LIE IN **DATA**

DATA OFFERS ENORMOUS UNTAPPED POTENTIAL TO CREATE COMPETITIVE ADVANTAGE, NEW WEALTH AND JOBS; IMPROVE HEALTH CARE; KEEP US ALL SAFER; AND OTHERWISE **IMPROVE THE HUMAN CONDITION**

ORGANIZATIONS ARE FAR FROM BEING DATA-DRIVEN. MOST COMPANIES:

1. DON'T FULLY KNOW WHAT DATA THEY HAVE OR EVEN WHAT DATA IS MOST IMPORTANT
2. CONFUSE "DATA" WITH "INFORMATION TECHNOLOGY" OR DIGITALIZATION, LEADING THEM TO MISMANAGE BOTH
3. LACK ANY SORT OF DATA VISION OR STRATEGY DEFINING HOW DATA CONTRIBUTES TO THEIR BUSINESS
4. UNDERESTIMATE THE EFFORT REQUIRED TO MANAGE DATA AND LACK THE ORGANIZATIONAL STRUCTURE TO DO SO

MANY COMPANIES ARE SUCCEEDING WITH SMALL-SCALE ANALYTICS, GOVERNANCE, QUALITY AND OTHER EFFORTS. STILL, WE FIND **NO EXAMPLES OF FUNDAMENTAL, LASTING, COMPANY-WIDE CHANGE** WITHOUT **COMMITTED LEADERSHIP** AND THE INVOLVEMENT OF EVERYONE AT **ALL LEVELS** OF THE ORGANIZATION.

… AND WE ARE FULLY AWARE HOW DIFFICULT IT WILL BE TO UNLOCK DATA'S POTENTIAL, UP AND DOWN THE ORGANIZATION CHART.

THEREFORE, WE URGE EVERYONE TO LEAD CHANGE

BOARDS, SENIOR EXECUTIVES AND SENIOR LEADERS: CHALLENGE YOUR PRECONCEIVED NOTIONS OF DATA.

See data not as the details buried in the bowels of IT and in your computer systems, but as a **source of unlimited, new opportunity**. Realize that data's potential isn't just for specialists, such as data scientists, but for everyone and a way for your company to **truly distinguish itself** from competitors. See data as a way for you personally to **leave an enduring legacy**. Consider what it would mean to put data assets on your balance sheet.

Leadership owes their shareholders and constituents a data vision. As a first step, focus on these areas:

1. Take better care of data, with a focus on the quality of your most important data. **2.** Try out the many ways to put your data to work and gain a competitive advantage. **3.** Advance a management system better suited to the rigors of data.

EVERYONE WHO NEEDS DATA TO DO HIS/HER JOB: BECOME DATA PROVOCATEURS TO DRIVE CHANGE.

Opportunities abound, so choose an area or two that interests you. It could be improving data quality; discovering a deeper analytic method; developing a new metric; delivering an idea that quantifies the hard-dollar value of data; or using data to build bridges with other departments.

DATA PROFESSIONALS:

Be more proactive, communicate with your business counterparts, sell the concepts, become a data mentor, and help people create their own success stories.

GET ON WITH THE WORK

These are exciting and perilous times: exciting because data offers opportunities to create competitive advantage, enhance existing products and services (and create new ones), better understand customers and reduce costs. And perilous because fixing what's broken will be arduous, and those who wait too long may find themselves severely disadvantaged.

Give this manifesto deep consideration.

SHARE IT. DEBATE IT.

And make it work in your organization.

www.dataleaders.org

Figure 1.1 The Leader's Data Manifesto.
Copyright © 2017 datalesaders.org. Used with permission.

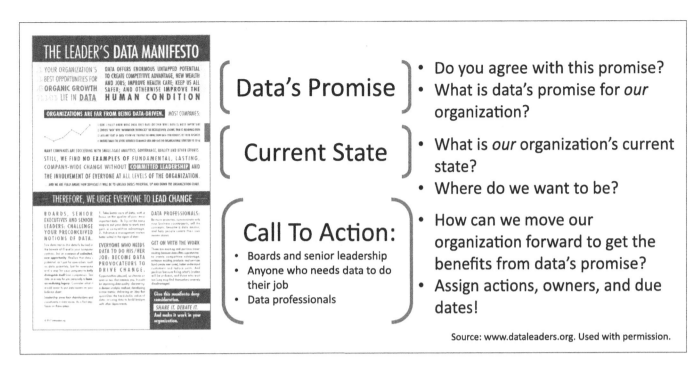

Figure 1.2 The Leader's Data Manifesto with discussion questions.

My call to all board members, executives, managers at every level, project and program managers, and individual contributors is to add data and information to the conversation. Since board members, executives, and senior managers are not the audience for this book, it will be up to the rest of you to spread the word. Give them a copy of this book and mark the first chapter for them to read. Follow up with them.

When you are part of the discussions that turn to people, processes, and technology, bring in data and information. To further the conversation, ask questions such as:

- What data and information are required to carry out <name the strategy, goal, issue, opportunity>?
- What information is needed to better serve our customers and provide products and services?
- Do we have the data we need?
- Do we trust the data and information that we have?
- What is the actual quality of the data and is it at the level needed?

This is not about paying *less* attention to processes, people, and technology. This is about *equal* attention to and investment in the quality of data and information upon which your organization depends. The broad approach to data quality shown in this book includes all aspects since all must work together. Let others know there is help available – the Ten Steps methodology. Some need to know the details. Others just need to know the right people are following a proven approach and turning out positive results.

Increase Data Literacy in the Workplace

At the time of this writing Data Literacy is a popular term. Data literacy is often compared to the general concept of literacy – the ability to read. But being literate is more than just being able to read the words. To be literate, people also need to comprehend and apply what they read. Given the importance of data in our lives,

many organizations are taking up the cause of data literacy. That is a good thing. However, definitions of data literacy vary and may depend on which organization is doing the defining or what product a vendor wants to sell. Most definitions include the ideas of working with data, analyzing data, representing data in context, communicating, and even arguing with data. These definitions emphasize being able to comprehend and interpret data. What is lacking in the definitions of data literacy is an acknowledgement of the need to understand the sources of the data and a means to determine if sources can be trusted. A person is not data literate if they use data from a source that is lying about the data or whose facts are inconsistent with more reputable sources or if they are not aware that they should even be checking these in the first place. The definitions also fail to recognize that the ability to adequately prepare the data for use is part of data literacy.

Without giving a definitive description of data literacy myself, and speaking broadly, there is a need to raise awareness, at every level in the organization, about the importance of data, everyone's role in it, what they should do, and the fundamentals of data quality as outlined in this book. These should be considered part of data literacy – at the right level of overview or detail depending on the audience, of course.

Until people enter the workforce with necessary data knowledge and skills, we have to rely on employers giving their employees the opportunity to learn and build their data skills. For example, managers and organizations can pay for in-house/on-site training, public training (in-person or online), conferences, certifications, and degree programs. Employers can encourage participation in industry associations and chapter meetings or arrange for consulting or coaching by qualified professionals. There are associations and conferences related to data for specific industries, such as insurance and finance, and for specific roles, such as Chief Data Officers. Don't reinvent the wheel. When employers invest in training and education to increase their employees' skills, their organizations also benefit from increased productivity and effectiveness. The Ten Steps methodology is part of the existing foundation of knowledge that any data professional can learn from and build upon.

Include Data (Quality) Management in Learning Institutions at All Levels

Ask for data quality management to be included in learning institutions at all levels: for older primary and secondary levels, higher education, and professional programs:

- **Coding and Data**. When young people are taught to code, include information about data management and quality so they understand why they are coding, the impact of the data that is created and used as a result of their programming, and their responsibility to do so in an ethical manner.
- **Degrees in Information Quality.** I want to see as many degrees for data and information professionals as there are engineering, accounting, and law degrees. As of this writing there is a large gap in higher education to provide degrees related to data and information quality. A noticeable exception and a leader in higher education is the Information Quality Graduate Program at the University of Arkansas at Little Rock, which is based in the US and provides distance learning for students around the world. (See https://ualr.edu/informationquality/) We need similar programs at more universities. Learn from what they are doing.
- **Data Management, Quality, and the MBA.** Include education about data management and quality in every MBA (Masters of Business Administration) program. MBA students become leaders who will make decisions about where their organizations focus time, money, and effort. Their studies expose them to such business areas as accounting, human resources, finance, economics, marketing, and organizational behavior. Yet when it comes to data and information, which underlie everything they must accomplish, the exposure is often limited to programming, computer science, or data science. Sadly, many of our leaders only learn about the importance of data and information and the skills required to manage them once they are in their organizations and are feeling the pain of poor-quality data. Including data quality as part of their education is the best way to prevent those problems.
- **Data Management, Quality, and Continuing Education.** Include data management and quality components in continuing education, short courses, and professional programs. When professionals, of any discipline, enhance their knowledge and skills, they need to be aware of how they impact the quality of the data they touch and how they depend on high data quality to do their jobs.

- **Data Quality Knowledge for Professionals.** At a minimum, any profession that relies on data and information (all of them) should have a section or module about data and data quality as part of their education. They need an understanding of what data – the right quality data – means to their particular profession, an appreciation of what it takes to manage data so they can trust it and use it, and their role in enabling quality. They must know enough about these things so they can prioritize resources necessary to ensure the quality of the data on which they depend.

I encourage everyone reading this to reach out to learning institutions at all levels, their alma maters, or those close to where they work. For the courses or degrees related to what you do, find out how information, data, and data quality are included. Offer to be a guest lecturer. Work with department heads and professors to appropriately include data quality into course work. Reach out to other universities who are already doing this and learn what has worked for them.

Are You Ready to Change?

The need for high-quality, trustworthy data in our data-dependent world will not go away. The pressure to create, improve, manage, and sustain the quality of data in our organizations will only increase. The question is, are you willing to do what is needed to meet these demands? Will you put as much emphasis on your data and information as you do on technology? Are you going to change in order to address the challenges, or will you keep doing whatever you are doing now – with no difference in the results?

I am reminded of a wonderful cartoon that came across my desk many years ago. The artist is B. Kliban. Imagine in your mind as I describe it. There are two men and one wagon full of round wagon wheels. With great effort, one man struggling to pull and one man pushing with all his might, they are moving the wagon full of round wagon wheels. But the wagon itself had square wheels! If you can get the visual of this, you recognize that had the men replaced the square wheels on the wagon with the round wheels they were transporting, they would reach their destination much more quickly and with much less effort than the effort it would have taken to change the wheels. They did not take advantage of the solution right in front of them.

This was a brilliant expression of what happens every day in our organizations. We move toward our destinations. With great effort we push and pull at the problems that get in our way, yet fail to use solutions that are right in front of us – solutions that would get us to where we need to be faster and with less effort. The Ten Steps methodology is the round wheel. Stop struggling and take advantage of the solutions offered in this book for the benefit of your organization. Turn the page and enjoy the journey!

Chapter 2

Data Quality in Action

*A growing economy; better health care;
a freer, safer, more just society;
and everything else I hold dear all depend on
better data and men and women
who can put that data to work.*

— Tom Redman
'The Data Manifesto: A TDAN.com Interview' (2017)

Improving the world one data element at a time.

— Navient Data Quality Program Tagline

In This Chapter

Executing Data Quality Projects. https://doi.org/10.1016/B978-0-12-818015-0.00002-5

Introduction to Chapter 2

"Doctor, my left arm hurts!" The doctor puts your arm in a sling, gives you an aspirin, and tells you to go home. But what if you were having a heart attack? You would expect the doctor to quickly diagnose your condition and take emergency measures to save your life. The first order of business is to keep the patient alive. After being stabilized, you would expect the doctor to run tests, get to the root cause of the heart attack, recommend measures to correct any damage done (if possible), and prevent another attack from occurring. You would then return for periodic tests and follow-up appointments so the doctor could monitor your condition and determine if what had been put into place was working. If not, adjustments would be made to medication, exercise, and lifestyle choices to enhance your health and prevent another heart attack.

Good health requires committed involvement from the patient with regular exercise, good eating habits, and smart lifestyle choices. The patient interacts with various people with knowledge (doctors, nurses, technicians) and makes use of test equipment and other technology available. Motivation on the part of the patient and healthcare professionals, along with the right information about the patient's condition are also essential. All aspects work together throughout the patient's lifetime, to give the patient the best chance of living a long and healthy life.

This seems like common sense when talking about our health. But when it comes to data and information, how often do we address the problem by only correcting a symptom of poor-quality data (the easy, yet inappropriate, fix which is like the aspirin and sling) and expect that to take care of everything? It is true that sometimes data must quickly be corrected in order to keep a critical business process going. This is similar to keeping the patient alive and, of course, that is a first priority. But after the emergency, no tests or assessments are run to determine the location or magnitude of the data quality problems, no root cause analysis is performed, no preventive measures are put into place, and no on-going monitoring is conducted. And then we are surprised when problems appear and reappear!

High-quality data and information do not happen by themselves. They require motivation where data quality work is tied into business needs – those strategies, goals, issues, and opportunities that must be addressed to satisfy customers and provide products and services. Four key components must work together – the data itself, processes, people and organizations, and technology – through the life cycle of the information.

Just as doctors are educated in the body, health, and dealing with disease, so those responsible for data must be educated in how to take effective action to ensure the quality of that data and information. This is where the methodology, Ten Steps to Quality Data and Trusted Information™, comes in.

To better put the Ten Steps methodology to work, it is useful to have some context before getting into the details. This chapter discusses tools, the many situations where the Ten Steps can be applied, and the Data in Action Triangle – how data quality is put into practice through programs, projects, and operational processes. Data quality cannot be put into action without skilled people and the right support, so resources for preparing your people are provided,

along with suggestions for engaging management. The chapter ends with a few key terms that will be used throughout the book.

A Word About Tools

A short comment about tools before we proceed. Many people think data quality is all about buying a tool. "If we just get a tool then all our data quality problems will be taken care of." Depending only on tools is like saying, "If we just get the right x-ray machine, we will all be healthy."

Of course, we do need a good x-ray machine to peer into the body and give information on which to act. Used at the right time and place in the hands of a skilled technician and directed by a qualified doctor, an x-ray machine will give us information to better manage our health, but more is involved than just the technology. The x-ray machine is just one aspect of many for what is needed to manage our health.

In the same way, the right tools are helpful, in some cases essential, to managing data quality, but they are not the end of the story. We are fortunate tools are available to aid in our data quality work, but additional skills and knowledge are required to know how and when use them well. That is where the Ten Steps methodology comes in. It addresses the processes, people, and organizational aspects of data quality, in addition to the technology. Think of the Ten Steps as a "wrapper" around your data quality tool. The Ten Steps approach is not specific to any particular tool, but it will help you better use tools on hand and make better decisions about tools you might need. Tools are further discussed in *Chapter 6*.

 Key Concept

Thinking the right tool will take care of all your data quality problems is like believing the right x-ray machine will make you healthy. The right tools are helpful, but they are not the end of the story. Tools are just one aspect of many needed to manage the health of our data and information.

Just as with your own health, you can prevent many data quality health problems. You can assess and take action if problems do appear. This chapter introduces you to the Ten Steps methodology which will help you manage your organization's data quality health. Think of the Ten Steps methodology as part of your wellness program for data and information.

Real Issues Need Real Solutions

Do any of these situations sound familiar? These are real situations, with real issues, that need real solutions. By applying the Ten Steps methodology, you can take action to help with all of them.

- Poor-quality data is causing issues for the organization, but no one is sure of their real impact and how much should be invested in dealing with those issues.
- The company has invested heavily in a data lake. Large amounts of data have been dumped there with the expectation that it can be used to provide valuable insights for the organization.

However, data scientists are spending the majority of their time finding and cleaning data before they can start their real jobs of helping to solve complex problems.

- Those who use reports from the business intelligence and analytics group don't trust the reports, complain about the quality, and are reverting to their own spreadsheets for verification.

- Your company is implementing (or has implemented) a third-party vendor application that brings together data from legacy sources for the first time. Poor-quality data is having an impact on project timelines and is hampering the migration and test results. Once in production, confidence in the information is low, and data previously used by only one business function is now being used in end-to-end processes, with poor results.

- Your new application development project goes live on time, maybe within budget, and the solution is being used. However, a few months later complaints start to surface. Additional staff are needed to handle data quality and reconciliation needs. It is discovered that the final solution does not have all the information users need in their operational processes. Or worse, incorrect information is presented to decision makers leading to costly mistakes.

- Because of mergers and acquisitions, your organization is starting a project to integrate data from the acquired companies. The project team has a tight schedule, yet you already know there are quality issues with the data to be integrated.

- A major division of your company has been sold. Data related to this division must be uncoupled from the existing systems and passed to the new owner.

- A division of your company has gone out of business. Before selling assets such as laptops and servers, data related to this division must be appropriately deleted or archived.

- As a worldwide organization, you must comply with varying (and sometimes competing) requirements related to data protection, security, and privacy.

- The organization purchases data from external sources but cannot depend on its quality to meet business needs.

- You have large amounts of data that need to be labeled, or need higher quality labels, in order to get the best use from it, such as in machine learning when training, validating, and tuning models.

- Your company invested in a major master data clean-up project, such as customer, vendor, employee, or product information. A few years later another clean-up project is started because the data quality declined and is once again causing issues for the business. A project focused on data quality which includes prevention and monitoring, in addition to clean-up, is a better use of resources so expensive clean-up will not have to be repeated again in a few years.

- Your organization has purchased a data profiling tool. Vendor training has shown how to use the tool, yet the tool is still not being used effectively. Use of the tool is not connected to the most important business needs and it is unclear which data is worth assessing. Once the profiling is complete, no one is looking at root causes or taking action on the results.

- You are involved in a Six Sigma project at the company and need more help regarding the information and data aspects of the project.

- Some aspect of data management (governance, quality, modeling, etc.) is an important part – or the full focus – of your daily responsibilities.

- Managing data quality is NOT part of your daily responsibilities, but you recognize data quality problems are hampering your ability to do your job.

This is only a short list of the many concerns this methodology can help address. It is imperative your people learn to recognize the data and information aspects of situations, and that they know how to take action to resolve them. Once again, the Ten Steps methodology can help!

About the Ten Steps Methodology

The Ten Steps methodology is an approach to creating, improving, managing, and sustaining the quality of data and information. The Ten Steps is all about taking action to deal with your critical business needs and their related data quality issues. The *Introduction* gave you a flavor of what is in the Ten Steps methodology. Let's discuss it further here. The methodology is comprised of the following main parts:

Key Concepts—Ideas crucial for the reader to understand in order to do data quality work well. Concepts are integral components of the methodology on which the Ten Steps Process is built. The reader needs to know how to think about data quality in order to apply the Ten Steps well. Just as you want a doctor who understands the theories and concepts of medicine so that specific actions can be correctly applied to your specific medical concerns, you also need to understand fundamental concepts (covered in *Chapter 3: Key Concepts)* so that the "how-to" (covered in *Chapter 4: The Ten Steps Process*) can be properly applied to your business needs and data quality concerns. Key Concepts include the Framework for Information Quality which is a conceptual framework visualizing the components necessary to have high-quality information, and POSMAD, the acronym for the fundamental phases of the Information Life Cycle (Plan, Obtain, Store and Share, Maintain, Apply, Dispose).

Ten Steps Process—The Ten Steps Process is how the Key Concepts are put into action. *Chapter 4: The Ten Steps Process* is the longest chapter in the book. There is a separate section for each of the Ten Steps. Each step provides business benefits and context for why that step is important, instructions, sample output, and templates. Also included are real examples of how other organizations have applied the Ten Steps. These all help readers put the concepts into practice and help them actually manage the quality of the data and information critical for the success of their organizations. When terms such as the Information Life Cycle or Data Specifications are used in the instructions, you already know what they mean. There are many techniques included within the Ten Steps Process. Additional techniques that can be used in more than one step are covered in *Chapter 6: Other Techniques and Tools*.

Structuring Your Project—This book uses projects as the vehicle for data quality work and how the methodology is applied. It is essential to structure your work well. How to do that starts in *Step 1.2 – Plan the Project* (in *Chapter 4*) along with *Chapter 5: Structuring Your Project*. The advice given here does not replace other well-known project management practices; instead, it applies those principles to data quality projects. It also helps make the transition from recognizing a data quality problem to actually addressing the problem.

Cooking Analogy

Let's deepen our understanding of the three main parts of the Ten Steps methodology using cooking as an analogy. See *Figure 2.1*. My mother made the world's best homemade caramels. As part of the recipe, the instructions said to bring a sugar syrup mixture to a boil and stir until it reached the soft ball stage. If you were making caramels for the first time, and soft ball stage was an unfamiliar term or concept, then you would have to research it. If you were already heating the syrup, by the time you researched the meaning I can guarantee the caramels would be overcooked and ruined. It pays to know the basic terms. (In case you are wondering, soft ball stage means the sugar syrup needs to reach 112°-116° C/ 234°-240° F. If you don't have a candy thermometer the temperature can be taken using a manual method, by dripping a small amount of the sugar syrup into a cup of cold water. A soft ball is formed when rolled between your fingers. Recipes for other types of candy call for the sugar syrup to be heated to other temperatures. When the sugar syrup is dripped into the cold water it reacts depending on its temperature – called firm ball stage, hard crack stage, etc.)

Let's assume you want to host a dinner party. You plan the event by considering the occasion, what will be on the menu, usual logistics such as where it will be held, how many people, who to invite, and any dietary restrictions. The day of the event you prepare the food. Having some background in cooking and knowing the applicable terms, you are able to follow the instructions and make the various menu items. You adjust the recipes for the number of people

to be served and one guest's special dietary requirements. The food is delicious, and the meal is a success – meeting your goal to gather together as friends and family, eat, and enjoy each other's company!

Similarly, in order to follow the Ten Steps Process (the recipe) you must understand key concepts (the basic cooking terms). With that background, along with properly structuring the project (planning the event), you will better apply the instructions, examples, templates and best practices in the Ten Steps Process. You are able to adjust the application of the Ten Steps Process for numerous situations where the quality of data is a factor. Of course, the goal is to make informed decisions and take effective actions in order to support your organization's business needs – to satisfy customers and provide products and services by addressing the data quality aspects of the organization's strategies, goals, issues, and opportunities. This illustrates the importance of all three aspects of the methodology working together in your data quality project.

The Data in Action Triangle

As mentioned, this book focuses on projects as a vehicle for data quality work and how the Ten Steps methodology is applied. It is helpful to expand that viewpoint for a moment and see how the Ten Steps methodology can be used in ways other than projects. In most organizations, work gets done through projects, operational processes, and programs. See *Figure 2.2 – Data in Action Triangle*. Data work is no different. All must be addressed in order to manage data quality well. These three aspects are different, yet complementary. All have a relationship with each other and are necessary to sustain data quality in any organization. Note that the triangle also applies to other functional areas of data such as data governance and metadata.

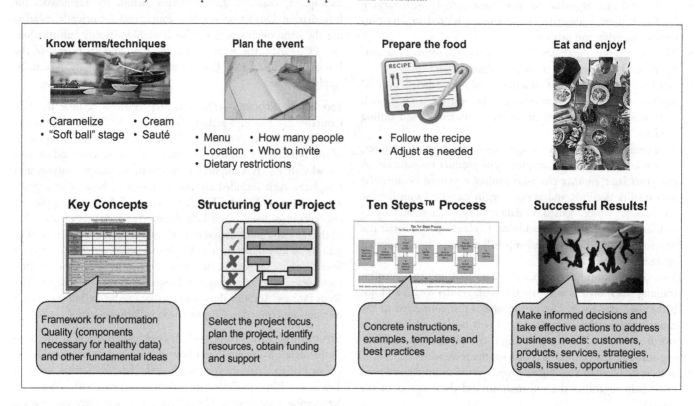

Figure 2.1 The Ten Steps methodology – from concepts to results.

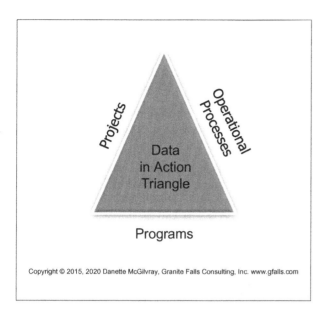

Figure 2.2 Data in Action Triangle.

Projects

A **project** is a one-time effort that addresses a business need. The duration of the project is determined by the complexity of the desired results. Project deliverables often include implementing what then become on-going production or operational processes. A project can be a structured effort to address an issue by one person, a large team, or it can include coordination across multiple teams. In the IT world, projects could be somewhat synonymous with work done by an Application Development team in software development projects.

In our context, a project applies data quality (DQ) activities, methods, tools, and techniques to address selected business needs. The project can be: 1) A focused data quality improvement project where the project concentrates on resolving specific data quality issues impacting the organization, 2) Where data quality activities are incorporated into other projects and methodologies, or 3) Ad-hoc use of data quality steps, activities, or techniques. The project aspect of the Data in Action Triangle is covered by this book.

Operational Processes

Generally, **operational processes** are series of activities directed toward a specific aim taken within an operational environment (as opposed to a project environment). In the IT world, Operational Processes could be somewhat synonymous with work done by an IT Operations team which supports software in the production environment. Here we are talking about incorporating activities that will enhance data quality or prevent data quality issues in day-to-day operations, "run" processes, or production support work. Examples include incorporating the awareness of data quality into new employee training, quickly applying Ten Steps thinking to an incident that arises in a supply chain process, or taking action on the results of data quality monitoring as a standard part of a person's role.

Programs

Generally, a **program** is an on-going initiative that manages related activities and/or projects in a coordinated way to obtain benefits that would not be available from managing them individually. A program avoids incurring duplicate time, effort, and costs from multiple business units developing their own services and data quality approaches. Having a program providing services that are used by many allows business units to spend their time adjusting those services to meet their own specific needs.

A data quality (DQ) program provides specialized data quality services that are utilized by projects or operational processes, such as training, managing DQ tools, and internal consulting using expert knowledge and skills to address data quality issues, conducting data quality health checks, raising awareness about data quality and gaining support for the work, adopting the Ten Steps as a standard or using it to develop your own data quality improvement methodology, etc.

A DQ program may be part of any organizational structure that makes sense for your company. For example, the DQ program may be part of a Data Quality Services Team, a separate program that is part of a Data Governance Office, a Data Quality Center of Excellence that is part of a data management function, a company-wide business function, or a branch of an enterprise data management team.

Having a data quality program is essential to sustaining the quality of data within an organization. Work on data quality can be started by implementing data quality projects, but projects eventually end. The program ensures the people with knowledge, skills, and experience with the data quality processes, methods, and tools used in the projects continue to be available to new projects and operational processes.

My experience is that without a healthy on-going program (and only focusing on projects), within two years the data quality work will start to wither and will eventually disappear. Later someone else wakes up to the importance of data quality and reconstructs what had been in place a few years before. This inefficient and costly way of managing data quality can be avoided by ensuring a foundational program is put into place. Though much of my work centers around helping organizations set up their data quality and governance *programs*, I have not written as widely about the program aspect as I have about projects, which is the subject of this book. See more on programs in my chapter "Data Quality Projects and Programs" in *Handbook of Data Quality: Research and Practice* (McGilvray, 2013).

How does a data quality program relate to a data governance program? Often, one of the main goals of a data governance program is to ensure data quality within the organization. Data quality can be *started* without formalized data governance, but it cannot be *sustained* without data governance. Whether it is called data governance or goes by another name, a level of focused management support is required to keep a focus on data quality. Because of this, data quality and data governance programs should be closely aligned within the organization. Options include having the data quality program under the overarching data governance program. Conversely, the data quality program could be the overarching program with data governance under it. Another option is having data quality and data governance being separate but equal "sister" programs that work closely together, but this means it may be harder to collaborate and keep them in sync.

No matter how a data quality program is structured or placed in your organization, it is still important to have it as a recognized program. There is a risk in absorbing it fully into data governance or data management, because there are detailed skills and knowledge needed to manage and sustain data quality.

Car Analogy

Let's use a car analogy to further illustrate the relationship between the three sides of the Data in Action Triangle. See *Figure 2.3*.

Build the car—In an automobile manufacturing plant, quality processes are in place to ensure that when the car rolls off the production line it meets requirements and specifications. We can be confident the brakes work and the steering wheel is in the right place.

In the same way, companies institute projects to build processes and practices that help the business support strategies and goals, address issues, or take advantage of opportunities. These projects are not focused specifically on data quality, yet data is an important component of the project. Critical data quality activities are incorporated into whichever methodology or approach is being used by the project. The success of these projects is increased because of the higher quality data that is supporting their goals. This is the type of project called "Data Quality Activities in Another Project."

Perform major repair—You purchase the car and drive it. After some period of time a clunking noise comes from under the hood. You try to ignore it for a while, but eventually you take it to the repair shop where it is diagnosed as needing a new transmission. The transmission is replaced, and you continue driving the car.

Replacing the transmission is similar to the type of project called a "Focused Data Quality Improvement Project." Use the Ten Steps as the basis for your project approach. This allows you to spend all your efforts applying the Ten Steps to create solutions for your particular needs. Otherwise, much time will be spent figuring out an approach or building a new methodology before you can get to

work addressing your specific needs. Use the Ten Steps to assess and fix data quality issues, identify root causes, and implement improvements (from both correction and prevention viewpoints), and implement controls. Often new or modified operational processes come out of these projects.

Fix a flat tire—You are driving down the road, hit a nail, and get a flat tire. Roadside service is called, they quickly repair the flat, and you are on your way again.

This is similar to data quality incidents where there is a standard process for handling them, such as first-level support provides a quick fix with little down time. However, work may move from operational support processes back to the project side of the triangle if the same fixes continue to occur or if there are bigger issues that cannot be resolved with the standard incident process.

Change the oil—Part of keeping a car running well includes regular maintenance such as oil changes, tune-ups, and rotating tires.

This is similar to when data quality activities are incorporated into established processes, such as procedures for creating data that will avoid creating duplicate records or technology modules that verify valid addresses. It also includes on-going controls such as data quality monitoring or dashboards.

Provide foundational services—Car manufacturers have certain responsibilities that apply to the plant as a whole such as instituting safety programs, managing recalls, designing new car models, retooling the factory, and training technicians to keep them current in new techniques. These initiatives are available to help no matter the particular model car and may help more than one factory.

Similarly, a data quality program provides specialized data quality services such as training, internal consulting, and managing data quality tools. This leaves the projects and operational processes free to apply them to meet their specific needs. For example, The Ten Steps methodology can be a standard provided by a data quality program,

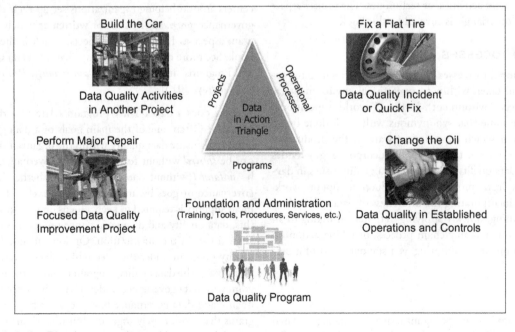

Figure 2.3 Data in Action Triangle – car analogy.

along with training. The program may have expert data quality practitioners who can help incorporate appropriate data quality activities from the Ten Steps into other projects, such as when migrating and integrating data from multiple legacy systems to a new platform. Practitioners from the program may lead or be part of a team for a business unit's focused data quality improvement project. A program may lead the change management and cultural aspects of data quality for the organization as a whole. A program may be the liaison for data quality tools with the vendor and/or an IT tool support team.

The Relationship

Figure 2.4 shows the relationship between the three sides of the triangle. Programs, which are on-going, provide services which can be used by both Projects and Operational Processes. Projects develop and implement operational processes that remain in place once the project goes into production. The project is then over, and the operational processes continue. In the course of business as usual (carrying out operational processes) business needs evolve, and issues or new requirements arise. A new project may be initiated to address these issues, moving the work back to the project side of the triangle.

When developing a data quality strategy (or any data strategy) account for each side of the triangle in your roadmap and execution plans. You can start on any side of the triangle, do the work in parallel or sequentially – whatever works best for you. But to sustain data quality in an organization all sides must be addressed at some point.

Why the Distinctions are Useful

Why do we even care about these distinctions? The only reason to make a distinction is if you do something different based on the distinctions. If projects, operational processes, and programs were treated the same there would be no reason to call out the differences. Categorizing as one or the other helps you make decisions about:

- **Prioritizing, planning, and executing the work**. When prioritizing activities within each side of the triangle, think of the differences between them and their dependencies on each other. Because the three are related, yet different, the priority of the

work and how the actual work will be done differs between them. Priority, planning, and execution are also affected by the following factors, which influence decisions about resourcing work in any organization.

- **Scope and complexity.** Is this a formal project or an activity on someone's to-do list? Is the work fairly straightforward or is it more complicated?
- **Money and funding.** How much money will this cost? Where does the funding come from and who makes the decision on how the money is spent? Often projects go through an approval process with a committee allocating money while operational processes are covered by budgets under the control of an individual manager.
- **Time and schedule.** How long will the work take and when will it happen? How long will the people resources be needed? Is the work going to end or become a part of on-going business-as-usual?
- **People resources.** What skills, knowledge, and experience are needed? Where are those resources found? This is closely allied to time and schedule in that projects will end, yet operational processes and programs are on-going, which informs how long people resources will be needed.
- **Support.** Who needs to support the work, particularly from management? What kind of support is needed – a cheerleader or evangelist, someone to convince colleagues, or someone to provide and manage resources?
- **Rules of engagement, decision rights, accountabilities.** These are often the purview of data governance, yet it is necessary to identify them for the scope of your data quality project. Is there a formal data governance program to work with? If not, as part of the project you will have to identify who is accountable for the data and who can make decisions. This adds time to your project, but it is essential to success. Whatever is put into place for the project can then become the starting point for a formalized data governance program, to be instituted separately after your project has ended.
- **Communication and organizational change management**. How will the effects of the changes brought about by the data quality work be managed? Who develops and executes a communication plan? Who needs to know what can vary between

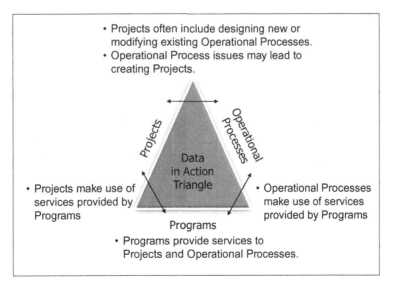

Figure 2.4 Data in Action Triangle – the relationship.

programs, projects, and operational processes. Programs and project communications often focus on the status of the work. Operational communications tend to focus on efficiency metrics and issue management.

- **How, when, and where to apply the Ten Steps methodology**. The Ten Steps can be used in different ways for different sides of the triangle. The Ten Steps Process can be the foundation for a focused data quality improvement project. Steps, activities, and techniques from the Ten Steps Process can be incorporated into other projects, SDLCs, or methodologies. A program can adopt the Ten Steps as a standard approach to addressing data quality and provide training. Once the Ten Steps methodology is learned it can be applied very quickly when dealing with data quality incidents. The Ten Steps can be used in a project to develop on-going monitoring of data quality. Once in production, the monitoring becomes an operational process.

When I was the enterprise data quality program manager at a global company, I wish I had been aware of the distinctions that eventually became the Data in Action Triangle. So many requests were coming my way that I was having a hard time deciding what to work on first, how to plan, and move forward. Others who are in similar situations have found the Data in Action Triangle useful to organize their work. For example, with any given request, ask yourself if this is a project, an operational process, or an element of a program. Then look at the distinctions just mentioned to help you understand what is needed to prioritize and schedule the request.

A Note about DevOps and DataOps

We've looked programs, projects, and operations which apply in almost all organizations. The basic idea of the Data in Action Triangle can also be applied in both a DevOps and DataOps environment. The term DevOps describes an approach that combines, or at a minimum encourages, collaboration and shared technologies between two historically separate Information Technology (IT) teams: Application Development, which develops software and releases it; and IT Operations, which deploys, maintains, and supports the software. The goal of DevOps is to accelerate the building of software by using automation, continuous integration, and continuous delivery by combining these teams and using Agile Development. The term DevOps was first used in 2009, when Patrick Debois

named a conference DevOps Days. It was popularized by the 2013 book, *The Phoenix Project*, by Gene Kim, Kevin Behr, and George Spafford (Mezak, 2018). While DevOps has gained in popularity, not all organizations use this approach. I see DevOps as a combination of the Project and Operational Processes sides of the Data in Action Triangle. If using a DevOps approach, the Ten Steps still apply when managing data quality.

DataOps is a more recent term and, as of this writing, definitions for DataOps vary. Most include the ideas that DataOps is about collaborative processes and use of tools, and partnerships between teams that might be separate (such as business users, data scientists, data engineers, analysts, and data management) to better manage data or deliver analytics. If your organization is applying DataOps, incorporate applicable steps, techniques, or activities from the Ten Steps into your work there.

Figure 2.5 shows the Data in Action Triangle applied to DevOps and DataOps, with the main activities performed in these approaches. While the words are different, the underlying ideas of the original Data in Action Triangle are the same. However, the cadence with DevOps and DataOps is more iterative than sequential. Thanks to Andy Nash for his input to this section on DataOps and DevOps and the corresponding figures.

Preparing Your People

Nothing can be put into action without people who have the knowledge and skills to do the job. Provide your people with the education, training, and support to be successful. Can you imagine a company telling each business unit's Finance team to just figure out how they want to manage finances, develop their own chart of accounts, report financials whenever they feel like it, and hire anyone who knows how to use an online tax program to be their controller? Yet, that is what happens when an organization expects those with other business or technology expertise to fill in for an information or data quality professional role. "Just get a good data entry person and our data quality will be fine" is a phrase often heard. But data quality requires much more than data entry. Of course, if someone does not currently have the skills, they can learn. Unfortunately, when someone has been put in charge of data, too often they don't realize that a profession exists with depth

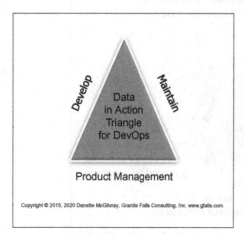

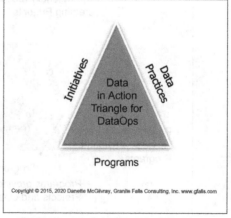

Figure 2.5 Data in Action Triangle for DevOps and DataOps.

of experience and knowledge. And the manager that put them in charge might not know it either.

Find resources to help gain the foundational knowledge necessary for people to do data quality work. Get training on and use a proven methodology like the Ten Steps, which gives everyone a jumpstart so the bulk of their efforts are spent applying the methodology to fit their particular needs, not reinventing the basics. Make use of industry associations and certifications, two of which are mentioned below.

As an individual, take the initiative to improve your skills. Read books, sign up for courses, in person or online, attend conferences and industry chapter meetings. Research opportunities to learn, proactively approach management to help pay for courses and/or time off work, and show how this benefits your organization. If you still don't get support, don't let it stop you from improving your skills on your own.

IQ International and the IQCP℠ Certification

IQ International (2004 – 2020) was a professional organization developed to improve business effectiveness through quality data and information. Even though nearly every department of an organization uses data to support the business (Finance, Legal, Operations), only one activity – data quality management – is applicable to almost every aspect of how an organization is run. To support organizational development, recognition and promotion of data leaders, IQ International developed the Information Quality Certified Professional (IQCP℠) focused on comprehensive mastery of the IQ field. All the materials and resources developed over the years will continue to be available. At the time of publication, the certification is transitioning to another organization. See links and information at www.iqint.org.

What came out of the development of the certification continues to apply to data quality professionals. I was invited to be part of a team, comprised of industry practitioners, academics, and consultants, who developed the original certification. We were led through the process by a company that specializes in creating certifications. One of the first steps was to define what it meant to be an information quality professional. We spent many hours together articulating, fundamentally, what an information quality professional does – not based on any one person's specific approach or methodology, but on the collective knowledge of the group.

This resulted in the identification and definition of six major areas of knowledge (called domains) considered essential to an information quality professional. It included the activities, knowledge, and skills necessary to successfully implement these domains. This was a significant contribution toward having data quality management recognized as a real profession, with real skills and knowledge required. It is important to retain and continue to give visibility to them.

See the first three columns in *Table 2.1* for a summary of the domains that make up the knowledge essential to an information quality professional. The last column indicates sections in this book that apply to the domain. Each of the domains and associated tasks are outlined in detail in the IQCP Framework at the website in the table. The domains and activities continue to be relevant and can be used in your data quality work:

- As an individual, you can assess your own knowledge and experience and identify areas for improvement. Dan Myers has created an assessment tool called "Know Thy Self" which can be used to evaluate your experience relative to each of the tasks within the IQCP Framework (Myers, 2018).
- If you are a manager building a data quality team, look at the domains. Within your organization, determine who is responsible for each task identified in the table. For those your team is responsible for, determine if they have the knowledge and skills required to meet the team's objectives, and use training and coaching to fill any gaps.
- If you are a data quality program manager, the domains can be used as a basis for developing capabilities related to data quality or services provided by a data quality program.

DAMA International, DAMA DMBOK, and the CDMP℠ Certification

DAMA (Data Management Association) International is a "not-for-profit, vendor-independent, global association of technical and business professionals dedicated to advancing the concepts and practices of information and data management." (See www.dama.org). There are DAMA chapters throughout the world and DAMA-I partners with Dataversity to provide conferences to its members and other interested parties. In addition, DAMA-I has developed the following bodies of knowledge and certification:

- **The DAMA Guide to the Data Management Body of Knowledge® (DAMA-DMBOK®) 2nd edition.** This reference book, often called DMBOK2, was written by leading thinkers in the field of data management and reviewed by DAMA members. It explains the "what" of data management. The DAMA-DMBOK® Framework, often referred to as the DAMA Wheel, visualizes the knowledge areas that make up the overall scope of data management. See *Figure 2.6*. Other emerging practices and technologies are referenced. These may be incorporated into the formal knowledge areas for Data Science and Data Engineering in future editions.
- **Navigating the Labyrinth**. Provides an executive's overview to the DAMA-DMBOK® 2nd edition.
- **DAMA Dictionary of Terms**. The DAMA Dictionary of Data Management (2nd ed.) provides a common data management vocabulary for IT professionals, data stewards, and business leaders.
- **Certified Data Management Professional (CDMP®) Certification**. The CDMP® requires a combination of education, experience, and a test-based exam. Since January 2019, all certification exams are based on DMBOK2. Data Quality is one of the Specialist exams available to supplement the base certifications.

Figure 2.6, often called the DAMA Wheel, shows the knowledge, or functional areas, within scope of the data management profession. What is the relationship between the DAMA Body of Knowledge and the Ten Steps methodology? The "how" of the Ten Steps methodology complements the "what" of the DMBOK2. As you can see, Data Quality is one knowledge area in the DAMA Wheel. I believe all the knowledge areas exist for the purpose of reliable, trustworthy data and information that support business

Table 2.1 Knowledge Essential to an Information Quality (IQ) Professional *

Domain	Description	Activities	Relevant Material in this Book
IQ Strategy and Governance	This domain includes the efforts to provide the structures and processes for making decisions about an organization's data as well as ensuring that the appropriate people are engaged to manage information throughout its life cycle.	Activities include working with key stakeholders to define and implement information quality principles, policies, and strategies; organizing data governance by naming key roles and responsibilities, establishing decision rights, and building essential relationships with senior leaders in order to improve information quality.	• *Chapter 2: Data in Action* ○ Data in Action Triangle, Engaging Management • *Chapter 3: Key Concepts* ○ The Framework for Information Quality • *Chapter 4: The Ten Steps Process* ○ *Step 1 – Determine Business Needs and Approach; Step 2 – Analyze Information Environment; Step 10 – Communicate, Manage and Engage People Throughout*
IQ Environment and Culture	This domain provides the background that enables an organization's employees to continuously identify, design, develop, produce, deliver and support information quality to meet customer needs.	Activities include designing information quality education and training programs; identifying career paths; establishing incentives and controls; promoting information quality as part of business operations; and fostering collaborations across the organization for the purpose of engaging people at all levels in information quality strategies, principles, and practices.	• *Chapter 2: Data in Action* ○ Data in Action Triangle, Engaging Management • *Chapter 4: The Ten Steps Process* ○ *Step 9 – Monitor Controls; Step 10 – Communicate, Manage and Engage People Throughout* • *Chapter 5: Structuring Your Project* ○ Roles in Data Quality Projects
IQ Value and Business Impact	This domain consists of the techniques used to determine the effects of data quality on the business as well as the methods for prioritizing information quality projects.	Activities include evaluating information quality and business issues; prioritizing information quality initiatives; obtaining decisions on information quality project proposals; and reporting results to demonstrate the value of information quality improvement to the organization.	• *Chapter 3: Key Concepts* ○ Business Impact Techniques • *Chapter 4: The Ten Steps Process* ○ *Step 4 – Assess Business Impact*
Information Architecture Quality	This domain includes the tasks that assure the quality of the data blueprint for an organization.	Activities include participating in the establishment of data definitions, standards, and business rules; testing the quality of the information architecture to identify concerns; leading improvement efforts to increase the stability, flexibility, and reuse of the information architecture; and coordinating the management of metadata and reference data.	• *Chapter 3: Key Concepts* ○ Data Specifications, Metadata, Data Standards, Reference Data, Data Models, Business Rules, Data Categories • *Chapter 4: The Ten Steps Process* ○ *Step 2.2 – Understand Relevant Data and Data Specifications; Step 3.2 – Data Specifications*

Domain	Description	Details

IQ Measurement and Improvement	This domain covers the steps involved in conducting data quality improvement projects.	Activities include gathering and analyzing business requirements for data; assessing the quality of data; determining the root causes of data quality issues; developing and implementing information quality improvement plans; preventing and correcting data errors; and implementing information quality controls.	• *Chapter 3: Key Concepts*
			  ○ Data Quality Dimensions, Data Specifications, Data Categories
			• *Chapter 4: The Ten Steps Process*
			  ○ Step 2 – Analyze Information Environment; Step 3 – Assess Data Quality; Step 5 – Identify Root Causes; Step 6 – Develop Improvement Plans; Step 7 – Prevent Future Data Errors; Step 8 – Correct Current Data Errors; Step 9 – Monitor Controls
			• *Chapter 5: Structuring Your Project*
			  ○ Types of Data Quality Projects; Comparing SDLCs; DQ and DG in SDLCs; Project Timing, Communication, and Engagement

Sustaining Information Quality	This domain focuses on implementing processes and management systems that ensure on-going information quality.	Examples include integrating data quality activities into other projects and processes (e.g. data conversion and migration projects, business intelligence projects, customer data integration projects, enterprise resource planning initiatives, or system development life cycle processes); and continuously monitoring and reporting data quality levels.	• *Chapter 3: Key Concepts*
			  ○ Framework for Information Quality; Information Life Cycle; Data Quality Improvement Cycle
			• *Chapter 4: The Ten Steps Process*
			  ○ Step 2 – Analyze Information Environment; Step 3 – Assess Data Quality; Step 5 – Identify Root Causes; Step 6 – Develop Improvement Plans; Step 7 – Prevent Future Data Errors; Step 8 – Correct Current Data Errors; Step 9 – Monitor Controls; Step 10 – Communicate, Manage and Engage People Throughout – Code of Ethics
			• *Chapter 5: Structuring Your Project*
			  ○ Types of Data Quality Projects; Comparing SDLCs; DQ and DG in SDLCs; Project Timing, Communication, and Engagement

Each of the domains and associated tasks are further detailed in the IQCP Framework at: https://www.iqint.org/certification/exam/iq-performance-domains/

*Columns 1-3 adapted from Information Quality Certified Professional (IQCP^{SM}) Domains. Used with permission of IQ International. Columns 1-3 appeared as Figure 6, in chapter "Data Quality Programs and Projects" by Danette McGilvray in *Handbook of Data Quality: Research and Practice*. Shazia Sadiq, editor (Springer, 2013).

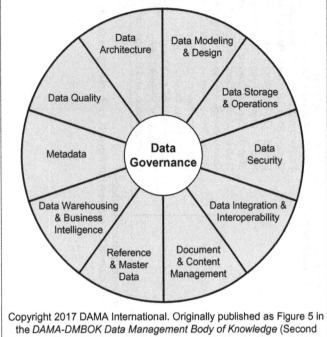

Copyright 2017 DAMA International. Originally published as Figure 5 in the *DAMA-DMBOK Data Management Body of Knowledge* (Second Edition), 2017, Technics Publications page 36. Used with permission.

Figure 2.6 The DAMA-DMBOK2 Data Management Framework (The DAMA Wheel).

needs. Therefore, there are aspects of the Ten Steps methodology that are important for all knowledge areas to be familiar with. For example, every functional area should know where they fit in the information life cycle. Those responsible for data modeling should produce high-quality models themselves and understand the impact they have on the quality of data. Those responsible for metadata, reference data, and master data need to understand the impact these have on transactional data and how they should work together. Because of the Ten Steps' broad view of data quality, many of the functional areas are touched upon in this book.

Engaging Management

The only way you will be able to put the ideas in this book into action is if you can engage your management. Support from the right level of management and suitable investments in time, money, and people are essential for success. The critical topic of obtaining management support is touched upon in this book, but it is a topic too broad to be covered completely. The following suggestions are presented to stimulate your thinking on this topic. I am indebted to Rachel Haverstick for her assistance in expressing these important ideas.

Best-case scenario—Engage the CEO and the board. In the best-case scenario, the board and executives of your organization will be completely convinced of the need to improve information and data quality and will allocate resources to support the culture-change activities that are necessary to create an environment that supports continuous quality improvement.

Right level of management—Not everyone who initiates an information and data quality improvement project has access to

executive level leadership. You don't have to have the CEO's support to get started. But you do need your manager's and project manager's support at the beginning. Keep working, show progress, and continue to obtain management support as high up in the organization as possible. A successful project can be a significant victory for a department; and engaging the right level of management is necessary to make a project successful.

Using the methodology—Use appropriate Business Impact Techniques in *Step 4 – Assess Business Impact* to help you show negative impacts from poor-quality data and the value from investing in resources to ensure high-quality data. Incorporate ideas from *Step 10 – Communicate, Manage, and Engage People Throughout* to help you engage executives, senior leadership, project managers, and managers of those doing the work in a way they can understand and relate to. Prepare managers for expected levels of resource commitment by communicating the business need and the improvement plan. This will increase the likelihood that you will receive the time, money, and participation needed. Likewise, provide regular status reports to managers and other working groups to enable them to see progress and continue to champion your project, and to prevent conflicting or duplicated work.

Communication techniques—As mentioned, the ideas presented in *Step 10 – Communicate, Manage, and Engage People Throughout* will help you optimize communication of important data quality concepts and project progress. Look at the suggestions in the *Communicate, Manage, and Engage callout boxes* at the end of each of the Ten Steps in *Chapter 4*. Use those ideas to plan your communication strategy. Of course, communication goes two ways and it is vital to open a dialogue, get feedback, listen, gauge reaction, and gain trust.

Know your audience—Knowing your audience's goals, values, and success criteria are some of the best ways to help you communicate effectively. Various audience groups need different communication formats and different levels of detail.

Right-size the message—Even though you may be excited about your project, your management audience rarely needs to hear the details of your data profiling or the impressive way in which you can now merge records to decrease redundancy. What they want to hear is that the improvement is working and that it is going to positively impact their work. Right-size the message to emphasize the topics that are most important to them.

Repeat—Remind your audience of the business needs the project is addressing. Repeat your project objectives and review milestones. Repeating your project objectives is especially important for communicating with managers, who need to be able to perceive the essentials of a project and track its pace and resource usage.

Broaden the scope—Be alert for opportunities to communicate your project goals and the information quality key concepts to a broader audience. The famous "elevator pitch" (a 30- to 60-second summary) is a good technique for communicating to any audience outside of a formal presentation. Also consider creating a four-slide project summary to make available in other presentations, such as department meetings or quarterly updates.

Manager as resource—Your manager can be a valuable networking resource, so keeping them informed performs double duty – ensuring support for your project and connecting you to other projects or efforts with which you can collaborate on shared goals.

Key Terms

In order to take effective action, we must be able to communicate. Having a common vocabulary or understanding of terms is a good starting point. Following are a few key terms which are helpful to understand before moving to the rest of the book. A list of all terms can be found in the *Glossary*.

Ten Steps—The full Ten Steps methodology is named Ten Steps to Quality Data and Trusted Information™. For brevity I use the term "Ten Steps" to refer to the methodology, which includes concepts, steps, and structuring your project. The "Ten Steps Process" refers to the steps themselves. The point to remember is that the methodology is not just about the Ten Steps Process (the instructions and examples in *Chapter 4*), but is also about understanding the key concepts that underpin the steps and structuring a project well to organize and manage the work.

Business Needs—I use the term "Business Needs" as my over-arching phrase to mean the most important things to an organization, driven by customers, products, services, strategies, goals, issues, and opportunities. Said another way, business needs include whatever is required to provide products and services to your customers and to work with your suppliers, employees, and business partners. Business needs also include the strategies, goals, issues, and opportunities that must be addressed to do this work. Data and information are needed to do this work. *High-quality* data and information are needed to do it well.

This term "business needs" is used frequently. It is a reminder that data quality work should NEVER be done only for the sake of data quality. Don't spend a moment on data quality for something no one cares about. There is too much important work to do. In a project, it is easy to get distracted by interesting, but possibly unnecessary, details or new issues that will not affect the goals at hand. Keep your organization and its business needs top of mind to select the project focus, inform and direct the work, and ensure your project stays on track.

Customer—Every organization has customers that make use of whatever products or services it provides. A customer is often thought of only as a prospective buyer or a client paying for services. Your end customer might be a police chief, a university president, a teacher, a student, a parent, a doctor, a patient, a hospital administrator, a soldier, a worthy charity, a politician, an artist, a patron of the arts, or someone giving or receiving humanitarian relief. Even more broadly, within your own organization, executives, managers, employees, suppliers, and business partners may be customers of the data and information you provide. They then use the information to provide products and services to the end customers. Realize all these types of customers are impacted by the quality of the data and information on which they depend to make informed decisions and take effective actions to help their organizations or their own personal lives.

Organization—An overarching word used to mean enterprises, institutions, agencies, establishments, and businesses of all sizes in any industry, such as for-profits, education, government, healthcare, nonprofits, charities, science, research, etc. The Ten Steps applies to them all because every organization is in the "business" of providing some kind of product and/or service and *every* organization depends on data and information to succeed.

Project—Generally, a project is a unit of work that is a one-time effort with specific business needs to be addressed and objectives to be achieved. In this book, the word project is used broadly to mean any structured effort that makes use of the Ten Steps methodology to address business needs. The duration of the project is determined by the complexity of the desired results. A project can apply the full Ten Steps Process or only selected steps and techniques. A project team can consist of one person, a small team of 3-4 people, a large team with several people, or can include coordination across multiple teams. A project can take four weeks, 3-4 months, or more than a year. No two data quality projects are the same, but the flexible nature of the Ten Steps means the methodology can be applied to all.

User—A general word to mean someone, in *any* role, who makes use of data and information. Synonyms for user include knowledge worker, information consumer, and information customer. For example, users can complete transactions, write reports, or make decisions on those reports. User roles include analyst, subject matter expert, service rep, repair technician, agent, marketing professional, scientist, researcher, programmer, executive, manager, customer, project manager, agent, broker, physician, hospital administrator, clinical research coordinator, scientist, teacher, data scientist, and the list goes on.

Stakeholder—As it applies to the Ten Steps methodology, a stakeholder is a person or group with an interest, involvement, or investment in or someone who will be impacted (positively or negatively) by the information and data quality work. Stakeholders may exert influence over the project and its deliverables. Stakeholders can be internal or external to the organization and represent interests related to business, data, or technology. For example, the person responsible for manufacturing processes would be a stakeholder for any data quality improvements that impact the supply chain. Stakeholders include customers, project sponsors, the public, or organizations whose personnel are most directly involved in doing the work of the project. Stakeholders can be accountable for all or portions of the project or responsible for specific deliverables. They may provide input to the project or simply be kept informed about the project progress and results.

Data—Strictly speaking datum is singular and data is plural. I used data as plural in the first edition ("data are"). Since that time, English usage has evolved to where data is used with either singular or plural verbs. I generally use data with the singular verb in this second edition ("data is"), with a few exceptions where "data is" just does not sound right. The majority of our data industry and my clients use "data is."

Data vs. Information—Data refers to known facts or other items of interest; information refers to those facts within context

(The data "09" and "20" and "752-5914" becomes information when put in context: "Order #752-5914 was shipped on September 20.") Data and information are often used interchangeably. There are a few exceptions where the distinction is important in the methodology and those will be called out. Use the words that resonate with your audience. For example, I tend to use the word information when talking to businesspeople and data with those in Information Technology, such as when discussing columns and rows in a database. But that is not a hard and fast rule. Use the term that will be most effective with whomever you speak.

Datastore—As used in this book, a datastore means any collection of data that is created or obtained, held, and used, regardless of the technology involved. A datastore can be a table in a SQL relational database, a full RDBMS (Relational Database Management System), a spreadsheet, a comma-delimited file, a data lake, or any of a variety of NoSQL (Not only SQL) non-relational databases. Datastores can be anywhere. A datastore can be located on-premises, where the software runs on an organization's own computers and servers, or cloud based, where the software is hosted on a vendor's servers and accessed by the organization through a web browser.

Dataset—As used in this book, a dataset is the set of data that is captured and used for assessment, analysis, correction, etc. and is often a subset of a full datastore.

Field or data field—As used in this book, a field is a location for storing a value. In relational databases, a field may also be called a column, a data element, or an attribute. Depending on the type of non-relational database, a field may be a key, a value, a node, or a relationship. Critical data elements (CDEs) are the data fields tied to the most critical business needs and deemed to be most important to assess for quality and manage on-going.

Record—In a relational database, a record is a row and is made up of a number of fields or columns. In the non-relational world, a record is not a consistently defined concept. You may hear "record" in a non-relational context. If you do, get a definition of what specifically is meant by that word. In this book, record is used generally to mean a group of data fields.

Chapter 2 Summary

This chapter started with comparing your own health and the health of data. It continued with a cooking analogy to describe how the three main parts of the methodology – key concepts, the Ten Steps Process, and structuring your project – work together. The idea of a data quality project was then put into context with other activities happening in your organization by introducing the Data in Action Triangle. The Triangle illustrates the relationship between projects, programs, and operational processes – three means of putting data quality into action. Suggestions were given for preparing your people and for engaging management, both of which are necessary for moving ahead in any data quality project.

The chapter concluded by defining key terms used throughout the book, since a common vocabulary is necessary to more easily put data quality into action. By having all this as a background, you are now ready for the rest of the book which covers the Ten Steps methodology, starting with key concepts in *Chapter 3*.

Key Concepts

He who loves practice without theory is like the sailor who boards ship without a rudder and compass and never knows where he may cast.

— Leonardo da Vinci

…data is now such a pervasive and mandatory aspect of organic growth that leadership needs to be more than just aware, they truly need to develop a solid level of understanding of … mandatory data concepts.

— John Ladley, *Data Governance* (2020)

Executing Data Quality Projects. https://doi.org/10.1016/B978-0-12-818015-0.00009-8

Introduction to Chapter 3

This chapter focuses on key concepts critical to managing data and information quality. For some, your eyes are glazing over and you are already turning to *Chapter 4: The Ten Steps Process.* After all, you think, "I'm a doer. I don't need no stinking concepts." Please reconsider. Understanding these concepts is essential to your data quality work. They are not unnecessary theory with no practical application to reality. Concepts are the foundation for the Ten Steps Process. Understanding them will help you decide which activities from the Ten Steps Process you should implement for any particular data quality-related situation. They will help you determine the right level of detail to go to for the steps you have chosen. Concepts will help you make better use of the Ten Steps.

Think of it this way: If you're going on a road trip through unfamiliar territory, you look at a map. This can be done by entering coordinates into a GPS system, finding the location on your smartphone, or unfolding a paper copy. Whichever way, you need to understand some basics to best use the map. A legend with symbols and their descriptions (the scale, types of roads, sites of interest, hospitals, etc.) will help you interpret what you see.

Similarly, the key concepts are broad ideas or guiding general principles that help you interpret and understand information quality. The specific activities in the Ten Steps Process are based on the principles outlined in the key concepts. Just as you can better plan and carry out your trip if you understand the basic concepts of how to read a map, you will make better decisions about applying the Ten Steps if you understand the basic ideas presented in this chapter. At a minimum, skim through the chapter to see what is included so you can return when you encounter unfamiliar terms in the rest of the book and as your project proceeds.

The Framework for Information Quality

The Framework for Information Quality (FIQ) provides a structure that visualizes and organizes the components necessary to ensure high-quality data.

Key Concept

The **Framework for Information Quality (FIQ)** A structure that visualizes and organizes the components necessary to ensure high-quality data. Using this framework helps make sense of the complex environments that create poor-quality information and enables organized thinking to recognize which components are lacking or missing all together. This helps identify root causes and determine improvements needed to correct existing problems and prevent the problems from reappearing.

Think of this framework as you would the graphic called My Plate in *Figure 3.1 – Visualizing the components – My Plate and the FIQ.* My Plate was introduced in 2011 (replacing the well-known Food Pyramid) and updated in 2020 by the United States Department of Agriculture's Center for Nutrition Policy and Promotion. Using the image of a place setting for a meal, it illustrates the five food groups that are the building blocks for a healthy diet. The graphic provides an easy high-level reminder of dietary guidelines. Additional instructions on the My Plate website describe concepts to help you further understand nutrition, build better eating habits, and encourage choices which support a healthy lifestyle. (See https://www.myplate.gov/.) My Plate is not one size fits all, but the basics are the same. You apply the concepts and details to make it work for your needs and situation.

Likewise, the Framework for Information Quality (FIQ) provides a visual of the components (concepts) necessary for healthy information. Applying the Framework enables organized thinking to help make sense of the complex environments that create poor-quality information and recognize which components are missing or not being done well. This helps identify root causes and determine improvements needed to correct existing problems and prevent them from reappearing. The FIQ summarizes a wealth of information that can be referenced in one glance.

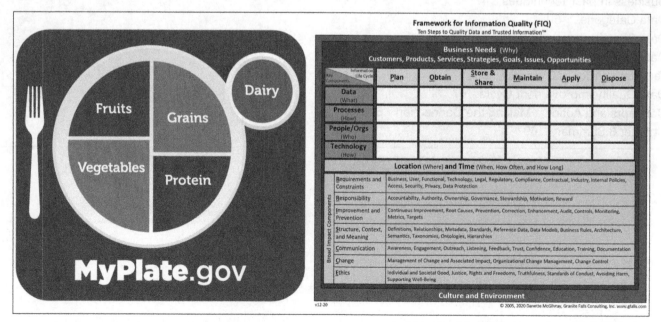

Figure 3.1 Visualizing the components – My Plate and the FIQ.

How to Use the FIQ

Once you understand the FIQ, use it as a quick reference and helpful tool for:

- **Diagnosis**. Assess your practices and processes; realize where breakdowns are occurring and determine if all components necessary for information quality are present; identify which components are missing and use them as input to project priorities and initial root cause analysis.
- **Planning**. Design new processes and ensure that components impacting information quality have been addressed; determine where to invest time, money, and resources.
- **Communication**. Explain what is required for high-quality data.

Remember, the FIQ shows the components necessary for high-quality information. *Chapter 4: The Ten Steps Process* provides the details for how to put these ideas into practice. Use what is learned from the FIQ and other key concepts in this chapter to make the Ten Steps Process work for you. Just like Choose My Plate, it is not one size fits all, but the basics are the same.

Sections of the Framework Explained

The **Framework for Information Quality** can be easily understood by considering seven main sections. See *Figure 3.2*.

1 – Business Needs – Customers, Products, Services, Strategies, Goals, Issues, Opportunities (Why)

Business Needs is an overarching phrase used to indicate whatever is important to an organization. Business needs are driven by customers, products, services, strategies, goals, issues, and opportunities. This section provides the context and backdrop to the other sections. All actions and decisions should be motivated and informed by business needs, particularly *critical* business needs. Projects should always start with the question, "Why is this important to the business?" Never do data quality only for the sake of data quality.

2 – The Information Life Cycle (POSMAD)

A life cycle is the process of change and development throughout the useful life of something. To get the full use and benefit from *any* resource, its life cycle must be understood and properly managed.

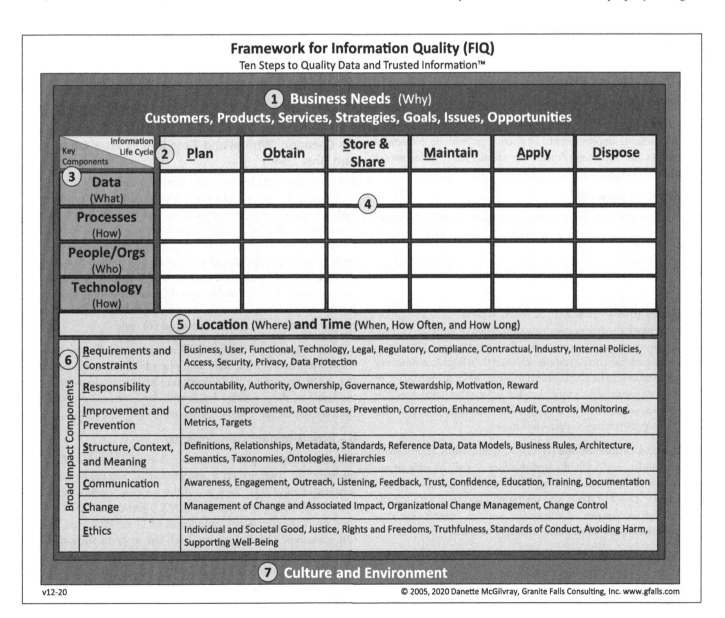

Figure 3.2 Framework for Information Quality with section numbers.

The acronym POSMAD represents the six fundamental phases in the *information* life cycle.

Plan—Identify objectives, plan information architecture, and develop standards and definitions; model, design, and develop applications, databases, processes, organizations, and the like. Anything done prior to a project going into production is part of the Plan stage. Of course, throughout design and development all phases of the life cycle should be accounted for so the information will be properly managed once in production.

Obtain—Data or information is acquired in some way, for example, by creating records, purchasing data, or loading external files.

Store and Share—Data is stored and made available for use. Data may be stored electronically such as in databases or files; it may also be stored in hardcopy such as a paper application form that is kept in a file cabinet. Data is shared through such means as networks or email.

Maintain—Update, change, and manipulate data; cleanse and transform data; match and merge records; and so forth.

Apply—Retrieve data; use information. This includes all information usage, such as completing a transaction, writing a report, making a management decision from a report, and running automated processes.

Dispose—Archive or delete data, records, or sets of information.

A solid understanding of the information life cycle is required for information improvement. This concept will be referenced throughout the Ten Steps Process. See details in the information life cycle section later in this chapter.

3 – Key Components

Four key components affect information throughout its life cycle. These components need to be accounted for in all of the phases in the POSMAD life cycle.

Data (What)—Known facts or items of interest. Here, data is distinct from information.

Processes (How)—Functions, activities, actions, tasks, and procedures that touch the data or information (business processes, data management processes, processes external to the company, etc.). "Process" is the general term used here to capture activities from high-level functions describing what is to be accomplished (such as "order management" or "territory assignments"), to more detailed actions describing how it is to be accomplished (such as "create purchase order" or "close purchase order") along with inputs, outputs, and timing.

People and Organizations (Who)—Organizations, teams, roles, responsibilities, and individuals that affect or use the data or are involved with the processes. They include those who manage and support the data and those who use (apply) it. Those who use the information are known as knowledge workers, information customers, information consumers, or simply as users.

Technology (How)—Forms, applications, databases, files, programs, code, and media that store, share, or manipulate the data, are involved with the processes, or are used by people and organizations. Technology is both high-tech such as databases and low-tech such as paper copies.

4 – The Interaction Matrix

The **Interaction Matrix** shows relationships, connections, or interfaces between the information life cycle phases and the Key Components of Data, Processes, People and Organizations, and Technology. The questions in each cell help you understand what needs to be known for each Key Component throughout the information life cycle. See *Figure 3.3* for sample questions for each cell of the matrix indicating the interaction between the life cycle phases and the four Key Components. Use the questions to prompt your thinking for additional questions relevant to your circumstances.

The questions can be answered from a current state (as-is) perspective to help you understand an existing situation. They can be answered again from a future state (to-be) perspective when modifying the existing situation to better manage the data. They can be used to design new processes to ensure nothing is missed. An experienced business analyst will immediately recognize these questions and see how the information perspective will enhance the work they would be doing anyway.

The output of the interaction matrix is not a huge matrix with tiny text answering each question. Rather use the questions to guide your thinking (and trigger additional questions) about what should be covered within the scope of your project, what is "just enough" information, how the answers will be documented, and the form of the resulting artifacts. Remember this is a framework with concepts. Put these concepts into practice using the instructions and examples in *Chapter 4: The Ten Steps Process*. Look for opportunities to reuse artifacts in subsequent projects.

5 – Location (Where) and Time (When, How Often, and How Long)

Always account for **location** and **time** – where and when events, activities, and tasks take place, when information will be available, and how long it needs to be available. For example, where are the users located? Where are those who maintain the data located? In which time zones are they? Does this impact their ability to access, update, or manage the data? Has the data been updated in a timely manner? Is there a required time period for which the data must be managed before it is archived or deleted? How long does it take for the data to move from system to system? Are adjustments to processes needed to account for location or time?

Note that the top half of the FIQ, along with the first bar, answers the interrogatives of who, what, how, why, where, when, and how long. Note: The Framework for Information Quality was developed independently of the Zachman Framework for Enterprise Architecture. Both address the same interrogatives, but for different reasons.

6 – Broad-Impact Components

Broad-impact components are additional factors that affect the quality of information. They are indicated as bars below the upper sections of the FIQ. These broad-impact components should be considered throughout the POSMAD Information Life Cycle as they affect the four Key Components of Data, Processes, People/Organizations, and Technology. Each bar contains the name of a category along with several words that describe the category. This is not meant to be a comprehensive list, but to provide enough context so you understand the topic. Think of how these broad-impact components are discussed in your organization and use the words most meaningful to your environment.

Interaction Matrix Detail with Sample Questions
From the Framework for Information Quality (FIQ)

Key Components / Information Life Cycle	Plan	Obtain	Store & Share	Maintain	Apply	Dispose
Data (What)	What are the business needs and project objectives? Which data supports them? What are the applicable business rules, data standards, other data specifications?	Which data is acquired (internal and external)? Which data is entered into the system (individual data elements and/or new records)?	Which data is stored? Which data is shared? What is the key data to be backed up for rapid recovery after a disaster?	Which data is updated and changed? Which data will be transformed for sharing, migration, integration? Which data is calculated or aggregated?	What information is needed/available to support business needs, requirements, transactions, automated processes, analytics, decision making, metrics, etc.?	Which data needs to be archived? Which data needs to be deleted?
Processes (How)	What are the high-level processes? Detailed activities and tasks? What is the training and communication strategy?	How is data acquired from sources (internal and external)? How is data entered into the system? What are the triggers for creating new records?	What is the process for storing data? What is the process for sharing data?	How is data updated? Monitored to detect change? Assessed for impact? How are standards maintained? Triggers for updates?	How is the data used? Triggers for use? How is information accessed and secured? How is information made available for those using it?	How is data archived? How is data deleted? How are archive locations/processes managed? Triggers for archival? For final deletion?
People/Orgs (Who)	Who identifies/prioritizes business needs and project objectives? Who develops project plans? Who assigns resources? Who manages those involved in this phase?	Who acquires information from sources? Who enters new data/creates records? Who manages those involved in this phase?	Who develops and supports the storing technology? Who develops and supports the sharing technology? Who manages those involved in this phase?	Who decides what should be updated? Makes changes in system and ensures quality? Who needs to know about changes? Who manages those involved in this phase?	Who directly accesses the data? Who uses the information? Who manages those involved in this phase?	Who sets retention policy? Who can delete data? Who archives data? Who does final disposal? Who needs to know? Who manages those involved in this phase?
Technology (How)	What is the high-level architecture within scope of the project? What technology supports the business needs, processes, and people?	How is the technology used to load new records or create new data in the system?	What is the technology for storing the data? What is the technology for sharing the data?	How is data maintained and updated in the system?	What technology allows access to information? How are business rules applied in the application architecture?	What technology is used to delete data or records from system? What technology is used to archive data and how is it used?

v12-20

© 2005, 2020 Danette McGilvray, Granite Falls Consulting, Inc. www.gfalls.com

Figure 3.3 POSMAD interaction matrix detail with sample questions.

The first letter of the first word in each bar creates the acronym RRISCCE (pronounced "risky"). This is a reminder that it is RRISCCE (risky) to ignore these broad-impact components. The risk of poor-quality data will be lowered by ensuring that components have been addressed. If they are not, the risk of poor-quality data increases.

Requirements and Constraints—Requirements are obligations that must be met. Data and information must support the ability of the organization to meet these obligations. Constraints are limitations or restrictions, that is, things that cannot or should not be done. Often looking from the point of view of "what I cannot do" uncovers additional considerations. The constraints then can often be stated in the positive to make a requirement. Sources of requirements and constraints can come from, or be based on, categories such as business, user, functional, technology, legal, regulatory, compliance, contractual, industry, internal policies, access, security, privacy, and data protection. Considering each of the categories will help uncover important items that must be met (requirements) or avoided (constraints) by the data itself or the project processes and outputs.

Responsibility—Responsibility refers to the fact that many people should answer for their part in ensuring high-quality data. Data work is done by people who, hopefully, know their roles and responsibilities. Expectations for participation are set. Avenues for interaction and decision-making are clear. Consider how to motivate and recognize people for the work they do. Other words which indicate these ideas include accountability, authority, ownership, governance, stewardship, motivation, and reward. Many organizations have formal programs around governance and stewardship that identify who is responsible for what data and who can make decisions about it. Governance organizes venues for interaction and communication so issues can be raised, decisions made, issues resolved, and changes implemented. The idea of stewardship means that whoever touches the data knows to care for it, not only for their own immediate needs, but also on behalf of others in the organization who also use the data. Motivation and reward highlight that if people are incentivized to take actions that ensure high-quality data, there is a greater likelihood they will do so.

Improvement and Prevention—Continuous improvement and prevention are reminders that having high-quality data is not accomplished through a one-time project or a single data clean-up activity. A client asked one of my colleagues, Bob Seiner, "How long do we have to do this data quality work?" His answer: "How long do you want high-quality data?" This encompasses continuous improvement, root causes, correction, audit, controls, monitoring, metrics, and targets. This category refers to the need to identify root causes and implement ongoing processes and activities to prevent issues from reappearing, in addition to correcting the data. Audits determine if requirements are being fulfilled. Controls are monitored, using metrics and targets to trigger notifications when something goes wrong. Metrics and targets also provide a point of comparison to help interpret data quality assessment results. Prevention is included in both the category name and the list to emphasize the importance of prevention, which is often overlooked.

Structure, Context, and Meaning—This broad-impact component lists topics that provide structure, context, and meaning to data. Generally, structure refers to the relationship and organization of parts and how they are arranged together. Context is the background, situation, or conditions surrounding something. Meaning refers to what something is or is intended to be, and can also include the purpose or significance of something. In order to manage the quality of data, we must understand how data is structured, how it relates to other data, the context in which it is used, and what it means. It is impossible to effectively manage anything that is not understood. Topics include definitions, relationships, metadata, standards, reference data, data models, business rules, architecture, semantics, taxonomies, ontologies, and hierarchies. *Table 3.1* briefly describes each of the terms.

Data Specifications is an overarching term used in the Ten Steps methodology when implementing these concepts. Data Specifications include any information and documentation that provide context, structure, and meaning to data. They provide information needed to make, build, produce, assess, use, and manage data and information. Without the existence, completeness, and quality of data specifications it is difficult to produce high-quality data and harder to measure, understand, and manage the quality of data content.

In this book, Data Specifications focuses on metadata, data standards, reference data, data models, and business rules. Yet any of the topics in this broad-impact component could be relevant to your business needs and project objectives. If so, include them within the scope of your project. Many resources are available for these topics if you need more depth and detail.

Communication—Communication is as essential to the success of any data quality effort as uncovering root causes. Communication is part of the work, not something that gets in the way of the work. Communication is required to build trust and confidence. This broad topic includes awareness, engagement, outreach, listening, feedback, education, training, documentation, etc.

Change—Change encompasses management of change and associated impact, organizational change management, and change control. Management of change or organizational change management (OCM) includes managing transformations within organizations to ensure culture, motivations, rewards, and behaviors are aligned and encourage desired results. People are often reluctant to change. "Oh, I'm fine with change, just don't do anything different!" Achieving high-quality data may trigger adjustments to roles and responsibilities, refine a process, fix a technology bug – all things that require change (large or small). Change control relates to technology and covers such things as version control and handling changes to a datastore and resulting impact on downstream screens or reports. If all kinds of change are not managed, they greatly increase the risk of NOT having improvements implemented and sustained. Data professionals need to increase their skills in managing change or partner with others who have this expertise.

Ethics—Ethics consider the implications of choices we make about the use of data on individuals, organizations, and society. Ideas which embody this broad-impact component of ethics include: individual and societal good, justice, rights and freedoms, truthfulness, standards of conduct, avoiding harm, and supporting well-being. Given the holistic approach to data quality in the Ten Steps methodology, these are also behaviors necessary for those who touch or use data in any way.

Table 3.1   Terms and Definitions for Structure, Context, and Meaning (an FIQ Broad-Impact Component)

Structure, Context, and Meaning. Generally, **structure** refers to the relationship and organization of parts and how they are arranged together. **Context** is the background, situation, or conditions surrounding something. **Meaning** refers to what something is or is intended to be, and can also include the purpose or significance of something. In order to manage the quality of data, we must understand how data is structured, how it relates to other data, the context in which it is used, and what it means. It is impossible to effectively manage anything that is not understood. The topics related to these concepts are briefly described in the remainder of this table. You will see how many are closely related to each other.

Note that Data Specifications is an overarching term used in the Ten Steps methodology when implementing these concepts. In this book, Data Specifications focuses on metadata, data standards, reference data, data models, and business rules. However, if any of the other topics in this broad-impact component are relevant to your business needs, include in the project scope and objectives. Use other resources for detail as needed.

Topics	Definitions
Definitions	A **definition** is a statement of the meaning of a word or phrase. It is a general term used here as a reminder that a basic aspect of high-quality data is that the data is defined, and the meaning is understood. Having a clear definition helps the data be created, maintained, and used correctly and consistently across the organization. Definitions relate closely to semantics and ontologies.
Relationships	**Relationship** is a general term for a connection or association between data. Understanding relationships is essential for managing data quality, as many expectations about data may be expressed in terms of relationships. Data models, taxonomies, ontologies, and hierarchies all show relationships.
Metadata	**Metadata** literally means "data about data." Metadata describes, labels, or characterizes other data and makes it easier to filter, retrieve, interpret, or use information. More on metadata can be found later in this chapter in a separate section of the same name and in the section *Data Categories*.
Standards	A **standard** is a general term for something that is used as a basis of comparison. With data quality the main focus is on data standards, which are agreements, rules, or guidelines on how data is named, represented, formatted, defined, and/or managed. They indicate a level of quality to which data should conform. A separate section on data standards can be found later in this chapter.
Reference Data	**Reference data** are sets of values or classification schemas that are referred to by systems, applications, datastores, processes, dashboards, and reports, as well as by transactional and master records. Examples include lists of valid values, code lists, and product types. Another example, ISO, International Organization for Standardization, has created a standard for country codes, known as ISO 3166. These codes can be downloaded and used as a reference table by business units across a global organization. More on reference data can be found in a separate section of the same name and in the section *Data Categories* later in this chapter.
Data Models	A **data model** is a visual representation, supported by text, of data structures in a specified domain. The data model may be either: 1) Business-oriented – representing what is important to an organization, visualizing the structure of an organization's data without regard to technology; 2) Technology-oriented – representing a specific collection of data in terms of a particular data management approach, showing where data will be held and how they will be organized (relational, object oriented, NoSQL, etc.). Data models are primary artifacts through which an organization represents its data to itself and through which it understands its data. A separate section on data models can be found later in this chapter.
Business Rules	A **business rule** is an authoritative principle or guideline that describes business interactions and establishes rules for actions. The behavior of data resulting from business actions can be articulated as requirements or data quality rules and then checked for compliance. Data quality rule specifications explain, at the physical datastore level, how to check the quality of the data, which is an output of the adherence (or non-adherence) to the business rules and business actions. Data is the output of a business process, and violations of data quality rules can mean that the process is not working properly – whether the process is carried out manually by people or automated with technology. It could also mean that the rule was incorrectly captured or misunderstood. Business rules can be collected to provide input for creating data quality rules, checking them, and analyzing the results of the assessments. The lack of well-documented business rules often plays a part in data quality problems. A separate section on business rules can be found later in this chapter. Ronald Ross, known as the "father of business rules," has several books on the subject for those wanting more detail.
Architecture	Generally, **architecture** refers to components of a structure or system, how they are organized, and their relationship to each other. Many are familiar with architecture as it applies to the design of buildings, open areas, and their environments. According to the DAMA-DMBOK® 2nd edition (DMBOK2), Enterprise Architecture encompasses the domains of: "1) Business architecture, which establishes requirements for data, application and technology, 2) Data architecture, which manages data created and required by business architecture, 3) Application architecture, which acts on specified data according to business requirements, and 4) Technology architecture, which hosts and executes the application architecture." For more information see *Chapter 4: Data Architecture* in the DMBOK2.

(Continued)

Table 3.1 Terms and Definitions for Structure, Context, and Meaning (an FIQ Broad-Impact Component) *(Continued)*

Topics	Definitions
	The Zachman Framework™ is a well-known structure for Enterprise Architecture which comprises a set of fundamental representations relevant for describing an enterprise. It indicates different types and levels of architecture within an organization (an enterprise). It was first developed by John Zachman in 1987, continued to evolve until the latest version in 2011, and is still in use today.
	All domains of architecture can establish requirements with which data must comply, but those dealing with data quality will look to data architecture as the guide, the master blueprint, for data within their organization. Information life cycle management, data models, definitions, data mapping, and data flows are elements of data architecture used within the Ten Steps Process.
Semantics	**Semantics** generally relates to the meaning of things, such as what a word, sign, or a sentence means, or is interpreted to mean. To manage the quality of data, what the data means and what people think it means must be known. Within the data and technology worlds, there are approaches based on semantics which are used to develop more flexible application software packages.
Taxonomies	**Taxonomies** classify things into ordered categories. For example, animals and plants are classified as kingdom, phylum, class, order, family, genus, and species. The Dewey Decimal system, used by libraries to classify books by divisions and subdivisions, is another taxonomy. These taxonomies must be understood in order to manage the data which supports them. Taxonomies are also created to better manage data itself, control vocabulary, build drill-down type interfaces, and to assist with navigation and search.
	A related term, **folksonomy,** is derived from "folk" and "taxonomy" and occurs primarily through tagging (adding metadata to content). It is also known as social tagging, collaborative tagging, social classification and social bookmarking. Users create digital content tags to categorize or annotate forms of data such as websites, pictures, and documents. These tags create an informal, unstructured taxonomy (as opposed to the structured taxonomies mentioned above) and are used to more easily locate content. Using the data in the tags gives improved content visibility, classification, and searchability. (See www.techopedia.com, folksonomy)
Ontologies	From the world of philosophy, **ontology** is the science or study of being or the existence of things. From a data point of view, data should represent what exists. In this context, an ontology is a set of formal definitions for concepts, including how the concepts relate to one another. Data can be understood and cross-referenced through ontologies.
Hierarchies	A **hierarchy** is a system of things ranked one above the other. It is a type of taxonomy. A parent-child relationship is a simple hierarchy. Other examples: an organizational chart, a chart of accounts in finance, or a product hierarchy. Some data relationships, and with them, expectations for quality, can be understood through hierarchies.

7 – Culture and Environment

The explanation of the FIQ started with section 1, which provides the context and backdrop to the other sections. This last section of Culture and Environment plays a similar role: it provides the context behind *all* the other sections and components in the FIQ. In other words, culture and environment impact all aspects of your information quality work. They should inform all your data quality work, but often they are not intentionally considered. **Culture** refers to an organization's attitudes, values, customs, practices, and social behavior. It includes both written (official policies, handbooks, etc.) and unwritten "ways of doing things," "how things get done," "how decisions get made," and so forth. **Environment** refers to conditions that surround people in your organization and affect the way they work and act. Examples are financial services versus pharmaceutical; government agencies versus publicly traded companies. Culture and environment can also refer to broader aspects of society, country, language, and other external factors, such as politics, that impact the organization and may affect the data and information and how they are managed.

This is not to say that you cannot be creative in how you approach your information quality work. However, you will better accomplish your goals if you understand and can work effectively with the culture and environment of your company. For example, a company that is highly regulated and is already used to following documented standard operating procedures will most likely have less difficulty accepting standardized processes to ensure information quality than will a company where everyone operates independently. Even within a company you may find differences. For example, discussing information quality with a sales team may take on a different look and feel than discussing it with an IT team.

Quick Assessment Parameters

The concepts in the Framework for Information Quality will be applied in various levels of detail throughout the Ten Steps Process. The FIQ can also be used at a high level to quickly ascertain a situation. The FIQ provides a logical structure for understanding the components that contribute to information quality. By understanding these components (along with the details in the POSMAD interaction matrix), you can better analyze a situation or complex environment where you are having information quality problems.

Suppose someone has contacted you regarding a data quality issue. You can immediately start asking questions such as:

- What business needs are associated with this situation?
- In which phase of the information life cycle is the problem appearing?
- Which data, specifically, is involved?
- Which processes are involved?
- Which people and organizations are involved?
- Which technology is involved?
- What happened to the data in the earlier phases of the life cycle?
- How will data in the later phases of the life cycle be impacted?
- Which broad-impact components have been addressed? Which areas need further attention?

Answers to these questions will help you understand the initial business impact, determine the scope of the issue and who needs to be engaged in solving it. Answers will help you uncover linkage points to other business areas and systems. Potential root causes may also be highlighted.

You can also use the FIQ to help when analyzing existing processes or developing new processes to ensure that you have accounted for the components that will impact data quality. Imagine how much more stable your processes would be (and how much better the resulting quality) if you could account for what was happening to your data, processes, people, and technology throughout the information life cycle.

Determine the phase(s) of the information life cycle that are within scope of your project. Realize that quality is affected by all phases but that real work must have manageable and specific boundaries. Of course, you cannot address everything at once and will need to prioritize your efforts. For example, one project team realized they had spent much time and effort in the Obtain phase of the information life cycle but had not spent any time managing the Maintain phase. They decided their next project would focus on how they were updating and maintaining their information. Knowing the larger picture can help you put together an approach to addressing what is most important now and what will be addressed at a later time.

The Information Life Cycle

As the information life cycle is so important to managing information quality, we will expand on the idea of the life cycle introduced earlier.

Information is a resource and is essential to performing business processes and achieving business objectives, just as money, products, facilities, and people are resources. Any resource should be properly managed throughout its life cycle in order to get the full use and benefit from it. In reality, you will have to make choices about which information life cycle phases you have the time and resources to address at any given time. Understanding the concept of a life cycle will help you make better choices about priority.

 Key Concept

Information is an asset that should be properly managed throughout its life cycle in order to get the full use and benefit from it.

The Life Cycle of Any Resource

In his 1999 book, *Improving Data Warehouse and Business Information Quality*, Larry English talks about a universal resource life cycle that consists of processes required to manage any resource – people, money, facilities and equipment, materials and products, and information. Many thanks to him for teaching me about the universal resource life cycle (Plan, Acquire, Maintain, Dispose, Apply). I modified the names and reordered the processes of the life cycle slightly from his original and call them phases. I added "Store and Share" and developed the acronym POSMAD (for Plan, Obtain, Store and Share, Maintain, Apply, Dispose). POSMAD is a reminder of the phases in the

information life cycle. Larry provided the examples for activities within each of the phases for financial, human, and information resources used in this section.

The high-level phases in the information life cycle, as I apply them, are described as follows:

- **P**lan – Prepare for the resource
- **O**btain – Acquire the resource
- **S**tore and Share – Hold information about the resource and make it accessible for use through some type of distribution method
- **M**aintain – Ensure the resource continues to work properly
- **A**pply – Use the resource to support and address business needs (customers, strategies, goals, issues, opportunities)
- **D**ispose – Remove or discard the resource when it is no longer of use

For financial resources you *plan* for capital, forecasting, and budgeting; *obtain* financial resources by borrowing through a loan or selling stock; *maintain* financial resources by paying interest and dividends; *store* financial information in systems or filing cabinets and *share* through networks, screens, reports, websites or mail; *apply* financial resources by purchasing other resources; and *dispose* of the financial resources when you pay off the loan or buy back the stock.

For human resources you *plan* for staffing, identify necessary skills and write job descriptions; *obtain* human resources by recruiting, interviewing, and hiring; *maintain* human resources by providing compensation (wages and benefits) and developing skills through training; *apply* human resources by assigning roles and responsibilities and putting people to work; and *dispose* of human resources through retirement or "downsizing" or through employees leaving of their own accord.

Phases of the Information Life Cycle

The information life cycle may also be called a data life cycle, information chain, data or information supply chain, information value chain, or the information resource life cycle. "Lineage" is currently a popular word, particularly used by vendors to describe tool functionality that documents and manages the information life cycle. Provenance, meaning what is the origin, is another word that indicates a subset of the life cycle. If you hear any of these words or phrases, recognize that they refer to what I call the information life cycle.

As mentioned, POSMAD refers to the six phases in the information life cycle. *Table 3.2* describes the phases and provides examples of activities within each phase of the life cycle as they apply to information.

Value, Cost, Quality, and the Information Life Cycle

It is important to understand value, cost, and quality in relation to the information life cycle (see *Figure 3.4*). Following are some key points:

- There is a cost to managing activities in all phases of the information life cycle.
- The quality of the data and information quality are affected by activities in all phases of the information life cycle. This includes activities to manage the data itself, the processes, people

Table 3.2 POSMAD Information Life Cycle Phases and Activities

Information Life Cycle Phase (POSMAD)	Definition	Example Activities for Information
Plan	Prepare for the resource	Identify objectives, plan information architecture, and develop standards and definitions. When modeling, designing, and developing applications, databases, processes, organizations, etc., many activities could be considered part of the Plan phase for information.
Obtain	Acquire the resource	Create records, purchase data, load external files, etc.
Store and Share	Hold information about the resource (electronic or hardcopy) and make it accessible for use through some type of distribution method	Store data electronically in a datastore, as hardcopy such as a paper application form, as a digital file such as a scanned copy of an application. Share information about the resource through networks or an enterprise service bus. Make available via screens, reports, websites or email. Make information in hardcopy available via mail, posters on the wall, or product tags on a store shelf.
Maintain	Ensure the resource continues to work properly	Update, change, manipulate, parse, standardize, validate, or verify data; enhance or augment data; cleanse, scrub, or transform data; de-duplicate, link, or match records; merge or consolidate records, etc.
Apply	Use the resource to support and address business needs (customers, products, services, strategies, goals, issues, opportunities)	Retrieve data; use information. This includes all information usage: completing a transaction, writing a report, making a management decision from information in those reports, running automated processes, etc.
Dispose	Remove or discard the resource when it is no longer of use	Archive information; delete data or records. Manage the disposition of data when a company goes out of business or an organization shuts down.

and organizations, and technology, plus the broad-impact components illustrated in the Framework for Information Quality.

- It is only when the data and information are applied that the company receives value from them. If the information is what the knowledge worker/information consumer/user expected and they can apply the information, then it has value to the company. If the quality is not what the knowledge worker needs, then that information has a negative impact on the business – from lost revenue, increased risks and costs, rework, etc.
- You can determine the costs of data and information and its value to the organization.

While the organization and its information consumers really only care about the information when they want to use it, appropriate resources must be devoted in every phase in the life cycle in order to produce the data and information at the right level of quality when it is needed. In reality, you cannot do everything at once. It may not be practical or feasible to address all phases of the life cycle at the same time. However, you should know enough about what happens in each phase and carefully consider how the information is being managed (or needs to be managed) in every phase so you can make informed decisions about investing in your information resource.

 Key Concept

"There is an economic formula for enterprise profitability and survival. The economic formula is simple. Economic Value occurs when the benefit derived from a resource's application is greater than the costs incurred from its planning, acquisition, maintenance, and disposition."

– Larry English, *Improving Data Warehouse and Business Information Quality* (1999), p. 2

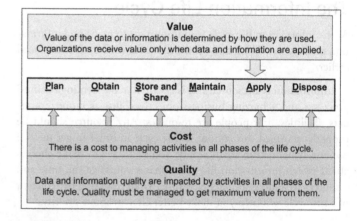

Figure 3.4 Value, cost, quality, and the information life cycle.

Information is a Reusable Resource

A major difference between information as a resource and other resources is that information is not consumed when it is used. This means multiple people or systems can use the same information – it is reusable. Once a product is purchased by a customer, it is no longer available for the next customer to buy. Once materials are used to build that product, they are not available to be used in the next manufacturing cycle. What happens with information? Just because Sam runs a report on the first of the month, does the information disappear when Maria runs her report on the tenth, or when Patel accesses the information to help a customer? Of course not! When information is used it is not depleted. The implications of this difference are important:

- **Quality is critical.** Information is used in many ways by many people, organizations, processes, and technology. If the information is wrong, the wrong information is used again and again – with negative results. And each time that poor-quality information is used, more costs are incurred, and revenue can be lost.

- **The value of the information increases the more it is used.** Many of the costs for planning, obtaining, storing, sharing, and maintaining the information have been expended. Often with little or no incremental cost, the data and information can be used in additional ways to help the organization.

The Information Life Cycle – Not a Linear Process

We have talked about the life cycle as if in the real world these activities happen in a very clear, recognizable order. This is not the case. See *Figure 3.5*. The graphic on the left illustrates the phases in the information life cycle. Note that the life cycle is NOT a linear process and is very iterative. The graphic on the right is a simplified example of an organization's architecture showing where data is stored and how it flows between systems – one way of indicating an information life cycle. I call this the "spider web" picture. Every organization has one and even at a high level, these flows are complex.

For example, suppose you purchase information from an external source. The data is received by your company and stored – maybe initially in a temporary staging area. The data is then filtered and checked before being loaded into the internal database. Once in the database the data is available for others to apply – some of the data is retrieved through an application interface. Other data may be shared through a mechanism called an enterprise service bus and loaded into another database where many in the company access and use it through yet a different application. Data can also be maintained in various ways – by updating individual fields and records through an application interface or by receiving and loading updates from a file sent by an external data provider. This is a simple example, but it is easy to see how the information path quickly becomes very complicated. There can be multiple ways that any piece of data or set of information is obtained, maintained, applied, and disposed of. The same information can also be stored in more than one place.

It is because activities in the real world *are* complicated and messy that knowing the information life cycle is so helpful. To manage the information and its quality, it is important to sort out where the data is going, how it is obtained/created, maintained, applied and disposed of and how it is impacted by the processes, people and organizations, and technology. Using the information life cycle helps us recognize what is happening to the information in a complex environment. For example, examine the various activities in a complicated process and place them in the various phases of the information life cycle to enhance your understanding of how those activities impact the quality of the data. Answering the questions in the POSMAD interaction matrix previously discussed (in *Figure 3.3*) is another way of providing clarity.

Information Life Cycle Thinking

If a data quality problem comes to light, place the issue in the phase of the information life cycle where it was first identified. This gives you a location to work backwards from to analyze the activities taking place, in which phases, that could have adversely impacted the data. You can also work forward to understand who else is using the data and could either be affected now by the same problems or should be consulted later before changes are made. I advocate the idea of "life cycle thinking," which can be applied in many ways. Using life cycle thinking helps you immediately start to understand (or start asking the right questions to discover) what is happening to your data from any view in your company. Let's look at a few examples.

Life Cycle Thinking from an Organizational Point of View.

Use the POSMAD information life cycle thinking as a framework for understanding who impacts information from a high-level organizational point of view. Assume you are newly responsible for the customer information that supports the Sales and Marketing functions in your company. You want to get an idea of where the customer information is used, and which organizations impact the quality. The head of Sales and Marketing for Europe in one global company was concerned about the quality of the customer data that supported his organization. He described his organization to me, and I drew a high-level organizational chart on the board. A Call Center, Marketing,

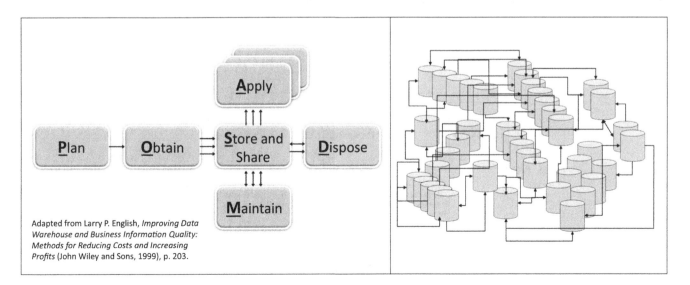

Figure 3.5 The information life cycle is not a linear process.

and Field Sales were the three main departments under the manager's geographical organization (in this case Europe Sales and Marketing). We chose to look further at the organizational structure under Marketing, which consisted of four teams – Business Intelligence, Customer Information Management, Marketing Communications, and Business Segments.

After a very brief tutorial on the information life cycle, I asked which teams impacted the customer information in each of the life cycle phases: Who uses or applies the customer information? Which have input into planning for their customer information? Which obtain or create the data? Who maintains the data? Who can dispose of the data? *Figure 3.6* shows the result of that 30-minute conversation. Examine it and see what you can learn about information quality – just with what is shown here and at this high level of detail.

Note that I asked the questions starting with the Apply phase (why we care about information quality) and did not discuss the Store and Share phase. You can use life cycle thinking without having to include every phase in every conversation. The purpose here was to understand, at a high-level organizational point of view, who was impacting the customer information in the relevant (for this conversation) phases of the information life cycle.

As shown in the figure, five of the six teams used or applied the customer information. Four teams have input when planning for the customer information. The Call Center, Customer Information Management, Marketing Communications, and Field Sales all obtain the information in various ways, but only three of these teams maintain or update it. This makes sense, as often the data obtained from Marketing Communications come from field events and this team sees each customer signing in as a new one. Therefore, we can already see that to avoid duplicate customer records there needs to be a process for identifying existing records in the customer database when adding new customer records obtained through Marketing Communications. At this early stage, we don't know if that is happening or not, but we have more information to guide additional questions.

A potential data quality problem can be seen when asking the question, "Do all teams that obtain the data receive the same data entry training and do they have the same set of data entry standards (whether manual or automated)?" If the answer is no, you can be sure you have a data quality problem – you just don't know yet how big it is or which pieces of data are most affected. You can also see that the Call Center obtains, maintains, applies, and disposes of the customer information, yet is not involved in the planning phase. Thus, important requirements could be missed and could impact data quality. There is more you can learn from this illustration, but it shows how you can start seeing potential impacts to data quality even at this point.

Life Cycle Thinking from a Customer Interaction Point of View.

Now let's look at the life cycle from another view – that of where the company has interaction with its customers. *Figure 3.7* starts with the customer and shows multiple communication methods between the company and the customer, the storage of the customer data in the database, and the various uses of customer information. Some uses of the information include re-contacting the customer. Once again, the various phases of the information life cycle are indicated. Note that this time we chose not to include the Plan or Dispose phases, but we did include Store and Share.

What can you learn from this viewpoint? If I am a customer and I register through the company website, a record is created in the customer database. Months later I attend a tradeshow and the sales rep in the same company's vendor booth scans my name tag. Another record is created. Both the records flow to the customer database. When records are loaded from different sources, are they checked to see if a record for that customer already exists and are the records merged? We don't know the answer to that question from this graphic. We do know that if they are not checked, there *are* duplicate records for customers in that database. We don't know the duplication rate or if it is causing a problem, but even at this level we can see potential sources of data quality problems which provide clues of areas to investigate as part of our project.

An unexpected lesson for the team during this exercise was seeing the list of ways their customer information was being used. If you were to ask, most managers would know that Account Management

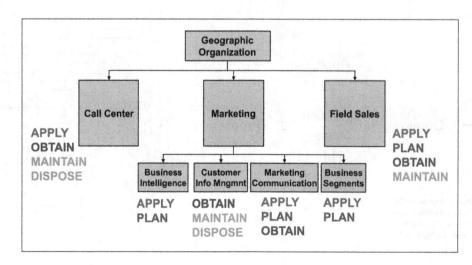

Figure 3.6 Organizational structure and the POSMAD information life cycle.

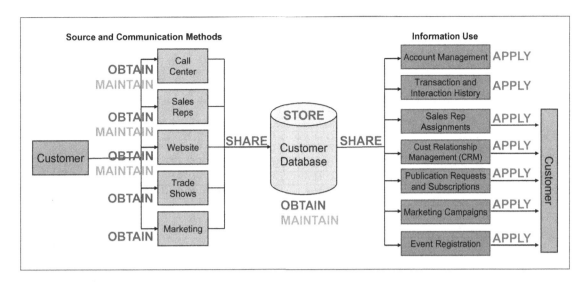

Figure 3.7 Interactions with customers and the POSMAD information life cycle.

uses customer information and Sales Rep Assignments also rely on it. But somehow just seeing this simple list of how customer information was used by both Sales and Marketing, and seeing these were critical activities for the year, built the business case for the data quality project.

Life Cycle Thinking from a Roles and Data Point of View.

You have seen how to apply life cycle thinking at a high level (the organizational and customer interaction points of view). Let's go to a different level of detail of life cycle thinking – yet another view – that of roles. *Figure 3.8* lists roles down the first column. Information is shown as headings in the columns to the right, with some being single data fields (e.g., Title) and others being multiple data fields grouped together (e.g., Address). Note that only three of the information life cycle phases are used (Obtain, Maintain, and Apply).

The team looked at each role and noted if the role obtained, maintained, and/or applied the corresponding customer information. Analyze each row and each column. The rows show the breadth of the data being impacted by each role. The columns show all the roles that impact a specific group of data.

A question can be raised similar to the one asked when looking at POSMAD at the organizational level: "Do all roles that obtain the data (e.g., create customer records) receive the same training and have the same set of data entry standards?" If not, once again, that means there *is* a data quality problem. You don't know the magnitude or which specific data is most affected, but you know the lack of consistent training and standards does result in lower quality data.

One project team knew that many departments could apply or use the same data, but they thought only one department could create or update them. Through applying life cycle thinking they found that people in other departments actually had the ability to create and update data. The impact to data quality could immediately be seen: No consistent training or standards for entering data across the teams means poor-quality data. This information gives you the knowledge to make some educated

statements about your information quality and where you want to focus your efforts.

In *Figure 3.8*, you can also see three roles that only apply the information; they do not collect or maintain it. What often happens in that situation is that the needs of those knowledge workers are not taken into consideration when obtaining the data. For example, pharmacists at one drug store chain needed to track information about customers but there was no place to enter it on their screen. So, they added codes to the end of the customer's name and a variety of symbols that indicated things like alternate insurance, suspected of shoplifting, and whether the patient had another record under a different name. Later the mailroom created labels for an offer that was sent to customers. Complaints started coming in from those who received letters with names on the mailing label that looked like "John Smith INS2 ! * check Rx comments to see alternate name." This is an example of what is called "hijacking" a field. Business and processes change, and people need to collect and use information that was not accounted for when the system was put in place. They make use of other data fields to fill their needs. This results in data quality problems, impacts other uses of the data and can have negative consequences, such as the one just described.

To summarize, the information life cycle is an essential concept and component of the Framework for Information Quality. It will be used throughout the Ten Steps Process. Every application, every set of information, and every piece of data has its own life cycle. Information life cycles intersect, interact with, and impact each other. One system's Apply is another system's Obtain. Information life cycle thinking applies to both internal data and external data brought into your organization. See *Figure 3.9*. Create and use the life cycle at the level of detail most helpful at any point in the project. The information life cycle will help you see what is happening to your information and the associated data, processes, people/organizations, and technology and how they impact the quality of the data. Using life cycle thinking helps you make better informed decisions and take effective action to manage the quality of your data.

Business Roles That Obtain, Maintain, or Apply the Information								
O = Obtain information								
M = Maintain information								
A = Apply information		Information						
		Contact Name	Site Name	Division	Dept.	Address	Phone	Title	Profile
Field Engineer	O, M, A	O, M, A	O, M, A	O, M, A	O, M, A	O, M, A	O, M, A	O, M, A
District Manager	O, M, A	O, M, A	O, M, A	O, M, A	O, M, A	A	O, M, A	O, M, A
Customer Service Reps	O, M, A	O, M, A	O, M, A	O, M, A	O, M, A	O, M, A	O,M	
Order Coordinators	O, M, A	O, M, A	O, M, A	O, M, A	O, M, A	O, M, A		
Quote Coordinators	O, M, A	O, M, A	O, M, A	O, M, A	O, M, A	O, M, A	O, M	
Collection Coordinators	A	A	A		A			
Business Center Mailroom		A	A		A			
On-line Tech Support	O, M, A	O, M, A	O, M, A	O, M, A	O, M, A	O, M, A	O, M, A	O, M, A
Sales Finance		A	A		A	A		
Information Management Team	O, M, A	O, M, A	O, M, A	O, M, A	O, M, A	O, M, A	O, M, A	O, M, A

(Business Roles)

Figure 3.8 Roles and the POSMAD information life cycle.

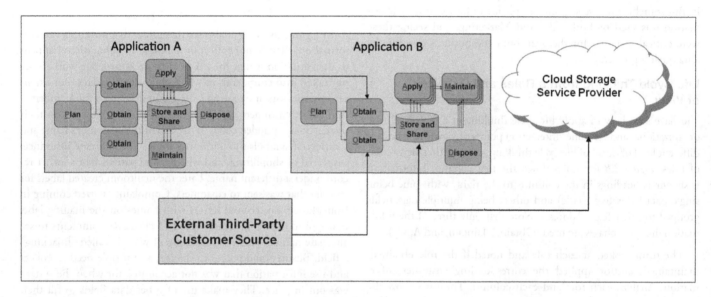

Figure 3.9 Information life cycles intersect, interact with, and impact each other.

Data Quality Dimensions

Data quality dimensions are characteristics, aspects, or features of data. They provide a way to classify information and data quality needs. Dimensions are used to define, measure, and manage the quality of data and information. This section introduces you to data quality dimensions and why they are important.

An easy way to think about dimensions is to think about a diamond. If you're purchasing a diamond for jewelry or investment purposes, you can understand its quality through a standard for describing diamonds, known as the 4Cs – color, clarity, cut, and carat weight. According to the GIA, a nonprofit source of gemological knowledge, "Until the middle of the twentieth century, there was no agreed-upon standard by which diamonds could be judged. GIA created the first, and now globally accepted standard for describing diamonds…Today, the 4Cs of Diamond Quality is the universal method for assessing the quality

of any diamond, anywhere in the world. The creation of the Diamond 4Cs meant two very important things: diamond quality could be communicated in a universal language, and diamond customers could now know exactly what they were about to purchase."

Consumers often add two more C's to their list: cost and conflict-free. Depending on what you want to buy (a ring, a necklace, or earrings, for instance) some of the C's will be more important to you than others. If the diamonds are for industrial use to cut, grind, drill, and polish, then hardness and heat conductivity are the most important, not the 4Cs.

In the same way, depending on the business needs, data quality issues, and how the data is used, some of the data quality dimensions will be more important than others. They provide a way to assess the quality of data and can be used to help those who use the data understand its quality.

Key Concept

Data Quality Dimensions – what they are and how to use them. A data quality dimension is a characteristic, aspect, or feature of data. Data quality dimensions provide a way to classify information and data quality needs. Dimensions are used to define, measure, improve, and manage the quality of data and information.

The data quality dimensions in the Ten Steps methodology are categorized roughly by the techniques or approach used to assess each dimension. This helps to better scope and plan a project by providing input when estimating the time, money, tools, and human resources needed to do the data quality work.

Differentiating the dimensions in this way helps to: 1) match dimensions to business needs and data quality issues, 2) prioritize which dimensions to assess and in which order, 3) understand what you will (and will not) learn from assessing each data quality dimension, and 4) better define and manage the sequence of activities in your project plan within time and resource constraints.

Reasons for Data Quality Dimensions

Each data quality dimension requires different tools, techniques, and processes to measure it. This results in varying levels of time, money, and human resources to complete the assessments. You can better scope your project by understanding the effort required to assess each of the dimensions. Select the data quality dimensions that, if assessed, will give you information to help address the business needs and project objectives within scope. Initial assessment of a data quality dimension results in setting a baseline. Additional assessments may be needed during the course of your project. After the project is completed, data quality dimensions can be built into your operational processes as part of ongoing monitoring and information improvement.

Differentiating the dimensions of data quality helps you:

- Match dimensions against business needs and project objectives
- Prioritize which dimensions to assess and in which order
- Understand what you will (and will not) get from assessing each data quality dimension
- Better define and manage the sequence of activities in your project plan within time and resource constraints

Data Quality Dimensions as Used in the Ten Steps

There is no universal standard list of data quality dimensions, though there are similarities between them. Each of the data quality dimensions as used in the Ten Steps Process is defined in *Table 3.3*. The dimensions included are those features and aspects

Table 3.3	Data Quality Dimensions in the Ten Steps Process – Names, Definitions, and Notes

Data Quality Dimensions – what they are and how to use them. A data quality dimension is a characteristic, aspect, or feature of data. Data quality dimensions provide a way to classify information and data quality needs. Dimensions are used to define, measure, improve, and manage the quality of data and information. Instructions for assessing the quality of data using the following dimensions are included in *Step 3 – Assess Data Quality* in *Chapter 4: The Ten Steps Process.*

Notes: The data quality dimensions in The Ten Steps methodology are categorized roughly by the techniques or approach used to assess each dimension. This helps to better scope and plan a project by providing input when estimating the time, money, tools, and human resources needed to do the data quality work. Differentiating the data quality dimensions in this way helps to: 1) match dimensions to business needs and data quality issues, 2) prioritize which dimensions to assess and in which order, 3) understand what you will (and will not) learn from assessing each data quality dimension, and 4) better define and manage the sequence of activities in your project plan within time and resource constraints.

Substep	Data Quality Dimension Name, Definition, and Notes
3.1	**Perception of Relevance and Trust.** The subjective opinion of those who use information and/or those who create, maintain, and dispose of data regarding: 1) Relevance – which data is of most value and importance to them, and 2) Trust – their confidence in the quality of the data to meet their needs. Notes: It is often said that perception is reality, and people act in accordance with their perceptions. Users' feelings about relevance and trust influence whether they readily accept and use the organization's data and information (or not). If users believe the data quality is poor, it is less likely they will use the organization's data sources or they will create their own spreadsheets or databases to manage their data. This leads to the proliferation of "spreadmarts" with duplicate and inconsistent data, often without adequate access and security controls in place. This dimension gathers the opinions of those who use and/or manage the data and information through a formalized survey (individual interviews, group workshops, online surveys, etc.). While in contact with users, it makes sense to ask questions about both the value/business impact and trust in data quality. Because the reason for surveying the users could be prompted from either the data quality or business impact viewpoint, it is included as both a Data Quality Dimension in *Step 3.1* and as a Business Impact Technique in *Step 4.7*. *Opinions* about the quality of the data can be compared to other data quality assessment results showing the *actual* data quality. This allows you to uncover and address any gaps between perception and reality. An assessment of the Perception of Relevance and Trust could be conducted on an annual or biennial basis much as employee satisfaction surveys are conducted. Results are compared for trends over time and to ascertain: 1) If the data being managed is still relevant to the users, and 2) If actions to prevent data quality issues are leading to expected increases in trust of the data.
3.2	**Data Specifications.** Data Specifications include any information and documentation that provide context, structure, and meaning to data. Data Specifications provide information needed to make, build, produce, assess, use, and manage data and information. Examples include metadata, data standards, reference data, data models, and business rules. Without the existence, completeness, and quality of data specifications it is difficult to produce high-quality data and harder to measure, understand, and manage the quality of data content. Notes: Data specifications provide the standard against which to compare data quality assessment results. They also provide instructions for manually entering data, designing data load programs, updating information, and developing applications.

(Continued)

Substep	Data Quality Dimension Name, Definition, and Notes
	Table 3.3 Data Quality Dimensions in the Ten Steps Process – Names, Definitions, and Notes *(Continued)*
3.3	**Data Integrity Fundamentals.** The existence (completeness/fill rate), validity, structure, content, and other basic characteristics of data.
	Notes: Most other dimensions of quality build on what is learned in Data Integrity Fundamentals. If you don't know anything else about your data, you need to know what is learned in this assessment. Data Integrity Fundamentals uses the technique of data profiling to assess basic characteristics of data such as completeness/fill rate, validity, lists of values and frequency distributions, patterns, ranges, maximum and minimum values, precision, and referential integrity. What other lists may call out as separate dimensions of data quality (e.g., completeness and validity) are part of this overarching dimension because all can be assessed using the same technique of data profiling.
	Note that this dimension *assesses* the quality, which is different than how you may choose to *report* results on a report or dashboard. You may want to report completeness and validity separately, for example, or you may combine results and report quality by a particular data field or dataset. Don't confuse the reporting categorization and presentation with the detail you need to know and learn from this data quality dimension.
3.4	**Accuracy.** The correctness of the content of the data as compared to an agreed-upon and accessible authoritative source of reference.
	Notes: The word accuracy is often used by some as a synonym for data quality in general. Data professionals know they are not the same. Data accuracy requires comparing the data to the real-world object it represents (the authoritative source of reference). Sometimes it is not possible to access the real-world object represented by the data, and in those cases a carefully chosen substitute for it may be used as the authoritative source of reference. The assessment of accuracy can be a manual and time-consuming process. Following are examples of what is learned through assessing Data Integrity Fundamentals using the technique of data profiling compared to what is learned in an Accuracy assessment:
	• Data profiling reveals if an item number contains a valid code indicating a make or buy part, but only an accuracy assessment using someone familiar with item #123 can determine if that particular item actually is a make item or a buy item.
	• Data profiling shows if a customer record has a valid pattern for a postal code, but only an accuracy assessment that contacts the customer or uses a secondary authoritative source such as a postal service list can tell if it is his or her postal code.
	• Data profiling displays the value for the number of products on hand in an inventory database and confirms it is the correct data type. But only by completing an accuracy assessment with someone manually counting or scanning products on the shelf and comparing that number to the record in the inventory system can you know if the inventory count in the database is an accurate reflection of the inventory on hand.
3.5	**Uniqueness and Deduplication.** The uniqueness (positive) or unwanted duplication (negative) of data (fields, records, or datasets) existing within or across systems or datastores.
	Notes: There are many hidden costs associated with duplicate records. For example, duplicate vendor records with the same name and different addresses make it difficult to ensure that payment is sent to the correct address. When purchases by one company are associated with duplicate master records, the credit limit for that company can unknowingly be exceeded. This can expose the business to unnecessary credit risks.
	Identifying duplicates requires different processes and tools than Data Integrity Fundamentals, Accuracy, or the other data quality dimensions.
3.6	**Consistency and Synchronization.** Equivalence of data stored or used in various datastores, applications, and systems.
	Notes: Equivalence is the degree to which data stored in multiple places are conceptually equal. The same technique of data profiling used in Data Integrity Fundamentals can be used on the same data as it appears in multiple datastores or datasets. Results are compared for consistency. Consistency and Synchronization is called out as a separate data quality dimension because each datastore that is compared adds time and work to your project. If it is necessary, it should be done, but knowing that you are assessing Consistency and Synchronization, in addition to Data Integrity Fundamentals will help you better plan for the additional resources and time required.
3.7	**Timeliness.** Data and information are current and ready for use as specified and in the time frame in which they are expected.
	Notes: This data quality dimension is easily added onto Consistency and Synchronization if the factor of how long it takes for the data to move from one datastore to another is a concern. It is called out separately here because you may or may not want to look at Timeliness. It is easy to add in or take out as needed.
	As the world changes, there will always be a gap between when the real-world object changes and when data representing it is updated in a database and ready to be utilized. This assessment can also examine the timing of data throughout its life cycle and determine if data is being updated in time to meet business needs.
3.8	**Access.** The ability to control how authorized users can view, modify, use, or otherwise process data and information.
	Notes: Access is often summed up as enabling the right individuals to access the right resources, at the right times, under the right circumstances. Defining the right individuals, right resources, right times, and right circumstances are business decisions, which need to balance enabling access against protecting sensitive data and information. Other functions such as Information Security or a separate Access Management team often typically manage access. Your data quality team should work closely with them if your project addresses this data quality dimension of Access.

Substep	Data Quality Dimension Name, Definition, and Notes
Table 3.3	Data Quality Dimensions in the Ten Steps Process – Names, Definitions, and Notes *(Continued)*
3.9	**Security and Privacy. Security** is the ability to protect data and information assets from unauthorized access, use, disclosure, disruption, modification, or destruction (US Department of Commerce, n.d.). **Privacy** for an individual is the ability to have some control over how data about them as a person is collected and used. For an organization, it is the ability to comply with how people want their data to be collected, shared, and used. Notes: Securing and protecting data require specialized expertise. This dimension does NOT replace that. However, data professionals should find and work with information security teams and others responsible for privacy in their organizations to ensure: 1) Appropriate security and privacy safeguards are in place for the data with which they are concerned, 2) They understand the security and privacy requirements with which the data they manage must comply. The data quality dimension of Access (*Step 3.8*) is focused on access for *authorized* users. Security also includes access, but it is focused on *unauthorized* access. The Information Security world (InfoSec) often talks about protecting through the CIA Triad: Confidentiality, Integrity, and Availability.
3.10	**Presentation Quality.** The format, appearance, and display of data and information support their collection and uses. Notes: Presentation quality applies to user interfaces, reports, surveys, dashboards, etc. Presentation quality can affect the quality of the data when it is *collected*. For example, does a dropdown list contain valid options or codes? Are questions framed in such a way that users understand what is being asked and can provide correct responses? Are the various methods for collecting the same data presented in a consistent manner? Presenting information in a way that is understandable from the user's perspective increases the quality of data from the time of collection. In this respect, good presentation quality is an excellent way to prevent data quality errors. Presentation quality also applies when *using* the data. For example, is the user interpreting a report correctly? Does it have descriptive column headings and include dates? Do the graphics, reports, or user interfaces correctly reflect the data behind them? If the data in the datastore is of high quality itself but is misunderstood when shown to a user, you still do not have data quality.
3.11	**Data Coverage.** The comprehensiveness of data available compared to the total data universe or population of interest. Notes: This dimension looks at how the datastore reflects the total population of interest to the business. For example, a database should contain all customers in North and South America, but there are concerns that the database really reflects only a portion of the company's customers. Coverage in this example is the percentage of customers actually captured in the datastore compared to the population of all customers that should be in it. This dimension is more in-depth than general decisions made about population, coverage, and selection criteria when developing the project data capture and assessment plans.
3.12	**Data Decay.** Rate of negative change to the data. Notes: Knowing data decay rates helps determine whether mechanisms should be put into place to maintain the data and what the frequency of those updates should be. This dimension is an example where just the idea of the dimension can spur you to action, often without the need for an in-depth assessment. Volatile data requiring a high reliability level requires more frequent updates than data with a lower decay rate or data where the quality level may not need to be so high. If essential data is already known to change quickly, then efforts should also quickly move to finding solutions. Determine how to become aware of the change in the real world. Develop processes where data can be updated within the organization as soon and as close to the real-world change as possible.
3.13	**Usability and Transactability.** Data produces the desired business transaction, outcome, or use for which it was intended. Notes: This dimension is a way to determine if the data is fit for purpose and is a final checkpoint of data quality. Even if the right people have defined business requirements and prepared data to meet them, the data must produce the expected outcome or use – or we still do not have high-quality data. Can the data be used to complete a transaction? Can the invoice be created? Can a sales order be completed? Can a lab order be produced? Can an insurance claim be initiated? Can an item master record be used properly when building a Bill of Materials? Can a report be correctly generated? If the answer is no, we still do not have high-quality data.
3.14	**Other Relevant Data Quality Dimensions.** Other characteristics, aspects, or features of data and information that are deemed to be important for your organization to define, measure, improve, monitor, and manage. Notes: There may be characteristics of data that are specific to an organization, uses of the data, or aspects of a data quality issue that are not already covered in the list of data quality dimensions. For example, within one corporate finance group, the main concern was reconciliation between systems. Some could call this completeness, but the word "reconciliation" is clearer to them and specific to their context. If another dimension is chosen, it can still be used within the context of the full Ten Steps Process, just like any of the others.

of data that provide the most practically useful information about data quality which most organizations are interested in, and are feasible to assess, improve, and manage within the usual constraints of most organizations. They have been proven through years of experience and are also based on knowledge learned from other experts.

Instructions for conducting an assessment for each of the dimensions can be found in *Step 3 – Assess Data Quality in Chapter 4*, with a separate substep for each of the dimensions as noted in the table. The dimensions are numbered for reference purposes and do not propose the order for completing the assessments. Suggestions

for helping you select the DQ dimensions most relevant to your needs and to include in your project are discussed below.

Many lists of data quality dimensions exist and may use different terms or categories for different purposes than shown here. Once again, the dimensions used in the Ten Steps are categorized roughly by how you would assess each dimension. For example, the dimension of Data Integrity Fundamentals includes what other lists may call out as separate dimensions (e.g., completeness and validity). Both, along with other characteristics of data, are part of the overarching dimension called Data Integrity Fundamentals because all can be assessed using the technique of data profiling.

Warning! Do not get overwhelmed by the list of data quality dimensions. You will not assess all of them. Having them categorized this way actually makes it easier for you to select the ones most relevant to your business needs and data quality issues.

Why Having Multiple Data Quality Dimensions is Helpful

Having multiple dimensions helps you make better choices about where and how to spend your time and effort. They help you:

- Select those dimensions that will help address the high-priority business needs, data quality issues, and project objectives within scope, while balancing them against available time and resources.
- Perform dimensions in the most effective order. Use the suggestions below to determine which dimensions should be done first.
- Better define and manage the sequence of activities within each chosen dimension using the instructions for each dimension in *Step 3 – Assess Data Quality* in *Chapter 4*.
- Understand what you will and will not learn from the various data quality assessments.

Considerations for Selecting Data Quality Dimensions

Choose the dimensions most meaningful to your situation. This is a simple statement, but it is often hard to know how to begin. At first glance, many of the data quality dimensions will seem pertinent.

As emphasized many times, always start with the business needs.

Know your business needs—If you are not sure where to focus your data quality project, use *Perception of Relevance and Trust* early in *Step 1 – Determine Business Needs and Approach*. Survey the users of the information to either: 1) uncover issues they are having which will provide an initial list of candidate issues for the project, or 2) prioritize an already-existing list of data quality issues and business needs to finalize the project scope. Remember that *Perception of Relevance and Trust* is both a data quality dimension (*Step 3.1*) and a business impact technique (*Step 4.7*).

Initial and final lists—Once the business needs and high-priority issues have been determined, develop a preliminary list of data quality dimensions to assess. This list may change once additional information is uncovered in *Step 2 – Analyze Information Environment*. At the start of *Step 3 – Assess Data Quality*, finalize the data quality dimension(s) to be assessed.

If you are looking in detail at the content of the data and once you are clear on the business needs, the following recommendations can help you decide which data quality dimensions to assess:

Data Specifications—Data Specifications (data standards, data models, business rules, metadata, and reference data) are important because they provide the standard against which to compare the results of the other data quality dimensions. If you have concerns that data specifications are missing or incomplete or if nothing was done on data specifications in *2.2 – Understand Relevant Data and Data Specifications*, you may want to start with *Step 3.2*. Once relevant data specifications have been collected,

decide if the quality of the specifications is good enough to meet the project needs. If you think they are good enough, move on to *Step 3.3 – Data Integrity Fundamentals*. If the quality of the relevant specifications is suspected to be poor, then you may decide to take time first to update them.

In practice, at this point most people are ready to look at the actual data and do not want to spend time on more specifications and requirements. If you really can't convince the team otherwise, try to have a minimum level of specifications and add to them as you go through your other assessments. If you begin with no specifications or requirements, just realize that you will have to get them at some point in order to analyze the results of other data quality assessments.

It is not unusual to find that poor-quality data specifications end up being one of the root causes of the data quality problems you find when assessing the other dimensions. Once you have proven the need for good data specifications, you can come back to this dimension. However, if you are fortunate enough to have support to start with data specifications, by all means do so!

Once you have your data specifications (at whatever level of detail), it is strongly recommended that you assess *Step 3.3 – Data Integrity Fundamentals*.

Data Integrity Fundamentals—If looking in depth at your data, start with *Step 3.3 – Data Integrity Fundamentals*. Here you learn the fundamentals of validity, structure, content, and other basic characteristics of your data. If you don't know anything else about your data, you need to know what this dimension provides. This assessment profiles the data and provides a snapshot of your data in time. It provides facts (not opinions) about your data, shows where the problems are, and the magnitude of those problems. Most other dimensions of quality build on what is learned from Data Integrity Fundamentals. Having said that, as important as Data Integrity Fundamentals is – and this dimension *is* essential and necessary – it is not always *sufficient* for what you need to know about your data. As needed, build on what is learned there by using other data quality dimensions.

Data Quality Dimensions work together—As mentioned, most other dimensions of quality build on what is learned from Data Integrity Fundamentals. It is tempting to skip this dimension because others may seem more important. Often people will say their major concern is duplicate records. You may want to jump to *Uniqueness and Duplication (*in *Step 3.5)* and skip Data Integrity Fundamentals all together. That would be a mistake. Even if understanding duplicates is your end goal, you should still profile your data first, because you need to know the basics about your data in order to understand duplication. Here is why.

Determining duplication requires an understanding of which data field, or combination of data fields, indicates uniqueness of a record. Whether using third-party tools or developing your own, algorithms to identify duplicate records are developed or configured. Those algorithms may be based on fields that are actually missing expected data (e.g., have a low completeness rate), that contain data that should not be there (e.g., an identification number is in a phone number field), or the quality of the data is poor (e.g., incorrect values in a country field). If the *input* is incorrect, then the *output* of your de-duplication process will also be incorrect. It is through Data

Integrity Fundamentals that you see the actual content of those data fields upon which deduplication efforts depend.

I learned this lesson years ago. The business was concerned about duplicates, so we went straight to Uniqueness and Deduplication where we chose the combination of data elements to indicate a unique record and configure the algorithms. Several times we modified the input, and still did not get valid results. After many cycles and lost time, we finally assessed Data Integrity Fundamentals where we found one of the fields we "knew" was essential for indicating uniqueness only had a 20 percent completeness/fill rate. That meant only 20 percent of the records had a value in that field. No wonder we could not get good results in identifying duplicates! Even if you're using sophisticated tools that claim to have algorithms needing minimal human intervention, know your data, look closely at the results, and make sure you understand what is behind the tool's deduplication approach.

Once Data Integrity Fundamentals has been completed, choose other dimensions based on your project scope and objectives and time available. For example:

- **Consistency and Synchronization** *(in Step 3.6)* can use the same techniques used in Data Integrity Fundamentals – just use them on multiple datasets and compare results.
- **Timeliness** *(in Step 3.7)* links closely to Consistency and Synchronization, by adding the time element to the assessment.
- To determine **Data Decay** *(in Step 3.12)*, you can do additional calculations on create dates and update dates after you complete Data Integrity Fundamentals or an assessment of Accuracy.
- After assessing **Coverage** *(in Step 3.11)*, you may determine that some of the issues there are the result of problems with *Access* (in *Step 3.8*) so you do further assessment there.
- **Presentation Quality** *(in Step 3.10)* relates to many of the other dimensions, because poor presentation when collecting the data or reporting the data can be a cause of perceived or real data quality problems.

Remember that you can use parts of various data quality dimensions to put together a plan to assess the most relevant aspects of the data within scope.

Another Method for Prioritizing Data Quality Dimensions

What if you are still having a hard time selecting which data quality dimensions to assess? Even using these suggestions, you may still have a list too long to be assessed within the schedule and using the resources available. In this case, use the prioritization technique in *Step 4.8 – Benefit vs. Cost Matrix*. Look at benefits and costs against the list of potential data quality dimensions to prioritize those dimensions of most benefit to assess for this project.

Don't make this too difficult. Simply list each quality dimension, quickly determine the possible benefit to the business (high to low) and estimated/perceived effort (high to low). The costs associated with assessing data quality dimensions can vary widely depending on the dimension you choose to assess and tools used.

Map your choices to the matrix. Don't do in-depth research; just make your best judgment based on what you know now. Balance the benefit against resources available for the assessment. Select the dimensions to assess. Document the dimensions chosen, the rationale behind the decisions, and assumptions on which the decisions were made. Then move quickly to begin your first-priority assessment.

Final Criteria for Selecting Data Quality Dimensions

To finalize which data quality dimensions to assess, ask yourself these two questions:

- ***Should*** **I assess the data?** Only spend time testing when you expect the results to give you actionable information related to your business needs, data quality issues, and project objectives.
- ***Can*** **I assess the data?** Is it possible or practical to look at this quality dimension? Sometimes you cannot assess the quality of the data, or the cost to do so is prohibitive.

Only assess those dimensions when you can answer yes to both questions!

If the answer to either question is "No," then do NOT assess that dimension – doing so will be a waste of time and money.

Remember, the assessment results should point to the nature of the data quality problems, where they are located, and the magnitude of the problems. This information guides where to spend time on root cause analysis and provides input to determining prevention and correction activities.

Business Impact Techniques

Business impact techniques are used to determine the effects of data quality on the business. They include both qualitative and quantitative measures and also methods for prioritizing.

Whenever a data quality problem is found, the first two words usually spoken by management are, "So what?" Management wants to know, "What impact does this have on the business?" and "Why does it matter?" Another way of saying it is, "What is the value of having information quality?" These are important questions. After all, no one has the money to spend on something that is not worthwhile. The business impact techniques help answer those questions and are the basis for making informed investment decisions for your information resource.

Business impact should focus on how the information is used – is it needed to complete transactions, create reports, make decisions, run automated processes, or provide an ongoing source of data for another downstream application? Information uses are part of the Apply phase of the POSMAD information life cycle discussed earlier in this chapter. Business impact can also look at costs in any phase of the information life cycle.

Details for the business impact techniques are described as part of the Ten Steps Process in *Step 4 – Assess Business Impact*. Each business impact assessment aligns with a business impact technique (e.g., anecdotes, usage, or process impact).

Key Concept

Business Impact Techniques – what they are and how to use them. A business impact technique is a qualitative and/or quantitative method for determining the effects of the quality of the data on the business. These effects can be good effects from high-quality data and/or adverse effects from poor-quality data. Results from the business impact techniques help make the usually intangible aspects of data tangible and meaningful to those who have to make tough investment decisions. Business impact is another way of expressing the idea that there is value in having quality information. It is only by showing business impact that management can understand the value of information quality. Use results from assessing business impact to gain support from management, establish the business case for data quality, motivate team members to participate in the project, and determine appropriate investments in your information assets.

Reasons for Business Impact Techniques

Results from the business impact techniques help make the usually intangible aspects of data tangible and meaningful to those who have to make tough investment decisions. Business impact is another way of expressing the idea that there is value in having quality information. It is only by showing business impact that management can understand the value of information quality. Use results from assessing business impact to:

- Gain support for data quality work and investments from wherever it is needed – boards, executives, senior leaders, and other managers
- Establish the business case for data quality work generally, specific projects, or necessary improvements
- Motivate team members to participate in the project and encourage their managers to support their participation
- Determine optimal levels of investment

Business Impact Techniques as Used in the Ten Steps

Each of the business impact techniques as used in the Ten Steps Process are defined in *Table 3.4*. Instructions for conducting an assessment of the techniques are in *Step 4 – Assess Business Impact* in *Chapter 4*, with a separate substep for each of the techniques as noted in the table. The dimensions are numbered for reference purposes and do not impose an order for completing the assessments. Suggestions for selecting the business impact techniques to use in your project follow the table.

Warning! Do not get overwhelmed by the list of business impact techniques. You will not use all of them. You may, however, use one

Table 3.4 Business Impact Techniques in the Ten Steps Process – Names, Definitions, and Notes

Business Impact Techniques – what they are and how to use them. A business impact technique is a qualitative and/or quantitative method for determining the effects of the quality of data on the organization. These effects can be good effects from high-quality data and/or adverse effects from poor-quality data. Instructions for assessing business impact using the following techniques are included in *Step 4 – Assess Business Impact* in *Chapter 4: The Ten Steps Process*.

Results from assessments using the business impact techniques help make the usually intangible aspects of data tangible and meaningful to those who have to make tough investment decisions. Business impact is another way of expressing the idea that there is value in having quality information. It is only by showing business impact that management can understand the value of information quality.

Use what is learned about business impact to help establish the business case for data quality improvements, gain support from management for data quality work, prioritize efforts, motivate team members to participate in the project, and determine appropriate investments in your information resource.

Substep	Business Impact Technique Name, Definition, and Notes
4.1	**Anecdotes.** Collect examples of the negative impact of poor-quality data and/or the positive impact of good-quality data. Notes: Collecting anecdotes is the easiest and most low-cost way of assessing business impact. Anecdotes are used to rapidly illustrate why focusing on data quality is important. The right example, told as an interesting story using your best communication skills and targeted for the audience, can stimulate interest and engage leadership and practitioners quickly.
4.2	**Connect the Dots.** Illustrate the connection between business needs and the data which supports them. Notes: A quick way to ensure the data being assessed or managed is actually the data that is relevant to the customers, products, services, strategies, goals, issues, or opportunities of concern to the business and within scope of the project.
4.3	**Usage.** Inventory the current and/or future uses of the data. Notes: An easy way to demonstrate the importance of data and information by listing the processes and people/organizations that rely on them.
4.4	**Five Whys for Business Impact.** Ask "Why?" five times to recognize the real effects of the quality of data on the business. Notes: A quality technique often used in manufacturing where asking "Why?" five times usually gets you to the root cause of a problem. This same technique can be used by asking deeper questions five times – of why, who, what, where, when – to get to the real business impact.
4.5	**Process Impact.** Illustrate the effects of data quality on business processes. Notes: Workarounds become a normal part of business processes and hide the fact that they are often a result of poor-quality data. Duplication of effort, costly problems, distractions, wasted time, rework, and lower productivity are other effects. By showing the impact of poor-quality data on the processes, the business can make informed decisions about improving issues that were previously unclear. Alternatively, high-quality data can be shown to make business processes more efficient and cost effective.

Table 3.4	Business Impact Techniques in the Ten Steps Process – Names, Definitions, and Notes *(Continued)*
Substep	Business Impact Technique Name, Definition, and Notes
4.6	**Risk Analysis.** Identify possible adverse effects from poor-quality data, evaluate the likelihood of them happening, severity if they do, and determine ways to mitigate the risks. Notes: Risk is often related to physical dangers at home or in the workplace. Risk analysis is included here as a business impact technique because poor-quality data has the potential of exposing an organization to damage.
4.7	**Perception of Relevance and Trust.** The subjective opinion of those who use information and/or those who create, maintain, and dispose of data regarding: 1) Relevance – which data is of most value and importance to them, and 2) Trust – their confidence in the quality of the data to meet their needs. Notes: This dimension gathers the opinions of those who use and/or manage the data and information through a formalized survey (individual interviews, group workshops, online surveys, etc.). While in contact with users, it makes sense to ask questions about both the value/business impact and trust in data quality. Because the reason for surveying the users could be prompted from either the data quality or business impact viewpoint, it is included as both a Data Quality Dimension in *Step 3.1* and as a Business Impact Technique in *Step 4.7*. Depending on where you are in the project, survey results help to determine which data (the most relevant) should have first priority to include in the project scope, to assess for quality, or to implement ongoing controls.
4.8	**Benefit vs. Cost Matrix.** Rate and analyze the relationship between benefits and costs of issues, recommendations, or improvements. Notes: This uses a standard quality technique of comparing benefits and costs. This technique can be used in several places within the Ten Steps Process to review and prioritize alternatives and provide answers to questions such as: • Which data quality issues should be the focus of our efforts? (*In Step 1 – Determine Business Needs and Approach*) • Which data quality dimensions should we assess? (in *Step 3 – Assess Data Quality*) • Which issues learned from a data quality assessment are impactful enough to continue to root cause analysis? (in *Step 5 – Identify Root Causes*) • Which recommendations for improvements (prevention and correction) should we implement? (In *Step 6 – Develop Improvement Plans*)
4.9	**Ranking and Prioritization.** Rank the impact of missing and incorrect data on specific business processes. Notes: Prioritizing indicates relative importance or value. Something with a high priority, then, implicitly has a higher impact on the business. The importance of data quality will vary for different data and will vary for different usage of the same data. This technique brings together those who actually use the data to rank the effect of incorrect and missing data on their associated business processes.
4.10	**Cost of Low-Quality Data.** Quantify costs and the impact to revenue due to poor-quality data. Notes: Poor-quality data costs the business in many ways: waste and rework, missed revenue opportunities, lost business, etc. This technique quantifies the costs and revenue impact that may have been understood only through stories or observation.
4.11	**Cost-Benefit Analysis and ROI:** Compare anticipated costs of investing in data quality to potential benefits through an in-depth evaluation, which may include calculating return on investment (ROI). Notes: Cost-Benefit Analysis and ROI are standard management approaches to making financial decisions. This detailed information may be required before considering or proceeding with any significant financial investment – and investments in information quality are often considerable. Management has the responsibility to determine how money is spent and will need to weigh investment options against each other.
4.12	**Other Relevant Business Impact Techniques:** Other qualitative and/or quantitative methods for determining the effects of the quality of data on the business that are deemed important for your organization to understand. Notes: There may be other techniques used by an organization to assess the effects of data quality that are not already covered in the list of business impact techniques.

or more at various points in your project. Having them defined this way makes it easier for you to pick and choose those most relevant to your project at any point in time.

Business Impact Techniques and Relative Time and Effort

Figure 3.10 shows a continuum with the relative time and effort needed to determine business impact for each technique, from generally less complex and taking less time (Technique 1) to more complex and taking more time (Technique 11).

Too often it is felt there is no time to show business impact – that all efforts must go toward the data quality assessments. However,

the importance of being able to show business impact cannot be stressed enough. It is essential to getting any kind of support (time, resources, money, expertise, etc.). When considering business impact, most people think only of fully-quantifying the Cost of Low-Quality Data (Technique 10) or a Cost-Benefit Analysis (Technique 11). Yet a business impact assessment does not always have to be so time-consuming and comprehensive. Much can be learned about business impact through other techniques that require less effort but still provide information to make good decisions.

Placing the techniques on the continuum shows that business impact can be assessed in a variety of ways which take varying levels of time and effort. Therefore, *every* project *can* and *should*

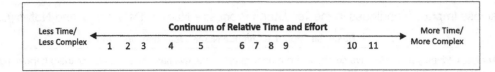

Figure 3.10 Business impact techniques on continuum of relative time and effort.

assess *something* related to business impact – even if done using techniques that take less time and effort. Every technique has been proven to show the value of high-quality data and has been used to gain support for the projects – in the right time and place.

Note that Technique 12 (Other Relevant Business Impact Techniques) is not shown on the continuum. Other techniques you may use could be placed anywhere along the continuum. Apply the idea of relative time and effort as input to planning the use of any business impact technique.

Considerations for Selecting Business Impact Techniques

Use the business impact techniques that you think will give meaningful results (within a reasonable time period, using available resources) to verify the need to take action on data quality. This requires experience and some experimenting to get the right balance. Use your best judgment to focus your efforts with the time and resources at hand, start moving, and adjust your approach if needed later.

Consider the following suggestions when choosing which business impact techniques to use:

Remember, the continuum shows relative effort, not relative results—Less complex techniques do not mean less useful results; nor do more complex techniques necessarily mean more useful results. Used in the right circumstances, *every* business impact technique has proven to show value, and used well, can help get the support you need.

That said, it is usually a good practice to start easy and move to the more complex as needed—If you don't have time to do anything else, start with *Step 4.1 – Anecdotes*. Almost everyone has some story to tell – they experienced it themselves or heard it from others. Something prompted you to start dealing with data quality, and that something is usually found in a situation that can be summarized and retold as an anecdote. Continue to quantify as you are able using other techniques.

Determine who needs to see the business impact and for what purpose—If you are describing business impact to a business analyst or subject matter expert for the purpose of gaining their willing participation on a data quality project, then a full cost-benefit analysis is overkill. If you are in the early stages of raising awareness about data quality, anecdotes or usage may be enough. If you have progressed to the point of getting budget approval, your financial approval process may require the more time-consuming quantification techniques. But even at this stage, don't ignore the power of the other techniques.

Decide if it is possible to assess business impact using a complex/time-consuming technique in a more limited fashion—It may be better to employ a technique against a smaller

scope such as quantifying one process using a small dataset in *Step 4.10 – Cost of Low-Quality Data* rather than quantify nothing at all.

Business Impact Techniques Work Together

The techniques can stand alone, but they are also complementary. Ideas from the various techniques can easily be combined to show business impact. For example, an anecdote can be effective even without quantitative data (*Step 4.1 – Anecdotes*). You can also expand on some aspect of your anecdote with quantitative information as your time permits to research. As you assess impact using other techniques, learn how to quickly tell a story using the facts and figures you have collected.

You may complete a list of the various business processes, people, and/or applications that use data (*Step 4.3 – Usage*) and then employ *Step 4.5 – Process Impact* to visualize the impact of poor-quality data for one or two specific business processes. Further, you can use the techniques in *Step 4.10 – Cost of Low-Quality Data* to quantify the costs associated with those few business processes. Once you have a list of how the data is used or a list of data quality issues, you can draw on *Step 4.8 – Benefit versus Cost Matrix* or *Step 4.9 – Ranking and Prioritization* to determine where to focus your data quality efforts.

Once you have been able to describe business impact through *Step 4.4 – Five Whys for Business Impact* you can use other techniques to further quantify or visualize impact.

Sometimes a full cost–benefit analysis is required (*Step 4.11 – Cost–Benefit Analysis*). It is relatively easy to gather costs (training, software, human resources, etc.). The difficult piece as it applies to data is showing the benefit. You can draw on any of the prior ten techniques to provide input to the benefit portion of a cost benefit analysis. For example, even though in *Step 4.10 – Cost of Low-Quality Data* we express the output as cost of poor-quality data, it can also be phrased as the benefit from having high-quality data.

Data Categories

Data categories describe common characteristics or features of data. They are useful for managing structured data because certain data may be treated differently based on their classification. Understanding the relationship and dependency between the different categories can help direct data quality efforts. For example (using terms that will be defined below), poor-quality master data may come from faulty reference data that was included in the master data record. By being aware of the data categories, a project can save time by ensuring the applicable data categories are included in initial data quality assessments. From a data governance and stewardship viewpoint (see section about the topic in this chapter), those responsible for creating or updating data may differ from one data category to another. Category is a generic term that can be used for any type of categorization. For example, data can be categorized according to sensitivity, medical vs. administrative data, Personally Identifiable Information (PII), etc. The data categories as used in the Ten Steps and discussed in this book (master data, transactional data, reference data, and metadata) are common terms used by those who work with data and are useful for managing data quality.

Key Concept

Data Categories – what they are and how to use them. Data categories describe common characteristics or features of data. They are useful for managing structured data because certain data may be treated differently based on their classification. The data categories as used in the Ten Steps (master data, transactional data, reference data, and metadata) are common terms used by those who work with data. Understanding the relationship and dependency between the different categories can help direct data quality efforts. For example, poor-quality master data may come from faulty reference data that was included in the master data record. For this reason, data from related data categories should be captured and assessed for data quality together.

Data Categories Example

See *Figure 3.11* as I describe a transaction using various data categories. Smith Corp., a US company, sells widgets to federal and state government agencies, commercial accounts, and educational institutions. ABC Inc. is one of their commercial customers (identified as Customer Type 03 in the Reference Data list)

and has been issued a customer identifier number of 9876 (in the master data record). ABC Inc. wants to purchase four blue widgets. The blue widget, product number 90-123, has a unit price which changes depending on the discount given based on customer type.

When the agent from ABC Inc. calls Smith Corp. to place an order, the Smith Corp. customer representative enters ABC Inc.'s customer number in the sales order transaction. ABC Inc.'s company name, customer type, and address are pulled into the sales order screen from its customer master record. The master data is essential to the transaction. When the product number is entered, the product description of "Blue Widget" is pulled into the sales order from the product master data. The unit price is calculated based on the customer type. The unit price for a commercial customer is $100. ABC Inc. purchases four blue widgets for a total price of $400.

Let's look at the data categories included in this example. We have already mentioned that the basic customer information for ABC Inc. is contained in the customer master record. The sales order is transactional data. Some of the data in the master record is pulled from controlled lists of reference data, customer type for example. Smith Corp. sells to four customer types. The four types with associated codes are stored in a separate reference list. Other reference data used in the customer's master record but not shown in the figure includes a list of valid US state codes, which is referenced when creating the address for ABC Inc. A list of shipping options is reference data used when creating the transaction.

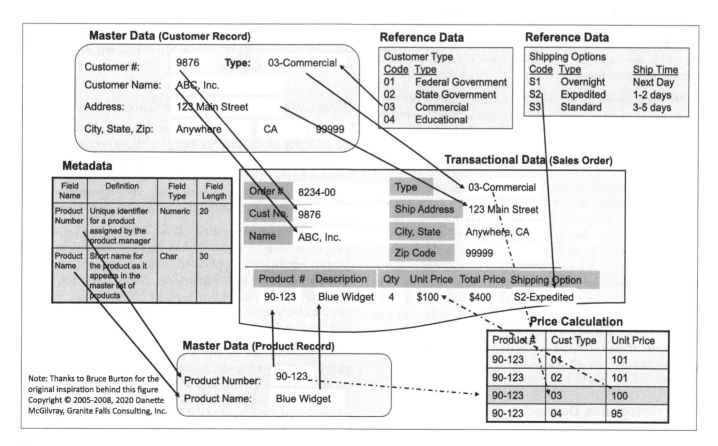

Figure 3.11 An example of data categories.

Reference data are sets of values or classification schemas that are referred by systems, applications, datastores, processes, and reports, as well as by transactional and master records. Reference data may be unique to your company (such as customer type). Reference data can also come from outside of your organization and be used by many companies, such as standardized sets of codes for currencies developed and published by ISO (International Organization for Standardization). In our example, the price calculations further emphasize the importance of high-quality reference data. If the code list is wrong, or the associated unit price is wrong, then the incorrect price will be used for that customer.

Master data describes the people, places, and things that are involved in an organization's business. Examples include customers, products, employees, suppliers, and locations. Gwen Thomas created a song to the tune of "Yankee Doodle" that highlights master data:

Master data's all around
Embedded in transactions
Master data are the nouns
Upon which we take action.

In our example, Smith Corp. has a finite list of customers and a finite list of products that are unique to and important to them – no other company will be likely to have the very same lists. While ABC Inc. is a customer of other companies, how its data is formatted and used by Smith Corp. is unique to Smith Corp. Likewise, Smith Corp.'s product list is unique to them, and the product master record may be structured differently from other companies' product masters.

Transactional data describes an internal or external event or transaction that takes place as an organization conducts its business. Examples include sales order, invoice, purchase order, shipping document, and passport application. In *Figure 3.11*, you can see that the sales order pulls in data from two different master data records. It also uses a list of shipping options, which is reference data specific to the transaction.

Metadata literally means "data about data." Metadata describes, labels, or characterizes other data and makes it easier to filter, retrieve, interpret, or use information. *Figure 3.11* also shows two fields in the product master record. Their definitions, field types, and field lengths are examples of metadata.

Metadata is critical to avoid misunderstandings that can create data quality problems. In the figure, you can see the product master record has a field containing "Blue Widget" that is called "Product Name," but the same field is labeled "Description" in the transactional record screen. In an ideal world, the data would be labeled the same wherever it is used. Unfortunately, inconsistencies such as the one in the figure are common and often lead to misuse and misunderstanding. Having clear documentation of metadata (showing the fields, their names, definitions, etc.) is important for managing the data, having clear screen titles and report headings, and understanding the impact of changes to the data fields. Well documented metadata can also help avoid errors when programming where the data is moved and used by other business functions and applications.

Data Categories Defined

Table 3.5 includes definitions and examples for each of the data categories discussed previously. These definitions were jointly created by the author of this book and Gwen Thomas, Founder of the Data Governance Institute.

Your organization may categorize its data differently than explained above. For example, some companies combine reference data and master data categories and call them master reference data (MRD). Sometimes it is difficult to decide whether a dataset, such as a list of valid values, is only reference data or is also metadata. It has been said that one person's metadata is another person's data. No matter how data is categorized, the important point is that you are clear on what you are (and are not) addressing in data quality activities. You may find that such data quality activities should include data categories not considered previously.

With every new generation of technologies that come out, it is likely that new words for data categories will be introduced. Chances are you will be able to map these new terms to one of the fundamental data categories discussed here. For example, geospatial data has become its own specialized subtype of master data.

Relationships Between Data Categories

Figure 3.12 shows the associations between the various data categories which is useful to understand from a business point of view. Note that some reference data is usually required to create a master data record and master data is usually required to create a transactional record. Sometimes reference data specific to the transaction is needed to create the transactional record and is not pulled in through the master records. Metadata is required to better use and understand all other data categories.

For historical data, corresponding metadata and reference data may need to be maintained and kept with the master and transactional records. If not, important context and the meaning of the data may be lost. Auditors will want to know who updated the data and when – for all categories of data. That is why audit trail data is part of metadata.

Data Categories – Why We Care

It is easy to see from the examples just given that the data categories are highly interrelated. Yet they are differentiated because how each data category is managed and who is responsible often differ. Knowing there are differences brings visibility to the need for coordination between the people, processes, and technology associated with each data category. Without this coordination, data quality will suffer.

High-quality reference data and metadata are key to interoperability, which is the ability to share data and exchange information between databases, applications, and computer systems, either within or outside of your organization. They can also help designate data that should not be shared. Errors in one data category have a multiplying effect as the data continues to be passed on and used by other data.

The quality of master data impacts transactional data, and the quality of metadata impacts all categories. For example, documenting definitions (metadata) improves quality because it transforms undocumented assumptions into documented and agreed-on meanings so the data can be used consistently and correctly. If you have a problem with transactional data, you may have to look at the quality of the master data and the reference data used to create it.

Table 3.5 Data Categories – Definitions and Notes

Data categories describe common characteristics or features of data.

Data categories are useful for managing structured data because certain data may be treated differently based on their classification. The data categories as used in the Ten Steps (master data, transactional data, reference data, and metadata) are common terms used by those who work with data. Understanding the relationship and dependency between the different categories can help direct data quality efforts. For example, poor-quality master data may come from faulty reference data that was included in the master data record. For this reason, data from related data categories should be captured and assessed for data quality together.

Data Category	Data Category Definitions and Notes
Master Data	**Master data** describes the people, places, and things that are involved in an organization's business. Examples include people (e.g., customer, employee, vendor, supplier, patient, physician, student), places (e.g., location, sales territory, office, geospatial coordinate, email address, url, IP address), and things (e.g., account, product, asset, device ID). Notes: Because master data is often used by multiple business processes and IT systems, standardizing master data formats and synchronizing values are critical for successful system integration. Master data tends to be organized as master records, which may include associated reference data. An example is a customer master record which contains an address with a field for state or geographical region. The reference data is the associated list of valid state or regions for that country.
Transactional Data	**Transactional data** describes an internal or external event or transaction that takes place as an organization conducts its business. Examples include sales order, invoice, purchase order, shipping document, passport application, credit card payment, insurance claim, medical visit, and grant application. Notes: Transactional data is typically organized as transactional records, which usually include associated master and reference data. For example, Smith Corp. (Vendor) sold 4 blue widgets (Product) to ABC Inc. (Customer). In this case Vendor, Product, and Customer are master data embedded within the Sales Order transactional record. Some people consider event data as a type of transactional data.
Reference Data	**Reference data** are sets of values or classification schemas that are referred to by systems, applications, datastores, processes, dashboards, and reports, as well as by transactional and master records. Examples include lists of valid values, code lists, status codes, territory or state abbreviations, demographic fields, flags, product types, gender, chart of accounts, product hierarchy, retail website shopping categories, and social media hashtags. Notes: Standardized reference data is key to data integration and interoperability and facilitates the sharing and reporting of information. Reference data may be used to differentiate one type of record from another for categorization and analysis, or they may be a significant fact such as country, which appears within a larger information set such as address. Organizations often create internal reference data to characterize or standardize their own information. Reference datasets are also defined by external groups, such as government or regulatory bodies, to be used by multiple organizations. For example, currency codes are defined and maintained by ISO.
Metadata	**Metadata** literally means "data about data." Metadata describes, labels, or characterizes other data and makes it easier to filter, retrieve, interpret, or use information. **Technical metadata** is metadata used to describe technology and data structures. Examples of technical metadata are field names, length, type, lineage, and database table layouts. **Business metadata** describes the non-technical aspects of data and its usage. Examples are field definitions, report names, headings in reports and on Web pages, application screen names, data quality statistics, and the parties accountable for data quality for a particular field. Some organizations would classify ETL (Extract–Transform–Load) transformations as business metadata. **Label metadata** is used to annotate data or information sets, such as tags, and are usually used with high volumes of data. While metadata for structured data is almost always stored separately from the data itself, with labeled data the metadata and content are stored together. See labeled data below. **Catalog metadata** is used to classify and organize collections of datasets. Examples include a music playlist, lists of available datasets, and smartphone apps. **Audit trail metadata** is a specific type of metadata, typically stored in a log file and protected from alteration, which captures how, when, and by whom the data is created, accessed, updated, or deleted. Examples include timestamp, creator, create date, and update date. Audit trail metadata is used for security, compliance, or forensic purposes. Although audit trail metadata is typically stored in a log file or similar type of record, technical metadata and business metadata are usually stored separately from the data they describe. These are the most common types of metadata, but it could be argued that there are other types of metadata that make it easier to retrieve, interpret, or use information. The label for any metadata may not be as important as the fact that it is being deliberately used to support data goals. Any discipline or activity that uses data will have associated metadata, even if that metadata is not recognized and documented as such.

(Continued)

Table 3.5 Data Categories – Definitions and Notes *(Continued)*

Data Category	Data Category Definitions and Notes
Additional data categories that impact how systems and databases are designed and data is used:	
Aggregate Data	**Aggregate data** refers to information that is collected from multiple records or sources and compiled into summaries. Recognizing the distinction between the detailed data and the aggregate data may be important when reporting or determining access to data. For example, the total number of medical staff deployed per month is reported publicly, but the names and other identifiers of individual staff are confidential.
Historical Data	**Historical data** contains significant facts, as of a certain point in time, which should not be altered except to correct an error. Historical data is important to security and compliance. Operational systems can also contain history tables for reporting or analysis purposes. Examples include point-in-time reports, database snapshots, and version information.
Reporting/ Dashboard Data	We see **reporting data** (that is, data used in reports and dashboards), not as a separate data category, but one of many uses of data. However, some may consider this its own data category. Challenges to the quality of data in a report or dashboard are typically addressed at the source of the data that is fed into the report. However, poor visualization of reports or dashboards can contribute to misunderstanding or misinterpretation, which is itself a form of data quality problem, even though the content may be correct.
Sensitive Data	Sensitive data (or restricted data) is information that must be protected against unauthorized access. Sensitivity labels are assigned to information sets to aid in implementing access, privacy, and security controls. Sensitive data is associated with elevated risk, if it is viewed by those who are not authorized to see it. Most organizations implement security and/or privacy controls to add additional protection for sensitive data to protect it from unauthorized viewing. It is important to note that "Sensitive Data" can have specific meanings in particular regulatory contexts (e.g., data protection/privacy laws). Also, while data about people might be considered "sensitive" in an organization, some data (e.g., health related data or data about religious beliefs or political opinions) may be subject to a higher standard of "sensitivity". Information may be considered sensitive for a variety of reasons. It might describe business deliberations, proprietary models, or trade secrets. It could describe investigations into criminal or ethical behavior, information subject to attorney-client privilege, or content subject to non-disclosure agreements. It could include information whose disclosure could compromise security or safety. Personally Identifiable Information (PII) is a unique type of sensitive data where privacy efforts work to ensure that individuals' PII is not shared or used inappropriately or without the individuals' consent. Certain subsets of PII such as health data may have further regulatory restrictions around their use. To protect sensitive data, military and intelligence organizations employ a system that matches sensitivity labels (top secret, secret, confidential, sensitive but unclassified, and unclassified) against formal clearance levels issued to individuals. Most organizations are not that formal, but they do employ terms to indicate the sensitivity of sets of data. An example is Public (meaning that it can be shared outside of the organization), Company Confidential (meaning that it can be shared within the company), or Highly Confidential (meaning that it should be shared only with those who have a clear reason to see it.) Individual facts, or discrete data elements, may be classified as sensitive. When combined with other data, the larger dataset would then be also considered sensitive data.
Temporary Data	**Temporary data** is kept in memory to speed up processing. It is not viewed by humans and is used for technical purposes. Examples include a copy of a table that is created during a processing session to speed up lookups.
The terms below are not data categories as used in the Ten Steps. They are uses of, or collections of, data which may include master data, transaction data, reference data, and metadata and can benefit from using what is covered in this book.	
Measurement Data	**Measurement data** is often captured in high volumes and at high velocity. It is captured via meters, sensors, radio frequency identification (RFI) chips and other devices and transmitted by machine-to-machine connections. These connections, along with the sensor devices are known as the Internet of Things (IoT). They may include crop sensors in corn fields, your internet-connected refrigerator, medical diagnostic tools, and electrical grid monitors. Unexpected values in measurement data often prompt systemic analysis and may lead to quality activities.
Event Data	**Event data** describes actions performed by things. Event data could be similar to transactional data or measurement data.
Big Data and Data Lakes	A data lake is a type of datastore that holds vast amounts of raw data. These large volumes of data are often referred to as Big Data. Your organization may use categories specific to the challenges of ingesting, storing, managing, retrieving, and analyzing data from a Data Lake. For example, labeled data (see below).
Labeled Data	Labeled data is data that has been tagged or annotated. While metadata for structured data is almost always stored separately from the data itself, with labeled data the metadata and content are stored together in a way that computers and/or human analysts can interpret and act upon them, for example for data used to train machine learning algorithms or models. Data labeling is a technique often used against large volumes of data held in non-relational databases.

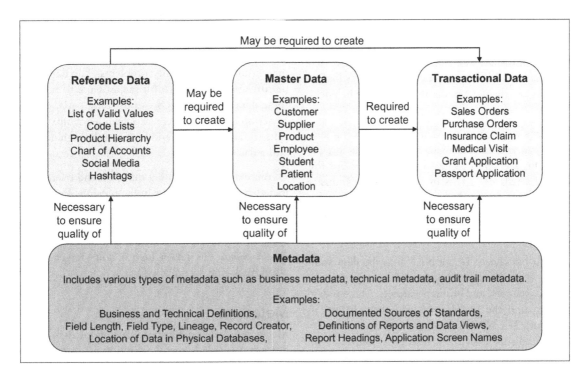

Figure 3.12 Relationships between data categories.

As mentioned previously, your company's data are unique (master product, vendor, customer data, etc., reference data, metadata). No other organization will be likely to have the very same data list. If correct and managed conscientiously, your data provides a competitive advantage because it is tuned for your company's needs. Imagine the cost savings and revenue potential for the company that has accurate data, can find information when needed, and trusts the information found. Quality must be managed for all data categories in order to gain that competitive advantage. Of course, you will have to prioritize your efforts, but consider all the data categories when selecting your data quality activities.

Data Specifications

Specifications generally provide information needed to make, build, or produce something. A floor plan specifies the layout of a house and electrical drawings indicate where light switches are placed in the home. **Data Specifications** is an overarching term used in the Ten Steps methodology to include any information and documentation that provide context, structure, and meaning to data and information. Data specifications provide information needed to make, build, produce, assess, use, and manage data and information.

Note that in this book, Data Specifications is used when implementing the concepts in the broad-impact component of Structure, Context, and Meaning in the Framework for Information Quality. (See *Figure 3.2*). The emphasis here is on metadata, data standards, reference data, data models, and business rules. However, if any of the other topics are relevant to your business needs, include them in the project scope and objectives. Use other resources for detail as needed.

Without the existence, completeness, and quality of data specifications it is difficult to produce high-quality data and harder to measure, understand, and manage the quality of data content. Data

specifications provide the standard against which to compare data quality assessment results. They also provide instructions for manually entering data, designing data load programs, updating information, and developing applications.

 Key Concept

Data Specifications – what they are and why we care. Data specifications is an overarching term used in the Ten Steps methodology to include any information and documentation that provide context, structure, and meaning to data and information. Data specifications provide information needed to make, build, produce, assess, use, and manage data and information. The Ten Steps emphasizes the data specifications of metadata, data standards, reference data, data models, and business rules.

You cannot ensure information or data quality unless you also understand and manage the data specifications that are needed to make, build, use, manage, or provide your information. Data specifications provide important guidance in the same way that an architect's drawings, electrical diagrams, and other plans specify how to build a house or what should be included in it. Use data specifications when building new applications (to help ensure data quality from the beginning) and to understand what constitutes data quality when assessing data in existing systems. Use them as input to instructions for manually entering data, designing data load programs, and updating information.

Problems with data specifications are often the cause of poor-quality data. For example, poor-quality master data may actually come from faulty reference data that was included in the master data record. The same techniques and processes presented in this book – most often applied to master and transactional data – can also be applied to reference data and metadata. For example, a metadata repository is just another datastore that can be assessed for quality, and reference data has its own information life cycle, which needs to be managed to ensure quality.

Relationships between Data Specifications

In the following sections we will look closely at the five data specifications emphasized in this book: metadata, data standards, reference data, data models, and business rules,. But first, let's look at the relationships between them. Consider the number 23 in a field. What does 23 mean?

- Without **metadata** we don't know what 23 means. Is it a temperature and, if so, is it in Celsius or Fahrenheit? Is it a patient number? One segment of a customer identifier? For this example, metadata tells us "23" is in a field called "Industry Code", defined as "A 2-digit code from NAICS which classifies business establishments. NAICS stands for North American Industry Classification System." The format for the field is 2 numbers.
- Our organization has chosen to use NAICS as the **data standard** to be used when classifying those with whom we do business – customers, vendors, and business partners. The standard tells us where to find the list of codes and their definitions (https://naics.com). The NAICS standard starts with a primary 2-digit code and tells us that "23" stands for "Construction." (The standard also drills down to 4- and 6-digit codes specifying additional levels of detail. Such as 2361 stands for Residential Building Construction and 236118 stands for Residential Remodelers. Each organization must determine which level of detail is needed to best understand and work with their customers, vendors, and business partners.)
- **Reference data** provides the list of valid NAICS Codes as used in our organization. The reference data is used by dropdown lists in application interfaces (such as when creating a customer master record and selecting the code pertinent to the new customer) and in analytics when preparing reports (such as using the code 23 when querying how many of our customers are in the construction industry). A data quality assessment will compare the codes in the company's reference data with the codes found in the customer master records.
- Our organization's **data model** tells us where the records we are assessing for quality are stored in the physical database, the relationship of the "Industry Code" code field to other data, and where to find the reference table with the list of valid NAICS codes.
- One of our organization's **business rules** states "Within our company, every customer must have a NAICS code which identifies the primary business of the customer's organization." The **business action** is "When creating a new customer master record, a customer service rep must ask the customer the primary business of their organization and select the corresponding code from the dropdown list in the Industry Code field." We can use this information to state **data quality rules** such as "It is mandatory for each customer master record to contain a valid 2-digit NAICS code." From that we can articulate two **data quality rule specifications**: 1) "In datastore XYZ, Table 123, the rule is true if fill rate for IND_CD field = 100%." This tells us completeness and covers the requirement of being mandatory, and 2) "The rule is true if, for all active customer master records, the list of unique values in IND_CD field match with active values contained in the NAICS_Table." This tells us validity and if the values comply with the NAICS standards.

You can see that what can be learned from data specifications will help when conducting a data quality assessment. The initial assessment sets a baseline so we can see the current nature and magnitude of data quality problems. The data quality rules can be run again as needed. If it makes sense to track compliance to these data quality rules on an ongoing basis, the same rules can be set up to run on a regular schedule, compared to previous results to show progress, and reported through data quality metrics and a dashboard.

You may have noted that metadata and reference data were also included as data categories in the previous section. Data specifications are put into practice as part of understanding the information environment in *Step 2.2 – Understand Relevant Data and Data Specifications* and as a data quality dimension in *Step 3.2 – Data Specifications*. The lesson here – don't forget data specifications when managing data quality!

Metadata

Metadata is often defined as "data about the data" – an accurate but not particularly useful definition on its own. Metadata labels, describes, or characterizes other data and makes it easier to retrieve, interpret, or use information. Metadata was discussed in the section *Data Categories* earlier in this chapter. Metadata is included here because it also specifies data. Examples of metadata include descriptive information about the name given to a data field, definition, lineage, domain values, context, quality, condition, characteristics, constraints, methods of change, and rules.

Metadata can be found in physical data (contained in software and other media such as hardcopy documentation, in tags associated with websites, pictures, documents, and other forms of data), and in the knowledge of people (such as employees, vendors, contractors, consultants, or others familiar with the organization).

 Definition

> Metadata labels, describes, or characterizes other data and makes it easier to retrieve, interpret, or use information.

These examples help explain metadata:

Example 1—Suppose you want to buy a book from an online bookstore or find a book on the shelf in a brick-and-mortar store, but you can't remember the complete title. You can look it up by entering the author's name or the subject. Books matching the criteria will be listed on the screen. You are able to find the book you are interested in because of metadata.

Example 2—Suppose you go into the grocery store and all the cans on the shelf have an empty label. How do you know what is in them? The name of the product, the picture on the label, the distributor, the number of calories and the nutrition chart – all are metadata that describe the food in the cans. Imagine how difficult it would be to do your shopping without this metadata. (From R. Todd Stephens, Ph.D. Used by permission.)

Metadata is important because it:

- Provides context for and aids in understanding the meaning of data
- Facilitates discovery of relevant information
- Organizes electronic resources
- Facilitates interoperability between systems
- Facilitates information integration
- Supports archiving and preservation of data and information

For descriptions and examples of technical metadata, business metadata, and other types of metadata, see *Table 3.5 – Data Categories – Definitions and Notes*.

Data Standards

Standard is a general term for something that is used as a basis of comparison. With data quality the main focus is on data standards, which are agreements, rules, or guidelines on how data is named, represented, formatted, defined, and/or managed. They indicate a level of quality to which data should conform.

Other standards, not necessarily called data standards, can also impact the quality of the data. For example, the International Organization for Standardization (ISO), has developed and published standards covering a huge range of activities, such as making products, managing processes, delivering services, and supplying materials. Because data and information support compliance with these standards, the standards themselves should also be understood by data quality practitioners. See *Chapter 6: Other Techniques and Tools* for an overview of ISO standards related to data quality.

Definition

Data standards are agreements, rules, or guidelines on how data is named, represented, formatted, defined, and/or managed. They indicate a level of quality to which data should conform.

Examples of standards include:

Naming Conventions for Tables and Fields—An example of a naming convention is: if the data in the field contain names, the column name should include the standard abbreviation "NM" along with a descriptive word for the name type – for example, "NM_Last" or "NM_First."

Data Definitions and Conventions for Writing Business Rules—You may have a standards document that describes the minimum set of information to be defined for each field. For example, each field must be documented in the data dictionary; documentation must include the field name, description, example of data content, a default value (if one exists), and whether the field is mandatory, optional, or conditional (with conditions noted).

Establishing, Documenting, and Updating Lists of Valid Values—It is important to agree on the values that are valid for any given field. Sometimes the valid value list is developed internally, and sometimes you may use an external standard list. In any case,

there should be a process that outlines how changes are made to the list and who is involved in those decisions.

Commonly Accepted Reference Values for Classification and Categorization—For example, NAICS (pronounced nakes), the North American Industry Classification System, was developed by the United States in cooperation with Canada and Mexico as the standard for use by federal statistical agencies in classifying business establishments. Use of the standard allows for a high level of comparability in business statistics among the three countries. NAICS can also be used to target and purchase marketing lists for specific industries. The codes can be appended to customer records to help evaluate industries of an organization's best customers. NAICS was adopted in 1997 to replace the older SIC (Standard Industrial Classification) system, yet the SIC system is still being used.

As it applied to data quality, you would ask: If your company was using the SIC system, did it change to NAICS? What is the standard being used now? If NAICS is being used, was all data in all systems in the organization updated from SIC to NAICS? Were the existing SIC codes correctly mapped and changed to NAICS? The NAICS codes can also be used as an example of reference data. The code list comprises the valid sets of values (reference data), but it is also the standard by which business establishments are classified.

Choice of Notation and Modeling Method for Data Modeling—Each data modeling method has a different emphasis and the methods are approximately interchangeable – but not quite. The modeling notation used should be based on your objective. See the section on *Data Models* later in this chapter for more details.

Reference Data

Reference data are sets of values or classification schemas that are referred to by systems, applications, datastores, processes, and reports, as well as by transactional and master records. Standardized reference data is key to data integration and interoperability and facilitate the sharing and reporting of information. Reference data may be used to differentiate one type of record from another for categorization and analysis, or they may be a significant fact such as country, which appears within a larger information set such as address.

An example of reference data is a list of valid values (often a code or abbreviation) that can be used in a particular field. Domain values that are defined and enforced ensure a level of data quality that would not be possible if any value was allowed in a field. The NAICS codes previously discussed as data standards are also an example of reference data. For more information on reference data, see the *Data Categories* section earlier in this chapter.

Analyzing the list of values appearing in a data field, using the frequency and validity of those values, and comparing them to associated reference data (usually stored in a separate table) are some of the most common data quality checks. These checks come under the data quality dimension of Data Integrity Fundamentals. See *Step 3.3*.

Definition

Reference data are sets of values or classification schemas that are referred to by systems, applications, datastores, processes, dashboards, and reports, as well as by transactional and master records. Examples include lists of valid values, code lists, status codes, territory or state abbreviations, demographic fields, flags, product types, gender, chart of accounts, product hierarchy, retail website shopping categories, and social media hashtags.

Key Concept

Data Models – What they are and why we care. A **Data Model** is a visual representation, supported by text, of data structures in a specified domain. The data model may be: 1) Business-oriented – representing what is important to an organization, visualizing the structure of an organization's data without regard to technology; 2) Technology-oriented – representing a specific collection of data in terms of a particular data management approach, showing where data will be held and how they will be organized (relational, object oriented, NoSQL, etc.).

Data models are primary artifacts through which an organization represents its data to itself and through which it understands its data. A good data model combined with documentation of constraints at every phase of system development – database design, application interaction, and accessibility – will help produce high-quality, reusable data and prevent many post-production data quality problems, such as redundancy, conflicting data definitions, and difficulty in sharing data across applications. Data models can even help with tasks like understanding information in third-party software. As noted in *Data Model Essentials*: "No database was ever built without at least an implicit model, just as no house was ever built without a plan" (Simsion and Witt, 2005).

Data models help anyone working with data become familiar with the underlying structure of data in order to understand the programs that capture, store, maintain, manipulate, transform, delete, and share them – all of which impact the quality of data. Better-quality data models support better quality data, so lack of a data model or a poor-quality data model may be one of the root causes of data quality problems.

If you are not a data modeler, find one to help you understand the data within scope of the project and ensure the relevant data is being captured for assessment. This section will show that differences exist in approaches to data modeling, so when discussing data models and associated terms, ask questions and understand the definitions that apply in your environment.

Another example of reference data: a list of valid values for gender could be M, F, or U, where M = Male, F = Female, U = Unknown. Some would point out that a list of gender values could also include such codes as MF, meaning previously male, now female, or FM, meaning previously female, now male – with these values needing some type of associated date field for when the new gender took effect. In a medical setting this is critical information. This illustrates the fact that the reference data must meet the needs of those using them. Historically "sex" and "gender" have been used interchangeably, but they are now seen as distinct and different attributes. So even the label attached to the reference data list may change. It is important to have a process in place so reference data can be discussed, agreed on, and changed when needed.

Data Models

A **Data Model** is a visual representation, supported by text, of data structures in a specified domain – a sphere, realm, or range of knowledge, or an area of responsibility, influence, or activity. The data model may either represent: 1) What is important to a business, government agency, or other type of organization; or 2) a collection of data in terms of a particular data management approach, showing where data will be held and how it will be organized (relational, object-oriented, NoSQL, etc.). Its scope may cover a single department or an entire industry or a branch of science.

My thanks to David Hay for his help and knowledge in writing this section.

Conceptual, logical, and physical are terms you may have heard to indicate different levels of detail for a data model. Even with those, there are multiple definitions for each. That is, there are different kinds of data models that come from different perspectives (business or technology), not just different levels of detail. Any business-oriented data model is called here "conceptual," and represents an organization, without regard to technology. A technology-oriented data model is developed from the perspective of a particular data management approach (relational, object-oriented, NoSQL, etc.) (Hay, 2018).

According to Steve Hoberman, "Data modeling is the process of discovering, analyzing, and scoping data requirements, and then representing and communicating those data requirements in a visual format called the "data model" (2015).

The terms entity, entity type, attribute, and relationship are central concepts in data modeling.

- An **entity** is an object of interest to the organization. For example, "John Doe," "Smith Corp.," and "Order 1234."
- An **entity type** (also known as an "entity class") is a category of those entities. For example, "Person," "Organization," and "Sales Order." The boxes on a typical data model represent entity *types*. In the object-oriented world, using a notation called UML (Unified Modeling Language), an "entity" is called an "object" and an "entity type" is called a "class."
- An **attribute** is the definition of a characteristic, quality, or property of an entity type. "First Name" and "Last Name" are attributes of "Person."
- A **relationship** associates an instance of one entity type with instances of another, defining their structure. An example of a relationship is "Each Organization may be the source of one or more Sales Orders." In the object-oriented world (UML) this is called an "association," and it has a different meaning.

There are multiple notations for data models, but they all use a rectangular box with rounded or square corners to represent an entity type, and an annotated line to represent a relationship between two entity types. Notations differ in how they represent the following characteristics of a relationship:

- **Cardinality** indicates the maximum numbers of instances of one entity type that can be related to instances of another entity type. For example, "A Company must be related to no more than one Address" or "A Company can be related to one or many Addresses."
- **Optionality,** for an instance of an entity type, indicates whether it is necessary (mandatory) for there to be an instance of a related entity type. For example, "A Company *must have* at least one Address." Attributes are also optional or mandatory.

Note that the model shows what *may* or *may not* exist. The model cannot be used to describe the *conditions* under which an attribute or relationship may exist. This is the domain of business rules.

Business-Oriented Data Models

Table 3.6 – Data Model Comparison compares the business-oriented and technology-oriented data models explained below, along with their sources.

A business-oriented data model is called a "conceptual" data model and represents the organization, visualizing the structure of an organization's data without regard to technology. There are three perspectives of a conceptual data model that have developed over the years:

Overview Data Model—An **overview data model** is a synopsis of the enterprise's information structure, based on organizational objectives, motivations, and other information concerns, such as employees, customers, products, services, etc. It provides context from top management, is wide-ranging, and has relatively little detail. It is a sketch or a simple entity/relationship diagram and shows the most important business concepts. There are many different names for the same kind of model. Steve Hoberman uses the phrase Business Terms Model (BTM) for the overview data model (2020).

Semantic Data Model—A **semantic data model** contains many elements, reflecting the complexity of the organization. It shows terms, concepts, and definitions. It does not directly represent business rules or inferences, but it does show the concepts required to describe them. The model captures the language actually used by an organization to describe the meaning of things of significance to it. The starting point is development of a glossary, clearly defining every term in the domain. These terms can be captured using the Resource Description Framework (RDF) in the Semantic Web. It is not unusual to find that the same word is used to mean different things and the same thing (or what appears to be the same thing) is described with different terms. At some point, these differences must be resolved. This resolution can be accomplished with an approach to evaluating how terms are used with respect to: 1) business rules, using Semantics of Business Vocabulary and Rules (SBVR), or 2) inferences, using the Web Ontology Language (OWL) in the Semantic Web. The semantic model can also be visualized using Entity Relationship Diagrams (ERD) and Object Role Modeling (ORM). Note that a semantic model is complex, and its visualization should be organized carefully in terms of meaningful subject areas.

Essential Data Model—Shows relatively simple, fundamental, underlying structures that are common across the enterprise. It shows entity classes, attributes, and relationships. It is more detailed than the overview model but is more abstract, and therefore simpler, and more compact than the semantic model. It can be derived from a semantic model or can provide the starting point for developing other types of data models. Note that the term "Essential Model" is used by David Hay (2018). The term "Universal Data Model" is used by Len Silverston (2001a,b).

Technology-Oriented Data Models

A technology-oriented data model is from the perspective of data management technology (relational, object-oriented, NoSQL, etc.) and specifies how data is to be represented in a datastore – which data will be held and how it will be organized. Let's consider them from two perspectives: logical and physical. Note that logical and physical data models are sometimes referred to as design models.

Logical Model—The **logical model** describes a body of data in terms of a particular data management technology, independent of a specific vendor's software. Categories of data management technology include:

- **Relational Databases**: Expressed in terms of tables and columns, with explicit references to primary and foreign keys. Tables are two-dimensional, organized according to Codd's Rules of Normalization (Codd, 1970).
- **Non-Relational Databases** (also known as NoSQL): Encompasses a wide variety of different database technologies that were developed in response to demands in building modern applications. These technologies can handle massive volumes of data, rapidly changing data types, and agility challenges. Moreover, they allow for accessibility from many different devices and scaling for millions of users globally. The bodies of data using these technologies are often referred to as data lakes. They are too large to be supported with SQL and so are built on non-relational technology. (SQL is the logic of relational databases, hence the name NoSQL meaning "Not only SQL"). These non-relational or NoSQL databases are usually grouped into four categories (Sullivan, 2015):
  - ○ **Key-value stores**. Every single item in the database is stored as an attribute name (or "key"), together with its value. Some key-value stores allow each value to have a type, such as "integer," which adds functionality. Key-value stores function similarly to SQL databases, but have only two columns (the 'key' and 'value'). More complex information is sometimes stored as BLOBs (Binary Large Objects) within the 'value' columns.
  - ○ **Graph stores**. Used to store information about networks of data, such as social connections.
  - ○ **Column stores**. Organizes data into collections of columns. A column is the basic unit of storage and is comprised of a name and its value. Collections of columns can be brought together providing more flexibility because they do not require a predefined schema. This approach can be optimized for queries over large datasets.
  - ○ **Document stores.** Pair each key with a complex data structure known as a document. Documents can contain many

different key-value pairs, or key-array pairs, or even nested documents. Document databases do away with the table-and-row model, storing all relevant data together in a single 'document' in JSON, XML, or another format, which can nest values hierarchically.

- **Dimensional**: A set of relational tables with some of them de-normalized to focus on **facts** and organized by identifying characteristics called **dimensions**. A fact is the assertion of the existence of something. A dimension is a descriptive characteristic of that fact, used to retrieve instances of it (Inmon, 2005; Kimball, 2005).
- **Object oriented**: Based on object-oriented programming, rather than on data management. Models are expressed in terms of classes, methods, and associations. UML (Unified Modeling Language) is the notation most commonly used (Booch, Rumbaugh, & Jacobson, 2017).
- **XML Schema**: XML (Extensible Markup Language) is a language for supporting data communications. The XML Schema is a description of a type of XML document, typically expressed in terms of constraints on the structure and content of documents of that type, above and beyond the basic syntactical constraints imposed by XML itself (Walmsley, 2002).
- **Data Vault:** Relational structures simplified for data warehousing, and to provide traceability for data changes (Lindstedt & Olschimke, 2016).

Physical Data Model—The **physical model** is derived from a logical model and is in terms of a particular vendor's data storage technology – how data is physically stored in a database. This could be in terms of **partitions** which are different physical files that segment an entire database. Smaller segments are sometimes called **tablespaces** or **clusters**.

Data Model Example

Figure 3.13 shows an example of an entity/relationship diagram (ERD). As mentioned, there are many notations for data models. This figure is rendered according to Approach A, the Row 2 "Semantic" model in *Table 3.6 – Data Model Comparison*, which follows further in this section. Cardinality and optionality are shown according to the discipline of Richard Barker and Harry Ellis, also used by Approach A. In the diagram:

- **Customer, Sales Order, SO Line Item, Product Type**, etc. are examples of entity types.
- Note that **City**, **State**, and **Country** are also entity types.
  - But each of these is also what is called a "sub-type of" the entity type **Geographic Area**.
  - That means that each of the sub-types (for example, City) is, by definition, also a definition of the super-type, Geographic Area.
- "SO Number", "SO Issued Date", and "SO Completed Date" are attributes of **Sales Order**.
  - The asterisk (*) means the attribute is mandatory.
  - A circle means it is optional.
  - A hashtag with underline (#) means the attribute is part of the unique identifier for the entity type. The attribute name is also underlined.
- The lines between pairs of entity types are examples of Relationships.
  - Cardinality and optionality of each relationship are further clarified by the text at each end of the line and can be stated in a sentence.
  - By naming relationships in this way, the resulting sentences must be either true or not true, when presented to someone in the business side of the organization.

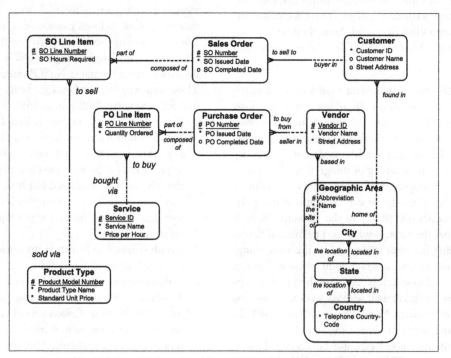

Source: David C. Hay. 2020. Updated from 2018. *Achieving Buzzword Compliance: Data Architecture Language and Vocabulary*. Technics Publications. Used with permission.

Figure 3.13 An Entity/Relationship Diagram (ERD).

- Examples of relationships with resulting sentences:
  - Each Customer may be buyer in one or more **Sales Orders**.
    - Optionality of "may be" is indicated by the dashed line nearest **Customer**.
    - Cardinality of "one or more" is indicated by the crow's foot nearest **Sales Order**. Note: For cardinality, the crow's foot notation indicates "many" by its many "toes." It was invented by Gordon Everest, who originally used the term "inverted arrow" (Everest, 1976).
  - Alternatively, each **Sales Order** must be sold to one and only one **Customer**.
    - The Optionality "must be" is indicated by the solid line nearest the subject entity type (in this case **Sales Order**).
    - The Cardinality "one and only one" is indicated by the absence of a crow's foot nearest the object entity type (in this case **Customer**).
- Example of relationship that is also part of the unique identifier:
  - A vertical bar next to a crow's foot means that the nearest relationship is also part of the unique identifier.
  - Each instance of a **Sales Order** is uniquely identified only by SO Number (indicated by #), whereas each instance of an **SO Line Item** is identified by a combination of the attribute # SO Line Number and the relationship "part of" **Sales Order**.

Data models at this level are usually used by data modelers only. A good data modeler will facilitate discussions and use simpler diagrams that can be understood by business audiences who need to verify the data and relationships, yet do not need to interpret a detailed model. If needed, someone on your data team with good communication skills can work with the data modeler to ensure those involved can provide input to and comprehend what the data model means to the business and how it can be used by the technologist.

Data Models – Why We Care

Data models are primary artifacts through which an organization represents its data to itself and through which it understands its data. In managing data quality, it is important to understand the underlying structure of the data in order to fully understand the programs that capture, store, maintain, manipulate, transform, delete, and share them. Conceptual data models are needed regardless of the underlying database technology.

According to Steve Hoberman in *Data Modeling Made Simple* (2016), data models ensure requirements for a new application are fully understood and correctly captured before the actual database is created. Communication and precision are two main benefits. He explains that data models allow you to understand an existing application (through "reverse engineering"); to manage risk through impact analysis (such as the impact of adding or modifying structures for an application already in production, which structures are needed for archival purposes, impact of modifying structures when customizing purchased software); to learn about the business (before application development to understand how the business works in order to understand how the applications that support the business will work); and to educate team members and facilitate training (to understand requirements).

Among other things, a data model can serve as a platform for discussing – and ultimately determining – a system's scope. Separately,

processes can be documented to show where they can or cannot be supported because the data does or does not exist. A business rule is an authoritative principle or guideline that describes business interactions and establishes rules for actions. Because business rules are concerned with interactions and actions, they do not appear on a data model. The structure of the data model may be important for accommodating the logic of a business rule.

NoSQL practitioners have claimed that they do not need a data model. In fact, now even with a data lake (a reservoir of large amounts of varying data, including unstructured data, which uses NoSQL to access) we need a picture of the underlying structure of the data.

But, as noted by David Hay, there are challenges. William of Ockham, a 14th century philosopher and friar developed the Maxim known as "Occam's Razor," a problem-solving principle, the most common English translation being "plurality should not be posited without necessity." A more direct translation is "Entities must not be multiplied beyond necessity" (Encyclopædia Britannica, 2017). In systems design, this means that simpler designs are easier to build, easier to change, less likely to need change in the first place, and easier to operate without error. Unnecessarily complex designs are difficult to build correctly, difficult to change, difficult to operate, and prone to error. "Complexity is the enemy of data quality." This raises the questions: "How complex is 'unnecessarily complex'? … How simple is 'too simple'?" (Hay, 2018, pp. 73-74).

Albert Einstein said that, "Everything should be made as simple as possible, but no simpler" (quoted in Sessions, 1950; see also Championing Science, 2019). Determining the right level of simplicity/complexity is at the heart of data modelers' and systems developers' jobs. It is their job to "defeat unnecessary complexity." To the extent that they do, it encourages and supports high-quality data (Hay, 2018).

A good data model combined with documentation of constraints at every phase of development – database design, application interaction, and accessibility – will help produce high-quality, reusable data and prevent many post-production data quality problems, such as redundancy, conflicting data definitions, and difficulty in sharing data across applications. Data models can even help with tasks like understanding information in third-party software.

Data models help anyone working with data become familiar with the underlying structure of data in order to understand the programs that capture, store, maintain, manipulate, transform, delete, and share them – all of which impact the quality of data. Better-quality data models support better quality data, so lack of a data model or a poor-quality data model may be one of the root causes of data quality problems.

If you are a data modeler, other resources for producing high-quality data models include Matthew West's *Developing High Quality Data Models* (2011) and Steve Hoberman's *Data Model Scorecard: Applying the Industry Standard on Data Model Quality* (2015).

Data Model Comparison

Table 3.6 – Data Model Comparison compares and summarizes the terms described above as used by four of several approaches

Table 3.6 Data Model Comparison

Level #	Data Model Level Description	Terms used by approach for corresponding data model level			
		Approach A Hay	Approach B Simsion, Witt	Approach C Hoberman	Approach D Object Management Group (OMG)
1	This model level is based on conversations with upper level executives. It: • Covers a few very high-level functions with information and data (a sketch of maybe a dozen primary entities, with many-to-many relationships and virtually no attributes). • Includes the vision (a statement of what it expects to be like a few years into the future) and mission (how it expects to get there) of the enterprise, which are used to establish priorities for future systems development projects.	Overview (Conceptual Level 1)	Context	Subject Area	Environment
2	This model level: • Describes, in detail, the language of the people operating the enterprise. • Includes all the entity types in the enterprise's language, along with most attributes. • With Approach A, it captures the extent of an enterprise's language which will uncover linguistic conflicts. There are: • Graphic versions of this level model, such as "entity/ relationship diagrams" [1] and "object role models" [2]. • Textual versions such as glossaries, the Object Management Group's "Semantics of Business Vocabulary and Rules" (SBVR)" [3] and various components of the "Semantic Web" [4]. The textual forms contain a more complete list of entity classes defining the language of the enterprise. To the extent that relationships are shown in the graphic versions, they are of the "one-to-many" variety.	Semantic (Conceptual Level 2)	Conceptual	Business Terms Model (BTM)	Class-of-Platform Independent Model (i.e., technology independent)
3	This level model is a consolidation of the Level 2 model, making use of patterns to describe the enterprise's semantics in terms of relatively fewer, more abstract, entity types. This model will resolve, as much as possible, the conflicts uncovered in the Level 2 Model.	Essential (Conceptual Level 3) [5]	Conceptual with patterns	Business Terms Model (BTM)	Not applicable
4	This level model arranges data to accommodate technical constraints and expected usage – in terms of a particular data management technology. It is a technology dependent model that is tuned for performance, security, and development tool constraints. Here, Level 2 and 3 models can be implemented using a relational database management system, object-oriented programs, XML schemas, NoSQL, etc. Remember, the Level 2 and 3 models are themselves independent of specific database software (Oracle, DB2, etc.) or reporting tools.	Logical	Logical	Physical Technology dependent	Class-of-Platform (Technology) Specific Model, Vendor Platform– Independent Model

5	This level model: • Organizes the data on one or more physical media. • Is concerned with physical table spaces, disk drives, partitions, and so forth. • Includes changes made to logical structures to achieve performance goals. • Is embedded in a particular vendor's database management approach.	Physical	Implementation	Vendor Platform-Specific Model

Approach Sources:

Approach A: Terms as used by David Hay. *Achieving Buzzword Compliance: Data Architecture Language and Vocabulary.* (Technics Publications, 2018).

Approach B: Terms as used by Graeme Simsion, Graham Witt. *Data Modeling Essentials, Third Edition* (Morgan Kaufmann, 2005), p. 17.

Approach C: Terms as used by Steve Hoberman. *Data Modeling Made Simple: A Practical Guide for Business and IT Professionals,* 2nd Edition. (Technics Publications, 2016) and *The Rosedata Stone: Achieving a Common Business Language* (Technics Publications, 2020).

Approach D: Terms as used by Donald Chapin. "MDA Foundational Model Applied to Both the Organization and Business Application Software," Object Management Group (OMG) working paper (March 2008).

Level 2 Sources:

[1]"**Entity/relationship diagrams**": Richard Barker. *Case*Method: Entity Relationship Modelling.* (Addison-Wesley, 1989).

[2]"**Object role models**": Terry Halpin. *Object-Role Modeling Fundamentals: A Practical Guide to Data Modeling with ORM.* (Technics Publication. 2015).

[3]**Object Management Group's** "**Semantics of Business Vocabulary and Rules**" (**SBVR**)": Graham Witt. *Writing Effective Business Rules: A Practical Method.* (Morgan Kaufmann, 2012). This book makes SBVR understandable.

[4]"**Semantic Web**". Dean Allemang and Jim Hendler. *Semantic Web for the Working Ontologist: Effective Modeling in RDFS and OWL.* (Morgan Kaufmann, 2011).

Level 3 Sources and Notes

[5]David Hay. *Enterprise Model Patterns: Describing the World.* (Technics Publications, 2011).

Notes: Len Silverston's approach is approximately row 3 above. He has published extensively on what he calls "Universal Data Models":

• **Volume 1** includes such topics as "People and Organizations", "Products", "Work Products", "invoicing", etc.
   ○ Len Silverston. 2001. *The Data Model Resource Book (Revised Edition): Volume 1: A Library of Universal Data Models for All Enterprises* (John Wiley & Sons).
• **Volume 2** is more specific. In each case, a subject is treated by a complete model.
   ○ Len Silverston. 2001. *The Data Model Resource Book (Revised Edition): Volume 2: A Library of Universal Data Models by Industry Types* (John Wiley & Sons).
• **Volume 3** shows the components that appear, modified, in the other two volumes. Included are such concepts as: Party "Roles", "Taxonomies" and "Hierarchies", states, and contact mechanisms. Also included is a section on "Business Rules", which is a bit trickier, since it is about "meta" data that constrain what an entity's value is permitted to be.
   ○ Len Silverston and Paul Agnew. 2009. *The Data Model Resource Book: Volume 3: Universal Patterns for Data Modeling* (Wiley Publishing, Inc.).
   ○ Volume 3 is closer to what David Hay previously called a "universal" data model. See David C. Hay. 1996. *Data Model Patterns: Conventions of Thought.* (New York: Dorset House), page 254.

available. As you will see, the terminology varies between the approaches described and not everyone agrees on the terminology shown in the table. It is not the purpose of this book to discuss the merits of the various approaches. It is only important to be aware that differences exist so when you are discussing data models and associated terms, you can ask about and understand the definitions that apply in your environment.

Whichever terms are used, it is important to distinguish between: 1) the viewing of data structures in casual terms, 2) the viewing of the fundamental structure of your data (and through that the fundamental structure of your business), and 3) the viewing of data structures that are based on technological constraints. The latter will change frequently. It is only by maintaining a solid understanding of the nature of the data you use that you will be able to rise above such changes and respond instead to changes in your business.

Business Rules

Ronald Ross, known as the "father of business rules," describes a business rule as "a statement that defines or constrains some aspect of the business … [which is] intended to assert business structure, or to control or influence the behavior of the business." He explains that "a real-world rule serves as a guide for conduct or action … and as a criterion for making judgments and decisions" (Ross, 2013, pgs. 34, 84).

For data quality, you must understand business rules and their implications for the constraints on data. See the *Definition callout box* for my definition of a business rule and related terms as they apply to data quality. Note that an authoritative principle means the rule is mandatory; a guideline means the rule is optional.

The relationships between business rules, business actions, and data quality rule specifications is seen in *Table 3.7*. In his book *Business Rule Concepts* (2013), Ronald Ross presents samples of business rules and informally categorizes each one according to the kind of guidance it provides. The first two columns are from Ron's book. The last two have been added to illustrate the business action that should take place and to provide an example of an associated data quality rule specification.

Data is an output of a business process, and violations of data quality rules can mean that the process is not working properly – whether it is carried out manually by people or automated with technology. A violation of a data quality rule could also mean that the rule was incorrectly captured or misunderstood. Collect business rules to provide input for creating necessary data quality checks and analyzing the results of the assessments. The lack of well-documented and well-understood business rules often play a part in data quality problems.

Table 3.7 Business Rules, Business Actions, and Data Quality Rule Specifications

Type of Business Rule**	Example of Business Rule**	Business Action	Data Quality Rule Specification
Restriction	A customer must not place more than 3 rush orders charged to its credit account.	A service rep checks customer's credit account to determine whether number of rush orders placed exceeds 3. If yes, customer can only place a standard order.	The rule is violated if: Order_Type = "Rush" and Account_Type = "Credit" and number of rush orders placed > 3.
Guideline	A customer with preferred status should have its orders filled immediately.	A service rep checks customer status. If designated as preferred ("P"), order should be shipped within 12 hours of being placed.	The guideline is violated if: Customer_Status = "P" and Ship_DateTime > Order_DateTime + 12 hours.
Computation	A customer's annual order volume is always computed as total sales closed during the company's fiscal year.	Not applicable – based on automated calculations.	The computation is correct if: Annual_Order_Volume = Total_Sales for all quarters in fiscal year.
Inference	A customer is always considered preferred if customer has placed more than 5 orders over $1,000.	A service rep checks order history of customer when placing order to determine if customer is preferred.	Preference is inferred when: Sum of 5 or more customer orders > $1,000.
Timing	An order must be assigned to an expeditor if shipped but not invoiced within 72 hours.	To ensure that the business transaction is finalized, service rep checks daily "Order Transaction" report and forwards to expeditor any orders shipped but not invoiced within 72 hours.	The rule is violated if: Ship_DateTime = 72 hours and invoice date = null and Expeditor_ID = null.
Trigger	"Send-advance-notice" must be performed for an order when the order is shipped.	The "Send-advance-notice" is automatically generated when order is shipped.	The rule is violated if: Send_Advance_Notice = null and Order_DateTime = not null.

**Source: Ronald G. Ross, *Business Rule Concepts: Getting to the Point of Knowledge*, 4th Edition (Business Rule Solutions, LLC, 2013), p. 25. Used with permission.

Definition

A **Business Rule** is an authoritative principle or guideline that describes business interactions and establishes rules for actions. It may also state the business process to which the rule is applied and why the rule is important to the organization. **Business Action** refers to action that should be taken if the business rule is followed, in business terms. The behavior of the resulting data can be articulated as requirements or **data quality rules** and then checked for compliance. **Data quality rule specifications** explain, at the physical datastore level, how to check the quality of the data, which is an output of the adherence (or non-adherence) to the business rules and business actions.

– Danette McGilvray and David Plotkin

Data Governance and Stewardship

Assume you live in a neighborhood of single-family homes. You know most of the people who live there. Every household maintains its home according to its own preferences – some people mow the lawn once a week; others work in their yards on a daily basis; some let the weeds grow wild. Now imagine that everyone on the street is packing their bags and leaving their homes. All the occupants of all the houses are moving in together!

Each household brings its own ways of living, preferences, and attitudes. We can immediately see the potential for conflict. Certainly, a different level of coordination and cooperation is required to live together productively and peacefully in the same house than was needed to live as neighbors in separate dwellings.

Any time your company integrates information, it is as though all of the source systems – with their associated people, business processes, and data – are packing up and moving in together. Organizations are living in a world that is much more integrated than it was in the past.

How are decisions to be made in this integrated world? In my example, each family has its own room in one large home. Occupants of a particular room have the right to put down new flooring and decorate the way they want. However, none of them can change the plumbing or redecorate the living room (a common area for all) without the agreement of the others who live in the building. In some cases, the occupants can bestow authority on someone to make the plumbing and common-area decisions. They trust that person to make decisions for the benefit of everyone who lives in the building. However, they expect to be informed of changes and to be able to raise any issues that need attention. There need to be roles, responsibilities, rules, and processes in place for managing the house. In other words, governance is required.

Data governance and data stewardship go hand-in-hand and are familiar terms to most. What do they have to do with data quality? It is outside the scope of this book to outline "how to do data governance." But the importance of data governance and stewardship to data quality requires a short discussion.

 Definition

Data Governance is the organization and implementation of policies, procedures, structure, roles, and responsibilities that outline and enforce rules of engagement, decision rights, and accountabilities for the effective management of information assets.

– John Ladley, Danette McGilvray, Anne-Marie Smith, Gwen Thomas

Data Governance and Data Stewardship Defined

My "go-to" definition for data governance is "the organization and implementation of policies, procedures, structure, roles, and responsibilities that outline and enforce rules of engagement, decision rights, and accountabilities for the effective management of information assets." I use this as a starting point with clients to discuss, understand, and modify as needed.

Robert Seiner defines data governance as "the formal execution and enforcement of authority over the management of data and data-related assets." Another definition highlighted in his book *Non-Invasive Data Governance* (Seiner, 2014) is "formalizing behavior around the definition, production, and usage of data to manage risk and improve quality and usability of selected data." Whichever definition you prefer, basic ideas within data governance include policy, authority, formalized behavior, accountability, management of data and information assets. In his book, *Data Governance*, John Ladley (2020b) points out that, "Principles, policies, and auditing accomplish for financial assets what data governance accomplishes for data, information, and content assets."

Data governance ensures that the appropriate people representing business processes, data, and technology are involved in the decisions that affect them. Data governance provides venues for interaction and communication paths to:

- Ensure appropriate representation when making decisions
- Actually make decisions
- Identify and resolve issues
- Escalate issues when necessary
- Ensure the right people are held accountable and responsible
- Implement changes
- Communicate and ensure the right people are appropriately engaged, informed, and consulted

 Definition

Data stewardship is an approach to data governance that formalizes accountability for managing information resources on behalf of others and for the best interests of the organization.

I promote governance and the idea of stewardship as it relates to data and information, but I do not generally promote the use of "ownership." Why? A steward is someone who manages something on behalf of someone else. Owner has two different meanings according to the Encarta Dictionary: English (North America): 1) possession, emphasizing that somebody or something belongs to a particular person or thing and not to somebody or something else; 2) responsibility for, acknowledging full personal responsibility for something. Too often people act as if they "own" the data as in the first definition. "This data is mine. You cannot have it. I get to decide what to do with it." This attitude is counterproductive to the well-being of the organization.

I do promote the use of "ownership" when it comes to business processes. Why? Because it is usually used as in the second definition – to acknowledge full personal responsibility for something. Those with the authority do "own" the processes in that sense. But even though the business may "own" a process, anyone who touches the data in carrying out that process is their "steward." They have to manage the data, not just to meet their own immediate needs or needs of a particular process or function, but also on behalf of others in the organization who also use the data or information.

I promote stewardship as an attitude and a way of acting. A data steward, on the other hand, can be the name of a particular role. There is no agreed-upon set of responsibilities for a data steward, though they have standardized somewhat over time. The title is often used for someone who is a subject matter expert or who fixes data at the application level. Others consider the data steward to be the person who is responsible for data names, definitions, and standards. Still others assign it a strategic role with responsibility for a data subject area across business processes and applications. There can be enterprise data stewards, business data stewards, technical data stewards, domain data stewards, operational data stewards and project data stewards. See David Plotkin's *Data Stewardship* (2020) for more detail on the subject. He summarizes data governance and stewardship as being "all about making sure that people are properly organized and do the right things to make their data understood, trusted, of high quality, and ultimately, suitable and usable for the enterprise's purpose."

Though I do help clients implement data governance and stewardship, the topic is outside the scope of this book. Governance and stewardship are included in the *Framework for Information Quality* as part of "Responsibility" – the second R in the RRISCCE broad-impact components, seen earlier in this chapter. What is important is that you do implement some level of data governance and stewardship. Whatever roles, responsibilities, and titles are used, ensure they are meaningful and agreed on by those within the organization.

Data Governance and Data Quality

Data quality is often seen as a one-time project. "Fix the data and we're done." Even if there is awareness that data quality requires ongoing attention, the lack of formal accountability for the data is a critical component that causes many data quality initiatives to dwindle over time or fail completely. It is also the reason that many application development projects, once in production, cannot uphold the quality of data required by the business. Data governance is the missing link that provides the structure and process for making decisions about a company's data. It ensures that the appropriate people are engaged to manage information throughout its life cycle. Implementing data governance and stewardship is important for the sustainability of data quality.

For any data quality work, you need to know:

- **Accountabilities**. Those accountable and responsible for the data through its life cycle
- **Decision rights**. Those who have the right to make decisions about the data throughout its life cycle
- **Rules of engagement**. How the various people/organizations will interact
- **Communication path**. Who needs to know what, and when and how
- **Escalation paths**. Who makes the final decision if those closest to the decision cannot come to agreement

Make use of a formalized data governance program if it exists in your organization to help with these areas during your data quality project. If one does not exist, you still need to know these to accomplish your project objectives. For example, you still need to find the right people who are responsible for the data within scope of your project, and you still need a process for making decisions about the data and ensuring the right people are involved in those decisions. It may take you longer to accomplish these tasks without a data governance program, but they must be done. The governance-type work done for a data quality project can then be used to form the foundation of a formal data governance program after the project is complete. To sustain data quality and before the project team dissolves, ensure people and processes are in place to govern the data as part of operational processes and a data governance program – either existing or (hopefully) newly formed.

Ten Steps Process Overview

The Ten Steps Process (in *Figure 3.14*) illustrates the steps for which the methodology is named. *Chapter 4: The Ten Steps Process* provides the details to help you assess, improve, sustain, and manage information and data quality and shows how to implement the concepts covered in this chapter.

While the process flow for the Ten Steps shows a natural progression from step-to-step, realize that successfully applying the steps takes an iterative approach. Project teams can return to previous steps to enrich their work, they can choose those steps that meet the business need, and they can repeat the entire Ten Steps to support continuous information improvement. *Step 10 – Communicate, Manage, and Engage with People Throughout* is so important that it is represented as a bar that runs under all of the steps. Something related to *Step 10* should be done in every other step because work here is critical to the success of every project.

The Ten Steps Process was designed as a pick-and-choose approach where various steps, activities, and techniques from the methodology can be applied to many different situations where data quality is a component. The steps will require varying levels of detail, depending on the business needs and project objectives. Each of the Ten Steps is summarized below.

1. Determine Business Needs and Approach—Identify and agree on business needs (related to customers, products, services, strategies, goals, issues, and/or opportunities) and data quality issues to be within scope of the project. Reference them to guide work and keep at the forefront of all activities throughout the project. Plan the project and obtain resources.

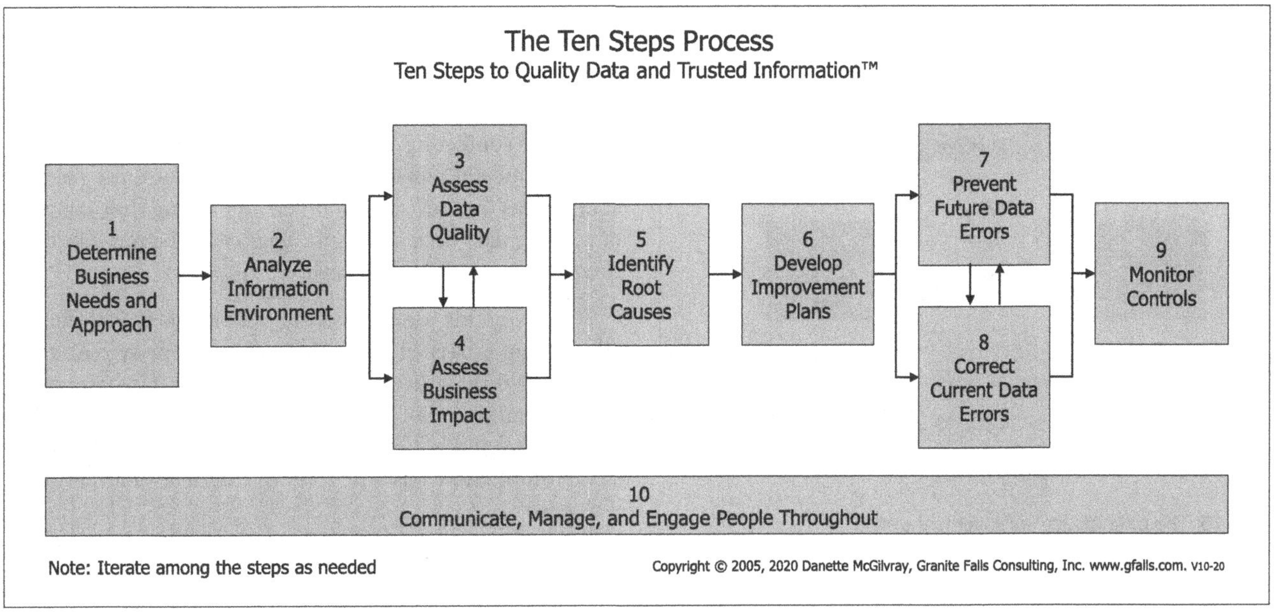

The Ten Steps Process
Ten Steps to Quality Data and Trusted Information™

Note: Iterate among the steps as needed — Copyright © 2005, 2020 Danette McGilvray, Granite Falls Consulting, Inc. www.gfalls.com. V10-20

Figure 3.14 The Ten Steps Process.

2. Analyze Information Environment—Understand the environment surrounding the business needs and data quality issues: analyze relevant requirements and constraints, data and data specifications, processes, people and organizations, technology and the information life cycle, at the appropriate level of detail. All provide input for remaining steps, e.g., to ensure only pertinent data will be assessed for quality, as a basis for analyzing results, identifying root causes, and implementing what is needed to prevent future data errors, correct current data errors, and monitor controls.

3. Assess Data Quality—Select the data quality dimensions applicable to the business needs and data quality issues within scope of the project. Evaluate data quality for the chosen dimensions. Analyze individual assessments and synthesize with other results. Make initial recommendations, document, and take action as needed at the time. Results from the data quality assessment(s) guide where to focus efforts in the remaining steps.

4. Assess Business Impact—Determine the impact of poor-quality data on the business. A variety of qualitative and quantitative techniques are offered, with each placed on a continuum from, relatively speaking, taking less time and being less complex to assess, to taking more time and being more complex. This aids in selecting the best technique(s) to fit the purpose of the business impact and within the time and resources available. Use any of the techniques at any time, in any step, whenever there is a need to gain support, establish the business case for data quality work, prioritize efforts, address resistance, and motivate others to participate in the project.

5. Identify Root Causes—Identify and prioritize the true causes of the data quality problems and develop specific recommendations for addressing them.

6. Develop Improvement Plans—Develop improvement plans, based on finalized recommendations, to prevent future data errors, correct current data errors, and monitor controls.

7. Prevent Future Data Errors—Implement improvement plans for solutions that address root causes of the data quality problems and will prevent data errors from reoccurring. Solutions may range from simple tasks to creating additional projects.

8. Correct Current Data Errors—Implement improvement plans that make appropriate corrections to the data. Ensure downstream systems can handle the changes. Validate and document changes. Ensure the data corrections do not introduce new errors.

9. Monitor Controls—Monitor and verify improvements that were implemented. Maintain improved results by standardizing, documenting, and continuously monitoring successful improvements.

10. Communicate, Manage, and Engage People Throughout—Communication, engaging with people, and managing the project throughout are essential to the success of any information and data quality project. These are so important that they should be included as part of every other step.

Data Quality Improvement Cycle

Once a data quality project is complete, we don't ignore the data and expect it to stay high quality on its own. The Data Quality Improvement Cycle, shown in *Figure 3.15,* illustrates the idea that managing data quality is a continuous process, done through three high-level steps: assessment, awareness, and action.

The Data Quality Improvement Cycle is a modification of the familiar Plan-Do-Check-Act (PDCA) approach, which is a basic technique for improving and controlling processes and products. A variation, PDSA, stands for Plan-Do-Study-Act. The basis of the circles started in 1939 and evolved in the early 1950s, mid-1980s, and 1993. Though accounts differ, Walter Shewhart, W. Edwards Deming (both pioneers in quality), and the Japanese companies

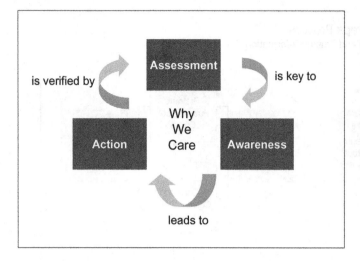

Figure 3.15 The data quality improvement cycle.

who were introduced to the ideas by Deming, all had a role to play in the development of PDCA and PDSA, which are still in use today (Moen & Norman, 2010).

The three steps in the Data Quality Improvement Cycle are:

Assessment - looking at your actual data and environment, then comparing them to requirements and expectations

is key to

Awareness - understanding the true state of your data and information, impact on the business, and root causes

which leads to

Action - prevention of future information and data quality problems in addition to correction of current data errors

which is verified by

Periodic assessments. And so, the cycle continues.

The statement "Why We Care" in the center reminds us that we don't do data quality for the sake of data quality. We do it because there is something we care about, a reason. Those are the business needs – our customers, products, services, strategies, goals, issues, and opportunities.

An Example of the Data Quality Improvement Cycle

One company profiled the data that supported order management. Everyone "knew" there should be no open sales orders older than six months, but the data quality assessment showed open sales orders dating back several years – some older than the company itself. Financial exposure was potentially in the millions of dollars.

Because of that assessment, an investigation was launched. Some of the orders that were older than the company were explained as leftovers from the parent organization, from which the company

had recently split. It was found that report parameters in the Business Center were not set to catch old orders so there was no visibility of open orders older than six months. Reports used by customer service reps in the Business Center and by management contained conflicting information. In addition, they found root causes of the old orders – for example, various order management applications "talked" to each other, and during this "conversation" of sending data back and forth, flags could be missed, data could become corrupted, and so forth.

Based on this awareness, the action taken included manually closing orders in the order management system and moving them to the order management history database, correcting report parameters to ensure visibility of open orders older than six months, and consolidating reports to make certain that the same information was sent to both managers and customer service reps.

So why was tracking older open sales orders so important? There was a financial impact to the company because the cost of manufacturing and selling the product or service had been incurred but the company had not been paid. And all this important work and resulting value to the company was triggered from a simple data quality assessment!

The Data Quality Improvement Cycle and the Ten Steps Process

The Data Quality Improvement Cycle helps illustrate the iterative and on-going nature of data quality management and can be mapped to the Ten Steps Process (see *Figure 3.16*). The Ten Steps Process (as introduced in the previous section) describes a set of methods for the continuous assessment, maintenance, and improvement of data and information. Included are processes for:

- Determining the most important business needs, associated data, and where to focus efforts
- Describing and analyzing the information environment
- Assessing data quality
- Determining the business impact of poor data quality
- Identifying the root causes of data quality problems and their effects on the business
- Correcting and preventing data defects
- Continuous monitoring of data quality controls

The Ten Steps are a concrete articulation of the Data Quality Improvement Cycle. Like the cycle, they are iterative – when one improvement cycle is completed, start again to expand on the results.

The idea of an improvement cycle comes into play again once controls are being monitored in *Step 9*. The responsibility for this moves into an operational process. If issues are uncovered from the monitoring, an improvement cycle comprised of *Steps 5, 6, 7, 8, and 9* begins with identifying root causes and moves through the remaining steps.

If issues require a new project to resolve them, then the improvement cycle may start again at *Step 1*.

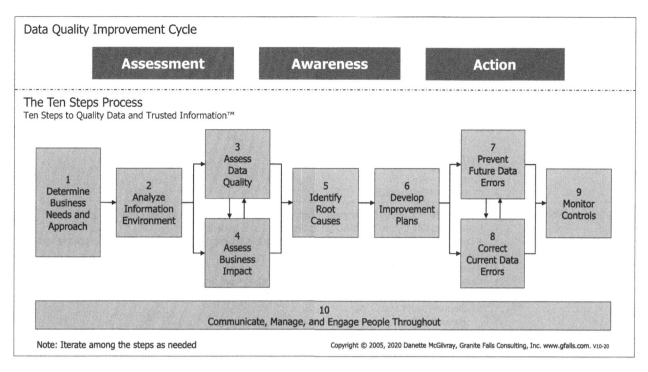

Figure 3.16 Data quality improvement cycle and the Ten Steps Process.

Concepts and Action – Making the Connection

Now that you are familiar with the concepts from the Framework for Information Quality and have been introduced to the Ten Steps Process, let's tie them together. *Table 3.8* and *Table 3.9* provide two ways of referencing and linking the concepts to where they are put into action in the Ten Steps, with one mapping the Ten Steps to the FIQ components and the other mapping the FIQ components to the Ten Steps.

In actuality, any of the concepts may show up in any of the Ten Steps and vice versa, but the tables highlight specific connections between the two. Use *Table 3.8* if you are working in one of the Ten Steps and want to see the concepts used there. You can then gather more information on those concepts. Use *Table 3.9* if you are looking at the concepts and want to see how they are put into action.

Chapter 3 Summary

Chapter 3: Key Concepts introduced you to fundamental ideas, the understanding of which, will aid your data quality work. High-quality data does not happen by magic. It takes a deliberate effort to

ensure that data meets the needs of the organization. Information, like financial and human resources, must be properly managed throughout its life cycle to get the full use and benefit from it. The acronym POSMAD is an easy way to remember the six phases of the information life cycle: Plan, Obtain, Store and Share, Maintain, Apply, and Dispose. You have been encouraged to apply life cycle thinking to all your data quality work.

POSMAD plus several other concepts were summarized in the Framework for Information Quality (FIQ), which provides an at-a-glance view of the components necessary to have high-quality information. Concepts in the FIQ were defined, along with others central to understanding and managing your data, such as data quality dimensions, business impact techniques, data categories, and data specifications (with a focus on meta-data, data standards, reference data, data models, and business rules). You were given just enough information about the concepts to get you started and given other resources for more detail when needed.

You were oriented to the Ten Steps Process and shown the relationship to the concepts. You are now ready to put the concepts to work using the instructions, examples, and templates in *Chapter 4: The Ten Steps Process*, *Chapter 5: Structuring Your Project*, and *Chapter 6: Other Techniques and Tools*.

Table 3.8 Mapping the Ten Steps Process to the Framework for Information Quality (FIQ)

Step in the Ten Steps Process	Section/Component/Concept in the FIQ Used in the Associated Step

Step 1 – Determine Business Needs and Approach	• Business Needs (Why) Customers, Products, Services, Strategies, Goals, Issues, Opportunities
	• Information Life Cycle POSMAD (at a high level)
	• All 4 Key Components of Data, Processes, People/Organizations, Technology (at a high level)
	• Subset of Broad-Impact Components (at high level):
	  o **R**equirements and Constraints
	  o **R**esponsibility
	  o **C**ommunication
	  o **C**hange
	  o **E**thics
	• Culture and Environment

Step 2 – Analyze Information Environment	• Business Needs (Why) Customers, Products, Services, Strategies, Goals, Issues, Opportunities
	• Information Life Cycle POSMAD (at appropriate level of detail)
	• All 4 Key Components of Data, Processes, People/Organizations, Technology (at appropriate level of detail for each)
	• Interaction Matrix
	• Location (Where) and Time (When, How Often, and How Long)
	• Subset of Broad-Impact Components (at appropriate level of detail):
	  o **R**equirements and Constraints
	  o **R**esponsibility
	  o **S**tructure, Context, and Meaning
	  o **C**ommunication
	  o **C**hange
	  o **E**thics
	• Culture and Environment

Step 3 – Assess Data Quality	• Business Needs (Why) Customers, Products, Services, Strategies, Goals, Issues, Opportunities
	• Information Life Cycle POSMAD
	• All 4 Key Components of Data, Processes, People/Organizations, Technology (at appropriate level of detail for each data quality dimension to be assessed)
	• Interaction Matrix
	• Location (Where) and Time (When, How Often, and How Long)
	• Subset of Broad-Impact Components (at high level):
	  o **R**equirements and Constraints
	  o **R**esponsibility
	  o **S**tructure, Context, and Meaning
	  o **C**ommunication
	  o **C**hange
	  o **E**thics
	• Culture and Environment

Step 4 – Assess Business Impact	• Business Needs (Why) Customers, Products, Services, Strategies, Goals, Issues, Opportunities
	• Information Life Cycle POSMAD (focus on Apply phase for biggest impact associated with revenue, other phases for impact associated with costs, all phases associated with risk)
	• All 4 Key Components of Data, Processes, People/Organizations, Technology (at appropriate level of detail for each business impact technique to be used)
	• Interaction Matrix
	• Location (Where) and Time (When, How Often, and How Long)
	• Subset of Broad-Impact Components (at high level):
	  o **R**equirements and Constraints
	  o **C**ommunication
	  o **C**hange
	  o **E**thics
	• Culture and Environment

Step 5 – Identify Root Causes	Use all components of the FIQ as a checklist. Anything that is missing is a potential root cause of data quality problems.

Table 3.8 Mapping the Ten Steps Process to the Framework for Information Quality (FIQ) *(Continued)*

Step in the Ten Steps Process	Section/Component/Concept in the FIQ Used in the Associated Step

Step 6 – Develop Improvement Plans	• Business Needs (Why) Customers, Products, Services, Strategies, Goals, Issues, Opportunities
	• Information Life Cycle POSMAD
	• All 4 Key Components of Data, Processes, People/Organizations, Technology
	• Interaction Matrix
	• Location (Where) and Time (When, How Often, and How Long)
	• All Broad-Impact Components (at high level):
	  o Requirements and Constraints
	  o Responsibility
	  o Improvement and Prevention
	  o Communication
	  o Change
	  o Ethics
	• Culture and Environment

Step 7 – Prevent Future Data Errors	• Business Needs (Why) Customers, Products, Services, Strategies, Goals, Issues, Opportunities
	• Information Life Cycle POSMAD
	• All 4 Key Components of Data, Processes, People/Organizations, Technology
	• Interaction Matrix
	• Location (Where) and Time (When, How Often, and How Long)
	• All Broad-Impact Components (at high level):
	  o Requirements and Constraints
	  o Responsibility
	  o Improvement and Prevention
	  o Communication
	  o Change
	  o Ethics
	• Culture and Environment

Step 8 – Correct Current Data Errors	• Business Needs (Why) Customers, Products, Services, Strategies, Goals, Issues, Opportunities
	• Information Life Cycle POSMAD
	• All 4 Key Components of Data, Processes, People/Organizations, Technology
	• Interaction Matrix
	• Location (Where) and Time (When, How Often, and How Long)
	• All Broad-Impact Components (at high level):
	  o Requirements and Constraints
	  o Responsibility
	  o Improvement and Prevention
	  o Communication
	  o Change
	  o Ethics
	• Culture and Environment

Step 9 – Monitor Controls	• Business Needs (Why) Customers, Products, Services, Strategies, Goals, Issues, Opportunities
	• Information Life Cycle POSMAD
	• All 4 Key Components of Data, Processes, People/Organizations, Technology
	• Interaction Matrix
	• Location (Where) and Time (When, How Often, and How Long)
	• All Broad-Impact Components (at high level):
	  o Requirements and Constraints
	  o Responsibility
	  o Improvement and Prevention
	  o Communication
	  o Change
	  o Ethics
	• Culture and Environment

Step 10 – Communicate, Manage, and Engage People Throughout	• Business Needs (Why) Customers, Products, Services, Strategies, Goals, Issues, Opportunities
	• Key Components of People/Organizations
	• Subset of Broad-Impact Components:
	  o Responsibility
	  o Communication
	  o Change
	  o Ethics
	• Culture and Environment

Table 3.9 Mapping the Framework for Information Quality to the Ten Steps Process

Section/Component/Concept in the FIQ	Step in the Ten Steps Process Where the Section/Component/Concept is Put into Action
All FIQ sections/ components/ concepts	• Used as a checklist in *Step 5 – Identify Root Causes*. Anything that is missing is a potential root cause of data quality problems.
Business Needs (Why) Customers, Products, Services, Strategies, Goals, Issues, Opportunities	• Specifically addressed in *Step 1 – Determine Business Needs and Approach* • Keep them visible at each step to keep activities focused • *Step 4 – Assess Business Impact* helps answer why
Information Life Cycle POSMAD	• *Step 1 – Determine Business Needs and Approach* (at a high level) as input to selecting project focus and input to project scope when planning the project • *Step 2 – Analyze Information Environment* (at appropriate level of detail when documenting and analyzing current processes) • *Step 3 – Assess Data Quality* (to determine where along the information life cycle path to capture data to be assessed for quality) • *Step 4 – Assess Business Impact* (as input to determining impact to revenue, costs, and risk) • *Step 5 – Identify Root Causes* (as input to root cause analysis) • *Step 6 – Develop Improvement Plans* (as input to deciding where along the information life cycle path improvements – both preventive and corrective – need to be made) • *Step 7 – Prevent Future Data Errors* (develop new processes to prevent future data errors) • *Step 8 – Correct Current Data Errors* (creating processes to correct data) • *Step 9 – Monitor Controls* (ensuring processes for ongoing monitoring are stable and sufficient)
Key Components of Data, Processes, People/Organizations, Technology	• *Step 1 – Determine Business Needs and Approach* (at a high level) • *Step 2 – Analyze Information Environment* (at appropriate level of detail for each substep) • *Step 3 – Assess Data Quality* (at appropriate level of detail for each data quality dimension to be assessed) • *Step 4 – Assess Business Impact* (at appropriate level of detail for each business impact technique to be assessed) • *Step 5 – Identify Root Causes* • *Step 6 – Develop Improvement Plans* • *Step 7 – Prevent Future Data Errors* • *Step 8 – Correct Current Data Errors* • *Step 9 – Monitor Controls*
Interaction Matrix	• *Step 2 – Analyze Information Environment* (when determining interactions between any of the substeps) • *Steps 3-9* (look at the interaction between the Information Life Cycle POSMAD and the 4 Key Components when documenting and analyzing current processes, developing new processes to prevent future data errors, creating processes to correct data, or ensuring processes for ongoing monitoring are stable and sufficient)
Location (Where) and Time (When, How Often, and How Long)	• *All steps* (to determine where activities should take place and when. If activities are to be repeated, how often and for how long they should be continued)
Broad-Impact Components	• Most of them will be applicable in most steps. • Specifics noted below.
Requirements and Constraints	• *Step 1 – Determine Business Needs and Approach* • *Step 2.1 – Understand Relevant Requirements and Constraints* • As input to any step to ensure what is being implemented adheres to requirements and takes constraints into account
Responsibility	• As input to any step
Improvement and Prevention	• *Step 5 – Identify Root Causes* • *Step 6 – Develop Improvement Plans* • *Step 7 – Prevent Future Data Errors* • *Step 8 – Correct Current Data Errors* • *Step 9 – Monitor Controls*
Structure, Context, and Meaning	Anywhere data specifications (metadata, data standards, reference data, data models, and business rules) show up in the methodology as input to understanding data content, requirements, and constraints, particularly: • *Step 2.2 – Understand Relevant Data and Data Specifications* • *Step 3.2 – Data Specifications* (a data quality dimension).
Communication **C**hange **E**thics	• All three should be considered in every step because they relate to *Step 10 – Communicate, Manage, and Engage People Throughout*. Since something from *Step 10* should be done in each of the prior steps, the broad-impact components of communication, change and ethics are a consideration for all steps in all projects.
Culture and Environment	• *Step 10 – Communicate, Manage, and Engage People Throughout* (as a consideration for how this step will be implemented) • Note that since something from *Step 10* should be done in each of the prior steps, culture and environment are a consideration for all steps in all projects.

The Ten Steps Process

I have been impressed with the urgency of doing.
Knowledge is not enough; we must apply.
Being willing is not enough; we must do.

— Leonardo da Vinci

In This Chapter

Executing Data Quality Projects. https://doi.org/10.1016/B978-0-12-818015-0.00006-2

Introduction to Chapter 4

Chapter 4 contains the step-by-step guide for creating, assessing, improving, sustaining, and managing information and data quality. It provides instructions for implementing the Ten Steps Process (see *Figure 4.0.1*) which puts the key concepts from *Chapter 3* into action. The Ten Steps are guideposts along your project path and they have stood the test of time.

Here you will find the details for carrying out each of the Ten Steps, starting with a "You Are Here" Figure which indicates where you are in the overall process. A Step Summary Table gives an overview of the main objectives, purpose, inputs and outputs, tools and techniques, communication suggestions, and checkpoint questions for each step. All the steps use the same format, with sections on Business Benefit and Context, Approach, and Sample Output and Templates. See *The Ten Steps Process Format* section in the *Introduction* for more information.

The Ten Steps Process was designed to be flexible so you can select the steps that will address the business needs and data quality issues of concern. A one-person, 4-week project can use the Ten Steps Process just as well as a multi-person, several-month project. The level of detail needed for each step, technique, or activity will vary depending on the project objectives, as will the time required to complete them.

It will be helpful to keep the Ten Steps Process visual readily available to stay oriented to where you are in the process while reading this chapter and executing your project. An overview is available in the *Appendix: Quick References* or can be downloaded from the companion website at www.gfalls.com.

The following advice will help when selecting and adjusting the Ten Steps to deal with the many and varied situations related to data quality that you will encounter: level of detail, just enough principle, document as discovered, and additional guidelines.

Level of Detail

Think of your project as a trip. Your "project" is to go from London to Paris. To get there, you will need information at different levels of detail during your trip. See *Figure 4.0.2*. Will you drive a car, take an airplane, a ferry, a train, or some combination? You decide to drive except for taking a ferry across the English Channel.

Showing how the project fits into the organization as a whole is similar to the world view map, which provides high-level context. A country level view, still high-level but with a bit more detail, shows beginning and ending points, the high-level route to be taken, and key cities along the way. This level view is useful when raising awareness about the project. It will help you orient others to the business needs and project objectives, how the team will proceed, and key milestones along the way.

The high-level views may be enough to get approval and resources, but project team members must have more detail to guide them through unfamiliar territory. A geographic area view will help the team drive efficiently through the various French regions and départements along the route. Once near Paris, your destination city, the geographic area maps do not provide the detail to get from the motorway or autoroute to the hotel. A street-level map is needed. Similarly, team members responsible for completing an assessment, analyzing results, making recommendations, or implementing controls require more detail to complete their tasks.

Different levels of detail are needed depending on business needs, where you are in the project, who is working on the various activities, and with whom you engage and communicate. The team lead may be using high to mid-levels of detail when communicating status to project sponsors while, at the same time, the team members are working at the street-level details to carry out an assessment. The point is to be cognizant of where you are in the project and only go to the level of detail needed to complete the work at any point in time.

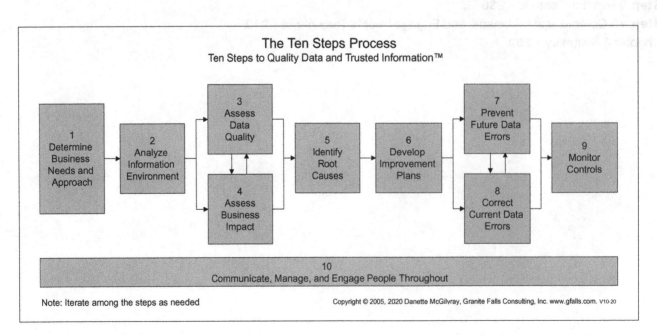

The Ten Steps Process
Ten Steps to Quality Data and Trusted Information™

Note: Iterate among the steps as needed

Copyright © 2005, 2020 Danette McGilvray, Granite Falls Consulting, Inc. www.gfalls.com. V10-20

Figure 4.0.1 The Ten Steps Process.

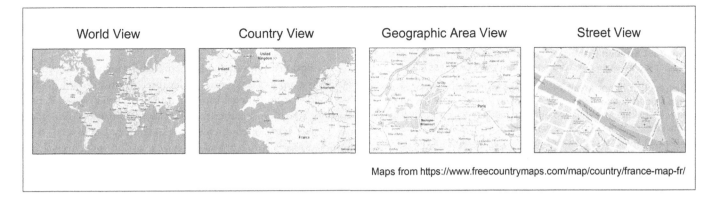

Maps from https://www.freecountrymaps.com/map/country/france-map-fr/

Figure 4.0.2 Maps – different levels of detail for different needs.

Think of the Ten Steps Process as the map for your trip. Select the steps to meet the business needs, data quality issues, and objectives within scope of the project – with different combinations of steps for different trips. Maps come in different levels of detail and you will use the level that best meets your needs at a particular moment. The instructions, techniques, examples, and templates in the steps provide directions to complete the steps. However, it is up to you to decide what is relevant, appropriate, and the suitable level of detail needed within a step and at any point in time.

Maps, like project plans, documentation, and other artifacts, not only let the team know where they are on their journey, they also keep the team coordinated in their efforts and moving forward.

 Best Practice

Level of Detail. Look to the business needs to determine what is relevant and focus there. For each step, start at a high level and work to lower levels of detail only if useful.

Use the following questions to help guide your decisions about the appropriate level of detail:

1) Will the detail have a significant and demonstrable bearing on the business needs, data quality issues, and project objectives?
2) Will the detail provide evidence to prove or disprove a hypothesis about the quality or business impact of the data?

Only if you can answer yes to both questions, should you go to the next level of detail.

Just Enough Principle

Too often project teams think they need to know everything about everything before they can do anything. This is known as analysis paralysis. Progress is slow because it takes too long to make decisions or show results. On the other hand, some people create inefficiencies by moving too quickly or chaotically in a way that causes unnecessary rework later. Use your good critical thinking skills to avoid both extremes by taking "just enough" time and expending "just enough" effort in each step. The Just Enough Principle provides crucial guidance by stating: "Spend 'just enough' time and effort to optimize results." This principle was inspired by Kimberly

Wiefling when she talks about "Just enough planning to optimize results. Not a drop more! . . . But not a drop less either" in her book *Scrappy Project Management™: The 12 Predictable and Avoidable Pitfalls Every Project Faces* (2007).

Just enough is not about being sloppy or cutting corners. It is about gathering enough information, making decisions based on what you know at the time, and moving on. If circumstances change or new knowledge comes to light, you can make adjustments from there. Whatever you are working on, spend just enough time on that step, technique or activity to optimize results. Not a drop more, but not a drop less either.

For example, at the beginning of the project you must have a good grasp of the business needs and the data quality issues, including the associated data subject areas (such as customer, product, or physician), the processes, people/organizations, and technology within scope – at a high level. This is done in *Step 1 – Determine Business Needs and Approach*. But you do not need to know every data field name, its description, other metadata, data standards, etc. at this point. If you do happen to have detail on any of these, set it aside for *Step 2 – Analyze Information Environment*. This is when you understand the data and data specifications at the field level. At that time, you may discover there are too many data elements to assess. It makes sense to prioritize them to the most important data elements (called Critical Data Elements or CDEs). These CDEs now become the focus of your project going forward and metadata is collected only for the CDEs. If you get to *Step 3 – Assess Data Quality* and find there are a few data fields that were missed, gather details at that time.

This approach is much better than using time in *Step 1* to gather *all* the detail about *all* the data fields, *all* the business processes, *all* the technology, and *all* the people that *might* be important. It is also better than mindlessly skipping *Steps 1 and 2* and rushing into the data quality assessment in *Step 3* without ensuring you are looking at the data that truly impacts the critical business needs.

Use just enough thinking to get what is needed at the right time. The Just Enough Principle will help you avoid both analysis paralysis and chaotic rework and will keep the project moving forward more effectively.

Document as Discovered

I am a major proponent of writing down ideas as you discover them. Capture "ah-ha" moments whenever they come. Have you ever been in a meeting when the team is thinking and working well together? Where everyone leaves the room energized by the progress and insights that came out of the meeting? But no one wrote them down! Two weeks later someone says, "Remember that great meeting we had and the good solutions we discussed? Do you remember what we decided?" No one remembers. The valuable knowledge is gone, time was wasted, and work has to be redone.

Maybe you are analyzing the information environment in *Step 2*. Possible root causes of data quality issues are uncovered at this early stage. The team knows that root cause analysis is *Step 5*. But do you say, "We cannot talk about root causes because we are only in *Step 2*?" Of course not! Document what you learn when you learn it. You will have many insights throughout your project – and not always when expected. That is the beauty of the Ten Steps process. It brings together information in new ways, showing relationships where they were previously hidden, sparking solutions that were not seen before. It is critical to document those ideas when they come to mind, even if they will be used later in the project. For more ideas and a template to help document when discovered, see *Analyze, Synthesize, Recommend, Document, and Act on Results* in *Chapter 6: Other Techniques and Tools*. Use tracking and documentation tools or applications if available. However, lack of a sophisticated tool is no reason not to document. Use a simple spreadsheet if that is what you have. Make documenting a priority. There is no excuse for not documenting!

Additional Guidelines for Using the Ten Steps

Iterative approach—Successfully applying the methodology takes an iterative approach. While the Ten Steps are represented by a linear progression from step to step, the process of information and data improvement is iterative. Through the iterations, the Ten Steps continue to provide the map to help you know where you are and the milestones or guideposts to keep you moving forward.

As additional information is uncovered throughout the project, earlier assumptions may need to be revisited and revised. It may be found that more detail is required from a previous step. Return to those activities to gather the necessary information. For example, project teams often discover that the root causes of their issues found in *Step 5 – Identify Root Causes* result in problems that are more widespread than they had originally believed. Suddenly the scope of the problem broadens, and the original data quality assessments seem inadequate. In this case, they can return to *Step 3 – Assess Data Quality* and repeat the assessment with a larger data set or choose another dimension to assess. Likewise, if the scope has broadened, they may turn to *Step 4 – Assess Business Impact* for a technique to help them show the value of additional work, present the business issue, and solicit more resources – or use business impact to identify the most critical of the most important to keep the scope narrow.

The whole Ten Steps Process itself is iterative in nature. If a project team has made use of applicable steps in one project, they can identify another business issue and start the improvement process again with a new project. Information quality improvement takes work and rework – it requires a true continuous-improvement mindset to institute long-term change. The beauty of the Ten Steps Process is that it can be applied to numerous situations where data quality is a concern and impacts critical business needs.

It is not unusual for one project team to assess data quality and business impact, identify root causes, and develop specific recommendations for improvement. Yet it is a different team who can actually effect change and implement the improvements. A different project may be initiated to focus just on the correction and prevention of data errors. Yet another team may be responsible for implementing controls such as metrics and scorecards based on what was learned from the first team's work.

It is possible that root causes are uncovered early in the Ten Steps Process. If there is a root cause that is urgent to address and can be easily implemented, jump ahead to *Step 7*, do the preventive work in parallel while the assessment work continues in *Step 3*.

Reference this book often—While you may not read the book cover to cover or apply it all at once, understand what is included so you can reference it when needed. Expect to cross-reference the various sections regularly and use the concepts when applying the Ten Steps in *Chapter 4*. Become familiar with the Framework for Information Quality and the information life cycle. Reference the sections on data quality dimensions, business impact techniques, and other key concepts in *Chapter 3* as needed. Become familiar with what is needed to successfully structure your project in *Chapter 5*. Be aware of the other tools and techniques in *Chapter 6* that can be applied in many steps. All are integral parts of the methodology.

Project management—Executing the Ten Steps Process successfully requires use of sound project management practices. A project is broadly defined as any use of the methodology to address a defined business issue related to data and information – whether by a single person or a team, as a standalone data quality improvement project, as data quality tasks integrated into another project or methodology (e.g., as a data migration project using a third-party methodology), or as ad hoc use of steps, techniques, and activities. Even if you are an individual, you can apply good project management practices in a much more abbreviated fashion than a project manager and team would need to.

Good judgement and your knowledge—I compared the Ten Steps Process to a recipe and a cookbook. Both provide instructions, but the Ten Steps are not applied the same way, every time they are used. As with a recipe, you will modify them to fit the occasion, number of people, and ingredients you have on hand. Its best use requires good judgment, knowledge of your business, and creativity

Pick and choose—The Ten Steps Process is designed to be flexible. Take a pick-and-choose approach to its use and execute only those steps applicable to your business needs, data quality issues, and project scope and objectives. While you should thoughtfully consider each of the Ten Steps, use your judgment to choose which of the steps and activities apply to your situation.

Scalable—The Ten Steps process can be used for everything from a one-person, few-week project to a several-month project with a multi-person team. The issues to be addressed, the steps chosen, and the level of detail needed greatly affect the length of time and the resources required. For example, a specific step could take one person two hours to complete while the same step used in a different project could take a project team two weeks.

Reuse (80/20 rule)—Many times the Ten Steps Process requires information that is already available within your organization. Supplement existing materials with original research only as needed. A general guideline is to expect that 80 percent of what is asked for in *Step 2 – Analyze Information Environment* already exists somewhere – formally documented or simply known by those who work there. Ensure that *your* discoveries, documentation, or updates are made available for re-use by other projects and teams.

Use examples as a starting point—Be aware that the actual output of the steps may take a different form than the examples shown. For instance, a template or sample output may use a matrix showing interaction between processes and data. However, the output of the step is not a matrix – it is knowledge about the processes and related data, their relationship, how they interact, and how that can impact data quality. Your output may take the physical form of a matrix, a diagram, a process or data flow, or a textual explanation. The format used should enhance understanding. What is important is the learning that comes out of completing the steps and resulting good decisions and effective actions.

Flexibility—Successful projects require the ability to deal with continuous change and to remain open to input from many stakeholders, both within and outside the project team.

Focus on process—Focus on why the problems exist, not on who is making them. "Blame the process, not the people." Know enough about what caused the problems to determine how to address them and then move quickly to solutions.

Tool independent—The Ten Steps process does not require any particular vendor tool. However, there are tools on the market that can make your data quality job easier. For example, there are tools available to help with cataloging, profiling, matching, parsing, standardization, enhancement, and cleansing of your data. Applying the Ten Steps Process can help you more effectively make use of these tools.

Improvement activities—Some of the improvement activities (root cause, prevention, and clean-up) can be implemented within the timeline and scope of your project. Others may generate additional activities or even separate projects which requires different people outside of your project team.

Analyze and document—Throughout the project be sure to capture in a central area the results of your analysis, suspected causes of issues you are finding, and suspected impact on the business. As the project proceeds, more will be learned to prove or disprove your early assumptions.

Broad perspective—Many information and data quality improvement projects happen in concert with other data management initiatives or company-wide improvements. Keep informed by contacting other project leaders so that you can produce and share documentation with each other that you can all use to inform your projects. Collaborate on communication and change management to bring clarity to others and avoid confusion.

Practice makes perfect—As with anything new, as you gain experience with the methodology (both concepts and process steps), subsequent uses of it will be easier and faster. Learning to select the steps and techniques, deciding the right level of detail, effectively applying the Ten Steps to the many, many situations where data quality is an important component – all are part of the *art of data quality*. Your ability to apply appropriately will increase with experience.

Step 1 Determine Business Needs and Approach

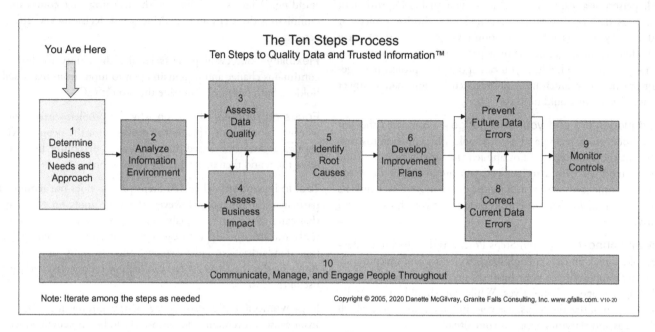

Figure 4.1.1 "You Are Here" Graphic for Step 1 – Determine Business Needs and Approach.

Introduction to Step 1

The importance of this step cannot be overstated. Your work *must* be, not should be, tied to one or more critical business needs. "Business Needs" is my overarching phrase for whatever is important to your organization – driven by customers, products, services, strategies, goals, issues, and opportunities. *Critical* business needs – meaning those that are the most important – must be the motivation behind your data quality project. The time, effort, and resources spent, and the project results should make a difference to your organization.

I have been told many times by those who skipped this step, "I spent 3-4 months working on a data quality project. Then I showed my business colleagues the results. They said it was interesting but nothing they really cared about." What a shame to waste time and talent on something that does not matter. For most, resources cannot be obtained to even start a data quality project unless that project is tied to critical business needs. That is how it should be. There is too much to do and too few resources to go around. If you are going to get support, attention, resources, and any chance of others taking action around data quality, your work must be tied to critical business needs.

Much time can be spent going after data quality issues that seem interesting. How much better to know what the business cares about, determine the data and information associated with those business needs, and use that as the starting point for your project. If you see data quality issues that are particularly troubling, determine if they tie into critical business needs. If yes, then that could also be the starting point for your project.

Table 4.1.1	Step Summary Table for Step 1 – Determine Business Needs and Approach
Objective	• Prioritize and finalize business needs (pertaining to customers, products, services, strategies, goals, issues, and/or opportunities) to be addressed by the project • Clarify project focus and benefits • Define project objectives and agree on expected results • Outline the information environment within scope at a high level – the data, processes, people/organizations, technology, and information life cycle • Plan and initiate the project using good project management practices • Communicate with and engage stakeholders from the beginning of the project

Purpose	• Ensure the project will add value by addressing only high-priority business needs
	• Ensure the data in question is connected to business needs
	• Increase the chance of success by managing the project well from the start
	   o Ensure necessary agreement with the project scope and objectives
	   o Guide project planning and scope by using the initial high-level snapshot of the information environment
	• Ensure support and necessary resources for the project

Table 4.1.1 Step Summary Table for Step 1 – Determine Business Needs and Approach *(Continued)*

Inputs	• Business needs where data and information are components • Known or suspected data quality problems • Knowledge and artifacts to help describe the high-level information environment within scope, e.g., organization charts and application architecture • Project management expertise using the selected project approach/SDLC

Techniques and Tools	• To gather/identify business needs and data quality issues, ensure data in question is connected with business needs, and prioritize which will be the focus of the project:
	  ○ *Template 4.1.1 – Business Needs and Data Quality Issues Worksheet*
	  ○ *Step 4.2 – Connect the Dots*
	  ○ *Step 4.7 – Perception of Relevance and Trust*
	  ○ *Step 4.4 – Benefit vs. Cost Matrix*
	  ○ *Friday Afternoon Measurement (FAM)*
	  ○ Other favored prioritization techniques used by your organization
	• To plan the project:
	  ○ See *Chapter 5: Structuring Your Project*
	  ○ Techniques for chosen project approach (e.g., create project charter, context diagram, features, user stories, etc.)
	  ○ *Template 4.1.2 – Project Charter*
	• To communicate and engage:
	  ○ See *Step 10 – Communicate, Manage, and Engage People Throughout*
	  ○ Other favored communication techniques
	• From *Chapter 6: Other Techniques and Tools:*
	  ○ Conduct a Survey
	  ○ Track Issues and Action Items (Start in Step 1 and use throughout)
	  ○ Analyze, Synthesize, Recommend, Document, and Act on Results (Start in Step 1 and use throughout)

Outputs	• Agreement and documentation of:
	  ○ Business needs, data quality issues, and project focus
	  ○ Project objectives and benefits
	  ○ Information environment within scope (high level)
	• Project plan and other artifacts "right-sized" for chosen project approach/SDLC (e.g., charter, context diagram, timeline, milestones, features, user stories)
	• Stakeholder analysis
	• Initial communication and change management plan
	• Completed communication and change management tasks appropriate at this point in the project

Communicate, Manage, and Engage	• Start building a stakeholder list and create an initial communication plan • If conducting surveys or interviews to gather/understand business needs and data quality issues, ensure respondents know the purpose and are prepared to participate • Meet with stakeholders, get feedback on the planned project, set expectations, and address their concerns • Listen to all feedback – positive and negative; make adjustments and follow-up • Finalize support and resources • Hold a project kickoff with the project team and management • Set up the structure for storing and sharing project documents • Set up processes for tracking issues and action items and documenting results
Checkpoint	• Are the business needs and data quality issues, project focus, benefits, and objectives clearly defined? • Have management, sponsors, stakeholders, the project team and their managers been appropriately engaged? Do they understand and support the project? • Have needed resources been committed? • Is the high-level information environment understood and documented – the data, processes, people/organizations, technology, and information life cycle within scope of the project? • Has the project been properly initiated, e.g., through a project kickoff? • Have the project plan, other artifacts related to the project approach/ SDLC, and file structure for sharing documents been created? • Has the initial stakeholder analysis been completed and used as input to the communication plan? • Has the communication plan been created and necessary communications in this step been completed?

Definition

Business Needs. An overarching phrase to indicate whatever is important to an organization and driven by customers, products, services, strategies, goals, issues, and opportunities. Critical business needs – meaning those that are the *most* important – should drive all actions and decisions and be the motivation behind your data quality projects.

Step 1 Process Flow

It is impossible to be strictly prescriptive about the sequence for carrying out the instructions in this step, because the starting point for this step varies widely from project to project. For some, the business needs and role data plays are clear, support is strong, and resources are available. All that remains in this step is to plan the project. For others, the idea of a data quality project is a new idea and much has to be done to identify the most important needs, prioritize them, finalize the project focus, gain support, and find resources before starting the project plan. See *Figure 4.1.2* as I describe what happens in this step. The order in which they are completed is up to you.

The emergence of a data quality project often starts as: 1) Business need(s) where data is a component, or 2) Known or suspected data quality issue(s). No matter the starting point, during this step you must identify the data underlying the business need or ensure there is a real business need associated with the known or suspected data quality issue.

The business needs of your organization (or business unit, department, team) and data quality issues are input to *Step 1.1*. As mentioned, for some the focus of the project is already clear. In others, there will be several issues or opportunities from which you can choose to focus your efforts. There are multiple ways to prioritize. Use techniques suggested here or a prioritization approach that has worked well in your organization.

As you discuss the business needs and data quality issues, connect them with the associated data, processes, people/organizations, and technology– *at a high level*. Out of these activities comes the selected project focus, which is input to devising your project plan in *Step 1.2*. Ideally, your selected project focus will be confirmed with the appropriate stakeholders *before* finalizing the project plan.

In *Figure 4.1.2*, *Step 1.1* illustrates that there are different starting points for a project. For some, a particular business need and/or data quality issue makes it clear where to point their efforts. Others have to prioritize and select from several possibilities before the focus of the project is finalized. *Step 1.2 – Plan the Project* is also important because any data quality work needs to be organized well. *Chapter 5: Structuring Your Project* provides helpful details to supplement this step so you set yourself up for success from the beginning.

This step forms the foundation for the remainder of the project. Make sure your project addresses something that people care about and will bring value to your organization.

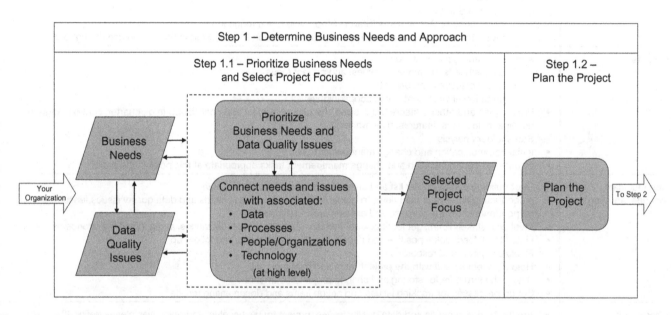

Figure 4.1.2 Process flow for Step 1 – Determine Business Needs and Approach.

Step 1.1 Prioritize Business Needs and Select Project Focus

Business Benefit and Context

It is imperative your project spends time only on something the business cares about. (Have I stressed that enough?) This step helps identify what is of most importance, if business needs are not already known. As mentioned, the order in which to carry out the instructions in this step are not prescriptive, but the critical business needs must be identified no matter the sequence of activities.

Approach

1. Identify business needs and data quality issues.

What motivates your company, agency, or institution? There can be many reasons that encourage them to act. These reasons can vary over time. An organization might have a long-term strategy or plan of action that is driving shorter-term goals. There may be particular issues or pain points that have arisen, sometimes unexpectedly, and are causing problems that need a solution. Maybe the motivation is tied to an opportunity where circumstances are allowing the company to move into a new market, for example. Or a government agency is now mandated to provide a new service. All require data and information, with the high-quality (we could also say the right-quality) data and information helping them to be the most effective.

Template 4.1.1 – Business Needs and Data Quality Issues Worksheet in the *Sample Output and Templates* section is useful to compile the business needs and data quality issues found before prioritizing.

The following methods can be used to uncover business needs and data quality issues or to learn more about those already known:

Research—Read your organization's internet site (available to public), their intranet site (available internally), annual report, and presentations at employee meetings. These can indicate what is vital to your team, your function, or the organization as a whole.

Interviews and Surveys—The goal of a survey in this step is to uncover critical business needs and/or data quality issues to help you decide the focus of your data quality project. Talk with your manager, your manager's manager, your colleagues and others in positions to know what is most important to the business right now. If you have access to C-level executives and a board of directors, include them. Invite business, data, and technical stakeholders to contribute their concerns and perspectives. You don't need to survey everyone, but ensure you are interviewing those with insight to the problems along with those who have authority to approve and pay for the project.

See *Step 4.7 – Perception of Relevance and Trust* for another business impact technique to uncover people's pain points, impacts felt from poor data quality, and which data is important to them, along with their perceptions of and level of trust in the quality of the data. Also see Conduct a Survey in *Chapter 6: Other Techniques and Tools* for additional help when developing and implementing a survey.

Documented data quality issues—If you or someone else has kept a list of complaints related to data quality, now is the time to review it. See if those data quality issues are associated with high priority business needs.

General business impact—Consider the following general types of business impact to spark people's thinking about business needs and data quality:

- **Lost revenue and missed opportunities**. Where revenue could increase if the data quality issue is addressed – for example, increasing the products or services purchased because the customer information was correct and therefore more customers were able to be contacted. Put another way, the customer did not get the chance or choice of doing business with your company because 1) they were never contacted as a result of incorrect contact data, or 2) were not given the offer due to incorrect demographic information that informed the segments of the population to whom the offer was made.
- **Lost business**. Where your company once had a customer or vendor, but they chose not to do business with you because of a problem where data quality was a contributing factor. For example, the inability to ship products correctly due to poor-quality data may cause the customer to order from another company. The inability to pay invoices in a timely manner due to poor data quality may influence a supplier's decision to refuse to provide parts, materials, or supplies to your company.

- **Increased risk**. Where data quality issues increase risk to your company. Examples are compliance and security failures due to poor-quality data or exposure to credit risks when purchases by one customer are associated with duplicate customer master records, causing the credit limit for that customer to be exceeded.
- **Unnecessary or excessive costs**. Where the company incurs costs due to wasted time and materials from rework, data correction, cost to recover lost business, impact to processes, and so forth. For example, manufacturing stops because materials were not ordered and available in a timely fashion due to incorrect inventory data.
- **Catastrophe**. Where poor data quality contributed to disastrous results such as legal repercussions, loss of property, or loss of life.
- **Shared processes and shared data**. Where several business processes share the same information, and quality problems in the data impact all of them; or one key business process central to the organization is affected by the lack of good data quality. For example, supplier (or vendor) master records affect the ability to quickly place an order with your supplier and the timely payment of that supplier's invoices. If your company only interfaces with its customer via the website, then the quality of information presented on the website is of critical importance.

Examples of actual data quality—Query and extract a few examples of actual poor-quality data from the organization's systems. See the *Best Practice callout box* for how to do a quick assessment that brings data quality issues to view.

 Best Practice

Do you have a data quality problem? The first step in solving a problem is admitting that you have one. Tom Redman has a technique to answer the question, "Do I have a data quality problem?" He designed it in response to the need for organizations to make a simple, defensible measurement of data quality without investing too much time or money. It is called FAM because many people can fit it into a Friday afternoon, hence Friday Afternoon Measurement.

Narrow your focus to the most recent data (the last 100 records used, created or processed), and the 10-15 most essential attributes (fields, columns, or attributes) to complete some task, such as signing up a customer, renewing a software license, and so forth. Put the data in a spreadsheet and print hardcopies. Invite 2-3 people who understand the data to a 2-hour meeting where they each mark errors with a red pen. Count a data record as "perfect" if there are no red marks.

Together summarize and interpret results. The most important step in doing so is counting the perfects. You'll get a number between 0 and 100 and it represents your "DQ score." Most are surprised by their low scores. When reporting results, don't generalize. Simply state, that "In the last 100 records, 42 failed." It means that 42 things got messed up in your business. Reporting results in this way helps close the gap between data quality and the work the organization does.

FAM was designed to be a physical activity and tactile in a way that helps data become more tangible. It is fast, cheap, and identifies whether you have a data quality problem and where to start targeting your efforts. It does not scale up, but it does usually provide motivation to take further action.

– Thomas C. Redman. Further details available in Getting in Front on Data: Who Does What (2016) and "Assess whether you have a data quality problem" (2016)

Note: Once the data quality problems are seen, address them by using relevant steps, techniques, and activities from the Ten Steps Process.

2. Prioritize the business needs and data quality issues.

The focus of your project may be clearly apparent. But don't be surprised if you uncover a long list of business needs and/or data quality issues. If so, you have to prioritize that list to answer the question: What are the most important goals, strategies, issues, and opportunities facing the business right now, and which should be the focus of the project?

There are many ways to prioritize. Your organization may have a preferred method, or you may have a favorite technique. See *Step 4.4 – Benefit vs. Cost Matrix* for one technique that works well when prioritizing a list of business needs. Selected business, data, and technical stakeholders may be invited to participate in a facilitated session to select the most critical business needs.

If the business need connected to a data quality issue is not critical and of high priority, then find something else as the focus for your data quality project.

3. Connect business needs and data.

See *Step 4.2 – Connect the Dots* for an easy and quick technique to help you link the business needs and the data. This technique also identifies the high-level processes, people/organizations, and technology associated with the business needs. You might want to do this only for the high-priority business needs and data quality issues. Alternatively, you make decide to do this before prioritizing. Remember you are only in Step 1 so high-level information is enough. You will go into more detail in these areas in *Step 2 – Analyze Information Environment*.

Key Concept

Look at the *Framework for Information Quality* in *Chapter 3: Key Concepts* or in the *Appendix: Quick References*. The first four boxes down the left-hand side are labeled Data, Processes, People/Orgs, and Technology. These are the four key components that affect information throughout its life cycle. The following outlines how the idea of the four key components are put into practice:

- We must understand, account for, and manage the four key components to get high-quality information.
- We first identify the key components at a high level here in *Step 1.1 – Prioritize Business Needs and Select Project Focus*.
- The specific four key components associated with the selected project focus provide boundaries which help us scope the project in *Step 1.2 – Plan the Project*.
- They will be explored in more detail in *Step 2 – Analyze Information Environment*.

4. Select or confirm the focus of the project.

Finalize the subject of your project. Ensure it will support a critical business need where the quality of the data is in question. The selected project focus and what you learned in this step is the starting point for planning your project in *Step 1.2*. It provides a basis for developing specific project objectives and as input to the project charter.

5. Document, communicate, and engage.

Ensure project sponsors and other key stakeholders are clear on the business needs, have realistic expectations, and support what the project is intended to accomplish. Document the output of this substep.

Sample Output and Templates

Business Needs and Data Quality Issues Worksheet Template

There are many ways to capture and prioritize issues. *Template 4.1.1* is a simple worksheet for capturing business needs and data quality issues at this early stage of the project. List business needs in the second column and known or suspected data quality issues in the third column. Business needs and data quality issues are separated to emphasize that these are not the same things.

Often people say something like, "My business need is to have high-quality employee records." Of course, you should capture it in the worksheet – but that is a data quality issue, not a business need. When you can answer the question, "*Why* do I need high-quality employee records?" then you have the business need.

The answer to "why?" may be that the company recognizes many employees will be retiring in the next 5-10 years. The Human Resources department has been tasked with developing and implementing a plan to determine which jobs will need to be filled and when, where they are located in the world, the knowledge and skills required, and how to train the employees who will fill those jobs. There is early evidence that employee records are outdated or do not contain the information needed to ensure the company continues to have people ready at the right time, in the right place for those jobs as other employees transition out. That is the business need.

Fill in the template and refine throughout this step. For example, what might originally be called a data quality issue will need to be expressed in business language, not data language. What started as a business need, may really be the data quality issue. Capture what is learned about the high-level data, processes, people/organizations, and technology associated with a specific business need or data quality issue.

Business Needs and Data Quality Issues Worksheet Examples

Figure 4.1.3 shows two examples using *Template 4.1.1* : 1) the initial list as business needs and data quality issues are first gathered and recorded, and 2) the refined list after items are clarified, along with additional information learned while doing this step. A few notes as you compare the two lists:

- In the initial list, line 2 started with a data quality issue, but did not have a business need. In the refined list, line 2 included the business need, in business language which was added later.
- In the initial list, Line 3 showed "Need high-quality employee data" as a business need, when it was really the data quality issue. This is a common mistake, yet the distinction is important. Business stakeholders are rarely moved to action when told, "We need high-quality data." It is only when they see how the data supports the business need that you will have a chance of them supporting data quality efforts. In the refined list, the data quality statement was moved to the column "Data Quality Issue" and the Business Need was added.

Template 4.1.1 Business Needs and Data Quality Issues Worksheet

			High-level Information Environment					
Item #	Business Need	Data Quality Issue	Processes	People/ Organizations	Technology	Data	Project Objectives *	Comments
1								
2								
3								
4								

* Project objectives will be finalized in Step 1.2, but document as discovered in Step 1.1.

Example 1: Initial List of Business Needs and Data Quality Issues

Item #	Business Need	Data Quality Issue	Associated with Business Need (High Level)				Project Objectives
			Processes	People/ Orgs	Technology	Data	
1	Research customer complaints about overcharges on invoices.		Billing	Finance Department			
2		Get rid of duplicate customer records				Customer master records	
3	Need high quality employee data					Employee master records	
Etc.							

Example 2: Refined List of Business Needs and Data Quality Issues

Item #	Business Need	Data Quality Issue	Associated with Business Need (High Level)				Project Objectives
			Processes	People/ Orgs	Technology	Data	
1	Address customer complaints about overcharges on invoices.	Quality of invoice data suspected to be part of the problem.	Billing	• Finance Dept • IT Ops	Finance Cloud-Based Software	• Invoice transactions • Customer Master Records	• Develop info life cycle for invoice • Assess quality of invoice records
2	Credit overextended to some customers, exposing us to credit risks. Customer credit limit exceeded when based on each of the separate (duplicate) customer master records.	Duplicate records. Business transactions for same customer linked to different master records for that customer.	CRM	• Sales • Marketing • Online Chat • Phone Reps • Credit Dept	• CRM application • Customer DB	Customer master records	• De-duplicate customer master records
3	Workforce is aging / retiring. Need to ensure business continuity	Unacceptable level of quality for employee data	• Hiring • Training	• Human Resources	HR Module in ERP	• Employee master records • Training Data	
Etc.							

Figure 4.1.3 Business needs and data quality issues worksheet with examples.

Step 1.2 | Plan the Project

Business Benefit and Context

Continuing the trip example from the *Introduction to Chapter 4*, once you have clarified the destination, there are several aspects to planning your trip. Who will be coming? Are you traveling alone, with a few colleagues, or a large tour group? What is the purpose – business or pleasure? You can plan the trip yourself using online travel sites or books. You can ask friends and family who have taken similar trips in the past. You can use an experienced travel agent to help with all or part of the trip. Once you reach your city, you can use GPS on your handheld device to provide step-by-step driving or walking instructions. You can hire a tour guide for a specific activity. Similarly, you plan the data quality project by considering various factors such as the business needs to be addressed, project objectives, who will be involved, the approximate size of the project, whether to bring in outside help, and so on.

The planning for your data quality "trip" starts in this step along with *Chapter 5: Structuring Your Project* which contains additional details for setting up your project. Let's start off with a few definitions. See the *Definitions callout box* for definitions of project, project management, project approach, and SDLC as used in this book.

Definitions

According to the Project Management Institute, "A **project** is a temporary endeavor undertaken to create a unique product, service, or result. **Project management**, then, is the application of knowledge, skills, tools, and techniques to project activities to meet the project requirements."

As it applies in this book, the word **project** is used broadly as any structured effort that makes use of the Ten Steps methodology to address business needs. A project can apply the full Ten Steps Process or selected steps, activities, tools, or techniques. A project team can consist of one person, a small team of 3-4 people, a large team with several people, or can include coordination across multiple teams. I have categorized the types of projects using the Ten Steps methodology into three broad groups. The **project types** are:

- Focused Data Quality Improvement Project
- Data Quality Activities in Another Project
- Ad hoc Use of Data Quality Steps, Activities, or Techniques

The type of project informs the project approach. The **project approach** refers to how solutions will be delivered, and the framework or model used. It provides the basis for the project plan, phases within the project, the tasks to be undertaken, resources needed, and structure of the project team. The model used can be the Ten Steps Process itself or any SDLC model that best fits the situation. The three project types and suggested approaches are further defined in *Table 4.1.2* and in *Chapter 5*.

SDLC refers to a Solution (or Software or Systems) Development Life Cycle. There are many SDLC options. For example, a linear sequential approach (often referred to as waterfall) has been around for many years. An Agile model (with several methodologies such as Scrum or Kanban) is a more modular, flexible, iterative, and incremental approach which has gained in popularity since the Agile Manifesto was introduced in 2001. DevOps is a recent approach which blends tasks of the historically separate IT application development and IT operations teams. All models and methodologies have their advantages and disadvantages. Models can be combined to create a hybrid approach. All approaches can benefit by including data quality and governance activities in them. SDLC is the overarching term, no matter which approach or model is used.

The selected project focus (based on business needs and data quality issues) informs the project objectives. **Project objectives** articulate specific results from the project aligned with the business needs and data quality issues to be addressed. While business needs should be in business language, project objectives can also include data language. Project objectives should be written in a way that they can be quantified with criteria used to determine if the objectives have been met. Often-used criteria make up the acronym SMART, meaning the project objectives should be Specific, Measurable, Attainable, Relevant, and Time-Bound.

As an historical note: Although often attributed to Peter Drucker, the first known use of SMART was by George T. Doran in 1981. See Doran (1981, p. 1) and Wikipedia.org, SMART_criteria (2020).

Good project management is essential to the success of any project. The intent of this step is not to teach project management in detail. If you are new to this topic, there are many websites, books, articles, and conferences that can help. However, this step will give you a jump start in applying good project management techniques when planning your project, since effective planning is essential to the success of any project.

While devising your project plan ensure there continues to be agreement with relevant stakeholders.

Quote to Remember

"From exciting new innovations to mundane yet necessary improvements, organizations institute projects to help the business address issues, support goals and objectives, or take advantage of opportunities.... The more effective those projects, the sooner they realize results.... Of course, the real benefits come, not from being able to say we have high-quality, integrated information, but the fact that the business can make informed decisions and take effective action. Focus ... on the data most important to your business."

– Danette McGilvray and Masha Bykin,

"Data Quality and Governance in Projects: Knowledge in Action," (2013), pgs.1, 3, 20, 21.

Approach

1. Determine the type of project and the approach to be used.

The selected project focus and what you learned about the business needs, data quality issues and associated high-level data, processes, people/organizations, and technology in *Step 1.1* are the starting points for planning your project here. These provide the basis for selecting the project type and developing the specific project objectives. They are also input to other standard project management artifacts.

Types of data quality projects that use the Ten Steps are categorized into the three broad groups described in *Table 4.1.2*. The type of project informs the project *approach*, which is the model to be used to develop the solution. Note: A more thorough explanation for each of the project types is found in *Chapter 5: Structuring Your Project*.

2. Build the project team.

Determine the skills needed to carry out the project, who should be involved, and the size of your project team (e.g., an individual, small team, extended team, data team as part of another project). See *Table 5.10 – Data Quality Project Roles* in *Chapter 5*. Gain approval from the managers of those you want on the team. Gain interest and commitment from those who will be team members.

3. Specify project objectives, develop the plan, and create other applicable project artifacts to fit within the approach chosen.

"Right size" the project management approach. Create a project charter that is right-sized for your project and a context diagram that visually represents the elements within scope. See *Sample Output and Templates* below. Agree on specific project objectives that, if completed, will address the business needs and data quality

Table 4.1.2 Types of Data Quality Projects

Focused Data Quality Improvement Project	
Description	Approach
A data quality improvement project concentrates on specific data quality issue(s) impacting the business. The goal is to improve the quality of the data through assessment, root cause analysis, correction, prevention, and controls. The Ten Steps can also form a foundation to create a data quality improvement methodology for your own organization.	Develop project objectives and choose which steps, activities, and techniques from the Ten Steps Process are relevant to addressing the business needs and data quality issues. The Ten Steps Process itself can be used as the foundation for the project plan/work breakdown structure, and as the structure for organizing files and project artifacts and documents. If using an Agile approach, use the steps and substeps in the Ten Steps Process to help determine features and the amount of work that can be done within any one sprint and the order of work to be done in the series of sprints.
Data Quality Activities in Another Project	
Description	Approach
Incorporate steps, activities, or techniques from the Ten Steps Process into other data-dependent projects, methodologies, or SDLCs. For example, in application development, data migration and integration, business process improvement projects, and Six Sigma or lean projects, data quality is not the primary focus, but data is integral to success. These projects will yield better results if data quality is addressed early in the project and built into the technology, processes, and roles/responsibilities that will be part of the system once in production. Any process, methodology, or framework that uses or impacts data or information can benefit from paying more attention to the quality of the data and how they manage that data. Addressing risks related to data will increase the overall success of such projects and using the Ten Steps will help. A variation is to integrate data quality activities from the Ten Steps into your organization's standard SDLC.	The overall project may be using a third-party vendor SDLC or an internal preferred SDLC (either of which could be sequential, Agile, etc.). Become familiar with the overall project and the approach being used. Then select the steps, activities, and techniques from the Ten Steps that are relevant to the data portion of the work. Determine specifically where they belong in the project plan and whichever methodology is being used. Do not expect anyone else to do this. Do not expect them to understand the Ten Steps Process the way you do. Make it easy for the project manager and team members to see where data quality fits and how it will benefit the overarching project. Incorporate data quality work into their project so it is seen as integral, necessary, and as important as the other project work. For a project using an Agile approach, scope the work to fit into the "chunks" of time by creating features and user stories with clear acceptance criteria.
Ad hoc Use of Data Quality Steps, Activities, or Techniques	
Description	Approach
Make use of any portion of the Ten Steps Process to address a business need or data quality issue, such as a support problem that arises in the course of daily work or in an operational process.	Though it may not be a formal "project" as the word is often used, the data quality work must still be organized. Ad hoc use tends to be limited in scope and time boxed. Select the few steps, activities, or techniques that apply, when they will be used, and who needs to be involved.

issues within scope. Develop a project plan – a right-sized work breakdown structure with dependencies, resources, estimated effort and/or duration, and timeline.

 Key Concept

Agile and Project Management. Too often those using an Agile approach dismiss the words or ideas that come from more traditional project management, such as project charter, work breakdown structure, or context diagram. Yet a project using an Agile approach still has to have a way of agreeing on objectives, getting work done, coordinating resources, tracking progress, and communicating with each other – through the product vision statement, product roadmap, release plan, sprint goals, and backlogs, among others.

If data quality issues are not resolved, they tend to become debt. This data debt causes deterioration over time that contributes to the system breaking down. Besides addressing data quality in an Agile project, operational teams using Agile methodologies can make data quality improvements and reduce debt as ongoing deliverables.

Look at the terms used by the preferred project approach and the intent of how the overall project is managed. Ensure your data quality work fits seamlessly into whichever approach is used.

4. Make use of other good project management practices, tools, and techniques.

For example, set up processes for:

Tracking issues and action items throughout the project— Your organization may have a software application or standard template for this purpose. If not, see the section *Track Issues and Action Items* in *Chapter 6: Other Techniques and Tools* for a template.

Documenting results of each step—Start now to help yourself document results and analysis of each step. Create a file structure where all team members have access. Get into the habit of ensuring that documentation is a completed deliverable at the end of each step. See the section *Analyze, Synthesize, Recommend, Document, and Act on Results* in *Chapter 6: Other Techniques and Tools* for additional information.

5. Communicate, manage, and engage throughout this step.

Early in the step identify the project stakeholders. Create and start executing a communication plan. See *Step 10 – Communicate, Manage, and Engage People Throughout* for techniques and templates.

For any type of data quality project, get approval and support from sponsors and stakeholders for the project focus, objectives, and resources. Ensure they understand and agree with the business needs that will be addressed by improving the quality of the data. Set expectations with stakeholders about their roles in the project and what will be accomplished. Confirm management support, necessary approvals, and committed resources. Use your project charter as input to your communications. Use the context diagram which visualizes the elements within and outside of the project scope to make it easier to discuss, get input, and finally agree on the project scope.

Consider the following for the three types of data quality projects:

- **For a focused data quality improvement project**. If working with a project team, communicate with and get support from IT and business management, sponsors, stakeholders, and team members. If you are a project of one, get support from your manager for the project's objectives, the business needs it fulfills, and time that will be spent.
- **For data quality activities in another project**. Work closely with the project manager and ensure data quality activities are integrated into the project plan and known by all team members.
- **For ad hoc use of data quality steps, activities, or techniques**. Ensure you know why you are using them, how they will be used, and the expected outcome from their use. Discuss with those whose help you will need and who will benefit from your work.
- **For all**. Engage with those from whom you will need input and those likely to be affected by your project. Listen to all feedback – positive and negative. Make adjustments and follow-up as needed.

Hold a project kickoff, which is a meeting or workshop for team members and management to officially start the project. A project kickoff happens at the end of the step, after the project focus, scope, plan, etc. have been agreed upon and resources have been committed. The project kickoff:

- Ensures all involved have a common understanding of the project, such as the business needs and data quality issues to be addressed, project objectives, benefits, roles and responsibilities, and other expectations
- Provides an opportunity for management and team members to meet and learn how each contributes to the project and how they will interact
- Offers the chance to confirm expectations, discuss issues, and clear up misunderstandings.

All these activities set the foundation for on-going support from and interactions with stakeholders and team members throughout the project. Communication and engagement are real work. They are as necessary to your success as formulating a solid project plan.

6. Away you go!

Sample Output and Templates

Project Charter

The purpose of a project charter is to ensure agreement between sponsors, stakeholders, and the team delivering the project. A project charter is applicable no matter the project approach or size. It is a key document even for an Agile project team, as clarity is needed so all resources are aligned toward the same goals and understand the approach to be used. Even if you are an individual addressing a data quality issue within the scope of your daily responsibilities, spend an hour writing the project charter for your one-person project. It provides a basis for discussion with your manager to ensure you both agree on goals and necessary activities within scope of your project.

If your organization does not have a template for project charters, use *Template 4.1.2* as a starting point. Discard those sections that do not apply and add sections relevant to your situation. Be concise and try to keep the charter to one to two pages. If you need a more detailed project charter than the one shown here, maintain a one-page summary version. Update it throughout the project to provide an at-a-glance view that anyone involved with the project can see to quickly understand the project. Refer to the charter for content when providing an overview of your project in various communications.

Context Diagram

In project management terminology, a context diagram visually represents the elements within scope and sometimes elements outside of the scope. A data professional can look at many context diagrams and know that they also represent a very high-level information life cycle. Create a context diagram that shows the high-level data, processes, people/organizations, and technology involved. A picture is really worth a thousand words at this point. A good context diagram is useful when discussing the elements being considered for the project and when deciding what should be in or out of scope.

Figure 4.1.4 is a high-level context diagram showing responsibilities internal and external to a utility company. For example, the smart meters on a home are owned by the utility. Originally the figure had the data from the smart meters going directly into the internal private cloud. Then I was told the data was first sent to a financial institution for processing and to bill the customers, then onto the utility company. So the bank was added to the context diagram. That was a good example of why a graphic is helpful. People can ensure it accurately represents the high-level flow and then have a discussion about what should be within scope of the data quality project. Where are the known issues and which data – in the data lake, data coming from the external cloud service provider, or smart

Template 4.1.2 Project Charter

Project Name Include name, abbreviation or acronym, if any.	
Date At a minimum, include last update date of the charter. Include creation date and subsequent revision dates if you need to track revision history	
Key contact/Prepared by Name, title, and contact information of the person who should be contacted if there are questions or concerns regarding the project charter	
Project Overview	
Project Summary and Background Executive summary easily understood by anyone. Include: • Situation leading to the project • Business needs (related to customers, products, services, strategies, goals, issues, opportunities) that triggered the project and/or will be addressed by the project • Brief description of project goals and purpose • Business justification or rationale for the project	
Benefits Expected benefits from the project. Include both quantitative benefits (e.g., cost savings, revenue growth, compliance) and qualitative benefits (e.g., decreased risk, customer satisfaction, employee morale) as you are able.	
Project Resources	
Include pertinent information such as name, title, department, team. Include contact information as needed. With geographically dispersed teams it is often helpful to include locations such as site name, country, and time zone.	
Executive Sponsor(s)	
Project Sponsor(s)	
Stakeholders	
Project Manager	
Project Team Members	
Extended Team	
Project Scope	
Goals and Objectives	1. 2. 3.
Major Deliverables	1. 2. 3.
The Project DOES include:	At a high level, the following are within scope of project: • Data • Processes • People and Organizations • Technology
The Project does NOT include:	If needed for clarity, describe what appears to be related, but is outside of the scope of the project: • Data • Processes • People and Organizations • Technology

(Continued)

Template 4.1.2 Project Charter *(Continued)*	
Project Conditions	
Success Criteria How we will know when the project is done and if the goals have been met.	
Critical Success Factors What must be in place for the project to be successful.	
Assumptions, Issues, Dependencies, Constraints Items that can impact the project scope, schedule, work to be done, or quality of deliverables.	
Risks Items that may negatively impact the project. For each risk, indicate the likelihood of it occurring and, if it does occur, the potential impact and action to be taken.	
Metrics, Performance Measures, and Targets Indicators of project success and what will be tracked during the project. These may be developed as the project gets underway.	
Timeline Summary of the timeline and major milestones.	
Costs and Funding Estimated costs and who is paying for the project.	

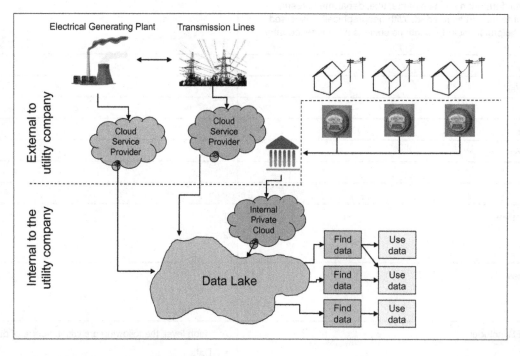

Figure 4.1.4 Context diagram/high-level information life cycle.

meters? etc. Draw circles around the parts that are in scope. Modify the graphic until everyone is satisfied it is a useful representation of the flow and environment. Add other graphics to show additional details, if needed, and supplement with explanatory text. The right graphics can be a useful point of reference throughout the project. When the team is talking about a particular datastore, data source, or process, the graphic can remind everyone of where they are in relation to the bigger picture.

Other Templates

See the following sections in *Chapter 6: Other Techniques and Tools* for templates that can be used throughout the project and should be started here in *Step 1*:

- Track Issues and Action Items
- Analyze, Synthesize, Recommend, Document, and Act on Results

Ten Steps in Action

The three *Ten Steps in Action callout boxes* illustrate the flexibility and scalability of the Ten Steps methodology and the various ways it can be put to use, in different countries and organizations – all with good results. The example from Seattle Public Utilities includes more detail than the others to show what a thorough use of the Ten Steps Process looks like.

Ten Steps in Action

Using the Ten Steps for Data Quality Education in Australia

An Information Management team of 60 people in an Australian state government organisation was built from the ground up. A data analyst within the team said, "To learn about and understand data quality, the team used the first edition of this book as a guidebook and bible on best-practice data quality processes. It was a very useful tool which helped to develop knowledge within the team. The Ten Steps Process provided input to our Data Quality Framework."

Ten Steps in Action

Various Uses of the Ten Steps in South Africa

Paul Grobler is a Principle Consultant in Altron's Data Management Practice and serves on the board of DAMA South Africa.

He explains how the Ten Steps have been used:

For data advisory engagements, which would normally result in a Data Strategy or Roadmap for a specific data-related solution, Step 1 was the inspiration for how we Define (or Articulate) the needs of that particular engagement. These engagements are normally technology agnostic.

We also used the outline of the Ten Steps Process for data quality assessments, using a variety of tools. Where possible, our project plans roughly echoed the steps in the Ten Steps Process where it made sense. Even though the Ten Steps method is geared more towards data quality, it helped to elevate the importance of DQ in an MDM (Master Data Management) initiative.

If I have to single out the most significant factor that the method highlighted, it is the importance of linking data quality with problems within the business. This focus caused us as consultants to really align closely with business and work hard together to actually find the right questions before getting the right answers. This helped build trust with our customers. It also helped greatly to align the thinking and engagement model within the team members, especially for those new to the discipline. The approach, as well as the categorisation of the data quality dimensions, helped simplify the discussions greatly.

Ten Steps in Action

Using the Ten Steps for a Data Quality Improvement Project at Seattle Public Utilities

Contributors—Thanks to the following who contributed to the project and agreed to share what they did:

- Duncan Munro, Utility Asset Information Program Manager, Seattle Public Utilities
- Lynne Ashton, Senior GIS Departmental Analyst, Seattle IT
- Scott Reese, Drainage and Wastewater Line of Business IT Liaison, Seattle Public Utilities
- Stephen Beimborn, Manager of Departmental GIS, Seattle IT

Project Name—Seattle Public Utility Asset Information Management– Drainage and Wastewater Mainlines Pilot Study (Wastewater Pipes)

Organization Overview—The core work of Seattle Public Utilities (SPU) is to provide Community-centered utility services (drinking water, drainage and wastewater, and solid waste) while protecting public health and the environment for Seattle, Washington (USA), Puget Sound, and surrounding areas (see http://www.seattle.gov/utilities).

Business Need—SPU has physical assets such as pipes, pumps, overflow control facilities, and many more. There were challenges when trying to determine which of the numerous data sources that describe those physical assets was most appropriate for solving a specific problem. Physical asset design, build, operations, and maintenance decisions were being made on the basis of data with unknown provenance. In several cases this led to additional costs for the agency.

Specifically, one of the main drivers for the data quality project came when a design process went forward using location data from non-survey-quality data. This caused rework during construction, at a cost of around $100,000. SPU did not want the situation to be repeated.

Another motivation for better quality data was challenges of working with inaccurate measurements of physical asset dimensions during hydraulic modelling.

Project Focus—The data quality pilot project focused on drainage and wastewater mainlines (referred to here as wastewater pipes). SPU sought a consistent and scalable approach to measure and communicate data quality, which included the design of processes to remediate data quality issues that could be owned and operated by business Subject Matter Experts (SMEs).

Project Overview—Duncan Munro, SPU Utility Asset Information Program Manager, was part of the design and implementation of a data management practice at SPU. The data quality pilot project identified a small subset of the data that characterizes one of their most challenging asset classes – wastewater pipes. The project took approximately 6 months as the core team of 4 people fit the work into their other responsibilities.

The team members' different backgrounds provided a holistic view of the data life cycle. The team examined each process in the cradle-to-grave data lifecycle for 12-14 attributes of Wastewater Pipes. Thirty SPU staff were surveyed and interviewed, representing multiple business areas (field operations, engineering, planning, project management, hydraulic modeling) that led and contributed to tasks in each phase of the physical asset life cycle. The data lives in two of SPUs major enterprise platforms: 1) Maximo – for Work and Asset Management, and 2) GIS – Geographic Information System, which manages spatial or geographic data. For analytical purposes, the data is integrated with the City of Seattle financial management platform, PeopleSoft. All the research allowed them to select a subset of the data based on which data was used most frequently and which was most important to the largest number of people.

(Continued)

Ten Steps in Action (Continued)

Business Value Realized—Benefits and outcomes from the data quality project:

- **Broader data management**. Laid the foundations not only for specific improvements to the data that describes SPU's wastewater pipes but also in broader data management for all subject areas at SPU.
- **Data quality analysis as a core business practice**. Heightened awareness of the value of establishing data quality analysis as a core business practice that underpins continuous improvement in data management. For example, the use of the data specification templates developed in the project have been extended to all data subject areas at SPU. These completed templates are leveraged by data stewards who use a newly deployed GIS Metadata Management tool that enables metadata to be viewed through each of SPU's GIS applications. Presentation of the metadata to users in the field allows them to:
  - Consume GIS data more efficiently in situations where rapid response is required
  - Identify where corrections are needed to individual data values – a process they refer to as Map Corrections – thereby improving the quality of their data
  - Ensure that they are adequately equipped and staffed to do the work assigned in the field
- **Reuse**. What was learned during the pilot project is being carried forward to other projects. They realized their specification process (*Step 2 – Analyze Information Environment*) was not mature and more careful data engineering up front was needed. They have identified other workflows and processes which could benefit from going through this methodology. The early stages of another project, assessing the work and dataflows for Catch Basin Inspection, is seeing an additional benefit from a focus on the specification process. With approximately 35,000 Catch Basins under SPU management, and given that data acquisition in field settings can be challenging, reducing the number of attributes for which values are captured and simplifying their observation protocols has the potential to bring large efficiency gains.

Following outlines how the project made use of the Ten Steps Process.

Step 1 – Determine Business Needs and Approach—Middle-tier SPU management identified anecdotally several ongoing challenges with data quality in the "apply" phase of the data life cycle.

Step 2 – Analyze Information Environment—The team:

- Created work and data flow diagrams in Microsoft VISIO for data in the "Obtain" phase of the data lifecycle
- Used and then redesigned the "Detailed Data List" template from the first edition of the book to capture specifications

The team called *Step 2 – Analyze Information Environment* the specification state of the data life cycle. At the conclusion of the pilot they realized how important this stage was. If they don't engineer carefully then subsequent metrics of data quality within specific Data Quality Dimensions are challenging. Without sufficient business engagement in specification there is a tendency for the IT perspective to be the sole focus.

Step 3 – Assess Data Quality—Data quality was assessed in the following areas:

- The Data Specification process was assessed, and the team identified gaps in standards, metadata, and reference data
- Profiled data tables in GIS to assess the DQ dimensions of Data Integrity Fundamentals and Data Coverage
- Created and conducted a survey of users to assess Perception, Relevance and Trust

Step 4 – Assess Business Impact—Leveraged the survey vehicle to have users identify several qualitative impacts of data quality issues which confirmed the drivers for the pilot study.

Step 5 – Identify Root Causes—Analyzed work and dataflows to identify where major gaps were creating data quality issues.

Step 6 – Develop Improvement Plans—Formalized a data specification process and developed templates and the review process to complete.

Step 7 – Prevent Future Data Errors—Updated editing tools and processes to include more integrity checks and auditing capabilities for additions and updates to datasets. Revised the workflows to contain more checks and balances. Created a new representation of where survey data is acquired in Seattle and a process to make survey data available to all GIS customers.

Step 8 – Correct Current Data Errors—Updated data errors using more logical integrity checks to remove data inconsistencies.

Step 9 – Monitor Controls—Established a review and approval process for standard business data specifications. Added audit capabilities to data editing processes and tools in GIS operations.

Step 10 – Communicate, Manage, and Engage People Throughout—As the pilot study team reached out to more parts of SPU, it became clear that the vocabulary of data quality was a foreign language to people doing their day-to-day jobs, who had no connection to the data life cycle. They consumed data by looking at map displays or apps that showed where crews were working. Users assumed the information they saw was exactly what they should see on the ground. The challenge was to create vocabulary around data that was understood by all. For example, the Ten Steps process uses POSMAD to represent the information life cycle, which SPU calls the data life cycle. The pilot team changed it to Specify, Acquire, Manage, Apply, Retire, which was verbiage that worked well with the broader SPU audience and was already being used as the phases of the physical asset life cycle. Currently, as more leadership becomes engaged in data management issues, they sometimes simplify the data life cycle further using Bob Seiner's stages of Define, Produce, Use (Seiner, 2014). One unexpected advantage of using this simplified data life cycle is that there is a lessened connection to technology and for many audiences that is a good thing.

Step 1 Summary

No matter the size or scope of your project, all of *Step 1* is critical. Here you spent just enough time prioritizing and selecting the business needs and data quality issues to be addressed by your data quality project. You determined the project approach, which sets the foundation for all project activities. All types of projects require some level of planning – whether as a focused data quality improvement project, as data quality activities in another project, or as ad hoc use of data quality steps, activities or techniques.

Ensuring the right level of communication and engagement is imperative. Many a project has failed because of misunderstanding between those involved (sponsors, management, teams, business, IT, etc.). Effective planning is essential to the successful execution of any project; and defining the business need and approach provides the necessary focus for your project activities. Don't let lack of clarity regarding what will be accomplished and why, keep your project from succeeding.

If you ignore this step or do it poorly, you have already guaranteed failure, no more than partial success, or lots of time and effort focusing on the wrong thing. But if you do it well, you have a springboard for a successful project and the real opportunity to bring value to your organization.

 Communicate, Manage, and Engage

Suggestions for working effectively with people and managing the project in this step:

- Start building a stakeholder list and create an initial communication plan
- If conducting surveys or interviews to gather and understand business needs and data quality issues, ensure respondents know the purpose and are prepared to participate
- Meet with stakeholders, get feedback on the planned project, set expectations, and address their concerns
- Listen to all feedback – positive and negative; make adjustments and follow-up
- Finalize support and resources
- Hold a project kickoff with the project team and management
- Set up the structure for storing and sharing project documents
- Set up processes for tracking issues and action items and documenting results

 Checkpoint

Checkpoint Step 1 – Determine Business Needs and Approach

How can I tell if I am ready to move to the next step? Use the following guidelines to help determine completeness of this step and readiness for the next step:

- Are the business needs and data quality issues, project focus, benefits, and objectives clearly defined?
- Have management, sponsors, stakeholders, the project team and their managers been appropriately engaged? Do they understand and support the project?
- Have needed resources been committed?
- Is the high-level information environment understood and documented – the data, processes, people/organizations, technology, and information life cycle within scope of the project?
- Has the project been properly initiated, e.g., through a project kickoff?
- Have the project plan, other artifacts related to the project approach/ SDLC, and file structure for sharing documents been created?
- Has the initial stakeholder analysis been completed and used as input to the communication plan?
- Has the communication plan been created and necessary communications in this step been completed?

Step 2 | Analyze Information Environment

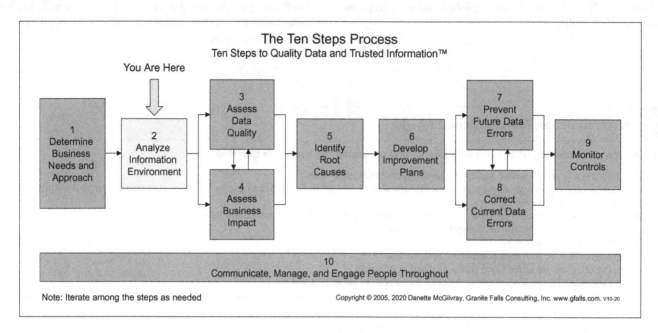

Figure 4.2.1 "You Are Here" Graphic for Step 2 – Analyze Information Environment.

Introduction to Step 2

Once the business needs and project focus are finalized in *Step 1*, the natural inclination is to jump right into the data quality assessment in *Step 3* and skip *Step 2*. Please don't!

Think of it this way – there has been a murder. There is a body lying in the park. Police come to investigate, what do they do? Do they just pick up the body and whisk it off to the coroner's office without another thought as to the surroundings? Of course they don't! They cordon off the vicinity to protect the area under investigation. They look around. What can they learn? What is the weather, the time of day? They want to know where the person was coming from. Where were they going and what were they doing in the park at that time? What was their purpose for being there? How long had the body been there? Were there any witnesses? There is much to be learned from the environment around the body that can help them solve the murder. Of course, more will be learned from the body itself when an autopsy is conducted. But right now, they are taking the first look at the body, the setting around the body, and the body's relationship to its surroundings to help them solve the crime.

Similarly, there are all kinds of data quality crimes! What often happens? People swoop in, clean up the data and don't do anything else. That is just as if the police come in, send the body to the coroner's office, and immediately bring in a crew to clean up the crime scene. We know that isn't the way to stop the criminal. Yet, I'm sure you have seen the "let's-clean-up-the-bad-data" project again and again in your organization. And then people wonder why data quality crimes continue to happen. Bad data continues to show up and have negative impacts on the organization. By not analyzing the information environment, much important evidence is missed that can help solve and prevent data quality crimes.

This step will help you understand the information environment – the settings, conditions, and situations that surround, may have created, or exacerbated, data quality problems. Data landscape or data ecosystem are other terms for similar ideas. Analyzing the information environment means looking at requirements and constraints, data and data specifications, processes, people and organizations, technology, and the information life cycle. Solving the "Case of Poor Data Quality" requires interpreting clues that can only be uncovered by investigating the information environment. Put on your investigator's hat! Whether you relate to one of the many crime solving television shows like NCIS or Midsomer Murders or to classic detectives like Sir Arthur Conan Doyle's Sherlock Holmes and Agatha Christie's Hercule Poirot, you can join their ranks and solve the mystery!

We live in complex environments that are a spider's web of systems, applications, program code, people and processes touching data and using information, data flowing here and there, and requirements that must be met. Using the structured thinking laid out in *Step 2* sorts out the conditions and forces that influence the quality of the data and information. Often these aspects of data, processes, people/organizations, technology, requirements, and the information life cycle are looked at individually. "It's a technology problem" or "Our business processes are broken." *Step 2* brings all of these aspects together in a holistic way, so we see relationships between them in a way that we did not before. When we understand the forces that shape the information, we can devise better solutions. We will ensure that the data captured and assessed for quality is actually the data associated with the business needs. Otherwise, it is not unusual to find that data has to be extracted multiple times before getting the data really needed. Completing this step at the right level of detail will also give you the background to interpret and analyze what you see from the data quality assessment. Though the pressure

Table 4.2.1 Step Summary Table for Step 2 – Analyze Information Environment

Objective	• Compile, analyze, and document each of the elements in the current information environment at the level of detail needed to address business needs and data quality issues within scope, achieve project objectives, and prepare for upcoming steps Note: The elements of the information environment are: requirements and constraints, data and data specifications, technology, processes, people and organizations, and the information life cycle
Purpose	• Understand the environment that created the data quality issues • Ensure data to be assessed is actually the data associated with the business needs and project objectives • Provide a foundation for all other steps and activities throughout the Ten Steps Process, and as input when: developing a data capture and assessment plan, analyzing data quality and business impact assessments, identifying root causes, developing and implementing improvement plans for both prevention and correction, monitoring controls, managing the project, and communicating and engaging with people
Inputs	• Learnings and artifacts from *Step 1*: business needs and data quality issues within scope; project focus, approach, plan, and objectives; information environment (high-level) • Knowledge in existing documentation, within tools, and from subject matter experts about the various elements of the information environment. For example, metadata repositories, business glossaries, business rules engines, architecture, data models, data flow diagrams, business process flows, organization charts, job roles and responsibilities, data acquisition/purchase contracts • Stakeholder analysis, communication and change management plans • Feedback from and adjustments as needed based on communication and engagement to this point

Techniques and Tools	• From *Chapter 3: Key Concepts* sections related to the elements of the information environment e.g., Framework for Information Quality, Information Life Cycle
	• From *Chapter 6: Other Techniques and Tools:*
	  o Information Life Cycle Approaches
	  o Conduct a Survey
	  o Ten Steps and Other Methodologies and Standards
	  o Tools for Managing Data Quality
	  o Track Issues and Action Items (started in *Step 1* and used throughout)
	  o Analyze, Synthesize, Recommend, Document, and Act on Results (started in *Step 1* and used throughout)

Outputs	Note: All outputs are at the appropriate level of detail and relevant to the business needs, data quality issues, and project objectives. Examples: • Finalized requirements (from *Step 2.1*) • Detailed data grid and data specifications; data mapping if assessing more than one data source, initial source to target mappings if migrating data (from *Step 2.2*) • Data model and metadata to understand the structure, relationships, and meaning of the data so the relevant data can be captured and analyzed (from *Step 2.2*) • Application architecture within scope (From *Step 2.3*) • Process flows (From *Step 2.4*) • Organizational structures, roles and responsibilities (From *Step 2.5*) • Information life cycle reflecting elements within project scope (from *Step 2.6)* • Matrices showing interaction between various elements in the information environment • Documented and analyzed results, lessons learned, issues uncovered, possible root causes, and initial recommendations • Updated project status, stakeholder analysis, communication and change management plan • Completed communication and change management tasks appropriate at this point in the project

Communicate, Manage, and Engage	• Refine the stakeholder list based on what was learned in *Step 2.5 – Understand Relevant People and Organizations* and update communication plan accordingly
	• Engage with stakeholders and team members:
	  o Provide periodic status reports
	  o Listen to and address suggestions and concerns
	  o Provide updates regarding what was learned in this step, such as potential issues that could impact scope, schedule, or resources
	  o Based on what was learned in this step, set expectations for potential impacts or changes to upcoming project work, team participation, or individual personal involvement
	• Track issues and action items; ensure deliverables are completed in a timely manner
	• Ensure resources and support for upcoming steps in the project

(Continued)

Table 4.2.1 Step Summary Table for Step 2 – Analyze Information Environment *(Continued)*

Checkpoint	<ul><li>Are the applicable elements of the information environment understood and documented, at the appropriate level of detail, to help perform the next project steps most effectively?</li><li>If conducting a data quality assessment in *Step 3:*<ul><li>Has the data been understood sufficiently that there is confidence a data quality assessment will focus on the relevant data?</li><li>For data to be assessed for quality, have requirements and constraints, detailed data grids and mappings, and data specifications been finalized?</li><li>Have any problems with permissions and access to data been identified?</li><li>Are tools available to conduct the assessment or must tools be purchased?</li><li>Have training needs been identified?</li></ul></li><li>If conducting a business impact assessment in *Step 4:*<ul><li>Are the business needs and information environment understood and linked sufficiently that there is confidence a business impact assessment will focus in the right areas?</li></ul></li><li>Have results from this step been documented? i.e., lessons learned and observations, known/potential issues, known/probable business impact, potential root causes, initial recommendations for prevention and correction</li><li>Have resources for the upcoming assessments been identified and committed?</li><li>Has the communication plan been updated and necessary communications for this step been completed?</li></ul>

is often there to skip this step, understanding just enough about your information environment actually makes your assessments go more quickly, provides many benefits, and avoids rework – see the *Key Concept callout box.*

Key Concept

Benefits of Understanding the Information Environment. *Step 2 – Analyze Information Environment* provides essential knowledge that will be used throughout the project. Use the Just Enough Principle to understand the relevant requirements and constraints, data and data specifications, processes, people/organizations, technology, and the information life cycle surrounding the data quality issue. By doing so you will:

- Make sense of the complex environments within your organization. Using the structured thinking laid out in *Step 2* sorts out the conditions and forces that influence the quality of the data and information.
- Make better decisions because you understand the relationships between the various aspects of the environment.
- Ensure the relevant data associated with the business issue is actually the data being assessed. Otherwise, data often has to be extracted multiple times before getting the data really needed – resulting in wasted time, effort, and money.
- Develop a realistic data capture and assessment plan in *Step 3 – Assess Data Quality.*
- Identify those who should be involved in the project, either as key resources or stakeholders.
- Uncover requirements. These become specifications against which data quality will be compared and highlight potential problem areas you should look for during the assessment.
- Interpret results of the assessments. The more you understand the context and the environment that affect the data, the better you will decipher what you see when you assess the data.
- Identify root causes. Elements of the environment (or combinations of them) caused the data quality issues. You must understand them to determine the true causes and how to prevent them from happening again.
- Devise solutions for preventing data quality problems from (re) occurring and determine where and when corrections to the data should be made.

All lay the foundation for high-quality data and information which our organizations can trust and depend upon to address their strategies, goals, issues, and opportunities. Are you convinced? Don't skip Step 2!

Step 2 Process Flow

There are six substeps to guide you through understanding the information environment. The process flow is shown in *Figure 4.2.2.* This step builds on what was learned in *Step 1* where you identified the high-level data, processes, people/organizations, and technology associated with the business issue and within scope of the project. We now expand on these to include requirements and constraints, data specifications, and the information life cycle. If you need a refresher on any of these terms, read *Chapter 3: Key Concepts* before proceeding. Can you find the elements in this step in the Framework for Information Quality?

IMPORTANT!!! Each of the substeps in Step 2 are interrelated. They are numbered for identification, not for the order in which they must be completed. Start with the area/substep in which you have the most information or with which you are most familiar. Work out from there in any order until you have obtained the relevant information at the appropriate level of detail. You will be most successful if you implement this step iteratively.

Think of putting together a jigsaw puzzle. Many start with the border pieces. This is similar to first sketching out a high-level information life cycle. You may have already done this in *Step 1.2 – Plan the Project* as a context diagram. If not, you can do it now in *Step 2.6.* This provides boundaries around work done in the other substeps. As you learn more from them, cycle back to *Step 2.6* and continue to add detail to the information life cycle.

Step 2.2 – Understand Relevant Data and Specifications is another substep to look at early. First narrow the detailed data within scope by prioritizing the most important items. These are referred to as Critical Data Elements (CDEs). The CDEs then guide work done throughout. For example, you only need to spend time gathering data specifications for the CDEs, not for all data elements within a business process or application. This greatly reduces the amount of time spent here and ensures you are focusing your efforts on that which is most important.

Some like to sort pieces of the puzzle by colors, patterns, or shapes. They then build each section, or work back and forth between them, and eventually connect them. You can do the same by analyzing each substep in whatever order makes sense to you and bringing them together by understanding the interactions between them.

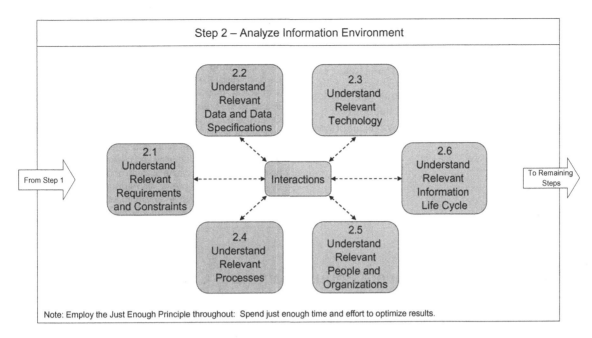

Figure 4.2.2 Process flow for Step 2 – Analyze Information Environment.

You will make many choices along the way about what is relevant to the business needs, data quality issues, and project objectives. As you explore the information environment, you may find the problem is broader than you imagined. This can feel overwhelming. Use the guidelines in the *Best Practice callout box* to help narrow your focus. To further assist your decisions, an example of what could be considered high, mid, and low levels of detail is included with the instructions in each substep.

Timing for Step 2

Estimating time to spend on *Step 2 – Analyze Information Environment* seems to be somewhat problematic for focused data quality improvement projects. The activities in this step are less familiar to some team members and project managers, and the level of detail needed can vary widely.

Obviously, the amount of time spent on *Step 2* depends on your scope. For focused data quality improvement projects, the following guidelines will help when estimating the time to spend analyzing the information environment in *Step 2*. Estimates below include work done in *Steps 1-6*. They do not include *Steps 7-9*, because time to correct data, prevent future errors, and implement controls will vary greatly depending on what is found in the earlier steps.

- If estimated time for *Steps 1-6* is 4 weeks, then approximate time for Step 2 is 3-5 days
- If estimated time for *Steps 1-6* is 4 months, then approximate time for Step 2 is 2 weeks
- If estimated time for *Steps 1-6* is 9 months, then approximate time for Step 2 is 1 month

As you actually work through *Step 2*, if you find yourself spending much more time on *Step 2* than the guidelines above, either you are going into more detail than is needed at this time or you underestimated the effort for the overall project.

You will uncover many items of interest. On one project team, we gave each other permission to ask at any time, "Are we going down a rat hole?" This was the signal to pause and ask ourselves if the level of detail or item of interest was actually relevant to the business needs and project objectives. If yes, we agreed to spend more time

 Best Practice

What is relevant? What is the right level of detail? Determining the answers to these questions will help you avoid analysis paralysis and keep you moving forward. Keep these questions in mind throughout the project. Using them in *Step 2 – Analyze the Information Environment* is particularly important. The answers to these questions will impact where you focus your efforts, how much time is spent, and the nature of your results.

- **Relevant**. In this context means that the steps or substeps selected, along with the techniques and activities chosen within them, have a bearing upon the business needs, data quality issues, and the project objectives within scope.
- **Level of detail**. Within each step, substep, technique and activity the level of detail needed will vary depending on where you are in the project and of course, the business needs, data quality issues, and project objectives. Start at a high level and work to lower levels of detail only as needed.

As you determine whether additional detail is warranted, ask yourself these questions:

- Will additional detail have a significant and demonstrable bearing on the business needs and project objectives?
- Will additional detail provide evidence to prove or disprove a hypothesis about the quality or the business impact of the data?

Employ the Just Enough Principle. Spend just enough time and effort in each step and substep to optimize results. Don't skip Step 2, but don't get too far into detail that may be unnecessary. The balance of determining what is just enough (what is relevant and the right level of detail) is part of the art of data quality.

Use your best judgment and move on! Make rapid decisions based on what you know at the time and move on. If circumstances change or new knowledge comes to light, make adjustments from there. If more information is needed later, gather it at that time.

in that area. If no, we refocused our efforts on the tasks that kept our eyes on why we were doing the project (the business needs) and what we were to accomplish (the project objectives). This practice helped us move forward, stay on track, and use our time well.

Spend just enough time to get the foundational information needed to proceed effectively. Don't skip this step, but don't get too far into detail that may not be used. You can always get additional detail later if needed.

Warning

Avoid Wasting Time and Money! This is so important it bears repeating – resist the temptation to skip *Step 2*! Learn just enough in *Step 2* to ensure that the data being assessed for data quality is actually related to the business needs and data quality issues to be resolved. Otherwise you run the risk of multiple extracts and rework before getting to the actual data relevant to the business issue. Understanding just enough about the information environment will also help you interpret results of data quality and business impact assessments. It will help you during root cause analysis and enable you to make better decisions about which preventive measures and controls to implement. Analyzing the information environment will usually be more in-depth for a data quality assessment than for a business impact assessment.

Step 2.1 | Understand Relevant Requirements and Constraints

Business Benefit and Context

Requirements are obligatory or demanded. They can be things necessary for the business to succeed, such as processes, security, or technology. Some requirements may be external – those with which the business is obligated to comply, such as privacy, legal, or governmental. Because the data should support compliance with all these requirements, it is important to understand them as soon as possible in the project.

Constraints are limitations or restrictions and those things we should NOT do. Considering what we cannot do often brings to mind more items that should be uncovered in this step. What we cannot do then could be articulated into requirements, i.e., what we must do to ensure we do NOT do what we are not supposed to do. Did you follow that?

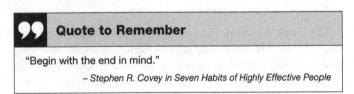
Quote to Remember

"Begin with the end in mind."
– *Stephen R. Covey in Seven Habits of Highly Effective People*

Approach

1. Consider the level of detail needed for requirements and constraints.

Ask, "At this point in our project, what do we need to know about relevant requirements and constraints in order to: Carry

out the next project steps most effectively? Address the business needs? Achieve the project objectives?" See *Figure 4.2.3* for examples of levels of detail.

2. Gather requirements and identify constraints.

Ensure the requirements and constraints are relevant to the business issues, associated data, and data specifications necessary for compliance with them and within scope of the project. Consider requirements and constraints related to the following areas: business, users, functional, technology, legal, regulatory, compliance, contractual, industry, internal policies, access, security, privacy, data protection. They may apply to your organization, your country, or internationally. For example, the General Data Protection Regulation (GDPR) was drafted and passed by the European Union (EU), but it applies to organizations anywhere in the world if they target or collect data related to people in the EU. In the US, the California Consumer Privacy Act (CCPA) addresses privacy rights for California consumers with specific criteria for the size of businesses which must comply. Many countries have passed laws related to how Personally Identifiable Information (PII) is handled. You may need to contact your organization's finance, legal, or other departments for help.

For the data to be assessed for quality in your project, identify any constraints such as who has permission to access and see the data. See *Sample Output and Templates* for *Template 4.2.1*, which can be used as a starting point to capture requirements, and *Table 4.2.2* for how the idea of data quality dimensions was used to gather more detailed data quality requirements.

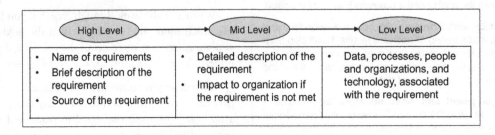

Figure 4.2.3 Example levels of detail for requirements and constraints.

3. Analyze, synthesize, recommend, document, and act on what you learned about requirements and constraints.

See the section of the same name in *Chapter 6: Other Techniques and Tools* for additional help.

Look at the various requirements for the same information, for the same organizations, and so on. These requirements will eventually need to turn into detailed data specifications to ensure that data supports adherence to them. This can take place in *Step 2.2 – Understand Relevant Data and Data Specifications* or in *Step 3* when assessing the data quality.

Synthesize results with what you have learned from other sub-steps within *Step 2*. Make initial recommendations based on what you know at this point and take action now if the time is right. Document results.

Sample Output and Templates

Gathering Requirements

The following explains what is included in *Template 4.2.1 – Gathering Requirements*. You can see the information is at a high- to mid-level of detail. Because data is essential to comply with most regulations, at some point the information gathered here will have to be turned into specific requirements to ensure the data itself is in compliance, or the quality of the data will support business processes being in compliance.

The first line under the column headings in the template provides an example from a bio-technology company. Look for data quality-related controls already built into the regulation mentioned, recognizing that they may not be called "data quality." Supplement them with others needed to ensure data quality.

Requirement—Brief description of the requirement.

Source of Requirement—The person who provided the information along with the specific source such as a particular law or internal policy.

Type of Requirement—Consider the following areas: business, users, functional, technology, legal, regulatory, compliance, contractual, industry, internal policies, access, security, privacy, data protection. They may apply to your organization, your country, or internationally. Other types may apply to your situation; discuss a meaningful way to categorize them.

Associated Information/Data—Information that must be in place in order to comply with the requirement OR the information itself that must comply with the requirement (if the requirement specifies the information). You decide if starting at a higher information level or more detailed data level is most useful.

Associated Processes—Processes that the requirements apply to or specialized processes already in place that support compliance. These processes are where data and information are used or obtained/created/captured/collected/maintained. You may decide to expand to processes that impact the information throughout the POSMAD life cycle at some point.

Associated Organizations—Organizations, teams, departments, and the like, impacted by the requirement.

Impact If Requirement Not Met—The result if the requirement is not met: legal action, risk of fines, and the like. Be as specific as possible with what is known at this time. This will drive decisions if trade-offs need to be made based on resources and time, or if there are conflicting requirements.

Using Data Quality Dimensions for Requirements Gathering

Regardless of the project approach used, every system implementation project has some kind of requirements gathering effort. This effort typically focuses on what users need to see in terms of interfaces or high-level data flows, but frequently does not get into the quality of the information itself. Data quality requirements can also be collected at the beginning of any project when gathering other requirements.

The *Ten Steps in Action callout box* shows a different approach to requirements gathering than shown in *Template 4.2.1*.

Template 4.2.1 Gathering Requirements

Requirement	Source	Type	Associated Information/ Data	Associated Processes	Associated Organizations/ People	Impact if Requirement is not met
Information captured to ship products must be specified formally and changes must be under formal change control	Current Good Manufacturing Practice (CGMP) Regulations*	Compliance	Customer Product Shipment	Order entry Returns management Recall management	Customer sales Shipping and logistics	Patient health Company reputation Financial penalties

* Current Good Manufacturing Practice (CGMP) is the main regulatory standard for ensuring the quality of human pharmaceuticals and is regulated by the US Food and Drug Administration (FDA). CGMPs provide for systems that assure proper design, monitoring, and control of manufacturing processes and facilities. Adherence to the CGMP regulations assures the identity, strength, quality, and purity of drug products by requiring that manufacturers of medications adequately control manufacturing operations. Source: US Food & Drug Administration (2018).

In this example, the same data quality dimensions described in *Step 3 – Assess Data Quality* are used to uncover data quality requirements. These requirements are then used as a point of comparison when assessing data quality in *Step 3*. If the current data quality is found to be unacceptable, data cleansing and necessary improvements should be built into the project. If the list of improvements is long, they may have to be prioritized and implemented over time through additional data quality projects.

Ten Steps in Action

Guidelines for Gathering Data Quality Requirements

Background—Mehmet Orun was the principal data architect and led Data Services at a large life sciences company. As part of his work with business and IT groups, he advised his colleagues on how to capture data quality requirements to develop innovative solutions while seeking to improve delivery quality, efficiency, and effectiveness.

In the following scenario, Mehmet shares an experience where a project team needed to make integration technology decisions. The business representatives knew what they needed from the Enterprise Resource Planning (ERP) system and there were a number of technology options. He met with people who represented the business on the project – the knowledge workers who applied the information in their jobs. Instead of focusing on the technology, Mehmet facilitated the session using information life cycle concepts and data quality requirements. He was then able to make a recommendation about interfaces (batch, real time, etc.) based on the specific business use.

The requirements gathering session—Mehmet provided background for those he was questioning. It sounded something like this: With today's technologies, we have many different data exchange options. We can exchange information in real time or on established schedules. Even for real-time exchange, we have the option to receive information as soon as it's available (publish-and-subscribe) or we can choose when to retrieve it, with an immediate turnaround time (request–response). To implement the right interfaces and maintain data quality across systems, we need to understand how business users will use the information, including indirect users of the application such as management. (Note: Technical terminology, such as publish-and-subscribe, was not a part of the dialogue but is included for readers in a technology role.)

Mehmet then used information life cycle concepts to understand how the information is used by discussing the following three points:

- Do you need to change this information in your application? Why?
- Does this change need to be sent back to the ERP? Why/Why not?
- "Let's talk about your information needs …"

He used selected data quality dimensions to find out how the users perceived data quality needs and the likely impact of poor data quality. *Table 4.2.2* outlines how he handled that discussion and provides a guide for others wanting to use the same approach. Note that the order in which the dimensions were discussed and the words used made sense to the audience. (These are different from the wording, full list, and order in which they are presented in *Step 3 – Assess Data Quality*).

Table 4.2.2 Data Quality Dimensions and Requirements Gathering

Dialogue	Data Quality Dimension	Example
How up to date does the information have to be? How long after a piece of information is available do you need access to it? Is a particular delay desired?	Timeliness	We need to know when new employees are hired on the same business day in order to create all appropriate accounts for them.
Which data elements must be correct in order to make the decision/ perform the transaction?	Accuracy	Vendor tax ID and billing address must be accurate to place a transaction. If the accuracy of a vendor's minority status is not required to complete a transaction, but it must be up-to-date each quarter for financial reporting, track this as a separate Timeliness / Accuracy requirement.
Are there other systems or data sources the data must match? How often must they be synchronized to other financial systems? Is there an external trigger to this?	Consistency and Synchronization	Finance and Sales organizations may be using different systems to track their capital spending. There may be a forecast schedule that drives the need for consistency.
How much of the total data universe must be available/ accessible? What are the criteria to subset the population?	Coverage	How many of all practicing prescribing doctors must be stored in the Sales Force Automation system? All oncologists, immunologists, etc.?
Is duplicate data acceptable? If not, but duplication is likely, what is the timeframe in which duplicates must be resolved?	Duplication	Duplicate data is not acceptable. Can existing records be identified in real time to avoid creating duplicates?
How formally must data specifications be captured and maintained? What are the policies or regulations that require this?	Data Specifications	FDA CGMPs (US Food and Drug Administration Current Good Manufacturing Practices) require pre-implementation documentation and formal change control of all design documents.

Ten Steps in Action *(Continued)*

Mehmet suggests the following best practices for capturing data quality requirements:

- Always provide a brief description of what you are trying to achieve and be ready to give examples. This will help your interview or workshop go more smoothly.
- Capture requirements at the business entity level (e.g., purchase order) using business terminology. Conceptual data models would support this effort effectively and allow you to see dependencies as well, to ensure that your requirements are complete.
- Use the terms consistently within and across projects, including the data quality dimensions.
- Compare the results of requirements gathering, per business entity and data quality dimension, to ensure that there are no conflicts. With regard to timeliness, for example, one person may want the entity to be updated within one business day, but not to be changed more than every 4 hours. Another person may want it

updated in real time. You have a requirements conflict that needs to be resolved. If you did not capture requirements at the business entity level with consistent terminology, you will rely on luck or work much harder to detect conflict.
- Capture requirements as distinctly as possible. The more specific you are in the requirements phase, the easier it will be to design and test solutions.
- Use business impact to prioritize the testing of your requirements. Remember that some of these requirements cannot be automatically tested and require specific coordination. For example, many projects test whether interfaces work properly but do not test their timing (the Timeliness data quality dimension).

This is a good example of how to use the idea of the dimensions, not to do a full assessment, but to gather requirements and to discuss the dimensions in such a way that they are understood by those with whom you are speaking.

Step 2.2 | Understand Relevant Data and Data Specifications

Business Benefit and Context

In this step, you will identify the data and related data specifications relevant to the business issue and within scope of the project. Data and information can be listed at a high level by common business terms, names seen on an application interface, or web app. These can then be divided into data subject areas or objects, which can be further broken down to the detail of field names, facts, attributes, columns, or data elements. If you are going to assess the quality of data content in *Step 3*, then you will need to go to the data field level. If doing a business impact assessment in *Step 4*, then the data field level might not be needed.

Remember that data specifications is an overarching term used in the Ten Steps methodology to encompass any information and documentation that provide context, structure, and meaning to data and information. Data specifications provide information needed to make, build, produce, assess, use, and manage data and information. This book focuses on the data specifications of metadata, data standards, reference data, data models and business rules. There are additional data specifications that may be of interest to the project such as taxonomies. For more detail on any of these see *Chapter 3: Key Concepts*.

To ensure high-quality data you must also manage and understand the data specifications which provide the information needed to make, build, use, manage or provide your information. Use data specifications

- When building new applications and designing new processes (to help ensure data quality from the beginning)
- When modifying applications or processes (to ensure data quality is taken into account)
- As a basis of comparison when assessing data quality so you know what constitutes high-quality data

This step is closely related to *Step 2.3 – Understand Relevant Technology*, so you may want to complete these two steps together.

Approach

1. Consider the level of detail needed for data and data specifications.

Ask, "At this point in our project, what do we need to know about relevant data and data specifications, in order to: Carry out the next project steps most effectively? Address the business needs? Achieve the project objectives?" See *Figure 4.2.4* for examples of levels of detail for data.

2. Identify critical data elements (CDEs).

In *Step 1*, information within scope of the project was probably identified at a high level. Now is the time to understand the data that makes up the information and quickly narrow the focus to what are often called critical data elements (CDEs) or key data elements. CDEs are the pieces of data which are the most important and have the most impact on the organization. You will want to know the data which is most important within the scope of your project.

Get to the CDEs as quickly as possible. See if CDEs have already been identified as part of another initiative. If not, one technique that works well in identifying CDEs can be found in *Step 4.9 – Ranking and Prioritization*. This technique uses business processes as the context for determining what is most important. For each of the data elements under consideration, the question is asked, "If this data field is missing or incorrect, what will be the impact to XYZ business process?" Use the business processes identified in *Step 1*. Those data elements ranked as A (or 1 or High) means complete failure of the process or unacceptable financial, compliance, legal or other risk is likely if the data is missing or incorrect. These are your CDEs.

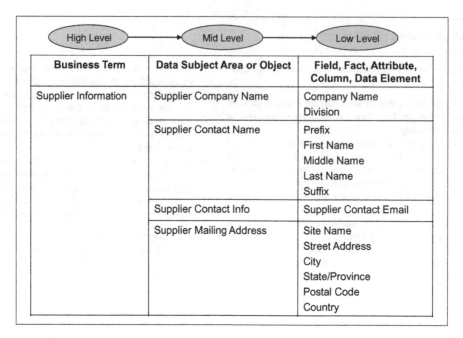

Business Term	Data Subject Area or Object	Field, Fact, Attribute, Column, Data Element
Supplier Information	Supplier Company Name	Company Name Division
	Supplier Contact Name	Prefix First Name Middle Name Last Name Suffix
	Supplier Contact Info	Supplier Contact Email
	Supplier Mailing Address	Site Name Street Address City State/Province Postal Code Country

Figure 4.2.4 Example levels of detail for data.

To shorten the time, facilitate the prioritization with a small group of people who know the processes and uses of the data. Take their list and obtain agreement on the CDEs from stakeholders. Finalize, document, and ensure appropriate team members and other stakeholders are informed. Use the CDEs to guide your work, such as only collecting data specifications associated with the CDEs. I will use CDEs going forward to mean whatever data you have determined is within scope of the project to be assessed for data quality.

See the *Best Practice callout box* for questions that may get you to CDEs even more quickly. One caution: when assessing data quality for the CDEs, don't be too narrow in your selection criteria – at least the first time you view the data content. For example, other fields in the same record might be less important to you, but should be looked at – at the least first time you view content – because they provide context to help you understand the CDEs and refine your selection criteria for additional data captures.

Best Practice

Identifying Critical Data Elements (CDEs). Melissa Gentile, DQR Consulting, suggests the following questions to quickly identify critical data elements.

- Does this information appear on a report for an executive or is it sent outside the organization (the data and anything in aggregate that created it)?
- Does it drive decisions that impact your customers?
- Is the information needed to comply with regulatory requirements?

Do you know the answer to the questions above? If not, you should! These are your CDEs.

For each of the CDEs, do you know how it is created, what it means, where it is logically and physically, who consumes it, what reports it is on, and how to fix it if its broken?

(Note from author: Using the Ten Steps will help you answer these questions.)

3. Connect CDEs and business terms.

It is critical that the terms used by the business are linked to the actual data to be assessed for quality. The business terms will most likely be associated with how the information is applied and how the business sees and thinks about the information. Business terms will not necessarily be the same as the names of columns in databases or field in applications. You will need to help make that connection in order to ensure that you are assessing data that the business cares most about. For example, you will need to identify the tables, fields, and databases where CDE data is stored. The business terms represent the language used by the business, which you will also want to use to ensure business audiences understand what is included in the project.

You may start with the business terms or with data subject areas (groupings of related data) within the project scope. Then move to the detail of where data is stored. Conversely, if you are more familiar with the fields where the data is held, start with those terms and trace them back to the business terms. Examine documents, reports, system screens and interfaces or conduct interviews as needed to ensure the business terms and data fields are linked.

See *Template 4.2.2 – Detailed Data Grid* to get you started. Often the information is documented in formats or locations not available or easily understood by those on the project team. The goal of the detailed data grid is to have a clear understanding of the data you plan to assess and make it easy to reference by the project team. If this information is already documented in a useable format, don't duplicate work. Start with what is known now and add to it as this step progresses.

4. Document CDEs in each datastore to be assessed and map between them.

If your data quality assessment includes looking at the same data in more than one datastore, that means you are assessing the data quality dimension of consistency and synchronization (*Step 3.6*).

Template 4.2.2 Detailed Data Grid

				Application/System/Datastore:					
Business Term	Table	Field Name	Data Type	Field Size/ Length	Description	Mandatory, Optional, Conditional *	Data Domain **	Format	Other

* If conditional, note the conditions under which the data should be added.
** The list of valid values. This may contain a table or file name where the values can be easily found.

Template 4.2.3 Data Mapping

Business Term	Application/System/Datastore 1				Application/System/Datastore 2				Notes
	Table	Field Name	Description	Other Info	Table	Field Name	Description	Other Info	Other *

* Differences found, items to look for when assessing for quality, initial transformation rules, etc.

Create a detailed data grid for the CDEs in each datastore and map between them. The mapping shows where data is held in one datastore and where the same data is held in another datastore. This will be important information to use as you develop your data capture and assessment plan for *Step 3*. See the Data Mapping template (*Template 4.2.3*) above.

You might be mapping from screen names in one application to the underlying database in the same application, to the field names in a different application and its underlying datastore. As you do, recognize that the mapping represents a subset of the information life cycle. The word lineage is often used as a synonym.

Source-to-target mapping is a typical activity in other projects where data is moved and integrated, such as data migration from an old legacy system to a new application. Similar mapping work may have already been done as part of what is called

source-to-target mapping (STM). Don't duplicate work – find and make use of any STMs that already exist. Recognize that many STMs are made based on field names and that the quality of the STMs can be increased by what is learned through profiling the data. This is covered in *Step 3.3 – Data Integrity Fundamentals*. Use existing mappings and continue to update them as more is learned.

5. Collect relevant data specifications for the CDEs.

A good data modeler is a valuable resource when collecting many kinds of data specifications, not just data models. Find one, get him or her on your project, and make use of his or her expertise!

Table 4.2.3 – Collecting Data Specifications below highlights information helpful to know about the metadata, data standards, reference data, data models, and business rules associated with the data in scope.

Table 4.2.3 Collecting Data Specifications

Data Specification	Information to Collect
Metadata	• Database/data store • Table names and descriptions • Field names and descriptions • Date type • Field size/length • Definitions • Indicators of validity (e.g., formats – a specified form, style, or pattern) • If the field is validated by the system and any associated reference tables • If the field is generated by the system • Data domains/valid values (also considered reference data) and where the approved lists of values can be found • If the data field is mandatory/required, optional, or conditional and the conditions for when data should be added
Data Standards	• Naming conventions for table and field names • Data entry guidelines – rules to follow when entering the data (can include accepted abbreviations, casing (upper, lower, mixed), punctuation, etc.) • External standards the company uses or with which they are required to comply

(Continued)

Table 4.2.3 Collecting Data Specifications *(Continued)*

Data Specification	Information to Collect
Reference Data	• Data domain – the set of allowed values • Names of reference tables containing valid values • Descriptions of values • Domain and format guidelines for lists of values
Data Models	• Data models applicable to the data that will be assessed, including identifying primary keys and foreign keys • Cardinality – how many instances of one entity class can be related to an instance of another entity class (zero, one, or many) • Optionality – if an instance of one entity class exists, if it is necessary for there to be an instance of a related entity class • Whether the field is mandatory, optional, or conditional (with conditions documented) as required by the technology • Higher-level information architecture plans related to the scope of your project
Business Rules	• Whether the field is mandatory, optional, or conditional (with conditions documented) as required by the business (which may or may not be enforced by the technology). Data quality issues are often found when the business requires data, but the technology does not, or cannot, enforce mandatory rules. • Explicit or implicit statements about how and when an instance (a record) or a particular data field should be treated throughout the POSMAD life cycle • Documented business rules and dependencies – conditions that govern business actions and establish data integrity guidelines (e.g., where major state changes can occur and rules for corresponding data behavior that state when a record is obtained/created, maintained/updated, or deleted)
Real-World Usage	• Data quality issues are often found when the technology requires data but the business does not have the information available when the record needs to be created or updated • Common business usage or "real-world" usage of which you are aware. For example, the system requires a physical address. If the physical address is not known when the record is created, a period is often put in the field. This technically fulfills the system requirement of a value in the field and allows the knowledge worker to complete the record. However, it creates data quality issues for downstream systems needing the address.
Other Learnings	• If it is clear that a particular field should or should not be included in an assessment, document this and the reasons.

Data specifications are often, though not always, associated with a particular physical application or system. Identify the systems, applications, and datastores where the data is used and stored. This activity is closely related to *Step 2.3 – Understand Relevant Technology*. Tools with data catalog functionality are helpful when discovering where, exactly, data resides.

Understand the data model. *Figure 4.2.5* shows an example of a context model that was useful for providing an overview of the data to be assessed for quality. Even at this high level it provided helpful information about the data and relationships within scope. Other more detailed data models can be useful to show system scope, processes that can and cannot be supported because data does or does not exist, and business rules supported by the data. Different levels of data models are described in *Table 3.6 – Data Model Comparison* in *Chapter 3*. You may need to simplify a detailed model when speaking with those in the business. At a minimum, you need to know data relationships at a very high level.

This is yet another case when you will have to use your judgment as to the level of detail needed at this time. Use existing data models to help. If there is no data model, developing one should be one of the first items on your recommendation list.

Sometimes data specifications are clearly documented and easily available. Other times research is required to uncover them. Look for data specifications in the following:

• Tools with data catalog, data governance, lineage, business process modeling, or workflow management functionality – and their artifacts may be lost or orphaned in files or network shares

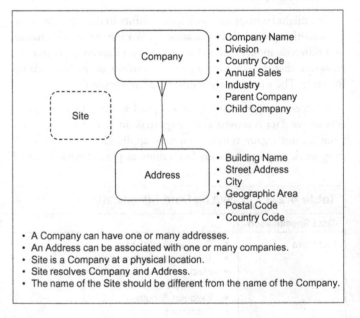

• A Company can have one or many addresses.
• An Address can be associated with one or many companies.
• Site is a Company at a physical location.
• Site resolves Company and Address.
• The name of the Site should be different from the name of the Company.

Figure 4.2.5 Context model.

• Application documentation and/or user guides
• Spreadsheet and diagramming files kept by subject matter experts or data stewards
• Knowledge of subject matter experts and users, especially for business rules, in their minds but not written down

- Other people knowledgeable about the data: business analysts, data analysts, data modelers, developers, database administrators (DBAs), and the like.
- Requirements and constraints gathered in *Step 2.1 – Understand Relevant Requirements*, which may be input to create specifications, such as metadata and business rules that support those requirements
- Data models, data dictionaries, metadata repositories, or business glossaries
- Embedded within interfaces and ETL transformation procedures
- In JSON texts, XML files, or otherwise stored in NoSQL documents or key/value pairs
- Other sources that provide the layout which best represents the data according to the most likely extraction method
- A relational database directory or catalog for data in a relational system for metadata on the column-level layout of the data
- Structural information within the database management system. For example, in relational systems primary key, foreign key, and other referential constraint information can be extracted.
- Any TRIGGER or STORED PROCEDURE logic embedded within the relational system to find data-filtering and validation rules being enforced
- The program specification block (PSB) in IMS, which defines the logical data structure and gives insight into the hierarchical structure being enforced by IMS
- A COBOL copybook or a PL/1 INCLUDE file that lays out the data if accessing an IMS or VSAM data source (Note: The death of the programming language COBOL has been pronounced for many years, yet it continues to live on.)

6. Analyze, synthesize, recommend, document, and act on what you learned about the data and data specifications within scope.

If you haven't already started systematically tracking results, do so now. See the section *Analyze, Synthesize, Recommend, Document, and Act on Results* in *Chapter 6: Other Techniques and Tools* for additional help. Document any potential effects on data quality or business impacts recognized at this time. For example, did you learn anything about real world usage that could impact the quality of the data and should be checked during the DQ assessment? Do you anticipate any problems with permissions and access to the data you want to assess?

Sample Output and Templates
Detailed Data Grid

Use *Template 4.2.2 – Detailed Data Grid* as a starting point for documenting the CDEs in a format that is easy to reference by the project team. Note that this template brings together the business terms and CDEs as they relate to specific technology.

Data Mapping

Use *Template 4.2.3* as a starting point for mapping data if you will be assessing data in more than one application or database or if you are creating source-to-target mappings as part of another project.

Collecting Data Specifications

Table 4.2.3 contains useful information to know about the metadata, data standards, reference data, data models, and business rules associated with the data in scope.

| Step 2.3 | Understand Relevant Technology |

Business Benefit and Context

Remember that technology is used broadly to include forms, applications, databases, files, programs, code, or media that store, share, or manipulate the data, are involved with the processes, or are used by people and organizations. Technology is both high-tech such as datastores and low-tech such as paper copies. Much of the information about technology will be discovered in the course of working on *Step 2.2 – Understand Relevant Data and Data Specifications*. You may want to complete these two steps in parallel.

A database management system (DBMS) is a software system that stores, organizes, and manages data in databases. There are several types of DBMSs and databases, a few of which are discussed below.

Relational databases, now considered traditional, were a revolutionary idea in 1970 when Edgar Frank "Ted" Codd published the seminal paper "A Relational Model of Data for Large Shared Data Banks." It described a new method for storing data and processing large databases which, "in plain terms, his relational database solution provided a level of data independence that allowed users to access information without having to master details of the physical structure of a database" (IBM, n.d.).

Between 1974 and 1977, two major prototypes of relational database systems were created, Ingres and System R. After learning about the relational model from Ted Codd, Don Chamberlin and Raymond Boyce invented SQL, for Structured Query Language, and by 1980 it was the most widely used computer language for querying relational databases – and remains so to this day. Even with the advent of NoSQL databases (for Not only SQL and discussed next), use of relational databases remain strong, in spite of predictions of their impending death.

The NoSQL technologies are usually grouped into four categories: key-value stores, graph stores, column stores, and document stores. A data lake has become somewhat synonymous with big data technologies and a data warehouse with relational databases. A recent combination of the two is a "data lakehouse." A discussion of types of data management technologies can be found in the section on *Data Models* in *Chapter 3: Key Concepts*. For a good overview of NoSQL databases, see Mohammad Altarade's "The Definitive Guide to NoSQL databases" (Altarade, n.d.). If your project includes big data, then you must have some understanding about the non-relational technology that is managing it.

Don't forget other database management systems such as IMS, one of the first database management systems. In 1965, IBM and North American Aviation, developed an automated system to track the millions of parts and materials used in NASA's (the US National Aeronautics and Space Administration) Apollo Space Program. In 1966 they were joined by Caterpillar Tractor and together designed and developed a system, ICS, which was the precursor to IMS. It was installed at NASA in 1968 and contributed to the first human landing on the moon in 1969. Two years later, ICS was relaunched as IMS and made available commercially.

It is possible some of the readers of this book have never heard of IMS, yet it is still in use today – and on a large scale. According to a 2017 article, over 95% of Fortune 1000 companies use IMS in some capacity, and "In a world where the relational database is an old workhorse increasingly in competition with trendy new NoSQL databases, IMS is a freaking dinosaur. It is a relic from an era before the relational database was even invented, which didn't happen until 1970. And yet it seems to be the database system in charge of all the important stuff." (Two-Bit History, 2017).

This brief history is included to emphasize the point that you will most likely be working with a variety of technologies in your quest for higher-quality data. It is also a reminder not to ignore technologies because they are not the latest getting attention. Any technology which touches the data throughout its life cycle can impact the quality, and may have to be taken into account in your project – such as database management systems, networks which move data, and tools specifically for managing data quality. See *Tools for Managing Data Quality* in *Chapter 6*.

The technology landscape and tools are rapidly changing. Do not think you can, or should, know all the details about every tool. Work with your technology partners to understand just enough about the technology used throughout the information life cycle for the data within scope. Learn about tools that can be used for

assessing data quality in *Step 3* and when improving and monitoring the data in *Steps 7, 8,* and *9*.

Having said that, there is no technology that ensures data quality *on its own*, so do not be misled into thinking that technology is the *only* thing we need to be concerned with to have high-quality data. I hope by now, between what you have learned from the Framework for Information Quality and the Ten Steps Process, that it is clear there are many other aspects that affect the quality of the data that must be managed, and they must each be addressed.

On the other hand again, though I just stressed that tools alone are not the answer to our data quality problems, I know that the right tools, used for the right purposes, in the right circumstances, are invaluable.

Approach

1. Consider the level of detail needed for this step.

Ask, "At this point in our project, what do we need to know about relevant technology in order to: Carry out the next project steps most effectively? Address the business needs? Achieve the project objectives?" See *Figure 4.2.6* for examples of levels of detail for technology.

If preparing for a data quality assessment, understanding technology at the data field level will usually be required. If preparing for a business impact assessment, knowing which information is accessed by users through a particular application may be enough to proceed. Use the Just Enough Principle to guide your decisions about which technology and the level of detail for each that is relevant for your project.

2. Gather information on the technologies and tools associated with data in scope of the project.

Start with the high-level technology from *Step 1*. Identify the applications, datastores, tools, technologies, and business events (manual or automated) which either create, modify, or employ the data in the scope of your project. It is outside the scope of this book to fully define all the technologies, so work with your IT partners to understand enough about the technologies to support the project objectives. Make use of existing documentation and partner with

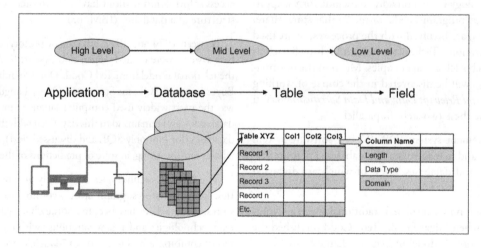

Figure 4.2.6 Example levels of detail for relational technology.

technology experts such as a developer, technical data steward, or DBA to provide the information or verify what you collect. Look for others who should be included in the project from the technology side as a stakeholder or team member. Include tools that will be used when improving the data and monitoring controls in *Steps 7, 8,* and *9.*

For each technology document the name of the software (the common name used by the business and the "legal name" used by the vendor if a third-party package), the version in use, the application owner, the teams responsible for supporting the technology, the platform, if the technology is on-premises or in the cloud, your contact for the project to answer questions, and so forth.

See the section *Tools for Managing Data Quality* in *Chapter 6* where *Table 6.3* and *Table 6.4* list various tool functionalities. Use them as a guide to determine if there are gaps between functionalities available in-house and those needed for the project (cleansing, prevention, controls and ongoing monitoring).

Following are additional considerations when determining which technologies are relevant to your project:

Data at rest—Data at rest refers to when data is stored and sitting still. As a reminder, a datastore as used in this book means any collection of data that is created or obtained, held, and used, regardless of the technology involved. Datastores can be anywhere. A datastore can be large or small. A datastore can be located on-premises, where the software runs on an organization's own computers and servers, or cloud-based, where the software is hosted on a vendor's servers and accessed by the organization through a web browser.

A variety of technologies are used for datastores. Examples of datastores include a table in a SQL relational database, a full RDBMS (Relationship Database Management System), a spreadsheet, a comma-delimited file, an XML document, a flat file, a file repository, a data warehouse, a hierarchical database (LDAP, IMS), or any of a variety of NoSQL non-relational databases.

Data in motion—When data moves between various datastores it is referred to as data in motion. The ability to move, transform and exchange data are essential to interoperability which is the ability for different technologies, tools, and devices to connect and communicate in a coordinated way. You may need to account for networks, messaging technology, or interfaces involved with sharing data. For more information, see April Reeve's book *Managing Data in Motion* (2013).

A data interface is an application written to facilitate the movement of data, the exchange of data, and to transform data as needed so it can be combined. ETL, or Extract-Transform-Load, is a process where data is obtained (extracted) from a source system, changed (transformed) to be compatible with the target or destination system, and then put into the target system (load). This is not the same as the user interface (UI) discussed below.

A Source-to-Target Mapping (STM) provides information to move data from a source to a destination along with needed transformation logic. The quality of the mappings and the resulting code in programs and ETL tools greatly impacts the quality of data.

Any time data is transformed, the chances of negatively impacting data quality increases.

Another technology consideration for data in motion relates to the timing and structure of the data being moved in large batch files being different from data moved as multiple, independent real-time transactions.

Data in use—Data in use refers to data used for business transactions, analysis, and decisions. These can happen at the micro level (e.g., a bank teller completes a deposit) all the way to a macro level (an executive sets strategies and policies). Data in use is where data becomes valuable – the Apply phase of the information life cycle.

Data is accessed by a user through a user interface (UI). A user interface is a broad term that connects a user with a particular technology. A graphical user interface (GUI) is a main type of interface. For example, the UI can be a screen for an application where the user creates records or a touch screen on a mobile device. The UI design can affect data quality and should support both: 1) the collection of data, and 2) uses of information.

When collecting data, the UI appearance and underlying code affect how easily the screen can be understood and accessed, constraints on values that can be entered into a field, and calculations for derived data. When data is in use, such as when the answer to a query is returned or when a report is displayed, the format should ensure the user can properly interpret the results. To prevent data quality issues, work with a UI team to design new applications and to update the UI if it is found to be one of the root causes of data quality problems.

Structured Data—Often thought of as "traditional" data that is easily organized in a rigid format such as relational databases with conventional data models. For example, master data, transactional data in business applications, and data consolidated into a data warehouse. Data in spreadsheets can also be considered structured data. Structured data may have fields that contain unstructured data such as free form text fields where anything can be entered without constraints.

Unstructured Data—Complex data such as text, business documents, presentations, blogs, social media posts, images, audio and video files. The development of NoSQL non-relational databases brought the ability to manage large volumes of unstructured data that are difficult to collect, store, and organize in relational databases.

Semi-Structured Data—Data with elements of both structured and unstructured data. The content itself is unstructured but has properties such as tags that make it easier to organize and find. For example, digital photos themselves are unstructured but may have tags with date, time, and geographic location.

Not everyone agrees on what is considered structured vs. semi structured data. Some consider emails unstructured data while others point out that though the message itself is unstructured, the email also contains structured data such as email address and date/time stamps for when the email was sent.

On-premises vs. cloud computing—At the highest level, with on-premises computing an organization hosts the data on software installed on its servers behind its firewall. With cloud computing the data is hosted on a third-party server. There are differences between the two in cost, security, control, compliance, and how they are deployed.

Cloud computing has a further distinction of public and private. The private cloud service is not shared with any other organization. A public cloud service shares computing services among different customers, with each customer's data and applications being hidden from other cloud customers. In addition, private clouds can be hosted (offered by a third-party cloud provider) or internal (managed and maintained internally by the organization itself). Hybrid cloud has a mixed deployment of on-premise, public and private cloud. Why should we care? Who is responsible for the data, and therefore can affect the quality of the data, may be accessible to the project team – or not. If data quality issues are found, being able to resolve, and possibly escalate, a problem may be more complicated, depending on how and where the data is stored.

POSMAD Information Life Cycle and CRUD—Those with a background in IT may be familiar with four data operations known as CRUD (Create, Read, Update, and Delete). CRUD indicates the four basic data operations – that is, how data is processed in the technology. Many IT resources will relate to the CRUD point of view. When working with them and researching the technology used throughout the POSMAD life cycle, it may be helpful to discuss using terms with which they are familiar. You can also take the opportunity to make them aware of the POSMAD view of the information life cycle. *Table 4.2.4* maps the six phases of the POSMAD information life cycle to the four data operations (CRUD).

From a data quality point of view, anything technology does to the data throughout its life cycle can impact the quality for good or ill – from planning for the technology (has the business point of view been represented?) to obtaining/creating/loading to storing and sharing to maintaining/updating to access and use to disposal/archiving. For example, if an issue is found during the

Maintain phase when a user is changing a record,' a starting point for investigating possible technical causes would be the UI and the application's update programs. If you are going to conduct a business impact assessment, see how many programs relate to the Read phase of CRUD. This can give you an idea of how the information is being applied.

Looking ahead—Look ahead at the types of data quality assessments you will be conducting in *Step 3*. What tools are already in the organization that could help with data quality assessments? Are you able to make use of them and who has to give permission? Do you anticipate the need to purchase any tools to help in the assessments? If yes, what is the cost and lead time for purchase? For any tools, what training is needed to use them effectively in the project?

What technology is associated with data specifications in scope? Where are metadata, data standards, reference data, data models and business rules stored? How are they made available for use?

3. Understand interactions between the technology and the other key components of data, processes, people/organizations.

Create mappings as needed. See *Step 2.2 – Understand Relevant Data and Data Specifications* for templates which also apply here:

- *Template 4.2.2 – Detailed Data Grid* which brings together business terms as seen by users and the critical data elements (CDEs) with respect to the specific technology where they are stored
- *Template 4.2.3 – Data Mapping* for a starting point to see where the same data is stored in more than one system

4. Analyze, synthesize, recommend, document, and act on what you learned about the technology.

See the section *Analyze, Synthesize, Recommend, Document, and Act on Results* in *Chapter 6: Other Techniques and Tools* for additional help. Capture any impact to the business or data quality seen

POSMAD Phase	Definition and Examples	CRUD Data Operation
Plan	Prepare for the information resource. Identify objectives, plan information architecture, model data and processes, develop standards, design processes, organizations, etc.	CRUD does not include Plan.
Obtain	Acquire the data or information. Purchase data, create records.	Create: Produce a record or attribute.
Store and Share	Hold data and make it available for use. Hold information about the resource electronically or in hardcopy and make available for use through a distribution method.	CRUD does not include Store and Share.
Maintain	Ensure that the resource continues to work properly. Update, change, manipulate, standardize, cleanse, or transform data; match and merge records, etc.	Update: Modify or change existing data.
Apply	Use information and data to accomplish goals. Retrieve data; use information. Includes all information usage such as completing a transaction, writing a report, making a management decision, running automated processes, etc.	Read: Access the data.
Dispose	Discard the resource when it is no longer of use. Archive information; delete data or records.	Delete: Remove existing data.

Table 4.2.4   Mapping the POSMAD Information Life Cycle to CRUD Data Operations

Key Concept

Principles of data quality are technology neutral, yet technology impacts the quality of data. Data can have sources/creators, manipulators, and users. Ideally, an item of data should only have one source, but in some situations, inevitably there could be multiple potential sources for a single fact. A fact can be *stored* in multiple places; though that has generally been considered bad database design for the past 35 years or more. Uncontrolled redundancy undermines DQ reliability and trust.

A fact can be *used* by multiple applications, multiple processes, and multiple people. Indeed, facts residing in data flows (data in motion) should be monitored for their quality before they come to rest and are available for business users.

From a cultural point of view many heads-down technologists are often distant from and unaware of the needs of data quality. Organizationally, it is often difficult for them to have access to those from the business who use the data. In addition, if they "don't know what they don't know" about data quality, they might not even know there are questions that should be asked.

– Michael Scofield, MBA, Assistant Professor, Loma Linda University

through understanding the technology. Did you learn anything about real world IT tools and operations that could impact the quality of the data and should be checked during the DQ assessment? Do you anticipate any problems with permissions and access to the data you want to assess? Any preliminary recommendations? Is this the right time (or not) to take action on them?

Sample Output and Templates

POSMAD and CRUD

Table 4.2.4 shows the information life cycle phases, using POSMAD, as they apply to 4 basic data operations (how data is processed in the technology), commonly known as CRUD – Create, Read, Update, Delete. When discussing the information life cycle with those in IT, use the terms most familiar to them.

Step 2.4 | Understand Relevant Processes

Business Benefit and Context

As a reminder, process is the overarching term used to mean functions, activities, actions, tasks, or procedures that touch the data or information. These can be business processes, data management processes, or processes external to the company; they include events that trigger a response or change the state of the data. Functions are major high-level areas describing *what* is to be accomplished, such as sales, marketing, finance, manufacturing, lead generation, vendor management, etc. Other levels of detail may be called processes, activities, actions, tasks, or procedures which describe *how* it is to be accomplished, such as detailed instructions for creating a purchase order. Sometimes functions or processes use titles similar to how an organization is structured. Processes are usually associated with people, so you might want to do this step along with *Step 2.5 – Understand Relevant People and Organizations.*

If planning for a data quality assessment, you may look at some or all phases of the POSMAD information life cycle since the quality of the data is affected by activity within any of the six phases – Plan, Obtain, Store and Share, Maintain, Apply, and Dispose.

If preparing for a business impact assessment, focus on the Apply phase – those processes that use the data for any reason. For example, the data may be used to complete a transaction, or it may be in the form of a report to support decision making. The data may also be used by an automated program such as electronic funds transfer where money is pulled from a customer's account on the date a payment is due. Some may consider this IT use, and it is, but it is also a process on which the business depends. If the business impact assessment includes cost, then any of the POSMAD phases can be included since there is a cost to all activities in the six phases.

Approach

1. Consider the level of detail needed for this step.

Ask, "At this point in our project, what do we need to know about relevant processes in order to: Carry out the next project steps most effectively? Address the business needs? Achieve the project objectives?" As with data, technology, and people/organizations, there are different levels of detail for processes. See *Figure 4.2.7* for an example showing levels of detail for processes. Use your best judgment to determine the level of detail most useful to address the business needs within scope.

2. Identify processes within scope at the chosen level of detail.

Start with the high-level business functions or processes from *Step 1*. Function versus process is a relative relationship, with function being higher level and process being more detailed. What could be called a function in one project may be a process in another. Determine which level of process detail is most helpful at this time for your project. Look for those experienced in Business Process Management (BPM) or workflow management.

3. Understand interactions between the relevant business processes and the other key components of data, technology, and people/organizations.

An interaction matrix is one way of showing the relationship between the key components. See the following tables for examples of matrices showing the relationship between data and processes at different levels of detail. Use the terms and definitions for business

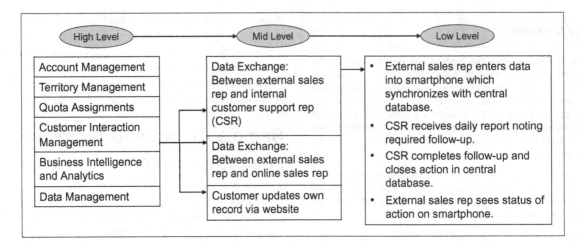

Figure 4.2.7 Example levels of detail for processes.

processes and the data or information that are recognized and used by the business:

- *Table 4.2.5 – Interaction Matrix: Data-to-Key Business Processes*
- *Table 4.2.6 – Interaction Matrix: Business Function-to-Data*
- *Table 4.2.7 – Interaction Matrix: Processes-to-Data*

These interaction matrices can be input to prioritize if resources are constrained, i.e., the data used by the most processes should be assessed first. They provide templates as starting points for your own work. They point to which processes should have input to decisions regarding the data.

When analyzing, look for patterns of similarities and differences across the rows and down the columns. For instance, in *Table 4.2.7* there are four processes that obtain the data but only three that maintain them. Since data from sales events only result in adding records, there is a possibility that duplicates could be created. Check if all processes that obtain and maintain data are similar and using the same standards. If not, training should be instituted to encourage consistency in data entry.

4. Analyze, synthesize, recommend, document, and act on what you learned about the processes.

See the section *Analyze, Synthesize, Recommend, Document, and Act on Results* in *Chapter 6: Other Techniques and Tools* for additional help. Capture lessons learned, impact to the business, potential impact to data quality and/or value, and initial recommendations learned from analyzing processes. Is there additional action related to processes that should be done at this time?

 Key Concept

Learning is the output. Be aware that the actual output of any of the substeps in *Step 2 – Analyze Information Environment* may be in a format different from the example interaction matrices shown. The output is not really a matrix; the output is knowledge about the processes and related data, how they interact, and how that interaction can impact data quality. Your output may physically take the form of a matrix, a diagram, or a textual explanation. The format used should enhance understanding. It is the learning that comes out of completing the step or substep that is important.

Table 4.2.5 Interaction Matrix: Data-to-Key Business Processes

	Key Business Processes (KBP)				
	Quote to Cash	Procure to Pay	Manufacturing	Product Lifecycle	Finance
Master Data					
Item	●	●	●	▶	●
Customer	▶				●
Price List	●	▶		●	▶
Supplier		▶	●	●	●
Etc.					
Transactional Data					
Sales Order	▶		●		●
Accounts Receivable Invoices	▶		●		●
Etc.					
▶ = process creates and uses the data ● = process uses the data					

Table 4.2.6   Interaction Matrix: Business Function-to-Data

Business Function	Sales Rep	Name and Address				Customer Profile			
	SR Code	Contact Name	Division	Street Address	Zip Code	Industry Code	Position Level Code	Department/ Function Code	Product Class
Account Management	X	X	X	X	X	X	X	X	X
Territory Management	X	X	X	X	X				
Quota Assignment	X	X	X	X	X	X			
Market Analysis/ Decision Support	X	X				X	X	X	X
Lead Generation	X	X	X			X	X	X	X
Deal Management	X	X	X			X	X	X	X
Data Management	X	X	X	X		X	X	X	X

X = Business functions that use the information

Table 4.2.7   Interaction Matrix: Processes-to-Data

						Function: Account Management							
Processes	Sales Rep	Name and Address					Customer Profile				System Codes		
	SR Code	Contact Name	Division	Street	City	Etc.	Industry Code	Position Level Code	Department/ Function Code	Etc.	Change Reason Code	Delete Reason Code	Etc.
Customer adds/ updates by sales rep	OM	OM	OM	OM	OM	OM	OM	OM	OM		OM	OM	
Changes from call center	OM	OM	OM	OM	OM	OM	OM	OM	OM		OM	OM	
Data from sales events		O	O	O	O			O	O				
District territory assignment	OMA	OMA	OMA	OMA									

O = Data is obtained/created by the process
M = Data is maintained/updated by the process
A = Data is applied/used by the process

Note: The activities in the interaction matrix can be further detailed if needed. For example, Obtain may be designated as C = manually created through application interface and L = load from external source.

Sample Output and Templates

Interaction Matrix: Data-to-Key Business Processes

If looking at data across an organization, where it gets complex very quickly, it is helpful to start at a high level, as in *Table 4.2.5*. It lists the key business processes (KBP) as developed by and recognized by the business side of the organization. A "●" symbol indicates which KBP uses the data. A "▶" symbol means the KBP creates the data, in addition to using it – meaning no other KBP should be able to create that same data. Note, this is something you will want to verify during your data quality assessment or as you research the information life cycle. Use the matrix as a guide to see where it makes sense to go into more detail. For example, it is easy to see that if you are concerned about Price List data, there is no need to look at the Manufacturing key business process (unless you do a quick check to confirm the table was created correctly). If you are concerned about Item, it will take longer to go into detail because it spans all key business processes. Because Item is used by all KBPs it would be a higher priority for checking quality if time is constrained.

Interaction Matrix: Business Function-to-Data

In *Table 4.2.6*, an X indicates which business functions use the information listed in the columns across the top. Analyze across the rows and down the columns. For example, look down the column for position level code. Several functions use that code. What is the source of the codes? Do all codes have clear definitions

and are they being used consistently? Do all functions that use the code have input into them or have the ability to request or modify codes? The function "Account Management" is further detailed in *Table 4.2.7*.

Interaction Matrix: Processes-to-Data

Table 4.2.7 continues the example from *Table 4.2.6* by detailing the Account Management function. Note that only three of the POSMAD phases (Obtain, Maintain, and Apply) are used. It is easy to see that several processes obtain/create and maintain/update the same data. If a data quality assessment in *Step 3* shows differences in the same data, use the matrix to point to processes for further research. See if those differences can be traced back to individual processes that created the data. Uncover what is impeding consistency in the processes and what can be done to encourage that consistency.

Step 2.5 Understand Relevant People and Organizations

Business Benefit and Context

As a reminder, people and organizations refer to organizations and their subdivisions, such as business units, departments, teams, roles, responsibilities, and individuals that affect or use the data or are involved with the processes. This includes those who manage and support the data and those who use (apply) it. Those who use the information are known as knowledge workers, information customers, information consumers, or simply as users.

The purpose of this substep is to understand people and organizations as they affect information quality and value. As with the other substeps in *Step 2*, start at a high level of detail and move to more detail as needed. Understanding organizations at a group/team/department level may be sufficient; knowing roles, titles, and

job responsibilities may be necessary. At some point, knowing the individuals who fulfill roles of interest, along with pertinent contact information, may be needed as well. Processes are carried out by people and organizations, so you might want to work on this and *Step 2.4 – Understand Relevant Processes* together.

Approach

1. Consider the level of detail needed for this step.

Ask, "At this point in our project, what do we need to know about relevant people and organizations in order to: Carry out the next project steps most effectively? Address the business needs? Achieve the project objectives?" See *Figure 4.2.8* for examples of levels of detail for people and organizations:

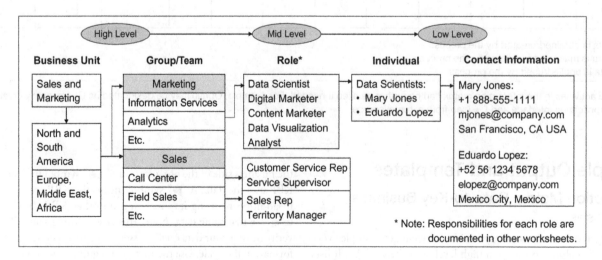

Figure 4.2.8 Example levels of detail for people and organizations.

2. Identify people and organizations within scope, at the chosen level of detail.

Start with the people and organizations within scope of the project from *Step 1*. Gather more information, beginning at a high level, and work down to details helpful to know at this time (organizations, teams, roles, responsibilities, individuals, and/or contact information).

Use existing documentation such as organization charts and job descriptions. Make use of a stakeholder analysis if you started that in *Step 1*. If not, see templates and instructions for identifying stakeholders and conducting a stakeholder analysis in *Step 10 – Communicate, Manage, and Engage People Throughout*.

Apply information life cycle thinking to uncover roles applicable to the project. Reference *Table 4.2.8* for the POSMAD phases with related job roles and sample titles. These provide a starting point for identifying roles in your organization that affect the quality of data. This may be the first time some roles are recognized as impacting data quality. Understanding the connection will lead you to people who impact the data in some way and could provide input to the project.

If preparing for a data quality assessment, any of the roles in the POSMAD phases may be included – it depends on which phases are within scope of your project. If preparing for a business impact assessment, focus on those who use the data and information – those in the Apply phase. For example, those who complete

Table 4.2.8 POSMAD Phases with Related Job Roles and Titles

General Role Information	Sample Titles *
POSMAD Phase: Plan	
Include a data quality perspective when planning: • Priorities and budgets which should include support for data quality activities through funding and other resources • Any project, program, or operational process where data is a component, e.g., creating new and refining existing business processes, development or purchase of technology that impacts data in its life cycle General planning roles include: • Managers who determine if and how data quality activities will be included in plans • Those involved with gathering requirements and designing processes and technology (systems, applications, databases, etc.) that impact the information throughout its life cycle	Executives and board members; senior, mid-level, program, and project managers Data analyst, business analyst, subject matter expert, enterprise architect, data modeler, developer, DBA (Database Administrator), business data steward, technical data steward, scrum master
POSMAD Phase: Obtain	
Source. The first origin of the information, which can be: • External to the company, e.g., the customer is the source of information about him/herself • Internal to the company, e.g., engineer is the source of information about a specific product • Non-person, e.g., a physical product may be measured to obtain its physical dimensions If the primary source is not available, an agreed-upon secondary source may be used as a substitute. **Producer**. Those who capture, create, acquire, or purchase data as a part of their job role and processes they perform. A producer can be: • Internal: originates data within the company • External: data is produced outside of the company • Intermediary: receives data from elsewhere and enters it into a database or application A person can be both a source and a producer.	Sources of data used by an organization include customers, policy holders, third-party vendor of address data, a country's postal agency. Almost anyone within an organization has the potential of being a data producer. Some have specific responsibilities related to data (e.g., data entry clerk, data steward). Others produce data in the course of daily responsibilities (e.g., purchasing agent, customer service rep, receptionist, office manager, agent, stockholder, nurse, physician, faculty member, dispatcher).
POSMAD Phase: Store and Share	
Technology is the focus of store and share; those who develop and support technology such as: • Hardware, software, networks, etc. that store and share the data. Affects data by determining how it will be available to users – security, synchronization, etc. • The code and queries used for accessing data and maintaining the required data sets to conform to regulations. • Those who ensure the information is held electronically and made available for use through some type of distribution method. Reminder: Technology can be low tech such as hardcopy forms and applications in a filing cabinet with distribution methods such as mail.	High tech: DBA, developers, IT support, operations, other technical support. Low tech: Print specialist, administrative assistant, mailroom clerk.

(Continued)

Table 4.2.8 POSMAD Phases with Related Job Roles and Titles *(Continued)*

General Role Information	Sample Titles *
POSMAD Phase: Maintain	
Those who update, change, manipulate, transform, standardize, validate, verify, enhance, or augment data. Those who cleanse, scrub, transform, de-duplicate, link, match, merge, or consolidate records.	The same people who produce data often maintain the data also. See titles under Obtain.
POSMAD Phase: Apply	
Those who use the information to accomplish their goals, as part of job responsibilities, or in performing a process. E.g., those who complete transactions, write reports, make management decisions from information in those reports. Those who depend on data to run their automated processes. General terms: knowledge workers, information customers, information consumers, users. Multiple Roles: Users can both obtain and maintain the data. • Buyer procures supplies and materials for the company and creates a vendor master record (role: internal data producer). • Buyer uses that master record to create a purchase order (role: knowledge worker – using the master information to purchase a product – and data producer – creating the purchase order). Quality Gap: Those who obtain data can be different from those who use it and may not be aware of the users' requirements, which often results in data quality problems.	Customer service rep, agent, policy holder, business analyst, data analyst, manager, supervisor, project manager, executive, data scientist, report developer. They can be internal to the company (employees) or external (contractors, consultants, other business partners).
POSMAD Phase: Dispose	
Those who delete or archive data or information. The archiving, storing, and later retrieval of the information can impact the quality of the data.	Any role that obtains, maintains, or uses data may have permission to delete it. Specialized roles related to archiving include records manager, archivist, change management specialist, DBA, third-party off-site records storage vendor, cloud-based archiving vendor.

* Typical titles used in organizations though some are not recognized as roles that impact data quality.

transactions, create reports, make decisions from reports, or use the output of automated processes. If the business impact assessment includes cost, then roles in any of the POSMAD phases can be included since there is a cost to all activities in the six phases.

3. Understand interactions between the relevant people and organizations and the other key components of data, processes, and technology.

An interaction matrix is one way to show how the various roles impact each of the data subject areas or fields. See *Table 4.2.9* in the *Sample Output and Templates* section for an example of a role-to-data interaction matrix. Use your best judgment as to the level of detail for both the people/organization axis and the data axis.

4. Analyze, synthesize, recommend, document, and act on what you learned about the people and organizations.

See the section *Analyze, Synthesize, Recommend, Document, and Act on Results* in *Chapter 6: Other Techniques and Tools* for additional help. Document lessons learned, potential impact to data quality and to the business, potential root causes, and initial recommendations in your results tracking sheet. Is there additional action related to people and organizations that should be done at this time? For example, did you find people who you would like to consult with as part of the project? Seek approval from them and their managers to participate.

 Best Practice

Identify Allies and Advocates. While working on *Step 2*, keep your eyes open for those who are friendly towards the idea of data quality and care about the business needs and project objectives within scope. They may be suffering from data quality issues themselves and you may be able to help solve their problems. Recognize good allies and advocates who can provide information for the project and in some cases support the project through additional money and people.

Sample Output and Templates

POSMAD with Job Roles and Titles

Use *Table 4.2.8* as input to identifying those who impact the quality of the data throughout the information life cycle. Determine who should be involved in the project as a core or extended team member, who can provide input, and who should be informed about progress.

Role-to-Data Interaction Matrix

Table 4.2.9 is an example of how to show the interaction between roles and how those roles impact specific data. When analyzing, look at the rows across and the columns going down for similarities

Table 4.2.9 Interaction Matrix: Role-to-Data

Business Role	Contact Name	Site Name	Division	Department	Address	Phone	Title	Profile
Sales Rep	O M A	O M A	O M A	O M A	O M A	O M A	O M A	O M A
District Manager	O M A	O M A	O M A	O M A	O M A	A	O M A	O M A
Customer Service Rep	O M A	O M A	O M A	O M A	O M A	O M A	O M	
Order Coordinator	O M A	O M A	O M A	O M A	O M A	O M A		
Quote Coordinator	O M A	O M A	O M A	O M A	O M A	O M A	O M	
Collection Coordinator	A	A	A		A			
Business Center Mailroom		A	A		A			
Online Tech Support	O M A	O M A	O M A	O M A	O M A	O M A	O M A	O M A
Sales Finance		A	A		A	A		
Data Management Team	O M A	O M A	O M A	O M A	O M A	O M A	O M A	O M A

The role: O = obtains/creates the data, M = maintains/updates the data, A = applies/uses the data

and differences. For example, one project team knew that many departments could apply or use the data, but they thought that only one could create or update them. Through this exercise the team found that people in other departments actually had the ability to create and update data as well. They could immediately see the impact on data quality – there were no consistent standards for entering data across the departments. Initial recommendations included looking at the organization to determine if it was appropriate that create and update ability were distributed across departments or if these should be centralized in one place. At a minimum, all teams creating and updating data should receive the same training.

Step 2.6 Understand Relevant Information Life Cycle

Business Benefit and Context

In this activity, you will describe the information life cycle from planning or creation to disposal – or a relevant subset of POSMAD. The goal is to represent and summarize the life cycle by bringing together what you have learned about the data, processes, people/organizations, and technology from the other substeps in *Step 2*. Focus on the POSMAD phases that apply to your business issue – Plan, Obtain, Store and Share, Maintain, Apply, and Dispose. If you need background or a refresher, see the *Information Life Cycle* section in *Chapter 3: Key Concepts*.

The information life cycle can be used, at various levels of detail, in the following ways:

- As a high-level context diagram to reference in team meetings, guide work done throughout the project, and ensure the project team is clear at which points work is taking place.
- See how the data currently flows, the "as is" view. This is input to determine at which point(s) along the life cycle path to assess for quality in *Step 3*. It forms the basis of the data capture and

assessment plan – see section of the same name in *Chapter 6: Other Techniques and Tools*.
- After a data quality assessment has highlighted where along the life cycle problems are occurring, track back through the life cycle to help identify the location of root causes.
- Show gaps, duplicate work, unnecessary complexity, unexpected problem areas, and inefficiencies in the process itself that can adversely impact the quality of data and provide input to *Step 5 – Identify Root Causes*.
- These same gaps, complexity, and inefficiencies may also put the organization at risk from a business impact point of view. The life cycle can show where information is applied and used – a revenue point of view. All provide input to *Step 4 – Assess Business Impact*.
- Based on what is learned through the project, the "as is" view of the life cycle can be changed or improved to show the "to be" view which will produce quality data, prevent quality problems, and increase the value of the information. The "to be" view may form the foundation for process improvements implemented in *Step 7 – Prevent Future Data Errors*.

- Further identify and improve key control activities needed. This will show where simplification and standardization may be possible and where to minimize complexity and redundancy (therefore minimizing cost and risk) and maximize the use of the information (therefore maximizing value).
- Determine if the data, processes, people/organizations, and technology within scope have been appropriately accounted for.

Key Concept

Apply Phase = Value. An organization receives value from information only during the Apply phase of the POSMAD information life cycle – when information is retrieved and used. All the other phases are important and necessary to manage the data and information and make them available for use, but only activities in the Apply phase provide real value.

Approach

1. Determine the scope and level of detail for the information life cycle.

Ask, "At this point in our project, what do we need to know about the information life cycle in order to: Carry out the next project steps most effectively? Address the business needs? Achieve the project objectives?"

Determine the level of detail needed to understand the process and identify problem areas. Your life cycle may be a simple high-level flowchart showing only sufficient information to understand the overall life cycle. Or it might be very detailed in some phases to show every action and decision point. If you are unsure which level is appropriate, start out at a high level and add detail later as needed. As mentioned earlier, a best practice is to start *Step 2* by sketching out the high-level information life cycle within scope of the project. This provides boundaries and guidance for your work. Even if detailed artifacts are already available which illustrate some aspects of the information life cycle, it is helpful to put them into context of a high-level life cycle.

Remember that every datastore, every dataset, every data field has its own life cycle. They intersect, interact, and impact each other. You can go high-level in one area and more detailed in another aspect of the life cycle. See *Figure 4.2.9* below for an example of a high-level information life cycle within a data lake, along with more details in the *Sample Output and Templates* section.

2. Gather/modify existing information life cycles or create a new information life cycle.

Make use of existing documentation as input to the information life cycle. Learn to recognize an information life cycle in whatever documentation you have (architecture, context diagram, data flow diagram), whether it is labeled an information life cycle or not. You may be able to use as is or modify to fit the needs of the project.

Determine the approach for illustrating and documenting the life cycle. Various methods for depicting the life cycle have been used successfully. See *Information Life Cycle Approaches* in *Chapter 6: Other Techniques and Tools* for details, templates, and examples. The approach used will be influenced by the level of detail and the scope of the life cycle.

Information life cycles can be created using tools such as Visio or PowerPoint or other diagramming tools. A life cycle can also be

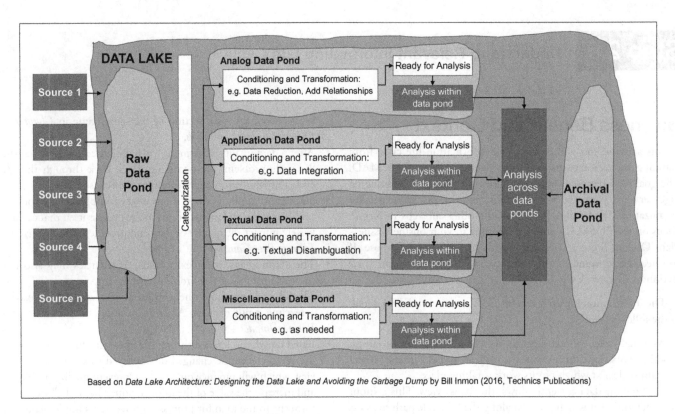

Based on *Data Lake Architecture: Designing the Data Lake and Avoiding the Garbage Dump* by Bill Inmon (2016, Technics Publications)

Figure 4.2.9 Example information life cycle within a data lake.

created in a low-tech manner. I like to use a white board, post-it notes, and markers. Decide first on the approach to be used (swim lane, SIPOC, table, etc.). Write the life cycle steps on large sticky notes. Move them around until you are satisfied with the sequence. Add different color notes to indicate decision points or relevant details learned while completing the substeps for data, processes, people/organizations, and technology. Use the markers to draw flows and dependencies between the steps. It is easy to erase and redraw lines and move the post-it notes around as the discussion evolves. Take a picture of your work to document later in your chosen tool. As you document or visualize the life cycle your understanding of it will deepen. This technique can also be replicated using functionality available in teleconferencing tools for teams not physically located in the same place.

Uncovering an existing complex life cycle can be automated using tools with functionality often called lineage. Whether automated or manual, you must still deeply understand the life cycle.

Expect to update the information life cycle as more is learned from the other substeps. To see the evolution of one organization's information life cycle, look at the *Ten Steps in Action callout box* in the *Sample Output and Templates* at the end of this step.

3. Analyze, synthesize, recommend, document, and act on what you learned about the information life cycle.

See the section *Analyze, Synthesize, Recommend, Document, and Act on Results* in *Chapter 6: Other Techniques and Tools* for additional help. Use the bullet points in the *Business Benefit and Context* section earlier to broaden your thinking during analysis.

Note hand-offs between operations. These are areas where there is potential for error, thus affecting the quality of the data. For example, the life cycle may show that more than one team is maintaining the same data. This is important to know so the business can determine if this is still the best organizational model. If so, the business will want to ensure that both groups receive the same training in data entry, updating, and the like. If the organizational model, roles, or responsibilities should be changed, the life cycle can help the business understand possible alternatives and serve as a high-level checklist to make sure various processes are being covered in the reorganization or realignment of duties.

If reviewed on a periodic basis, the information life cycle will provide a systematic way to detect change. The life cycle can be used to answer the following questions:

- Has the process changed?
- Did any of the tasks change?
- Did the timing change?
- Did the roles change?
- Did any of the people filling the roles change?
- Did the technology change?
- Did the data requirements change?
- What impact do the changes have on the quality of information?

Document lessons learned, potential impact to data quality and to the business, potential root causes, and initial recommendations

in your results tracking sheet. Is there additional action related to the information life cycle that should be done at this time? After the quality and/or value assessments have been completed, one of the recommendations may be to return to this step to create and implement a more effective life cycle.

4. Continue to use what has been learned about the information life cycle and other elements of the information environment throughout the project.

What you have learned about all the elements in the information environment provide input to:

Step 1 – Determine Business Needs and Approach. Even though this step has been completed, there may be additional information about the information environment that comes to light in other steps which would prompt you to review and adjust the business needs and data quality issues within scope; project focus, approach, plan, and objectives.

Step 2 – Analyze Information Environment. This step has been completed, but once again, there may be additional information from other steps that may prompt you to review and adjust any of the elements of the information environment.

Step 3 – Assess Data Quality. To determine where data should be captured and assessed for quality.

Step 4 – Assess Business Impact. To understand where in the information life cycle work is happening that affects costs and revenue as input to a business impact assessment.

Step 5 – Identify Root Causes. Use the information life cycle as needed to track and trace the location of root causes.

Step 6 – Develop Improvement Plans, Step 7 – Prevent Future Data Errors, and *Step 8 – Correct Current Data Errors.* As input to where along the life cycle preventive measures and controls should be put into place and where data corrections should be made.

Step 9 – Monitor Controls. To determine where in the information life cycle controls should be monitored. Develop the information life cycle for the on-going monitoring itself.

Step 10 – Communicate, Manage, and Engage People Throughout. To understand where people are involved along the information life cycle and the work they do, as input to how to best communicate and engage with them.

Sample Output and Templates

See *Information Life Cycle Approaches* in *Chapter 6: Other Techniques and Tools* for other examples and additional information.

Example – Information Life Cycle in a Data Lake

Figure 4.2.9 shows a high-level information life cycle within a data lake. The graphic is based on what Bill Inmon describes as a well-managed data lake in his book, *Data Lake Architecture* (2016). Some could say this visualizes the data architecture – and that is true. Using our life cycle thinking we can look at any data architecture and recognize elements of a high-level information life cycle.

Step 2 might have started with an existing, well-documented architecture that you used as you finalized the boundaries of your project which included the data lake. On the other hand, it is possible you had to research and document the information life cycle even to understand it at a high level, and Figure 4.2.9 might be the end result of your work in *Step 2*, not the beginning. Whatever your starting or ending points, a high-level visual such as this illustrates where the data is sourced and how it proceeds through various stages before it is ready to be used, in this case for analysis.

This visual can be used to discuss where it makes sense for data quality assessment to take place – where along the information life cycles are concerns being raised? Do you want to assess the quality first at each of the sources? If so, go into more detail for each source to be assessed. These are important decisions that affect what you need to know about the data and data specifications, the processes, the technology, and the people/organizations within scope. Answers also affect the amount of time and resources needed for your data quality assessment in *Step 3*. Having a visual helps to direct the discussions.

Ten Steps in Action

Evolution of an Information Life Cycle

Organization Overview—Central banks or reserve banks perform functions not normally carried out by commercial banks. Their responsibilities vary depending on the country, but often include encouraging economic growth by formulating and implementing monetary policy, protecting the value of the country's currency, managing interest rates, and maintaining price stability. There are hundreds of central banks around the world – this case is from one of them.

Business Need—A key asset of central banks is the information at their disposal. An earlier assessment highlighted where business issues could be resolved through data management and also triggered a wide-ranging data quality (DQ) assessment. This DQ assessment provided recommendations to address the data quality issues found.

Statistics (STS) was one of the departments included in the overall DQ assessment. STS provides input to bank decisions. For example, they collect data from within the bank and externally from various industry sources, such as automotive, insurance, pension funds, etc. STS analyzes the economy and provides input to the committee which sets monetary policy. This committee ultimately decides what should happen to the interest rate. Better quality data from any research and statistics contributes toward better monetary policy decisions.

Project Background—A data quality specialist was hired into the information management (IM) team to address the recommendations from the DQ assessment. While the DQ assessment had been done throughout the bank, IM was a small team so they had to prioritize which departments would have the most success and start there. The DQ specialist was assigned to work with STS and did so through the business data steward who was the touchpoint into that department.

Use of the Ten Steps and Data Lineage—Several of the Ten Steps were used by the DQ specialist to address the data quality issues. Much work was done in *Step 2 – Analyze Information Environment*.

This example focuses on the information life cycle, referred to in their organization as the data life cycle or lineage.

In the words of the DQ specialist: "Visualizing data lineage to see the flow of information, sources, and a view of the landscape was particularly important. The information life cycle often started as a drawing on a piece of paper when speaking with a business data steward. This was then transferred to Microsoft PowerPoint so it could be shared with others. It was a good start, but not sustainable, so we moved to a tool that allows a person to visualize business processes, use cases, data flows, data models, etc. In addition, terms can be defined, and the tool automatically links the definition to wherever a term is used."

See *Figure 4.2.10* to see three versions of the information life cycle. It is not meant to be read in detail but to illustrate the evolution of the information life cycle from paper to Excel to Visual Paradigm. It was found Excel did not work well for this purpose, so PowerPoint was used before finding a better tool.

Business Benefit—By understanding the information environment, particularly the data lineage, STS can now:

- See what data and components of the data go into final reports. It was discovered that some data was not being used so they could stop collecting it, which saves time for both the data provider and STS. It also identified potential duplicate data being collected.
- Tie in data that STS needs to data that is being collected elsewhere in the bank because of legal mandates.
- Consider purchasing data and investigate if that is a more cost-effective option.

Note from Danette: Expect your information life cycle to develop and change before settling on the expression of the life cycle(s) at the level(s) of detail most helpful to your project. Once you learn where to get input for the life cycle and which tools and approach work for one project, developing the information life cycle will go faster for subsequent projects.

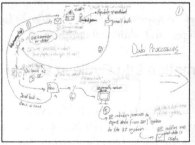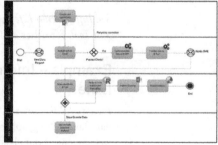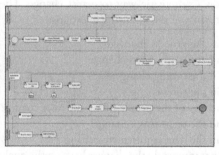

Figure 4.2.10 Evolution of an information life cycle.

Ten Steps in Action

What we learned from Step 2 – Analyze the Information Environment

The team from one data quality improvement project summarized what they learned in *Step 2* and how they used it:

We researched, learned about, and documented:

- The information life cycle within scope of the project
- Descriptions of each environment where the data landed throughout its life cycle
- Technology involved, including various third-party vendor tools, and where transformations were being made to the data as it moved through the life cycle
- Timing of when data was received, processed, and available for use
- How the data was actually being used and planned future use

This knowledge was used to determine:

- The final scope of the project
- Which data within which environments would be assessed for quality in *Step 3* (our final selection criteria)
- Input to the data quality assessment plan, with division of work and who would:
  o Capture the data
  o Profile and analyze the data and which tools would be used
  o Determine next steps such as root cause, prevention, and correction
- We created visuals that were referenced throughout the project for:
  o Management, to explain and sustain support for scope and deliverables
  o Project team, to keep track of where the various project activities were taking place

Step 2 Summary

From *Step 1* you learned, at a high-level, something about your data and data specifications, something about your processes, something about your technology, something about your people and organizations, and possibly something about the information life cycle. Here in *Step 2*, you delved into more detail as necessary, in whatever order made sense, and uncovered gaps where additional information needed to be gathered. This step gave you the opportunity to see all this knowledge in new and interrelated ways. You have made, and will continue to make, better decisions about information quality because of it.

You were given guidelines to determine what was relevant and the right level of detail and were encouraged to follow the Just Enough Principle. If followed, these helped you avoid feeling overwhelmed and kept the project focused and moving in the right direction.

At the end of every substep you were given the opportunity to synthesize results from other steps and make preliminary recommendations based on what you knew at each point. You looked at the recommendations and determined if anything could be done about them now, or they were saved for action at a later time. You were encouraged to document findings as discovered so important learnings would be available as input for other steps and rework to re-discover could be avoided. You may have created visuals of your information life cycle that will be used to keep the project team oriented as to where work is taking place.

If you have not yet done so, take the time now to organize your thoughts, your files, and document your results. (If I mention it enough times you might actually do it!) You will be glad you did. You are now ready to assess data quality in *Step 3* and/or assess business impact in *Step 4*.

Communicate, Manage, and Engage

Suggestions for working effectively with people and managing the project in this step:

- Refine the stakeholder list based on what was learned in *Step 2.5 – Understand Relevant People and Organizations* and update communication plan accordingly
- Engage with stakeholders and team members:
  o Provide periodic status reports
  o Listen to and address suggestions and concerns
  o Provide updates regarding what was learned in this step, such as potential issues that could impact scope, schedule, or resources
  o Based on what was learned in this step, set expectations for potential impacts or changes to upcoming project work, team participation, or individual personal involvement
- Track issues and action items; ensure deliverables are completed in a timely manner
- Ensure resources and support for upcoming steps in the project

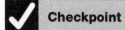

Checkpoint

Checkpoint Step 2 – Analyze Information Environment

How can I tell if I am ready to move to the next step? Use the following guidelines to help determine completeness of this step and readiness for the next step:

- Are the applicable elements of the information environment understood and documented, at the appropriate level of detail, to help perform the next project steps most effectively?
- If conducting a data quality assessment in *Step 3*:
  - o Has the data been understood sufficiently that there is confidence a data quality assessment will focus on the relevant data?
  - o For data to be assessed for quality, have requirements and constraints, detailed data grids and mappings, and data specifications been finalized?
  - o Have any problems with permissions and access to data been identified?
  - o Are tools available to conduct the assessment or must tools be purchased?
  - o Have training needs been identified?
- If conducting a business impact assessment in *Step 4*:
  - o Are the business needs and information environment understood and linked sufficiently that there is confidence a business impact assessment will focus in the right areas?
- Have resources for the upcoming assessments been identified and committed?
- Have results from this step been documented? I.e., lessons learned and observations, known/potential issues, known/probable business impact, potential root causes, initial recommendations for prevention and correction.
- Has the communication plan been updated and necessary communications for this step been completed?

Step 3   Assess Data Quality

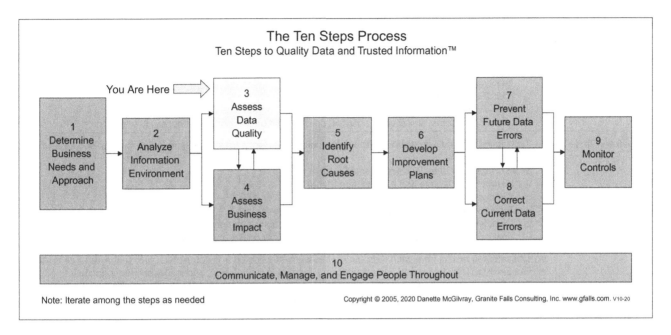

Figure 4.3.1 "You Are Here" Graphic for Step 3 – Assess Data Quality.

Introduction to Step 3

Assessing data quality is often the only thing people think about when tackling data quality issues. I hope you have seen that everything prior to this step is necessary to be able to do this step well. And everything that comes after assessing the quality (root causes, improvements through prevention and correction, sustaining data quality through monitoring controls) is the reason for doing this step. In other words, conducting a data quality assessment is not the end – it is a means to the end of having the right quality data to support business needs related to customers, products, services, strategies, goals, issues, and opportunities.

Orient yourself to this step by reading through *Table 4.3.1 – Step Summary Table.* You were introduced to the concept of data quality dimensions, the dimensions as used in the Ten Steps Process, and guidelines for selecting dimensions in *Chapter 3: Key Concepts.* The list of dimensions and their definitions are repeated in *Table 4.3.2* for your quick reference.

There is one substep for each dimension. The substeps are numbered for ease of reference, not because they must be done in that particular order. You will select and assess quality for those dimensions that will help address your business needs and data quality issues and may change from project to project. Each substep contains three main sections: Business Benefit and Context, Approach, and Sample Output and Templates, which provide just enough detail to assess the quality of the particular dimension.

With few exceptions, data quality should not be viewed in terms of obtaining a state of "zero defect" or perfect data. This very high level of quality entails cost and can take considerable time. More

cost efficient is a balanced, risk-based approach that defines data quality needs and investments in improvements based on business impacts and risks. Whenever needed, use business impact techniques from *Step 4* to help make those decisions.

Definition

A **Data Quality Dimension** is a characteristic, aspect, or feature of data. It provides a way to classify needs related to information and data quality. Dimensions are used to define, measure, improve, monitor, and manage the quality of data and information.

The benefit of data quality assessment(s) will be concrete evidence of the problems that underlie the business needs and data quality issues that were identified in *Step 1.* As input to this step, make use of what was learned in *Step 2 – Analyze Information Environment.*

Results from your data quality assessment provide a picture of the nature of the data quality problems, their magnitude, and location. This knowledge helps focus your efforts during subsequent steps as you investigate root causes (*Step 5*), develop improvement plans (*Step 6*), correct data errors (*Step 7*), and prevent future data errors (*Step 8*). If assessing data quality for the first time, a data quality assessment sets a baseline against which to compare future progress. What is learned here can also be used when detecting data quality issues through monitoring controls (*Step 9*).

If you skipped *Step 2,* please reconsider! Feedback from project teams always confirm that spending just enough time analyzing the information environment is essential before jumping into data

Table 4.3.1 Step Summary Table for Step 3 – Assess Data Quality

Objective	• Assess and evaluate data quality for the dimensions applicable to the business needs, data quality issues, and project objectives
Purpose	• Identify the type and extent of data quality errors • Confirm or refute opinions of data quality

Inputs	• Output, learnings, and artifacts from:
	  o *Step 1* – updated, as needed, based on what has been learned so far in the project: business needs, data quality issues, project scope, plan, or objectives
	  o *Step 2* – the information environment analysis
	  o *Step 4* – if business impact was needed before starting the data quality assessments
	• Current project status, stakeholder analysis, communication and engagement plans

Techniques and Tools	• Techniques and tools applicable to the data quality dimensions to be assessed (see substeps, one for each data quality dimension)
	• From *Chapter 6: Other Techniques and Tools:*
	  o Design Data Capture and Assessment Plans
	  o Conduct a Survey
	  o Tools for Managing Data Quality
	  o Track Issues and Action Items (use and update throughout the project)
	  o Analyze, Synthesize, Recommend, Document, and Act on Results (use and update throughout the project)

Outputs	• Documented results from each data quality assessment selected and completed, with synthesis of all results • Documented lessons learned, issues uncovered, possible root causes, and initial recommendations • Artifacts from *Steps 1 and 2,* updated as needed based on data quality assessment results • Documented data capture and assessment plans, for future reference and use • Actions taken, based on what was learned about data quality, that could be completed during this step • Completed communication and engagement activities needed at this point in the project • Updated status, stakeholder analysis, communication and engagement plans based on feedback and data quality results • Agreement on next step in the project – can the team go directly to *Step 5 – Identify Root Causes* or will business impact of specific data quality issues found need to be completed first?

Communicate, Manage, and Engage	• Ensure deliverables are completed in a timely manner; track issues and action items
	• Engage with project sponsors, stakeholders, management, and team members to:
	  o Work cooperatively as data quality assessments are conducted
	  o Remove roadblocks, resolve issues, and manage change
	  o Stay appropriately involved (accountable, responsible, provide input, informed only)
	• Communicate status, assessment results, likely impacts, and initial recommendations; get feedback and complete needed follow-up
	• Based on learnings from data quality assessments:
	  o Adjust project scope, objectives, resources, or timeline
	  o Manage expectations of all involved
	  o Anticipate change management needed for likely improvements to be implemented and accepted
	• Ensure resources and support for upcoming steps in the project

Checkpoint	• For each selected data quality dimension, has the assessment been completed and results analyzed?
	• If conducting multiple assessments, have results from all been synthesized?
	• Have the following been discussed and documented?
	  o Lessons learned and observations
	  o Known/potential issues
	  o Known/probable business impact
	  o Possible root causes
	  o Initial recommendations for prevention, correction, and monitoring
	• If there are changes to the project, have they been finalized and agreed-upon by sponsors, stakeholders and team members? E.g., If additional people are needed for the next steps, have they been identified and committed? Is funding continuing?
	• Have activities to communicate, manage, and engage people during this step been completed and are plans updated?
	• Have action items not completed during this step been logged with assigned owners and due dates?

Table 4.3.2 Data Quality Dimensions in the Ten Steps Process

Data Quality Dimension. A data quality dimension is a characteristic, aspect, or feature of data. Data quality dimensions provide a way to classify information and data quality needs. Dimensions are used to define, measure, improve, and manage the quality of data and information. Instructions for assessing data quality using the following dimensions are included in the Ten Steps Process in *Step 3 – Assess Data Quality*.

Substep	Data Quality Dimension Name and Definition
3.1	**Perception of Relevance and Trust.** The subjective opinion of those who use information and/or those who create, maintain, and dispose of data regarding: 1) Relevance – which data is of most value and importance to them, and 2) Trust – their confidence in the quality of the data to meet their needs.
3.2	**Data Specifications.** Data Specifications include any information and documentation that provide context, structure, and meaning to data. Specifications provide information needed to make, build, produce, assess, use, and manage data and information. Examples include metadata, data standards, reference data, data models, and business rules. Without the existence, completeness, and quality of data specifications it is difficult to produce high-quality data and harder to measure, understand, and manage the quality of data content.
3.3	**Data Integrity Fundamentals.** The existence (completeness/fill rate), validity, structure, content, and other basic characteristics of data.
3.4	**Accuracy.** The correctness of the content of the data as compared to an agreed-upon and accessible authoritative source of reference.
3.5	**Uniqueness and Deduplication.** The uniqueness (positive) or unwanted duplication (negative) of data (fields, records, or datasets) existing within or across systems or datastores.
3.6	**Consistency and Synchronization.** Equivalence of data stored or used in various datastores, applications, and systems.
3.7	**Timeliness.** Data and information are current and ready for use as specified and in the time frame in which they are expected.
3.8	**Access.** The ability to control how authorized users can view, modify, use, or otherwise process data and information.
3.9	**Security and Privacy. Security** is the ability to protect data and information assets from unauthorized access, use, disclosure, disruption, modification, or destruction. **Privacy** for an individual is the ability to have some control over how data about them as a person is collected and used. For an organization, it is the ability to comply with how people want their data to be collected, shared, and used.
3.10	**Presentation Quality.** The format, appearance, and display of data and information support their collection and uses.
3.11	**Data Coverage.** The comprehensiveness of data available compared to the total data universe or population of interest.
3.12	**Data Decay.** Rate of negative change to the data.
3.13	**Usability and Transactability.** Data produces the desired business transaction, outcome, or use for which it was intended.
3.14	**Other Relevant Data Quality Dimensions.** Other characteristics, aspects, or features of data and information that are deemed to be important for your organization to define, measure, improve, monitor, and manage.

quality assessments. Start at a high level and work down to more detail only if needed. It is more efficient to get some background prior to the assessment. If you decide to move in *Step 3* without any work in *Step 2*, the exact data to be assessed still has to be identified. You still need just enough background to help you interpret and analyze results of the data quality assessment(s). This can be done while here in *Step 3*, usually less efficiently.

 Quote to Remember

"One accurate measurement is worth a thousand expert opinions."
– *Grace Hopper (1906-1992), Admiral, United States Navy*

How Data Quality Dimensions are Categorized

The data quality dimensions used in The Ten Steps methodology are categorized roughly by the techniques or approach used to assess each dimension. This helps to better scope and plan a project by providing input when estimating the time, money, tools, and human resources needed to do the data quality work. Differentiating the data quality dimensions in this way helps to: 1) match dimensions against a business need and prioritize which dimensions to

assess and in which order, 2) understand what you will (and will not) learn from assessing each data quality dimension, and 3) better define and manage the sequence of activities in your project plan within time and resource constraints.

Note: There are other ways to categorize data quality dimensions. For more information, see Dan Myers's compilation of research on the dimensions of data quality (Myers, n.d.). Dan has also developed his own list called the Conformed Dimensions of Data Quality. I have learned from all of them. Since this book is about putting the ideas of dimensions into action, I categorize the dimensions in the Ten Steps methodology for the reasons explained above.

Step 3 Process Flow

The overall approach to Step 3 is straightforward. See the process flow for *Step 3* in *Figure 4.3.2*. First select the dimensions that will be most helpful to assess for any particular situation; second, design data capture and assessment plans; third, assess data quality for the chosen dimensions; fourth, synthesize results if more than one assessment has been done, make recommendations, and take action! This high-level process flow applies to all data quality dimensions and is explained here to avoid repeating within each substep.

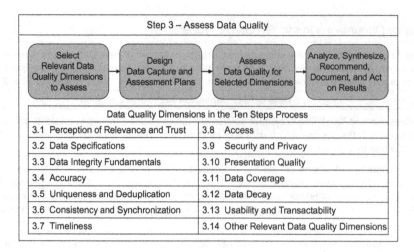

Step 3 – Assess Data Quality			
Select Relevant Data Quality Dimensions to Assess	Design Data Capture and Assessment Plans	Assess Data Quality for Selected Dimensions	Analyze, Synthesize, Recommend, Document, and Act on Results

Data Quality Dimensions in the Ten Steps Process	
3.1 Perception of Relevance and Trust	3.8 Access
3.2 Data Specifications	3.9 Security and Privacy
3.3 Data Integrity Fundamentals	3.10 Presentation Quality
3.4 Accuracy	3.11 Data Coverage
3.5 Uniqueness and Deduplication	3.12 Data Decay
3.6 Consistency and Synchronization	3.13 Usability and Transactability
3.7 Timeliness	3.14 Other Relevant Data Quality Dimensions

Figure 4.3.2 Process flow for Step 3 – Assess Data Quality.

Select Relevant Data Quality Dimensions to Assess—Familiarize yourself with the various data quality dimensions and what is required to complete an assessment for each one. It is important to select the dimensions most meaningful for each project, but it may be hard to know where to begin. See the section on *Data Quality Dimensions* in *Chapter 3: Key Concepts* for suggestions when choosing which dimensions to assess. Quickly revisit your business needs and project objectives from *Step 1 – Determine Business Needs and Approach*. Ensure the business needs, available resources, etc. have not changed. If they have, modify your project focus, scope, and objectives as needed and select the data quality dimensions to meet the updated situation. Ensure everyone involved is informed and supportive of modifications.

Design Data Capture and Assessment Plans—Data capture is how the data to be assessed will be accessed (e.g., extracting data to a flat file and load to a secure database for testing or connecting directly to a reporting database). An assessment plan is how you propose to evaluate the quality of the data. Design the data capture and assessment plans for each of the dimensions chosen. See details for designing your data capture and assessment plans in *Chapter 6: Other Techniques and Tools* in section of the same name.

Account for the tools and technology to be used when capturing and assessing the data and reporting results. See *Tools for Managing Data Quality* in *Chapter 6*. Make use of what you learned in *Step 2.2 – Understand Relevant Data and Data Specifications* and *Step 2.3 – Understand Relevant Technology*.

Develop and document the sequence of tasks to capture and assess. Ensure those involved are aware of and agree to their responsibilities. Remember to include the managers of those who will be doing the work. The simplicity or complexity of data capture and assessment plans will vary from project to project. Make good use of resources by spending "just enough" time to ensure the relevant data is captured and assessed at the right time, from the right datastores, by the right people.

Assess Data Quality for Selected Dimensions—Each of the dimensions has a separate substep within this chapter with details specific to assessing that dimension. Implement your data capture and assessment plans, and complete the assessment using the specific instructions and examples for each data quality dimension within scope.

Analyze, Synthesize, Recommend, Document, and Act on Results—Analyze results of each data quality assessment and synthesize by bringing all assessment results together. Use what you learned in *Step 2 – Analyze Information Environment* to help interpret results and understand what could have caused problems found. Make initial recommendations based on what was learned. Recommendations can be for which data should be corrected, various controls for preventing data quality errors from reoccurring, specific business rules or data quality rules or general controls that should be monitored. Document it all to ensure knowledge and insight from each step are retained and used in the next step. Take action when the time is right. See the section *Analyze, Synthesize, Recommend, Document, and Act on Results* for general instructions and a template that apply to all the dimensions in *Chapter 6: Other Techniques and Tools*.

 Best Practice

Final Criteria for Selecting Data Quality Dimensions. To finalize which data quality dimensions to assess, ask yourself these two questions:

- *Should I assess the data?* Only spend time testing when you expect the results to give actionable information related to the business needs, data quality issues, and project objectives.
- *Can I assess the data?* Is it possible or practical to look at this quality dimension? Sometimes you cannot assess the quality of the data, or the cost to do so is prohibitive.

Only assess those dimensions when you can answer yes to both questions! If the answer to either question is "No," then do NOT assess that dimension – it will be a waste of time and money.

Step 3.1   Perception of Relevance and Trust

Business Benefit and Context

It is often said that perception is reality. If users believe data quality is poor, it is less likely they will use the organization's data sources or they will create their own spreadsheets or databases to manage their data. This leads to the proliferation of "spreadmarts" with duplicate and inconsistent data, often without adequate access and security controls in place.

This dimension gathers the opinions of those who use and/or manage the data and information through a formalized survey (individual interviews, group workshops, online surveys, etc.). While in contact with users, it makes sense to ask questions about both the value/relevance/business impact of information and the trust/confidence in the quality of the data.

Because the reason for surveying the users could be prompted from either the data quality or business impact viewpoint, it is included here in *Step 3.1* as a Data Quality Dimension and also in *Step 4.7* as a Business Impact Technique.

I want this dimension/technique to be clearly visible in both the data quality and business impact lists as options for assessment. The definition, whether as a data quality dimension or business impact technique, is the same.

 Definition

Perception of Relevance and Trust (Data Quality Dimension). The subjective opinion of those who use information and/or those who create, maintain, and dispose of data regarding: 1) Relevance – which data is of most value and importance to them, and 2) Trust – their confidence in the quality of the data to meet their needs.

Approach

The *Approach* section, with instructions that apply to perception of relevance and trust as both a data quality dimension and business impact technique, can be found in *Step 4.7* (under *Step 4 – Assess Business Impact*).

Sample Output and Templates

The *Sample Output and Templates* section, with examples that apply to perception of relevance and trust as both a data quality dimension and business impact technique, can be found in *Step 4.7* (under *Step 4 – Assess Business Impact*).

Step 3.2   Data Specifications

Business Benefit and Context

You cannot ensure the quality of data unless you also manage the data specifications which provide the information needed to make, build, produce, assess, or use the data and information. Data Specifications include any information and documentation that provide context, structure, and meaning to data. The data specifications focused on in this book are metadata, data standards, reference data, data models, and business rules. (Note: There are others that can also impact the quality of your data, e.g., taxonomies, ontologies, and hierarchies, which are outside the scope of what could be covered in this book. Please use other resources if they apply to the data within scope of your project.)

Without the existence, completeness, and quality of data specifications it is harder to measure and understand the quality of data content. Problems with data specifications are often causes of poor-quality data. See the *Data Specifications* section in *Chapter 3: Key Concepts* for more on this topic.

 Definition

Data Specifications (Data Quality Dimension). Data Specifications include any information and documentation that provide context, structure, and meaning to data. They provide information needed to make, build, produce, assess, use, and manage data and information. Examples include metadata, data standards, reference data, data models, and business rules. Without the existence, completeness, and quality of data specifications it is difficult to produce high-quality data and harder to measure, understand, and manage the quality of data content.

Data specifications provide:

- Context for analyzing data quality
- Standards against which to compare data quality assessment results
- Instructions for manually entering data, updating data, designing data load programs, developing applications, etc.

At a minimum, if you did not collect data specifications applicable to the CDEs in *Step 2.2 – Understand Relevant Data and Specifications*, this step gives you another chance to do so. These will be used as you conduct assessments for other data quality dimensions.

In addition, you may need to assess the quality of the specification content and/or the documentation of those specifications. This step may be as simple as ensuring that the associated reference data is identified and will be extracted as part of your data integrity fundamentals assessment. Or it may be an in-depth articulation of business rules with which to test data being migrated as part of an ERP implementation.

Note: The same techniques and processes for assessing other data content, such as in master and transactional data, can also be applied to many of the data specifications. For example, a metadata repository is just another data store which can be assessed for quality. Metadata has its own information life cycle which needs to be managed to ensure quality. Metadata can be profiled using *Step 3.3 – Data Integrity Fundamentals* and checked for duplication using *Step 3.5*.

Approach

1. Collect the specifications needed.

This step goes hand-in-hand with *Step 2.2 – Understand Relevant Data and Data Specifications*. Use the instructions there and output from that step as a starting point. If you did not collect existing data specifications earlier, now is the time.

If the specifications exist as hardcopy, which ones will be collected? Who will collect them and by when? Where will copies of those specifications be stored so they will be available for the project team?

If the specifications are held electronically, do you need a login for access? Who provides permission for access? Will you access them yourself or do you need to have someone else access the specifications? Do they exist in files that can be copied to a project share drive?

Make a list of the specifications and note which specifications are needed but missing or not documented.

2. Complete a data quality quick evaluation to determine if an in-depth assessment is needed.

Use *Template 4.3.1 – Data Specification Quality – Quick Evaluation* and instructions in the *Sample Output and Templates* section. It provides a way to quickly ascertain the quality of the data specifications and determine if a more in-depth data quality assessment is needed for them or not.

The results from the quick evaluation are qualitative, such as an opinion of the quality (or lack thereof) of the specification and how that impacts the quality of the data. For example, a metadata repository may be available, but you already know most of the definition fields are blank or specifications are documented in a hardcopy binder on someone's shelf and have not been updated for ten years. For both we can assume that:

- The specification content is out-of-date or non-existent and they will need to be created/updated which will add time to the project and should be reflected in the project plan.

- The data content (not the specifications) will be inconsistent when checked for quality and will reflect the low quality of the specifications.
- For the specifications to be used, they need to be made easily available, in a way other than hardcopy. If this is the case, an initial recommendation can be added to your results document to resolve at a later time.

3. Conduct an in-depth data quality assessment of the specifications, if needed.

Apply the other data quality dimensions—Remember, a data store holding specifications (such as a metadata repository or business glossary) is just another data store. The same techniques and processes for assessing master and transactional data can also be applied to many of the data specifications. You can use the technique of data profiling against a metadata repository to learn about Data Integrity Fundamentals such as completeness, fill rate, and validity. Use *Table 4.3.3* as input to your assessment.

Determine your source of reference for comparison—This applies the ideas from the Accuracy data quality dimension. Will you be comparing your data specifications within the database itself, to organizational-unit or enterprise-wide specifications, or to external sources of reference? For example, you may use ISO (International Organization for Standardization) codes as the source of reference for some of your domain values.

If a definitive enterprise-wide standard does not exist, look for common databases used in your particular part of the business. For example, is there a regional or worldwide data store that is used by several business groups that could be considered a source of reference for naming standards or valid code lists?

Determine who will do the evaluation—Appropriate reviewers are internal auditors, data management, or data quality professionals from within the business unit whose data are being assessed. Reviewers could also come from outside the business unit. A reviewer must not have a vested interest in the specifications being reviewed – for example, the reviewer should not be the creator of the data definition.

You can expect the data to be entered inconsistently if data entry standards have not been updated in five years, if the documentation is not easily available to those doing the data entry, or if you find conflicts in data entry standards from team to team. These predictions of possible inconsistencies should be looked for when assessing the quality of the data itself. Quantify results, if possible, such as by reporting percentage of specifications that conform to standards or percentage of existing versus expected specifications.

4. Create and/or update the specifications, as needed.

If the specifications do not exist, which ones specifically need to be written or created? Who will create and/or update them and by when? What is the method of documentation? Use *Table 4.3.3* again, this time as input to what should be included when creating or updating specifications. Ensure all who are creating the specifications are creating them consistently according to standard.

Quality-check the work to ensure the new or updated specifications meet expectations. This action item is not one to put on the action list to be done later, because the specifications provide the level of quality needed against which to compare results from other data quality assessments. Do this as quickly as possible, but ensure the specifications created/updated are of high quality themselves.

5. Track progress.

Track the progress of assessing, creating, and updating data specifications. Ensure the work is going according to schedule. Keep this step tightly scoped for specifications related to the CDEs.

It is possible that you actually need an organization-wide effort to collect data specifications and ensure they are stored, managed, and made easily available. What you find in this step may underscore that need. List that as a recommendation coming out of this step. But don't let the fact that you don't have an organization-wide metadata repository stop you from moving forward with your project. Collect/create/update those data specifications needed for your project and use them as a starting point when a separate metadata repository project is launched.

6. Analyze, synthesize, make recommendations, and document results.

See the section of the same name in *Chapter 6: Other Techniques and Tools* for more details. Highlight data specifications that you may want to test in other data quality dimensions to prove or disprove assumptions. Document key observations, lessons learned, issues uncovered, and positive discoveries, along with known or probable impact to the business or quality of the data. Capture potential root causes and preliminary recommendations.

Remember that results include the immediate next steps that must be taken to keep the project moving forward. Does what was learned in this step impact your project timeline, resources needed, or deliverables? If so, how? Has that been communicated? Decide when the time is right to act on results from this step or results from other steps.

Quote to Remember

"You cannot tell if something is wrong unless you can define what being right is."

– Jack E. Olson in Data Quality: The Accuracy Dimension (2003)

Sample Output and Templates

Data Specification Quality – Quick Evaluation

At a minimum, you will need applicable data specifications for the critical data elements (CDEs) within scope of the project. Whether you can use the specifications and their documentation as is, or if

they are suspect and must be addressed before proceeding to other data quality assessments, is up to you. Use *Template 4.3.1* to help with those decisions:

- Be clear on the data for which specifications are needed. This is the data within scope of your project, the most important data that supports the business needs, which could be the CDEs from *Step 2.2.*
- In the first column, list the data specifications needed for the data within scope. List the name of the document and/or where it is located in the rows. For example, name of a business glossary or metadata repository; a data catalog, data governance, or data modeling tool; a spreadsheet maintained by a data steward; title of a hardcopy manual at each customer service rep's desk; on-line help features in an application; or in the mind of a subject matter expert.
- For each document listed, collect basic information.
- For each document listed, look at the quick evaluation questions in the middle section of the table. Then answer the overall question in the middle column: "Based on the quick evaluation questions below, do you think the quality of the specification is good enough to use in other data quality assessments?" Make a conclusion of Good Enough, Unknown, or Unacceptable.
- Determine next steps based on the quick evaluation conclusions and actions in the last section of the table. For example, do you need to create the specifications by interviewing a SME – and where will that knowledge be documented, stored, and made accessible to others? This requires additional effort and should be accounted for in your project plan.
- Document results and assumptions made. Capture why an item was included or excluded if in-depth discussion took place before reaching agreement.

The quick evaluation is just that – quick. Don't labor over the answers. If the right people are in the discussion, the appropriate conclusion should be apparent. But if there are strong disagreements, then default to "Unknown" and investigate further.

Data Specification Quality – Input When Assessing, Creating, and Updating

Use *Table 4.3.3* when looking at data specification quality in more detail than the quick evaluation. The table does not include everything that should be considered, but provides a good starting point when:

- Assessing the quality of the specification, for what should be in place for a specification to be determined to be of high quality
- Creating or updating the specification, as part of instructions and training to help ensure the resulting specification is of high-quality

Template 4.3.1 Data Specification Quality – Quick Evaluation

Quick Evaluation Summary

Type of Data Specification	Conclusion – Good Enough, Unknown, Unacceptable Based on the quick evaluation questions below, do you think the quality of the specification is good enough to use in other data quality assessments?	Next Steps
Metadata		
Undocumented-ask Mary Jones		
Documentation 2		
Data Standards		
Documentation 1		
Documentation etc.		
Reference Data		
ISO country codes in Table XYZ		
Documentation etc.		
Data Models		
Documentation 1		
Documentation etc.		
Business Rules		
Documentation 1		
Documentation etc.		

Basic Information

For each type of specification and each type of documentation capture:

- Type of specification (metadata, data standards, reference data, data models, business rules)
- Name of documentation
- Brief description and purpose of the documentation
- Location of documentation (master and copies)
- Type of documentation (online help feature in the application, hardcopy manual at each desk, data modeling software, etc.)

Quick Evaluation Questions

Questions for quick evaluation:

- Who has ownership and responsibility for updating the documentation?
- Who *currently* uses the documentation and is it for the stated purpose or another purpose?
- Who *should* use the documentation and is it for the stated purpose or another purpose?
- Do those who need to reference the documentation know it is available?
- Is the documentation easily accessible?
- Is the documentation easy to understand?
- How is the documentation updated? E.g., file from external source sent monthly, direct connect to external source and updated real-time, business data steward
- Who decides when the specification should be updated? E.g., users notify data stewards, business data steward brings new codes to data governance council for final approval
- How often is the documentation supposed to be updated? When was it actually last updated?
- Is the version of the data specification documentation consistent with a supported application version? Is there a history of them being consistent?

Quick Evaluation Conclusions and Action

Based on the questions above, do you think the quality of the specification/documentation is good enough to use in other data quality assessments? Determine if the quality of the data specifications is:

- **Good Enough.** Good enough to use in the remainder of the project, therefore make sure they are available to the project team and move on to other data quality assessments
- **Unknown.** Not known or unclear and further assessment is needed before proceeding to other data quality assessments. Use *Table 4.3.3* to further assess the quality of the data specifications:
  - o For critical data elements (CDEs) only at this time
  - o Add to project recommendations – assess the quality of other specifications
- **Unacceptable.** Poor and not good enough to use as is, therefore the specifications need to be updated before proceeding with other assessments, e.g.,
  - o Update specifications for CDEs only at this time
  - o Add to project recommendations – update other specifications

Table 4.3.3 Data Specification Quality – Input When Assessing, Creating, and Updating

Type of Data Specification	Input when assessing quality of existing specifications or when creating or updating specifications
Metadata	For data definitions, ensure each *field* includes the following: • Title, label, or name and a description that is complete, accurate, understandable • Fields are identified as mandatory, optional, or conditional (with conditions documented) • Aliases or synonyms • Valid patterns or formats • Lists of valid values (see reference data and data standards) • An example of usage is helpful Ensure each *table* has a name and description. Definitions are not the only consideration for metadata, but they are the essential starting point. For more information on what to include in a data definition, see *Principles of Data Management: Facilitating Information Sharing*, Second Edition (2013) by Keith Gordon, Chapter 5.
Data Standards	For table and field names: • Compare actual physical structure names to naming conventions. Physical structure can mean tables, views, fields, etc. • Ensure any abbreviations used in names are accepted standard abbreviations. • If there are no stated naming conventions, look for any consistency within and across the names themselves. Data entry guidelines: • Rules to follow when entering the data, such as use of reference data, accepted abbreviations, casing (upper, lower, mixed), punctuation, etc. Lists of valid values: • As set by an authoritative internal or external source. These are also referred to as reference data.
Reference Data	• Review the set of valid values and the definitions for the values. • Check if values include a high-quality definition (see metadata). • Check if lists of values contain only valid values. • Determine if the list of values is complete (that is, includes all values needed). • Determine if the values are mutually exclusive (so there will be no confusion when selecting the value, and the meanings of the values do not overlap).
Data Models	• Look for names and definitions that are clear and understandable. • Review data models to ensure that entities and data relationships are consistent. • Identify how the data model is being communicated and used. • Ensure the naming structure within the data model (including casing and punctuation) is consistent with naming conventions. For an in-depth look at ensuring data model quality, see *Data Model Scorecard: Applying the Industry Standard on Data Model Quality* by Steven Hoberman (2015).
Business Rules	• Review business rules for accurate and complete definitions. • Look for policies that govern when instances/occurrences/records should be created, updated, or deleted. • Look for explicit or implicit statements about how and when a record or data field should be treated throughout the POSMAD information life cycle, such as where major state changes can occur and how the data should behave as a result. The corresponding data behavior can then be stated as requirements or a data quality rule. The data quality rule can be checked for compliance. • For example, the business rule is: "Prospects become customers when they purchase a product." The behavior by the online order rep is: "When a prospect becomes a customer, change the customer indicator flag to A (for active customer)." When testing the data for adherence to the rule, you may create a data quality rule: "Every record with a customer indicator flag of A must also have an associated order record." Or "Any record with an indicator flag of P (for prospective customer) must not have an associated order record." Look for opportunities to automate the change of the flag which will help enforce the business rules. If the process is already automated, test the rule anyway to ensure the programs are working correctly.

Step 3.3 | Data Integrity Fundamentals

Business Benefit and Context

Data Integrity Fundamentals focus on the existence, validity, structure, content, and other basic characteristics of data. The technique for assessing Data Integrity Fundamentals is called data profiling. I use Data Integrity Fundamentals as an umbrella term which includes essential characteristics such as completeness/fill rate, validity, lists of values and frequency distributions, patterns, ranges, maximum and minimum values, and referential integrity. If you don't know anything else about your data, you need to know what is learned from this data quality dimension. Most of the other dimensions build on what is learned from Data Integrity Fundamentals. I will spend more time on this dimension because you *must* know the basics about your data.

This data quality dimension uncovers the structure, content, and quality of data by using a technique called data profiling. Tools are available to profile data, but they continue to change and there may be another technique with a different name that replaces the term data profiling in the future. However, no matter what the tool functionality is called, we will always have the need to understand the fundamentals of our data, hence the reason this dimension is called Data Integrity Fundamentals, not data profiling.

Definition

Data Integrity Fundamentals (Data Quality Dimension). The existence (completeness/fill rate), validity, structure, content, and other basic characteristics of data.

Quote to Remember

"When it comes to data if you buy it, sell it move, transform it, integrate it, or report from it you must know what the data really means and how it behaves."

– Michael Scofield, MBA, Assistant Professor, Loma Linda University.

Typical Profiling Functionality

Data profiling looks at your data from different viewpoints. See *Figure 4.3.3* for three essential views of data made possible by a profiling tool. Note that specific data profiling capabilities, terms, and results vary depending on the tool used and that a column refers to a field, data element, or attribute.

1. Column profiling—Analyzes each column in a record, surveying all records in the dataset. Column profiling will provide results such as completeness/fill rates, data type, size/length, list of unique values and frequency distribution, patterns, and maximum and minimum ranges. This may also be referred to as domain analysis or content analysis. It enables you to discover true metadata and content quality problems, validate if the data conform to expectations, and compare actual data to target requirements.

2. Profiling within a table or file—Discovers relationships between data elements/columns/fields/attributes, within a table or file. This enables you to discover actual data structures, functional dependencies, primary keys, and data structure quality problems. You can also test user-expected dependencies against the data. This is also referred to as dependency profiling.

3. Profiling across tables or files—Compares data between tables or files, determines overlapping or identical sets of values, identifies duplicate values, or indicates foreign keys. Profiling results can help a data modeler build a third normal form data model, in which unwanted redundancies are eliminated. The model can be used to design a staging area that will facilitate the movement and transformation of data from a data source to a target database such as an operational data store or data warehouse. Cross-table or cross-file analysis can be extremely powerful when used properly.

The same principles apply when profiling big data in NoSQL datastores. The main difference is in number 3, profiling across tables or files, the technique for checking foreign key relationships and data redundancy. Even though NoSQL stores by nature do not maintain foreign key relationships between tables, the ability to "join" files by keys still exists. However, the whole idea of

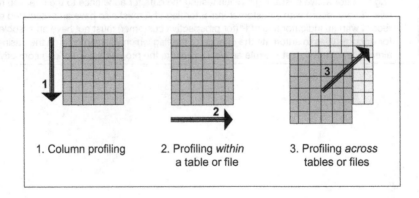

1. Column profiling
2. Profiling *within* a table or file
3. Profiling *across* tables or files

Figure 4.3.3 Typical profiling functionality.

NOSQL is to flatten all of the data so it can be processed faster, i.e., denormalize the data, which actually creates data redundancy. This is part of the tradeoff between a traditional relational database and big data file processing.

In a relational database, the focus is on minimizing redundancy by storing single instances of entity information in separate tables. For example, an employee database would have a master employee table, but each row (employee record) would reference (by a foreign key) a separate table with information about the employee's department. When processing the employee table, SQL can be used to automatically join the information in the two tables together. In big data processing, you may elect to maintain this in a single employee record. So if several employees are in the same department, all of the department information (name, location, billing codes, etc.) for each employee is repeated in each employee record.

It is important to understand the underlying structure when analyzing profiling results.

Data Profiling Tools

Tools with data profiling capabilities look at, but usually do not change, the data. Data can be profiled using a commercial data profiling tool, a report-writing program, a statistical analysis tool, or by writing queries such as using SQL. Some open source software is available for profiling. These are helpful initially if you have never used a data profiling tool before. Most have basic functionality for free and more in-depth functionality can be purchased. Traditional profiling tools work against relational databases and most are now able to profile big data in NoSQL databases. Look for data profiling capabilities that are built into other tools, such as integration tools.

At times, commercial data profiling tools are looked at with disdain or suspicion by developers or others who enjoy writing queries. ("I can write a profiling application this weekend.") However, for large-scale or ongoing quality efforts you cannot, within a reasonable time period, write a profiling application that will run the multitude of queries needed, present the results, and store them for future use the way existing profiling tools can. Let the profiling tools do the basics, which they are very good at.

Put your developers' skills to work supplementing what cannot be automatically done by the profiling tools, such as in-depth checking of business rules or relationships. Some of the advanced work can be done within the profiling tools, but using the results requires human intervention; sometimes it requires work outside the tools. This is a much more effective use of the deep knowledge of your data and your business. I would much rather see people spend their time analyzing and taking action on the profiling results instead of writing queries to obtain them.

If building the business case for data quality work, you may write a few queries just to bring visibility to actual data quality errors. But, if establishing a data quality baseline that will be monitored, if data quality activities are part of a large-scale integration project, or if you are serious about an ongoing data quality program, I highly recommend purchasing a tool with data profiling functionality.

Key Concept

Machine Learning, Artificial Intelligence, and Data Profiling. Machine Learning can be used in powerful tools to support profiling. However, Machine Learning and AI cannot replace human analysis and action.

Two main relevant broad categories of machine learning are supervised and unsupervised machine learning. Supervised learning bears many similarities to the profiling activities involved in data quality management. Briefly, supervised learning algorithms produce inferred rules from datasets of human-labelled training examples including inputs and outputs. Unsupervised learning algorithms infer structure and rules from a dataset of inputs by identifying patterns and structures in the data. With a large enough dataset of reasonably good and homogenous data, unsupervised machine learning can infer and extrapolate business rules, but any mistakes made or incorrect rules inferred can result in entrenched automation of mistakes faster and at scale.

No matter how sophisticated the algorithm in identifying patterns and extrapolating inferred rules, "artificial intelligence" is incapable of understanding context. For instance, unsupervised machine learning applied to a dataset involving US personal information might identify the pattern of a social security number, but this pattern recognition would break down immediately in a dataset involving equivalent social insurance numbers from more than one country, as other countries use different formats. Unless the machine learning process was made aware (by a human) that there were other patterns from other countries for things that mean the same as social security number it is likely it would not recognise the error.

Human insight is needed to understand whether a rule generalized from patterns in the dataset (unsupervised learning) is a desired business rule that will promote consistency, or a red flag exposing existing quality issues in the dataset or in problems with a business rule which result in poor-quality outcomes. Human insight is also needed for supervised learning, as algorithmic optimisation may not result in optimal outcome for your business needs. Subject matter expertise is necessary to understand the meaning and structure of your organization's data no matter how you apply the process, whether using humans or machine learning.

– Dr. Katherine O'Keefe, Director of Training and Research, Castlebridge

Data Profiling Uses and Benefits

Data Integrity Fundamentals, using the technique of data profiling, should be the first data quality dimension assessed when looking at the data content itself. Data profiling can be used to assess any data set to provide insight for any of the three types of data quality projects: 1) Focused data quality improvement project, 2) Data quality activities in another project, and 3) Ad hoc use of data quality steps, activities, or techniques.

Most of the other dimensions build on what is learned from this dimension. For example, even if your top priority is to determine duplicate records, in order to get valid results from a matching algorithm, fill rate and validity at the field, column, or data element level must be high. Any issues at the field level will be made visible using the technique of data profiling.

Data profiling complements Extract–Transform–Load (ETL) processes and tools because profiling results help create better source-to-target mappings in a shorter time than the traditional method of producing mappings based only on column headings without knowledge of actual content. Creating correct source-to-target mappings is a good reason for using a data profiling tool. Understanding the basics of source data before mapping data and writing code to transform and load the data is one of the most important data quality activities to include in any project that moves data from a source to a target.

Table 4.3.4 – Know Your Data through Data Profiling is particularly helpful when incorporating data quality activities into another project. The first column lists what is learned through data profiling and the second column the benefits from knowing that information and how to make use of it.

Table 4.3.4 Know Your Data through Data Profiling	
What You Learn	**Benefits – Use the Information in the Following Ways**
Are there any data quality problems that pose a risk to our scope, schedule, resources, and the success of our project? Are we focusing our efforts where they are really needed?	Data profiling provides the first visibility to the magnitude and location of data quality problems. Knowing this, you can be confident you are spending your time in the areas that really need your attention. Equally important, you can be confident where you do NOT have to spend time.
Do we have the right selection criteria for which data (records and data fields) will be extracted and moved?	When profiling data for the first time, use broad selection criteria – you don't know what you don't know. Profiling uncovers data that may be unknown to a subject matter expert. It provides the visibility to make good decisions on data (both fields and records) that should or should not be migrated. Once the data is profiled you have better input to refining or confirming the final selection criteria. Having the right selection criteria ensures that all the pertinent records and data fields are selected and loaded to the target system.
Are there any gaps between our source data and what the new target system requires?	Profiling highlights the differences between what is in the source data and what the target system requires. Decisions can then be made regarding which activities will best close the gap: creating data, cleansing data, transforming data, and/or purchasing data. Closing the gap helps the data load properly with fewer rejects and in a shorter amount of time. Having the high-quality data helps ensure business continuity and fewer issues after go-live.
What data do we have? What data is missing?	Data profiling provides rapid assessment of which records exist and which fields are consistently populated, which are then compared to expectations or requirements. Determine the impact on business and specific uses from missing data. Determine if data needs to be created or purchased to supplement missing data.
What data needs to be created?	Profiling uncovers if data is missing. If creating data to fill that gap, after the data is created profile the newly-created data to ensure it has been created correctly and meets target requirements.
What data needs to be cleansed?	Cleansing the data is one option for closing the gap between source data and target requirements. Use profiling results to determine if data can be cleansed at the source or other points along the information life cycle.
What data needs to be transformed?	Transforming the data is one option for closing the gap between source data and target requirements. Using profiling results leads to more accurate and comprehensive transformation rules.
What data needs to be purchased? What is the quality of data we have purchased, or are thinking about purchasing, from external data sources? Will the external data really meet our needs?	Profiling provides input to determine which external data sources have better-quality data and which best fit the target system needs. Work with external vendors to do a proof-of-concept and assess the quality of their data. Work with your procurement group to include criteria for the vendor's data quality in contracts and service level agreements. Once data is purchased, profiling can be used to check the external data as it is received and prior to loading to the company's databases.
Is there a way to do better and faster source-to-target mappings?	Profiling shows the content of data fields and if there are inconsistencies between column headings and content. This information yields better source-to-target mappings in a shorter time than a traditional mapping method in which only column headings are looked at. Without visibility of the data content, incorrect mappings are often not discovered until testing. Source-to-target mappings are common in most projects and anything that helps them be completed more quickly and accurately is greatly helpful.
Is there data in source systems that we do NOT need in the target system?	Once the data content is visible, some data may not be needed in the target system. If migrating data, being able to identify data that will not be moved reduces the volume of data, which in turn reduces the amount of time whenever data is extracted, test loads are done, and final move to production takes place.
Have we chosen the correct system of record?	If you have multiple systems from which to pull the same data, profiling provides input to decisions about the best system or source to use.

Table 4.3.4 Know Your Data through Data Profiling *(Continued)*

What You Learn	Benefits – Use the Information in the Following Ways
Is there any data we can use with no changes?	If data is of the quality needed, is nice to have good news. You can be confident in the data and not worry about unpleasant surprises that can impact your project.
How can we better control our test data?	When application functionality testing fails, too often too much time is spent investigating causes that end up being problems with the test data, not the software functionality. Manage the variables by profiling the data to be used in testing. By knowing the quality and content of the test data, less time is spent searching for errors and there is more focus on the application's functionality needs.
Are there other ways we can use the data profiling results?	• Create or validate a data model. Profiling, in the hands of a good data modeler, allows the creation of new models that support data to be moved into a new application, and it exposes structural differences between an existing target data model and the source data to be moved. • Compare, analyze, and understand source, target, and transitional data stores (e.g., files, staging areas). Profiling source, target, and transitional data stores shows the state of the data in any system, highlighting differences and their magnitude and pointing out where to focus cleansing, correction, transformation, or synchronization. • Support ongoing data quality monitoring. Profiling results provide the basis for continuous improvement and the same profiling tools can often be used for regular monitoring. • Identify opportunities for business process improvement. Bad data means the business processes that create the data can be improved. Process improvements done right will help prevent poor-quality data. • Help document previously unknown business and data quality rules.

Is there anything in this table that a manager or project manager would not want to know as soon as practically possible for the project? Said another way, I think every manager or project manager would like to know the answers to the questions in column 1 as quickly as possible in any project. Profiling is the best first step to answering them.

The answers will impact resources needed, timeline, costs, and possibly the scope of the project. Avoid increasing the risk of rework, lost time, and negative impacts to the schedule and resources from unpleasant data quality surprises. Instead, use data profiling to increase the chances of success by learning about your data, making informed decisions, and taking effective action. This can make the difference between success and failure of your project. Of course, other data quality dimensions may be needed, but Data Integrity Fundamentals, using the technique of data profiling, should be the first.

In summary, knowing your data through data profiling allows you to:

- Develop a realistic project plan
- Keep to your schedule by avoiding surprises later in the project due to poor data quality
- Have more successful test loads
- Lower the risk of design changes late in a project
- Make better use of resources
- Avoid rework
- Focus efforts where really needed – the magnitude and location of the problems have been uncovered, so you can be confident your time and effort will be spent in the areas that really need your attention, and feel equally confident where you do NOT have to spend time
- Ensure resulting information will allow the business to make good decisions and take effective action regarding their data

Approach

1. Finalize the data capture and assessment plans.

If assessing more than one data quality dimension, overall data capture and assessment plans may have been created earlier. If so, confirm specifics of that plan for Data Integrity Fundamentals. If not, create and finalize your plans now. See the section *Design Data Capture and Assessment Plans* in *Chapter 6* for more details. Use *Template 6.2 – Data to be Captured* in that section as a guideline for the decisions that need to be made when finalizing which data will be captured and how.

Document the process for capturing and assessing the data. Communicate with those involved. Ensure all are clear on their responsibilities and the timing.

2. Capture the data according to plan.

It is often easier to capture all the fields in a data set than pulling out only (the CDEs) identified in *Step 1*. And the additional data fields can provide important context when analyzing the data considered most important.

3. Profile the data according to plan.

Use the tools that best meet your needs. If you have to purchase a tool for profiling, this should have been accounted for in your project plan, so the tool is available to use when needed. Get training on tools to be used and apply best practices from the tool vendor.

If writing your own queries reference *Table 4.3.5* below for the types of checks to be done against the data. Depending on the tool used, those who profile the data may be different from those who analyze the output of the profiling.

4. Analyze and document results.

See the section *Analyze, Synthesize, Recommend, Document, and Act on Results* in *Chapter 6* for helpful details.

If you are using an automated tool, all the fields may be quickly profiled. Focus analysis on the most critical data, while realizing that less critical data can still provide context to help you better understand the data you most care about.

You may hear claims that no human intervention is needed for tools that make use of artificial intelligence/machine learning to profile (and possibly to update/correct) large volumes of data. Do not take the word of a vendor. Analyze a sampling of the results to verify the claims and ensure results are valid.

Reference *Table 4.3.5* again as you analyze the results and determine what action should be taken. Include subject matter experts, data experts, and technical experts to interpret what is seen in the profiling results.

Document what is found while looking at each data field. Start asking now why the data looks the way it does. Conduct additional profiling or write other queries to answer additional questions that arise. Include confirmation or non-verification of opinions about the data. Document any possible impact to the business revealed during analysis. Document potential root causes and use them when analyzing root causes in depth in *Step 5*.

Develop initial recommendations for addressing issues found for correcting the data, for preventing future data errors, and for controls that should be monitored.

Take action when the time is right. For example, do data errors found need to be corrected right away or are there additional data

Table 4.3.5 Data Integrity Fundamentals – Data Quality Checks, Sample Analysis and Action	
Number of records	Total count of records in the data set being assessed.
<ul><li>Compare the total number of records to the number expected. Investigate the causes of both missing records and if there are more records than expected.</li><li>Confirm desired population and selection criteria. Re-capture the data and profile the dataset again.</li></ul>	
Completeness/ fill rate	A measure of the fields that contain a value by count (#) and percentage (%).
Completeness or fill rate is based only on the *existence* of a value. Additional checks are needed to determine if the values are *valid*. To interpret results, you must know which fields are required/mandatory, optional, or conditional and the conditions. If the field is required (by the application, by the business, or if it is a primary key) the fill rate should be 100 percent. If the fill rate is less than 100 percent for a required field, investigate causes: <ul><li>If the field *is* required by the business but the application *does not* require it, see if the application can be modified to require the data. If the application cannot be modified, document data entry requirements and train those who enter the data as to what should be entered and why. In this case, the data should be monitored closely for quality.</li><li>If the field is *not* required by the business but the application *does* require it, expect to see data quality issues. If the data is not important or the data to be entered is not known, often meaningless data is entered just to get past the technical requirement for a value in the field.</li><li>Check the feasibility of enforcing a not null constraint in the database, which can be used to enforce business logic. Not null means that in a column of a relational database table, every row must contain a value – it cannot be left blank. Null is the absence of a value – not a zero or a blank space – and implies a value has not been stored.</li></ul>Check the completeness/fill rate at two different levels: <ul><li>For a single column or field: Determine if any data exists in the field (e.g., 80 percent of the employee records have a code in the department field).</li><li>For a grouping of data: Determine the fill rate for a set of fields required to complete a specific essential process. For instance, mailings in the United States require a street address or Post Office Box and a city, state, and zip code. Determine the number and percentage of records where all the required fields have a value (e.g., 75 percent of the patient records have the required data to ensure delivery of mail).</li></ul>	
Nulls	A measure of the fields that are empty (i.e., it is null because the field contains nothing) by count (#) and percentage (%).
Null is the absence of a value – not a zero or a blank space – and implies a value has not been stored. Nulls are the opposite of completeness or fill rate. The same analysis under completeness/fill rate applies here, but you will be looking at it from the opposite point of view.	
Content	Actual data content matches column or field names or labels.
Compare the column or field names with the actual data content. Does the field contain the data expected (e.g., does the phone number field actually contain phone numbers or are they numbers that actually indicate a government-issued personal identifier)?	
Validity	Values in the field conform to rules, guidelines, or standards.
<ul><li>Define and document what "valid" means for each field; what constitutes validity will vary from field to field.</li><li>Indicators of validity include format or patterns, domain values, valid codes, type (e.g., alpha or numeric), dependencies, maximum and minimum ranges, conformance to business rules or data entry standards.</li><li>For example, do the records contain a valid format for United Kingdom postcodes? Do all the records contain valid codes as defined by the business in code tables in the system? If the field is numeric, are there characters in the field? Does the date in a date field fall within the required range?</li><li>Be clear on date formats. Does 09/05/2020 mean September 5, 2020 or May 9, 2020?</li><li>Validity tests may be reported along with completeness/fill rates (e.g., UK postcode field has a 95% fill rate; of those records with a value, 90% conform to a pattern indicating a valid UK postcode).</li></ul>	

(Continued)

Table 4.3.5 Data Integrity Fundamentals – Data Quality Checks, Sample Analysis and Action *(Continued)*

Unique values	A list of distinct or unique values within a field.

- Review the list of values to ensure they are valid or allowed. The set of valid values may also be referred to as a data domain or a set of domain values.
- Check the *number* of distinct values against the number of valid values for that field.
- Compare the list of *actual* values to a list of expected valid values, if available.
- Expected valid values may come from a list of values in a reference table, a governed code list, an external standard to which your company adheres, or from consulting a subject matter expert.
- If an approved list of valid values does not exist, use the list from your profiling as a starting point to develop one.
- Look for *default* values, e.g., the application automatically inserts a value into a blank field such as "999-999-9999" if no telephone number is entered. Some decide to consider any field with the default value as not filled because it does not supply any meaningful information. Document default values.
- Look for values with *duplicate* meanings (e.g., varying abbreviations for the same company name: ABC Inc, ABC-INC, abc, co.).
- If changes are made to the list of values, document any mappings of values (code Y is now = code 3), and update records with the values that need to be changed.
- The list of unique values applies to those fields with a manageable number of unique values (e.g., it does not work well with free-form text fields or names).

Frequency distribution	The rate of occurrences of distinct or unique values within a field by count (#) and percentage (%).

- Sort by distribution. The frequency gives an idea of usage. Look at the values with the highest and lowest counts.
- For values with a low frequency, consider dropping them and changing to another comparable value that is used more often.
- Research any constants found. A constant is any column that has the same value for every record. This may be an indication of a field that was never used or is no longer used.
- Determine if the distribution of values is what you expect (e.g., if looking at order records across countries, does the frequency distribution of the country code align with your expectations of percentage of sales in each country?)
- Look for occurrences of unusual values that were learned about when analyzing your information environment and are being used generally by the business. For example, those creating the records tell you they rarely know the information for a certain field, but the system requires a value, so they enter a period (.) in the field to finish adding the record. Look for the number of periods (.) in that field.
- Look at the frequency distribution of default values or false values such as "999-999-9999" in a phone number field or "Mickey Mouse" in a name field.
- Use frequency distribution to determine candidates for primary keys in a relational database. "100 percent unique" or "near 100 percent" may be candidates – still check for bad data.
- If there is a low percent of distinct values, fields with equal value may be related. Many nulls or zeroes (0) can be a problem.
- A mid-range percent of distinct values may identify pure business data that will be determined by other columns.
- Fields that have only 1 distinct value (i.e., all records always have the same value in the field) are potentially unused or constant attributes. Determine if space should be taken in the database for this. Consider putting in a constant table.

Recency	Frequency distribution of critical date fields and/or date ranges by count (#) and percentage (%).

A type of frequency distribution related to date fields and/or date ranges – e.g.,"20 percent of the records were updated in the last 0-12 months; 25 percent updated in the last 13-24 months, etc." or "Based on the create date, 50 percent of the records were created in the last year."

May also be used to simulate or provide input to two other Data Quality Dimensions: Timeliness (the degree to which data is current) and Data Decay (the rate of negative change to the data).

Patterns	Unique patterns or formats of the values by count (#) and percentage (%).

- What constitutes a valid, or expected, pattern will vary depending on the field.
- Look for unexpected patterns, e.g., there are only a few valid patterns for US zip codes: nnnnn, nnnnn-nnnn, nnnnn nnnn, nnnnnnnnn. If a pattern in the field is any other than these, there is a data quality problem to investigate.
- Look for identical patterns for identification (ID) fields.
- Some may consider patterns a type of validity check.

Range of values	The boundary of values as shown by upper (maximum) and lower (minimum) limits.

- Look for values outside the expected or documented range.
- Any values at the top or bottom of the value range may indicate data quality problems, e.g., "ZZZZZ" in a name field, or "111-111" or "999-999" in an Identification Number field.
- Look at maximum and minimum values for key date fields, e.g., dates on open invoices or purchase orders to determine if they fall within business guidelines, such as, "There should be no open purchase orders older than six months from today's date."
- Some may consider range of values a validity check.

Precision	The level of detail, specificity, or granularity of a value.

- For numeric data, determine whether the number of places to the right of the decimal point are at the level of precision needed.
- Determine if date/time fields are at the level of precision needed. Does year only suffice, is month/day/year needed, or does time to the tenth of a second need to be included?
- Determine if a code or classification system has been captured at the level of detail or precision needed by the business. For example, the North American Industry Classification System (NAICS) is used by the United States, Canada, and Mexico to classify business by industry. It is a six-digit code with three levels. Do all records contain a full 6-digit code or do some contain the less precise 4-digit or 2-digit codes? What level of precision is needed by the business to conduct their work?
- Some may consider precision a type of validity check.

(Continued)

Table 4.3.5 Data Integrity Fundamentals – Data Quality Checks, Sample Analysis and Action *(Continued)*

Data type	The kind of data that a value can have, such as String for alphanumeric characters; Integer for whole numbers; Float for numbers with a decimal point; Boolean for logical values; BLOB (Binary Large Object) a collection of binary data stored as a single entity to store data files like images, videos, or other multimedia objects; CLOB (Character Large Object) for character data with very high size limits, etc.

- A data type in computer programming constrains values that the field can take, defines the operations that can be done on the data, and how values of the type can be stored.
- A profiling tool may show the documented data type (or expected data type per the metadata) and compare to the data type inferred from the actual data content. Look for differences between expected and actual.
- Look for differences between source and target data types that need to be addressed when migrating and integrating data.
- For data modeling, the tool may show the data type and examples of alternate data types that could be used in the model.
- Some may consider data type a validity check.

Size or length	Length of data in the field.

- Look for differences between actual data size and expected data size.
- Look for a large number of records with exactly the same size. This could indicate that the data in the field was truncated when it was loaded.
- If the size of a field in source data is longer than what is allowed in a target system where the data will be moved, some data will be lost through truncation. Determine the count and percentage of source records that exceed the target size:
  - If a small number, you may be able to update the records manually.
  - If a large number, you need to understand the impact to the business if the data is truncated when migrated and loaded. Research tools that can automate these types of complex updates.
- Some may consider size a type of validity check.

Referential Integrity	Consistency of data within a relationship; reasonability tests for related fields.

- In relational databases referential integrity has a specific meaning where it is enforced through foreign keys and primary keys.
- Referential integrity is also used here in a general way to recognize relationships between related fields. Use the idea of referential integrity to highlight relationships that can be understood through a data quality check.
- Look at consistency of data within a record or across records (e.g., order date must always be before ship date).
- Review business rules to understand relationships and look for conformance. For example, if a party record code is C (for contact) the business needs certain information on that person, so certain fields should contain specific values; if the party record code is O (for organization) the business needs different information, so other fields should have other values.
- Look for other dependencies. The value in one field is in the correct format relative to the value in another field (e.g., addresses in the United States have postal codes within the valid formats).
- Look for calculations. A stored calculated value is correct as per the input fields and formula (e.g., Sales Item Total Amount is equal to Sales Item Price multiplied by Sales Item Quantity).
- Look for dates such as current date, birthdate, and corresponding ages, e.g., must be 18 years or older to apply, but dates indicate the person is only 2 years old.
- These types of checks are closely related to conformance to business rules.

Consistency and Synchronization	Equivalence of data stored or used in various data stores, applications, and systems.

- Profile the same records in separate datastores throughout the information life cycle. Compare profiling results for differences.
- Some tools compare and show overlaps between distinct data values in different tables or columns, usually based on exact string matches. Tools may visualize the relationship with a Venn diagram which shows how much the different groups have in common. E.g., the master record dataset shows 100 unique values in one field and 60 unique values in the associated reference table. Of the 100 unique values, 45 are also in the reference table. This leaves 55 values not in the reference table but contained in the master records, and 15 values in the reference table not used by any master records. This raises the question of how values not in the reference table got into the master records, particularly if allowed values are supposed to be selected from a dropdown list when records are created or updated. Verify the values in the dropdown list with the values in the reference table and the values in the master records.
- A separate data quality dimension called Consistency and Synchronization is further detailed in *Step 3.6*, which helps when planning for the extra time and resources needed to profile, compare, and analyze each datastore. When actually assessing the data, the two dimensions (Data Integrity Fundamentals and Consistency and Synchronization) may be assessed together, depending on the best way to coordinate the work.

Uniqueness and Deduplication	Determine if unwanted duplication exists.

This is not the same as the data quality dimension by the same name, which uses other tools and techniques for an in-depth assessment of duplication. This is a quick view of duplication or redundancy shown through standard data profiling. For example:
- Look at the list of unique values in a data field for duplicate values and meanings. See Unique Values in this table.
- Some profiling tools may include functionality which highlight duplicate data using "fuzzy matching," where various algorithms identify non-exact matches. Other more sophisticated techniques are most often used in separate tools meant for in-depth matching and deduplication.
- If profiling NoSQL datastores, realize that the "flattening" of the data so it can be processed faster creates data redundancy. E.g., all department information for each employee in that department is repeated in each employee record. This is expected redundancy, not unwanted duplication.
- Understand the types and limits of matching within any data profiling tool used.

(Continued)

Table 4.3.5 Data Integrity Fundamentals – Data Quality Checks, Sample Analysis and Action *(Continued)*	
Business Rules	Determine if data values indicate conformance to business rules, which are authoritative principles or guidelines that describe business interactions and establish rules for actions and resulting data behavior and integrity.

- It is useful to consider business rules and what the resulting data should look like. You can then articulate data quality rules to be checked for compliance. Using a business rules perspective can help uncover important data quality checks that might otherwise be overlooked. For more on business rules, see *Chapter 3*. These checks may be done by writing queries either within or outside of a data profiling tool.
- Determine if business and data rules not embedded in the data structure are being enforced by the application program logic. This is usually done against a subset of the data that has its own rules. For example, you may have different party types (organization, contact, etc.) with specific rules that require some columns to be null and others to be populated.
- Some consider conformance to business rules as validity.

quality dimensions to be assessed where it would be better to wait for those results first and make all corrections at the same time?

5. Share results and get feedback.

When sharing results, think through how to categorize and report on the various data quality checks. For example, what is considered valid will vary from field to field. Validity can be indicated by a valid pattern, level of precision, or whether a code conforms to a list of valid values. Do you want to report all under the label of validity or call out precision separately, for example?

If using a data profiling tool, consider how the tool reports, labels, and categorizes the profiling results. Report and show results in a way that makes sense for your organization. Once your baseline is set, these data quality checks may eventually become data quality rules and metrics that are run on a periodic basis to monitor the state of data quality (in *Step 9*).

Sample Output and Templates

Testing Data Integrity Fundamentals

Table 4.3.5 provides a list of data quality checks, along with considerations when analyzing results and action that could be taken. The title and definition of each check are in the grey rows.

If writing your own queries, use it as a guide for the queries to write and again when analyzing query results. For any data quality check that does not match expectations or requirements, the next question is, "Why or how did this happen?" and investigate from there. The data quality checks can also provide input when comparing functionality offered by third-party data profiling tools.

 Warning

Data profiling does not equal data quality! In spite of the emphasis on data profiling, and as helpful and important as it is, data profiling does not equal data quality. Data profiling in and of itself will not guarantee high-quality data. Data profiling is a means to an end, not the end in itself. The purpose of data profiling is to understand the data so you can make informed decisions and take effective action regarding your data. It is what you do with the critical information uncovered by data profiling that makes the difference.

Remember, data profiling is not the only consideration for data quality. For example, if you are concerned about duplicates or accuracy, there are separate data quality dimensions that use different techniques, tools, and approaches to assess them. But data profiling is the best start to your data quality efforts.

Step 3.4 | Accuracy

Business Benefit and Context

It is easy to associate the words "data quality" with "accuracy." It seems obvious that the goal of data quality should be to produce accurate data. Some use accuracy as a synonym for data quality in general. Data professionals know they are not the same. For the purpose of assessing and managing data quality it is important to make the distinction between the dimension of accuracy and other data quality dimensions, particularly data integrity fundamentals. An assessment of *data integrity fundamentals* tells us the basic measures of completeness, validity, structure, and content using the technique of data profiling. Data *accuracy* tells us the correctness of the content of the data. This requires comparing the data to what it

represents – to the authoritative source of reference. Following are examples of what is learned through assessing data integrity fundamentals using the technique of data profiling compared to what is learned in an accuracy assessment:

- *Data profiling* will reveal that every item record in a dataset contains a valid code of M (Make) or B (Buy) in the "Part Source" field, along with a count and percentage of records with each code. These are fundamentals of data quality and are important to know. However, to assess *accuracy*, we must have an authoritative source of reference for comparison. In this case, it could be a design document or someone from engineering or procurement who knows the items well enough to determine if the code assigned to each part reflects if it is actually made internally (M) or purchased externally (B).

- *Data profiling* of customer records shows that postal codes are actually in the postal code field and that they conform to acceptable patterns indicating valid postal codes. You can also check if each city, geographic area, and postal code creates a valid combination. But only the customer or a secondary authoritative source such as a postal service list can tell us if a particular postal code is the correct postal code for that particular customer – once again, this is *accuracy*.

- *Data profiling* displays the value for the number of products on hand in an inventory database and confirms it is the correct data type. But only by completing an *accuracy assessment* with someone manually counting or scanning products on the shelf and comparing that number to the record in the inventory system can you know if the inventory count in the database is an accurate reflection of the inventory on hand.

Definition

Accuracy (Data Quality Dimension). The correctness of the content of the data as compared to an agreed-upon and accessible authoritative source of reference.

See *Figure 4.3.4* for a decision flow which illustrates that in order to assess accuracy, you must be able to identify, access, and agree on an authoritative source of reference, and be able to afford to conduct an accuracy assessment. Accuracy requires an agreed-upon and authoritative source of reference and a comparison of the data to it. That comparison can take the form of a survey (such as a phone call to a customer or an emailed questionnaire) or an inspection (such as a comparison of the inventory count in the database to the actual inventory on the shelf).

Sometimes it is not possible to access the real-world object represented by the data, and in those cases a carefully chosen substitute for it may be used as the authoritative source of reference. It is also important that there is agreement among team members and stakeholders in the project as to the appropriate authoritative source of reference or you risk distrust in assessment results.

Sometimes all or part of an accuracy assessment can be automated, but more often it is a manual, time-consuming, and therefore more expensive process. In this case, determine if a smaller number of records or fewer data fields can be assessed and still get meaningful results. Unless you can answer yes to all the questions in the figure, you cannot or should not assess accuracy. You can still use other data quality dimensions to assess quality and these will be helpful, but they will not tell you whether your data is accurate, as defined here.

Why am I making such a point of these distinctions? It is because of the misunderstanding of the general use of the word "accuracy" and because assessing accuracy can be more expensive than assessing other dimensions. It is best to know early if you can or should actually assess accuracy or not. Data professionals must know what they will and will not get from each type of assessment. It is also their responsibility to ensure others understand what they will and will not get. This is particularly important for accuracy so there is no misunderstanding.

Approach

An accuracy assessment has three main parts: prepare for the assessment, execute the assessment, and score and analyze results. In the instructions below, the word survey is used to indicate the method of assessment. The survey instrument refers to the questions to be asked or comparisons to be done. You will see that many of the instructions relate to preparation. The time spent preparing will

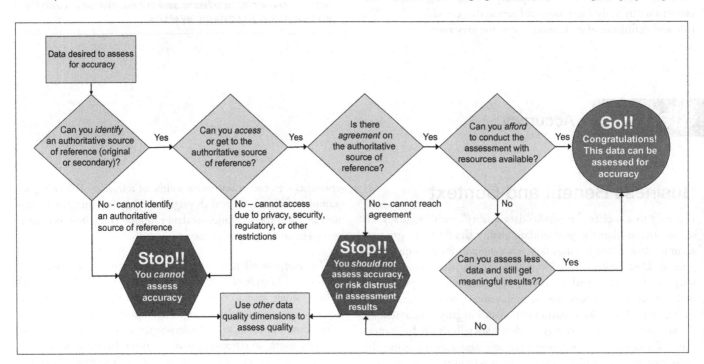

Figure 4.3.4 Determine ability to assess accuracy.

help ensure a smooth assessment and avoid costly rework or errors during what is usually an expensive assessment.

1. Verify the data to be assessed for accuracy and the authoritative source of reference.

Use Figure 4.3.4 to discuss and confirm that an authoritative source of reference can be identified, accessed, and agreed upon. In addition, ensure you can afford to conduct an accuracy assessment.

Identify—Identify what or who is the authoritative source of reference for the data. Examples:

- A customer may be the authoritative source of reference for customer information.
- A scanned or online application and resume may contain the authoritative data for personnel-recruiting information.
- An administrative contact may be able to verify site information.
- Product itself may be the source for a product description. Alternatively, a product engineer could be an authoritative secondary source.
- Manually counting or scanning products on a shelf, in storage, and/or at a distribution warehouse to verify product inventory.
- An upstream order system may contain authoritative data about orders that are passed onto a warehouse.
- A generally accepted "Golden Copy" (controlled and validated version) might serve as an authoritative source of reference.
- A recognized industry-wide standard, such as Dun and Bradstreet, for company names and hierarchies.

It is possible that the same source of reference can be used for all fields in a record. Other times, different sources of reference can apply depending on the data field.

Access—Is the authoritative source of reference (either original or secondary) available and accessible? There may be no way to corroborate data gathered too far in the past. Another issue may be regulations that constrain direct contact of customers to verify their information in your database. Are there any constraints (such as privacy or security) that would prevent you from accessing the source for an accuracy comparison?

Agree—Do the team members agree on the source of reference? Are there stakeholders who need to agree on the source(s) before going further? If there is not agreement, you risk distrust in assessment results. Distrust means you run the risk of people not taking action needed and then the money spent on the accuracy assessment would be wasted.

Afford—Do you know the number of records which can be checked for accuracy? Because of the expense of determining accuracy, the assessment is usually done against a sampling of records, while with profiling tools you can often check all records. Work with a statistician to ensure you have a valid sample and the number of records that must be verified for accuracy. If a problem with accuracy is found in the sample, at that point the business can determine if accuracy updates on all the data are worth their cost. Are there business processes already in place that can be utilized? For example, taking inventory is a common business process. Can you participate in or use results from the standard inventory process to show the level of accuracy?

Adjust and Finalize—Adjust the scope, if necessary, by assessing fewer records or fewer data fields. Document which records and fields will be assessed for accuracy and their source(s) of reference. You may decide not to assess for accuracy.

2. Determine the method of assessment.

You will use tools to capture the results of the assessment, but sometimes the assessment itself cannot be performed by an automated tool. See *Conduct a Survey* in *Chapter 6: Other Techniques and Tools* for help.

Examples of survey and inspection methods include:

- **Internet survey**. Use a website to collect assessment data. May require a way to authenticate those providing the information and a way to keep respondents' data private.
- **Telephone survey**. Expensive, but has a greater chance for confirmation.
- **Mailed survey**. Less chance for confirmation. Some contacts may not respond or may not be reached because of address errors. Telephone follow-up, if allowed, can offset a lack of response.
- **Physical inspection of objects.** Manual and time-consuming.
- **Manual comparison**. Of data in the database against a printed source of reference.
- **Automated comparison**. Of data in a digital authoritative source of reference to the data being assessed.

Consider the following factors when finalizing the method of assessment:

- **Cultural**. What is acceptable in your environment?
- **Response**. What is the best way to obtain input from the authoritative source? What method will increase response rates?
- **Schedule**. How quickly do you need a response? For example, mailed surveys or phone surveys would have a slower turn-around time than internet surveys.
- **Constraints**. Are there any legal requirements that restrict you from using a particular assessment method?
- **Cost**. What are the costs for the various assessment methods?

3. Develop the survey instrument, survey scenarios, record dispositions, update reasons, and scoring guidelines.

Depending on the survey instrument and the type of data to be assessed, use the following to determine how to track progress and understand how the assessment is going. These apply whether accuracy is assessed manually or automatically:

Survey instrument—The survey instrument is the set of questions used for assessing accuracy, whether by questioning a respondent, having the respondent complete them independently, or by manually checking against a source of reference.

- For a telephone survey, develop the set of questions and the script for obtaining input from respondents.
- For an internet/website, hardcopy, mailed, emailed, or website survey, develop the questionnaire to be completed and submitted by respondents.
- For manual comparisons, decide what forms will be used to capture results and how the data from the database will be presented to facilitate easy comparison to the source.

- Determine if questions should have predefined answer choices. For instance, product questions may correspond to a product table in the database. If so, ensure that your list of choices matches the valid reference in the database and that both the list and corresponding codes are correct and complete.

Survey scenarios—Survey scenarios are possible situations the surveyor might encounter throughout the survey period. An example for a survey of customers includes the following: "Unable to contact customer"; "Contacted customer but customer declines to participate"; "Customer starts survey but does not complete it"; and "Customer completes survey."

Record dispositions—Determine how to track the status of each record throughout the survey. Assign a code that corresponds to each status. For example, if the surveyor is able to verify the status of each data element within the record, the disposition for that record is "fully checked." Other record dispositions include "partially checked" or "not checked," "contact not located," "declined," and so forth. Only those records with the disposition "fully checked" are later scored for accuracy. However, tracking ALL record disposition types can yield additional important quality measures.

Update reasons—Update reasons explain why the data as held by your organization was different (or not) from the data supplied by the source of reference. The updated data is captured in some way (manually or automatically) and compared to the original data (manually or automatically). Update reasons are noted while the inspection is being performed or the survey is being conducted. You may want to track an update reason for each field that is compared for accuracy. For example, the update reasons could be:

- **Correct**. No updates are needed; the information provided by the source of reference is the same as that contained in the database.
- **Incomplete**. The information in the database is blank; the source of reference provided the missing information.
- **Wrong**. The information provided by the source is different from the information in the database.
- **Format**. The content of the information is correct, but the formatting is incorrect.
- **Not applicable**. The information was not validated with the source.

Scoring guidelines—Scoring quantifies the results of the accuracy assessment. Scoring guidelines are the rules that determine whether the update reasons will be scored as correct or incorrect. Each field compared for accuracy will be scored as correct or incorrect. The scoring guidelines are applied to the survey or inspection results after the survey or inspection has been completed. In order to score the accuracy results, follow these steps:

- **Prioritize and weight the data**. Decide which data are the most important and assign a ranking of value relative to other data elements (e.g., low, medium, high, or 1, 2, 3).
- **Create scoring guidelines**. The scoring guidelines are the rules that determine the score to be assigned to each update reason. For example, a field with an update reason code of "correct," "blank," or "format" may be assigned a score of 1,

while a field with an update reason code of "wrong" may be assigned a score of 0. Whether the record is a 1 or a 0 is determined when the scoring is completed. The scores are put into the scoring mechanism (such as a spreadsheet) to calculate accuracy statistics.

- **Create a scoring mechanism**. This may be a spreadsheet that calculates the data element, record level, and overall accuracy statistics based on the assessment.

4. Develop the survey or inspection process.

The survey or inspection process is the standard process that will be used for comparing the data with the source of reference and capturing the results. Determine:

- **Overall process flow**. If the survey is to be sent, determine where and how it is to be distributed, returned, and processed. If the accuracy assessment involves inspection, determine when and how the inspection will take place. Ensure all details for the survey have been finalized and documented.
- **Overall timing.** Account for key dependencies that may affect timing. For example, the data in the database should be extracted at a time as close as possible to the time the assessment starts.

5. Develop reports and the process for reporting results.

Clarify reporting needs up-front to ensure the correct information is collected during the survey or inspection and will be readily available on the back end. Reports should include how the data from the database will be extracted and formatted, and in what form the information will be available for those conducting the inspection or survey. At a minimum, ensure the output for every record shows a before and after picture of each data field. Output should account for the status of every record assessment; for example, it should describe the number and percentage of records for each record disposition status – fully checked, partially checked, no basis for comparison, etc. Mock-up the reports to ensure agreement on the content and format of the information to be reported. Finalize the reports.

6. Extract the appropriate records and fields for assessment.

Verify that the extracted data meet your selection criteria and that the sample is random and representative of the population. See *Design Data Capture and Assessment Plans* in *Chapter 6* for additional help.

7. Train those who are conducting assessments.

If carried out by multiple people, the assessments must be conducted consistently to ensure correct results.

8. Run and test the inspection or survey process from beginning to end.

Make changes, as needed, to the process, survey instrument, survey scenarios, record dispositions, update reasons, scoring guidelines, reports, and training.

9. Execute the survey.

Complete the following while the accuracy assessment is being conducted:

Ensure the latest data is being used—Re-capture the data to be assessed if too much time has passed between preparation and when the assessment begins.

Collect results—Capture assessment results throughout the survey period according to the process. Capture the correct values while inspecting or conducting the survey in the survey instrument. But do not perform updates to the actual data source unless those updates can be done in a separate field. Important context and information needed when researching root causes may be lost. Capture the updates separately and make corrections at a later date.

Monitor the progress of the assessment throughout the survey period—This will allow you to confirm if the work is on schedule and is being done correctly and consistently. It is important to find problem areas early on. If needed, stop and make adjustments to the survey instrument, provide additional training to surveyors, and so forth.

Know when to stop the survey—Stop the assessment when the desired number of completed (fully checked) records has been reached.

10. Analyze, synthesize, make recommendations, and document results. Act on results when the time is right.

Finish the following items after the survey has been completed.

Score the survey according to scoring guidelines—Obtain final reports. Scoring refers to evaluating the differences between what was originally in the database with what was found during the assessment, assigning a score, and calculating the accuracy levels.

- You may program this comparison to be done automatically as part of the assessment process. If not, it will be done manually.
- Choose an objective third party to do the scoring.
- Prepare materials and document the process for scoring so it can be done consistently.
- Only score records that have been "fully checked" – those for which every question in the survey was asked and compared to the existing records.
- Compare what is in the database against the assessment or survey results and apply a score for each data element.

Analyze results of the survey—Look at accuracy at both the data field and record level. Also look at overall sample accuracy. Analyze the record disposition-statistics – the number and percentage of records for each disposition. Other considerations:

- What is the accuracy level? If you have targets for accuracy, compare the actual results to them.
- How do results compare with your expectations? Any surprises?
- Do accuracy results vary by country, geographic region, or some other category that is meaningful to your company?
- Has anything been learned during the assessment that provides enough information about impact to determine if it is worthwhile to periodically monitor accuracy? Did you expect this to be a one-time assessment only? Have you learned anything about accuracy that will change that plan?

- How will you handle the correction of records found to be inaccurate? Who will do this and when?
- How can you prevent the creation of inaccurate records? Any ideas on root cause?
- Look at accuracy results in relation to other data quality assessments, if any.
- Based on analysis, make initial recommendations on what action should be taken.
- Document results and analysis.

See *Analyze, Synthesize, Recommend, Document, and Act on Results* in *Chapter 6*.

Sample Output and Templates

 Ten Steps in Action

Accuracy Assessment

One data quality team conducted an accuracy assessment of customer information in their customer master database. The authoritative source of reference was the customers themselves. They were to be contacted via phone. Part of the preparation included developing a script that was approved by the sales manager in charge of the territories where the customers were located. The sales reps were informed of the survey so they would not be caught by surprise if a customer asked them why they were being called.

A telemarketing company was hired to call the customers and confirm the information in the customer master. If the customer could not be reached with the phone number on file, there were procedures for looking for alternate phone numbers. In spite of that, one surprising result from the assessment was that 36 percent of their contacts could not be located. The sponsor of the project, who was also the owner of the customer database, could have tried to hide this bad news. But she was vocal in sharing results and said, "If we don't share results, nothing will get fixed." This was a good example of the courage it takes to be willing to talk about problems that will come up, at some time or another, during a data quality project. There was also good news. The accuracy rate was high for records that were fully validated, meaning all data fields in the customer records were verified with the customer.

The project illustrates the cost, time, and important communications that were part of the accuracy assessment. This type of survey worked well and provided valuable insights which influenced what data quality actions were taken to improve the quality of the customer master. However, in today's environment, I would be very cautious about repeating this survey because many customers would be suspicious of someone calling and claiming to be with the company. That is why it is vital to carefully identify the authoritative source of reference and take into account any privacy, security, regulatory, or other factors that may prevent you from using a particular source or even the ability to conduct an accuracy assessment. An alternative would be to find a secondary source that could suffice.

Having said that, while writing this second edition, I received an email from an association who wanted me to purchase their mailing list. The email claimed the records were "updated by our staff of marketers by phone...Each record has been phone verified for accuracy...All contacts info are assured and updated within the last 10 days." Once again, the art of data quality requires you to make judgements about what will work best for your business needs and within your environment.

Step 3.5	Uniqueness and Deduplication

Business Benefit and Context

There are many costs associated with duplicate records. Some examples:

- Duplicate patient records can put people's health and lives at risk
- Duplicate vendor records with the same name and different addresses make it difficult to ensure that payment is sent to the correct address
- Duplicate customer records create risks that decisions may be made on incorrect information. For example, as a customer's credit limit changes, the limit may be updated on one record but not the others. If multiple records, with multiple credit limits, are being used, the credit limit for that customer can unknowingly be exceeded, which then exposes the business to unnecessary credit risks.
- Decreased ability to link multiple devices (phones, tablets, laptops) to one consumer which prevents obtaining insight needed for personalized marketing.
- Duplicate records take up storage space and eat up processing time.

Thanks to John Talburt, PhD, Acxiom Chair of Information Quality and Director, Entity Resolution and Information Quality (ERIQ) Research Center, University of Arkansas at Little Rock, for his help and expertise in updating this step.

 Definition

Uniqueness and Deduplication (Data Quality Dimension). The uniqueness (positive) or unwanted duplication (negative) of data (fields, record, or data sets) existing within or across systems or datastores.

Goal of Uniqueness and Deduplication

The goal of this data quality dimension is to identify the data that is unique, meaning that one and only one version of the data field, record, or dataset that exists; it has no duplicates. Another way of saying it is to identify and resolve unwanted duplication of data. Entity resolution is another term used for the same idea, where entity is the real-world object, person, place, or thing, and resolution is the process for identifying records that represent the same real-world entity. For more details, see John Talburt's book *Entity Resolution and Information Quality* (2011).

In John's terminology, records referring to the same real-world objects are called "equivalent records," but here we will use "duplicate records" to mean the same thing. A master data management (MDM) initiative is all about creating a single system to identify duplicate (equivalent) records describing a particular master entity such as a customer or a product. Each master entity is assigned a unique identifier by the MDM system, and these identifiers are appended to the records as they flow through to other operational systems in the organization. In this way, there is a consistent and accurate identification of duplicate records in one place in the organization. In addition, the entity identifier assigned by the MDM system to each record makes it easier for downstream systems to identify and handle duplicate records appropriately for a particular process. This is outside of what this data quality dimension covers, but what is included here as useful input to any project with concerns about duplicate records. A good resource for MDM and big data projects is Talburt and Zhou (2015), *Entity Information Life Cycle for Big Data: Master Data Management and Information Integration.*

General Process

Identifying duplicates and resolving them by creating a survivor record are usually done with tools meant for that purpose. I have been involved in one project where it was all done manually against a small dataset, but that is not the norm. Even though tools will do the heavy lifting for this data quality dimension, a basic understanding of the underlying concepts, terms, and processes is helpful.

I will explain the overall process assuming a tool is being used, against records within a dataset, to answer the question: Do multiple records represent the same or different real-world objects? There are three basic processes involved: 1) prepare the data, 2) define uniqueness, and 3) resolve the duplicates. First, let's discuss the following basic terms related to these three processes.

Record Matching—Records that have a high degree of similarity. For example, records having the same or similar values for several shared attributes such as "Johnson" vs. "Johnston" for a Last Name attribute. Matching (similarity) is the primary tool for identifying records representing the same real-world object, such as multiple records representing the same customer, employee, supplier, patient, facility, or product. The assumption is that the greater the similarity between two records, the greater the likelihood they are duplicates, i.e., that they represent the same entity. Conversely, it is assumed the less similar they are, the less likely they are duplicate. However, similarity measures only give a likelihood or probability the records are duplicates. Very similar records could be for different customers. For example, "Bill Smith, 123 Oak St" and "William Smith, 123 Oak St" are very similar, but could be a father and son living at the same address. A generational suffix attribute value (Jr. or Sr.) or age attribute value would be needed to make the distinction. Also "Jane Smith, 345 Elm St" and "Jane Eyre, 678 Pine St" could be the same patient, but after marriage and moving to another address. As noted above, I am using the term equivalent records to refer to duplicate records, as opposed to similar records. In some contexts, the term matching records is used to refer to duplicate records. A set of matching records is called a match set or cluster. More on matching later.

Record Linking—Process of assigning the same identifier to two or more records to indicate and preserve an important relationship, yet keeping individual records separate. For example, householding is a linking concept often used by banks to understand the relationships among various customers. All records associated with a particular household are linked with a common identifier. For example, a young adult with a new checking account may be linked to that of his or her parents, who may have a number of accounts with the bank. Linking is also used to identify households with multiple investment accounts with the same company so only one privacy notice is sent to each household, therefore saving printing and mailing costs (yes, mailing still happens) and helping our environment along the way. However, record linking most commonly refers to linking duplicate (equivalent) records together. In some cases, the duplicate records are retained after linking, creating what is called a "cluster" or "match set." In other cases, the information from the individual linked records is "merged" into a single record (the "survivor record"), and the other duplicate records are "purged" (deleted) from the system. The latter case is often called a "merge-purge" process.

Survivorship/Merge/Consolidation/Deduplication— Synonyms for the process of resolving duplicate records. Different methods can be used such as: 1) Select one record as the "master" and merge additional information into it from duplicate records, 2) Build a new "best-of-breed" record by selecting the best data from the various duplicate records.

Equivalent Records—Records referencing the same real-world entity such as a customer or product. While this is usually what is meant by the term "duplicate records," there are cases where duplicate can mean an exact copy of a record. Using three different terms helps to clearly distinguish among the three concepts of (1) two records referring to the same object (equivalent records), (2) two records having a high degree of similarity (matching records), and (3) two records being an exact copy of each other (duplicate records). The term "matching" is sometimes used to mean any one of these three things, so it is important to understand each writer's definition.

Entity Resolution/Record Matching/Record Linking/Record Deduplication—These terms are often used interchangeably, but technically are somewhat different. Entity resolution is the process of determining if two records are equivalent or not (i.e., duplicate records or not). While record matching is the most commonly used technique to accomplish entity resolution. New artificial intelligence (AI) methods such as machine learning (ML) are emerging as alternatives to traditional deterministic and probabilistic matching techniques. While it is true that an entity resolution system will link the records it determines to be equivalent, linking may be done for other reasons than entity resolution. Also, from a purely technical perspective, record linking is defined to take place between two different files or datasets and not within the datasets. For example, linking records for the same patient between Hospital A's database and Hospital B's database, while assuming (perhaps optimistically) there are no duplicate patient records within each of the two databases.

Note that these terms are not always used consistently. For example, some use entity resolution to mean only matching, and deduplication to mean both matching and merging. Ensure your project team and the vendor providing the tool are using the same words to mean the same things and that everyone involved has a common understanding of the process.

Prepare the Data

This could also be called "know your data and prepare as needed." There are many approaches to identifying duplicates. Some tools determine matches using the data as is, others standardize the data first.

Standardization is a general term used to indicate data being changed to adhere to rules and guidelines, such as a similar format or approved values. Standardization can also include parsing. Parsing is the ability to separate multi-valued fields into individual pieces, such as separating character strings or free form text fields into their component parts, meaningful patterns, or attributes, and moving the parts into clearly labeled and distinct fields. For example, separating out product attributes from product description in a freeform text field.

No matter which approach is used, the better the quality of the data in the records, the better the matching results will be. The more you know about your data, the better you will be able to customize standardization routines, if needed, and matching algorithms used by your tool. Profiling is a great way to understand the data. See *Step 3.5 – Data Integrity Fundamentals* for more on understanding your data.

In one project early in my career, we had to identify which combination of fields indicated a unique record. This was configured into the tool and the matching routine was run. Manual review showed poor match results. The cycle of "adjust algorithm-run routine-review" continued for a number of weeks, still with unacceptable results. It was at this point we decided to fully profile the data. We found that one of the fields used to indicate a unique record, that we "knew" had a 100% fill rate, actually only had values in 20% of the records. No wonder we could not get good matching results! It pays to know your data.

Another project, in hindsight, recommended keeping the standardized data in a separate field from the original data field. The standardized data was used to help with the matching. If the team made adjustments to the standardization routines, the data could be re-standardized using the updated algorithms. If you don't have the original data, it will not be possible to do this.

Define Uniqueness

Determine how the business looks at uniqueness and document the rules. How does the business determine if a record is a duplicate of another record? What combination of data elements constitutes a unique record? What is the level of similarity (match threshold) between two records that must be met for the records to be considered duplicate? Refer to your review of the data model in *Step 2.2—Understand Relevant Data and Data Specifications* for input. For example, does a unique combination of sold-to, ship-to, and bill-to addresses constitute one unique record? Should there be only one occurrence of a particular customer name in the database? From a technical point of view, what is considered acceptable redundancy in a NoSQL database would be unacceptable in a relational database.

Most systems use one of two styles of matching: deterministic (Boolean) or probabilistic (scoring). In the deterministic approach, rules are developed describing agreement and disagreement of different combinations of attribute values. For example, one match rule could require First Names agree, Last Names agree, and Dates-of-Birth agree. However, another could require First Names agree, Dates-of-Birth agree, and Phone Numbers agree. The second rule is needed for cases where a last name may have changed. Other rules could be added for other cases.

There is a misconception that "deterministic" requires an exact match, but that is not true. Deterministic rules can allow for so called "fuzzy" matching at the attribute level. For example, First Names agree could mean the two first names are exactly the same or they are common nicknames of each other. Deterministic only means a rule is satisfied (True) or not satisfied (False). For this reason, deterministic rules are sometimes called Boolean rules.

Another common matching technique is called probabilistic matching. In this method, the corresponding attribute values are compared. If the values agree, the comparison is assigned a numerical value called an agreement weight. If the values disagree, then the comparison is assigned a disagreement weight typically smaller than the agreement weight. To get the match score, the assigned weights from each attribute comparison are added together. If the total score is above a given threshold value, the records are considered matching records (duplicates), otherwise they are considered a nonmatch. For this reason, this technique is also called a "scoring rule."

The scoring approach offers several advantages: 1) By setting a high threshold, the matching will be more precise creating fewer false positive errors at the expense of false negative errors. Vice versa, a lower threshold will reduce false negatives while potentially increasing false positive errors. See *Figure 4.3.6.* 2) Pairs of records with scores near the threshold, slightly below or slightly above, can easily be identified as belonging to the Gray Area, see *Figure 4.3.5*, and set aside automatically for manual inspection, which is sometimes called "clerical review" or "remediation." 3) Perhaps the most important, the agreement and disagreement weight can be assigned at the value level, not just at the attribute level. For example, in addition to having an agreement weight for First Names

in general, it is possible to generate an agreement weight for specific First Names such as "JOHN". Because "JOHN" is such a common (frequently used) first name in most US populations, it should be assigned lower agreement weight than the general First Name agreement weight. This is because two records sharing the First Name "JOHN" are less likely to be equivalent (for the same person), than two records sharing a less common first name. When the weights are assigned in this way based on the frequency of particular values, then the scoring technique for matching become truly probabilistic matching.

Decide at which level to test for uniqueness:

Record level—For instance, there should only be one occurrence of a particular customer in the database. Do you care about sites and/or contacts? For uniqueness of sites, you may want to look at combinations of address fields. For uniqueness of persons, you may want to look at combinations of name and address fields and demographic information.

Field level—For instance, phone numbers should generally be unique unless you are assessing site phone numbers where there is one central number for all contacts at that site. Identification numbers should be unique. Simple field level uniqueness based on exact string matches can be accomplished using a data profiling tool. If you need a more sophisticated algorithm, use an entity resolution or record linking tool. For example, the Python programming language popular for data analysis has available a very rich Record Linkage Toolkit for implementing matching rules.

Following are concepts and terms related to identifying matches.

- **Match.** Two or more records in the dataset have been identified as equivalent, i.e., representing the same real-world thing, using the business rules/algorithms as implemented within the tool. The group of records determined to be duplicates are called a match set.
- **Nonmatch.** No other records in the dataset represent the same real-world thing; that is, the record is identified as being unique (non-equivalent), using the business rules/algorithms as implemented within the tool.
- **False Negative.** Records have been classified as unmatched (non-equivalent), but they should have been matched (equivalent); that is, they are missed matches.
- **False Positive.** Records have been incorrectly classified as matches (equivalent). They are actually non-matches (non-equivalent); that is, they are mismatches.

When records are run through a tool, results will show those records that are not matches and those records that are. There is always a "gray" area where the matches and nonmatches overlap, which means that it is not clear if the records are a match or a nonmatch. The further you move away from the gray area (in either direction), the more confident you are that the matches are true matches and the nonmatches are really nonmatches (as illustrated in *Figure 4.3.5*). But again, this is only a confidence or likelihood based on the level of similarity. While most of the false positive and false negative errors will occur in the gray area, there can still be errors in the high confidence regions.

Look closely at the gray area in *Figure 4.3.6.* When examining the detail, you can see the difference between the false negatives

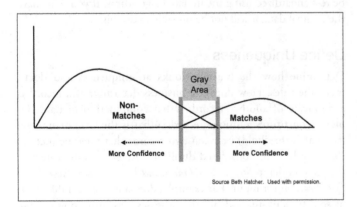

Figure 4.3.5 Matching results – matches, nonmatches, and the gray area.

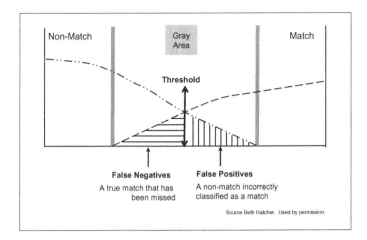

Figure 4.3.6 Matching – false negatives and false positives.

(the matches that have been missed) and the false positives (non-matches incorrectly classified as matches). The threshold line is the point at which two objects are sufficiently alike to be considered potential duplicates. The threshold can be adjusted.

Setting the threshold is a balancing act and is as much an art as a science. The following list contains a few ways to think about the trade-offs:

- Moving the threshold to the left maximizes matches but increases the risk of incorrect matches (false positives) while decreasing missed matches (false negatives).
- Moving the threshold to the right increases the number of missed matches (false negatives) while minimizing the number of incorrect matches (false positives).
- If the business does not want to miss the true matches, it must see more incorrect matches (false positives).
- Is it more important have fewer false negatives or fewer false positives? What is the impact to your business and processes from one or the other?
- Think forward to merging the records. Is there more risk in merging records that should not be merged or in not merging records that should be merged? This decision will vary with the type of application. For example, most financial systems prefer false negative errors over false positives. A bank would rather explain why they didn't know a customer had both a home loan and a car loan, than to explain why they deducted money from the wrong customer's account. On the other hand, most security and law enforcement applications prefer false positive errors over false negative. They would rather stop and verify the identity of several people who actually have access rights, than to let one bad actor who does not have access rights get into the system. Perhaps the most difficult is healthcare. For example, there could be significant adverse events connected with both false positive and false negative errors on a medical record used by a physician for diagnosis and treatment. Many times, once a record is merged, it cannot be easily unmerged. Find out from your tool vendor what options, if any, are available for unmerging should that be needed.

Resolve the Duplicates

If the goal of the matching was to identify related records and link them, then no records will actually be merged, and this step would not apply. Ensure the appropriate links are made. A good resource is the book *Data Quality and Record Linkage Techniques* by Herzog, Scheuren, and Winkler (2007).

Resolving the duplicates means that the set of matched records needs to become one record. As mentioned, this can be done by: 1) Selecting one record as the "master" and merging additional information into it from duplicate records, or 2) Choosing which source provides the best data for each field and build a new "best-of-breed" record from the various duplicate records.

Carefully plan the merge process:

- Identify all systems that will be impacted by the merging of records. Are there any changes to those systems that must be accounted for? Can you delete or change master records if open transactional records, such as invoices or sales orders, are still associated with it? If not, how will the record be handled (e.g., flag the duplicate master record so that it will no longer be used, and then delete it after all the associated transactional records have been closed). Whatever the approach, ensure time and resources for these activities are included in the project plan.
- Maintain a complete cross-reference of old to new identifiers throughout the project and retain for future reference. One operational team used the cross-references created during the project for months after the project was over.

Tools

Recognize that some tools may have combined functionalities of profiling, standardization, matching, and merging in one tool.

A data profiling tool can provide some high-level checks for uniqueness (usually based on an exact string match). It can easily show if all records in an identification field are unique. Anything more rigorous than that usually requires a specialized tool.

Third-party tools that perform match and merge are sometimes referred to simply as data cleansing tools, and they include other functionality besides identifying duplicates. See *Tools for Managing Data Quality* in *Chapter 6* for more information. Some of the same functionality used to dedupe records can be built into the front end when capturing data such as searching for existing records through an application interface before creating a new record.

There have been automated match and merge algorithms for many years. Often these algorithms were run against a dataset, manually reviewed, and then automated once the results were felt to reflect what looked like legitimate matches. Then the tool was used to merge the records and create survivor records. Once again, manually reviewing and then automating only after the output of merged records were acceptable. Another option is testing and automating the match process, with the merging process always being manual. With the advent of machine learning and artificial intelligence being applied to deduplication, much more of the process has been automated.

You will often be told that you don't have to do anything – the tool will take care of it all. Don't believe it. Make sure you review examples of both matches (duplicates) and also of survivor records after merging. Ensure the algorithms are resulting in legitimate matches or nonmatches and that records are being appropriately merged.

Approach

1. State the expected goal from this data quality dimension.

Be clear on the desired outcome. For example, in one company a high-level duplicate assessment was conducted to provide input to decide which application should be considered the source of reference for the particular data. This was a one-time only assessment lasting about one month. In another project, a new customer master was being created from several sources. The records from this customer master were to be migrated into a new platform. This required months of work and intensive use of a tool to match and merge records. In another project, the goal was to uncover relationships and link records, but not to merge records. However, if the objective is a first look at duplication rates to determine if further work in this area is needed, then resolving the duplicates may not be done initially. The goal influences the amount of time and who should be involved.

2. Determine the tool(s) to use for finding and resolving matches.

This is where you will most likely use a third-party tool or one that may have already been developed in-house. Knowing how the business looks at duplicates and how the data is held within the data model goes hand-in-hand with how a particular tool identifies duplicates.

If a tool has to be purchased, this step can be quite time-consuming as you will go through whatever process your company requires for software acquisition (research options, determine tool selection criteria, schedule demos, make a purchase decision, negotiate and finalize the contract, obtain and install the software). If a tool is currently available, check your licensing agreement and ensure that the contract is up-to-date.

In either case, you will need training in order to use the particular tool. Remember, all explanations in this data quality dimension are for a general understanding of the concepts behind duplication. Features and a particular approach to deduplication will vary depending on the tool you use – understand them.

3. Analyze and prepare the data for matching.

Most tools come with out-of-the-box algorithms, but they need to be tuned to your specific data. You will translate business needs to the rules and algorithms the tool requires. For example, you may have to make decisions, such as which combination of fields indicates a unique record, which fields will be compared and criteria for matching, standardization rules, deduplication algorithms, weights, and thresholds. Expect several rounds of testing to get your standardization and matching routines to an acceptable level.

Expect difficulty in preparing the data and matching across languages. In countries like Switzerland, where multiple languages are spoken and multiple languages are reflected in the data, it may be difficult to programmatically see what language is being used in order to standardize the data. You will have to use different algorithms and thresholds for different languages and address formats.

You will also have to deal with differences in how the data was entered and the point of reference and knowledge of the person who performed the data entry. For example, a person in France entering a French address and a person in Germany entering the same French address often do so in very different ways.

Allow plenty of time for analysis activities. Analysis is critical to obtaining successful results when you are ready to perform the matching.

4. Design the data capture plan and the process for identifying and resolving duplicates.

See *Design Data Capture and Assessment Plans* in *Chapter 6*. Include the following:

- Understand the approach for the underlying algorithms, the process, and the terms used by the chosen tool.
- What is the population of interest and associated selection criteria (both business and technical)?
- Who will extract the data and when; what output format is needed?
- Who will run the data through the tool and when?
- Will the process only identify matches, or will records also go through the merge/survivorship process?
- At what point will results be reviewed before going to the next step?
- Who will analyze results and share them?
- What metrics will be gathered and what reporting is required?
- What training is required to use the tool(s)?

5. Capture the data.

Extract, access, or capture the data according to plan.

6. Identify the matches and analyze results.

Run the tool to uncover potential duplicates or matches. Review results. Modify tool as needed, for example adjusting standardization routines, threshold levels, and matching algorithms. Flag records that show as duplicates but are acceptable to leave as is.

I realize the promise of all automation with no human intervention is appealing. Still, look at some of the results from the matching and ensure you are satisfied with them before moving to merge/survivorship.

7. Resolve duplicates.

Once duplicates are identified, following are options for resolving duplicates through the merge process:

- **Manual merging.** Done by a person using a standard application interface, an application developed specifically for manually merging the duplicates, or through a third-party tool with the capability to manually merge records. Rules for manual merging should be tested and documented. Train all those who will be merging the records. It is unlikely that large numbers of records would be manually merged as part of the standard process.

- **Automated merging**. Run the matched records through the tool. Analyze results and make adjustments as needed. Review-adjust-repeat until satisfied that records will be merged correctly. Only then should the process for merging records be fully automated.

- **Combination manual and automated merging**. Automated merging for the majority of the records and manually merge for records where merging would be more complicated. For example, records that fall in the "grey area" discussed earlier may always have to be handled manually. Ensure resources are planned to handle these in a timely manner. Be clear on the criteria for what will be automated vs. manually merged and how the match sets will be classified as one or the other. Also, manual merging is helpful while experience is gained in how to automate the merging process.

- **Non-merging (virtual merging) systems**. Merging duplicate records into a survivor record is primarily the legacy of limited and expensive storage. With the advent of low-cost storage and Big Data tools, it is feasible to keep every match set (cluster) of duplicate records. While it costs in storage, this approach provides many other positive advantages. (1) It preserves the unique variations of attribute values in each record. For example, previous customer addresses, name variations, and phone numbers. Often such variations could be important, but they are lost when creating a merged (survivor) record with a limited number of fixed attributes. (2) It is much easier to recover from a false positive (over-merge) error. Because the original records are still intact, they can be sorted out (re-linked) and re-clustered correctly. (3) Creating a single "golden record" for all application many not always work. While one application might want the best billing address, another might want the best mailing address, and another the best winter or summer occupancy address. Creating business rules to analyze all of the historical records for the same customer can sometimes be a better approach than trying to anticipate and create special fields for all of these contingencies. (4) Under some regulations, data governance requires more transparency and the ability to trace the lineage of the data as it moves through the system from source to final product. Merging and consolidating data reduces this visibility. The extreme of this non-merge approach is sometimes called the Data Lake. It requires all source information to be preserved in its original form in a large repository (the lake) prior to any operations on the data. Because data is only transformed when reading from the lake, it is sometimes called "transform on read" versus the traditional "transform

on write" where data first goes through an ETL (extract, transform, load) process before writing the data into a fixed database schema. For this reason, it sometimes called ELT (extract, load, transform), i.e., load into the lake before transforming it.

For any of the options, put cross-references and audit trails in place. Ensure you know how, and if, merged records can be unmerged.

8. Analyze, synthesize, recommend, document and act on results.

See the section by the same name in *Chapter 6*. Keep the goals of your deduplication effort in mind. Consider the following questions:

- What level of duplication was found? Does duplication vary by country, geographic region, product line, or some other category that is meaningful to your organization?
- Is the level of duplication significant? What is the impact of the duplicates to the business? Has anything learned during the assessment provided enough information about impact to determine if it is worthwhile to continue addressing duplicates?
- How will the resolution of duplicate records be handled? If merging master records, will there be any issues with open transactional records associated with them? How will the merging of records affect other downstream processes?
- How can duplicates be prevented? What potential root causes and initial recommendations for prevention and correction should be documented for use in future steps?
- If this was an initial assessment, what have you learned that will determine how match and merge will be handled in the future? On an ad-hoc basis? As a scheduled batch job on a regular basis? Integrated into another application and used in real time? Manual vs. automated merging? Which tools?

Tools and processes can be built into production processes to prevent future data errors (*Step 7 – Prevent Future Data Errors*) or used to correct current data errors (*Step 8 – Correct Current Data Errors*). They may also be used when implementing ongoing controls (*Step 9 – Implement Controls*).

9. Communicate and engage throughout this step.

This is particularly important if this step takes longer than a few weeks. Update stakeholders. Let them know progress and keep them informed of any roadblocks. Remind them why addressing duplicates is important. Engage with those providing input to match rules and reviewing results. Keep in contact with tool vendors and technology partners who may be running the tool itself or supporting the tool from the back end. Ensure all stakeholders that will be impacted by merging duplicate records are kept informed early and throughout this process.

Sample Output and Templates

Ten Steps in Action

Using Data Quality Dimensions to Improve Reports

As I was writing the book, an email came from a workshop attendee as to how he successfully leveraged the Ten Steps Process. Success was demonstrated in various ways: improved reports for the institution, positive recognition by his Director, acceptance of the approach by teammates, the ability to reuse in other situations, and the resulting personal satisfaction and recognition.

I will let Phil Johnston, Special Projects Administrator, tell it in his own words:

A couple of months ago my Director asked me and a colleague to review some new departmental reports and dashboards and conduct some quality assurance (but didn't specify much about how). Our department had created some new reports and arguably released them prematurely for external testing beyond our Department but within our institution. Initial feedback had suggested that they needed much more cautious review before being shared so myself and a colleague were to conduct the QA on them.

Having remembered attending your workshop, I looked at my notes, the workshop manual and used the Ten Steps Process, specifically *Step 3 – Assessing Data Quality*, using various data quality dimensions including Presentation Quality, Data Specifications, Duplication, Consistency and Synchronization. This approach, demonstrating rigour and grounded in learnings and professional development from conferences attended, was received really well by teammates and especially by my Director.

The review conducted, the approach, and the changes identified has led to much improved reports for us to share within our institution in terms of clarity of terminology, consistency with other data, and accuracy in presentation. My Director is eager to apply the model, or something similar to it, to other aspects of a Data Governance program we have going. Last week in my Annual Performance Review, the Director specifically identified this (along with other successful work throughout the year) as evidence of very desirable behaviour and I received a glowing review. I thought you would appreciate hearing a specific example of how your work has been used and brought back for use / integration.

Step 3.6 | Consistency and Synchronization

Business Benefit and Context

The data quality dimension of Consistency and Synchronization refers to the equivalence of data stored or used in various datastores, applications, and systems. This assessment compares data at points throughout its life cycle when stored or used in various data stores, applications, processes, and the like, and determines if it is consistent. Consistency refers to the idea that if the same data is stored and used in various places in the organization, the data should be equivalent – that is, the same data should represent the same fact and be conceptually equal. It indicates that the data have equal values and meanings or are in essence the same. Synchronization is the process of making the data equivalent.

When data is stored in multiple places it is considered redundant. Whether redundancy in detailed records is wanted or unwanted, necessary or unnecessary, is usually determined in *Step 3.5 – Uniqueness and Deduplication*. When assessing consistency and synchronization, as you learn about the information life cycle and environment around each datastore it may become clear that some datastores are unnecessarily redundant, and others are required. Recommendations to do further research to resolve the unnecessary redundancy should be captured in the results from this step.

For example, your company makes (manufactures) some parts for building products and buys other parts. A make part is indicated in the first database as M. In another database a make part is coded as 44. Any make part record moved from the first database with a value of M should be stored in the second database with a value of 44. If it is, the data is equivalent and still consistent. If not, the data is different and not consistent.

An example of being consistent, but not directly equivalent, may be in a hierarchy where one system shows medical specialty as breast cancer and another shows medical specialty as oncology. They are not equivalent but they are consistent.

Consistency and synchronization are important because the same data is often stored in many different places in the company. Any use of the data should be based on those data having the same meaning. It is not uncommon for management reports on the same topic to have different results. This leaves management in the uncomfortable position of not really knowing the "truth" of what is happening in the company and makes effective decisions difficult.

The same technique of data profiling used in *Step 3.3 – Data Integrity Fundamentals* is also used here against each datastore and results compared for consistency. The measures of completeness and validity are particularly pertinent to consistency and synchronization. This dimension is called out separately from Data Integrity Fundamentals so you can better plan and coordinate for the additional resources that are required to look across multiple data sets. Each datastore that is profiled and compared adds time and may require different people to capture and analyze the data.

Definition

Consistency and Synchronization (Data Quality Dimension). Equivalence of data stored or used in various datastores, applications, and systems.

Approach

1. Identify the datastores that will be compared for consistency.

Use what you learned about the information life cycle, the data, and technology in *Step 2 – Analyze Information Environment*. If you haven't already, create a visual to show the various locations where the data is stored. This will help guide your decisions when developing the data capture and assessment plan.

2. Identify the detail for each field of interest in each datastore where it resides.

This is a detailed mapping of the same data as they are stored in each datastore. Refer to *Step 2.2 – Understand Relevant Data and Data Specifications*.

3. Develop the data capture and assessment plans.

See section on this topic in *Chapter 6: Other Techniques and Tools*. Planning is particularly important for this dimension since you will be capturing data from multiple datastores. Be clear on the population (selection criteria) of the records to be captured and assessed. You will capture a subset of data from the first datastore and select the corresponding records from each datastore as those records flow through the information life cycle, so the timing is vital. You may capture complete records for the population of interest but decide to compare only a subset of the data fields in those records.

If you also care about the impact of timing between the two data stores, you may want to do this together with *Step 3.7 – Timeliness*.

4. Capture the data according to plan.

Capture the data from the first datastore and select the corresponding records from each additional datastore.

5. Assess and analyze the data according to plan.

Use the technique of data profiling from *Step 3.3 – Data Integrity Fundamentals* against the data in each additional datastore. Compare results between the datastores. Comparisons may be done manually or programmatically using custom code. Make use of already-existing programs or third-party tools that could be used for the comparisons.

Determine if one datastore (probably the one as close to the original source data as possible) is considered the authoritative source of reference against which the others should be synchronized. You may decide to compare each data store against the authoritative source and also against the datastore which is the source of the data immediately prior to it in the information life cycle. Realize that you are probably looking at completeness and validity, not accuracy.

Note the differences and where in the information life cycle those differences occur. Understand and document the distinction if the data is conceptually equal (e.g., different codes used in different datastores for the same record, but the codes mean the same thing) versus the data is different (e.g., the codes in the same record in different datastores mean something different). Look at the technical process of synchronization between the datastores to understand why the data is different. Look at the business processes, people/organizations, and technology to see how these may create those differences.

Use the results of the comparisons and what you learned about the information life cycle and environment around each datastore to determine if the redundant datastores are necessary or not.

6. Synthesize, make recommendations, document, and act on results.

See the section of the same name in *Chapter 6: Other Techniques and Tools* for more details.

Compare results from this dimension against results from other dimensions that may have been assessed. Make preliminary recommendations based on what you know now. Highlight if it is clear that the redundancy is unnecessary and unwanted. Document lessons learned such as potential impact to the business and possible root causes. Act on results when the time is right – some actions can be taken immediately while others may have to wait.

7. Share results.

Determine who needs to hear results, such as other core team members, extended team members, project manager, sponsors, other stakeholders, and owners of the datastores where data was assessed. Ensure communications are at the appropriate level of detail and focus on the interests of the audience. Obtain feedback such as their reactions to the results. Were they expected or unexpected? Outline initial recommendations and possible timing for implementation. Obtain support as necessary for your next steps in the project.

Sample Output and Templates

 Ten Steps in Action

Consistency and Synchronization

Background—Sales reps in the company were one of the main vehicles for obtaining customer information. That information eventually made its way through various processes and ended up in the Customer Master Database, where it was further moved and used in transactional and reporting systems. The project team looked at the high-level information life cycle (an output of *Step 2 – Analyze Information Environment*) to determine all systems where the data was stored. Because of resource constraints they could not assess consistency for every system at the time.

Focus—The team decided to focus on the front end of the information life cycle and assess data for consistency between the Customer Master Database and just one of the transactional systems that used the customer data – the Service and Repair Application (SRA).

Inquiry, the "override" flag—The project team paid particular attention to what is called the "override" flag. When phone reps created service orders, the SRA allowed them to override data pulled in from the Customer Master Database. The team wanted to understand the magnitude of the differences for those records where the override flag was set to yes (Y) and the nature of the differences in the data.

(Continued)

Ten Steps in Action *(Continued)*

Capture the data—The project team extracted records from the SRA where the override flag was set to Y. They then extracted the associated records from the Customer Master Database. When performing the comparisons, the Customer Master Database was considered the system of record. The project team used a data profiling tool to profile each dataset and then compared them for equivalence.

Method – random sample and manual comparison—For some data elements (such as company name and address) the comparison

was done manually. In addition, the team wanted to further segment the results to see if there were significant differences between countries in the SRA. A random sample of the population from profiling for each country was selected for the manual comparison.

See *Step 3.7 – Timeliness* for a continuation of this example that includes the timeliness dimension.

Results—*Template 4.3.2* shows the template used to report results of the manual comparisons for consistency.

Template 4.3.2 Consistency Results

Summary: Consistency for Country 1*		
	Count (#)	Percentage (%)
Total closed orders from Service and Repair Application		
Orders with override flag = Y		

Analysis of Orders with Changes	Number of Overrides	% Type of Overrides	% of Total Records
MAJOR – Company names and address completely changed			
MAJOR – Address attributes changed; indicates different physical location or different site			
Minor or no changes			
Impact: 35 percent of orders have major changes to company name and/or address. This data, which is assumed to be the most up to date, is lost when the repair order is closed and is not reflected in the Customer Master Database.			

Summary: Consistency of Repair Addresses	Country 1	Country 2	Country 3
Total number of service orders in Quarter 1			
Total number of service orders with override flag			
Sample size			
Company name and address completely changed			
Address attributes changed			
Override flag on, but no changes to name or address			
SRA number not in Customer Master Database			

* There was one consistency report for each country examined.

Timeliness

Business Benefit and Context

Data values change over time, and there will always be a gap, however large or small, between when the real-world object changes and when data representing it is updated in a database and ready to be utilized. This gap is referred to as information float. There can be manual float (the delay from when a fact becomes known to when it is first captured electronically) and electronic float (time from when a fact is first captured electronically to when it is moved or

copied to various databases that make it available to those wanting to access it). This assessment examines the timing of information throughout its life cycle and shows if data is up to date and available in time to meet business needs. As Tom Redman points out, "Timeliness is related to currency – data are current if they are up-to-date and are the usual results of a timely information chain" (2001, p. 227). Latency, the time interval or delay between a data packet moving from one node to another, is another word used in relation to timeliness.

Assessing timeliness may be quite detailed as in the example in *Sample Output and Templates*. Other times, just the idea of timeliness may spur us to action. As I write this book, with the number of businesses being partially or fully closed at various times during the worldwide COVID-19 pandemic, keeping store hours updated on their websites is very important. From a consumer point of view, I want to know that at any time I look at a store's website, that the correct hours are there, no matter how often they changed during these uncertain times. That is timeliness. In this case, a full assessment of data as it traverses the information life cycle is not needed. What is needed is to immediately put a process into place so when decisions are made about the store hours, they are quickly passed onto the person who can reflect those changes on the website. The purpose of the data quality dimensions is to provide information about our data so we can make informed decisions and take effective action. The quicker we get to the right actions the better.

> **Definition**
>
> **Timeliness (Data Quality Dimension).** Data and information are current and ready for use as specified and in the time frame in which they are expected.

Approach

1. Confirm the information life cycle within scope.

Review the information life cycle developed in *Step 2.6 – Understand Relevant Information Life Cycle* and update if necessary. See the *Ten Steps in Action callout box* for an example.

2. Develop the data capture and assessment plans for assessing timeliness.

See section on this topic in *Chapter 6: Other Techniques and Tools*.

You may want to assess timeliness together with *Step 3.6 – Consistency and Synchronization*.

Determine which phases of the information life cycle to assess for timeliness. Ideally, you will be able to look at the complete life cycle, but you may need to focus on only a portion. If possible, start at the source and move forward.

Determine the process for measuring information float between each step. Work with your information technology group to understand the timing of updates and load schedules of the various datastores. See if this can be done automatically. If not, then document manually. If necessary, have data producers keep a log of date and time when specific occurrences of data become known during the assessment period.

Work with a statistician to determine the number of records to trace for a valid sample. Work with technology partners to determine how a random sample of records will be captured at the first point in the information life cycle and traced forward.

3. Capture data and assess timeliness according to plan.

Select a random sample of records to trace through the information life cycle.

Determine the time elapsed between the steps in the process for each of the records. Document the start time, stop time, and elapsed time for each step in the process. Be sure to take geographic locations and time zones into account.

4. Analyze, synthesize, recommend, document and act on results.

See the section of the same name in *Chapter 6: Other Techniques and Tools* for more details.

What are the timeliness requirements? When does the information need to be available at each point in the life cycle? Are processes and responsibilities completed in a timely manner? If not, why not? What can be changed to ensure timeliness?

Document results and recommended actions. Include lessons learned, possible impact on the business, and potential root causes.

Sample Output and Templates

 Ten Steps in Action

Timeliness

The Situation—This continues the example from *Step 3.6 – Consistency and Synchronization*. The assessment for consistency was completed. Next the business wanted to understand the timing of events as the data moved through the information life cycle. A subset of the life cycle for one country was examined in detail for timeliness. The process started when the change was made in the real-world and continued through several steps to when the information was available for use in the Service and Repair Application (SRA).

The Requirements—Changes to customer information must be reflected in the Customer Master Database and made available for transactional use within 24 hours of knowledge of the change. All sales reps should synchronize their personal handheld databases with the central database every evening (Monday through Friday) by 6 p.m. US Pacific Time.

Table 4.3.6 shows the results of tracking one record through the process. *Table 4.3.7* shows results after compiling and analyzing output from all records tracked for timeliness.

Table 4.3.6 Tracking and Recording Timeliness

Information Life Cycle Process	Date	Time	Elapsed Time	Notes
Customer changes location	Unknown	Unknown		
Company notifies sales rep of change – via email	Monday, March 5	8:00 am		
Sales rep reads email	Monday, March 5	11:30 am	3.5 hours	
Sales rep updates personal handheld	Monday, March 5	6:00 pm	6.5 hours	

(Continued)

Ten Steps in Action *(Continued)*

Table 4.3.6 Tracking and Recording Timeliness *(Continued)*

Information Life Cycle Process	Date	Time	Elapsed Time	Notes
Sales rep synchronizes data with central Customer Master Database	Friday, March 9	8:00 pm	98 hours (4 days and 2 hours)	
Customer Master Database batch processing starts	Monday, March 12	8:00 pm	72 hours (3 days)	Synchronization missed Friday processing.* Records not processed until Monday evening.
Updates available for transactional systems (when batch processing completes)	Monday, March 12	11:00 pm	3 hours	
Used by Service and Repair Application (SRA) **				
Total			183 hours	

Note: All times US Pacific Standard Time

* Customer Master Database starts batch processing daily (Monday – Friday) at 8:00 pm. When processing is complete (approximately 3 hours), the changes are available for transactional systems.
** Time tracking forward to various transactional and reporting uses (e.g., sales reps taking calls from customers and creating service orders) was determined to be out of scope at this time.

Table 4.3.7 Timeliness Results and Initial Recommendations

Number of records tracked:
Number of associated sales reps:
Timeliness Assessment Period:

	Average	High	Low
Length of time from customer changes known by sales rep until changes available to be used by transactional and reporting systems			
Sales rep's time to complete synchronization	35 min.	90 min.	15 min.
Number of times a month sales reps synchronize personal databases with Customer Master Database	2	4	0

Findings	Suspected Root Causes	Initial Recommendations
Longer than expected delays occur between when sales reps learn about changes and when data can be used by rest of the company.	See below	Assess impact to business use of transactional data when changes are delayed, to determine if recommendations should be pursued.
Most sales reps rarely synchronize databases more than two times a month.	Sales reps generally synchronize personal databases with central Customer Master Database at end of day – usually after 6:30 pm US Pacific. Technical problems often prevent reps from completing synchronization. IT help desk is not open after 7:00 pm. No technical help available when needed.	Investigate and correct causes of technical issues that prevent synchronization. Is there a way to simplify the synchronization process?
Updates from Friday evening's synchronization often miss Friday's batch processing, thus delaying the availability of the updates until Monday evening.	Daily batch processing starts at 8:00 pm. Most sales reps don't synchronize their databases until after that time.	Check into update schedules for the Customer Master Database. Are there any changes to the processing schedule that better fit into sales rep timing for synchronization?
New sales reps synchronize databases less than once a month.	New sales reps do not know how to complete the synchronization.	Train sales reps in synchronization process.
Some sales reps do not synchronize their databases at all.	Sales reps don't know what happens to their data once it leaves their personal databases. There is distrust of the central system.	Do we need to survey some of the sales reps to understand more about their distrust before finalizing recommendations? Document and educate sales reps on use of their customer data. Work with sales managers to devise incentives for synchronizing databases.

Step 3.8 | Access

Business Benefit and Context

Access, as a Data Quality Dimension, refers to the ability to control how authorized users can view, modify, use, or otherwise process data and information. It is often summed up as enabling the right individuals to access the right resources, at the right times, under the right circumstances. The term can refer to a discipline, set of tools, processes, practices, or a combination. Access Management (AM) is sometimes referred to as Access Control, Identity and Access Management (IAM), or Identity and Access Governance (IAG).

Who defines the right individual, right resources, right times, and right circumstances? These are business decisions, which need to balance enabling access against protecting sensitive data and information. Most organizations have high-level policies which define principles for access and specify how decisions are made. Business and/or compliance teams then create specific business rules or requirements to define access to types of resources for types of authorized users. Technical teams are involved in translating those business requirements into controls that work to manage how authorized users of systems can access the data and information made available through user interfaces.

This data quality dimension of Access also affects other dimensions. For example, data cannot be considered usable and transactable if the people who must use the data are not authorized to have necessary access to it. See *Step 3.13 – Usability and Transactability*.

Thanks to Gwen Thomas, Sr. Compliance Officer, The World Bank Group, for her help and expertise in writing in this section.

 Definition

Access (Data Quality Dimension). The ability to control how authorized users can view, modify, use, or otherwise process data and information.

Relationship with Other Teams Who Manage Access

See *Figure 4.3.7* for functions that typically manage access. Your data quality team should work closely with them if your project addresses this data quality dimension of Access.

Data quality teams working with other data quality dimensions learn how to translate principles into business requirements and technical or process controls. While these teams may never work on access-related projects, it is common for the same sets of business stakeholders to define multiple types of requirements. And so, workshops may reveal both data quality requirements and requirements for users' access to data and information through systems' user interfaces. It is helpful for those who collect or interpret

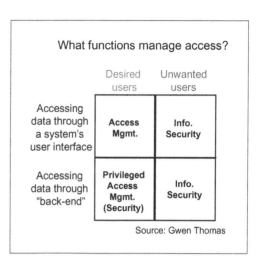

What functions manage access?

	Desired users	Unwanted users
Accessing data through a system's user interface	**Access Mgmt.**	**Info. Security**
Accessing data through "back-end"	**Privileged Access Mgmt. (Security)**	**Info. Security**

Source: Gwen Thomas

Figure 4.3.7 Functions typically managing access.

data quality requirements to understand the basic concepts behind Access Management.

Access Management teams frequently work with Information Security (InfoSec) teams that manage risks associated with privileged users. This class of users includes database administrators and others whose jobs require special levels of access, often bypassing system controls and accessing data through back-end technologies. The activities for managing risk for this type of users is referred to as Privileged Access Management (PAM).

InfoSec teams also manage risks associated with unwanted or unauthorized users. Staff Security Training often includes use cases in which someone pretending to be an authorized user (a "phisher") asks to be provided data or sign-on credentials. It is good practice for data quality teams to reinforce security good practices when working with stakeholders.

Protecting data and information against unauthorized users ("hackers") who break into systems is also the purview of InfoSec teams. See *Step 3.9 – Security and Privacy* for more details.

Understanding Access Requirements

Understanding access management requirements involves understanding users, the types of access they are being granted under different conditions, the data they are being granted access to, and the granularity of access rights for that data. *Figure 4.3.8* illustrates how those who might attempt to access data stored or processed in IT systems can be classified.

Classifying Data Users—For the purposes of access management requirements, users may be sorted into personas or types. "Desired Users" versus "Unwanted Users" is a simple form of classification. There can be many ways to sub-classify desired users, each with their own requirements. Examples are Staff vs. Non-Staff, Active vs. Inactive, Managers vs. Non-Managers, Retail Customers

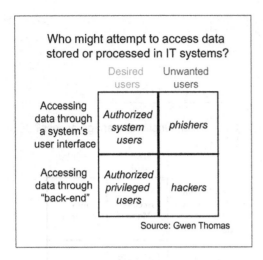

Figure 4.3.8 Classifying data users.

vs. Wholesale Customers. Often, classification of a user involves choosing between more than two options: examples are by the user's Country, Employer, Profession, Job Classification, Project, Work Location, Assignment, Membership in a Group, or Role they are playing. When this is the case, access requirements probably pull these values from data sets that are collected and maintained as reference data or master data. The quality of those data sets is an assumption often made by Access Management teams. It may be worthwhile to check the quality of those datasets as part of the assessment of Access.

Classifying Actions and Guidelines—Access requirements specify what authorized individuals can do with data or information. Often, high-level principles will include words like "use" or "view" which need more precise definition in practice. Well fleshed-out access requirements might answer questions such as: Can the user view the data ONLY on the screen, or can they also print out a copy? Does the time of day or day of week matter? Does using the data mean the individual can share it with a teammate? How about with a project member who is not an employee? If the data is editable by anyone, should THIS type of user be able to edit it?

Classifying Data—Just as with users, there are many ways to classify data. It may be classified according to functionality, subject area, status in a workflow, or other criteria. See examples of types of data (underlined) embedded in the requirements below. Terms marked with an asterisk (*) refer to data that probably exists as reference data and has unique values that must be factored into access requirements (e.g., which Shift).

- A Physician can modify the <u>Physician Notes</u> of her own Patients.
- A Nurse can view the <u>Patient Charts</u> of all Patients in her unit.
- A Technician can view the <u>Prescription Schedule</u> for a Patient that has been assigned to him, but only during his Shift*, and using his unit's Equipment*.
- No Hospital Staff can access <u>Patient Records</u> from Personal Devices*.
- Official Devices holding <u>Corporate Data</u> must be powered off and locked while going through Security Procedures* at any Transportation Hub*.

Good definitions are essential for translating access requirements into actionable controls. In the examples above, all capitalized terms would need to be clearly defined. Good data quality practices include validating whether definitions used in access management requirements match those used for other dimensions of data quality.

Aggregation of Data—Aggregate data refers to information that is collected from multiple records or sources and compiled into summaries. In some circumstances, aggregate data may not be considered sensitive, but the *details* that have been rolled up into the aggregate *are* sensitive. Example rules:

- We publicly disclose the number of medical staff deployed by country, but not by city.
- The total number of medical staff deployed per month is not sensitive, but the names or other identifiers of individual staff are considered Strictly Confidential and are not to be made available to any type of user through the dashboard.
- If the dashboard user is staff but does not have the role of Statistician, the dashboard must not allow drilling down past city-level summaries.
- If the dashboard user is staff and also has the role of Statistician, the user can drill down through counts of deployed medical staff by region, country, city, hospital, and even isolation wards within each hospital.

From the above example rules, we can infer that detailed hospital-level data is stored in the dashboard's data source. Dashboard functionality allows data to be displayed at its most detailed level to some users, or to be rolled up into aggregate summaries for other users.

Levels of Access—Now imagine that a physician is given a key card that enables physical access to a hospital. What access rights does the key card grant? Does it merely get the physician into the building? Or does it both open the building and unlock the entrance to patient floors? Does it also open another lock, for the isolation ward? Does the key card even unlock the medicine cabinet in the isolation ward?

We could say that the key card provides only "course-grained access" if it only authorizes the physician to enter the building. We could say it authorizes "medium-grained access" if it enables the physician to also enter patient floors. And, we could say the key card provides "fine-grained access" if it authorizes the physician to enter the isolation ward, and perhaps even open the medicine cabinet.

Access requirements for data can similarly address course-grained, medium grained, or fine-grained access rights. An IT system with coarse-grained data access follows an "all or nothing" pattern. Every authorized system user can view all data within the system. If the system employs medium-grained data access, some segmentation is in place. Users might have access to some system modules, but not to others. If an IT system employs fine-grained data access, then detailed rules enforce access to selected data. It might be specified records in a database ("my patients" but not "all patients"). It might be certain types of data in the database ("prescription information" but not "billing information"). It might mean that only certain fields in a record are made visible ("prescription name" but not "prescription price").

When applying the "just-enough" principle to access management requirements, it is important to reach agreement on the level of access needed. After all, a key card programmed with only course-grained access could be freely handed out to physicians of all specialties. On the other hand, hundreds of business rules might be required to specify individualized fine-grained access that distinguishes between types of departments, and locked rooms within those departments mapped against physicians' specialties and other factors.

Key Concept

"Leadership expectations are moving toward **fine-grained access**. This capability allows organizations to share more data with staff, while protecting sensitive information. Staff who are skilled in collecting Data Quality requirements can be invaluable to Access Management programs."

– Gwen Thomas, Sr. Compliance Officer, The World Bank Group

Approach

1. Determine whether Access Management teams are stakeholders in Data Quality projects.

When undertaking a project to improve data quality for a set of data, determine whether Access requirements apply to that data. If so, the Access Management team should be included as stakeholders.

2. Determine whether Access issues are affecting perceived data quality.

Sometimes consumers of information are not authorized to access the golden source of data that has been subjected to quality controls. Instead, they are accessing copies that do not have the same controls applied. The data consumer may perceive a data quality issue, when the fix could be gaining access to a better source.

3. Share data definitions.

Many data quality and data governance teams have great expertise and experience in developing actionable definitions. Consider whether Access Management teams are aware of standardized terms and how they might be leveraged in Access Management projects. This is a good place to make use of metadata and other data specifications that were uncovered in *Step 2.2 – Understand Relevant Data and Data Specifications* or *Step 3.2 – Data Specifications*.

4. Share standards for access requirements.

Many organizations consider moving from medium-grained access to fine-grained access as part of updating IT systems. However, technical resources might not be trained in writing precise and actionable access business requirements. If this skill is a strength of your data quality team, consider sharing your expertise and standards with technology teams.

5. Share access requirements in a concise format.

One key tool for project managers for any type of project is a matrix that shows who has what type of responsibility for what task within a project. Such matrices place individuals (or roles or business units) on one axis, and tasks on another, with assigned responsibilities in the boxes of the grid. See *Figure 4.3.9* for an example of a Responsibility Matrix.

Similar matrices can be used to concisely collect and display access rights. A note: all terms used in any responsibility matrix or access rights matrix should be carefully and clearly defined (e.g., Provide, Collect, Data Owner, Conduct Gap Analysis).

6. Analyze, synthesize, make recommendations, document, and act on results.

See the section of the same name in *Chapter 6: Other Techniques and Tools* for more details.

After this point, a data quality team would probably not be expected to assess whether current access rights are compliant with the access requirements defined in this step. Rather, they might be expected to share their findings with the appropriate Access Management or Security Teams, who would then be responsible for acting upon them.

Sample Output and Templates

Access rights matrices can address course-grained, medium grained, or fine-grained access rights. They are also useful for visualizing potential gaps in requirements. See *Figures 4.3.10* and *4.3.11* for examples of Access Control Requirements. The roles are listed down the left-hand side, with each row representing a role. The columns represent the data to be accessed. The interaction matrix indicates the type of access allowed. The first figure shows gaps (in bold). The second figure shows the same matrix with access requirements plus corresponding controls at the bottom.

Example Responsibility Matrix				
Roles \ *Tasks*	*Collect Requirements*	*Conduct Gap Analysis*	*Propose Solution*	*Build Solution*
Data Owners	**Provide**	**Validate**	**Approve**	**Accept**
Analysts	**Collect**	**Conduct**	**Concur**	**Test**
Technical Team	**Review**	**Contribute**	**Propose**	**Build**
Standard Font = Roles, *Italic = Tasks*, **Bold = Responsibility**				Source: Gwen Thomas

Figure 4.3.9 Example responsibility matrix.

Data / Role	Physician Notes	Patient Charts	Prescription Schedule	Patient Records	Official Devices holding Corporate Data
Example Access Requirements - with Gaps Noted					
Physician	Can modify, but only for own Patients	**Rule is needed**	**Rule is needed**	Physician must be prevented from accessing Patient Records from Personal devices. **Does this need exception for Physicians?**	Must power off and lock while going through Security Procedures at any Transportation Hub
Nurse	**Rule is needed**	Can view, but only for Patients in Nurse's Unit	**Rule is needed**	Must be prevented from accessing from Personal devices	
Technician	**Rule is needed**	**Rule is needed**	Can View, but only for Patient assigned to Technician, and only during the Technician's shift, and only via Unit Equipment	Must be prevented from accessing from Personal devices	
					Source: Gwen Thomas

Figure 4.3.10 Example access requirements – with gaps noted.

Data / Role	Physician Notes	Patient Charts	Prescription Schedule	Patient Records	Official Devices holding Corporate Data
Example Access Requirements - with Gaps Noted and Corresponding Controls					
Physician	Can modify, but only for own Patients ①	**Rule is needed**	**Rule is needed**	Physician must be prevented from accessing Patient Records from Personal devices. **Does this need exception for Physicians?**	Must power off and lock while going through Security Procedures at any Transportation Hub ⑤
Nurse	**Rule is needed**	Can view, but only for Patients in Nurse's Unit ②	**Rule is needed**	Must be prevented from accessing from Personal devices ④	
Technician	**Rule is needed**	**Rule is needed**	Can View, but only for Patient assigned to Technician, and only during the Technician's shift, and only via Unit Equipment ③	Must be prevented from accessing from Personal devices ④	

Notes for controls:
① Relies upon matching Physician ID from Physician's login with Physician ID in Patient Record
② Relies upon matching Unit ID in Nurse Shift Records with Unit ID in Patient Record
③ Relies upon multiple data points from multiple records
④ Relies upon technology that recognizes Corporate Devices
⑤ Process control dependent upon user discipline

Source: Gwen Thomas

Figure 4.3.11 Example access requirements – with corresponding controls.

Step 3.9 | Security and Privacy

Business Benefit and Context

Security is the ability to protect data and information assets from unauthorized access, use, disclosure, disruption, modification, or destruction. Privacy for an individual is the ability to have some control over how data about you as a person is collected and used. For an organization, it is the ability to comply with how people want their data to be collected, shared, and used.

Security and privacy are distinct, yet related, and so are together in this data quality dimension. Privacy encompasses security because that is one of the common areas where organizational and technical controls are implemented. For your purposes, you may decide to work with them separately. Privacy and security are often focused on Personal Data (any data relating to a person that could identify them either directly or indirectly) and Personally Identifiable Information (PII). But privacy and security can include other data that does not relate to people or identify them.

Definition

Security and Privacy (Data Quality Dimension). Security is the ability to protect data and information assets from unauthorized access, use, disclosure, disruption, modification, or destruction. Privacy for an individual is the ability to have some control over how data about you as a person is collected and used. For an organization, it is the ability to comply with how people want their data to be collected, shared, and used.

A word about data protection: Data protection is a broader concept over security and privacy. It looks at minimizing risks and harms to people arising from a misuse or abuse of data about them or relating to them. It encompasses the downstream implications of the potential uses of data in the context of the choices people are presented and make and the potential impact that can have on their other rights and freedoms as people. For example, automated processing of data puts you on a watch list and results in your right to travel being curtailed until you get the data quality problem sorted out. Data protection includes privacy (right to be left alone/control over how data is used) but also includes consideration of impacts on other rights and freedoms.

Thanks to Daragh O Brien and Katherine O'Keefe of Castlebridge for their help and expertise in this step.

Security and privacy often require specialized expertise to protect data. This dimension does NOT replace that. I do not expect a data professional to have the skills to protect your organization from malicious internal or external cyberattacks. Data professionals *are* often well positioned to assess who has what type of access to data and to set levels of security, such as public access vs. restricted accesses because of confidentiality, sensitivity, or legal obligations.

Note that the data quality dimension of Access (*Step 3.8*) is focused on access for *authorized* users. Security also includes access, but it is focused on *unauthorized* access.

Data professionals should find and work with information security teams and those responsible for privacy, such as legal, in their organizations to ensure: 1) Appropriate security and privacy safeguards are in place for the data with which they are concerned, 2) They understand the security and privacy requirements with which the data they manage must comply.

This data quality dimension may also encompass the data category of sensitive data. See *Table 3.5* in the *Data Categories* section of *Chapter 3: Key Concepts* for a definition and examples.

Readers may already be familiar with the traditional CIA triad of Confidentiality, Integrity, and Availability that are traditionally considered to be crucial components of information security. In that context, Confidentiality is usually understood as the business and policies that restrict access to data, Integrity is the assurance that the data is trustworthy and accurate, and Availability is the guarantee of access to the information by authorized people.

However, in the context of data protection, confidentiality is one of a number of concerns to be considered, with the focus of data protection and privacy being more on why the data is being processed rather than how confidential it is. Daragh O Brien describes it as follows: "Confidentiality is the price of admission to the game. Data Protection requires you to think about what the game you are playing is, and who the winners and losers might be."

Likewise, the information security concept of Integrity differs from how data quality professionals might understand it. To an information security professional, integrity means that the data has not been altered or deleted during its life cycle so that it is consistent, accurate, and trusted. As such, it spans several of the data quality dimensions discussed in this book, including data integrity fundamentals. From a data protection and privacy perspective, the dimensions of accuracy and consistency, among others, are also important.

Availability in the information security context is focused on the challenges of managing the hardware and infrastructure necessary to ensure authorized access to information in a timely manner, and to ensure timely recovery from outages or disruption to that data access. This is an important consideration in data protection as well, but from the perspective of the impacts on people arising from the disruption to availability, such as not being able to access their bank account because their bank's IT systems are off-line. However, if a systems outage is remedied using a backup that doesn't have the orders from this week's customer purchases, it might be available from an information security perspective, but it does not meet the data quality threshold for timeliness and availability.

Approach

1. Define business needs and approach.

Around the world, data protection laws require organizations to process data for specified purposes – and to refrain from using it for other purposes. Fundamental ethics principles call on people to treat each other as an "end in and of themselves, not simply a means to an end." Therefore, the "Define Business Needs and Approach" step in the Ten Steps is used to define, in clear terms, what the objective of the proposed data processing is and what the target benefits are to both the organization and the people whose data is going to be processed.

Formulating this idea follows a simple problem statement, similar to that described in the Ten Steps:

- We want to do this processing…
- So we can execute this process…
- So we can deliver these benefits to the organization AND
- So we can deliver these benefits to the people whose data we are processing.

If there are other stakeholders who will benefit from the outcomes of the processing, they should also be recognized as part of this problem statement.

Defining the business needs is an iterative process that may be revisited a number of times during a data protection/privacy impact assessment, as often the initial statement of the processing that an organization is proposing can encompass several sub-processes which may present different data protection, privacy, security, or ethical issues or risks. For example, in a data analytics process there may be objectives that can be met without processing identifiable personal data or PII data, but other objectives might present serious risks to privacy or other rights.

Also, this definition serves a second purpose of ensuring time or other resources are not invested in proposed processing which has not been properly thought through by the organization. This is a corollary of W. Edwards Deming's comment that, "If you can't describe what you do as a process, you don't know what you are doing."

2. Analyze the information environment.

Because data protection, privacy, and ethics require us to take our heads out of the data and consider the process that will use that data and the outcomes that will be delivered from that processing, the information environment needs to be considered from a broader perspective.

Legal—What is the legal basis for the processing you are planning to do and for the outcome that it will deliver? Are there any legal reasons why you might not be able to do those things? This means that data management people need to go to their colleagues in legal or in their privacy office early and be able to explain their plans for the data so that the relevant legal environment can be understood correctly.

Process and People—Who are the actors in this process? What are their roles and responsibilities with respect to the data? Are any of the functions going to be outsourced? What will the handovers

between actors be (e.g., file transfer, access to a shared database, or a spreadsheet attached to an email)? What are the critical-to-outcome data quality characteristics that might impact the process? These are just some of the questions that need to be considered as part of the assessment of the process environment and the people and organizations involved. This is especially important if the processing will use a new technology or an existing technology in a novel way.

However, the answers to these questions help us to identify what issues and risks might arise in this process environment. For example, if the process requires data to be transferred to a supplier in another country, this may give rise to data protection issues or additional legal requirements to ensure compliance with data protection and privacy laws.

Data—Consider the following when assessing the data aspects of the information environment in this context:

- What type of data is being processed? Does any of it fall into a protected category of data which might require a higher standard of care? Is there any linking or merging of data that would allow individuals to be singled out in the data which might have privacy or data protection implications?
- How long does this data need to be kept to achieve the goals of the process? Are there other related purposes the organization might need the data for (e.g., regulatory compliance)?
- What are the relevant data quality characteristics for this data? How precise does it need to be (for example, do you need a full date of birth or would a month/year combination suffice)? Do you have sufficient data coverage or completeness of data to meet the objectives of the process? How will errors in the data that are identified be corrected so that impacts on the rights and freedoms of the people whose data is being processed are avoided?
- Are you proposing to process any data that is not necessary for the business need or purpose which has been identified? Can the objective be met with less data (the inverse of data coverage)? Is it necessary to process data that can directly or indirectly identify individuals to achieve the objective of the process?

This is not an exhaustive list of considerations and the specific circumstances of a project or initiative may require other questions to be asked. For example, if a machine learning process is being implemented, you might need to consider the risks of quality, quantity, or bias in the training data that was used to develop the machine learning model, which in turn will result in bias or errors in the implemented algorithms which may have implications for the risks to individuals. The challenges of facial recognition accuracy, particularly with different ethnic groups, is a good example of this.

Social—Because data protection, privacy, and data ethics issues require consideration of the concerns or expectations of the categories of people whose data may be processed, it is important to include an assessment of the social aspects of the proposed processing.

- Does the processing raise any issues that might be the subject of discussion in the media? Do these issues potentially arise in the context of your proposed processing?

- What might be the downstream implications for people arising from the processing? What might they be prevented from doing or be denied access to as a result of the processing?
- Are there any representative groups for categories of individuals who you might consult for their perception of the potential issues and risks to their constituents or members? Bear in mind that the determination of "quality of data protection" should be defined from the point of view of the people who will be affected by the outcomes of the processing. Indeed, in certain circumstances, this can be a legal obligation in some jurisdictions such as the EU.
- What is your organization's internal data management culture or maturity? When implementing new processes or technologies for processing personal data, your existing data management maturity may be a cause of, or potentially a mitigation for, risks to the rights or freedoms of the people whose data you are processing.

Techniques that can be used in this step include a media review, surveys, or focus groups. The objective is to identify any ethical issues that might arise from the processing and to ensure that the interests and rights of affected individuals are appropriately considered. This is in line with the principle of 'User-Centric Design' in the Privacy by Design ethos developed by Dr Ann Cavoukian, former Privacy Commissioner of Ontario, and the Privacy Engineering methods developed by Michelle Dennedy and others (see Cavoukian, 2011 and Dennedy et al., 2014).

3. Assess quality of data protection/privacy/ethics and business impact.

Here the objective is to review the analysis of the information environment to identify the overall impact on data protection and privacy from the individual's perspective, and also to identify the impact on the business objective of any issues identified in the analysis.

Issues to be considered include the necessity and proportionality of the processing, the external stakeholder perspective of the potential issues and risks inherent in the processing, and any legal barriers to executing the process in the proposed manner. The decision that needs to be made is whether there are any "show-stoppers" that would require the scope of the business need and approach to be reviewed to address the critical issues identified.

This evaluation may involve the gathering of more information about how the processing will work, changing the proposed approach to achieving the business objective to address the issues identified, or reviewing the legal basis for the processing to ensure that there is sufficient clarity. This cycle of iterative review should be repeated until there is sufficient clarity on the proposed approach and the issues and risks that might arise and the show-stoppers have been addressed.

4. Analyze, synthesize, make recommendations, and document results. Act on results when the time is right.

It is important to conduct a root cause analysis (see *Step 5*) of data protection, privacy, or security risks that remain following the elimination of show-stoppers. This is to ensure that the correct triggers for the risk are identified so that correct mitigations and controls can be defined and implemented.

A common mistake that can arise is for a mitigation to be proposed which doesn't actually address the underlying root cause. This can give a false sense of remediation. For example, under the EU's GDPR, organizations need to clearly identify the legal basis for their processing. Consent is just one basis that can be relied upon but often it is selected without considering if the elements of valid consent are actually possible (it needs to be freely given, specific to a particular processing activity, informed, and unambiguous) and where another legal basis might be more appropriate.

Based on the root cause analysis, a remediation or improvement plan needs to be developed (see *Step 6*) which will put in place the appropriate mitigations and controls. This plan may need to address existing issues in the data processed by the organization or may require additional steps to be taken to mitigate the potential future issues and risks identified in the analysis. It will also need to identify the preventive, detective, and reactive controls that will need to be implemented to ensure that the organization can properly manage the identified data protection, privacy, and security risks. These may be a restatement of existing organizational or technical controls in the context of this new processing activity, or it may require the specification of and implementation of new organizational (people/process) controls or technical controls to address those issues appropriately.

Standard root cause analysis and data quality management techniques such as Five Whys analysis (*Step 5.1*) are used in this stage of the process.

A key part of the adapted Ten Steps in this context is a cost/benefit analysis (*Step 4.11*) of the proposed improvement plans and mitigations in the context of the scale of processing, the nature of the data, and the potential severity of impacts to individuals arising from the processing of data. If the cost of the mitigations is disproportionate to the level of risk (*Step 4.6*), it may be appropriate to revisit the proposed business needs and approach to determine if the plan can be further evolved to find an appropriate "win-win" balance between the objectives of the organization and the rights of individuals.

Finally, these recommendations need to be communicated into the project team implementing this proposed change to processes or introduction of new processes so that the correct scope and requirements for implementation are addressed in the project planning and execution. During the life cycle of the project the impact assessment may need to be revisited if there are changes to scope, approach, functionality, or suppliers, so having the outputs documented and communicated is a critical factor in ensuring quality outcomes for all stakeholders.

Sample Output and Templates

Ten Steps in Action

Castlebridge 10 Steps Data Protection/Privacy Impact Assessment (DPIA)

Castlebridge offers services related to governing information as an asset. This includes strategic planning, assessments and reviews, consulting, and training. They have a strong emphasis on data privacy and protection and have led the way in what they call "Ethical Enterprise Information Management" which is the discipline of applying ethical principles and practices to information management and governance. See https://castlebridge.ie.

Daragh O Brien, Founder and Managing Director, tells how they have used the Ten Steps:

We began using a 'fork' of the Ten Steps about seven years ago to help clients put structure on Data Protection/Privacy Impact Assessments (DPIA) and move them away from a 'templates and tick-boxes' mindset. In one organisation we worked with they had a 37 tab excel spreadsheet to document data privacy impacts on projects. That kind of complexity may be required, but it is ultimately unworkable when you are dealing with an aspect of data management and governance that people often struggle to get their heads around.

Our evolution of Danette's Ten Steps started from our view that the experience of the stakeholder of information and process outcomes is the ultimate arbiter of quality, and that data protection and privacy considerations are another quality characteristic of data (or at least of how data is managed). So, 'beginning with the end goal in mind' is a key missing piece in how many organisations have approached DPIAs.

One of the biggest challenges with doing data protection or data privacy impact assessments is getting organisations to move out of a 'solutionist' mindset and actually apply privacy by design. All too often the process is approached as an affirmation of a technical or process approach that has already been adopted. What our evolution of the 10-steps framework has allowed us to do is to first get the people in the organisations to define, in simple terms, what they want to do, why they want to do it, and the benefits that they want to achieve for their organisation *and for the people whose data they are processing.* That's where the 'Define Business Needs and Approach' starting point of the 10-steps comes into its own. We then iteratively elaborate the processing activities within the proposed system or process into distinct and discrete sub-processes, each of which may have different data protection/privacy challenges or requirements to address.

As shown in *Figure 4.3.12*, Castlebridge's adaptation, the Ten Steps Process provides a structure for framing and asking key questions during the development of an assessment of data protection impacts, privacy issues, or ethical implications of proposed processing.

Examples of where the 10 Steps has been used by Castlebridge with clients include the analysis of a remote patient monitoring application for supporting the response to Covid-19 in Ireland and the United States. This project involved us examining the processing activities involved in implementing remote monitoring for patients using a smartphone app, pulse oximeters, and in-hospital dashboards that would allow clinicians to monitor the clinical observations being logged by patients who were self-isolating at home. When the Business Need and Approach was analyzed, we identified that there were at least 10 sub-processes that needed to be considered.

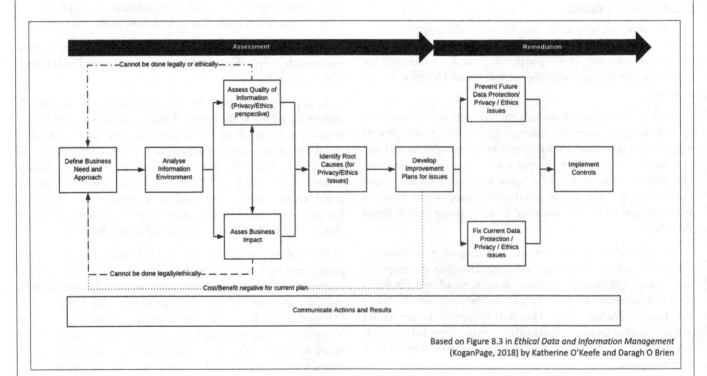

Based on Figure 8.3 in *Ethical Data and Information Management* (KoganPage, 2018) by Katherine O'Keefe and Daragh O Brien

Figure 4.3.12 Castlebridge 10 Steps Data Protection/Privacy/Ethics Impact Assessment (DPIA).

Ten Steps in Action *(Continued)*

Each of these processes had different information environment considerations, ranging from the use of analytics to support push notifications, to the use of third-party couriers to distribute pulse oximeters to patients, to the fundamentals of customer support for users of the application – both clinicians in the hospital setting as well as patients in their own homes. The data protection issues and impacts on the healthcare system of NOT being able to move lower-risk patients out of hospitals for monitoring were assessed and the key issues and risks were identified.

Based on the objective assessment of the issues and an assessment of the root causes, a clear plan for remedial actions was defined so that it could be aligned into the product roadmap, so that weaknesses could be resolved through the application release life cycle. Some of the identified issues were data and technology related, while others were process and governance related.

Another application of the methodology was in the assessment of remote skin temperature measurement systems for infection control in a post-lockdown scenario. This was undertaken as a research project by Castlebridge to help clients 'jumpstart' their own assessments of the pros and cons of this kind of technology from a data protection and privacy perspective. The identified business need was the prevention of disease spread in a workplace, with the approach being defined as the use of skin temperature measurement using infra-red

scanners. The analysis of the information environment highlighted key issues like the:
- Range of potential causes of false-positive temperature measures (everything from menopause to physical activity)
- Range of causes for false-negatives (hormonal conditions, use of medicines to suppress a fever)
- Level of virus spread from asymptomatic or pre-symptomatic carriers

The analysis showed that organizations would be making significant decisions affecting staff or customers based on potentially very poor-quality data that could not be a trusted source for the declared purpose. The impact of those decisions would depend on the processes or actions that followed from that decision (e.g., denying entry to workplace, refusing a customer entry to a store). However, the data quality issues mean that there is no certainty that the objective would be met, and other infection control measures (e.g., masks/social distancing) potentially have a better or equivalent outcome without the need to process personal data. Our analysis of the social aspects of the information environment also suggested that technologies such as thermal checking could give rise to a false sense of security in places where it was used.

The summary guidance report we produced based on this research is available on the Castlebridge website www.castlebridge.ie/resources-category/guidance.

Step 3.10 | Presentation Quality

Business Benefit and Context

Presentation quality refers to the appearance of data and information and how they are formatted and displayed, such as on application screens and user interfaces (UI), in reports, and on dashboards. The visual layout should be functional, easy to use, and created with users in mind. Presentation quality can affect the quality of data and information when: 1) they are collected, and 2) they are used.

When data is collected, the interface, whether electronic or hardcopy, should be intuitive and easy to follow, and questions should be understandable. If there is a list of options from which to select when answering a question, the options should be clearly defined and mutually exclusive, that is, each option should have a distinct meaning which does not overlap with other options.

When information is used, the format of the report or the user interface helps users correctly interpret and understand the information being presented. Data visualization is another term that is popular at the moment. There is a profession dedicated to user interface design. I do not expect this data quality dimension to replace that. But just as a data quality perspective could enhance a UI designer's work, so can a presentation quality perspective enhance a data professional's work. To prevent data quality issues, work with a UI team when designing new applications, and to update the UI

if it is found to be one of the root causes of data quality problems. From an assessment point of view, this dimension can often be assessed more quickly than other dimensions.

Definition

Presentation Quality (Data Quality Dimension). The format, appearance, and display of data and information support their collection and uses.

The list of options in a dropdown list seems like a simple idea, but it can have a big impact. For example, the day I was writing this section, I found a free report on another subject I was researching. Before downloading the report, I had to provide my name, address, and answer questions. That was fine because I was getting something of value and giving them something of value in return. The problem began with the first list of options where none of them applied to me. I chose something that sounded close, which led to another set of options and, once again, none of them applied. When I finished selecting the option for the third dropdown list, a page of recommended subscriptions popped up. I was not even remotely interested in any of them. I did download the report which was my original goal. Within an hour, I received an email suggesting something that looked very similar to the subscriptions that had been recommended. Again, nothing of interest. As a consumer, I am not happy because I can expect to receive more emails of no interest to me and I am not getting something that could be helpful. The company who is sending the emails is not be happy either, even though they don't know it. Why? Because the information they have on me is wrong, so they have zero chance of getting any kind of positive response from me no matter how many emails they send. And it was all because of presentation quality and their dropdown lists.

> ### Quote to Remember
>
> "While Data Governance understands how data quality can be degraded by a poorly-designed interface, the UI designers know how to turn that information into an interface that safeguards the quality."
>
> – *David Plotkin, "Designing in Data Quality with the User Interface," (2012)*

Approach

1. Prepare for the presentation quality assessment.

Select the data and information to be assessed for presentation quality. For example, if data profiling showed that certain data has quality issues and it is known there are several venues for collection, this data would be a candidate for a presentation quality assessment. If users are complaining about the usability of a dashboard then that is also another candidate. If an application development project is underway, you may skip the assessment piece and work with the UI team to design the UI from the beginning. If the screens have already been developed, but not finalized, an assessment can be a useful first step.

Decide if the assessment is from the collection and/or use point of view. Identify and gather the various media through which the data within scope is collected and/or used. Some UIs can be points of both collection and use. Refer to the information life cycle for activities and people involved in the Obtain phase of POSMAD (for collection) and in the Apply phase (for uses).

> ### Definition
>
> **Media** are the various means of presenting information, including (but not limited to) user guides, surveys, forms, and reports – whether electronic or hardcopy, dashboards, application screens, and user interfaces.

A single medium can be assessed or multiple media that collect or use the same information can be compared. For example, you may want to compare all the ways that customers provide information about themselves, and the media may be an email campaign, an online Web survey, and a hardcopy response form completed during an in-person customer seminar. See *Table 4.3.8* in *Sample Output and Templates*.

Outline a consistent process for assessing presentation quality. Decide who will perform it. This can be as simple as one person reviewing four types of media or entail a small team reviewing several media. Ensure that all those performing the assessment are trained and that they and their managers understand and support the activity. Your process may include assigning someone from the data quality team to work directly with a UI designer.

2. Assess presentation quality according to plan.

Always take into account who uses the media, their purposes, and what presentation makes sense for them. Understand the users' perspectives – how the information is being applied (its purpose) and the context of that usage (what happens when and where it is used). Interview users to find out how well the medium works for them – what works and what causes problems. In one project, users knew they should be updating information but to do so required several clicks down through multiple screens before getting to the field where the data could be updated. No wonder the information was rarely captured or updated.

Compare information in various media to determine if the information is collected consistently and impact to the quality – for good or bad. Look for inconsistencies, mistakes, or a design that encourages misunderstanding. Use the following list as a starting

---

Table 4.3.8 Presentation Quality – Comparison of Media that Collects Data

Data Field: Number of Employees

Type of Media	Email campaign (name and date)	Online survey (name and date)	Response form from in-person seminar (date)
Team Responsible for Media	Marketing	Marketing	Sales
Specific Question	How large is your company?	How many employees are there in your company?	Number of employees
Possible Responses	1 2-10 11-50 51-100 101-500 501-1000	1-100 101-1000 1001-10,000 10,001-100,000 Over 100,000	1-10 11-100 101-1000
Analysis	• Question in email campaign is confusing – not clear that "large" refers to number of employees. • Response ranges vary greatly across the media. Check with users: are these the right ranges and helpful to the business? Does it make sense, or not, to standardize the response ranges across all media? • Does the database allow for the different response ranges?		

point for developing your own set of questions and criteria for evaluating the presentation quality.

Collecting data and information:

- Is the form design easy to follow?
- Are the questions clear? Does the respondent understand what is being asked?
- Are there redundant questions?
- Is it mandatory that the field/question be completed/answered? If so, will the respondent have the knowledge to answer the question correctly?
- Does the question or field have limited options for response?
  - Are the options provided, e.g., as a dropdown list on a screen or a list with checkboxes on a hardcopy?
  - Are the options complete – do they cover all potential responses?
  - Are the options mutually exclusive – is there only one applicable option?
  - Are these the right options?
  - Is there a default value? This seemingly innocent question can wreak havoc with data quality if not used correctly. When profiling data, see how many times the default value appears and how many times, upon further inspection, it is not applicable to the record. I'm not saying don't use default values. I'm saying be thoughtful about where they are used and what the default value should be.
- Does the presentation require interpretation that could introduce errors?
- Are there complete process instructions?
- Are field labels clear and consistent? Do labels need definitions? If so, how are these made available, (e.g., by a pop-up window when the mouse hovers over the label)?
- Is there someone to contact if the user has questions?

Using the information, such as reports or dashboards:

- Are report or screen titles concise and representative of the content?
- If using tables, are column and row headings concise and representative of the content?
- Are there graphics that could present the information better than text and numbers in tables?
- Do the graphics encourage meaningful comparisons and discourage meaningless comparisons?
- Are the colors, resolution, font style and size, conducive to readability and aesthetically pleasing?

- Are last update dates and source of information included?
- Is there someone to contact if the user has questions?
- See additional ideas and resources in *Chapter 6* in the *Visualization and Presentation* section of *Metrics*

3. Document results and recommended actions.

Include lessons learned, possible impact to the business, suggested root causes, and initial recommendations. For example, you may want to meet with the contacts responsible for each of the media, discuss the differences, determine what needs to be changed, and ensure that the database can support what is needed.

Partner with those who have expertise in survey design or UI design to improve presentation quality.

See section on making recommendations and documenting results in *Chapter 6*.

Sample Output and Templates
Comparing Presentation Quality

Through data profiling and root cause analysis, one company determined that some of the data quality problems were due to the many different methods of collecting customer information, particularly company revenue, number of employees, department, position level, and so on. Each of the various media presented the questions and offered possible responses in a different way. There was no process for standardizing responses and developing the questions. *Table 4.3.8* gives an example. No consistency in how the data was gathered led to issues with how the data was entered and issues with being able to use the data later.

In one project, the root cause of many data quality issues was found to be a variety of methods through which customer information was collected. Analysis showed that the same question was often asked in different ways with different options for answering. Other times, questions were unclear. Customers did not know what to answer and so provided inaccurate information. In this case, the project could 1) improve the clarity, content, and phrasing of questions so customers could understand how to answer each question; 2) standardize questions for consistency and effectiveness of data collection and use; and 3) obtain buy-in to change the various forms, websites, and so forth. This recommendation was ranked as having a high impact but being fairly low cost to implement as compared to other recommendations. It could not be done in just a few days, but it could be accomplished over weeks with a small project team.

Step 3.11 | Data Coverage

Business Benefit and Context

The data quality dimension of Data Coverage is the comprehensiveness of data available compared to the total data universe or population of interest. In other words, how well does the datastore capture the total population of interest and reflect it to the business? Coverage also applies when determining the population of interest and selection criteria for data to be included when capturing data to assess, correct, and monitor it. See *Design Data Capture and Assessment Plans* in *Chapter 6*.

Coverage is included here as a separate data quality dimension goes more in-depth than just simple selection criteria. This dimension is useful if there are concerns that a datastore does not actually represent the population of interest to the business. For example, the database should contain all customers in North and South America, but there are concerns that the database really reflects only a portion of the company's customers from those areas. Coverage in this example is the percentage of customers actually captured in the database compared to the population of all customers that should be in it.

> **Definition**
>
> **Data Coverage (Data Quality Dimension).** The comprehensiveness of data available compared to the total data universe or population of interest.

Approach

1. Define coverage for the project, total population, and goals as it relates to business needs.

The following are examples of specific project definitions for coverage and total population:

Coverage – an estimate of the percentage of active installed equipment collected in the customer database.

- Total population: This is the installed base market (customers and installed products) that exists in Asia Pacific.
- Goal: Determine how well the database being measured captures and reflects the total installed base market within the region.
- Business needs: This information is input to general marketing decisions, number of personnel needed to support product questions, and if plans for personalized marketing can go forward with the information currently on hand or if additional data collection is needed.

Coverage – an estimate of the percentage of all sites collected in the customer database.

- Total population: All US sites within strategic account ABC that purchase our company's products.
- Goal: Assess how many of the US sites are actually captured in the customer database and document the processes that capture the data.
- Business needs: Strategic account manager needs accurate information about the number and status of the sites in order to assign accounts and sites to individual salespeople as part of the organization's territory management process. If the information about the sites is incomplete or has changed, then this will impact which salespeople are assigned particular accounts. The information is also used to know which sites were actually purchasing.

2. Estimate the total size of the population or data universe.

For example, assume you want to determine the installed market (either customers or installed products) that exists in a country for each product line. This will give you an idea of how large your database

should be if all customers and /or installed products were captured in it. You may look at orders and shipments over the past few years to determine the number of customers. Work with the Sales and Marketing department and utilize the figures they already have.

3. Measure the size of the database population.

Perform record counts for records that reflect the population of interest.

4. Calculate coverage.

Divide the actual database population (number of records from #3) by the estimated total population (from #2) and multiply the answer by 100. This provides the percent coverage in your database.

5. Analyze the results.

Determine if the coverage is enough to meet business needs. It is possible that the coverage will be greater than 100 percent. This indicates as much of a problem as a very low figure, such as 25 percent. Specifically, coverage numbers greater than 100 percent could indicate other data quality problems such as duplicate records.

6. Analyze, synthesize, make recommendations, document, and act on results.

See *Sample Output* for a template to capture and report results. Document assessment results, lessons learned, possible impact on the business, suggested root causes, and initial recommendations. Share and act on results when the time is right.

Sample Output and Templates

Template 4.3.3 provides a form for reporting results of a coverage assessment for 2 populations, in this case customers and installed products. Note that there can be separate analysis and recommendations for each population and additional recommendations for both after the results are synthesized.

Template 4.3.3 Coverage Results		
Goal of Coverage Assessment		
Business Needs		
	Customers	Installed Products
Datastore Name		
Datastore Description		
Total Population of Interest Description		
Estimated Total Population of Interest (number or count)		
Actual Population of Interest (number of records)		
Percent Coverage		
Analysis and Recommendations	• • •	• • •
Synthesis and Recommendations	• • •	

Step 3.12 | Data Decay

Business Benefit and Context

Data decay refers to the rate of negative change to the data. It is also known as data erosion. It is a useful measure for high-priority data that is subject to change as a result of events outside a system's control. Focus on high-priority data that changes quickly AND is critical for your organization. Knowing data decay rates help determine whether mechanisms should be installed to monitor the frequency of updates and notify stakeholders of the changes, and whether staff should be trained in how to update the data. Volatile data requiring high reliability requires more frequent updates than less important data with lower decay rates.

This dimension is an example where just the idea of the dimension can spur you to action, often without the need for an in-depth assessment. If it is already known that essential data will decay quickly because of events outside your system's or organization's control, then move quickly to find solutions. Determine how to become aware of the change in the real world. Develop processes where data can be updated within the organization as soon and as close to the real-world change as possible. As of the time of this writing and to prevent the spread of COVID-19, many small businesses had to close. It remains to be seen how many of them will be able to open again. If you are a supplier of goods to these businesses, it is fair to assume that data about your customers (the small businesses) has already decayed. Part of your strategy as the economy reopens should be to ensure you update the data about your customers.

 Definition

Data Decay (Data Quality Dimension). Rate of negative change to the data.

This step is less about the actual measure of data decay than it is about situations that may cause that decay and which data may decay most quickly. Combine that with your understanding of which data are most important and you can spend more of your efforts on data quality prevention, improvement, and correction, often with less time on assessment.

Approach

1. Quickly examine your environment for general processes that cause data to decay and for data already known to decay quickly.

Arkady Maydanchik, in his book *Data Quality Assessment*, presents 13 categories of processes that cause data problems (2007, p. 7). Five are processes causing data decay:

- Changes Not Captured
- System Upgrades
- New Data Uses
- Loss of Expertise
- Process Automation

If you see these processes in your environment, you can be sure your data is decaying. Use what you learned about the information life cycle within scope of your project and other factors when analyzing the information environment in *Step 2*.

2. Look for general decay rates relating to the data of interest.

If actual data decay rates are needed, make use of data already captured elsewhere. For example:

External sources—Look for government or industry statistics related your high-priority data of interest. Do a quick internet search. For example, if you care about address changes, does the postal service in your country publish rates about how quickly addresses change?

Another external source example, statistics referring to employee turnover rates are indicators of potential resulting data decay of employee data in your organization. The US Bureau of Labor Statistics runs a Job Openings and Labor Turnover Survey (JOLTS) program. One of the statistics relates to separations which is defined as "all employees separated from payroll during the month." They also provide a full definition for that term with what is and is not included. According to one JOLTS table, the annual total separation rates ranged from 42.3% in 2015 to 45.0% in 2019. The rates were higher or lower depending on industry and region of the country. (US Bureau of Labor Statistics, 2020, Table 16). From a data quality perspective, a separation means every time a person leaves an organization, their status within the company changes and contact information may change. If the data about that person is not updated to reflect those changes, the data has decayed.

Other data quality assessments—Reference statistics that include changes over time from previous data assessments. Having create dates and update dates by record or field can provide useful input for analysis. You may have the data from these fields as part of data integrity fundamentals, accuracy, consistency and synchronization, or timeliness assessments. Categorize by useful date ranges. If you have conducted an accuracy survey, use the data samples and assessment results for accuracy. (See *Figure 4.3.13* in the *Sample Output and Templates* section below.)

While data decay focuses on the rate of negative change to the data, also consider the rate of change from a data creation point of view. How quickly are records being created? If you are analyzing last update dates, you may want to analyze create dates at the same time.

Other internal current tracking and reporting processes—For example, one marketing group surveys their resellers every four months to update reseller profiles, contact name and job title information, and product sold. The vendor that administers the survey determines during data entry if the contact name has been added, deleted, or modified, or if it is unchanged. This information is used to see percent changes (data decay) to reseller data.

3. Determine actual data decay rates, if needed.

If the general results are not enough to move into planning and implementing improvements (i.e., someone does not believe their organization is similar to the statistics), then a more thorough assessment can be done.

4. Analyze, synthesize, make recommendations, and document results. Act on results when the time is right.

See the section of the same name in *Chapter 6: Other Techniques and Tools* for more details. If you are also looking at create dates, look at the rate of new records being created. Is it more than you expected? Are you staffed to handle the rate of creation? Are new records being created because existing records are not being found? If so, are duplicate records increasing? Include lessons learned, possible impact on the business, suggested root causes, and preliminary recommendations.

Sample Output and Templates

Customer Contact Validation Date

Figure 4.3.13 compares the results of updates in two countries for customer data in the same application. The application had a field called Customer Contact Validation Date. This field was supposed to be updated whenever the customer information manager contacted the customer and verified their information. By looking at that field, some assumptions could be made about the rate of the data decay of customer data.

Based on the dates in the field, in Country One, 88 percent of the records had not been verified with a customer for more than 60 months (5 years) and only 12 percent had been verified in the last 18 months. It appears that Country One had contact activity more than 5 years ago, yet the efforts had languished until 18 months prior to the analysis, when contacts with customers were taking place again.

Contrast that with Country Two, where 63 percent of the records had been verified with customers in the last 18 months and only 22 percent of the records had not been verified for more than 5 years.

Using this example, if you only had time to assess the quality of customers records for one country, how could the data decay be useful input? Without any other information, I would focus on Country One since 88 percent of their records had not been validated with the customer for over 5 years, with the assumption that the longer it has been since a record is validated with the customer, the more likely it is that the quality of the data has decayed.

As part of the assessment, it was found another factor came into play (which the numbers do not show). The customer contact validation date had to be manually updated. This was different than a standard update date which was automatically updated whenever any change was made. The Customer Contact Validation Date field was not easily accessed. It was known that customers had in fact sometimes been contacted, but the date had not been updated. This led to one recommendation that user screens be changed (presentation quality) to make the Customer Contact Validation Date field readily available to those contacting customers.

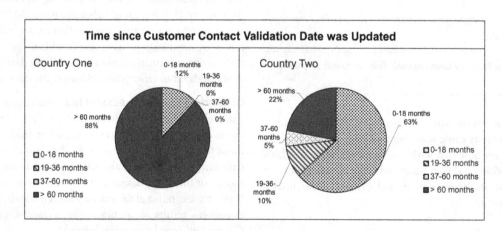

Figure 4.3.13 Use of Customer Contact Validation Date field to analyze data decay.

Step 3.13 | Usability and Transactability

Business Benefit and Context

Data and information exist to be used. They are inserted into transactions and records that are part of business processes. They are analyzed to inform business decisions and presented in reports and dashboards to communicate information. Even if the right people have defined business requirements and prepared data to meet them, the data must produce the expected outcome or use – or we still do not have high-quality data.

Can the invoice be correctly generated? Can a sales order be completed? Can a lab order be produced? Can an insurance claim be initiated? Can an item master record be used properly when building a Bill of Materials? When data is used in other processes (such as downstream usage in reports, dashboards, and transactions), does the end result meet their needs? Does a report contain the expected information? If the answer is no (in spite of all we have done to ensure the data can be used), and if an information consumer or an automated process has difficulty retrieving, understanding, interpreting, using, or maintaining data, it means the data has not fulfilled its purpose. Therefore, in our broad definition, we do not have the quality needed.

Definition

Usability and Transactability (Data Quality Dimension). Data produces the desired business transaction, outcome, or use for which it was intended.

This dimension is a final checkpoint of data quality. This type of assessment could be included in an SDLC as part of testing, often user acceptance testing. Those developing requirements, creating transformation rules, and cleaning source data need to be involved with those who are testing the data for usability – that same data they helped clean or create. None of the data quality work done is any good if the business processes cannot be completed satisfactorily.

The following are closely related to Usability and Transactability. This dimension may be expanded to include:

- **Access**. People must have the necessary access to do the work for which they are responsible. Include *Step 3.8* if you think lack of access is adversely impacting usability. For example, the person is supposed to have write access through a UI, but only has read access, so the transaction cannot be completed. Or a person does not have authority to run a particular report. This is a potential root cause of a usability problem.
- **Creation and maintenance**. Creating and maintaining data is often done using the same user interfaces (UIs) and processes as when data is used. While looking at them, look for a connection between usage, creation, and maintenance, and opportunities to make improvements that will help all of them.

- *Ease* **of use, creation, or maintenance**. How easy, or difficult, is it to use, create, or update the data? What can be done to make the processes more user-friendly? Difficulties in this area can impact transactability. For example,
  - It takes a small team of people several days to pull together what appears to be a simple report.
  - The process for creating a product master record has so many steps that the chance of having a record with no mistakes is highly unlikely.
  - The process for updating customers' preferences for being contacted is so time-consuming that it is skipped by many salespeople, which leads to unwanted emails and unhappy customers.

Approach

1. If working with a project testing team or a software quality assurance team.

Enlist their support. This data quality dimension cannot be done in isolation. Ensure the team and its manager are open to this collaboration.

Work with the testing team to understand their testing process and determine how the data team fits into that. It may be having someone from the data team sit in on the testing and observe. It could be setting up a feedback loop between those testing the data and the data team that created, cleansed, or transformed the data. It is not unusual to find that data is changed in the course of testing to complete the transaction successfully. However, this fact does not always make it to those responsible for the data so they can learn from what happened during testing and make appropriate changes to the data or the requirements. Once the data team is aware of the problem, the two most common causes are:

- Data was not changed per the creation, transformation, or cleansing specifications or requirements. The data team should find out why and ensure the data is re-created, transformed, or cleansed correctly and then given to the testing team for another round of testing.
- Data was changed per the specifications/requirements, but the specifications/requirements were wrong. The data team should update the specifications and ensure the data is re-created, re-transformed, or re-cleansed according to the new requirements and then given to the testing team for retesting.

To avoid the issues just mentioned, once the data has been created, transformed, or cleansed according to requirements it can be helpful to quickly profile the data set just prior to testing to ensure the data meets requirements. It should be profiled during every testing cycle after data changes and before testing.

Quick action needs to be taken because it is part of a testing cycle where time is usually limited. There will be much pressure to charge forward and move to production. It is not unusual for testing cycles to take place, yet the schedule does not allow for taking action on the results of that testing. Use your best persuasion skills to avoid this and ensure there is time to fix the data itself and/or the requirements. If not, all the trouble the testing team had will be multiplied for every user once the application has gone live. This is a place where an ounce of prevention is really worth the pound of cure.

Once the testing team has seen the benefits of including attention to data quality for one project, try to make it a standard part of all their testing – an excellent data quality control to include in *Step 7* and/or *Step 9*. One manager of a software quality assurance group estimated the team's overall testing time was increased by 1/3 due to poor-quality data. In addition, one week of post-production testing was added to the software testing cycle due to poor-quality data.

2. If evaluating the processes for *ease* of use, creation, or maintenance.

Make use of anything you have learned about the information life cycle up to this point. Gather process documentation. Interview those who use, create, or maintain the data about the processes and tools they employ. Even better, have them show you their processes. You may also want to spend time observing how they work and interact with the UI.

Look for differences between what the documentation says should happen and how the processes are actually carried out. Analyze the documented process for inefficiencies, rework, and redundant tasks. Work together with the users, creators, and maintainers to develop more efficient processes.

Ensure any recommended improvements are moved forward to *Step 6* to be included in the improvement plans and implemented in *Steps 7, 8,* or *9*. If the improvements can be made immediately and you are sure the changes will not have adverse effects on other areas, start now. There is no need to wait.

Use what you know about other data quality dimensions that have been assessed for additional insight into where problems have been found.

3. Analyze, synthesize, make recommendations, and document results. Act on results when the time is right.

As with the other dimensions, analyze results and synthesize with results from other assessments. Document lessons learned,

potential business impact and root causes, and recommendations for prevention and correction.

Sample Output and Templates
When Multiple Dimensions Apply

As an example of the relationship between multiple data quality dimensions, think of a situation where a sales rep is the source of customer information. The only way the data gets into the central customer master database is by syncing the database and the rep's handheld. It is general knowledge that many sales reps do not want to share their customer information. The question then is, "Why don't the sales reps want to share their information?" The following answers help us learn more, which would lead us to various data quality dimensions:

- When data comes back from the central database, my customer information has been changed. Now I have lost important information about my customers (the basis of my sales, commissions, and my livelihood) and I cannot take care of my customers the way I should. (Usability and Transactability)
- I don't trust the central database. I know the data is updated and transformed in some way, but I have no visibility as to why. (Perception of Relevance and Trust)
- It is too difficult to complete the synchronization process between my handheld and the central customer database. (Ease of use, creation, and maintenance)
- Could any of this be affecting what information actually gets into the central database and how big (or little) of a problem is this? (Coverage)

Having the list of data quality dimensions helps a team identify which aspects could affect the quality of the data. The team could decide to speak with more of the sales reps to understand how widespread the problem is and ask questions about usability, ease of use, and trust within the survey or interview.

Alternatively, maybe the data quality team first did an assessment on coverage and the aspects of usability, ease of use, and trust came out as potential causes for lack of coverage. From here they could: 1) decide they have enough information to identify root causes, or 2) decide they don't know enough about the problem to know if it is widespread or not, and they want to do a survey to understand more.

Step 3.14   Other Relevant Data Quality Dimensions

Business Benefit and Context

Even with the many data quality dimensions already provided in previous steps, this step is added as a placeholder for other data quality dimensions that have not been included in the previous dimensions and would be helpful to assess for your project. For example:

- Within one corporate finance group, the main concern was reconciliation between systems. Some could call this completeness, but the word "reconciliation" is clearer to them and specific to

their context. You may decide to do a separate assessment called "Reconciliation" or use different wording in another assessment to make results more relevant to the finance group.
- An assessment of duplication has been completed. You found that the users create duplicates because it is easier to create a new record than it is to find an existing one. This would be a reason to look closely at the process to assess *ease* of use, creation, and maintainability, which was included as a potential related aspect of Usability and Transactability in *Step 3.13*.

> **Definition**
>
> **Other Relevant Data Quality Dimensions**. Other characteristics, aspects, or features of data and information that are deemed to be important for your organization to define, measure, improve, monitor, and manage

If another data quality dimension is chosen, remember to use it within the context of the full Ten Steps process. You still need to connect business needs with the data to be assessed. You still need to learn just enough about the information environment to provide insight when analyzing assessment results and ensuring they are used when identifying root causes, preventing future data errors, correcting current errors, and monitoring controls.

Approach

The instructions will be dependent on the additional data quality dimension to be assessed.

Sample Output and Templates

Output will be dependent on the additional data quality dimension to be assessed.

Step 3 Summary

Congratulations! You have completed your data quality assessments (or have learned about them in preparation for an assessment).

You may have done one quick assessment or assessed multiple data quality dimensions over a longer period of time. Either way, completing this step is an important milestone in your project. Everything you learned during the assessments provides input to the next steps.

Remember that you can also use the *concept* of the data quality dimensions, even without doing a step-by-step detailed assessment. For instance, see *Step 2.1 – Understand Relevant Requirements and Constraints* for an example of how the idea of data quality dimensions was used in requirements gathering.

Step 3 required communication and engagement to ensure team members, managers, project sponsors, and other stakeholders were aware of the work, heard results and initial recommendations, and had a chance to give feedback. It is your job to educate others so they are clear on what was learned or not learned from each assessment, and action that should or should not be taken as a result. Do not mislead your stakeholders!

You will face many future situations where the data quality dimensions can help. For any given scenario, use the list of dimensions and select which ones apply. How you decide to assess the dimensions, separately or together, in-depth or high-level, is up to you. If you are doing a good job of analyzing, synthesizing, and documenting results throughout, the relationships, impacts, and potential root causes will start coming together to provide a more complete picture of the actual quality of the data and what is truly causing the problems. All of which helps you decide what, specifically, should be done in *Steps 5, 6, 7, 8,* and *9,* and how quickly you can start them.

Communicate, Manage, and Engage

Suggestions for working effectively with people and managing the project in this step:

- Ensure deliverables are completed in a timely manner; track issues and action items
- Engage with project sponsors, stakeholders, management, and team members to:
  - Work cooperatively as data quality assessments are conducted
  - Remove roadblocks, resolve issues, and manage change
  - Stay appropriately involved (accountable, responsible, provide input, informed only)
- Communicate status, assessment results, likely impacts, and initial recommendations; get feedback and complete needed follow-up
- Based on learnings from data quality assessments:
  - Adjust project scope, objectives, resources, or timeline
  - Manage expectations of all involved
  - Anticipate change management needed for likely improvements to be implemented and accepted)
- Ensure resources and support for upcoming steps in the project

---

Checkpoint

Checkpoint Step 3 – Assess Data Quality

How can I tell if I am ready to move to the next step? Use the following guidelines to help determine completeness of this step and readiness for the next step:

- For each selected data quality dimension, has the assessment been completed and results analyzed?
- If conducting multiple assessments, have results from all been synthesized?
- Have the following been discussed and documented: lessons learned and observations, known/potential issues, known/probable business impact, possible root causes, initial recommendations for prevention, correction, and monitoring?
- If there are changes to the project, have they been finalized and agreed-upon by sponsors, stakeholders and team members? E.g., If additional people are needed for the next steps, have they been identified and committed? Is funding continuing?
- Have activities to communicate, manage, and engage people during this step been completed? Are plans updated?
- Have action items not completed during this step been logged with assigned owners and due dates?

Step 4 Assess Business Impact

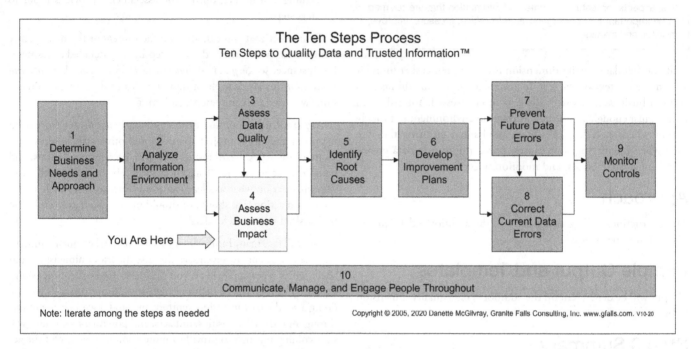

Figure 4.4.1 "You Are Here" Graphic for Step 4 – Assess Business Impact.

Introduction to Step 4

Let's turn our attention from the *quality* of the data itself to the *value* of the quality of the data. Imagine the following scenario: You have a desk, a chair, and a laptop with the only copy of your organization's customer or product or supplier master records and all transactions for the last two years. There is a fire. You only have time to save one of them. Which do you save? The desk, the chair, or the laptop with the only copy of critical information? When I pose the question, I am usually met with silence and faces with an expression of, "That is a stupid question. The answer is obvious!" Why do we all know we would save the information on the laptop? We can easily replace the desk or the chair. Even your favorite ergonomic chair can be replaced. How difficult and costly would it be to replace the information? In many cases we could not replace the information at all. If my organization has been taking water samples for the last 40 years to track levels of pollutants as input to water management, and that information is gone and not found elsewhere, we cannot replace it.

If we intuitively know that we would save the information because it is most valuable, why do we continue to meet resistance when asking for time, money, and people to manage our data and information?

When a data quality issue is recognized, the "So what?" and "So why?" questions are immediately raised. "What impact does this have on my organization? On my team? On me?" and "Why does this matter?" "What is the return on my investment?" Early in my career when asked these questions, I got prickly inside and thought, "Don't they understand that data quality is important? It is obvious! Why do I need to spend time answering them? I should be spending all my time working on the quality of the data." At some

point, thankfully, I had an "ah-ha" moment where I realized that executives and managers are *supposed* to ask those questions. It is their job to sort through the many requests for resources coming to them. So… if these are the right questions and executives and managers are doing *their* jobs, what is *my* job? My job is to be able to answer those questions! It may sound silly now, but that realization had a big effect on me. I didn't need to spend a moment's time resisting the effort it took to answer their questions. I could spend my energy figuring out how to answer them!

Historically "So what?" and So why?" questions have been difficult to answer. But help is here! This step provides a variety of techniques, called Business Impact Techniques, that can answer those questions. Review the section on business impact techniques in *Chapter 3 – Key Concepts*, if needed. See *Table 4.4.2* for a list and definitions of the business impact techniques included in this step. There is one substep with detailed instructions for each of the business impact techniques (*Steps 4.1–4.12*).

 Definition

A **Business Impact Technique** is a qualitative or quantitative method for assessing the impact of data quality on an organization.

Even though these techniques are presented in *Step 4* of the Ten Steps Process, use them *anytime and anywhere* in your project, during any step, when the need arises, to:

- Answer questions, such as "Why should I care about data quality (or your project) and why are they important?" "What difference will data quality have on our organization, on my team, on me?"

- Address resistance when it is seen, heard, or felt, such as vocal disagreement ("We have better places to spend our money than on data!") or hear words of support but see no action.
- Establish the business case for data quality improvements
- Determine appropriate investments in data quality activities
- Gain support from management
- Motivate team members and others to participate in the project
- Prioritize efforts

Some techniques help prioritize what to work on. When asked why those are included, think of it this way. If I prioritize something as a 1 or high importance, vs. a 10 or low importance, what have I just said? The item prioritized as 1 has more business impact than the item prioritized as 10. We always have more to do than we have the time, money, and other resources in which to do them. Therefore, it is essential that data professionals have good prioritization techniques to apply against their work. With the variety of techniques presented here, there is no excuse for not understanding business impact when it is needed.

Anytime you hear, see, or feel resistance, that is a clue to look at the techniques and see what can help you address it. If you are incorporating data quality activities into another project using any Agile or other SDLC, if you hear words of support, but see no action, turn to *Step 4* and find a technique to help. If running a focused data quality improvement project using the Ten Steps Process, following are typical places where the Business Impact Techniques can be useful:

- In *Step 1*, when identifying and prioritizing business needs, selecting the project focus, and looking for funding and support for your project
- After completing *Step 2* and additional data quality issues have been uncovered, to determine the focus of the in-depth data quality assessment in *Step 3*
- After doing an in-depth data quality assessment in *Step 3*, to decide which of the issues found are important enough to continue with root cause analysis in *Step 5*
- After identifying root causes in *Step 5* and there is a long list of specific recommendations for prevention, correction, or for controls to be monitored, to decide which are most important to put into place in *Steps 6, 7, 8* and *9*.
- When you see, hear, or feel resistance anywhere and anytime during the project

The most significant business impact often comes from how the information is used, since that is when its value is realized. Remember the Apply phase of the Information Life Cycle? However, impact can also be shown in other phases of the information life cycle, such as impact from growing costs to correct the data (the Maintain phase) or increased operational costs to store the data because no archiving is done (the Dispose phase).

As a reminder, using these techniques can show business impact, not only for data quality projects, but for programs and operational processes. See the Data in Action Triangle in *Chapter 2*.

Table 4.4.1	Step Summary Table for Step 4 – Assess Business Impact
Objective	Assess business impact using techniques applicable to the situation
Purpose	At any time in the project, during any step, to: • Answer questions, such as "Why is data quality important?" "What difference will data quality have on our organization, on my team, on me?" • Address resistance when it is seen, heard, or felt, such as vocal disagreement or hear words of support but see no action • Establish the business case for data quality improvements • Determine appropriate investments in data quality activities • Gain support from management • Motivate team members to participate in the project • Prioritize efforts

Inputs	• Output, learnings, and artifacts from:
	  o *Step 1* – updated, as needed, based on what has been learned so far in the project: business needs, data quality issues, project scope, plan, or objectives
	  o *Step 2* – analyzing the information environment
	  o *Step 3* – especially if business impact will be based on specific issues found during data quality assessments
	• Anything else known about the situation that caused the need to assess business impact
	• Current project status, stakeholder analysis, communication and engagement plans

Techniques and Tools	• Techniques and tools applicable to the business impact techniques to be used
	  o See details in substeps, one for each business impact technique
	• From *Chapter 6: Other Techniques and Tools:*
	  o Design Data Capture and Assessment Plans
	  o Conduct a Survey
	  o Tools for Managing Data Quality
	  o Track Issues and Action Items (use and update throughout the project)
	  o Analyze, Synthesize, Recommend, Document, and Act on Results (use and update throughout the project)

Outputs	• Documented results from each business impact assessment selected and completed, with synthesis of all results – quantitative and/or qualitative • Documented lessons learned, issues uncovered, possible root causes, and initial recommendations • Artifacts from *Steps 1* and *2,* updated as needed based on business impact results • Documented data capture and assessment plans, for future reference and use

(Continued)

Table 4.4.1	Step Summary Table for Step 4 – Assess Business Impact *(Continued)*	
	• Actions taken, based on what was learned about business impact, that could be completed during this step • Completed communication and engagement activities needed at this point in the project • Updated status, stakeholder analysis, communication and engagement plans based on feedback and business impact results • Agreement on next steps in the project, dependent on when and where in the project the business impact assessment took place	

Communicate, Manage, and Engage	• Help team members work cooperatively as business impact assessments are conducted
	• Work with project sponsors and relevant stakeholders to remove roadblocks and resolve issues
	• Track issues and action items; ensure deliverables are completed in a timely manner
	• Ensure project sponsors, team members, management, and other technical and business stakeholders have been:
	   o Appropriately engaged during business impact assessment (some may be actively involved, others provide input, yet others only informed)
	   o Apprised of results and initial recommendations based on what was learned about business impact
	   o Given the opportunity to provide reaction and feedback
	   o Informed of changes to project scope, timeline, and resources and know the plan going forward
	• Based on learnings from the business impact assessments:
	   o Adjust project scope, objectives, resources, or timeline
	   o Manage expectations of stakeholders and team members
	   o Anticipate change management needed to ensure potential future improvements are implemented and accepted
	• Ensure resources and support for upcoming steps in the project	

Checkpoint	• For each selected business impact technique, has the assessment been completed?
	• If using multiple business impact techniques, have results from all been synthesized and documented?
	• Have results from this step been documented?
	   o Lessons learned and observations
	   o Known/potential issues
	   o Known/probable business impact
	   o Potential root causes
	   o Initial recommendations for prevention, correction, and monitoring controls
	   o Actions or follow-up needed that were not completed during this step
	• If there are changes to the project, have they been finalized and agreed-upon by project sponsor, relevant stakeholders, and team members? E.g., are additional people needed for the next steps? If so, have they been identified and committed? Is funding continuing?
	• Have the communication and engagement plans been kept current? Do they include change management?
	• Have necessary activities to communicate, manage, and engage people during this step been completed?	

Table 4.4.2	Business Impact Techniques in the Ten Steps Process	
Business Impact Techniques. A business impact technique is a qualitative and/or quantitative method for determining the effects of the quality of data on the organization. These effects can be good effects from high-quality data and/or adverse effects from poor-quality data. Instructions for assessing business impact using the following techniques are included in the Ten Steps Process in *Step 4 – Assess Business Impact*.		
Substep	**Business Impact Technique Name and Definition**	
4.1	**Anecdotes.** Collect examples of the negative impact of poor-quality data and/or the positive impact of good quality data.	
4.2	**Connect the Dots.** Illustrate the connection between business needs and the data which supports them.	
4.3	**Usage.** Inventory the current and/or future uses of the data.	
4.4	**Five Whys for Business Impact.** Ask "Why?" five times to recognize the real effects of the quality of data on the business.	
4.5	**Process Impact.** Illustrate the effects of data quality on business processes.	
4.6	**Risk Analysis.** Identify possible adverse effects from poor-quality data, evaluate the likelihood of them happening, severity if they do, and determine ways to mitigate the risks.	
4.7	**Perception of Relevance and Trust.** The subjective opinion of those who use information and/or those who create, maintain, and dispose of data regarding: 1) Relevance – which data is of most value and importance to them, and 2) Trust – their confidence in the quality of the data to meet their needs.	
4.8	**Benefit vs. Cost Matrix.** Rate and analyze the relationship between benefits and costs of issues, recommendations, or improvements.	
4.9	**Ranking and Prioritization.** Rank the impact of missing and incorrect data on specific business processes.	
4.10	**Cost of Low-Quality Data.** Quantify costs and the impact to revenue due to poor-quality data.	
4.11	**Cost-Benefit Analysis and ROI.** Compare anticipated costs of investing in data quality to potential benefits through an in-depth evaluation, which may include calculating return on investment (ROI).	
4.12	**Other Relevant Business Impact Techniques:** Other qualitative and/or quantitative methods for determining the effects of the quality of data on the business that are deemed important for your organization to understand.	

Use what is learned about business impact to help establish the business case for data quality improvements, gain support from management for data quality work, prioritize efforts, motivate team members to participate in the project, and determine appropriate investments in your information resource.

Do *something* related to business impact! Too often it is heard, "I don't have time to look at business impact. I need to work on the data quality problem." Or "I don't know how to determine business impact." This step gives you choices. Some business impact techniques are quantitative, others qualitative. Some take less time and are less complex, relatively speaking, than others which will take more time and are more complex. No matter the time constraints, you can do *something* related to business impact. Maybe all you can do right now is collect a few anecdotes and tell a story. Do that! Maybe you need to fully quantify the impacts, but you don't have time. Select one technique that you can fit with the time and resources available now. Tackle the more time-consuming techniques later, if needed.

Many of the techniques presented here work together. They can also be used alone. Assess the business impact using *only* the techniques that are the *most appropriate* in a *particular* situation and with the time and resources available. It is worthwhile to note that even though these techniques are focused on data quality, they work equally well when showing the business impact of data governance, metadata, data standards, etc. There is no excuse not to show business impact in some way.

Each of the business impact techniques have been numbered for ease of reference, not because they must be done in any particular order. There is one substep for each business impact technique. Each substep contains three main sections providing details to help you complete the assessment: Business Benefit and Context, Approach, and Sample Output and Templates.

Step 4 Process Flow

The overall approach to *Step 4* is straight-forward. First select the techniques to use that will be most helpful for any particular situation; second, plan for the assessment; third, assess business impact using those chosen techniques; and fourth, synthesize results if more than one assessment has been completed, make recommendations, and take action! See *Figure 4.4.2 – Process flow for Step 4*. This high-level process flow applies to all business impact techniques and is explained here to avoid repeating within each substep.

Select Relevant Business Impact Techniques—Think of the list of techniques as a menu of choices. You never order everything on the menu at your favorite restaurant. You make choices about what to eat based on how hungry you are, what you feel like eating, and sometimes how much the meal costs or how much time you have to eat.

The Business Impact Techniques are presented in order of the relative time and effort to assess. Each is placed on a continuum with the techniques that take less time and are less complex (starting at 1 on the left) to those, relatively speaking, that take more time and are more complex (ending at 11 on the right). The last technique *4.12 – Other Relevant Business Impact Techniques* is not on the continuum, because what additional technique someone may use could be placed anywhere depending on the time and complexity the technique involves.

Note that *all* techniques have proven to be effective. The continuum shows relative *effort* – not relative *results*. You can understand business impact even without completing a full cost benefit analysis. Less complicated does not necessarily mean less useful results; more complex does not necessarily mean more useful results. The techniques can be used alone or in various combinations.

Become familiar with the various techniques, what is required for each, and where they are placed on the continuum. When the need to show business impact arises, you can open this step (your toolkit) and select which technique(s) will best help with the current situation. See the *Business Impact Techniques* section in *Chapter 3* for more considerations when selecting techniques.

Design Data Capture and Assessment Plans—This step is often simpler than the planning for a data quality assessment. It is a checkpoint for yourself to do the right level of planning if you are combining multiple techniques. For example, if you are only collecting anecdotes then this can be skipped completely because there is one technique, no data capture, and you can do your planning

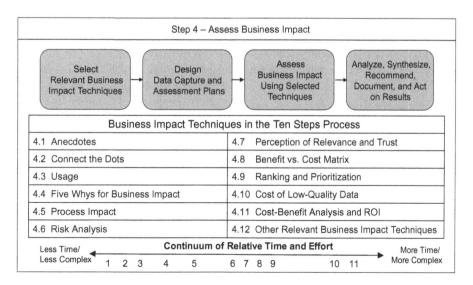

Figure 4.4.2 Process flow for Step 4 – Assess Business Impact.

within *Step 4.1 – Anecdotes*. If you are doing *Step 4.10 – Cost of Low-Quality Data*, and data content will need to be accessed from datastores to help with calculations, then it is important to give more thought to data capture and assessment. Likewise, if using multiple techniques, spending just enough time to plan is well worth what you gain in being more efficient in using the techniques.

If you have results from a data quality assessment (such as specific errors, their magnitude, and location), use that as input to your plans. You may want to assess data where there are a high number of errors or where the subject matter expert has already assigned a high priority.

Assess Business Impact Using Selected Techniques— Complete the business impact assessment for each technique chosen using the instructions provided in the substeps (*Steps 4.1–4.12*).

Analyze, Synthesize, Recommend, Document, and Act on Results—Analyze results from the techniques you have used. Combine and synthesize results from multiple business impact assessments. Compare results against any potential business impacts documented as a result of any data quality assessment.

Make initial recommendations based on what you have learned. You may find that data quality issues have more impact than thought. Use these results to determine your next steps (e.g., communication needed, business action required, adjustments to project scope, timeline, and resources needed, priority for assessing root causes or which improvements to implement).

Document it all to ensure knowledge and insight from each step are retained and used in the next step. Take action when the time is right. See the section *Analyze, Synthesize, Recommend, Document, and Act on Results* for more information in *Chapter 6: Other Techniques and Tools*.

> ### 🎯 Best Practice
>
> **Business Impact Concerns Vary.** Be aware of what business impact means to different people and organizations and how they might want to see results in terms of:
>
> - Increased revenue (data quality will help us make more sales)
> - Money saved (data quality will save us x dollars in costs)
> - Operational efficiency (data quality will decrease production time by two days)
> - Headcount (data quality will save us x number people)
> - Risk (data quality will lower the risk of xyz)
> - Other concerns where business impact of data quality can be shown
>
> Share and express business impact results in the ways most meaningful to those from whom you need support. See more in *Step 10 – Communicate, Manage, and Engage People Throughout*.

Step 4.1 | Anecdotes

Business Benefit and Context

Collecting anecdotes is the easiest and most low-cost way of assessing business impact. However, it can still produce good results. Use the anecdotes, along with your best storytelling and communication skills (see *Step 10*), to make data quality more tangible and to provoke interest in a topic in a way that listeners can relate to their own experiences. Use them to engage leadership quickly – especially when it provides context for facts and figures. Even without quantitative data, an anecdote can still be useful. Let them help you capture attention so management will discuss data quality and your project in more depth.

 Definition

Anecdotes (Business Impact Technique). Collect examples of the negative impact of poor-quality data and/or the positive impact of good-quality data.

Approach

1. Collect anecdotes.

Anecdotes are useful for immediate issues where the business is trying to get a first understanding of data quality impact. You can also document and save anecdotes as you collect them. When you hear about problems at your company caused by data quality, investigate and find out the specifics – who, what, when, where, and why. The anecdotes will be useful for future communication.

Collect examples or stories from external news sources, websites, and industries that relate to your organization, and internal specific company examples about actual business events.

Create a place and process for collecting the anecdotes so they are available at short notice to start off an important meeting or presentation. *Template 4.4.1 – Information Anecdote Template* works well for this purpose, see the *Sample Output and Templates* section. *Template 4.4.2* shows an example of how the template can be used. Encourage team members to use it to quickly capture the situations heard during the project. Caution: Use the template for *collecting* results, not for *presenting* them. Use the content from the template to tell the story in an interesting way to articulate the points to be made and which will resonate with each audience.

2. Be as specific possible.

You don't have to know everything right now but capture what you do know. The high-level data, processes, people/organizations, and technology that are relevant to the anecdotes may also provide pointers for additional research into the impact on those areas.

Use the following questions to stimulate your thinking about business impact. Get more specific about a particular incident or situation that applies to:

Critical business decisions—What information is required to make those decisions? What happens if the information is wrong? How does that impact the business?

Key processes or key business flows—What information is required to carry out those processes? What happens if the information is wrong – to the immediate transaction, to other processes, to reporting, to decisions made from those reports, and so forth?

Incorrect data and information—What is the impact if particular data is wrong (e.g., poor decisions, impact to customers, lost sales, increased rework, data correction)?

Master data—Such as customer, vendor, item master, bills of material. What processes or other transactions are dependent on the integrity of the master data? What will happen to the transactions if the master data is wrong? Are other categories of data also impacted?

Transactional data—What will happen if the transactional records are wrong, e.g., if the purchase order or the invoice is wrong?

Required fields—How does the user get the data? What happens if they are not available at the time the record is created? What will happen if incorrect data is entered just to satisfy a system requirement for an entry in a field?

3. Quantify the impact, if possible.

Quickly quantify parts of the anecdote, if possible. This technique is all about what you can learn with the least amount of time and effort, but you may be able to quantify the impact by asking questions such as, "How often does this happen?" and "How many people were affected?" You can further analyze the impact of what you have found by using other business impact techniques.

4. Generalize the impact.

Take the isolated anecdote and determine the impact if the same experience were to be applied across the organization.

5. Determine how to tell the story.

Be creative. See the *Sample Output and Templates* section for an example of how Aera Energy used anecdotes to obtain funding for an Enterprise Architecture Plan supported by a comprehensive data quality program.

Use the anecdotes to support your communication needs. For example, do you have 30 seconds, or 3 minutes to tell the story? What does the audience need to hear? What point are you emphasizing? (See *Step 10 – Communicate Actions and Results*.)

 Key Concept

One manager explained how often management and investment decisions are based on real anecdotes and said, "Never underestimate the power of a good story!"

Another manager told me that many important business decisions are based on stories, meaning stories are what make the situations real and relatable. Collecting and using anecdotes is a low-cost way of obtaining content to build stories which show real business impact.

6. Analyze, synthesize, recommend, document, and act on results.

Document the anecdotes along with sources and supporting information. Include the qualitative and more intangible results. Capture tangible impact that can be *quickly* quantified in numbers and dollars.

Any of the anecdotes could be a starting point for other business impact techniques such as detailing processes in *Step 4.5* that are part of the anecdotal situation or more fully quantifying impacts in *Step 4.10 – Cost of Low-Quality Data*. See *Chapter 6 – Other Techniques and Tools* for the section of the same name for additional suggestions.

Sample Output and Templates

Information Anecdote Template

The Information Anecdote template (*Template 4.4.1*) is an easy way to collect facts about data quality issues. See *Template 4.4.2* for an example. Make the template available to your team so each can quickly capture situations that will arise throughout the project and in their daily work. Caution: Use the template for *collecting* content, not for *presenting* the information. Use the content from the template to develop the story and tell it in a way that will engage your audience.

The template can also be used after completing other business impact techniques to condense what was learned and provide summarized content to help tell the story from those results.

Business Impact – Using Anecdotes and Perception of Relevance and Trust

The following describes one company's experience showing business impact by using both anecdotes (*Step 4.1*) and a survey of knowledge workers (users) to understand their perception of relevance and trust (*Step 4.7*).

C. Lwanga Yonke, Information Quality Process Manager at Aera Energy LLC, recounts the narrative. A popular story used at Aera Energy LLC, an oil company based in Bakersfield, California, revolved around the Winchester Mystery House in San Jose. As the story goes, Sarah Winchester, widow of the inventor of the Winchester rifle, believed her family was cursed and was told by a medium that she was being haunted by the ghosts of individuals killed by the Winchester rifle. The medium further advised her to move, build a new house, and keep that house under perpetual construction as a way to appease said ghosts. And so, she did, spearheading a 38-year construction project with no apparent master plan; it only stopped when she died.

The result was a jumbled floor plan and strange features such as stairs that lead directly to ceilings, doors that opened to walls, and so on. In his book, *Enterprise Architecture Planning*, Steven Spewak draws an analogy between that house and information systems in most organizations, asserting that those systems are built like the Winchester Mystery House: a bunch of components poorly connected, poorly integrated, redundant, and disparate because there was no plan, no architecture, just a commitment to build (1992, pp. xix–xx).

Template 4.4.1 Information Anecdote Template	
Title:	
Data:	**People/Organizations:**
Processes:	**Technology:**
Situation:	
Impact (quantify where possible):	
Suggested action, potential root causes, initial recommendations, or next steps:	
Submitted by:	**Date:**
Contact information:	

Template 4.4.2 Information Anecdote Example – Legal Requirements for Pricing	
Title: Legal Requirement to Prove Pricing	
Data: Pricing for Government Contracts	**People/Organizations:** Purchasing Agents
Processes: Procurement	**Technology:** ERP (Enterprise Resource Planning)
Situation:	
For government contracts, the company has a legal requirement to prove pricing for the last ten years from the expiration of a contract. The only way to prove compliance is through pricing history.	
In the system, the pricing history is not created automatically – the audit trail is a single layer, meaning that it only tracks one previous change. Therefore, in the system the only way to create the required history is to create a new price list line instead of changing the data for the existing line.	
The users (purchasing agents) have quickly figured out that an *existing* price list line can easily be updated – and much faster than *adding* a new one. There is no technical edit. Unless they know the reasons for adding the new price list line, they will take the quickest route (modifying the existing line), with the result that pricing history is missing or incomplete. The company is legally required to have this information.	
Impact (quantify where possible):	
When pricing history is missing or incomplete, the company cannot comply with the legal requirement to prove pricing for the last ten years from the expiration of a contract. Compliance to legal requirements is at risk if this manual process is not followed.	
Suggested action, potential root causes, initial recommendations, or next steps:	
Investigate technical solutions (modifications to system) to support this requirement. For example, can the issue be addressed through complete audit trails at the database level so that complete histories are generated, regardless of training or access method?	
Assess how often this happens and the magnitude of the problem.	
Address the issue through training. Train users in *why* new price list lines must be added (to meet legal/contractual requirements) in addition to *how* to add them.	
Check with legal about the penalty for noncompliance.	
Submitted by:	**Date:**
Contact information:	

Members of Aera's Enterprise Architecture Plan (EAP) team used the story and Spewak's analogy to build a case for enterprise architecture. The story became well known and popular in the company because it illustrated in simple terms that everyone could understand the importance of developing an information systems architecture. Aera also used internally generated data to assess the financial impact of poor information quality.

As part of the process, the EAP team conducted an assessment of the amount of time that enterprise knowledge workers spent finding, cleaning, and formatting data before they could analyze them and make decisions that create value. The average time quoted was 40 percent. This statistic convinced Aera management of the need to implement the Enterprise Architecture Plan. The salary cost alone for everyone in the enterprise spending that much non-value-added time would pay for the project. However, the real opportunity was the increased time available for knowledge workers to spend on analysis and decision making.

The assessment consisted of a survey of well-respected engineers, geoscientists, and other knowledge workers in the company, chosen because of their credibility with their peers and with company leaders – the executives who had final authority over whether Aera was going to invest in enterprise architecture implementation and data quality.

Each of those interviewed was asked: (1) their opinion about the data quality at Aera, and (2) specifically what percent of their time they spent looking for, reconciling, and correcting data before they could use it for analysis and decision making. Survey participants were also individually photographed in their work environments.

The stories and pictures were compiled and presented in a very creative way. Imagine a series of slides, each one containing the picture of one knowledge worker, the person's name, a pithy quote about data quality at Aera, and the percentage of time that person spent dealing with bad data. In the various presentations where the slides were used, their cumulative impact was the same: For most managers, knowing that their valuable engineers and geoscientists were spending 40 percent of their time dealing with bad data instead of making value-adding decisions provided a convincing argument for a radical change.

With the Winchester Mystery House anecdote and the internal pictures and interview results, Aera built compelling business impact stories, which resulted in the approval of a five-year,

multimillion-dollar project. The core of the subsequent Enterprise Architecture Implementation (EAI) program was an ambitious system development schedule, supported by a comprehensive data quality process. During the eight years after its EAI began, Aera has successfully replaced hundreds of disparate legacy systems with robust applications, as defined in their Application Architecture. Each project included specific plans to standardize work processes, prevent future data quality errors, and correct the existing data errors. Time spent finding, cleaning, and formatting data was reduced significantly.

See another example from Aera Energy of a different survey of knowledge workers in *Step 4.7 – Perception of Relevance and Trust.*

Price Tag of Poor-Quality Data

This example is included with the Anecdotes technique to show how estimates of impact can sometimes be quickly quantified. *Template 4.4.3* uses figures from industry research and examples of calculations. Add your own figures and calculations. Of course, the actual numbers may be smaller or much larger than

Template 4.4.3 Price Tag of Poor-Quality Data

Formula	Calculations (Example using conservative %)	Estimated Impact of Poor-Quality Data (Example)	Additional Questions or Calculations
REVENUE: Estimated cost of bad data for most companies is 15-25% of revenue (SMR)			
Revenue x 15-25%	$100 million x 15% = $15 million	In 2019, the estimated cost of bad data to our organization was $15 million USD.	What do you think the percentage is for your organization? What else could your organization do with the money saved if you increased data quality and lowered the cost of bad data?
WASTED TIME: Up to 50% of the time of knowledge workers (those who use the data and information) is wasted due to poor-quality data (SMR). This comes from time spent trying to find the data they need, correcting errors, looking for data from other sources or reworking the data because they don't trust what they have, and dealing with mistakes that result from the poor-quality data.			
Number (#) of knowledge workers x # of hours worked per knowledge worker each week x 50%.	Team: 10 team members x 40 hours week x 45% = 180 hours a week Organization: 15,000 employees x 40 hours week x 45% = 270,000 hours a week	Within our team, an estimated 180 hours a week is wasted due to poor-quality data. Within our organization an estimated 270,000 hours a week is wasted due to poor-quality data.	Extrapolate to one month, quarter or year. Use salaries and calculate $. Calculate for your organization as a whole. What else could your team or organization accomplish if wasted time could be decreased?
ERRORS IN CREATED DATA: On average, 47% of newly created data records have at least one critical (e.g., work impacting) data error (HBR)			
# data records created weekly x 47%	10,000 x 45% = 4500	Of the 10,000 records created every week, an estimated 4500 of them have at least one critical error that then adversely impact our business.	Extrapolate to one, month, quarter or year. Specifically, how do those errors impact your business?
TRUST IN DATA: 16% of managers fully trust the data they use to make important decision (SMR)			
# managers x 16%	5000 managers x 20%	Of the 5000 managers in our company, only 1000 of them fully trust the data they use for decision-making	What do you think the percentage is for your organization? Why don't they trust the data? What does that mean to the quality of decisions being made?

Sources:

(SMR) = https://sloanreview.mit.edu/article/seizing-opportunity-in-data-quality/ by Thomas C. Redman (Nov 27, 2017)

(HBR) = https://hbr.org/2017/09/only-3-of-companies-data-meets-basic-quality-standards by Tadhg Nagle, Thomas C. Redman and David Sammon (Sept 11, 2017)

the example here. Whatever the numbers, these provide an excellent starting point for discussions on how poor-quality data could be impacting your organization. Make choices that will be meaningful within the context of your organization. Note that the second column calculations use percentages that are lower than the research percentages in the first column. I recommend being conservative when doing these types of estimates. Even so, the numbers usually end up being much larger than expected.

Step 4.2   Connect the Dots

Business Benefit and Context

Before embarking on a data quality project, always ensure the data and the quality issue is actually associated with something the business cares about. Too many times I have been told, "I spent four months on a data quality assessment. Then I talked with the business people and they said, 'That's interesting, but it isn't anything that matters to me.'" How much better to spend a short amount of time using this technique to connect the data of interest to business needs. Of course, communicating and engaging with others early in the project will also help avoid going down the wrong path.

Many of us have seen connect-the-dots puzzles when we were children. See *Figure 4.4.3*. If a child completed the puzzle on the left, she would be surprised, "It's an apple!" But we are adults and we can simply look at the puzzle without drawing the lines and know what it is. Look at the puzzle on the right. It's a bit more complicated. What is it? Most people say a swan, but a few times I have gotten the answer, "It's a frog – look at the lily pads." Even if something seems obvious to one person, it is not always obvious to

another. (And some people, like our friend who focused on the lily pads, can be very confident in an answer that turns out to be incorrect.) In our complex environments, it is not always easy to connect the dots between the business needs and the data. This technique helps you do just that.

> **Definition**
>
> **Connect the Dots (Business Impact Technique).** Illustrate the connection between business needs and the data which supports them.

This technique establishes the connection between business needs and the data which supports them. It works well in *Step 1*, before going too far into the project, to uncover or verify that the data quality issue is connected to something the business cares about or which data should be within scope for the business needs of concern.

Figure 4.4.3 Connect the dots puzzles.

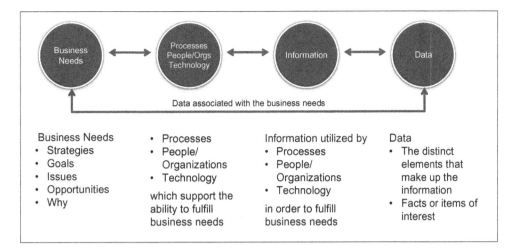

Figure 4.4.4 Connect the Dots technique.

The connect the dots technique can be done in an hour or less, depending on your background or if a little research is needed. Knowing the connection helps you describe, in business terms, why someone would care about the project you are proposing. It is a first look at seeing which data should be assessed for quality.

Reference *Figure 4.4.4* as the technique is explained.

Situation—First state, in a few sentences, the situation under discussion (not shown in the figure).

Then describe the following areas as they apply to that situation:

Business Needs—What is the specific business need or needs? Every organization has business needs. The business needs could be related to customers, products, services, strategies, goals, issues, or opportunities, or some combination.

Processes, People/Organizations, Technology—Processes, people/organizations, and technology support the ability to fulfill business needs. Which business processes support the ability to fulfill the stated business needs? Who are the people or organizations that are involved in the processes and support the ability to fulfill the business needs? What technology (i.e., applications, systems, databases) is used in the processes, by the people/organizations, in order to fulfill the stated business needs?

Information—What information is utilized by the processes, people/organizations, and technology in order to fulfill the business needs? For example, what information is in the reports or on a user interface or application screen?

Data—What data makes up the information? The information is made up of distinct elements, facts, or items of interest that we call data. This is one of the few places where I do make the distinction between data and information.

Once the business needs, on the left, follows the path to the data, on the right, there is now a connection directly between the data and the business needs.

Any of the four dots can be the starting point. For example, look first at the data and then work your way backwards to the business needs. Remember, we never do data quality for the sake of data quality. We must ensure if we have a data quality problem, that if

we address that problem, it will actually make a difference to something the business cares about. Alternatively, start with the data and ask the questions in reverse order:

- Describe, in a few sentences, the data quality issue. This is the situation.
- List the data and information of concern.
- Which technology (i.e., applications, systems, databases) houses the data and makes the information available? Which processes and people/organizations make use of that information?
- How are the processes and people/organizations using the information and why? This leads to the business needs.

This technique works well at a high level in *Step 1 – Determine Business Needs and Approach* as a quick confirmation that the data quality issue you are considering for your project is actually connected to needs that the business cares about, or if starting with the business needs, to ensure you will be looking at the data connected with it. See the *Sample Output and Templates* for examples.

Approach

1. Setup the session.

This works well with a small group of 3-5 people. You can also do it individually. No fancy tools needed. Draw the four dots on a piece of paper, flip chart, white board, or a virtual meeting alternative.

Provide an overview of the technique. Use the information and examples from this step.

2. Work through the process of connecting the dots.

Decide which "dot" is your beginning point. Start with whichever of the four areas, or dots, that you know best and work out in either direction until they are all connected. Work through each dot, in whatever order, using the instructions for *Figure 4.4.4* and the examples in the *Sample Output and Templates*.

Start at a high level, which is what you see in the examples. If using this in *Step 1*, remember you are early in the project. You don't need all the details, but you do need to show that there is a connection between data and business needs. This is a first easy opportunity to show business impact. The high-level dots can be enough to help scope the project by characterizing the business needs and the associated high-level data, processes, people/organizations and technology.

If needed, you can drill down into more detail. This technique can be used for anything related to data, such as a metadata or data governance.

3. Articulate, document, and use the results.

Describe what you learned by connecting the dots. Watch out for "data speak." Talk the language of non-data people – the language of business. See the examples for how to talk about the results.

Use results in an "elevator speech," meaning if someone asks why data quality is important in this project, you can summarize it in 30 seconds or less. Use the results in presentations or hallway conversations. The goal is not to know everything there is to know about business impact, but to take a first step to ensure you are on the right track and able to show potential project sponsors and stakeholders why the data quality project is worth pursuing.

Sample Output and Templates

Connect the Dots Example – Retail

See *Figure 4.4.5* for an example of using this technique for an online retail company.

- Situation: concern about the accuracy of turnaround time reports. These reports are generated twice a day and track the time between receiving an order and when the order is shipped.
- The starting point is information in reports.
- How are the reports used? Managers in the shipping department analyze reports and make adjustments to the shipping processes as needed. The reports are generated from system ABC.
- What business need is met by the work of these managers and the shipping processes and the fact that we are using system ABC? They support the ability of the company to keep the promise in its "principles of doing business" to ship all items within 24 hours of receiving the order. If needed, you could further describe why shipping within 24 hours is important, which might lead you to answers such as, "This differentiates us from our competitors." or "Our customers demand it."

- There is one piece still missing from our connect-the-dots sequence and that is the data. Which data goes into the twice-daily reports that track turnaround time? It is data such as order date, ship date, shipping location, etc.

We now have a connection between the data and the business need. Why is that helpful? Instead of saying, "We need accurate reports," you can explain that, "As you know, this company is proud of our promise to ship all items within 24 hours of receiving an order. We live by it and our customers count on it. What you may not know is that our managers depend on a turnaround time report to help them see if products are going out within the 24-hour time period. The information in those reports is critical so they can make necessary adjustments to their processes and personnel. Without trustworthy data in those reports, we cannot be sure we are actually meeting our promise to our customers." Showing that connection greatly increases the chance of that person responding with, "I didn't realize that. Can we set up a time to talk about this further?"

What if the data quality issue was a concern about the ship date? Others challenge the importance of spending resources to look into it. We could have started with the data and worked through to business needs. Instead of waving my hands and exclaiming, "We need high-quality ship dates!" I can say, "I know you are familiar with the twice-daily turnaround time reports managers use to monitor the shipping processes. What you may not realize is that the ship date is an integral part of those reports. Without trustworthy data in those reports, we cannot be sure we are actually meeting our promise of shipping all items within 24 hours of receiving the order, which we all know is a fundamental principle for how our company conducts its business."

Can you see the difference? Remember, this technique will not answer all questions about business impact. But it is one of the first and easiest ways to easily show business impact at a high level. It allows you to talk about the value of the project much more effectively than running around saying, "The ship dates are bad! The ship dates are bad!" and wondering why no one is listening.

Connect the Dots Example – Metadata

See *Figure 4.4.6* for an example of using the Connect the Dots technique to connect metadata with business needs.

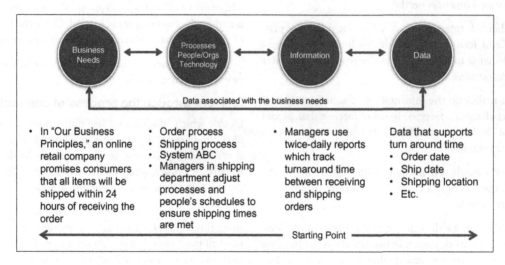

Figure 4.4.5 Connect the Dots example – retail.

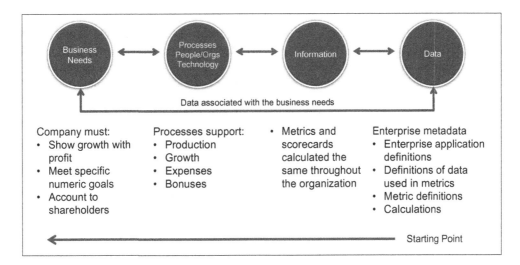

Figure 4.4.6 Connect the Dots example – metadata.

- **Data**. Our starting point this time is the data, in this case metadata. For this company their definition for enterprise metadata is any data that's used by two or more parts of the organization. Two important aspects of their metadata are the definitions and specific calculations that are done.
- **Information**. That data is used in metrics and scorecards, with the hope that they are calculated consistently throughout the company.
- **Processes**. Those scorecards and metrics are used in processes necessary to support production, manage expenses, pay bonuses, and track progress toward goals within the company.
- **Business Needs**. All of which help management understand if the company is growing, if it is growing profitably, and if they are meeting other numeric goals. This information is also required to account progress accurately to shareholders.

Metadata has now been connected to business needs. Instead of bemoaning the fact that no one will listen to how important metadata is, you greatly increase your chances of interest in metadata by being able to say, "Understanding if our company is growing profitably depends on the information in the metrics and scorecards related to production, growth, expenses, and bonuses. Those all depend on high-quality metadata to help ensure the calculations are done consistently across the company so we can trust the results to make management decisions and report to our shareholders."

 Best Practice

Business Language vs. Data Language. Recognize the difference between business language and data language. "We need high-quality billing data" is NOT a business need. The business need is *why* you need the high-quality data: "Our customers are complaining that they are being overcharged on their invoices, and the additional phone calls are increasing our support time and costs. There is early evidence that some customers are being undercharged, which leads to a loss in revenue." Is the business language or data language more compelling?

Confusing business language and data language is a common mistake, yet the distinction is important. Business stakeholders are rarely moved to action when told, "We need high-quality data." It is only when they see how the data supports the business need that you will have a chance of them supporting data quality efforts that ultimately will benefit them.

Step 4.3 | Usage

Business Benefit and Context

Usage is another easy way to show business impact. This technique takes an inventory of how the data and information are currently being used and their planned future uses, if applicable. This technique is to the left of the continuum as a technique that takes less time and is less complex. This is a low-cost way to show that the data has an impact on the business simply because of the number of ways it is used.

Current uses come from the Apply phase of the POSMAD information life cycle. The Apply phase refers to any use of the information, such as completing transactions (e.g., taking orders, creating invoices or shipping documents, closing insurance claims, scheduling appointments, filling prescriptions), creating reports, making decisions from those reports, running automated processes (e.g., electronic funds transfers, automated credit card payments), or providing an ongoing source of data for another downstream application.

Future uses can be found in business long-term strategic plans, current year road maps, and business unit or team goals and objectives.

 Definition

Usage (Business Impact Technique). Inventory the current and/or future uses of the data.

Approach

1. List current uses of the data and information within scope of your project.

Reference the Apply phase of the information life cycle. Include actual uses of the information, the people and/or organizations using it, and the technical applications where it is accessed.

2. List future uses.

Look at business plans and road maps. Talk to the managers of the business process areas or the technical applications.

3. Quantify uses as much as possible.

Try to quantify current uses as much as possible. For example, if listing a widely used report, determine the number of people using it and how often. Be aware that the number of users is not the only indicator of importance, since in one company the report they cared about was the one the CEO used each week to report to the stock market. Remember that those who run the reports often pass them on to others who make decisions and take action on the content, so you will want to account for them also.

Remember CRUD that was discussed in *Step 2.3 – Understand Relevant Technology*? Work with your technology partners to see how many people have what type of access (Create, Read, Update, Delete) to the data within scope. Pay particular attention to the Read operation which can give you clues as to usage of an application.

4. Analyze, synthesize, recommend, document, and act on results.

Capture the uses along with the sources and supporting data, tangible and intangible impact, any aspects that can be quantified, what was learned (any surprises?), and initial recommendations.

Even though most people know, at some level, that the information supports what they are doing, often even a simple list can startle the business into paying attention. One company, just by highlighting all the uses of customer data – account management, sales rep assignments, inquiry/interaction history, Customer Relationship Management (CRM), literature requests, direct mail projects, and event registration – needed very little additional motivation to support a project that would address known data quality issues.

Sample Output and Templates

The *Ten Steps in Action callout box* illustrates how two very different organizations were each able to utilize the business impact technique of Usage.

 Ten Steps in Action

Business Impact Technique of Usage

Global Company—A global company was focusing on the data in their customer master. A quick investigation, talking to a few people, uncovered the following current uses and users of that data:

- By marketing for market planning and web marketing
- By sales for targeting new customers
- By product launch teams to identify potential customers when a new product was released
- By brand teams
- By data acquisition when purchasing additional customer data
- By finance for compliance
- As the base universe of customer records for other projects

When discussing this with the sponsor of the project, it was found he was already aware of how the information was currently being utilized. He indicated the real value of the customer master data was that it was a foundational building block of the business strategy for the upcoming year. It was this future use that was important enough to spend money on the customer master data quality project. As a result, the future uses were included in any communication about business impact of this project.

Water Resource Management—A governmental water management district was raising awareness that the district could not fulfill its mission without data which was a vital asset to be managed. They wanted to communicate the importance of data governance to managing the district's data and needed to maintain support for the program goals. The technique of Usage was one of four techniques (the others being Anecdotes, Five Whys for Business Impact, and Process Impact) which were used to show business impact and value of the data. These quick assessments provided content for their communications to raise awareness and gain support. Following are examples of how data about water quality is used:

- Calibrate models
- Fulfill mandated reporting requirements
- Perform ad-hoc analysis
- Create reports
- Make decisions from the reports
- Run automated processes
- Provide an on-going source of data for another downstream application or use
- Comply with legal requirements and be defensible in court
- Test hypotheses

Note: It is often helpful to give an example for each, such as an example of a model. Reports, automated processes, and downstream applications, etc. could be further named and listed. But even having this short list is a way to quickly show business impact.

Step 4.4 | Five Whys for Business Impact

Business Benefit and Context

The Five Whys for Business Impact is an easy technique that can be used with an individual, group, or team. The technique was developed at Toyota and was originally used in manufacturing to get to root causes (it will be used for that purpose in *Step 5 – Identify Root Causes*). The same idea is applied here to get to real business impact. This technique is essentially an interview with some structure to back-and-forth questions and answers, starting with a known data quality issue and asking "Why?" five times to determine business impact. By the time the fifth "Why?" is answered, you should be able to articulate how the business will really be impacted by the low-quality data.

Definition

Five Whys for Business Impact (Business Impact Technique). Ask "Why?" five times to recognize the real effects of the quality of data on the business.

Someone once asked, "Isn't this going to be irritating – to be asked why, why, why?" This is not the 2-year-old interview with a child peppering the parents with, "Why is the grass green? Why is the sky blue?" The point is to drill down and ask the next deeper question. The question may not always be "why?" It may be "who?" "what?" "where?" "when?" "how?" "how often?" or "how long?"

This technique can be used against a general data quality issue or against a specific data quality problem found during a data quality assessment in *Step 3*.

Best Practice

Use along with gathering anecdotes. Combine the Five Whys for Business Impact with gathering anecdotes (*Step 4.1*). Once you get to the final "why?" collect details about the specific situation and use the content to better tell the story.

Approach

1. Articulate the issue associated with poor-quality data.

This can be an issue uncovered during a data quality assessment (see *Step 3 – Assess Data Quality*) or some other known data quality problem where the specific data has not yet been assessed.

2. Prepare for the interview.

Determine who will be involved. If you have the right background, you may work through the Five Whys yourself. It works well as an interview with another person or a small group of people. Schedule logistics. Explain what you are trying to accomplish. Ensure those involved have necessary background and are ready and willing to participate.

3. Conduct the interview.

Set the tone at the beginning of the meeting and make those attending feel at ease. See the *Best Practice callout box*. Ensure that everyone knows what problem is being explored. Take notes or write answers on a whiteboard so they are visible to all. Make it an easy conversation. You don't have to use the word "why" each time if another interrogative (what, where, when, who, etc.) will accomplish the same result.

Best Practice

Set the right tone. Help the respondents feel at ease from the start. You don't want those answering the questions to feel like it is a criminal interrogation. It is natural to feel defensive when asked questions and wonder, "What do they want? What if I don't give the right answer? Where is this questioning going?" Prevent those feelings by making them feel comfortable. For example:

"Good afternoon! Thanks for taking the time to meet with me. As I mentioned in my email, we are seeing that every single week, tens of thousands of products are sold as unidentified in our stores. This is due to a product code that does not scan at the Point of Sale when the customer is checking out and paying for their merchandise. We know that problems with the quality of the item master data contribute to the issue.

"We need to know more about why this issue matters to the company. I understand you have experience in this area, and I hope you can help. I'm going to ask you some questions. I will be probing a bit – asking why, who, when, where, etc. But I don't want you to feel defensive. There are no right or wrong answers – this is an investigation. It is all about helping us understand the business impact of this particular data quality issue. If you don't know the answer, that is all right, too, and we can dig into the issue together. Is that all right? Shall we put on our investigators hat and do some exploring together? Do you have any questions before we begin?"

How much better to give some background on why you are there, be relaxed yourself, help them be relaxed, and have fun with it.

4. Analyze, synthesize, recommend, document, and act on the results.

See section in *Chapter 6* for additional ideas. Capture what you learned along with the source and supporting data, tangible and intangible impacts found, any aspects that could be quantified, what was learned – confirmations or surprises, and initial recommendations.

Sample Output and Templates

The following two examples summarize the outcome of using the Five Whys for Business Impact. Caution: these examples are showing the *end* result of the conversation. They do not show the back-and-forth dialogue, all the interrogatives that were used in addition to "why?" and the discussion that got them to the business impact.

Example 1 – Quality of Reports for Compensation

Issue: There are complaints about the quality of information in reports coming out of the data warehouse

Ask: Why does the data quality matter?

Answer: The data is used in reports.

Ask: What reports?

Answer: The weekly sales reports.

Ask: Why do the weekly sales reports matter?

Answer: Compensation for sales reps is based on these reports.

Ask: Why does that matter?

Answer: If the data is wrong a highly effective sales rep may be undercompensated or another may be overcompensated.

Ask: Why does that matter?

Answer: If the sales reps do not trust their compensation, they will spend time checking and rechecking the compensation figures – time better spent selling.

Being able to discuss poor information quality in terms of impact to sales reps is much more meaningful than saying, "The report is wrong."

Example 2 – Incorrect Inventory Data

Issue: Inventory data is incorrect.

Ask: Why does the inventory data matter?

Answer: Inventory data is used in inventory reports.

Ask: Why do the inventory reports matter?

Answer: Procurement uses the inventory reports.

Ask: How does procurement use the inventory reports?

Answer: Procurement makes decisions about purchases based on the inventory reports. Procurement orders (or does not order) parts and materials for manufacturing.

Ask: Why do procurement decisions matter?

Answer: If the inventory data is wrong, then procurement may not purchase at the right time. Lack of parts and materials can impact the manufacturing schedule and delay products being sent to customers. This affects company revenue and cash flow.

Once again, being able to discuss poor information quality in terms of the impact of bad data on inventory levels, manufacturing schedules, and product time to customer is much more meaningful than saying, "The report is wrong."

Step 4.5 — Process Impact

Business Benefit and Context

Workarounds hide poor-quality data. Once workarounds become a normal part of business processes, people don't realize that change is possible. They don't see that poor-quality data causes costly problems and unnecessary distractions. By showing the effect of poor-quality data on the processes and the resulting costs, the business can make informed decisions about addressing issues that were previously unclear. Addressing process issues not only results in better quality data, it also increases efficiency.

This technique will most likely be done by a single person working with other individuals or by a small team with knowledge of the business processes. This technique is closer to the middle of the Continuum of Relative Time and Effort.

 Definition

Process Impact (Business Impact Technique). Illustrate the effects of data quality on business processes.

Approach

1. Outline the business process when good data is used and again with bad data.

Use the information life cycle from *Step 2 – Analyze Information Environment* or other business process flow as a starting point. Illustrate:

- First, with what the business process looks like when it is working well using high-quality data
- Next, with what the same business process looks like with poor-quality data

Be sure to include additional support roles and activities that may only be needed to deal with results from the bad data. See the *Sample Output and Templates* section.

2. Analyze the differences to the process with good data and compromised data.

Often just by illustrating the differences, it becomes clear that action needs to be taken. It does not always require that costs be quantified. Capture any recommendations for improving the business processes.

3. Quantify the impact, if needed.

Look at steps in the process that lend themselves to quantifying. Using the example in the *Sample Output and Templates* section, how much time is spent investigating and resolving rejection issues? Who is responsible and how much is that person's time worth?

If going in-depth with calculations, you could be combining this technique with *Step 4.7 – Cost of Low-Quality Data.*

4. Make recommendations and document the results.

Ensure that your documentation includes supporting data needed to understand the results, any tangible and intangible impact, and quantified impact. Include initial recommendations for improving the business processes.

Sample Output and Templates

Supplier Master Data Example.

Background—In one global company, all the enterprise data stewards were responsible for determining what work should be done in the upcoming year to improve the quality of the data for which they were responsible. After attending my workshop, the supplier enterprise data steward used the process impact technique and developed two process flows – one with high-quality data and the other with poor-quality data.

Process with good data—*Figure 4.4.7* shows the process of the supplier master record from creation to use. A major decision point in the process asks, "Is the request to set up the supplier master record OK?" indicated by the diamond in the middle of the figure. From previous work, the supplier enterprise data steward, knew that setup requests could be rejected for a number of reasons: incomplete or wrong information, duplicate requests, not approved, no documentation, incorrect employee request, and other.

It was known that 75% of the setup requests were rejected because of incomplete or wrong information, in other words poor-quality data. If you were to look closely at the standard process, recognizing it was the current/as-is process, you could see areas for improving and making the process more efficient. These could, and should, become recommendations for improvement at another time, but the purpose for now was looking at the current process with both good and bad data.

Process with bad data—*Figure 4.4.8* shows the same process of the supplier master record from creation to use, only this time with poor-quality data (when the answer to "Request OK?" is no). Rejected setup requests resulted in the following impacts:

- Time delay in placing orders with suppliers, paying supplier invoices, and reimbursing employees for expenses
- Rework by the central data administration team (rejecting the request, ensuring investigation and resolution, re-reviewing the updated request)

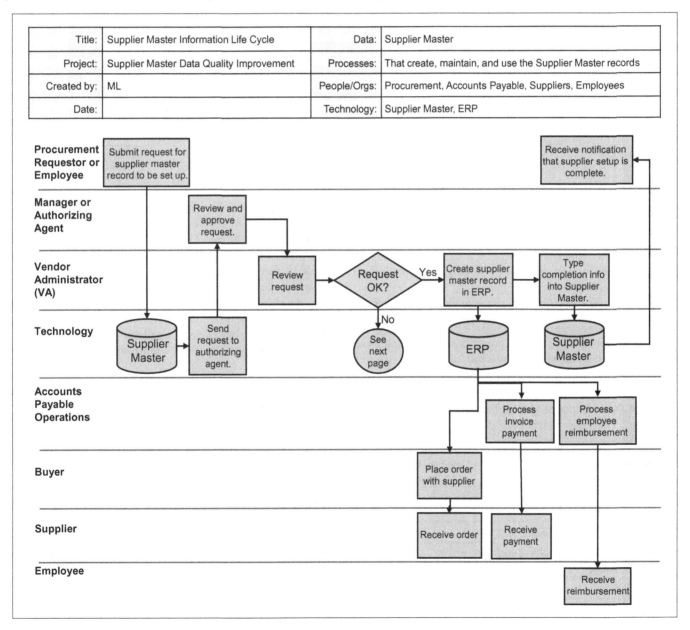

Figure 4.4.7 Process impact example – supplier master record, with high-quality data.

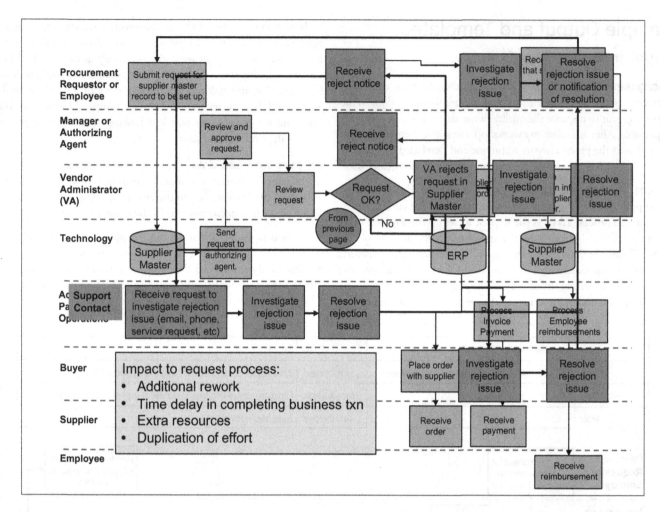

Figure 4.4.8 Process impact example – supplier master record, with poor-quality data.

- Rework by the requestor who submitted the original request (to investigate and resubmit)
- Rework by the support employee (to investigate and resolve)
- Frustrated employees
- Frustrated suppliers, many of whom are also customers of the company
- Loss of service to the company because payment has not been made

The two figures clearly show the processes when data was good (standard process) versus when data was bad (new support role and different processes which affected multiple roles).

Quantifying impacts—The supplier enterprise data steward quantified some of those impacts by interviewing some of the people in the roles that were part of the process (named in the swim lanes). She found out how long it took to complete tasks, determined the type of employee, and what they were paid based on the role and location. *Table 4.4.3* shows the spreadsheet – with fictitious numbers for illustration only. She quantified the costs for a month and then extrapolated for a year.

Table 4.4.3 Supplier Master Record – Costs of Rework from Poor-Quality Data

A	B	C	D	E	F	G
Cost of rework because of rejected requests due to incorrect or incomplete information	Amount of Time per Reject (in hours)	Cost Per Hour	Cost per Reject (B x C)	Number of Rejects per Month **	Total Number Rejects per Year (E x 12)	Total Cost Per Year (D x F)
1 US employee (to submit original request, investigate, resubmit)	3	$50	$150	150	1800	$270,000
1 US employee (to support/investigate)	2	$50	$100	150	1800	$180,000
1 <other country> employee (to review request and reject)	2	$20	$40	150	1800	$ 72,000
Total estimated annual labor costs for rework of requests that were rejected due to poor-quality data						$522,000
In $USD. Sample numbers for illustration purposes only						
Assumptions: ** Total rejected requests per month = 200 and 75% of all rejected requests are due to incorrect or incomplete information						

Results—The visual impact to the process differences between good and bad data was eye-catching. The visual along with the total impacts that were able to be quantified was significant enough that the supplier enterprise data steward was able to get funding for her data quality projects that year. Even though not all impacts could be quantified, such as frustration, it is important that they are included when presenting results.

Step 4.6 | Risk Analysis

Business Benefit and Context

The Oxford English Dictionary defines risk as: "the possibility of loss, injury, or other adverse or unwelcome circumstance; a chance or situation involving such a possibility" (OED Online, 2020).

We often think about risk as it relates to physical dangers at home or in the workplace. Risk analysis is included here as a business impact technique because poor-quality data has the potential of exposing an organization to damage. A risk analysis evaluates possible adverse effects from poor-quality data (the hazards or hazardous situations), the likelihood of them happening, severity of the damage if they do occur, and ways to mitigate the risks.

Definition

Risk Analysis (Business Impact Technique). Identify possible adverse effects from poor-quality data, evaluate the likelihood of them happening, severity if they do, and determine ways to mitigate the risks.

In their 1981 paper, "On the Quantitative Definition of Risk," Stanley Kaplan and B. John Garrick point out important ideas about risk still used today: Risk includes both uncertainty and some kind of loss or damage. Risk is subjective and relative to the person assessing the risk – which means that, qualitatively, risk depends on what a person does, knows, and does not know. For example, if a person is simply aware of a risk, the risk is reduced for that person. Risk can be large or small, but it can never be zero. Fundamentally, a risk analysis involves answering three questions: "1) What can happen? i.e., What can go wrong? 2) How likely is it that that will happen? and 3) If it does happen, what are the consequences?" (Kaplan and Garrick,1981).

This business impact technique offers one approach to analyzing risk which can be applied to your data and information quality work. It uses people's experiences and quantifies the answers in such a way that risk levels can provide input to decisions.

Approach

1. Prepare for the risk analysis.

As with any activity involving more than yourself, preparation is key to success. Identify those to be included in the risk analysis. The session may be a few people at an in-person meeting or several in an online video conference call. Invite attendees and inform their managers as needed. Ensure attendees know why they are there and are ready and willing to participate!

Determine who will facilitate the session. Schedule the venue (in-person or virtual) and have technology ready to go. Distribute any background or preparation materials *prior to* the session and prepare materials to use *during* the session. For the questions to be discussed, providing examples is always helpful. Do you want your audience to provide content from a blank template or review and give feedback on the work you have already done?

See *Data Capture and Assessment Planning* in *Chapter 6: Other Techniques and Tools* for more information about planning for a business impact assessment.

2. Discuss and complete the information in the risk analysis template.

Use the instructions and templates in the *Sample Output and Templates* section below, and adjust based on where you are in the project when the risk assessment is conducted.

3. Finalize, document, make recommendations, and use what is learned from this step.

Finalize, document, and assign actions as needed. Track issues and action items resulting from this step. Use results here as input to the appropriate spot in your project and the Ten Steps Process. See additional detail in *Analyze, Synthesize, Recommend, Document, and Act on Results* in *Chapter 6: Other Techniques and Tools*.

For a detailed look into risk management for information, see *Total Information Risk Management: Maximizing the Value of Data and Information Assets* (2014) by Alexander Borek, Ajith K. Parlikad, Jela Webb, and Philip Woodall.

Sample Output and Templates

Risk Analysis

Use *Template 4.4.4 – Risk Analysis* and the instructions below to help you analyze risk. Of course, document logistics such as the date the analysis was done, attendees, location, facilitator, etc. Which columns are used may vary depending on where you are in the project when doing the risk analysis. For example:

- If in *Step 1 – Determine Business Needs and Approach,* if using risk as input to which business needs and data quality issues should be addressed in your project, use columns 1-5 and 8.

Template 4.4.4 Risk Analysis

1	2	3	4	5	6	7	8
What can go wrong?	What is the likelihood of it happening?	What are the consequences if it does happen?	Risk Score	Risk Level	How can the risk be mitigated or controlled?	What is the impact of the mitigation?	Final decisions and actions
Identify the risk which is a hazard, hazardous situation, or source of harm. Who or what can be harmed?	The possibility that the risk will convert to some form of actual damage. Use the following scale: 5 = Almost Certain 4 = Likely 3 = Possible 2 = Unlikely 1 = Rare	The severity of the damage. Use the following scale: 1 = Insignificant 2 = Minor 3 = Moderate 4 = Major 5 = Catastrophic	Multiply Columns 2 and 3.	Assign the risk level using the Risk Score and Risk Level Charts	Identify actions (countermeasures) that can be taken to lessen the chances of the risk occurring or lessen the potential damage. There may be several countermeasures. Indicate what is already being done to mitigate the risk. List each on its own line under the associated risk.	The actions will reduce the risk significantly, somewhat, or have little impact.	Use as input to decide which business needs and data quality issues to address in *Step 1 – Determine Business Needs and Approach.* List actions to be taken to mitigate the risk OR decide to tolerate the risk when identifying root causes and specific recommendations for improvement in *Step 5 – Identify Root Causes and/or Step 6 – Develop Improvement Plans*
1.							
2.							
Etc.							

Based on Mansfield (2019), *How to Write a Business Plan (Your Guide to Starting a Business).*

- If in *Step 5 – Identify Root Causes* or *Step 6 – Develop Improvement Plans*, use columns 1-8.

Column 1. What can go wrong? Identify the risk which is a hazard, hazardous situation, or source of harm. Who might be harmed (The organization as a whole? A business unit? A team? An individual? A customer?). How will they be harmed?

Column 2. What is the likelihood of it happening? Determine the possibility that the risk will convert to some form of actual damage. Use the following scale: 5 = Almost Certain; 4 = Likely; 3 = Possible; 2 = Unlikely; 1 = Rare.

Column 3. What are the consequences if it does happen? Rank using the following scale. The severity of the damage will be: 1 = Insignificant; 2 = Minor; 3 = Moderate; 4 = Major; 5 = Catastrophic

Columns 4 and 5. Risk Score and Level. Multiply Columns 2 and Columns 3 to get the Risk Score and place in Column 4. Assign the Overall Risk Level by referencing *Figure 4.4.9* Risk Score and Risk Level Charts and place in Column 5.

If using the risk analysis to prioritize a list of items in *Step 1*, you might skip Columns 6 and 7 because you do not have enough information to determine how to mitigate the risks.

Always discuss and document final decisions and actions in Column 8. If you are determining root causes, identifying specific recommendations to address them, or developing improvement plans in *Steps 5* and *6*, you may also want to use Columns 6 and 7.

Column 6. How can the risk be mitigated? Identify actions (countermeasures) that can be taken to lessen the chances of the risk occurring, control the risk in some way, or lessen the potential damage. There may be several countermeasures. List each on its own line under the associated risk.

Column 7. What is the impact of the mitigation? Rank the actions based on if the actions will: Reduce the risk significantly; reduce the risk somewhat; have little impact.

Column 8. Final decision and actions. In *Step 1*, use as input to decide which business needs and data quality issues to address. Document your decisions. Always assign an owner and due date for any action to be taken.

If in *Step 5* and/or *Step 6*, decide:

- If actions (countermeasures) will be taken to mitigate the risk, or
- If the risk will be tolerated, and therefore no action will be taken.

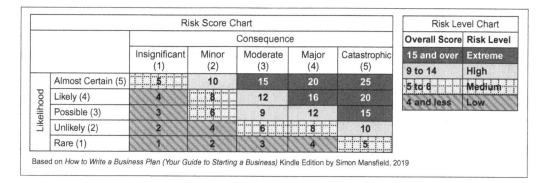

Based on *How to Write a Business Plan (Your Guide to Starting a Business)* Kindle Edition by Simon Mansfield, 2019

Figure 4.4.9 Risk score and risk level charts.

Step 4.7 Perception of Relevance and Trust

Business Benefit and Context

This dimension uses a formalized survey, such as individual interviews, group workshops, online surveys, etc. to gather the opinions of those who use and/or manage the data and information. If the trigger for the survey is to understand what data or information is most important, useful, or valuable to those using or managing the data (an indicator of business impact), then the design of the survey will focus there. However,

while you have the opportunity to be in contact, it makes sense to uncover their opinions of and trust in the quality of the data as well.

Because the reason for surveying the users could be prompted from either the business impact or data quality viewpoint, it is included here in *Step 4.7* as a business impact technique (with full instructions and examples), and also in *Step 3.1* as a data quality dimension (with minimal instructions and pointed to this step).

The definition, whether as a data quality dimension or business impact technique, is the same.

Definition

Perception of Relevance and Trust (Business Impact Technique). The subjective opinion of those who use information and/or those who create, maintain, and dispose of data regarding: 1) Relevance – which data is of most value and importance to them, and 2) Trust – their confidence in the quality of the data to meet their needs.

Depending on where you are in the project a survey can fulfill different purposes. For example:

1) Relevance – which data is of most *value and importance* to them, in order to:
   - Uncover data quality issues affecting users
   - Prioritize which issues should be the focus of the project
   - To decide which data should have first priority to assess, manage, and maintain
2) Trust – their *confidence in the quality* of the data, in order to:
   - Understand the impact of poor-quality data on user's job responsibilities and use this to help build a business case for data quality efforts.
   - Understand how users feel about the data and compare their *opinions* about the quality to *actual* results from other data quality assessments. This allows you to address any gaps between perception and reality through communication.

As part of an ongoing control after your project is complete, an assessment for this dimension could be conducted on an annual or biennial basis, much as employee satisfaction surveys are conducted. Results are compared for trends over time and to ascertain: 1) If data being managed is still relevant to the users, and 2) If actions to prevent data quality issues are leading to expected increases in trust of the data.

Approach

1. Prepare for the survey.

See *Conduct a Survey* in *Chapter 6: Other Techniques and Tools* to help. Adjust and apply the general instructions there along with those in this step to meet your specific goals. If needed, solicit the help of someone experienced in creating and administering surveys.

Determine the purpose of the survey—Determine what decisions will be made based on survey results. What questions need to be asked to get the relevant input? What do you need to know and at what level of detail? Decide if answers need to be on a general business level and/or on a more detailed data subject level. Many times, a survey from the business impact point of view will have more general questions than those driven by data quality.

To support the purpose, be clear against which set of data or information, from which datastore or application, and at what level of detail, the questions should be asked. A field-by-field survey is

often not effective; you may find resistance to participate and will not get more useful results than you would if you asked questions from a broader perspective. For example, the survey could ask perception of relevance and trust by:

- How user sees the information on a report or dashboard
- Label on the screen of the application or software
- Data subject or object level, e.g., just address or types of addresses, e.g., customer address, shipping address, billing address, patient address, hospital address
- Data element level, e.g., Address line 1, Address line 2, City, State or Province, Postal Code, Country (which, as mentioned, is often too detailed)

Identify those to be surveyed—Determine whether you will survey only those who apply the information or also those who manage (create, update, delete) the data. It might be helpful to have one survey showing the information at a higher level for managers who use reports and analytics for decisions and a separate survey with a more detailed level of the same data for those who use it to complete transactions.

If the complete population of interest cannot be surveyed, select a representative sample to participate. Document the name of the respondent, job title, functional area/business unit/department/team, and total number of similar roles within the group. Ensure the survey respondents have the right knowledge and experience to answer the questions.

Keep in mind the people being surveyed and how they are using the data. Some will not have a tolerance for detail. You may have different surveys for different audiences. For instance, a survey for someone doing data entry or using the data at the field level may be more detailed than a survey of a sales rep using the information to understand their assigned customers or an executive who uses the information in a variety of reports. Even for those creating data, it may be more helpful to understand their perceptions at a higher level than at a detailed level.

One project decided to survey knowledge workers who used a particular application. The results were going to be used to prioritize the data quality issues to address in the project. The project team pulled a list of those with logins to the application, only to find that the list was outdated. People had left the job, changed responsibilities, or shared logins and passwords with coworkers. In other words, the quality of the user list was so poor that we did not know who to include for our data quality survey. A clean-up effort on the logins and the list of users had to be completed before the survey about data quality could be started!

Select the survey method and prepare the survey instrument—The reasons for the survey, desired respondents, number of participants, etc. will inform the design of the survey instrument. In order to obtain usable results, ensure information is presented clearly and that the respondents will understand what is being asked. The data quality dimension of Presentation Quality applies here (see *Step 3.10*).

Think of the survey from the respondent point of view. Explain why the survey is being conducted, and how the results will be used.

Describe the benefit to the respondent and to the organization represented by the respondent. Call attention to the confidentiality of the survey and that individual's responses will not be identified – if that is true. Include a deadline for returning the survey and who to call with questions.

Capture pertinent information that will help analyze survey results such as respondent name, position/title, function/business unit/team within the organization. If conducting the survey in-person or via phone, document the date, time, location, respondents, those conducting the interview, and others listening in.

Depending on the number of people being surveyed, an effective method is to interview people directly either in-person or via video conferencing. Ask some questions to be answered using a measurable scale. This helps quantify responses when analyzing results. In addition, including open-ended questions will encourage additional dialogue. This often reveals important details, providing a more complete picture of the challenges people are facing.

If the number of people being surveyed does not allow for direct interviews, surveys can also be conducted electronically, with follow-up phone calls as needed to clarify answers.

Your survey may be a few open-ended questions, where you want to encourage a conversation, rather than a structured set of questions, or it may go more in-depth into the data and require more structure. See the *Sample Output and Templates* section for examples of surveys, both high-level and detailed, and how to use the perception survey results as input to prioritization.

Outline the process and timing for the survey—Decide when in the project timeline the survey will be conducted. Take into account time needed for preparation or when the results need to be available for use. Determine how and when:

- Survey participants will be notified and invited to participate
- The survey will be conducted
- The responses will be collected
- Responses will be analyzed
- Results will be communicated

2. Conduct the survey.

Carry out the survey according to plan. Monitor responses and response rates. Make adjustments if needed during the survey period. Stop the survey when the criteria for completion has been met (e.g., time deadline or number of responses).

3. Analyze, synthesize, recommend, document, and act on survey results.

See section of the same name in *Chapter 6: Other Techniques and Tools* for more details. Analyze results. What do you know about perceptions of data quality and business impact that you did not know before? What planned actions were confirmed? What new actions need to take place? What actions need to be taken now and what can wait?

If a survey of perception was done prior to the data quality project (see examples in *Sample Output and Templates*), be sure to compare the perception survey results to the actual data quality from other assessment results. Assuming the data in question is of high importance:

- **If perception of quality is low and actual quality is high.** Use communication and engagement to close the gap between perception and reality to help knowledge workers know they can use the data with confidence
- **If perception of quality is low and actual quality is low.** Admit there is a problem, put plans into place to address them, and share what is being done
- **If perception of quality is high and actual quality is low.** The organization is at risk. Immediately address the quality problems and share what is being done
- **If perception of quality is high and actual quality is high.** Share the good news!

When sharing results, don't just present what was found, allow time to gauge reaction. What did they expect and what were surprises? Ensure they know decisions and actions resulting from the survey. See *Step 10* for additional ideas when communicating and engaging with people. Consult your stakeholder list to decide who to engage with both before the survey and when analysis is complete:

- Project sponsors
- Other stakeholders, such as process or application owners that could be impacted by survey results
- Project team members
- Survey respondents
- Managers of survey respondents

Always document and make available for future reference. Some learnings will be used later in the project.

Sample Output and Templates
Survey – Uncovering Business Needs and Data Quality Issues

If the goal of a survey is to uncover critical business needs and/or data quality issues to help you decide the focus of your data quality project, it could consist of questions such as:

- What business needs (related to customers, products, services, strategies, goals, issues, opportunities) are of most importance to you? Your team? Your business unit? This organization as a whole?
  - Why are these important?
  - What data is associated with the business need?
  - What processes, people/organizations, and technology are associated with the business need?
- Please tell us about a specific situation or pain point where the lack of data quality caused problems.
  - What was the impact?
  - What data is associated with this situation?
- What does data quality mean to you?
- From your perspective, what are the most important business needs and/or data quality issues for this project to address?

Of course, modify to fit your needs, use the words meaningful to those you are questioning, and give examples to help them understand the questions. These types of surveys are often done as individual interviews.

Survey – Understanding Business Impact of Data Quality

To show the impact of data quality from a knowledge worker's point of view, C. Lwanga Yonke, Information Quality Process Manager at Aera Energy LLC, conducted a survey of stakeholders. The survey was sent to more than 60 knowledge workers (engineers, geoscientists, technicians, etc.) and consisted of two questions: "1) Describe an example where bad things happened because of poor-quality information. If possible, describe the impact in operational terms, then quantify it in terms of production loss and in terms of dollars; and 2) Repeat, but provide examples of good things that happened because you had quality information available."

The anecdotes and examples received were compiled into one document, which was then widely distributed throughout the company. The power of the document came from the fact that it captured the voice of the information customers, not that of IT or the information quality team. All the anecdotes were from knowledge workers – the people best placed to describe the impact of information quality on their ability to execute the company's work processes.

The survey results document served several purposes:

- It helped build the case for action for various data quality improvement projects.

- It helped solidify wide support for Aera's data quality process in general.
- It was used in a training manual to show others how to quantify the cost of poor-quality information and the return on investment of information quality improvement projects. Lwanga fondly recalls, for example, how the leader of one Enterprise Architecture Implementation project drew on several stories to rally support for incorporating specific data quality process improvements and data remediation work into his project plan.

Also see *Step 4.1 – Anecdotes* for another example of how results from a similar survey were used to secure approval and funding for Aera's Enterprise Architecture Implementation program.

Detailed Survey of Data Quality and Business Impact

Template 4.4.5 shows a structured way to ask detailed questions about both relevance and trust.

The top part of the survey provides an introduction for the respondents and provides a way to capture demographic information about them.

The body of the survey has two statements where respondents consider specific data, using the scale provided, to provide their opinions:

Template 4.4.5 Perception of Relevance and Trust Survey							
Introduction to the Survey:							
Name:							
Function/ Business Unit/Team:							
Position/ Title:							
Brief description of job responsibilities:							
Relevance or Value							
This information is important to me in performing my job:							
	Strongly Agree	Agree	Neutral/ Undecided	Disagree	Strongly Disagree	Not Applicable – I do not use this information	How do you use this information?
Customer Name							
Customer Email							
Etc.							
Etc.							
Trust in the Quality							
In my opinion, the quality of this information is suitable for performing my job:							
	Strongly Agree	Agree	Neutral/ Undecided	Disagree	Strongly Disagree	Not Applicable – I do not use this information	Why or why not?
Customer Name							
Customer Email							
Etc.							
Etc.							

- This information is important to me in performing my job (indicates relevance or value).
- In my opinion, the quality of this information is reliable and suitable for performing my job (indicates perception of data quality).

Relevance, importance, business impact, and value are roughly synonymous here. Trust, confidence, quality, and reliability are also roughly synonymous for these purposes. Use the words that are most meaningful to those to be surveyed.

Note that open-ended questions are also included. If open-ended questions are used, ensure there is enough room for the respondents to type in their answers.

Modify the questions and use the level of detail for the data or information to best suit your purposes. Format to fit the audiences and survey method (e.g., electronic or hardcopy).

Determine the response scale. You may assign a number to each of the options in the survey response scale to help when analyzing results (e.g., strongly agree = 5 down to strongly disagree = 1). See options for survey response scales in *Conduct a Survey* in *Chapter 6*.

Using Perception Survey Results to Prioritize

Use *Table 4.4.4* when analyzing results from a survey of the perception of both relevance/importance/value of the data and trust/confidence in the quality of the data. Use as input to deciding which data should be included in a data quality project.

Table 4.4.4 Analyzing Perceptions – Relevance vs. Trust

Perception of Relevance/ Value of the Data			Perception of Trust in/Quality of the Data			
Of what importance is this data to performing your job?			In your opinion, what is the quality of the data?			Analysis
Low 1	Medium 2	High 3	Low 1	Medium 2	High 3	Action to take based on the perceptions:
x			x			Low importance/low quality: Do not spend time on this data.
x				x		Low importance/medium quality: Do not spend time on this data.
x					x	Low importance/high quality: Do not spend time on this data.
	x		x			Medium importance/low quality: Possibility of spending time on this data, if data is connected to a current critical business need.
	x			x		Medium importance/medium quality: Possibility of spending time on this data, if data is connected to a current critical business need.
	x				x	Medium importance/high quality: Verify the actual quality.
		x	x			High importance/low quality: Highest priority data to include in a data quality project if data is connected to a current critical business need. Verify actual quality through other data quality assessments.
		x		x		High importance/medium quality: High priority data to include in a data quality project if data is connected to a current critical business need. Verify actual quality through other data quality assessments.
		x			x	High importance/high quality: If the data can be verified as high-quality, then no need to be included in a data quality improvement project.

Step 4.8   Benefit vs. Cost Matrix

Business Benefit and Context

The Benefit vs. Cost Matrix technique prioritizes lists of issues, recommendations, improvements, or opportunities by rating and analyzing the relationship between the benefits and costs of each item, and placing them on a cost-benefit matrix. It is a standard quality technique that also works well with data and information quality.

> 📖 **Definition**
>
> **Benefit vs. Cost Matrix (Business Impact Technique).** Rate and analyze the relationship between benefits and costs of issues, recommendations, or improvements.

This technique can be used at several points within the Ten Steps Process. It can be used to review and prioritize alternatives and provide answers to questions such as:

- Which issues or opportunities should be the focus of our data quality project? (In *Step 1 – Determine Business Needs and Approach*)
- Which data quality dimensions should we assess? (in *Step 3 – Assess Data Quality*)
- Which issues learned from our data quality assessments are impactful enough to continue to root cause analysis? (in *Step 5 – Identify Root Causes*)
- Which recommendations for improvements – prevention, correction, detection – should we implement? (In *Step 6 – Develop Improvement Plans*)
- Which goals are the most important for our data quality program (not project) to accomplish next year and should be included on our program roadmap?

Approach

1. Select and prepare participants for the benefit vs. cost prioritization session.

This technique could be done with the project team during a regular meeting, but it is often conducted as a facilitated session with a number of stakeholders. Select a neutral facilitator to lead the discussion and a scribe to take notes. Invite those who have background in the items to be prioritized, such as project team members, sponsors, business process owners, application owners, subject matter experts, and stewards. Limit the number involved to a few people who can represent the larger groups.

Prepare those attending so that they have the background they need, they support what you are trying to accomplish, and they are prepared to participate. Determine the method for discussing and capturing ratings. Be creative. This can be done via video conferencing or with a presentation program such as PowerPoint. It can be as low-tech as placing sticky notes or dots on a whiteboard or large sheets of paper. Any method is suitable that allows a quick change to ratings based on the discussion, and that will enhance, not hinder, the flow of the prioritization.

2. Finalize and define the list of items to be prioritized.

List and clarify each item to be prioritized. Give each a title and include a brief description so everyone will be clear on what is being prioritized. See *Figure 4.4.10 – Benefit vs. cost matrix template with list.* Each attendee should have a copy of the list for easy reference and to take notes during the session.

3. Determine scales for benefit and cost

Define each axis on the matrix and determine the scales to be used when prioritizing, in other words, what is meant by benefit and cost?

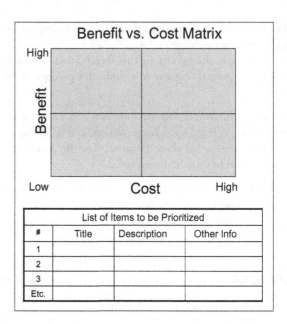

Figure 4.4.10 Benefit vs. cost matrix template with list

Consider the examples below to get you thinking.

Examples of benefits include:

- Impact – positive impact to the business if the recommendation is implemented, with examples for low, medium and high
- Expected profits or savings
- Payoff – performance and features
- Improved customer satisfaction
- Specific items that support business needs
- Report availability – decreased time from receiving data to having them available in reports
- Simplified business or data management processes
- Some other indicator of benefit to your organization

Examples of costs include:

- Time to implement a recommendation, e.g., this improvement can be implemented in x amount of time: low = 1 month, medium = 3 months, high = 6 months or more.
- Cost – the relative outlay in dollars, e.g., this recommendation will take x dollars to implement: low = $100,000 or less, medium = $500,000, high = $1,000,000 or more
- Specific skills, knowledge, or experienced resources required to implement the solution
- Some other indicator of cost meaningful to your organization

The scales can be qualitative (e.g., customer perspective) or quantitative (e.g., effects on cycle time). When finalizing the scales, terms, definitions, and examples for each side of the matrix, ensure they are applicable to what is being prioritized and meaningful to those doing the prioritizations.

4. In the session, rate each item and place on the benefit vs. cost matrix.

Use the information finalized prior to the meeting. For example, if customer satisfaction is an important criterion for benefit, you would ask when ranking, "What is the impact of recommendation number one on customer satisfaction (low to high)?"

If time to implement is an important criterion for cost, ask, "What is the time to implement for recommendation one (from low to high)?" You can have multiple criteria to consider when rating but make the set manageable (not too many).

Rating can be done by the team as a whole or individually. One approach is to let each individual quickly write down his or her rating and then discuss as a group. Another is to place the various options on the matrix so the varying opinions can be seen and discussed and then agreement reached on final placement. The goal is to reach agreement for each of the placements fairly rapidly. Ensure that the final ranking is visually placed on the matrix.

This technique is not meant to take many days while calculating exact figures. It is most useful with a first-pass "gut feeling" approach, which is actually based on the knowledge and experience of those in the room. Once the list has been prioritized, more in-depth calculations can be done on the high-priority items as needed.

5. Evaluate ratings, select final priority, and document results.

Discuss the results of the placement of the items on the matrix. Evaluate each one according to the definitions within each quadrant. (See *Figure 4.4.11* in the *Sample Output and Templates* section.) If the evaluation causes the initial rating to be changed, agree on final placement on the matrix. At this point during the discussion, the items are often ranked against each other to get to the final priority. For example, several items could have been rated and placed in Quadrant 2 and it is not possible to implement all of them. Of those, relative to each other, which are the highest priority?

The scribe should document any assumptions or considerations used to determine the placement on the matrix and final priority. Every point of conversation does not need to be written down, but if there is long discussion or disagreement on an item, be sure to capture the main ideas and how the final decision was reached. You will have to report the results of the session to others not in the room, often to get approval. They will ask questions and you will be glad to have these details to better answer them.

6. Communicate and use the results.

Determine, specifically, what will be done now that priorities have been finalized. Use what you have learned to guide your actions:

- What will now be done and who is the owner
- What will NOT be done, what not to do

- What is an activity vs. a project
- What you can start now
- What requires more planning

Share results of the prioritization. Get feedback, and ultimately support, for the choices made.

Sample Output and Templates

Benefit vs. Cost Matrix Template

Figure 4.4.10 shows a blank benefit vs. cost matrix. As described in the instructions above, modify each axis to fit your needs and prepare the list of items to be prioritized.

List for Prioritization

Use *Template 4.4.6* to compile the list of the items to be prioritized. These may be:

- A list of data quality issues, to select which should be the focus of the project in *Step 1 – Determine Business Needs and Approach*
- A list of data quality dimensions, to choose which should be assessed in *Step 3 – Assess Data Quality*
- A list of issues uncovered during a data quality assessment, to determine which are impactful enough to go forward with root cause analysis in *Step 5*
- A list of specific recommendations for improvements, to decide which should have detailed plans outlined in *Step 6*, and implemented in *Steps 7, 8,* and/or *9*
- A list of activities or goals for a data quality program, to decide which are of the highest priority to be part of the program roadmap
- Any time when needing to prioritize a list of options where considering benefit and cost is helpful

Provide items to be prioritized to those attending the session (listed in the first three columns). After the session, complete the remaining columns to document results of the prioritization.

Benefit vs. Cost Matrix – Evaluating Results

Once each item has been rated and placed on the matrix, the results must be further evaluated. *Figure 4.4.11* describes what each of the four quadrants means. Use this to analyze results and help determine the final priority.

Template 4.4.6 Benefit vs. Cost Matrix Worksheet

	Items to be Prioritized		Ratings		Outcome		
No.	Title	Brief Description	Benefit	Cost	Final Priority	Rational for Decision/Assumptions	Owner
1							
2							
3							
Etc.							

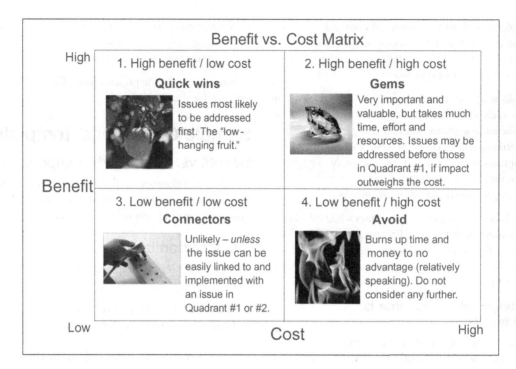

Figure 4.4.11 Benefit vs. cost matrix – evaluating the results

Benefit vs. Cost – Prioritized Data Quality Dimensions

Very often, selecting which data quality dimensions to assess is easy. However, if you are having difficulty deciding which would be the best to assess within the resource constraints, this technique can be used. *Table 4.4.5* shows the results from one company which used the matrix to prioritize which data quality dimension should be assessed during their project. Note that the matrix was called a "Payoff Matrix" and the terms "Possible Payback" and "Perceived Effort" were used for benefit and cost, respectively.

Table 4.4.5 Benefit vs. Cost – Prioritized Data Quality Dimensions

Data Quality Dimension	From Payoff Matrix (Low, Medium, or High)		Decision * (Yes or No)	Rational for Decision/Assumptions on Which Decision Was Made
	Possible Payback	Perceived Effort		
Data Specifications	High	Medium	Yes	• Consensus on high payback but level of effort not clear • Will evaluate only those standards documented and readily available • Will evaluate data domains, business rules, and data entry guidelines • Will not evaluate detailed data model or naming conventions for tables and data fields
Data Integrity Fundamentals	High	High	Yes	• Can use profiling tool to help automate the effort • Profile data for two countries
Accuracy	High	High	Yes	• Authoritative source of reference still to be decided (e.g., direct contact with customers via phone or other means)
Consistency and Synchronization	High	Medium	No	• Not enough resources or time available • Consider for next project
Timeliness	High	Medium	No	• Not enough time to look at two countries' data in two systems • Consider for next project

* Decision based on ranking, discussion, and answer to: Will we assess the data quality dimension as part of this project? Yes or No

Ten Steps in Action

Benefit vs. Cost Matrix – One Technique, Two Companies

Figure 4.4.12 shows the output of facilitated prioritization sessions from two different companies where the Benefit vs. Cost Matrix technique was used. These are shared to illustrate that this technique works well in both a low-tech and high-tech manner. Both examples successfully used the technique to make better decisions and guide their actions.

Example 1—The example on the left shows how the Benefit vs. Cost technique was used to prioritize which items were most important for a data quality program to work on during the upcoming year. You can see that it was simply a flipchart with one sticky note, numbered, for each of the recommendations being prioritized. Note that the vertical axis was called "Business Impact" (not Benefit). After the initial prioritization, each quadrant was named: 1 = Optimal, 2 = High Potential, 3 = Low Potential, 4 = Unlikely. The results from this session were used

to guide the data quality program for the next few years. The fact that it was done in a low-tech manner had no bearing on the good results.

Example 2—The example on the right shows the prioritization for 34 specific recommendations that came out of a data quality project. The result was nine top "Must-Do" recommendations to implement and four "Very Important" recommendations. Having then a shorter list to work with, the team and management came to agreement on the improvements to be implemented. The project sponsor had originally planned only for data cleanup. She had been convinced to try another approach and look at data quality more holistically. At the end of the project, she said, "I appreciate the project for guiding my funding decisions. 44% of the recommendations were quick wins – cost little but made definite improvements. Instead of embarking on a cleanup project it helped me prioritize and know where to spend my money." An excellent reminder of benefits from a data quality project!

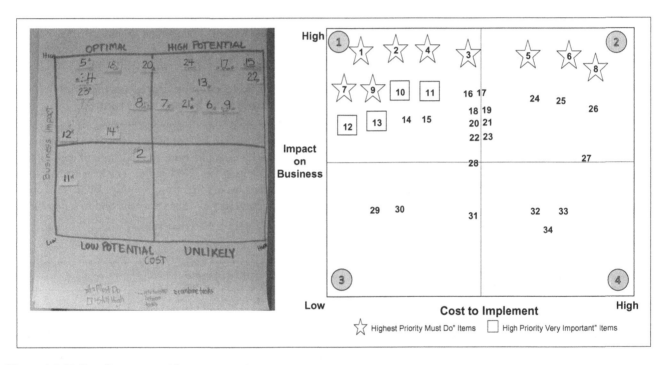

Figure 4.4.12 Benefit vs. cost matrix – two examples.

Step 4.9 — Ranking and Prioritization

Business Benefit and Context

Many times, a business person is asked, "Which data is most important to your business?" Often the quick answer is "I don't know." Actually, they do know, but we haven't asked the question in the right way. This technique is an excellent way to facilitate a conversation with your business people and provide context so they can answer that question. The context this technique provides is

the business processes in which they are involved and how they use the data. Prioritization is based on the impact of those business processes when specific data is missing or incorrect. Priority will vary for the different uses of the same data. Ranking and determining business impact are best performed by those who actually use the data or those who are designing new business processes and practices that will re-shape data usage.

This technique works well in:

- *Step 1 – Determine Business Needs and Approach*, to identify Critical Data Elements (CDEs), the most important data, on which to focus for the project overall.
- *Step 9 – Monitor Controls*, as input to setting targets for data quality for specific data fields.

 Definition

Ranking and Prioritization (Business Impact Technique). Rank the impact of missing and incorrect data on specific business processes.

Approach

1. Determine the specific information, along with business processes and its uses, to be prioritized.

Preparation is required to determine business focus and the specific processes and data to rank. Focus on the business processes that use and retrieve the information. Refer to the Apply phase in the Information Life Cycle POSMAD.

The ranking can be applied at whichever level of detail will be useful: field level, groupings of data consisting of several related elements, or sets of information. Examples:

- To complete a mailing to a customer, one must have complete name and address information.
- To make a sale of a high-priced product, one must know the technical buyer name, the decision maker, the sales cycle state, and so forth.

- To establish a CRM program, in addition to customer name and address, one must know the customer profile with attributes about a customer's behavior.
- To pay a vendor, one must have complete and current invoice information.

2. Identify and prepare those to be involved in the prioritization session.

A facilitated session is the most effective method for conducting the ranking. Decide who to invite to the session based on the business processes, who uses the information, and the data to be prioritized. It helps to involve people representing different interests, including senior managers. Then the very process of considering these questions becomes a way to facilitate understanding of the various uses of and importance of data, build data quality awareness, and support data quality improvement.

Prepare those attending so they have the background needed, they support what you are trying to accomplish, and they come ready and willing to participate. Determine the process for discussing and capturing the rankings. Make sure you can quickly change the rankings if needed. The method should enhance, not hinder, the flow of the prioritization. Have a neutral facilitator, scribe, and timekeeper.

3. In the ranking session, agree on the final processes and information to be ranked.

Ensure that there is understanding and agreement among the participants on what is to be ranked and why. Explain the process of ranking and give examples from your business of each ranking on the scale to be used (see *Table 4.4.6*). For instance, an incorrect prefix in a name would not cause complete failure of the mailing process (i.e., the ability to deliver the mail) and so it may be ranked

Table 4.4.6 Example – Impact of Missing or Incorrect Data on Business Processes

| Business Process | Individual Process Rankings | | | |
| | Mailings | Reports | Territory Management | |
Department	Marketing	Data Management	Sales	Final Overall Ranking
Sales Rep Code	C	A	A	A
Prefix	C	C	C	C
Contact Name	B	A	B	A
Site Name	C	A	A	A
Division	C	B	B	B
Department	B	B	B	B
Address	A	A	B	A
City, State, Zip	A	A	A	A
Email	A	C	A	A

Scale:

A = Complete failure of the process or unacceptable financial, compliance, legal, or other risk will result.

B = Process will be hampered, and significant economic consequences will result.

C = Negligible effects on process, minimal economic consequences will result

N/A = not applicable

a C or a D. However, in the US an incorrect zip code would cause complete failure (i.e., mail could not be delivered) and so it would be ranked an A.

4. Rank the data for each business process.

The facilitator will lead the attendees through the ranking. For each process, discuss the impact of poor-quality data by asking, "If this information were missing or incorrect, what would the impact be on the process?" The questions can apply to the organization as a whole, to a specific division, or to business processes. Determine the scale to be used prior to the session. Scale for ranking data:

A (or 1 or High) = Complete failure of the process or unacceptable financial, compliance, legal, or other risk will result.

B (or 2 or Medium) = Process will be hampered, and significant economic consequences will result.

C (or 3 or Low) = Negligible effects on process, minimal economic consequences will result

N/A = not applicable

For example, if "Contact Name" were missing or incorrect, what would the impact to the Territory Assignments process? To the reporting process? As each of these questions is answered, a value judgment is made by the individual attendees. Go through each piece of information and each process. Discussion should be encouraged as the ranking continues.

If needed, to further provide context for those doing the ranking, ask the following additional questions:

- What decisions do you make that rely significantly on the data?
- What are the impacts of these decisions in terms of
  - Lost revenue?
  - Increased costs?
  - Delays in responding to changing business conditions?
  - Regulatory and legal exposure and risk?
  - Relations with customers, suppliers, and other external parties?
  - Public embarrassment and corporate standing?
  - Business process halts or unacceptable delays?
  - Substantial misapplication of resources?

This is a subjective process, but it has proven to be very effective, because it ultimately relies on the knowledge and experience of people who use the data. There is no "correct" ranking; it depends on the use of the data and personal opinion. The process does not call for in-depth analyses. The initial "gut feel" ranking is usually correct and should be the one used. Avoid analysis paralysis by moving quickly through the rankings and relying on your initial reactions. At the same time encourage discussion and understanding between the participants.

Participants in the exercise will not always rank data the same way. If you are ranking for different uses or processes, let each participant rank the data individually. For instance, customer name may be given a high ranking by a sales rep who personally contacts them, but lower by someone concerned with reporting. Important: After all the rankings are completed, determine the final overall ranking. Realize that the given data should be managed to the highest level of business impact indicated. A ranking of C by one business process and a ranking of A by a different process indicates that the data should be treated as an A.

5. Rank the ability to collect and maintain the data, but only if needed.

Rank the data based upon the ability to collect and maintain it – but only if you think the knowledge gained will help you make decisions and take action in some way. 1 = easy; 2 = medium; 3 = difficult. Rank the ability to collect vs. the ability to maintain the data separately only if the processes for doing so are significantly different. See *Table 4.4.7* for input when analyzing results if this additional level of ranking is completed.

6. Assign a final overall ranking and analyze results.

There will be differences in the individual rankings. The final overall ranking is the highest one given by any of the processes. Look for differences between those who use the data and those who create or maintain it.

7. Make recommendations and document the results.

Make recommendations based on what was learned. The results can be used to prioritize what information is important enough to improve. It can also provide input when setting targets for data quality for metrics. Capture what was learned (including both surprises and confirmations of opinion) and initial recommendations based on the results. In one session, the area sales manager found that his sales reps were responsible for collecting information that they didn't use, but which they passed through to marketing. The information was essential to the marketing processes. This knowledge resulted in a promise by the area sales manager to convey and motivate his sales reps to spend the time required to ensure the accuracy of the information.

 Key Concept

While the rankings themselves are very useful, one of the biggest benefits from this technique is the conversation between those who utilize or affect the quality of the same information, yet who may not usually interact with each other. A successful session will result in increased understanding and cooperation between those who are responsible for the quality of the information and those who depend on the information.

Sample Output and Templates

A global high-tech company wanted to understand the impact of poor-quality customer data on its processes. One manager from each team (Marketing, Sales, and Data Management) participated in a facilitated session. Prior to the session, an individual meeting was held with each of the managers to educate them about the reasons for the session and finalize which of their business processes was most important to include in the prioritization. Each chose one critical business process to be used in the ranking session:

- Marketing chose mailings (for special events, promotions, subscriptions, etc.).
- Sales chose territory management (for maintaining sales rep geographic assignments within each district).
- Data management chose reports (for making business decisions, such as account lists and territory assignments).

Each agreed the time spent would be worthwhile. They came to the session knowing why they were there and were ready and

Table 4.4.7 Ranking Analysis

Impact of Non-Quality Data on the Business Process	Ability to Collect/ Maintain the Data	Considerations When Analyzing
A (or 1 or High) = Complete failure of the process or unacceptable financial, compliance, legal, or other risk will result.	Easy	The data is very important to the business process and is easy to collect. This implies the business is actually using, collecting, and maintaining the data on a regular basis. Is this being done?
	Medium	The data is very important, but it is not easy to collect and maintain. This implies there will be some possibility of data quality problems and a potential need to improve the processes for managing the data.
	Difficult	The data is very important, but it is hard to collect and maintain. There is a high probability of poor data quality and a high possibility of and need for process improvement.
B (or 2 or Medium) = Process will be hampered, and significant economic consequences will result.	Easy	The data is somewhat important to the business and is easy to collect and maintain. This implies the business is using the data and that the data is actually being collected and maintained. Is this being done?
	Medium	Determine if the consequences of not having the correct data are great enough to warrant the extra effort to collect and maintain them.
	Difficult	Determine if the consequences of not having the correct data are great enough to warrant the extra effort to collect and maintain them.
C (or 3 or Low) = Negligible effects on process, minimal economic consequences will result	Easy	May want to continue collecting/maintaining this data as long as it is easy to do so. Appears data provides no value to the business. Continue to collect/ maintain data only if it is easy to do so as part of processes that already collect/maintain critical data.
	Medium	May not want to spend resources to collect/maintain data. Appears data provides no value to the business. However, double-check yourself by asking, "If you could get data more easily, would it be more important?" If yes, should the business find better ways to collect and maintain data? If not, why spend any resources collecting this data in the first place?
	Difficult	May not want to spend resources to collect/maintain data. Appears data provides no value to the business. If data provides no value and is difficult to collect/maintain, why spend any resources collecting this data in the first place? Is it worthwhile to keep the data? Can the data be removed or a warning set for knowledge workers so that it is clear the data is not reliable?

willing to participate. Each piece of information was discussed, using the approach outlined in this step. Table *4.4.6* summarizes the outcome. The column Final Overall Ranking uses the highest-ranked impact from any of the processes. For example, if one process ranked the impact of missing or incorrect data as A and another

ranked it as C, the final overall ranking was A, not the average (B). Team used the results to decide which data to assess for quality.

Use *Table 4.4.7* to analyze results if doing additional ranking based upon the ability to collect and maintain the data.

Step 4.10   Cost of Low-Quality Data

Business Benefit and Context

Poor-quality data costs the business in many ways: waste and re-work; missed revenue opportunities; lost business, and so forth. This step quantifies the costs that may have only been understood by stories or observation. Quantifying costs shows impact with a measure best understood by the business – money.

 Definition

Cost of Low-Quality Data (Business Impact Technique). Quantify costs and the impact to revenue due to poor-quality data.

This technique is the next to the last business impact technique on the far right of the Continuum of Relative Time and Effort, meaning there are nine other options that can help you show business impact which will take less time and effort – and may be just as effective.

As you consider the Cost of Low-Quality Data, think of the POSMAD information life cycle. Activities in every phase of the life cycle have a cost and affect the quality of the data. Costs of these activities and how they are affected by low-quality data are quantified in this step. The real value comes from the Apply phase (where data is used) and this step also quantifies how poor-quality data impacts revenue.

In *Step 4.1 – Anecdotes* and *Step 4.5 – Process Impact*, examples were given when impacts could be quickly quantified. This step will be used if going into more depth.

Study the tables and templates referenced in the Approach below, along with the example in the Sample Output and Templates section which explains how a marketing group quantified costs and impact to revenue of poor-quality address data.

Another example comes from Navient who quantified the costs of poor-quality data, calculated the costs each month based on real results from their data quality metrics, and reported on their dashboard as "Business Value from Data Quality." See the Metrics section in *Chapter 6* for more information.

Approach

1. Identify key indicators of (poor) quality and performance measures.

The key indicator of quality is the data that, if wrong, adversely impacts the business. The performance measure refers to the uses of, or processes that use, the data. Together these provide the basis for your calculations and will be used to quantify the costs of poor-quality data.

One or more critical data elements (CDEs) already identified can be key indicators and the uses of/processes involved with those CDEs can become performance measures. Alternately, you may start with a particular use or business process which is feeling pain from poor-quality data. Then identify the data that is part of the process and use as your key indicator. Ensure your key indicators and performance measures are associated with something the business cares about, such as a diagnostic code in healthcare or the most important data in a critical report.

2. Define/verify the information life cycle of the key indicator.

Reference work from *Step 2 – Analyze Information Environment* to help identify activities with costs, and uses or processes involving the key indicator(s) which can be used as performance measures and included in the calculations.

3. Determine the types of costs to include in the calculations.

Identify the types of costs most important to your organization and therefore where you should concentrate your business impact assessment. Use the costs in *Table 4.4.8* and *Table 4.4.9* as a starting point. Select which costs apply and modify the wording to make them meaningful to your organization. For example, a compliance group may care about regulatory risk and state the type of cost as it applies specifically to potential GDPR fines.

Table 4.4.8 outlines costs due to poor-quality data from David Loshin (2001): (1) hard impacts – those that can be measured, and (2) soft impacts – those evident to the observer but difficult to measure. He explains there are impacts to operational, tactical, and strategic domains and further characterizes the impacts of poor-quality data in four categories, those that (3) decrease revenue, (4) increase costs, (5) increase risk, and (6) lower confidence.

Table 4.4.9 lists costs due to poor-quality data from Larry English (1999) for three categories: (1) process failure costs – a process does

Table 4.4.8 Loshin's Types of Costs from Poor-Quality Data

Category	Types of Costs
(1) Hard impact – effect that can be measured	• Customer attrition • Costs attributed to error detection • Costs attributed to error rework • Costs attributed to prevention of errors • Costs associated with customer service • Costs associated with fixing customer problems • Time delays in operation • Costs attributed to delays in processing
(2) Soft impact – effects evident to the observer, but difficult to measure	• Difficulty in decision making • Costs associated with enterprise-wide data inconsistency • Organizational mistrust • Lowered ability to effectively compete • Data ownership conflicts • Lowered employee satisfaction
Impacts by Domain	• Operational • Tactical • Strategic
(3) Decreased Revenue	• Delayed/lost collections • Customer attrition • Lost opportunities • Increased cost/volume
(4) Increased Costs	• Detection and correction • Prevention • Spin control • Scrap and rework • Penalties • Overpayments • Increased resource costs • System delays • Increased workloads • Increased process times
(5) Increased Risk	• Regulatory or legislative risk • System development risk • Information integration risk • Investment risk • Health risk • Privacy risk • Competitive risk • Fraud detection
(6) Lowered Confidence	• Organizational trust issues • Impaired decision making • Lowered predictability • Impaired forecasting • Inconsistent management reporting

Based on David Loshin, Economic framework of data quality and the value proposition in *Enterprise Knowledge Management: The Data Quality Approach*, (Elsevier, 2001), pp. 83-93. Used with permission.

not perform properly as a result of poor-quality information; (2) information scrap and rework costs – where scrap means rejecting or marking data in error and rework means the cleansing of defective data; and (3) lost and missed-opportunity costs – revenue and profit not realized because of poor information quality.

Table 4.4.9 English's Types of Costs from Poor-Quality Data

Category	Types of Costs
Process Failure Costs	• Irrecoverable costs • Liability and exposure costs • Recovery costs of unhappy customers
Information Scrap and Rework Costs	• Redundant data handling and support costs • Costs of hunting or chasing missing information • Business rework costs • Workaround costs and decreased productivity • Data verification costs • Software rewrite costs • Data cleansing and correction costs • Data cleansing software costs • Difficulty in decision making
Lost and Missed Opportunity Costs	• Lost-opportunity costs (e.g., alienate and lose a customer – customer chooses to take business elsewhere) • Missed-opportunity costs (e.g., customer did not get the chance or choice of doing business with your company; missed prospects that an unhappy customer could have influenced) • Lost shareholder value (e.g., accounting data errors)

Adapted from Larry P. English, *Improving Data Warehouse and Business Information Quality: Methods for Reducing Costs and Increasing Profits*, (John Wiley and Sons, 1999), pp. 209-13.

I recommend reading these two sources to further understand the items listed. We have more data, more different kinds of data, and more sophisticated technology than when these lists were first published, but the types of costs and categories are still applicable today.

If you are part of a non-profit or government agency that does not look at revenue the same way or have the same goals as for-profit organizations, you still have to be concerned with where your money comes from and how much you spend. The costs also apply to you.

4. Calculate the costs that have been chosen.

Use *Template 4.4.7 – Calculating Direct Costs* and the example in the *Sample Output and Templates* section as a starting point.

5. Calculate the impact to revenue.

Use *Template 4.4.8 – Calculating Missed Revenue* and the example in the *Sample Output and Templates* section as a starting point.

6. Analyze and document results. Take action when the time is right.

See *Analyze, Synthesize, Recommend, Document, and Act on Results* in *Chapter 6*.

Document all assumptions and formulas upon which the calculations were made. In every project, it has been difficult for people to accept the large numbers from both the cost and revenue side, but particularly the revenue. Do not be surprised if you meet resistance, "That cannot be right!" Discuss and clarify the assumptions, then update and recalculate if needed.

Template 4.4.7 Calculating Direct Costs

Key Indicator of Quality	
Event	
Date	
Prepared by	

Include background or notes about the key indicator, performance measure, processes involved, and other information that puts the results into context. Be clear on the time period used (1 month, 1 quarter, 1 year)

This template can also be used to calculate the cost of unusual cases, such as costs resulting from an event where the company received bad publicity due to poor-quality data.

1	2	3	4	5
Type of Cost	Description	Cost per Instance	Number of Instances per Time Period	Total Costs per Time Period (3 * 4)
List applicable types of costs on a separate line. For each, determine: • Time • Materials • # People • Other				
Totals				

Adapted from Larry P. English, *Improving Data Warehouse and Business Information Quality: Methods for Reducing Costs and Increasing Profits*, (John Wiley and Sons, 1999).
See Chapter 7 in Mr. English's book for a detailed process for calculating non-quality information costs.
Additional details can also be found in *Information Quality Applied* (Wiley, 2009), by Larry P. English.

Template 4.4.8 Calculating Missed Revenue – Example

1	2	3	4	5	6	7	8	9	10	11	12
	From marketing statistics	From marketing statistics	From marketing statistics	4/3	From marketing statistics	6/3	6 x 5	From sales and marketing	8 x 9	From direct cost worksheets	10 + 11
Mailing Event	Drop date	Total mailed	Number of positive responses	Percent positive responses	Number of returned mail pieces	Percent returns	Number of missed opportunities	Average revenue per response	Total missed revenue	Total direct costs	Total missed revenue and direct costs
M1		100,000	10,000	10%	3000	3%	300	$250	$75,000		
M2											
…											
M10											
					Total number of returns (sum column 6)		Total number missed opportunities (sum column 8)		Total all missed revenue due to poor quality data (sum column 10)	Total all direct costs due to poor quality data (sum column 11)	Total all missed revenue and direct costs due to poor quality data (sum column 12)

Sample Output and Templates

Calculating Costs

One marketing group was concerned about their mailing process, where catalogs and other promotional materials were sent to customers. To ensure the mailings reached the intended recipient, a good mailing address was required. As part of their standard business processes, the marketing group tracked the specific mailing events, the nature of the mailing (catalog, letter, brochure, etc.), the total pieces mailed, the number of returns (undeliverable mail) and positive responses. The key indicator of quality was address data. The performance measure was undeliverable mail due to poor-quality address data. Other process issues caused by poor-quality addresses, such as when completing insurance claims, could also have been included as performance measures. Note that even if your organization is not concerned with mailings, this provides a good example of how to quantify costs.

Let's use an example of ten mailings sent in a one-month time period (M1-M10). To calculate the costs of poor-quality data, they created a spreadsheet using *Template 4.4.7* with a separate tab for each mailing. They researched and documented costs for each mailing, such as costs to design and print the piece (a catalog, a brochure, etc.), postage costs, labor costs, etc. If the mailing activity in that one month represented an average month, costs for a year could be further estimated by multiplying the monthly results by 12. A summary sheet outlined the totals for all events and all costs. The cost totals

were added to the spreadsheet where they calculated missed revenue (see next section).

Calculating Missed Revenue

Template 4.4.8 shows an example of calculating missed revenue based on the mailings example. The first row indicates the column number. The second row shows the source of the data or the formula for the calculation. Columns 1-7 came from their marketing statistics or are simple calculations.

Column 8 contains the calculation for the number of missed revenue opportunities, which represented an important assumption that had been agreed upon: customers who *would have received* the mailing but did not (because of bad addresses) would have the same positive response as those who *did receive* the mailing. For Mailing 1, this showed 300 missed revenue opportunities due to poor-quality address data. Column 9, average revenue per response, required research with the various sales and marketing teams who used the mailings to support sales of their products. Total missed revenue due to poor quality data is calculated in Column 10. Column 11 brought in costs from the separate worksheets using the direct cost template described earlier. The last row sums the calculations in Columns 6, 8, 10, 11, and 12. The three bottom right-hand cells contain the total impact to revenue and costs (in dollars) due to poor-quality address data.

Information from this step was used to help management make better decisions about where to invest their money because it made visible the value of ensuring high-quality address data.

Step 4.11	Cost-Benefit Analysis and ROI

Business Benefit and Context

Generally, a cost-benefit analysis evaluates if the benefits of a new investment or business opportunity over a given time frame outweigh its associated costs. Cost-benefit analysis and return on investment (ROI) are standard management techniques as input to making financial decisions. As it applies to data quality, a cost-benefit analysis compares the potential benefits of investing in data quality with anticipated costs. In addition, return on investment (ROI) compares the benefit (or return) on an investment compared to the cost or amount of money invested and is the profit calculated as a percentage of the amount invested. Cost-benefit analysis and ROI can be used to determine if a single investment (such as a project or data quality activity) is worthwhile or to compare multiple investments.

This technique can be used if formally submitting a request for funds that must go through standard company approvals. Your organization may require this type of information before considering or proceeding with any significant financial outlay – and investments in information quality improvement can be significant. Management has the responsibility to determine how money is spent and will need to weigh its investment options. While this

technique may be needed for very large investments, I have also seen large investments approved for data quality based on results from less time-consuming techniques. This technique can also be used by an individual or small team to weigh options over which they have control.

This technique is placed to the far left of the Continuum of Relative Time and Effort because, historically, it has been difficult to articulate benefits from high-quality data and the reasons for investing in that work. This step is made easier by using some of the other ten business impact techniques already discussed. But each technique used adds effort, so this technique, relatively speaking, may take more time and be more complex.

Definition

Cost-Benefit Analysis and ROI (Business Impact Technique). Compare anticipated costs of investing in data quality to potential benefits through an in-depth evaluation, which may include calculating return on investment (ROI).

Approach

1. Use the standard cost-benefit template employed by your organization.

Use the standard form from your organization. The form may not be called a "Cost-Benefit" form, but may be labeled another way, such as a "Project Request Form" that asks for the same information on costs and benefits. Make it easy for approvers to understand your request and see it as equally valid as other requests by using a form with which they are familiar.

2. Clearly articulate the purpose for the request.

Your request may be to fund the overall data quality project itself or for money to implement specific improvements that will prevent data quality problems, correct data, and/or detect data quality issues through monitoring controls.

3. Identify the costs associated with the investment in data quality.

Include such things as human resources, hardware, software, licensing, maintenance, support costs, training, and travel expenses. Consider one-time and recurring costs. Are you calculating project costs and/or on-going operational costs?

You might also look at costs incurred if you do *not* undertake the project. *Step 4.10 – Cost of Low-Quality Data* can help here. If your organization is concerned about risk, look at *Step 4.6 – Risk Analysis*.

4. Identify the potential additional revenues and other benefits that will result from this request.

Being able to identify the benefits of high-quality data and put them in monetary terms has been a perennial challenge, but the business impact techniques are here to help. The value of data improvements and the cost of poor-quality data are opposite sides of the same coin. Use output from the other business impact techniques to present the benefits. Once again, look at *Step 4.10*.

5. Include benefits and costs that cannot be quantified.

Though the form may not ask for these, include them in a comment area or cover letter. Benefits and costs that cannot be quantified, such as decreased customer satisfaction or lower employee morale, should still be made visible. Include a brief statement that characterizes what they mean and an example. Even for benefits that cannot be quantified in terms of money, you may be able to quantify number of users, number of reports, number of business processes, etc. that make use of the data within scope. Most organizations require quantitative costs and benefits. Even so, always include the qualitative or soft costs and benefits expected.

6. Compare the benefits and costs.

Determine if the benefits outweigh the costs or not. Consider timeframes for benefits to be realized vs. when the costs are incurred. If quantified costs outweigh quantified benefits are there ways to decrease costs and increase benefits to make the request more practical? Are the qualitative costs and benefits as important, or even more important, that the quantitative ones? If the final result shows that the costs cannot justify the benefits, it is still important to know so ill-advised investments are not made.

7. Calculate ROI, if needed.

Return on Investment or ROI is one of the key financial metrics widely used to evaluate and rank different investment options. It is a ratio of the gain or loss from an investment relative to its cost. It can also be used to evaluate potential return from a stand-alone investment.

If an ROI calculation is used, it will most likely be needed by those deciding how funds will be allocated – an executive, manager, or council. You may be the one to choose how to spend money and other resources on various data quality-related opportunities; if so, you could use ROI yourself to help determine which data quality projects or activities will provide the best return.

ROI is a calculation that starts with the Cost of Investment being subtracted from the Gain from Investment and dividing that number by the Cost of the Investment. Then multiply by 100 to get the ROI as a percentage. This is shown by the formula:

$$\text{ROI} = (\text{Gain from Investment} - \text{Cost of Investment}) / \text{Cost of Investment} * 100$$

As it applies to a data quality project:

Investment = the amount of money needed for the proposed data quality activity (e.g., for the overall data quality project itself, or for specific improvements that will prevent data quality problems, correct data, and/or detect data quality issues by implementing ongoing controls to monitor data quality)

Gain from investment = benefits received from using the funds for the proposed data quality activity (for the project, preventive measures, corrections, controls, etc.)

Cost of investment = what it costs to carry out the proposed data quality activity (run the project, deploy preventive measures, make data corrections, monitor controls, etc.)

What is included in gains and costs can be modified to suit your situation. You may look at cost savings, incremental profit, value appreciation, and timeframe. Use input from the cost-benefit analysis to calculate ROI.

ROI can be either positive (total returns exceed total costs) or negative (total costs exceed total returns). Obviously, a positive return is desired. But if the calculation shows negative that is also important input into investment decisions.

8. Share, communicate, and sell your request.

Having a positive ROI may not be enough. Be aware that your request is competing against all the other requests for money and resources. Many of those who allocate funding will be unfamiliar with data quality and why it is important. Use your best communication and presentation skills to tell the story and engage your audience, realizing the story will probably have to be told both verbally and in writing.

Sample Output and Templates

I do not include a template for a Cost-Benefit Analysis because, as mentioned, you should use the standard form from your organization which asks for costs and benefits, and may be used when requesting funds or approvals from management or committees. The forms might have another label, such as "Project Request Form" or "Project Prioritization Form" that requires costs and benefits. If you are not aware of the form used in your organization, check with your manager or someone involved in finance or the budgeting process.

Step 4.12	Other Relevant Business Impact Techniques

Business Benefit and Context

It is possible that even with the business impact techniques outlined in this step, there are other techniques with which you are familiar or are used by your organization that can be applied to data quality.

Definition

Other Relevant Business Impact Techniques. Other qualitative and/or quantitative methods for determining the effects of the quality of data on the business that are deemed important for your organization to understand.

If using another technique, remember you are still doing the assessment within the context of the Ten Steps Process. This means you still need to ensure the work you do here in *Step 4* applies to the business needs and project objectives. You still need to prepare your data capture and assessment plans. After the assessment you still need to do root cause analysis and take action to both prevent future data errors and correct the current errors. Following are other approaches to assessing business impact not detailed in this book:

Data Debt—John Ladley (2017, 2020a) has presented about data debt, a concept related to technical debt. Technical debt, in software development, is the idea that there is a negative impact from choosing easy/short-term/limited/stop-gap software solutions at the expense of taking a better, long term approach and the implied cost of additional rework that comes with those decisions. Not all technical debt is bad and some is taken on as a calculated risk. But it can accumulate "interest" by increasing costs associated with changes that are needed, but not completed because a better, more stable approach was not instituted. The same idea is applied to data. For data quality, data debt can be the amount of money required to fix data problems. It can also be the additional burden the organization has taken on due to the cost of poor-quality data, because they chose not to address the data quality problems (through prevention, detection, correction). From this perspective, what you have learn from other business impact techniques can often be positioned as data debt or input to calculating data debt. Data debt is an example of my personal axiom in action, which is true on many levels: "Pay now or pay later, but if you pay later you always pay more."

Business case for data governance—John Ladley, in *Data Governance*, Second Edition (2020b), outlines the data governance business case in Chapter 5. What applies to data governance also applies to data quality. Note that his chapter has a short paragraph about costs of data quality issues – come back to *Step 4* in this book and use the business impact techniques to help there.

Business Driver Analysis—Irina Steenbeek, in *The Data Management Toolkit* (2019), provides a template and instructions for a business driver analysis that identifies and scores the main drivers and benefits for developing a data management function. These can be applied to a data quality program or project.

Information Asset Valuation—Doug Laney, in *Infonomics* (2018), shares how to value and monetize information assets that can also apply to data quality.

Approach

The approach is dependent on the other business impact technique chosen.

Sample Output and Templates

The output is dependent on the other business impact technique chosen.

Step 4 Summary

Congratulations! Assessing business impact is yet another important milestone in your project. You may have used this step multiple times in your project. The techniques here can be used in various situations such as when there is a need to:

- Answer questions, such as, "Why is data quality (or this project) important?" "What difference will it have on our organization, on my team, on me?"
- Address resistance when it is seen, heard, or felt, such as vocal disagreement or hear words of support but see no action
- Establish the business case for data quality improvements
- Determine appropriate investments in data quality activities
- Gain support from management
- Motivate team members to participate in the project
- Prioritize efforts

Use the results to make good decisions about your next steps – business actions and effect on business needs, data quality issues, project goals, scope, timeline, and resources, communication and engagement. Wherever you are in the project after using business impact to further the work, keep moving!

Communicate, Manage, and Engage

Suggestions for working effectively with people and managing the project in this step:

- Help team members work cooperatively as business impact assessments are conducted
- Work with project sponsors and relevant stakeholders to remove roadblocks and resolve issues
- Track issues and action items; ensure deliverables are completed in a timely manner
- Ensure project sponsors, team members, management, and other technical and business stakeholders have been:
  o Appropriately engaged during business impact assessment (some may be actively involved, others provide input, yet others only informed)
  o Apprised of results and initial recommendations based on what was learned about business impact
  o Given the opportunity to provide reaction and feedback
  o Informed of changes to project scope, timeline, and resources and know the plan going forward
- Based on learnings from the business impact assessments:
  o Adjust project scope, objectives, resources, or timeline
  o Manage expectations of stakeholders and team members
  o Anticipate change management needed to ensure potential future improvements are implemented and accepted
- Ensure resources and support for upcoming steps in the project

Checkpoint

Checkpoint Step 4 – Assess Business Impact

How can I tell if I am ready to move to the next step? Use the following guidelines to help determine completeness of this step and readiness for the next step:

- For each selected business impact technique, has the assessment been completed?
- If using multiple business impact techniques, have results from all been synthesized and documented?
- Have results from this step been documented?
  o Lessons learned and observations
  o Known/potential issues
  o Known/probable business impact
  o Potential root causes
  o Initial recommendations for prevention, correction, and monitoring controls
  o Actions or follow-up needed that were not completed during this step
- If there are changes to the project, have they been finalized and agreed-upon by project sponsor, relevant stakeholders and team members? E.g., are additional people needed for the next steps? If so, have they been identified and committed? Is funding continuing?
- Have the communication and engagement plans been kept current? Do they include change management?
- Have necessary activities to communicate, manage, and engage people during this step been completed?

Step 5 | Identify Root Causes

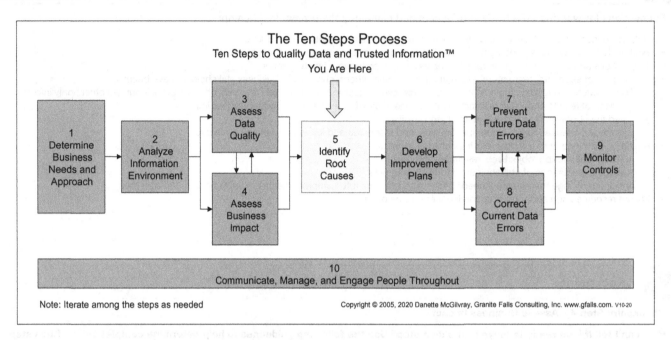

Figure 4.5.1 "You Are Here" Graphic for Step 5 – Identify Root Causes.

Introduction to Step 5

There is a tendency to jump to a solution that appears to be the most expedient in order to deal quickly with a data quality problem. The result is that the *symptoms* are often treated rather than the fundamental *underlying problems, i.e., the root causes* of the data quality issue.

Root cause analysis looks at all possible causes of a problem, issue, or condition to determine its actual cause(s). Often time and effort are spent treating symptoms of a problem without determining its actual causes, which would prevent the problem from recurring. The primary goals in this step are to find out why a problem happened and what can be done to prevent it from happening again.

Unfortunately, it is not unusual to find that when a data quality issue is uncovered, the company only corrects the data – sometime at great cost for large clean-up efforts. Then it is back to business as usual until a few years later, when those same issues cause the business to once again invest in data clean-up. This costly and unproductive cycle misses root cause analysis – which is essential for prevention.

Some people think there will be only one root cause of a data quality problem. I disagree. Expect more than one root cause. Some root causes, however, may be more impactful than others. Some root causes will work in concert with each other. Just as a fire requires oxygen, heat, and fuel, and the fire can be prevented or extinguished by removing any one of the three, you may find similar dependencies in the root causes uncovered.

Root cause analysis often follows an in-depth data quality assessment in *Step 4*. Other times, if the business needs and data

quality issues are clear and the right experts are working on the problem, root cause analysis may start right away without an in-depth assessment. If additional information is needed that would have been gathered in *Steps 2, 3,* or *4*, iterate back through those steps as needed.

Sometimes the issue needing attention is related to an urgent problem that has recently caused major impacts to the business – services cannot be provided, a production line is down, products are not shipped, orders cannot be taken – and it is suspected that data quality is a significant factor. Once the issue itself has been addressed, management wants to ensure that it will not happen again, so root cause analysis happens at that time. Alternatively, it may be that the specific issue did not cause an emergency but is a long-time problem everyone is aware of and has accepted as a cost of doing business. You may decide to spend time on root cause analysis to address the issue with the hope of stopping the constant waste of time and money it creates.

Once root causes are identified, ensure results are shared, along with the recommended improvements that need to be planned for and implemented in *Steps 6-9*, and potential impacts to the project plan, timeline, and resources.

 Definition

Root Cause Analysis is the study of all possible causes of a problem, issue, or condition to determine its actual cause(s).

Table 4.5.1	Step Summary Table for Step 5 – Identify Root Causes
Objective	• Identify the true origins of data quality issues and/or specific data quality errors • Develop specific recommendations for improvements that will address the root causes • Identify final owners who will be accountable for ensuring improvements are implemented or interim owners to move the work forward until final owners are found
Purpose	• Ensure the recommendations and future improvements focus on the true causes of the data quality issues • Make the best use of money, time, people by focusing on those things that will make the biggest difference to the quality of the data

Inputs	• The business needs and data quality issues within scope and project objectives from *Step 1*
	• Output from *Step 2 – Analyze the Information Environment*, such as the information life cycle and other artifacts
	• Output from *Step 3 – Assess Data Quality*, results of completed assessment(s)
	• Output from *Step 4 – Assess Business Impact*, results of completed assessment(s)
	• For all work completed to this point, analysis and synthesis with:
	  o Key observations/lessons learned/issues uncovered/positive discoveries
	  o Known or probable impact (qualitative and/or quantitative; to revenue, costs, risks, business, people/org, technology, other data and information, etc.)
	  o Potential root causes
	  o Initial recommendations
	• Current project status, stakeholder analysis, communication and engagement plans

Techniques and Tools	• Prioritization techniques from *Step 4 – Assess Business Impact* • Other prioritization techniques used within the organization • Facilitation techniques • Root cause analysis techniques in this *Step 5* – Five Whys for Root Causes, Track and Trace, Cause-and-Effect/Fishbone Diagram • Other root cause analysis techniques used by the organization

Outputs	• For each of the data quality issues within scope:
	  o Root causes identified
	  o Specific recommendation(s) for improvement that will address the root causes
	  o Owners for implementing the improvement(s)
	• Completed communication and engagement activities needed at this point in the project
	• Updated project status, stakeholder analysis, communication and engagement plans

Communicate, Manage, and Engage	• Use a neutral facilitator who is not invested in the outcome of root cause analysis sessions, but who will lead the participants through a process where everyone can be heard, root causes are identified, and ownership for next steps is established • Ensure those attending root cause analysis sessions know why they are there and come ready and willing to participate • In any root cause analysis session, quickly review the purpose for being there and the process for the session. Ensure people are comfortable and feel they can talk freely with no repercussions. Set a tone of openness and trust so people are more likely to look for good solutions, be less defensive, and not revert to placing blame. • After any root cause analysis session, follow up with action items, talk with owners who were identified to take responsibility for specific improvements – both those who were in the session and others who were not • Continue to engage with project sponsors and other stakeholders to ensure agreement for root causes and recommendations and improvements to be implemented in upcoming steps

Checkpoint	• Have the root causes for each of the data quality issues been identified and documented?
	• Have specific recommendations for addressing those root causes been determined and documented?
	• Have owners, who will be accountable for ensuring improvements are implemented, been identified?
	• Have the communication and engagement plans been kept current?
	• Have necessary activities to communicate, manage, and engage people during this step been completed? For example:
	  o Have you shared the root causes and specific recommendations from this step and obtained agreement to proceed from project sponsors and other stakeholders?
	  o Are you starting to include management of other teams who could be called upon in the future to help implement recommendations? Don't wait too long to let them know what is happening.

Root Cause Analysis – the Beginning of the Improvement Cycle

Think of *Steps 5* through *10* as an improvement cycle (see *Figure 4.5.2*). These five steps are called out separately because each has different processes, activities, and technology that need to be planned for, but they should be looked at holistically because of their relationships with each other. The various improvements will often have different owners and people who are part of the

implementation – and may or may not be part of the data quality project team who know which improvements should be put into place and why.

Once controls are being monitored (in *Step 9*) ensure they are part of operational processes. When issues are identified, standard operating procedures should include the five steps in the improvement cycle: identify root causes, and, when needed, develop improvement plans, prevent future data errors, correct current data

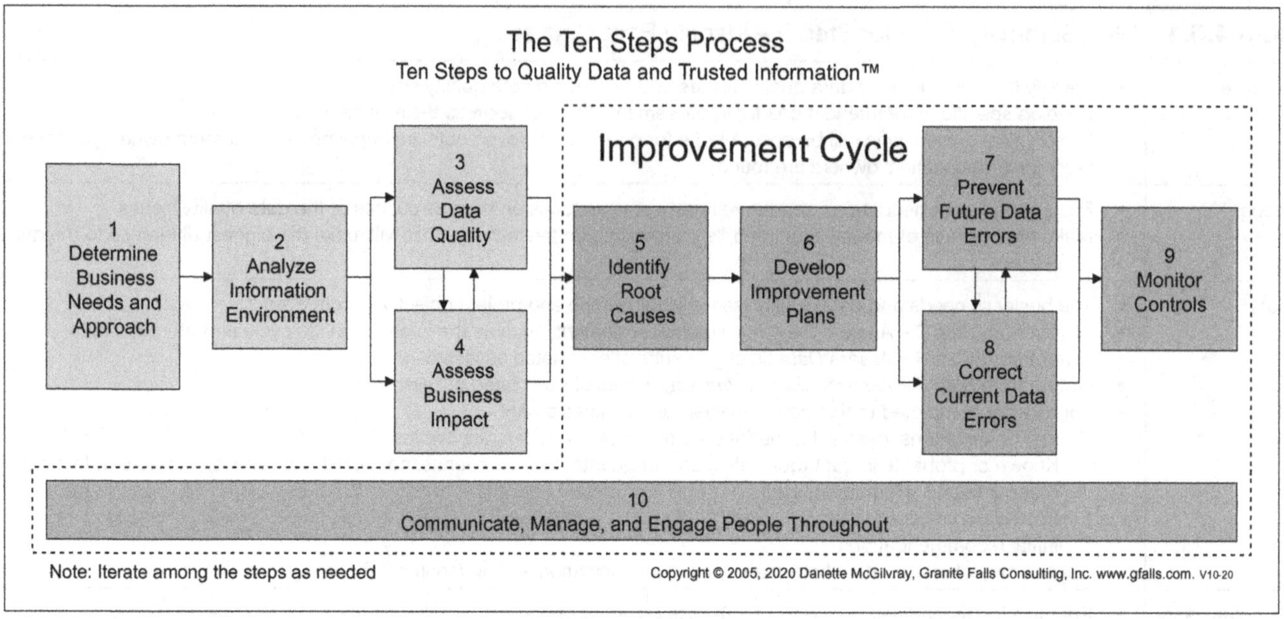

The Ten Steps Process
Ten Steps to Quality Data and Trusted Information™

Note: Iterate among the steps as needed

Copyright © 2005, 2020 Danette McGilvray, Granite Falls Consulting, Inc. www.gfalls.com. V10-20

Figure 4.5.2 The Ten Steps Process with improvement cycle highlighted.

errors, and make adjustments to the controls. Of course, communication and engagement continue to be important to ensure the right people are notified and taking action.

Prepare for Root Cause Analysis

You may have several issues where root causes should be identified. If there is not enough time to explore them all, you may have to prioritize which should move forward to root cause analysis. Use *Step 4.8 – Benefit vs. Cost Matrix* or other business impact techniques to select the highest-priority issues, should that be needed.

For the selected issues, prepare yourself for root cause analysis by compiling what has been documented and learned prior to this point in the project. If you have been documenting results and managing the project artifacts this will be easy. If not, plan on extra time. Use the information life cycle that should have been documented in previous steps to help determine where in the life cycle the root causes are happening. Everything learned to this point sheds light on the processes, people/organizations, and technology that affect the data in those locations – any of which are potential root causes. You may have to go to an additional level of detail in your life cycle to get to the root causes.

Three techniques that can be used to identify root causes are detailed in this step with a placeholder for other root cause analysis techniques you may already be using, see *Table 4.5.2*. Each of the root cause analysis techniques listed in the table has their own substep with further explanation specifically for that technique.

Depending on the urgency of the business issue and the complexity of the root causes you discover, you may use just one approach, combinations, or the fastest approach, the Five Whys, to get started.

Select which root cause analysis techniques will be used. Determine which data quality issues and which technique, or combination of techniques, will be used for any particular root cause analysis session. Prepare materials and schedule the venue and time

Table 4.5.2 Root Cause Analysis Techniques in the Ten Steps Process

Root Cause Analysis is the study of all possible causes of a problem issue or condition to determine its actual cause(s).

Substep	Root Cause Analysis Technique Name and Definition
5.1	**Five Whys for Root Causes**. Asks "Why?" five times to get to the real root causes of the data and information quality problem. It is a standard quality technique often used in manufacturing which also works well when applied to data and information quality.
5.2	**Track and Trace.** Identifies the specific location of a problem by tracking the data through the information life cycle, comparing the data at entry and exit points of processing, and identifying where the problem first appears. Once the location is identified, other techniques can be used to determine the root causes for the data quality problem in each location where the greatest number of problems are found.
5.3	**Cause-and-Effect/Fishbone Diagram**. Identifies, explores, and arranges the causes of a data quality problem in which the relationships between causes are graphically displayed according to their level of importance or detail. It is a standard quality technique often used in manufacturing to uncover root causes of an event, problem, condition, or outcome which also works well when applied to data and information quality.
5.4	**Other Relevant Root Cause Analysis Techniques**. Other applicable techniques that will help identify root causes.

for the root cause analysis session. Find a neutral facilitator and a scribe. Facilitators guide people through the process to get answers (in this case the root causes), but do not provide answers themselves. The scribe documents decisions, action items, and reasoning behind the decisions, particularly if there is long discussion before coming to agreement.

Identify who needs to be involved. Getting to root causes takes the insight of people who can represent expertise in the data itself, the business processes, the people/organizations, and the technology within scope. The root cause analysis techniques can be applied by yourself as an individual, with the data quality project team, through 1-1 interviews, or in a facilitated session with a small group or several people.

Ensure those attending the root cause analysis sessions know why they are there and come ready and willing to participate. During the session, ensure people are comfortable and feel they can talk freely with no repercussions. This is a session to find root causes which will lead to good solutions, not to point fingers and place blame. Determine what participants need to know:

- Prior to the meeting
- At the beginning of the meeting to quickly provide a common foundation
- At the end of the meeting so action items and owners are clear
- After the meeting as follow-up to the session

Recommendations – Between Root Causes and Improvement Plans

It is hard to jump from a list of root causes in *Step 5* to detailed improvement plans in *Step 6*. Specific recommendations for addressing each root cause are the segue between the two steps. A recommendation is an action statement that indicates how a root cause can be addressed. Recommendations can vary greatly. A recommendation can be a simple item on someone's to-do list, involve a few people to update a business process, or may initiate a new project.

The recommendation may address the overall solution to the root cause, such as in the first and second recommendations in *Figure 4.5.3*. If the solution is not clear, the specific recommendation is a statement indicating the immediate next step, as seen in the third recommendation, which assigns an owner to further research the solution. To ensure that progress continues to be made, an owner should be assigned for each recommendation. The owner might be the final owner for overseeing implementation in a later step or someone who agrees to find the final owner. It is usually helpful to develop the recommendations at the end of *Step 5* when the root causes are fresh in everyone's minds. However, they can also be developed at the beginning of *Step 6*.

If there are several recommendations moving forward to *Step 6* where implementation plans will be developed, it is helpful to assign someone to coordinate and track them.

If the list of recommendations is long and it is not reasonable to expect they can all be implemented, once again prioritization may be necessary. A prioritization technique such as *Step 4.8 – Benefit vs. Cost Matrix* works well to narrow down which recommendations should be included in the improvement plans. Using *Step 4.6 – Risk Analysis* can also be helpful to understand the risk if a particular recommendation is not implemented.

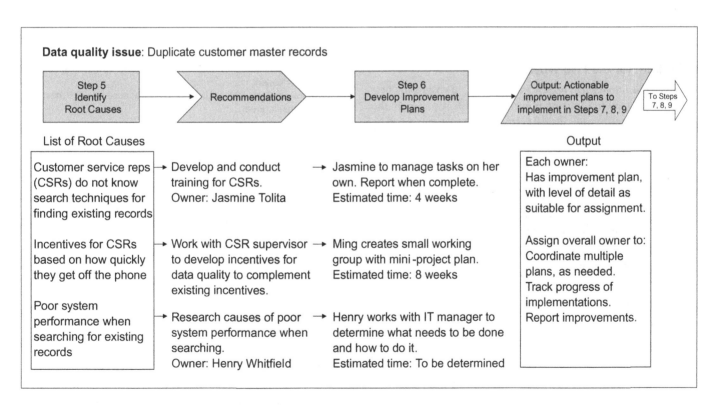

Figure 4.5.3 Specific recommendations – segue between root causes and improvement plans.

Step 5.1 — Five Whys for Root Causes

Business Benefit and Context

The Five Whys is a standard quality technique often used to get to root causes in manufacturing and which also works well when applied to data and information quality. This technique can be used by an individual, project team or group of experts. The Five Whys technique is also applied in *Step 4.4 – Five Whys for Business Impact*.

Think of the word "Why?" as helping you get to the next deeper level and closer to the root cause. Additional interrogatives such as What? Who? When? Where? How? How long? How often? provide context and insight to root causes. For example, Why did this data quality problem occur? Why did the process fail? What happened? Who was involved? When did it happen? Where did it happen? How did it happen? How long did it last? Has this happened before and if so, how often?

Definition

Five Whys for Root Causes is a technique which asks "Why?" five times to get to the real root causes of the data and information quality problem.

Approach

1. Prepare for the Five Whys analysis.

Reference the *Introduction to Step 5* to prepare and ensure any pertinent background information is readily available. Be clear on the data quality issue(s) or specific data errors where root causes will be identified. The more clearly the issue is stated, the better to focus the analysis and find the root causes.

2. Ask "Why?" five times.

Start with the stated issue and ask, "Why did we get this result?" or "Why did this situation occur?" From that answer repeat the question again five times. See the *Sample Output and Templates* section for an example.

3. Analyze the results.

Are there multiple root causes? Are there common features found among the root causes?

If needed, use the techniques in *Steps 5.2 – Track and Track* and *5.3 – Cause-And-Effect/Fishbone Diagram* to get additional detail about the root causes.

4. Develop recommendations to address the root causes.

Develop specific actions to address the root causes found, which will prevent the problems from reappearing. If there is a long list of recommendations, you may need to prioritize which to tackle first.

5. Document the results and take action when the time is right.

State the data quality issue with the root causes found, specific recommendations for addressing them, and how conclusions were reached. Also include any additional impacts to the business, tangible and intangible, that were uncovered or verified while going through this process.

Simple action items to address root causes may be assigned to owners in this step to start their work immediately. Other recommendations are more complex to implement and may need more research. All results from this step are input to *Step 6 – Develop Improvement Plans*.

Key Concept

Be clear on the difference between symptoms and root causes. In one company a new product had been promised, with ship dates and corporate sales goals to meet. Revenue could only be recognized if the product was shipped. It was a Friday at the end of the quarter, the product was ready to go and customers were waiting, but the necessary paperwork to ship could not be produced:

- Why couldn't the product be delivered? The pick-pack-ship could not be generated.
- Why couldn't the pick-pack-ship be generated? A sales order could not be generated.
- Why couldn't the sales order be generated? The material could not be released.
- Why couldn't the material be released? Because the item master data was incorrect.

Those who could review the data and find the mistakes had to be found. Different people had to update the master data in the system. All the transactions had to be created again. The cause of the problem was found, and the product was shipped. But was the true root cause found? The urgent matter of shipping product on time was solved. But this was similar to keeping the patient alive after a heart attack. To get to the true root causes, the critical question of "Why was the item master data incorrect?" should be asked, answered, and addressed after the crisis was averted. If the root cause is not understood and addressed, it is highly likely the problem will reappear, putting the ability to ship products at risk yet again.

Sample Output and Templates

Using the Five Whys for Root Causes of Duplicate Customer Master Records

See *Table 4.5.3* for a simple example of the Five Whys for Root Causes. You may find more than one potential contributing factor and need to continue questioning separately to get to the root cause for each. Decide which root causes can be addressed immediately and which require further investigation before a solution can be implemented.

In this example, there is enough information to put together a short training course on search techniques for the reps. However, further investigation is needed to understand the real root cause of any system performance problems and to develop solutions. Remember, a specific recommendation is a statement that indicates how a root cause root cause can be addressed or if the approach is not clear, the specific recommendation is an action statement indicating the immediate next step.

A note of caution: the table shows a nice, neat example of how the results of the Five Whys were documented. The Five Whys technique does work, but the actual process of finding the root causes is rarely as clean and straightforward as the table with the end results might imply.

Management and Process Root Causes

This example shows responses to a process failure which are potential root causes of data quality problems. In this situation, an employee on the manufacturing floor takes parts out of inventory. He is supposed to log the transaction in the system at the same time. He is in a hurry and decides to log the transaction in the system later when there is more time. The transaction does not get logged at all (or until several days later).

Table 4.5.3 Example Five Whys for Root Causes of Duplicate Customer Master Records

Data Quality Issue: Duplicate customer master records. Note this technique works whether: 1) the duplication of customer master records is a general concern, or 2) If an assessment has been completed and the actual percentage of duplicate records is known.
Why are there duplicate records? Answer: Customer service reps create new master records instead of using existing ones.
Why do the reps create new records instead of using existing records? Answer: The reps don't want to search for existing records.
Why don't the reps want to search for existing records? Answer: It takes too long to enter the search request and get results back.
Why is the long search time a problem? Answer: Reps are measured by how quickly they finish the transaction and get off the phone. They work around anything that slows them down. Creating a new record each time is faster. Reps have no visibility or understanding of why duplicate records are a problem to other parts of the business. **Root Cause:** Competing motivation, incentives, and key performance indicators (KPIs) **Specific Recommendation:** Develop KPIs and incentives to avoid creating duplicate records. **Next Steps and Notes:** Meet with manager of reps. Understand phone call turn-around time and other KPIs for reps. Do not expect business KPIs to change. Create data quality KPI(s)/incentives to help offset the pressure to get off phone that causes duplicate records. **Owner:**   **Due Date:**
Why does it take too long to get results back? Answer 1: Customer service reps do not know how to search for existing records. Answer 2: System performance is poor.
1: **Why** don't reps know how to search for existing records? Answer: Reps have not been trained in proper search techniques **Root Cause:** Lack of training in proper search techniques. **Specific Recommendation:** Develop and conduct training for customer service reps. **Next Steps and Notes**: Ask Customer Service Manager if a short (15-minute) training for reps can be included in: 1) next team meeting, and 2) new hire training to teach: • *How* to do search techniques and how using them avoids creating duplicate records. • *Why* duplicate records are a problem. **Owner:**   **Due Date:**
2: **Why** is system performance poor? Answer: It is unknown why system performance is poor in this situation. **Potential Root Cause:** Poor system performance. **Specific Recommendation:** Research causes of poor system performance when searching for existing customer master records. **Next Steps and Notes**: Work with technology partner to uncover why system performance is poor when looking for existing customer master records. **Owner:**   **Due Date:**

There is no immediate effect on the manufacturing line because they have the parts needed – but there is frustration ahead. Now the data does not reflect the need for parts. The inventory system still thinks those parts are available for use, so when the manufacturing resource planning system is run, the parts are not ordered.

Two weeks later, another employee needs the part and discovers the parts are not there. The ability to manufacture is affected, possibly to the extent of shutting down the line. This results in lost time, missing deadlines for products, higher costs to expedite ordering of parts, and so forth.

We trace back and see that we didn't have the data. We didn't have the data because the employee did not log the transaction. So we ask ourselves, "Why didn't the employee log the transaction?" Following are potential answers to those questions. You can then continue asking "why?" for each answer and formulate specific recommendations to address them.

"I didn't know I was supposed to do it"—The employee didn't know he was supposed to log the transaction in the system when the parts were taken out of inventory.

"I didn't know when I was supposed to do it"—The employee didn't know the transaction was supposed to be logged immediately after the parts were taken out of inventory. Logging can take place by scanning or manually entering into the system.

"I don't know how"—The employee did not know how to debit the inventory for the parts taken.

"I can't do it"—The system wasn't working; the employee could not log on or forgot his password, etc.

"I didn't know why I was supposed to do it."—The employee didn't know that logging the transaction was important to another function or process and wasn't motivated to do it.

A negative consequence follows positive action—Conflicting message – previously, the employee logged the transaction and the manager chastised him for taking the time to do so.

No negative consequence follows negative action—No feedback loop – the employee does not see how his actions (or inaction) caused parts not to be ordered.

– Example inspired by Coaching for Improved Work Performance by Ferdinand F. Fournies (2000)

Step 5.2 | Track and Trace

Business Benefit and Context

This technique identifies the specific location of a problem by tracking the data through the information life cycle. Data as it enters a point of the information life cycle for processing is compared to the data as it exits that point after processing. If there are differences between the two, you have found at least one of the locations with an issue. You may find more than one location with issues, some causing more problems than others. Other techniques can be used against the data in that spot to dive into detail and identify root causes there.

 Definition

Track and Trace is a root cause analysis technique that identifies the specific location of a problem by tracking the data through the information life cycle, comparing the data at entry and exit points of processing, and identifying where the problem first appears. Once the location is identified other techniques can be used to determine the root causes for the data quality problem in each location where the greatest number of problems are found.

Approach

1. Prepare to use the Track and Trace technique.

Use the information in the *Introduction to Step 5* to prepare. Be clear on which data quality errors you will be tracing. Ensure any pertinent background information is readily available, particularly anything known about the information life cycle and work done in *Step 2*. If no work was done on the information life cycle previously, you will need to research and document it now. Use tools that help uncover lineage, if available. If you completed *Step 3.6 – Consistency and Synchronization*, you will already have much of the background needed to track and trace.

Decide which dataset(s), specifically, will be tracked. Focus on the data where the most errors were found in *Step 3* and/or are the most impactful to the business. Agree on the starting point in the information life cycle and route for tracing the data. The route may be short and simple or long and complex.

Plan the work carefully and assign owners to get the work done as efficiently as possible. See *Figure 4.5.4* for a visual of the Track and Trace idea.

2. Compare the data at the entry and exit points for each step throughout the Information Life Cycle.

This is another place where you can use the technique of data profiling, see *Step 3.3 – Data Integrity Fundamentals*. Capture and profile data at the entry and exit points and then compare for differences. You will eventually find the place where the data is correct when entering a process step but incorrect when exiting it. For each point in the Information Life Cycle ask:

- Is the data correct in < process/location >?
- Is the same data correct in < next process/location >? Remember to account for any expected, legitimate transformations.
- If yes, keep tracking. If no, capture how many are incorrect and describe the nature of the problem.
- Continue tracking as needed.

3. Analyze what is found.

Analyze activities at the problem location. Identify the activities impacting the data between the point of entry (where correct) and the point of exit (where incorrect). Apply other root cause techniques as needed, such as the Five Whys for Root Cause, the Cause-and-Effect/Fishbone diagram, or other favored root cause analysis technique here.

Issues may be found in more than one location. Focus on the location with the greatest number of problems and apply the Five Whys or other techniques to get to root causes. Each location will have different processes, people and organizations, and technology which influence the quality of the data and are potential root causes.

4. Develop specific recommendations to address the root causes found.

Determine what needs to be changed to ensure that the data will be correct. Use the other root cause analysis techniques to get to the root causes. Discuss solutions and develop specific actions to address the root causes found, that if implemented, will prevent the problems from reappearing. Prioritize as needed, as explained in the introduction to this step.

5. Document results and take action when the time is right.

Document the data quality issue addressed, the process used, locations where problems were found, and the environment surrounding the locations where the greatest problems were found (the data itself, processes, people/organizations, and technology).

Document root causes found, specific recommendations for addressing them, and how conclusions were reached. Also include any additional impacts to the business, tangible and intangible, that were uncovered or verified while going through this process.

Simple action items to address root causes may be assigned to owners in this step to start their work immediately. Other recommendations are more complex to implement and may need more research. All results from this step are input to *Step 6 – Develop Improvement Plans.*

Sample Output and Templates

Routes for Track and Trace

Figure 4.5.4 shows an example of a high-level information life cycle where the Track and Trace technique was used. The letters A through E indicate locations between the major stages in the information life cycle where data was processed. This was used to decide where to compare date between exit and entry points in order to identify the location with the most data quality problems. Your information life cycle may show more detailed processes within a stage of the life cycle. In this case, the comparison might be between data entering and exiting a particular process.

See the section *Design Data Capture and Assessment Plans* in *Chapter 6* for examples of data capture and assessment plans when capturing, profiling, and comparing data at multiple points along the information life cycle.

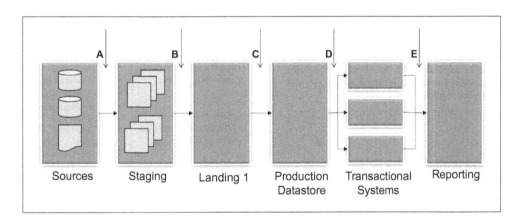

Figure 4.5.4 Select the route(s) for track and trace.

Step 5.3   Cause-and-Effect/Fishbone Diagram

Business Benefit and Context

The Cause-and-Effect diagram comes from Kaoru Ishikawa, a Japanese quality control statistician and highly regarded quality management expert. It is also known as the Ishikawa diagram, or Fishbone diagram. The term "fishbone" comes from the graphical

nature of the output, with the stated problem being the head and the causes the bones of a fish. See *Figure 4.5.5.* This technique is used to identify, explore, and arrange the causes of an event, problem, condition, or outcome in which the relationships between causes are illustrated according to their level of importance or detail. The approach is well known and has been effectively used in

Figure 4.5.5 Structure of a cause-and-effect/fishbone diagram.

manufacturing. It can be applied to information as well. As it applies to data quality, the specific defect refers to a particular data quality issue or a specific data quality error.

You may want to use this technique once the specific location of the problem has been isolated through the Track and Trace technique. The Cause-and-Effect diagram considers more than the most obvious causes and takes advantage of the knowledge of the group.

Definition

The **Cause-and-Effect/Fishbone Diagram** technique identifies, explores, and arranges the causes of a data quality issue or error in which the relationships between causes are graphically displayed according to their level of importance or detail. It is a standard quality technique often used in manufacturing to uncover root causes of an event, problem, condition, or outcome which also works well when applied to data and information quality.

Approach

1. Prepare for the root cause analysis (RCA).

Use the information in the *Introduction to Step 5*. Identify those who should be part of the root cause analysis. Gather any information pertinent to the issue (most of it output from previous steps). Provide any needed background prior to the meeting so the team comes to it supporting the goals and are prepared and willing to participate. Ensure that the physical setup of the meeting space is conducive to discussion and encourages collaboration – whether in-person or virtual.

2. State the issue associated with the poor data quality.

Explain the purpose of the meeting. The more clearly you state the issue, the more easily you can find the root causes. Allow time for discussion so everyone understands the data quality issue to be analyzed. State the defect/issue/problem. This is indicated as the "effect," which appears as the head of the fishbone. Start drawing the diagram by writing the effect/data quality issue in a box on the right side of the diagram. Use real or virtual whiteboard or a large sheet of paper that everyone can see.

3. Categorize the potential root causes of the data quality issue/error.

You may start with categories of common causes in *Table 4.5.4* below or categories based on the Framework for Information Quality in *Template 4.5.1* in the *Sample Output and Templates*. Include possible causes found and document throughout the project.

Alternatively, take a brainstorming approach and have attendees list all possible causes on sticky notes. Include possible causes documented throughout the project and then categorize and place them together on the diagram.

Draw a horizontal line to the left of the stated effect/data quality issue/error (the head). Then draw bones off the line and label them with the major categories. Use the categories that fit the problem – there is no perfect set or number. You may have to prioritize with which of the major categories to continue your questioning.

4. Continue questioning until the root causes are identified.

For each of the categories and/or potential causes identified, use the Five Whys for Root Cause to ask the next deeper questions that will help you identify root causes. "What is affecting or

Table 4.5.4	Common Categories of Root Causes
The 4 M's – often used in production processes***	• Machines (tools and equipment) • Methods (how work is done) • Material (components or raw materials) • Manpower or people (the human element)
The 4 P's – often used in service processes***	• Policies (higher-level decision rules) • Procedures (steps in a task) • People (the human element) • Plant (equipment and space)
Production and service processes often also use***	• Environment (buildings, logistics, space) • Measurement (metrics, data collection)
Other	• Management (management involvement, employee involvement, processes, communication, training, recognition)
From the Framework for Information Quality	The sections may be used as categories in root cause analysis: • Business Needs • The Information Life Cycle POSMAD • Key Components: Data, Processes, People/Organizations, and Technology • Location and Time • Broad-Impact Components: Requirements and Constraints; Responsibility; Improvement and Prevention; Structure, Context and Meaning; Change; Ethics • Culture and Environment See *Template 4.5.1* for details.

***Source: Brassard, M. and Ritter, D. (1994, 2018). Reprinted with permission of GOAL/QPC, Salem NH 03079; www.memoryjogger.com.

causing the problem? Why does this happen?" "What people/ organizational issues are causing the problem?" List these as smaller bones off the major bones. Reference the root causes collected throughout your assessment.

When analyzing root causes, also consider the distinction between chronic and acute problems. Chronic problems have been around for a long time and have been ignored. Acute problems have come up recently and are putting new pressures on the system or the business.

See the *Sample Output and Templates* for two fishbone diagrams with root causes identified when using this technique: *Figure 4.5.6* which answered the question "Why is the item master wrong?" and *Figure 4.5.7* which answered the question, "Why is information not managed as a business asset?" Root causes for information assets are often the same as those for data quality issues.

5. Develop specific recommendations to address the root causes found.

Develop specific recommendations for the major root causes. Such recommendations, if implemented, will prevent the problems from reappearing. Prioritize as needed, as explained in the *Introduction to Step 5*.

> ### Best Practice
>
> **Often Overlooked Root Cause – Architecture and Constraints**
>
> A good data model, combined with constraints at every level of its execution (database design, application interaction, and accessibility), will help produce quality, reusable data, and prevent many postproduction data quality problems (e.g., redundancy, conflicting data definitions, and difficulty in sharing data across applications). An optimum architecture and constraint design puts the appropriate constraints at the correct levels of the data and application architecture. Rules about validation and constraints should be considered and implemented across the enterprise, whether for applications developed in house or for those purchased from vendors.
>
> - Constraints at the database level must be general enough for all uses of the data by all applications, but only the DBA should be able to override them.
> - At the application layer, nuances of usage may be enforced.
> - Some accessibility rules may be enforced in the middle layer(s).

6. Document results and take action when the time is right.

State the data quality issue with the root causes found, specific recommendations for addressing them, and how conclusions were reached. Also include any additional impacts to the business, tangible and intangible, that were uncovered or verified while going through this process.

Simple action items to address root causes may be assigned to owners in this step to start their work immediately. Other recommendations are more complex to implement and may need more research. All results from this step are input to *Step 6 – Develop Improvement Plans*.

> ### Best Practice
>
> **Acute vs. Chronic Problems**
>
> When determining the cause of the problem, David Loshin suggests looking for
>
> - Chronic problems – those that have been around for a long time and have been ignored
> - Acute problems – those that have cropped up recently and are putting new pressures on the system
>
> For additional questions to ask when tracking the source of chronic and acute problems, see Loshin's book *Enterprise Knowledge Management: The Data Quality Approach* (2001), pp. 389–391.

Sample Output and Templates
Common Categories of Root Causes

Table 4.5.4 shows common categories of root causes used in production and service processes which could also apply to data and information quality. It also highlights sections from the Framework for Information Quality that could be categories of root causes.

Input to Root Cause Analysis Using the Framework for Information Quality

Template 4.5.1 provides a worksheet for considering potential root causes of data and information quality problems, using the sections in the Framework for Information Quality (FIQ). See *Chapter 3: Key Concepts* for the visual of the FIQ. The FIQ lists the components needed to ensure high-quality data and information. If any of these are missing or not done well, they are potential root causes for data and information quality problems.

Knowing Culture Leads to Root Cause

Suppose you were employing a set of demographic data for people who had immigrated to the US in the past fifty years. In examining the data, you notice something interesting: a statistically impossible number of individuals have January 1 listed as their birthday.

You check their birth years. If a statistically unlikely percentage also have the same birth year listed, you might doubt the integrity of the data. Perhaps something happened to a subset of records that replaced valid and accurate values with this data. But suppose the data in the Year-of-Birth field looks okay. What's happening with Day-of-Birth and Month-of-Birth?

You might filter out the suspect records and examine the country from which the individuals emigrated. Aha! "Somalia" jumps out at you. You remember reading somewhere that many Somali-Americans celebrate their birthday on Jan. 1. Another look shows that a great many of the individuals are from countries that you recognize as having experienced wars or famine. You realize that you have just come face-to-face with the result of a "just enough" principle in action.

Who put that principle into action? Probably many people, all working in refugee resettlements over the past fifty years. Recognizing that actual birthdates may not be considered important or memorable in some countries, these officials faced a dilemma: many refugees did not know the month and day of their birth, but

Template 4.5.1 Input to Root Cause Analysis Using the Framework for Information Quality

The FIQ lists components needed to ensure high quality data and information. If any of these are missing or not done well, they are potential root causes for data and information quality problems.

FIQ Ref #	Section in the Framework for Information Quality (FIQ)	Could anything in this category be a contributing factor or a cause of data quality problems? Explain.
1	**Business Needs.** Customers, Products, Services, Strategies, Goals, Issues, Opportunities	
2	**The Information Life Cycle.** POSMAD – Plan, Obtain, Store and Share, Maintain, Apply, Dispose	
3	**Data.** Known facts or items of interest. The distinct elements that make up information.	
3	**Processes.** Functions, procedures, activities, actions, steps, or tasks that affect or use data or information – including business, data management, technology, and third-party processes.	
3	**People and Organizations.** Organizations, teams, roles, responsibilities, or individuals that affect or use the data or information or are involved with the processes.	
3	**Technology.** Forms, applications, databases, files, programs, code, or media that store, share or manipulate the data, are involved with the processes, or used by the people and organizations – high tech and low tech.	
4	**Interaction Matrix.** Activity and relationship between data, processes, people/organizations, and technology across the information life cycle POSMAD.	
5	**Location.** Where.	
5	**Time.** When, How Often, and How Long.	
6	**Requirements and Constraints.** Business, User, Functional, Technology, Legal, Regulatory, Compliance, Contractual, Industry, Internal Policies, Access, Security, Privacy, Data Protection	
6	**Responsibility.** Accountability, Authority, Ownership, Governance, Stewardship, Motivation, Reward	
6	**Improvement and Prevention.** Continuous Improvement, Root Causes, Prevention, Correction, Enhancement, Audit, Controls, Monitoring, Metrics, Targets	
6	**Structure, Context, and Meaning.** Definitions, Relationships, Metadata, Standards, Reference Data, Data Models, Business Rules, Architecture, Semantics, Taxonomies, Ontologies, Hierarchies	
6	**Communication.** Awareness, Engagement, Outreach, Listening, Feedback, Trust Confidence, Education, Training, Documentation	
6	**Change.** Management of Change and Associated Impact, Organizational Change Management, Change Control	
6	**Ethics.** Individual and Societal Good, Justice, Rights and Freedoms, Truthfulness, Standards of Conduct, Avoiding Harm, Supporting Well-Being	
7	**Culture and Environment.** The organization's attitudes, values, customs, practices, and social behavior. Conditions that surround people in the organization and affect the way they work and act.	

this data is required by resettlement processes. And so, officials from the US State Department and the United Nations began recording "January 1" when actual dates were unknown. While the data may cause issues for other purposes by other users, it has come to be considered "good enough" for this purpose. Mystery solved!

Using Multiple RCA Techniques and Developing Recommendations

Let's continue the example of the item master from the *Key Concept callout box* in *Step 5.1 – Five Whys for Root Causes*. If you recall, the

Five Whys showed the item master data needed to be fixed in order to create the documents so products could be shipped. Once the products were out the door, the real root causes of why the item mater data was wrong still needed investigating. *Figure 4.5.6* shows a fishbone diagram with answers to the question, "Why was the item master wrong?" The root causes were numbered for ease of reference.

Table 4.5.5 continues the example by showing the specific recommendations to address the root causes. Note that some of the root causes had similarities in how they could be addressed and were grouped under one recommendation and assigned an owner.

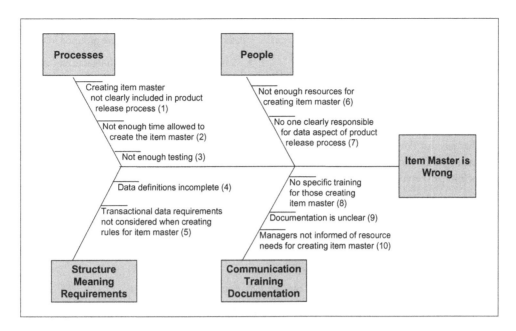

Figure 4.5.6 Item master example using a fishbone diagram.

Table 4.5.5	Item Master Example with Recommendations		
Issue: Item master data used in the product release process was wrong, which ultimately stopped products from being shipped. At the time, data was corrected in order to ship the products. Root cause analysis has now been completed. The following recommendations, if implemented, will ensure correct item master data – that is, product shipments will not be delayed in the future due to incorrect item master data.			
Root Causes	**Recommendations**	**Owner**	**Due Date**
• No one clearly responsible for data aspect of product release process (7)	• Assign data steward to work with product release team • Get buy-in from data steward's manager	Data Governance Manager	
• Creating item master not clearly included in product release process (1) • Not enough time allowed to create the item master (2) • Not enough testing (3) • No specific training for those creating item master (8) • Documentation is unclear (9)	• Update data aspects of product release process. Include specific steps for creating material master, estimating time needed, testing scenarios, training, and documentation	Data Steward	
• Data definitions incomplete (4) • Transactional data requirements not considered when creating rules for item master (5)	• Data steward to work with analysts to update rules and requirements	Data Steward	
• Managers not informed of resource needs for creating item master (10) • Not enough resources for creating item master (6)	• Product release manager to get support from managers of data steward and analysts for time needed to address root causes and for on-going process	Product Release Manager	

Barriers to Managing Information as a Business Asset

A research project was conducted by Dr. Nina Evans of the University of South Australia and James Price of Experience Matters into the barriers and benefits to organizations of effectively managing their Information Assets. Every organization studied recognized that they have data, information and knowledge i.e., their Information Assets, that are vital to their business. However, despite the recognized value and the large potential benefits, every organization studied acknowledged that their Information Assets were not managed as well as they could or should be.

Amongst others, participants in the research included Board members and C-Level executives of organizations from Australia, South Africa, and the United States, in industries as varied as utilities, oil and gas, legal services, banking, finance and insurance, manufacturing, and state and local governments.

Their findings, "Information Assets: An Executive Management Perspective," were published in the *Interdisciplinary Journal of Information, Knowledge, and Management* (Evans & Price, 2012). The full paper is also available through the dataleaders. org website.

Danette McGilvray, James Price, and Tom Redman added their deep experience and knowledge to this research to create a cause-and-effect diagram, which shows the barriers that slow/hinder/prevent companies from managing their information as a business asset. *Figure 4.5.7* shows the detailed barriers that slow/hinder/prevent companies from managing

their information as a business asset – the most commonly observed root causes. Detailed root causes were grouped into five main categories:

- Lack of awareness by both executives and practitioners
- Lack of business governance
- Difficulty in justification
- Lack of leadership and management
- Inappropriate or ineffective instruments

Note that the box to the far right further highlights the effects when information assets are not properly managed. The root causes and the effects shown are often the same for data quality issues.

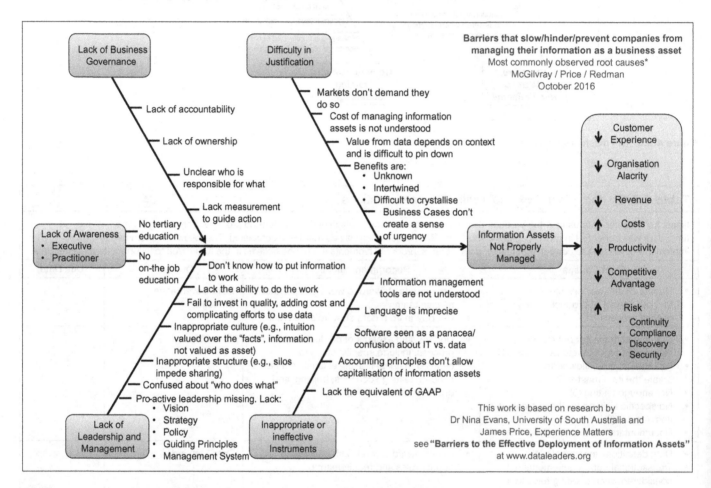

Figure 4.5.7 Barriers to managing information as a business asset – detailed fishbone diagram.

Step 5.4 Other Relevant Root Cause Analysis Techniques

Business Benefit and Context

The root cause analysis techniques detailed in this book are included because they are fundamental, proven techniques that can be used to find root causes of data quality defects. If there are other RCA techniques that work in your organization, use them!

For any technique, remember to use what you have learned and documented throughout the project. Use of these other techniques will be most effective within the flow of the Ten Steps Process. You still need to have done "just enough" of the previous steps to ensure if you address those defects in *Steps 6, 7, and 8,* that you will also be addressing the business need(s) and project objectives. Following is a sampling of other RCA Techniques which your organization may use but are not detailed in this book:

Failure Modes and Effect Analysis (FMEA)—FMEA subjectively lists all the possible failures (modes) that could happen and then assesses the consequences (effect) of each failure. Sometimes a relative score is given to how critical the failure mode is to the operability of the system or component.

Change Analysis—Describes the event or problem. The same situation is then described without the problem. The two situations are compared, differences are documented and analyzed. Consequences of the differences are identified.

Barrier Analysis—Identifies barriers used to protect a target from harm and analyzes the event to see if the barriers held, failed, or were compromised in some way. This is done by tracing the path to the threat from the harmful action to the target.

Commercial RCA Techniques—Such as Kepner-Tregoe Root Cause analysis and Apollo Root Cause Analysis™ methodology.

Step 5 Summary

Discovering root causes of data quality problems is one of the most important milestones in your project – a main goal for all of your previous work. Now you can make informed decisions about your next steps – business actions and communication needed. Update project goals, scope, timeline, and resources as needed based on root causes discovered. Get to root causes as quickly as possible in any project. Remember do just enough in *Steps 1-4* so you have selected the right problem on which to focus and get enough background to do root cause analysis well. Root cause analysis can be done either with or without an in-depth data quality assessment.

After root cause analysis, you may need to spend more time conducting tests to verify potential root causes or you may be confident enough that you can institute changes based on what you discovered. In either case, your recommendations should flow naturally to developing improvement plans.

Of course, remember to document results and recommendations. Review the questions in the checkpoint box to help you determine if you are finished or ready to move to the next step.

 Communicate, Manage, and Engage

Suggestions for working effectively with people and managing the project in this step:

- Use a neutral facilitator who is not invested in the outcome of root cause analysis sessions, but who will lead the participants through a process where everyone can be heard, root causes are identified, and ownership for next steps is established
- Ensure those attending root cause analysis sessions know why they are there and come ready and willing to participate
- In any root cause analysis session, quickly review the purpose for being there and the process for the session. Ensure people are comfortable and feel they can talk freely with no repercussions. Set a tone of openness and trust so people are more likely to look for good solutions, be less defensive, and not revert to placing blame.
- After any root cause analysis session, follow up with action items, talk with owners who were identified to take responsibility for specific improvements – both those who were in the session and others who were not
- Continue to engage with project sponsors and other stakeholders to ensure agreement for root causes and recommendations and improvements to be implemented in upcoming steps

 Checkpoint

Checkpoint Step 5 – Identify Root Causes

How can I tell if I am ready to move to the next step? Use the following guidelines to help determine completeness of this step and readiness for the next step:

- Have the root causes for each of the data quality issues been identified and documented?
- Have recommendations for addressing those root causes been determined and documented?
- Have owners, who will be accountable for ensuring improvements are implemented, been identified?
- Have the communication and engagement plans been kept current?
- Have necessary activities to communicate, manage, and engage people during this step been completed? For example:
  - Have you shared the root causes and specific recommendations from this step and obtained agreement to proceed from project sponsors and other stakeholders?
  - Are you starting to include management of other teams who could be called upon in the future to help implement recommendations? Don't wait too long to let them know what is happening.

Step 6 | Develop Improvement Plans

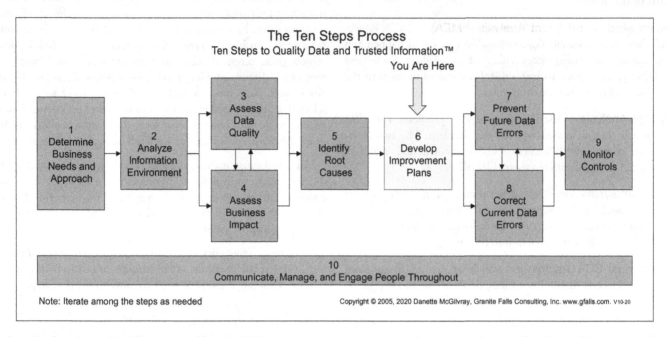

The Ten Steps Process
Ten Steps to Quality Data and Trusted Information™

You Are Here

1 Determine Business Needs and Approach

2 Analyze Information Environment

3 Assess Data Quality

4 Assess Business Impact

5 Identify Root Causes

6 Develop Improvement Plans

7 Prevent Future Data Errors

8 Correct Current Data Errors

9 Monitor Controls

10 Communicate, Manage, and Engage People Throughout

Note: Iterate among the steps as needed

Copyright © 2005, 2020 Danette McGilvray, Granite Falls Consulting, Inc. www.gfalls.com. V10-20

Figure 4.6.1 "You Are Here" Graphic for Step 6 – Develop Improvement Plans.

Business Benefit and Context

Step 6 is an important next step in the improvement cycle as this is where accountable owners are identified for the various improvements to be implemented. Decisions are made about who oversees, coordinates, and tracks the progress of multiple improvements. Detailed plans will be made for improvements to be implemented by the data quality team. For those improvements to be made by those outside of the project team, a handoff of documents and knowledge must take place between the project team and the new owners.

The improvements planned in this step are actually implemented in *Step 7*, *Step 8*, and/or *Step 9*. These three steps are separate in the Ten Steps Process because too often the only improvements people think about involve correcting current data errors (*Step 8*). It is also critical to prevent errors from reoccurring (*Step 7*), some of which should be monitored ongoing (*Step 9*). All three steps should be taken into account when finalizing improvements to be made.

In addition, often different people or teams are responsible for implementation and different processes and tools are required to do the work. For any of the improvements, who implements them will be based on skills needed, availability of resources, and how your organization is structured. For some, there is a clear division of responsibilities between who originally implements a control in *Step 7* and who would support and act on that control ongoing in *Step 9*. If working in a DevOps environment, then there is less of a distinction between the two. *Step 6* is where all these points are taken into consideration so the improvement plans can actually be implemented effectively within your organization's environment.

 Best Practice

Continue Management Support. *Step 6* is a critical point in the project where communication and engagement are key to ensuring that final recommendations are implemented. Too often short attention spans and the "next big thing" affect the memory of management, who forget why the data quality project was done in the first place. It is your job as the project team to remind them of the benefits that will result from implementing the improvements. This is a place where it is not unusual to look again at the business impact techniques in *Step 4* and communication and engagement in *Step 10* to ensure the various improvements have owners, support, and will actually be implemented. Do not underestimate the effort that may be required. Unless plans are made and improvements actually implemented in the upcoming steps, all prior work is wasted.

Improvement Plans in Context with Other Steps

Let's remind ourselves how we got to this step and where we are going. Look at *Figure 4.6.2* as I discuss the points. You have completed relevant activities within *Steps 1, 2, 3 and/or 4*, in whichever order and at the level of detail that makes sense, so your project is addressing the business needs, data quality issues, and project objectives within scope. The work could have taken 4 weeks or 6 months – the figure shows activities, not time.

After each step (e.g., after the information environment was analyzed, after each data quality dimension was assessed, after business impact techniques were used) or at major milestones, you should have done the items listed in the white box.

Table 4.6.1	Step Summary Table for Step 6 – Develop Improvement Plans
Objective	• Develop plans to implement improvements, which include prevention, correction, and detection controls, communication and change management • Confirm owners who will be accountable for ensuring plans are implemented
Purpose	• Ensure the business needs and data quality issues within scope that started the project and the project objectives are addressed by the improvements being planned • Ensure plans are based on root cause analysis and final recommendations • Ensure owners are committed to implementing the improvements • Ensure the work done so far in the data quality project is given the best chance of realizing benefits for the organization • Ensure those affected by changes will support, participate, and accept them

Inputs	• The business needs and data quality issues within scope and project objectives from *Step 1*
	• Any initial recommendations from *Steps 2, 3, or 4* that were not included in root cause analysis in *Step 5*
	• From *Step 5 – Identify Root Causes*, for each of the data quality issues within scope:
	  ○ Root causes identified
	  ○ Specific recommendation(s) for improvement that will address the root causes
	  ○ Final and/or interim owners for implementing the improvement(s)
	• Current project status, stakeholder analysis, communication and engagement plans

Techniques and Tools	• Prioritization techniques if list of recommendations is too long for all to be implemented • Communication and engagement techniques to help ensure improvement plans have owners and support (see *Step 10*) • Project management techniques for whichever approach will be used when implementing improvements
Outputs	• Plans to implement preventive, corrective, and/or detective controls based on final recommendations from the project and root cause analysis • Final owners responsible for implementations • Detailed plans for improvements to be implemented by the data quality project team • For improvements to be implemented by those outside of the project team, high-level plans if available, documentation and knowledge transferred to identified owners who have accepted their accountability • Completed communication and engagement activities needed to "sell" the improvements and obtain owners and commitment to implement them • Updated project status, stakeholder analysis, communication and engagement plans
Communicate, Manage, and Engage	• Ensure project sponsors and other stakeholders understand the benefits from, agree with, and support the recommendations and the improvement plans for implementing them • Obtain owners and commitment for those accountable for implementing the improvements, who may be within or outside of the current project team • Raise awareness of the plans among those who will be impacted by the improvements
Checkpoint	• Have the recommendations been finalized? • Have owners who will be accountable for ensuring improvements are implemented been identified and have they accepted the accountability? • If the project team is responsible for implementation, have improvement plans been completed? • Has the project team completed documentation and done a handoff/knowledge transfer to those outside the project team who are responsible for implementation? • Have the communication and change management plans been kept current? • Have necessary activities to communicate, manage, and engage people during this step been completed?

For each step, results should have been analyzed, synthesized, and documented, with initial recommendations developed. If so, you will be well prepared for root cause analysis in *Step 5*. Documenting provides the best chance of remembering and using what has been learned. Recommendations are listed as those that prevent, correct, or detect (monitor) data quality issues or errors to ensure each category has been considered.

Acting on results when the time is right is included because some prevention or correction may have been done prior to *Step 5*, such as in an emergency situation where operational processes were stopped or key reports were wrong and had to be immediately addressed. Any of these actions should be taken into account when identifying root causes as you will want to determine if additional work in these areas still needs to be done or not.

The initial recommendations will probably cover correcting data – that is always the first inclination. But they should also in-

clude recommendations for how those errors can be prevented, which may include monitoring. As a reminder, a recommendation states the overall solution or the immediate next step needed to keep the action moving forward. If you need to know more about specific recommendations, please re-read *Step 5*.

The change in terms is subtle, but meaningful. What needs to be done starts out as initial recommendations, then become final recommendations for improvements. The final recommendations are turned into improvement plans. Remember that your improvements apply to a range of situations. Plans may quickly address one small issue, or they may spinoff a separate project to address root causes that are difficult, complicated, and have been entrenched in business processes and increasing costs and risk for many years. Many of the improvements will be able to make use of the Ten Steps Process again in some way.

Improvement plans are then carried out to implement controls. Control is used here to indicate various activities that check, detect,

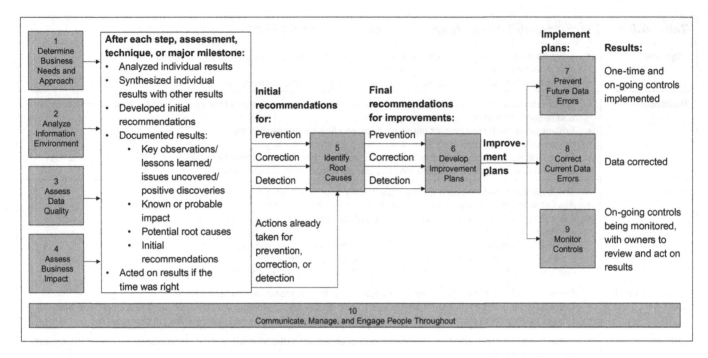

Figure 4.6.2 From initial recommendations to implementing controls.

verify, constrain, reward, encourage, or direct work that will ensure high-quality data, prevent data quality issues or errors, or increase the chances of producing high-quality data. These controls can be one-time implementations or may continue to be monitored over time. Once again, three general types of data quality controls are those that prevent errors, correct errors, and detect errors. Errors refers to where the data itself is wrong which may then highlight larger data quality issues which must be addressed.

When implementing improvements, those that address prevention, correction, and detection can be done separately or together. They can be implemented by the data quality project team itself, separately by those outside of the project team, or through a combination. As mentioned, some are simple tasks on someone's to-do list, others may be complex activities that require a separate project to manage the work. When multiple improvements will be implemented, consider assigning an owner to provide oversight, coordinate the work, and track overall progress.

 Quote to Remember

"If a pipe breaks, we'll fix it. We won't organize a permanent wiping team. If the tap water would be mixed with sewer, we will redesign the system. We won't invest in another cleaning facility."

– *Håkan Edvinsson, Author and Data Management Advisor, at DG Vision, Washington DC, December 2019*

Input to Building Improvement Plans

Figure 4.6.3 outlines factors to take into account when putting together plans for implementing various recommendations for improvement: timing, complexity of the solution, certainty, and ownership and involvement. Each are placed on a continuum. Where any recommendation lands on the various continuums is input to the actual plan for implementing that improvement: when

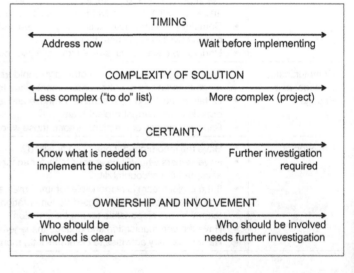

Figure 4.6.3 Considerations when building improvement plans.

it should be done, who should own it, who else should be involved, and how quickly it can be put into place. Have I emphasized enough to think broadly and account for prevention, correction, and detection activities?

Approach

1. Gather all recommendations for improvement that are under consideration.

If you have been making recommendations and documenting results throughout the project, then compiling your list will be quite easy. If you have not, then it will take longer assemble the list. It is possible you will have to do a bit of rework to analyze and synthesize results first, if what was learned has been forgotten. Look at the section *Analyze, Synthesize, Recommend, Document, and Act on Results* in *Chapter 6: Other Techniques and Tools* for help.

Your list of recommendations will most likely include correction activities, prevention activities from root cause analysis, and monitoring of controls to detect data quality issues. Expect the items on the list to range from small to large, and that they will take varying levels of resources and time when ready to implement.

2. If recommendations were not made previously, develop them now.

If recommendations were not made previously, particularly those based on root causes, then develop them before proceeding. Remind yourself of the root causes identified in *Step 5* and revisit the instructions for developing recommendations.

3. Prioritize the list of recommendations, if needed.

It is possible the list of recommendations is short, and you anticipate being able to implement all of them. If so, no prioritization is necessary. Otherwise, they need to be prioritized. You can use business impact techniques such as *Step 4.8 – Benefit vs. Cost Matrix* or *Step 4.6 – Risk Analysis*, where risks and consequences that could arise due to *not* implementing a recommendation are taken into account.

Before prioritizing, remind yourself of the business needs and data quality issues that started the project, the project objectives, and any new data quality issues found. Look for similarities across the recommendations. You may want to group them before prioritization. For example, if they are part of the same business process.

Prioritization may be done by the project team and then results discussed and finalized separately with the project sponsors. Alternatively, project sponsors and/or other stakeholders could participate in the prioritization. It is usually best to have a neutral facilitator lead these types of sessions. The facilitator will ensure a good process has been followed and that attendees participate. This increases the chances that the results of the prioritization will be accepted and implemented.

4. Identify who is accountable for the implementations.

Determine who should be involved in prioritizing and finalizing recommendations, developing and approving improvement plans to address them, and taking ownership of implementation. Make use of any formalized data governance structure and stewards that exist. If there is no formalized data governance in place, the following questions still have to be answered. For example:

- Who is accountable for implementing the improvement?
- Who is responsible for helping with the implementation?
- Who provides input and needs to be consulted? Who has the knowledge?
- Who needs to be informed of the plans?
- Who has the authority to make decisions?
- Who will be responsible for change management?

For every recommendation that has been finalized and agreed to, identify who will be accountable, or at least who should take initial ownership.

5. Develop the improvement plans.

Remember, this is the planning step. The recommendations/improvements will actually be implemented in upcoming steps *Step 7* for prevention, *Step 8* for correction, and *Step 9* for detection through monitoring controls. These steps are called out separately because often different people or teams are responsible for different kinds of improvements. But your plans may have them being done by one team, separate teams, in parallel or one after the other.

Of the prevention activities in *Step 7*, some may be one-time. Others will be on-going, which requires a handoff between *Step 7* and *Step 9*. The monitoring of controls which detect anomalies will make data quality issues visible so they can be handled quickly and early. Corrections done in *Step 8* can also inform ongoing metrics implemented in *Step 9*.

Don't try to fix everything at once, but be sure the plans you put in place will address root causes. Not every improvement requires a full project to be implemented. Look for quick wins and short-term activities that will provide benefits.

To best ensure improvements will be implemented in the upcoming steps, the following summarizes work to be done by:

The *existing* data quality project team—Overall, ensure that if the plans implemented – no matter who is accountable for doing so – that the business needs, data quality issues, and project objectives will have been addressed. Ensure the plans include necessary prevention, correction, detection, and/or communication.

For improvements assigned to the project team, develop detailed plans for implementing. Use the same good project management skills to organize and manage how the work will be done. Include time for communication and engagement. Ensure funding, resources, and support for the work to be done. If implementing controls to be monitored, plan to handoff support to operational teams and confirm who will act on the results if issues are detected.

For improvements assigned outside of the project team, the project team will still need to prepare to transfer knowledge and documentation about the project to others. The project team may also have developed high-level implementation plans based on what was learned in the project, which will give the new owners a jump start with their work. Schedule time together to hand off the materials and ensure ownership has been agreed to. These handoffs may have to be made to several individuals or teams, depending on how the ownership of the implementations have been assigned.

A conscious effort to raise awareness and "sell" the plans to others to implement will need to be made to turn assigned accountability into action. Ideally, those you suspect will be impacted will have been kept informed throughout the project and the fact that they are being asked to help implement recommendations will come as no surprise. The more involved people are throughout the project, the less likely they will be to reject efforts to include them in solving the problems found.

By those *outside* the data quality project team—Make use of results, documentation, and anything the data quality project team has to offer to help. Commit to implementing the improvements and supporting data quality efforts.

If there is an ongoing data quality program or data governance program (remember the Data in Action Triangle), the program may want to track the status of the implementations, no matter who is accountable, and provide encouragement and help to ensure they are completed.

 Ten Steps in Action

Planning Improvements – A Magic Moment

What I call a "magic moment" occurred during one of the final team meetings to prioritize specific recommendations from a data quality project. As responsibility for the recommendations was being assigned, the data management manager agreed her team should institute some of them. But she lamented that there was no money to spare for implementing these recommended improvements.

The marketing manager, the project sponsor, was also in attendance. Because she had been appropriately involved and informed throughout the project, she was aware of the recommendations' value to the goals of the company and her marketing department. She asked, "How much will it cost for your team to institute these recommendations?" The data manager replied with an estimate. The marketing manager laughed, "I waste more money than that in one marketing campaign. I'll pay to implement those recommendations!" Magic happens when the people who can implement recommendations are linked with the people who can pay for the improvements. As you can see from this true story, it is well worth the effort required to communicate and ensure that the right people are engaged throughout the project.

6. Document and communicate results.

Document detailed improvement plans to be implemented by the project team. Document the handoff and final ownership for plans to be implemented by those outside of the project team. See suggestions in the Communicate box at the end of this step.

Sample Output and Templates
Multiple Ways to Improve Data

Following is an example of improvements that were focused on getting source data ready for migration. It also illustrates how different improvements, or changes, require different plans.

In one large global project, data from hundreds of source systems, was being moved to and integrated in a new system. Data profiling had been done against the source systems (the legacy systems) by data subject area, such as item, customer, sales order, etc. The profiling results, which showed current data quality, were compared to the requirements in the new target system. Data readiness activities were put into place to close the gap between the current state of the data in the source systems and what was needed in the new platform to run the business. Depending on the situation (source, data subject area, data quality issues found, resources needed), data was handled in various ways as outlined in *Table 4.6.2*.

 Ten Steps in Action

Implementing Data Quality Identification in a New Zealand Public Sector Infrastructure Agency

Liz is a new Data Quality Specialist in the Transport Sector in New Zealand. Her agency is at the earliest stages of developing a data quality framework and an enterprise data management programme.

She shares her experiences using the Ten Steps:

Business Problem—There were many complaints about poor data quality, but our agency had no real evidence base to understand priority or urgency of data quality issues. Several software projects had generated a collated list of 'pain points,' but little supporting documentation of where the problem had arisen, or which business processes were impacted by the issue. In general, we had dozens of decades-old operational systems, many with documentation buried on internal servers in siloed parts of the business, and a Help Desk to report system faults but no mechanism for logging data related problems.

We recently developed an Enterprise Data Warehouse and hired dozens of new data scientists, dashboard developers, and business intelligence analysts. Data is now being combined and presented in new ways, and the specialist staff were spending a large part of their days 'preparing data for use,' that is, profiling data and cleaning up data sets. The specialists had to find the business owners for the data as there was no central record keeping at the data or dataset level. This was incredibly time-consuming, wasteful of their talents, and led to huge turnover rates. Further, the data issues never got better since there was no capability for root cause analysis or development of an effective remediation plan to fix data at the relevant source system(s).

Use of the Ten Steps—I selected one recently re-developed system as a pilot project to establish a data quality baseline, selected because it had very fresh technical artefacts and tight synchronization between instances in the source database and the satellite data warehouse copies. I had the expectation that with a new system, completing the integrity checks using the data quality dimension of Data Integrity Fundamentals (in *Step 3*) would be straight-forward, and researching the information environment (*Step 2*) would go smoothly. We also had the support of the business owner and technical data stewards identified.

I ran workshops with different groups of stakeholders to show the goals of the pilot project, and to enlist their participation to report data quality problems as they arose when they were applying data to a business process, such as processing an analytics or dashboard request. This methodology was adapted from the Ten Steps framework POSMAD alignment discussion. The outcomes were (1) further identification of the stakeholder groups, (2) improved understanding of data quality dimensions and agreement to use the conformed dimensions of data quality as outlined by DQ Matters, and (3) agreement on how to use the data quality issue reporting service.

Business Value Realized—The immediate benefit from logging data quality issues is that we can assess and address issues in terms of value to the business. The evidence base helps our team assign priority and urgency as we work through the Root Cause Analysis phase of assessment and prepare remediation plans.

Another important benefit is improved understanding of the effectiveness of our stewardship model. Positioning the data quality issue reporting at the point of data application with the specialist analysts has also identified gaps in functional stewardship for several of our key datasets.

Ten Steps in Action *(Continued)*

There is also new awareness that the current technical ticketing system is inadequate to record data incidents. While the Manager of Data and Information is collecting requirements for an enterprise data catalogue, I have submitted a requirement that each data entry in the catalogue have links to the log of issues for that data set, and to record the key relationships with the data, e.g., the effective stewards and business owner contacts.

Further Development Plans—Next steps in our Data Quality project are to build a central register for data quality issues, including services to automate the incident form, facilitate storage of the relevant artefacts, and perform logging to the central data quality issue file. Our goal is to make the Data Quality Issue Log accessible to our whole agency via dashboard technology (QLIK). We will likely use Office 365 tools e.g., Forms, Flow and SharePoint for record keeping in the data management team.

Expected Outcomes / Actions to Resolve Data Quality Issues—The project, using the Ten Steps Framework, has made the emerging stewardship model visible and functional. We now have more effective conversations and can address issues because we started logging data quality issues. Specifically:

- Business impact assessment will be improved by involving the business owner. Issues raised can now be categorised and prioritised by the business owner in terms of value and impact.
- Root cause analysis workshops can now be held with technical data stewards, using fishbone techniques to group specific issues into root cause categories and help focus remediation activity. The six categories are User Knowledge, Standards Compliance, Technical Platform, Business Process, Data Sources, System Design.
- Remediation plans can be co-created with the business owners and technical data stewards.

Table 4.6.2 Data Readiness Plans

If the quality of the data in legacy systems ...	... then the following data readiness activities took place	Improvement Plan Notes
Met requirements of target system	None needed	
Was so poor it could not be used or the data did not exist at all	Data was created or purchased	A plan for data creation was put into place and progress tracked separately Responsibility for purchasing data was assigned
Did not meet requirements	Clean data at source in legacy system OR Transform data during ETL process	These were the preferred options and carried less risk than any of the others in this table. Good communication was required between team and source analysts and between team analysts and developers.
Did not meet requirements – large number of records and changes needed were complex	Create new master records from multiple data sources before loading to new platform	Due to the number of customer data sources and complexity to combine them, it could not be done via ETL. A separate data quality project, requiring in-depth deduplication, was initiated to combine all the sources of the customer data into a master first, before being loaded to the new platform. A separate project plan was created with deadlines that were synchronized with the overall project plan.
Did not meet requirements – small number of records and changes needed were complex	Manual changes after loading to production but before new platform released to users	This was done for only a very few data sets where the changes were complex and required human judgement.

Step 6 Summary

In *Step 6* you may have completed any of the following:

- Developed specific recommendations for improvement, if not already done at the end of prior steps
- Prioritized the recommendations, if the list was longer than could be reasonably implemented with available time and resources
- Identified owners for the high-priority recommendations
- Developed detailed plans for improvements that can be implemented by the existing project team

- Prepared background information on improvements, possibly with high-level plans, and transferred ownership to those outside of the project team who are, or should be, responsible for implementing

In addition, you probably found that increased communication and engagement were required with project sponsors and other stakeholders to confirm ownership and support for the plans made.

You are now ready to continue through the improvement cycle by actually implementing the improvements in *Steps 7, 8,* and *9* – in whichever order makes sense.

Communicate, Manage, and Engage

Suggestions for working effectively with people and managing the project in this step:

- Ensure project sponsors and other stakeholders understand the benefits from, agree with, and support the recommendations and the improvement plans for implementing them
- Obtain owners and commitment for those accountable for implementing the improvements, who may be within or outside of the current project team
- Raise awareness of the plans among those who will be impacted by the improvements

Checkpoint

Checkpoint Step 6 – Develop Improvement Plans

How can I tell if I am ready to move to the next step? Use the following guidelines to help determine completeness of this step and readiness for the next step:

- Have the recommendations been finalized?
- Have owners who will be accountable for ensuring improvements are implemented been identified and have they accepted the accountability?
- If the project team is responsible for implementation, have improvement plans been completed?
- Has the project team completed documentation and done a handoff/knowledge transfer to those outside the project team who are responsible for implementation?
- Have the communication and change management plans been kept current?
- Have necessary activities to communicate, manage, and engage people during this step been completed?

Step 7 Prevent Future Data Errors

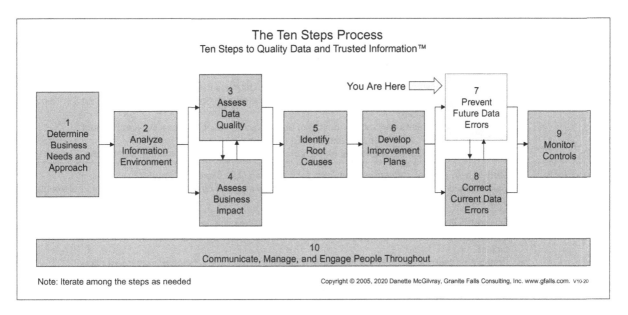

Figure 4.7.1 "You Are Here" Graphic for Step 7 – Prevent Future Data Errors.

Business Benefit and Context

We are now in *Step 7* of the Ten Steps Process. This is one of the steps in the improvement cycle where you will see the fruits of your assessment labors. You will note that there are fewer instructions in this step than others in the Ten Steps Process. This does not mean it is less important. It does not mean it will take less time, though it might, depending on what needs to be done. It is shorter because by this point what you need to do is entirely dependent on what was found in the previous steps, your recommendations, and improvement plans. If other steps were done well, what you need to do is clear, and this step is where you actually put into place whatever is needed to stop the data errors from reoccurring.

Data quality project team members and stakeholders will be encouraged by success – and preventing future data errors is ongoing success. While not every error can be prevented, vastly improved information will raise morale throughout the business and raise expectations for the success of subsequent improvement projects.

There is a reason that proverbs are repeated over time, and "An ounce of prevention is worth a pound of cure" is a truth that certainly holds up under scrutiny. In spite of that, too often the tendency is to skip prevention and start immediately correcting current errors. I hope to bring attention to doing it a different way, which is why prevention is first in *Step 7* before correction in *Step 8*. Prevention reaps long-term benefits and increases trust in information quality. If a company is going to ignore prevention, it should do so consciously only after it has been able to justify cleansing the data without any effort to prevent those problems from reoccurring. And a good justification for correction without prevention is rare.

Preventing future data errors means that a business has processes that produce quality data, instead of facing the time and cost of future data-cleansing activities. In one case an organization had dealt with severe impacts from data quality issues reaching company-wide and up to the highest-level executives. An extremely expensive data cleansing activity, which was called a data blitz, had just been completed when I started working with the organization. I met with the person in charge to learn more about what had happened. She told me that they completed a retrospective after the project. I was impressed because often that does not happen. When asked about results from the retrospective she said proudly, "We now have a fully documented process for a data blitz." I replied, "OK, but wouldn't it be better to figure out how to avoid a data blitz in the first place?" She was silent for a few moments and then said, "Well, that is a good idea, but we are now on to other things." This further confirmed my experience that prevention is not top of mind. Don't be surprised if you have to educate others in the value of prevention – especially the cost of prevention being less than the cost of data cleanup again … and again … and again.

Some prevention activities implemented in *Step 7* are controls that are candidates for monitoring in *Step 9*. *Steps 7, 8,* and *9* can be done in any order, in parallel or sequentially. Just don't forget prevention!

> ### 99 Quote to Remember
>
> "Once a company realizes that its data quality is below par, its first reaction is typically to launch a massive effort to clean up the existing bad data. A better approach is to focus on improving the way new data are created by identifying and eliminating the root cause of the errors."
>
> *– Thomas C. Redman, in Data's Credibility Problem, Harvard Business Review, December 2013*

Table 4.7.1   Step Summary Table for Step 7 – Prevent Future Data Errors

Objective	• Implement solutions that will address root causes of data quality issues/errors
Purpose	• To prevent data errors from reoccurring • Ensure that what has been learned so far in the project is put to use for the benefit of the organization • Ensure that investments in clean-up or correction of data errors are not wasted • Ensure those affected by changes will support, participate, and accept them

Inputs	• Plans for preventive controls to be implemented by the data quality project team (from *Step 6*):
	   ○ Detailed implementation plans that are also coordinated with *Step 8* (correction) and *Step 9* (detection and monitoring controls)
	   ○ Note: Improvements may range from tasks on a person's "to do" list to a separate project
	• Final owners responsible for implementations
	• Current project status, stakeholder analysis, communication and change management plans

Techniques and Tools	• Tools to help prevent data errors (see *Tools for Managing Data Quality* in *Chapter 6*) • Communication and engagement techniques to ensure support, funding, and resources for implementations (see *Step 10*)
Outputs	• Completed implementations of controls/solutions for addressing root causes and preventing future data errors • Completed communication, engagement, and change management activities appropriate at this point in the project • Updated project status, stakeholder analysis, communication and change management plans
Communicate, Manage, and Engage	• Ensure continued support and resources throughout the implementation • Track and report status of implementations • Continue to keep in touch with those implementing improvements outside of the project team to offer help and encouragement, track progress, and coordinate work as needed • Train personnel affected by controls to ensure a consistent understanding of changes, expectations, new or modified roles, responsibilities, processes, etc. • Complete documentation and ensure signoff/approvals of implementations • Share and celebrate successes and accomplishments from this step and acknowledge those involved • Ensure others understand benefits the organization will see as a result of the preventive solutions and controls implemented
Checkpoint	• Have the solutions for addressing root causes and preventing future data errors been implemented? • Have changes to the roles, responsibilities, processes, etc. been documented and shared and do those affected have a consistent understanding of the changes, new expectations, etc.? • Has necessary training been completed? • Have other necessary activities to communicate, manage, and engage people during this step been completed? • Have the communication and change management plans been kept current?

Remember the Data in Action Triangle from *Chapter 2*? The three sides of the triangle (programs, projects, and operational processes) indicate how data quality is put into action. Your data quality project has been working the project (left-hand) side of the triangle. Some controls to prevent data quality errors may be done one time, as part of the project. For example, implementing a drop-down list with valid codes to ensure those creating a record can only select from approved reference data, instead of entering free form text. But others need to be implemented as part of operational processes (the right-hand side of the triangle).

If the project team needs to ensure continuation through operational processes, they generally fall into two categories: 1) data quality controls incorporated into standard business operational processes, such as updating business processes to include how to prevent creating duplicate records and training customer service reps in the new procedures and why they are important, and 2) data quality specific controls that are on-going and therefore operational processes themselves, such as a data quality dashboard with metrics that detect data quality errors.

If a data quality program does not exist, one of the recommendations out of the project could be to implement one. This is a connection into the third side of the triangle – programs. A data

quality program is a good place for tracking progress of all implementations. It is also an excellent way to ensure continuity so people with data quality knowledge and skills have a home and are available to other teams and projects.

Approach

1. Confirm the implementation plan for each of the prevention improvements.

This is particularly important if some time has passed since the original assessments and root cause analysis were completed and when beginning to implement the preventive measures. Ensure that the improvement activities still apply to the current environment.

Ensure that improvement activities or projects focus on root causes. Review the root causes discovered in *Step 5* and the plans from *Step 6*.

Remember every piece of data has a life cycle. Ensure preventive measures are put into place in the right place in the life cycle. Preventing data quality problems at the time of creation should be the first priority.

Carefully implement your improvements to ensure that harmful side effects do not result from your work. Reference the Framework for Information Quality to ensure that you have accounted for components that will affect the plan. For example, make sure that you have accounted for the people/organizations that will be responsible for improvements. Look at the *POSMAD Interaction Matrix Detail – Sample Questions* in the *Appendix: Quick References* or *Figure 3.3* in *Chapter 3* to help you implement effective improvements.

Expect many of the improvements to be related to processes. After all, data are products of business processes. As mentioned, some improvements will take the form of "quick-win" activities that can easily be implemented; others will require more resource-intensive effort.

Remember training! See additional suggestions in *Sample Output and Templates*. Include awareness of the dependency that other parts of the business have on the quality of the data they collect, and awareness of the impact to the organization if the quality is poor. I believe that most people want to do a good job, so even this level of awareness can go a long way. I worked on a project with a woman responsible for determining rebates to be paid to resellers based on sales data from a particular system. She recognized that the data she was using in this job was the same kind of data she entered into the same system in a prior job some years earlier. She noted, "If I would have known *then* what I know *now* about how this data is used, I would have been a lot more careful!"

2. Ensure that responsibilities are assigned and training completed.

All the same principles for good project management addressed in *Step 1 – Determine Business Needs and Approach* apply here. Of course, you don't need a project charter for small improvement activities, but you may need one for large-scale improvements.

Train personnel affected by controls to ensure a consistent understanding of changes, expectations, new or modified roles, responsibilities, processes, etc.

3. Complete the implementation.

Just do it! Track and report progress. Finalize documentation. Obtain acceptance and signoff when implementations are complete.

4. Ensure continuity for controls to be monitored.

Ensure a handoff of documents and knowledge transfer from those who implemented the controls to those who will support the controls as they are monitored and take action on results. This may be done here or in *Step 9 – Monitor Controls*.

5. Document and communicate results.

Continue to communicate and engage with project sponsors, other stakeholders, and anyone recently identified who will be impacted by these improvements. Include change management to help everyone deal with the adjustments to their processes, roles, responsibilities, the way they work together, etc. Ensure they know why the changes were done and how they will benefit from them. Use the ideas from *Step 10 – Communicate, Manage, and Engage People Throughout*.

Sample Output and Templates

Examples of Preventing Future Data Errors

Following are sample activities that will prevent future data errors:

- **Focus on data creation**. Identify the processes that create data along with the roles and responsibilities of those who create data. Implement accountability and rewards for data producers. Institute

procedures that enforce or encourage good data quality practices and include in training and process documentation. Ensure the training includes not only how to create high-quality data, but also why high-quality data is so important. Bring together data producers and data users to discuss issues and determine how the needs of both groups can be met. Standardize questions for consistency and effectiveness when collecting/creating data.

- **Training**. Almost every person in an organization affects the quality of data in some way. Many users create and maintain data in the course of doing their jobs. Yet how many of them have any awareness that the data they create is being used by other people? Do they realize that the quality of the data they touch can have either a positive or negative impact as it flows throughout the company? That it can actually affect costs and revenue and customer satisfaction? Most do not. Data users do not need to know all about the Ten Steps Process and key concepts. But they do need to know something about data quality. New employee orientation, often called on-boarding, can take place at organizational, department, team, or job levels. A data quality message can be tailored for all of them. Incorporate into standard training they receive about standards of conduct, safety and security, etc. Why not a short section about how and why to be careful about data they touch? Be specific about the data they create. Equally important tell them why to take good care of the data that crosses their desk. Provide general examples of data and where it flows. Illustrate how interconnected they and their jobs are through data, how they help or hurt each other depending how they take care (or not) of data that crosses their path. Give examples of how specific data they touch is used by others and what impact it has on them. Help them understand why ensuring quality data is important.

- **Incentives**. Implement incentives/metrics for data quality that complement business metrics or KPIs that may inadvertently negatively impact data quality. For example, quick customer call turnaround (i.e., time per support call) is often the only metric for customer service reps. The pressure to get off the phone can mean that data entry suffers. Work with managers to ensure alignment between business and data quality metrics. Help everyone understand the benefits from them. Motivate and reward those who support data quality.

- **Accountability for data quality**. Ensure that data quality-related activities are included in job responsibilities and are part of annual performance reviews. Implement service level agreements for the level of quality for data from internal data providers. Work with your procurement department to build data quality criteria into contracts with external data providers.

- **Trust**. Increase trust in, and thus usage of, critical data. Let users know results of baseline assessments and get feedback. Share prevention activities currently under way, correction activities already completed, and business impact results that created the motivation for improvement.

- **Communication**. Get management at all levels to show their support of data quality work in both words and actions and show impact to the organization.

- **Technology bugs**. Fix any technology bugs uncovered during the project that contribute to poor data quality.

- **Big Data**. Examine the ingestion process and data quality activities that sanitize data coming from its origin before landing in a data lake.

- **ML and AI**. Ensure that data used to train algorithms is of high enough quality to be used in machine learning and artificial intelligence.
- **Data quality in your organization's SDLC**. Incorporate data quality activities from the Ten Steps into your organization's standard SDLC, its approach for managing projects. Obtain approvals for the changes. Raise awareness about the changes with teams who will be using the revised SDLC in upcoming projects. Work with current projects to incorporate as many of the data quality activities as possible. Ensuring high-quality data when new systems are put into production is one of the most effective means of preventing data quality problems.
- **Standard data quality improvement**. Create a standard data quality improvement methodology based on the Ten Steps. Modify the Ten Steps Process to fit your organization, using terms and language most meaningful to those who will use it.

 Ten Steps in Action

Artificial Intelligence Project to Automate a Business Solution

Mary Levins, Principal, Sierra Creek Consulting, worked with an artificial intelligence (AI) project to solve a customer-facing business problem.

She explains how the Ten Steps Process was critical to the project's success:

Background and Business Need—A very large cable and internet provider wanted to explore ways to use AI and Machine Learning to improve customer service. Current processes to quote new services were inconsistent, costly, and had unpredictable and unacceptable turnaround times for the customer. A real time automated cost estimate using AI could solve the business problem with a greater prediction rate than what currently existed through manual processes. However, a successful business solution using AI depends on relevant and quality data and is itself only as relevant as the data used to train the model. The Ten Step Process was critical for a trusted sustainable solution.

Business leaders and their teams did not have a consistent or predictable view of their business data needed to make a variety of business decisions. Many operational teams across the organization had multiple solutions to meet their data visibility and reporting needs. These solutions ranged from many different expensive systems to low cost manual tools and spreadsheets. Reports and data differed within and between these solutions so business leaders could not get a consistent or predictable view of the data. This presented a great challenge when identifying available and trusted data for an AI solution.

Use of the Ten Steps—Because of the situation just described, one of the specific business problems needing to be solved was to better predict real time cost estimates, using many factors as input. First, the business need was clearly defined (*Step 1 – Determine Business Needs and Approach*) and then the information environment was analyzed (*Step 2*). From this analysis, it was clear there were many gaps, including lack of data governance processes and lack of consistent or shared data definitions across departments. Improvement plans were developed (*Step 6*), which included a recommendation to implement a Data Governance program and team to lead the definition of critical data elements across sources.

Final Result—The use of the Ten Steps enabled clear identification of the business problem and of the relevant data for an effective AI algorithm. The algorithm was developed for real time cost estimates that solved the business problem with a greater prediction rate than what currently existed through manual processes. The accuracy of the algorithm will be refined and improved as the volume and quality of data improves over time through implementation of new Data Governance processes and other improvement plans identified using the Ten Steps approach.

Step 7 Summary

In this step you completed the implementation of controls meant to address root causes and prevent future data errors from occurring. How, when, and who was responsible should be coordinated with the corrections made in *Step 8* and monitoring of controls in *Step 9*. I hope you have taken the time to congratulate all those involved with the implementation and share your successes with others. Feel good knowing that you have contributed to your organization's success by supporting its business needs through better quality data.

 Communicate, Manage, and Engage

Suggestions for working effectively with people and managing the project in this step:

- Ensure continued support and resources throughout the implementation
- Track and report status of implementations
- Continue to keep in touch with those implementing improvements outside of the project team to offer help and encouragement, track progress, and coordinate work as needed
- Train personnel affected by controls to ensure a consistent understanding of changes, expectations, new or modified roles, responsibilities, processes, etc.
- Complete documentation and ensure signoff/approvals of implementations
- Share and celebrate successes and accomplishments from this step and acknowledge those involved
- Ensure others understand benefits the organization will see as a result of the preventive solutions and controls implemented

Checkpoint

Checkpoint Step 7 – Prevent Future Data Errors

How can I tell if I am ready to move to the next step? Use the following guidelines to help determine completeness of this step and readiness for the next step:

- Have the solutions for addressing root causes and preventing future data errors been implemented?
- Have changes to the roles, responsibilities, processes, etc. been documented and shared and do those affected have a consistent understanding of the changes, new expectations, etc.?
- Has necessary training been completed?
- Have other necessary activities to communicate, manage, and engage people during this step been completed?
- Have the communication and change management plans been kept current?

Step 8 | Correct Current Data Errors

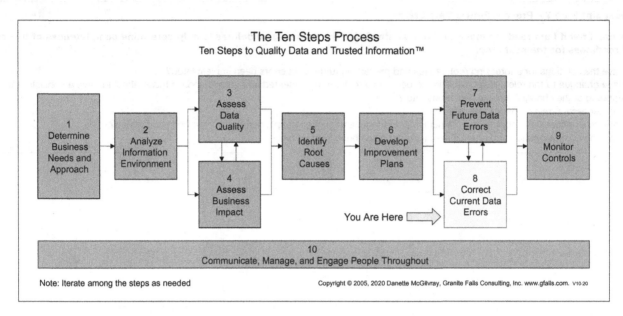

Figure 4.8.1 "You Are Here" Graphic for Step 8 – Correct Current Data Errors.

Business Benefit and Context

The correction of current data errors is an exciting milestone in the information and data quality improvement process. However, for continuous improvement it is important not only to correct current data errors, but also to prevent future ones. Larry English strongly recommends that data correction activity should be a "one-time event only, coupled with process improvement to prevent occurrence of those defects" (1999).

What if data errors are stopping business processes? In this case they should immediately be corrected, as in the example in *Step 5 – Identify Root Causes* where incorrect master data records were halting product shipments. Once the critical records are updated, determine root causes of the problem and implement preventive measures so they do not reoccur.

 Quote to Remember

"Rule 1: Focus on those data most critical to the organization's most important strategies first, ignore data that are not used.

Rule 2 (prevent, then clean): Prevent future errors by improving upstream information chains and suppliers first. When these data sources are of acceptable quality, target clean-ups at important pockets of long-lasting data.

Rule 3: Data clean-up by itself is almost never a viable long-term strategy.

Rule 4: If clean-up is required, make sure it is NEVER repeated."

– Thomas C. Redman, in Data Quality: The Field Guide, (2001), p. 66

Approach

1. Confirm the records to be updated and the specific changes needed.

Use results from data quality assessments in *Step 3* to confirm specifically which records and changes are to be made.

2. Determine the method and process for making the changes.

See *Template 4.8.1* for options for correcting data. The method, or combination of methods, chosen for corrections will drive the process for how and when those changes will be done. What is the best way to make the changes? Who will be involved? How long will it take? Are there other timing constraints that will affect the data correction efforts, such as software updates to the application or needed resources that are unavailable?

Consider changes to master data versus transactional data. For example, merging duplicate master records may not be possible until all associated open transactional records are closed. In this case, a duplicate record may have to be flagged so it will not be used while related transactional records are still open. Once closed, the duplicate record can be merged or deleted.

Document instructions and train those involved in the changes, whether the work is being done manually, through written programs, or by configuring and running data quality tools. Apply life cycle thinking as it applies to the correction process.

3. Make the changes.

Use the documentation to ensure consistency of changes done manually – particularly if more than one person is making them. Use an analysis of data dependencies to make sure that the changes

Table 4.8.1 Step Summary Table for Step 8 – Correct Current Data Errors

Objective	• Implement solutions that correct existing data errors • Use what has been learned about the location, magnitude, and impact of data errors to update the most critical data
Purpose	• Ensure data being used by the organization can continue to support business needs

Inputs	• Improvement plans for correcting data from *Step 6*:
	  o Informed by data quality assessment results from *Step 3*
	  o Detailed implementation plans that are also coordinated with *Step 7* (prevention) and *Step 9* (detection and monitoring controls)
	  o Note: Improvements may range from tasks on a person's "to do" list to a separate project
	• Final owners responsible for implementations
	• Current project status, stakeholder analysis, communication and change management plans

Techniques and Tools	• Tools to help with data corrections and cleansing (see *Tools for Managing Data Quality* in *Chapter 6*) • Communication, engagement, techniques to ensure support, funding, and resources for corrections (see *Step 10*)
Outputs	• Data corrected according to specifications, with documentation and signoff • Completed communication, engagement, and change management activities appropriate at this point in the project • Updated project status, stakeholder analysis, communication and change management plans
Communicate, Manage, and Engage	• Ensure continued support and resources to complete the corrections • Track and report status of corrections • Keep in touch with those making corrections outside of the project team to offer help and encouragement, track progress, and coordinate work as needed • Train personnel who will be making manual corrections to ensure consistency in the updates • Document work done and obtain approvals for completed corrections • Share and celebrate successes and accomplishments from this step and acknowledge those involved • Ensure others understand benefits to the business from the corrections made
Checkpoint	• Have the current data errors been corrected and approved? • Have the results been documented and communicated? • Have necessary activities to communicate, manage, and engage people during this step been completed? • Have the communication, engagement, and change management plans been kept current?

Template 4.8.1 Options for Correcting Data

Option	Notes	Which options apply?
Manual	Individuals use standard application interfaces, screens, and keyboard. Data corrected with this method takes advantage of any edits built into the user interface, but the possibility of human error exists. It is much slower than other options and not practical when there are large volumes of updates.	
Keystroke emulation	This automates the use of a keyboard by replicating the keystrokes as if done manually. As with manual corrections, it takes advantage of edits built into the user interface. Tools such as these still require human monitoring and may have poor error handling.	
Mass updates directly to the database	This is a quick way to update large numbers of records and, unfortunately, is done too often when there is time pressure. This is a high-risk option and the caution with this method is that edits, validations, and triggers that are part of the application interface are bypassed. This can cause additional data quality problems and issues with the database's referential integrity. There is often no good audit trail for the changes made.	
Data cleansing tool	Many data cleansing tools are available on the market, some of which take advantage of machine learning and artificial intelligence. When comparing data cleansing tools, different terms may describe the same functionality. For example, data wrangling or data munging, often used in the data science world, refer to cleansing, transforming, enriching, or structuring raw data to make it more useable for analytics.	
Deduplication and entity resolution	Tools that provide the ability to determine if more than one reference to a real-world object (a person, place or thing) are referring to the same object or to different objects and the process for merging records that represent the same real-world object.	

(Continued)

Template 4.8.1 Options for Correcting Data *(Continued)*

Option	Notes	Which options apply?
Custom interface programs	Sometimes the complexity and volume of changes require a custom interface program. It can be very time-consuming to build and test these interface programs, but the resulting changes are of high-quality.	
Decide not to make corrections	Sometimes the choice is to fix the root causes and only focus on creating good data moving forward instead of fixing existing data.	
Overall	Select the option(s) which work best for the situation. Be wary of spending too much time on corrections and ensure they will not come at the expense of preventing problems over the long term.	
Factors Which Influence Options Chosen		
Think through the following factors that can influence which option will best meet your needs:		How do these apply to the data corrections needed?
Volume. Small volumes of records can be updated manually. Determine how many can realistically be manually updated in your environment. Large volumes (Big Data) may require specialized tools. Find out if there are limits to the volumes that can be processed.		
Complexity of changes. Will there be changes to one or several data fields? Are the changes to be made clear and straightforward or will complex algorithms, calculations, or human judgement be required? Are there dependencies that should be taken into account, such as changes to supplier attributes that could impact the product master?		
Time to make changes. The time needed to make changes must be feasible and practical with the resources (tools and people) available and fit within the project schedule.		
Skills required. What skills and training are needed to use the correction tools? Are those with knowledge about the data content/changes able to access systems and use tools or must others be involved?		
Impact on system performance. Some changes will have more impact on system performance than others and should be scheduled during times of lower usage.		
Availability and cost of tools. What tools are already available to use? Do you need to purchase new tools? If yes, how much will they cost and how quickly will you be able to procure them? Do you have funding needed?		
Life of the solution. Balance the investment in the particular solution with how long you, or others, anticipate being able to use it.		

themselves don't produce data quality problems. And stay alert – the changes may have effects on downstream processes that you did not predict.

Caution

Do not introduce new errors or adversely affect business processes when correcting data! Carefully make changes so that harmful side effects are not created as a result of the corrections. Ensure changes to upstream data do not adversely affect data being used in downstream systems. Prepare users and processes to expect and accept the corrections. Avoid slowing system performance by timing the changes to coincide with lower usage of the production system. For example, do not strain the system by making data changes during holidays when retail website traffic is already high and poor system performance could affect the ability to process orders. The main point here is – ensure changes do not cause other problems!

4. Document the changes.

Describe the changes in structured documents so that future improvement teams can follow the data correction process. Structured documents mean an organized method of collecting, storing, and sharing the information such as through an enterprise knowledge management system or website. It does not mean storing documents on your hard drive, making them accessible only to you. Obtain approvals from those who have to accept the work done.

5. Communicate results.

Results of data correction should also be communicated to project sponsors, other stakeholders, and users of the data. Describe how corrections will benefit the business. Find out if there were unexpected impacts from the corrections and address them. Inform technical teams and provide documentation about the changes. What was learned when correcting the data is valuable input to *Step 9 – Monitor Controls* as the same processes, tools, and people used here may also be used to correct errors that are detected through operational controls.

Sample Output and Templates

Options for Correcting Data

To correct data, it is likely you will need to use tools other than what can be updated manually through an application user interface. Different tools may be needed depending on the data sets and changes to be made. *Template 4.8.1* summarizes options for correcting data, along with factors that can influence which option will best meet your needs. See the section *Tools for Managing Data Quality* in *Chapter 6* for additional information.

How data can be corrected generally falls into two categories: manual and automatic. Automatic will be more accurate than manual – if the programs are written correctly and tested prior to final changes. Though machine learning and artificial intelligence methods claim to replicate human judgement, these are still only as good as the algorithms used and the quality of the data which trained those algorithms. Understand what they are based on.

 Key Concept

Automation in data quality tools. There is a movement toward automation in data quality tools, with much research going into "automated data curation," which is the ability to take raw datasets and put them through an entirely automated (unsupervised) process to clean and integrate the data. Rich Wang has coined the term "data washing machine" for this concept.

The first step is to automatically generate data quality rules (validation rules). But some tools are going farther and looking at actual data correction. Data editing is a term used in the production of official statistics for detecting and correcting errors in survey data. There is also a well-established practice of "data imputation." Data imputation is filling in a missing value, primarily for numeric survey data, and is usually based on statistical methods.

There is a lot of research around unsupervised entity resolution and how machine learning and master data management can work together. With the ability to cluster records for the same person, product, etc. without human-made rules, then it is also possible to compare and replace values within a cluster. For example, if you have a high confidence a cluster of 10 records are for the same patient, and 9 of the 10 records have a street number of 123, and the tenth record has 124, then there is a high confidence 124 should be changed to 123.

This automation in data quality tools is being driven by Big Data, digital transformation initiatives, more complex information environments, and the availability of new technologies. Innovations and changes in this space are rapid. More to come!

– John Talburt, PhD, IQCP, Professor, University of Arkansas at Little Rock

---

Step 8 Summary

You have now completed updates to current data errors found during the data quality assessments. You should have coordinated your work with preventive controls being implemented in *Step 7* and monitoring of controls in *Step 9*. Take the time to congratulate all those involved with the corrections and share your successes with others. Feel good knowing that, through correcting the data supporting business needs, you have contributed to your organization's success.

 Communicate, Manage, and Engage

Suggestions for working effectively with people and managing the project in this step:

* Ensure continued support and resources to complete the corrections
* Track and report status of corrections
* Keep in touch with those making corrections outside of the project team to offer help and encouragement, track progress, and coordinate work as needed
* Train personnel who will be making manual corrections to ensure consistency in the updates
* Document work done and obtain approvals for completed corrections
* Share and celebrate successes and accomplishments from this step and acknowledge those involved
* Ensure others understand benefits to the business from the corrections made

---

 Checkpoint

Checkpoint Step 8 – Correct Current Data Errors

How can I tell if I am ready to move to the next step? Use the following guidelines to help determine completeness of this step and readiness for the next step:

* Have the current data errors been corrected and approved?
* Have the results been documented and communicated?
* Have necessary activities to communicate, manage, and engage people during this step been completed?
* Have the communication, engagement, and change management plans been kept current?

Step 9 | Monitor Controls

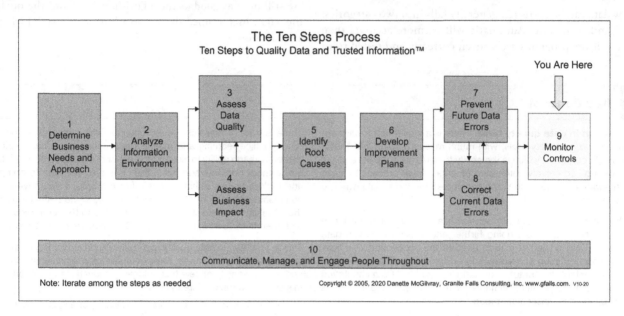

Figure 4.9.1 "You Are Here" Graphic for Step 9 – Monitor Controls.

Business Benefit and Context

Many standard quality principles and practices can be applied to data. Controls are yet another area where we can learn from quality experts. Joseph M. Juran, a world-renowned expert in management studies and author of leading international reference literature on quality, notes: "The control process is a feedback loop through which we measure actual performance, compare it with a standard, and act on the difference" (Juran, 1988, p. 24.2).

While this step is focused on monitoring controls, understand that quality does not come from inspection and quality is not a monitoring process. Rather, quality should be incorporated into business processes and when building information systems. The best prevention is to build in data quality as new solutions are created and deployed. Monitoring controls is a back-end process to let us know how business processes and information systems are working.

This step looks at controls/preventive measures that may have been implemented in *Step 7*, or for critical data that was corrected in *Step 8* that should be monitored for quality, another type of control. Some of the activities in those steps may have been looked at as one-time efforts. Here we determine which are important enough to track on an on-going basis. Organizations need visibility to what is important to them to be managed and therefore measured. Any control should help us understand what is working and what is not and let us know if action needs to be taken. We then need clear directions for those actions – what needs to happen under each circumstance, when, and by whom.

 Definition

Control is used generally in this book to indicate various activities that check, detect, verify, constrain, reward, encourage, or direct work that will ensure high-quality data, prevent data quality issues or errors, or increase the chances of producing high-quality data. The controls can be one-time implementations or may continue to be monitored over time.

More specifically, "A **control** is a form of feedback built into a system to keep it stable. A control has the ability to detect conditions that indicate a lack of stability (most often in the form of a measurement) and initiate action based on this observation."

– *Laura Sebastian-Coleman, Measuring Data Quality for Ongoing Improvement: A Data Quality Assessment Framework (2013), p. 52.*

Controls related to data quality offer the following benefits:

- Provide visibility to data quality issues so we can react quickly when they arise
- Show us where things are working so we can confidently turn our attention to other priorities
- Monitor and verify improvements that were implemented
- Determine if the improvement actions achieved the desired effect
- Standardize and continuously monitor successful improvements
- Encourage the improvements
- Avoid returning to old processes and behaviors

A particular type of control, metrics, often in the form of a dashboard, is one of the most familiar types of data quality controls. *Chapter 6: Other Techniques and Tools* has additional detail on metrics that supplement this step.

Table 4.9.1 Step Summary Table for Step 9 – Monitor Controls

Objective	• Develop new controls or monitor controls previously implemented
Purpose	• Determine if improvements made are achieving the desired effect • Maintain successful improvements by standardizing, documenting, and continuously monitoring them • Encourage continuous improvement and avoid returning to old processes and behaviors • Ensure that what has been learned so far in the project is put to use for the benefit of the organization • Ensure those affected by changes will support, participate, and accept them
Inputs	• Plans for monitoring controls to be implemented by the data quality project team (from *Step 6*) • Detailed implementation plans that are also coordinated with *Step 7* (prevention) and *Step 8* (correction), • Final owners responsible for implementations • Current project status, stakeholder analysis, communication and change management plans
Techniques and Tools	• Tools used dependent on controls (see *Tools for Managing Data Quality* in *Chapter 6*) • *Metrics* in *Chapter 6* • Communication and engagement techniques to ensure support, funding, and resources for implementations (see *Step 10*)
Outputs	• Controls to be monitored are implemented, with documentation, signoff, and assigned owners • Completed communication, engagement, and change management activities appropriate at this point in the project • Updated project status, stakeholder analysis, communication and change management plans
Communicate, Manage, and Engage	• Ensure support and resources to continue monitoring • Continue to keep in touch with those implementing improvements outside of the project team to offer help and encouragement, track progress, and coordinate work as needed • Train personnel affected by controls to ensure a consistent understanding of changes, expectations, new or modified roles, responsibilities, processes, etc. • Complete documentation and ensure signoff/approvals of implementations • Share and celebrate successes and accomplishments from this step and acknowledge those involved • Ensure others understand benefits the organization will see as a result of the controls being monitored
Checkpoint	• Have the controls been implemented and are they being monitored? • Have results from monitoring, both positive and negative, been documented and addressed? • Have improvements been verified? • Have successful improvements been standardized? • Have necessary activities to communicate, manage, and engage people during this step been completed?

An excellent resource for a deep dive into monitoring controls and ongoing improvement in operational processes is Laura Sebastian-Coleman's book *Measuring Data Quality for Ongoing Improvement: A Data Quality Assessment Framework* (2013).

Approach

1. Determine which controls should be monitored.

Monitoring refers to controls that should be checked on an ongoing or period basis vs. a one-time control that is implemented

 Best Practice

Working with Audit and Compliance teams. In this book, most examples and good practices are described using the language of business or IT. For example, we might say:

"Financial reports for international organizations often include aggregate data based on country totals. And so, it is important that country codes be managed and governed as corporate reference data. Good practices should be followed for standardizing the codes and ensuring that non-standard data does not skew report totals."

Colleagues who work in Compliance or Audit functions would probably not challenge such a statement. However, they might express their concerns more precisely, using different language. They might say:

"Management is expected to implement controls to prevent inaccurate financial reporting and to detect issues prior to publishing financial reports. For example:

The impact of aggregating data based on inaccurate country totals would be high, and the likelihood of errors would also be high without assurances that only standardized data is employed. Our expectation is that a standardized set of country codes is defined. We expect process controls and technical controls to be in place to prevent the use of nonstandard values, to detect them should preventative controls fail, and to correct data prior to its presentation in published financial reports. We expect to see evidence that a formal reference data governance function is in place and empowered to establish and enforce reference data standards."

When assessing, measuring, or monitoring data quality, select the controls and data quality dimensions that best address your business needs and project objectives and are within the time, budget, and other resources available. When you do, ensure you are speaking, and understanding, the language of those with whom you are working.

– Gwen Thomas, Sr. Compliance Officer

and then assumed to work. Appropriate controls, which detect conditions and initiate action, will vary widely depending on your business needs, project scope and objectives, and previous work done. Following are candidates for controls:

- Recommendations that addressed root causes discovered in *Step 5* and implemented in *Step 7*, if they are more than one-time efforts and should be monitored over time
- Data that was corrected in *Step 8* that is high enough priority to track the quality ongoing
- Existing controls in operational processes, such as standard reconciliations, that can be enhanced or expanded to include data quality, or already enforce or encourage data quality, but may not be called "data quality controls"
- Include data quality rules in machine learning and AI algorithms, business rules engines, and processes based on business rules
- Metrics – which themselves can take many forms such as a single data quality check or a data quality dashboard combining many metrics
- Because metrics focus on specific data, it can be worthwhile to institute a periodic data quality assessment against the larger dataset so as not to lose visibility into the wider context for the data.
- Incorporate data quality checks into ETL (Extract-Transform-Load) processes
- Integrate data quality assessments, activities, or techniques into your organization's standard project approach (SDLC such as Agile or sequential), with processes to ensure they are being followed in each project
- Periodic surveys of those who use the data to determine if the data being monitored is still important to them and if their confidence and trust in the quality of the data has increased. See *Step 3.10 – Perception, Relevance, and Trust.*
- Controls for reference data – once allowed values are specified and translated into edits, monitor usage of the various values, to spot trends or detect misuse

2. Plan and implement the controls.

Review the data quality and business impact assessments done to this point. Which of the initial assessments are worth monitoring on an ongoing periodic basis? Can any of those assessments be used as a baseline against which to monitor progress? Make use of the processes, people, and technology used for the initial assessments. What worked and what did not? Modify the processes as needed to accommodate the ongoing nature of the controls. Ensure a smooth handoff from those on the project team who implemented the controls to those who will be responsible for the controls in an operational environment.

Statistical quality control (SQC), also referred to as statistical process control, was invented by Walter Shewhart in the 1920s and is an established practice in manufacturing. The purpose of SQC is to predict future process performance and to judge process stability by examining current and past performance. You can learn more about how Tom Redman has applied SQC to information quality in *Data Quality for the Information Age* (1996), pp. 155–183.

Employ some of the business impact techniques in *Step 4* to validate the value of the controls to the business.

Gain commitment to ensure action will be taken when indicated by controls. Monitoring without action is a waste of money and produces no useful results.

3. Obtain buy-in for what is to be implemented.

Develop incentives for supporting the controls and for ensuring data quality. If your data quality is dependent on action from knowledge workers (such as taking the extra time to check that contact information is updated when support reps talk to customers on the phone), be sure that the responsibility is supported by their management and is a recognized part of their job description and performance evaluation.

4. Evaluate the improvements that have been implemented.

See if the expected results have occurred and determine next steps. If you (and, more important, those in the business and other stakeholders) are satisfied, and there are no negative side effects, then standardize the improvements. Ensure that the processes and controls become part of standard operating procedures, and are included in training, documentation, and job responsibilities.

If there are any issues, such as satisfactory improvements with harmful side effects or unsatisfactory improvements (because of poor implementation or because the control itself was not a good idea), return to *Step 6 – Develop Improvement Plans, Step 7 – Prevent Future Data Errors*, or *Step 9 – Implement Controls* to reassess your implementation plan or the improvement itself.

5. Communicate, communicate, and communicate some more!

Market the benefits through education and feedback. Celebrate and advertise success. Adjust where the controls are not working. Promote the value provided to the business and the team's success with the project.

6. Identify the next potential area for data and information quality improvements.

Start again with new issues that arise and use the Ten Steps Process. Consider reviewing other recommendations that did not get implemented, from *Step 5 – Identify Root Causes* and *Step 6 – Develop Improvement Plans*. Determine whether the recommendations still apply to the current environment, reprioritize, and implement more improvements.

Sample Output and Templates

Metrics Worksheet.

If implementing metrics, *Template 4.9.1* can act as a checklist to ensure you are developing a stable, sustainable metrics process. It provides a guide for thinking and planning, as well as for documenting metrics. It can also be used to evaluate existing metrics. See *Metrics* in *Chapter 6* for more details on this subject. Apply the concepts in the template as needed, depending on the type of metric and the level of detail for the metric. Always identify the reasons behind the metric, especially the behaviors that will be influenced by the metric.

Template 4.9.1 Metrics Worksheet

Item	Description	Apply to Your Metrics
Metric Title	Name of metric.	
Metric Definition	A clear, understandable description of what is to be measured.	
Business Impact and Beneficiaries	Business impact from the metric. Primary beneficiary from metric positive results. Other or indirect beneficiaries from the process.	
Behavior	Behavior that will be changed as a result of the metric. List both positive and negative.	
Data and Sources	Data associated with the metric and sources of the data.	
Responsibilities, Processes, and Tools	Summary of how the measurement will be conducted and at what frequency. Tools to be used. Who is responsible for various tasks throughout the process.	
Targets, Status Criteria, and Control Limits	Goal or standard for the metric. Status assigned (e.g., red, yellow, green) based on results, which triggers action to be taken. If the target is not met, at what point action will be taken. Upper and/or lower control limits.	
Metric Usage and Action	Summary of who will receive and use the metric and what action will be taken.	
Notes	Any applicable background information.	

Ten Steps in Action

Data Quality Control in a Bank

Ana Margarida Galvão, an area coordinator at a bank, was involved with developing and implementing the data quality controls described here. She and her team used the Ten Steps Process as input to improving the Framework Data Quality in the Third Level.

Background—This European bank, through its 5000 employees and 387 branches, services approximately 1.3 million customers. The bank had taken significant steps against its commitment to efficiency, process improvement, and digital transformation in order to differentiate them from their competition. They recognized the important role of high-quality data in decision making and the ability to comply with regulatory requirements, such as BCBS 239 guidelines.

BCBS 239, standard number 239 from the Basel Committee on Banking Supervision, is a principle-based standard with the objective of strengthening banks' risk data aggregation capabilities and internal risk reporting practices. Adoption of the principles should enhance the risk management and decision-making processes at banks. (The term "risk data aggregation" means defining, gathering and processing risk data according to the bank's risk reporting requirements to enable the bank to measure its performance against its risk tolerance/appetite. This includes sorting, merging or breaking down sets of data. See https://www.bis.org/publ/bcbs239.pdf.)

To support their goals, the organization developed a quality certification environment that consists of five levels of defense, which allows the global validation of the information flow to be carried out in a more efficient way. See *Figure 4.9.2*.

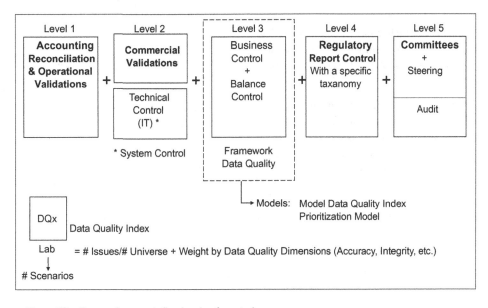

Figure 4.9.2 Data quality certification environment: five levels of controls.

(Continued)

Ten Steps in Action *(Continued)*

First Level—Accounting Reconciliation & Operational Validations

- Accounting Reconciliations are performed on a daily basis between Application Sources and Accounting Systems.
- Operational Validations apply recurrent rules and procedures in the operational phase with the main objective ensuring the correct characterization and operations input.

Second Level—Commercial Validations

- Information from data warehouse/golden source is acceded on a daily and monthly basis by the commercial areas (branches and commercial central units). In case of errors or incidents, immediately a defect is open for clarification/resolution, fulfilling the Commercial Validations.

Third Level—Data Quality Certification Process

- Data Quality Certification Process, occurs daily and monthly and it is composed of a reconciliation process (balance control). Also, here is the Framework Data Quality, improved with the Ten Steps approach.

Fourth Level—Regulatory Report Control

- AnaCredit (Analytic Credit Datasets), COREP (Common Reporting Framework), and FINREP (Financial Reporting) reports are subject to recurrent validations prior to being accepted by the regulators. The Bank has tools that ensure the mandatory validations and checks defined in the European Central Bank (ECB) taxonomy.

Fifth Level—Committees and Audit

- Some committees are in place and monitoring the Themes of Data Governance and Data Quality. The external and internal audits are part of this last line of defense.

- This is the last line of control of the organization's data quality monitoring governance.

On the third level, the Framework Data Quality is composed of business controls. These controls are distributed in a tree model: the data quality dimension is the lowest level; then the validation, which can include more than one dimension; then the control, which can consist of more than one validation; and the theme, that is composed of more than one control. In addition this framework has specific calculation models: Model Data Quality Index (model that measures a unique index of Data Quality DQx, calculated based on number of exceptions, target universe, weight, and data quality dimension type, such as accuracy, integrity, etc.) and Prioritization Model (model that allows us to prioritize the monitoring based on the Data Quality Index, the impact and risk defined in the control).

This framework also has a laboratory that allows us to simulate the calculation of the Data Quality index based on different scenarios, scenarios with different weights in the quality dimension and/or exception weight.

Benefits—Through this framework it is possible to proceed with an effective monitoring of the certification process, from the origin of the information to the final report. In this way, with the detection of problems closer to the origin and with the prioritization of monitoring that the model gives us, it is possible to proceed with the correction of information ever closer to its origin, avoiding contamination of several processes, in more efficient way.

It is possible to observe, over time, an improvement in the quality of information, which means that all regulatory reports, or internal bank calculation processes, result in fewer errors and lower costs from tax/fines imposed by regulators in the delivery of information. For example, in one on-site inspection performed by ECB on BCBS239, they were very satisfied and commented about the great advancement in this area.

Step 9 Summary

Congratulations again! Depending on your project, this may be the last step, you have completed your project and are celebrating your success.

In this step you determined which controls implemented in *Step 7* should be monitored. You also identified and implemented additional controls that should be monitored if they had not been done in previous steps.

Monitoring controls implies that they will continue even after the project is over and the team disbanded, which means they are part of an operational process. It is imperative there is a clear handoff from those who implemented the controls to whomever will be responsible for monitoring the controls. Even more important is the assurance that action will be taken when issues are detected. Launching the continuous improvement cycle (root cause analysis, prevention, correction, detection, communication in *Steps 5-10*) can be standard operating procedure.

As a project team, you will do everything in your power to ensure there are owners who have accepted these responsibilities. They will have received training on the controls themselves, what should be done when problems are found, and been given background documents from the project. They should know that when data quality problems are detected, root cause analysis should take place so the underlying causes can be tackled, not just the symptoms that may have been highlighted. They should know to plan the improvements and prevent future data errors, in addition to the more obvious correction of data errors that will take place. Adjustments may need to be made to the controls themselves and the process for monitoring.

Over time, the same issues sometimes continue to arise, so a new project may be launched to address them. Put on your investigator hat and start with *Step 1 – Determine Business Needs and Approach* to use the Ten Steps Process again. Select applicable steps for the new situation and use the experience, knowledge and skills gained from the previous project to solve another data quality crime!

Communicate, Manage, and Engage

Suggestions for working effectively with people and managing the project in this step:

- Ensure support and resources to continue monitoring
- Continue to keep in touch with those implementing improvements outside of the project team to offer help and encouragement, track progress, and coordinate work as needed
- Train personnel affected by controls to ensure a consistent understanding of changes, expectations, new or modified roles, responsibilities, processes, etc.
- Complete documentation and ensure signoff/approvals of implementations
- Share and celebrate successes and accomplishments from this step and acknowledge those involved
- Ensure others understand benefits the organization will see as a result of the controls being monitored

 Checkpoint

Checkpoint Step 9 – Monitor Controls

How can I tell if I am ready to move to the next step? Use the following guidelines to help determine completeness of this step and readiness for the next step:

- Have the controls been implemented and are they being monitored?
- Have results from monitoring, both positive and negative, been documented and addressed?
- Have improvements been verified?
- Have successful improvements been standardized?
- Have necessary activities to communicate, manage, and engage people during this step been completed?

Step 10 | Communicate, Manage, and Engage People Throughout

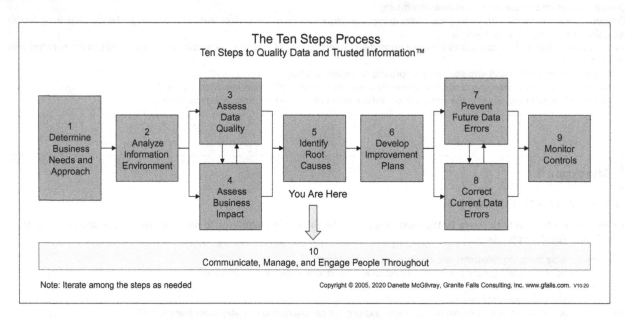

Figure 4.10.1 "You Are Here" Graphic for Step 10 – Communicate, Manage, and Engage People Throughout.

Business Benefit and Context

The name of this step describes some of the range of what is included. It accounts for the human element of a data quality project, along with the project management aspects – broad subjects indeed. It puts into action the concepts of communication, change, ethics, culture, and environment from the Framework for Information Quality. Doing *Step 10* well is essential to the success of any data quality project. *Step 10* should be referenced and applied as needed in every other step, which is why it is visualized as a bar that is underneath all the preceding nine steps.

The topics are so wide-ranging, yet important, that I can only give brief advice and hope you are inspired to get additional help from other resources. It is up to you to determine, at any point in time, when they should take place, the nature of the engagement, and with whom – all part of the art of data quality.

Instructions and guidelines based on real experience are given throughout the book, yet I don't give many hard and fast rules because of the variety of situations you will face. But this is one place where I say "must." You *must* do *something* related to communication, management, and engagement throughout your project. You may not completely fail without them, but if ignored, the best you can do is achieve limited results.

This step is about more than sharing PowerPoint slides and holding a few meetings. You will want to use your best skills to engage with:

- **Sponsors of your data quality project and other stakeholders**. To gain/sustain support and keep them apprised of progress throughout and demonstrate the value of information and data quality improvement

- **Team members, contributors to the project, and their managers.** To gain support and encourage collaboration
- **Process and application owners.** To gain cooperation for correcting data, improving processes, monitoring controls, incorporating data quality into training, etc.
- **Users**. For those dependent on information to perform their jobs and who often impact the quality of the data while doing their jobs, to let them know how continuous improvement will help the data they use and how their own actions impact data and other people who use it.
- **Everyone.** To listen carefully, get feedback, act on their concerns, and follow-up

 Warning

Do not skip this step! If you don't communicate, manage, and engage with people throughout your project, you will fall somewhere between failing miserably and receiving only limited acceptance of your results, recommendations, improvements implemented, and other actions. Ignoring this step won't get you anywhere near success.

Communication is part of the work, not something that gets in the way of your work! Recognize that communicating and engaging appropriately with people is as integral to your data quality work as doing a data quality assessment.

Approach

1. Identify stakeholders.

Identify stakeholders early in the project. As defined earlier in the book, a stakeholder is a person or group with an interest, involvement, or investment in, or who will be impacted (positively or negatively) by information and data quality work. Stakeholders may exert influence over the project and its deliverables. Stakeholders can be internal or external to your organization and represent interests related to business, data, or technology. For example, the person responsible for manufacturing processes would be a stakeholder for any data quality improvements that impact the supply chain.

Stakeholders can include customers and clients, project sponsors, the public, regulatory agencies, individual contributors, subject matter experts, board members, executive leadership teams, project team members and their managers, process owners, application owners, business partners, committees, organizational units such as divisions or departments, and those whose personnel are most directly involved in doing the work of the project.

The list of stakeholders may be long or short depending on the scope of the project. Stakeholders may change throughout the course of a project. The list may expand over time to include anyone influencing or affected by the changes, recommendations, or improvements made as a result of the project. I use the term stakeholders broadly, but I will occasionally call out specific stakeholders such as team members, those providing input to the project and their managers if the nature of the engagement with them differs from the larger group.

Of course, direct managers will be stakeholders but what about their peers, their boss, their boss' boss? What about your colleagues or those who report to you and their peers? Take a 360-degree view from where you and your project team sit. Not everyone you think of will be a stakeholder, but it is better to think broadly and be selective than to think narrowly and miss out on someone who should be included.

2. Conduct a stakeholder analysis

Once stakeholders are identified, conduct a stakeholder analysis to learn more about them and their roles in data quality work – either specific to the project or to the broader data quality program.

 Key Concept

Board members, executives, and other senior managers affect data quality because they set priorities for the organization as a whole. They make decisions about funding and allocation of other resources. Their attitude about the importance of data quality sets the tone and example for the rest of the organization and are picked up by others. We often forget about the boards – of directors or trustees – that set the direction for an organization as a whole. Once board members get on board (pun intended), data quality work can proceed much more rapidly and with the right resources than if they are unaware or resistant. They are the ultimate level of accountability within an organization and influence what the executives and other senior members place as a priority.

A great advocate for data quality work at the executive or senior level, if your organization is fortunate to have one, is that of Chief Data Officer. A Chief Data Officer is responsible for organization-wide data governance and utilizing information as an asset. This role is related to the CIO (Chief Information Officer) whose title reflects information but is usually focused on technology. An organization needs both. A CDO should work closely with the CIO, along with other members of the executive team.

A CDO usually determines what kind of information the organization needs, what will be captured, and for what purposes. As such, a CDO can yield much influence in helping others understand how poor-quality data affects an organization and can push for the appropriate attention and resources to ensure the right level of quality to support business needs.

Table 4.10.2 in *Sample Output and Templates* provides questions that will help you gain that insight.

Understanding stakeholders of your project will help:

- Uncover expectations for and concerns about the project
- Discover their influence and interest in the project and desired level of participation
- Better meet the needs of those providing resources for the project

Table 4.10.1	Step Summary Table for Step 10 – Communicate, Manage, and Engage People Throughout
Objective	• Include appropriate communications and engagement activities in every step of the Ten Steps Process and throughout every data quality project • Identify project sponsors, team members, and other stakeholders early, keep them informed, and provide opportunities for them to provide input • Apply good project management practices to the data quality project • Promote the inclusion of negotiation, facilitation, decision making, listening, change management and other skills related to working with people; inspire project managers and team members to increase their skills where needed • Raise awareness and educate about the importance and impact of data quality • Celebrate and share successes; learn from mistakes
Purpose	• Increase the likelihood of success by addressing the human factors, change management, and project management aspects of data quality projects • Avoid misunderstandings which, if they arise, increase the risk of delays to the project and the risk that project results will not be implemented or accepted • Obtain and sustain support for the project • Understand needs and concerns of stakeholders and interact with those impacted by the project, at the right times, using the most effective methods • Increase the chances that recommendations, action plans, and improvements will be implemented, standardized, and embraced • Manage the data quality project effectively and efficiently
Inputs	• Results from any of the steps

(Continued)

Table 4.10.1 Step Summary Table for Step 10 – Communicate, Manage, and Engage People Throughout *(Continued)*

Techniques and Tools	• In this *Step 10* under *Sample Output and Templates*: o Stakeholder analysis o RACI o Communication and engagement plan o 30-3-30-3 of Selling Data Quality • Any communication, engagement, change management, or project management techniques that work well in your organization's culture and environment • From *Chapter 6: Other Techniques and Tools*: o Conduct a Survey, if needed for input to the stakeholder analysis o Track Issues and Action Items (Start in *Step 1* and used throughout) o Analyze, Synthesize, Recommend, Document, and Act on Results (Start in *Step 1* and used throughout)
Outputs	• Stakeholder analysis and communication plan – done early in the project, kept updated, and used throughout the project • Communications and engagement completed based on timeline and plan • Communications and engagement reacting to ad hoc situations as they arise • Project plan, artifacts, and status created and kept updated throughout the project
Communicate, Manage, and Engage	• Consider the following related to working with people and managing a project. Use your best judgment to include in your project and apply appropriately throughout: o Communication and Engagement: awareness, out-reach, feedback, listening, education, training, documentation, negotiating, facilitating, writing, presentation skills, business storytelling, decision-making, internal consulting, networking, learning theory, and the list goes on o Change: management of change and associated impact, organizational change management, change control o Ethics: individual and societal good, justice, rights and freedoms, truthfulness, standards of conduct, avoiding harm, supporting well-being o Project management: managing teams (in person and virtually), holding effective meetings, status reports, basic skills related to the SDLC and project approach used (Agile, vendor SDLC, hybrid, etc.)
Checkpoint	• For *each step* in your project: o Are results, learnings, recommendations, and completed actions documented, shared, feedback encouraged, and adjustments made as needed? o Is appropriate training provided to those who need it? o Are you getting necessary support, and if not, are you addressing it? o Are you soliciting help as needed from those with skills in the various aspects of communication, management, and engagement? o Generally, are you completing necessary activities to communicate with and engage people and manage the project? o Are you personally helping to create an atmosphere of cooperation and fun, where the project team is being productive and enjoying the journey? o Are you personally setting an example of and encouraging ethical behavior? • At the *end* of the project: o Were project results documented and appropriately shared? o Was a project retrospective held, results shared and documented, and made available for future reference? o Were successes recognized and project sponsors, team members, other contributors and stakeholders thanked? o Have owners been identified, with support and resources committed, for ongoing processes, action items, and/or projects that resulted from the data quality project and are to be continued after it is concluded?

• Provide input to communications and training and how to best engage with them
• Avoid misunderstandings which, if they arise, increase the risk of delays to the project and the risk that project results will not be implemented or accepted

You may decide to interview a few or several sponsors, stakeholders, and/or users to provide input to the stakeholder analysis. If so, ideas under *Conduct a Survey* in *Chapter 6: Other Techniques and Tools* can help.

A management technique called RACI can be used to further identify stakeholder roles based on designations of Responsible, Accountable, Consult, and Inform. See *Template 4.10.1* in *Sample Output and Templates*.

2. Create a communication and engagement plan.

Develop a communication and engagement plan early in the project. Use *Template 4.10.2* in Sample Output and Templates as a starting point. I want you to broaden your thinking about communication. An impromptu Zoom meeting or a chat in the hallway can go a long way in building relationships with your stakeholders, but it is often not thought of as communication. Your plan may include activities to manage change. Remember that communication goes two ways, so be sure to include venues and vehicles for obtaining feedback from your stakeholders, listen carefully, create the opportunity for dialogue, and deal with questions and concerns. Use the plan, refer to it, and update it throughout the project. Use it as a reminder to communicate. Document completed communication and engagement efforts.

Communications must be adapted to fit various audiences, situations, and time available. See the *30-3-30-3 of Selling Data Quality* in *Sample Output and Templates* for one technique to help. The RACI technique just mentioned can provide input to determine the frequency and level of detail helpful for those in various roles. For example, those in an Inform role often receive communications at a summary level, after work is completed, and less frequently than those in Responsible, Accountable, or Consult roles.

3. Improve communication, management, and engagement skills.

Think of the word communication as the starting point for the various soft skills that come into play with any information or data quality project. After all, companies are "just a collection of people" (Conley, 2007) so the human factor cannot be ignored if you expect to be successful.

Improve your skills in communication and related areas – anything that will help you deal with the human element of your data quality work. Following are a few to consider: presentation skills, negotiation, facilitation, decision making, consensus building, listening, writing, project management, managing teams and fostering teamwork, internal consulting, change management, resolving conflict, collaborating, ethics, and networking.

Even consider sales and marketing since you are selling information quality and marketing your project or program. For many years, teams have worked remotely from each other. As I am writing this book much of the world is still in shutdown mode from the 2020 COVID-19 worldwide pandemic. We don't know yet what the new normal will look like, but we can be assured that less direct face-to-face, with more virtual meetings and events, can be expected. Therefore, increasing your ability to manage virtual teams and get buy-in when you cannot walk down the hall for an in-person chat will be useful skills.

I cannot cover all the items just mentioned, so the list will have to be just enough to spark your interest. Don't get overwhelmed. Select one area where you want to increase your skills. Resources like coaches, mentors, books, classes, professional organizations, and websites abound to help increase your skills in any of these areas. No one can be the best at everything, so find others (inside or outside of your project team) who have skills to complement yours. Offer to help them and they will usually help you.

You will notice that "management" is also part of this step. A colleague told me that you don't manage people, you manage projects, programs, processes, etc. Whether you use the word management as applying to people or not, the project does have to be managed to initiate it and see it through to successful completion. All project roles have important parts to play throughout the project. All are people where appropriate communication and engagement are essential.

I will call out a few areas which are worth paying particular attention to:

Ethics—Ethics is an important concept in the Framework for Information Quality as a broad-impact component, which includes ideas such as individual and societal good, justice, rights and freedoms, truthfulness, standards of conduct, avoiding harm, and supporting well-being. I highly recommend *Ethical Data and Information Management: Concepts, Tools, and Methods* by Katherine O'Keefe and Daragh O Brien for a deep dive into this subject.

Quote to Remember

"Increasingly the tools and technologies we have at our disposal as information management professionals have the potential to bring benefit or cause harm to people. All information that is processed, with very few exceptions, impacts on people in some way.

With the incredible increase in computing power, data-gathering capabilities and machine-learning technologies, the potential for harm to be caused to individuals or to groups of society, either by accident or by intentional design, is significant.

As a result of this significant power and significant risk, it is more important than ever that information management professionals have an appropriate grounding in ethics so that decisions that are made in relation to the management and use of information are based on sound ethical principles."

– *Katherine O'Keefe and Daragh O Brien, Ethical Data and Information Management (2018) p. 1.*

Many organizations and professions have defined standards of business conduct. IQ International (2005-2020), was a not-for-profit organization that promotes best practices in managing information quality. Their Code of Ethics and Professional Conduct is included in the *Best Practice callout box*. I think it is a code that should be lived by *anyone* who works with data and information and should be discussed and adapted as needed.

Best Practice

Code of Ethics and Professional Conduct. The purpose states that, "The IQ International Code of Ethics and Professional Conduct is an important component of a broader effort to build the information/data quality discipline on a solid and honorable foundation. The need for the code is based on a belief that we are individually and collectively responsible for the image and reputation of the information/data quality discipline. As we set out to serve our organizations and society in general, the Code defines a high standard of professional excellence, highlights a set of desired behaviors, and provides a framework to guide day-to-day decision-making. Because it makes explicit a set of expectations we are establishing for ourselves and for each other, we hope the Code serves as a catalyst for a dialogue about ethical issues in our

discipline and that it encourages ethical decision-making and professional conduct by everyone engaged in information/data quality work."

Code of Ethics and Professional Conduct

1. **Honesty and Integrity**
   1. Be clear, concise and truthful in all forms of shared information.
   2. Ensure your advertisements, research or other published materials supporting or promoting a theory, position, product or service are based on complete, accurate and factual information.
   3. Openly communicate corrections or clarifications in a timely and professional manner.

(Continued)

Best Practice *(Continued)*

4. Clearly and accurately represent your professional credentials and limitations in all employment and service engagements.
5. Build a professional reputation based on the merit of services provided and achievements attained.

2. **Respect, Fairness, Confidentiality and Trust**
   1. Proactively and fully disclose any potential conflicts of interest with the appropriate stakeholders.
   2. Abstain from opportunities where a conflict of interest cannot be mitigated.
   3. Give credit where credit is due. In particular, credit contributing parties in your published works.
   4. Respect and abide by copyrights, patents, trademarks and all the intellectual property rights held by others.
   5. Make your professional services and skills available on a fair and equitable basis.
   6. Vigorously protect all proprietary, private and confidential information entrusted to you.
   7. Promptly notify stakeholders of any intentional or inadvertent breach of confidentiality, privacy or misuse of proprietary information.

3. **Professional Growth**
   1. Seek professional growth as an individual through ongoing education, practical experience, research and study.

2. Support the growth of our professional community through ongoing advocacy, communication, collaboration, mentoring, publications or other shared contributions.
3. Openly share non-proprietary knowledge, skills and experience with peers.
4. Encourage and provide opportunities for the professional development of others.
5. Strive to increase the prestige and competency of our profession through exemplary leadership and conduct.

4. **Community and Public Service**
   1. Hold paramount the safety, health and welfare of the public in the performance of your professional duties.
   2. Seek opportunities to volunteer professional information/data quality services for the public welfare and common good.
   3. Promote and encourage adherence to information/data quality best practices in all forms of communications that are intended to influence public opinion.
   4. Comply with all laws, regulations, statutes and policies that govern your business, work, professional activities or volunteer service.

Source: https://www.iqint.org/about/code-of-ethics-and-professional-conduct/. Used with permission.

What's In It For Them—You may be familiar with WIIFM, or what's in it for me. What's In It For Them (WIIFT) is my slight twist on the same idea. We spend a lot of time figuring out the details of *our* projects, asking for money and resources so *we* can do what *we* need to do. But even if we have carefully tied our project to business needs, we must continually remind ourselves that it is NOT about us. We must shift our focus to others, *their* specific needs and figure out what's in it for *them*. How does high-quality data in general or this project specifically make their life better? Their team's day-to-day work better? Help them fulfill their responsibilities, meet their performance measures, or keep their boss happy? Before meeting with anyone ask, and answer, the question, "What's in it for them?"

Change management—"I'm OK with change – just don't do anything different!" Human beings resist change – some more than others. Early in my career I wondered why it was challenging to get people to take action on the results of a data quality assessment and root cause analysis that would address important issues. Then I realized that almost everything I requested meant they had to do something different – correct the data, update business processes, create or modify existing roles and responsibilities, modify the technology, make time for a new activity, etc., etc., etc. This naturally put pressure on their already-limited resources and often made it difficult to make progress.

Realize that your data quality project will initiate change. If change is not managed, it greatly increases the risk of NOT having improvements implemented and sustained. Data professionals need to increase their skills in managing change or partner with others who have this expertise. Depending on the scope of the change, additional help may be warranted. But even small changes should be acknowledged and managed.

Margaret Rouse (n.d.) defines change management as "a systematic approach to dealing with the transition or transformation of an organization's goals, processes or technologies. The purpose of change management is to implement strategies for effecting change, controlling change and helping people to adapt to change. To be effective, the change management process must take into consideration how an adjustment or replacement will impact processes, systems, and employees within the organization." She sees organizational change management (OCM) as "a framework for managing the effect of new business processes, changes in organizational structure or cultural changes within an enterprise" and that successful OCM strategies should include:

- Agreement on a common vision for change – no competing initiatives
- Strong executive leadership to communicate the vision and sell the business case for change
- A strategy for educating employees about how their day-to-day work will change
- A concrete plan for how to measure whether or not the change is a success – and follow-up plans for both successful and unsuccessful results
- Rewards, both monetary and social, that encourage individuals and groups to take ownership for their new roles and responsibilities

There are many approaches to managing change. Following are some you might want to explore further:

- John P. Kotter (2012) has an eight-stage process: Establish a Sense of Urgency; Create the Guiding Coalition; Develop a Vision and Strategy; Communicate the Change Vision; Empower Employees for Broad-Based Action; Generate Short-

Term Wins; Consolidate Gains and Produce More Change; Anchor New Approaches in the Culture.
- William Bridges (2016) has three phases: Ending, Losing, Letting Go; The Neutral Zone; and The New Beginning.
- The Gleicher Change Equation:

$$\text{Change} = (D)(V)(F) > R$$

where D = Dissatisfaction with status quo;
V = Vision of the change; F = First steps, and R = Resistance.

For change to happen, dissatisfaction with the status quo, vision of the change, and first steps have to be greater than the resistance to the change (Beckhard & Harris, 1987).

- Kathleen D. Dannemiller and Robert W. Jacobs (1992) built on the Gleicher equation:
  - What happens if an element of the equation is missing?

    (D) with no (V) and no (F) = Frustration

(Dissatisfaction but no Vision or First Steps)

(D) with no (V) but with (F) = "Flavor of the Month"
(Dissatisfaction and First Steps but no Vision)

No (D) with (V) and with (F) = Wishful thinking that evolves into passivity
(Vision and First Steps but no Dissatisfaction)

Look at yourself—Are you setting the example and tone, yourself, personally that you would like to see from those with whom you work? Are you modeling the behavior you would like to see from your stakeholders and project team? The buck stops here.

Company cultures—William E. Schneider (1999, 2017) writes about different types of company cultures. He helps the reader identify causes of conflict and sources of competitive strength and use these to make cost-effective decisions concerning change and improvement within their organizations.

 Ten Steps in Action

Business Storytelling and the Ten Steps

According to Lori Silverman, The Shift Strategist, Founder/CEO of Partners for Progress®, "The only form of narrative that has the ability to influence and shift people into action is a story."

The output from all the steps are just that, output. It is up to you to use your best communication skills to put the output into context, make it meaningful, and bring it to life through business storytelling.

See what Lori has to tell us about storytelling and the Ten Steps:

Reflect on a couple meetings you've recently attended. How do people react when they see numbers, bulleted information, or data visualizations, versus someone telling a story that brings to life what the numbers are communicating? We now know that the brain dislikes data. Yes, you read that correctly. Data, facts, figures, data visualizations in the form of bar charts, pie charts, run charts – all of which are forms of persuasion – do not move people to act; they frequently cause debate and slow down the decision-making process. The only form of narrative that has the ability to influence and shift people into action is a story – not an example, anecdote, case study, description, or the like – but a story about a singular main character, that people can easily relate to, who experiences conflict (a problem or series of problems) and attempts to work through it.

What does this mean to you in the Ten Steps Process? You can use story to humanize the business need in *Step 1* – remember to separate it from any data you might have. This is where a real-life story about a customer/consumer could be utilized. So might a co-created vision story about what life will be like for someone in the enterprise (who is representative of those impacted by the problem) when the data quality issue is mitigated.

In *Steps 2 and 3*, how might you craft a mystery story about the data quality crime scene, ensuing investigation, suspected root causes and potential ways to mitigate them, perhaps this time, through your eyes as a private detective? You can come back to this story and expand upon it in *Step 5* when you reveal the root causes. When you convey impact in *Step 4*, the main character of the story becomes whoever is most impacted by the data quality issue. If there are multiple issues impacting multiple stakeholders, you could tell a story of a main character who, in a series of interactions with others, comes to realize the magnitude of the issue(s). Keep in mind when you're constructing the story that loss is more motivating than benefit – better to expand upon what people stand to lose versus telling them what they stand to gain. The same is true for the stories you convey in *Steps 6, 7, 8, and 9* to ensure that final recommendations actually get implemented and controls are monitored. Some of the earlier stories that you developed once again become useful in any of the steps when training others.

Where do you get these stories? They may come from internal and external customers/consumers, from stakeholders, from previous experiences that you and others have had. And, you may create them too, from previous life experience.

All along this path, you also want to collect and share stories of small successes – employees who were able to save time or be more nimble in their work, a leader who begins to see cost savings drop to their bottom line, and individual consumer feedback that signifies you're on the right track.

For more details on how to find, construct, and tell stories, see *Business Storytelling for Dummies* (Wiley, 2013) by Karen Dietz, PhD, and Lori L. Silverman.

 Best Practice

Decision-making. Decisions will be made throughout your project. If you have formal data governance, make use of it to bring together decision makers. If you don't, decisions still have to be made and will likely take longer. See what Lori Silverman has to say about decision-making:

"In our work, we make hundreds, if not thousands, of decisions each day. The Ten Step Process is no different – embedded within each step, as shown in this book, are myriad decisions that need to be made by all different kinds of stakeholders. Of utmost importance is being clear on what each one is (and the context surrounding it),

(Continued)

Best Practice (Continued)

documenting it, recording the answer and who made it, when. This information needs to be transparent and visible to everyone on the project. Don't forget that every decision – yes, every single one – implies an action will be taken. Record this too.

"The entire Ten Steps Process itself is also a decisioning mechanism. With this in mind, fleshing out the context, the presenting problem, and communicating it (via a story) in *Step 1* is absolutely key. There are two reasons for this. First, you cannot glean "meaningful" insights about a problem unless you are very clear upfront what it is. Keep in mind that observations about the data are rarely insights; insights are true ah-hah's that come from your synthesis about what you learn after studying the data and blending human reasoning with it. Second, it's important to ask some questions we may be prone to avoid. Questions like: whether the sponsor (and key stakeholders) believe they already know the causes of the data quality problem

and whether they are open to hearing what you learn in your investigations. If they believe they already know what actions should also be taken to mitigate them, you want to learn this, too. In all of these instances, their intuition is a form of data based on past experiences, rightly or wrongly. Knowing the answers will keep you from being blind-sided later on.

"When communicating your insights, you'll be able to accelerate the process of decisioning surrounding them during each step in the Ten Steps Process by storifying the insight. Some ideas on how you might do this are presented in the callout box on business storytelling."

– Lori L. Silverman, The Shift Strategist, Founder/CEO of Partners for Progress®

For more information on Making S.M.A.R.T.E.R.™ Decisions With Data, see Episode 10 of "Level Up With Lori," on YouTube (Silverman, 2020).

---

4. Communicate, manage, and engage people throughout.

Not much more can be said here except – do it!

Sample Output and Templates

Stakeholder Analysis

Once the stakeholders for the project have been identified, conduct a stakeholder analysis to understand more about each one. What are their concerns? How might they be affected by the project? What do you need from them?

Use *Table 4.10.2 – Stakeholder Analysis* to help understand your stakeholders. It was created by John Ladley and appeared in his book, *Data Governance*, Second Edition (2020b). Even though developed with data governance in mind, it can be easily adjusted for data quality or any aspect of data management. It can also be used when looking at stakeholders for an overall data quality program. Expect stakeholders to overlap between data governance and data quality programs and projects.

To use the table:

- Add a column with the stakeholder name. Document other basics such as contact information, title, where they sit within the organization chart (business unit/department/team), and role as it relates to the data quality project or program. Include external contractors, consultants, or other business partners as applicable. Physical location is useful for time zones when scheduling meetings.
- For each stakeholder, answer the questions in the table. The term "the change" in the table means whatever you are trying to accomplish. For example, the change might refer to the project as a whole, a request for funding and people, or changes expected from recommendations to be implemented.
- In addition to the questions in the table, it is often helpful to note what each stakeholder knows about data quality and its importance (from unaware to basic understanding to fully knowledgeable) and/or their level of support (from negative/opponent to neutral to positive/ally/advocate).

RACI

RACI is a management technique, originally used to identify roles and responsibilities in a change process. It can be applied to your data quality project when identifying roles and responsibilities, decision rights and accountabilities, and escalation paths. It is input to communications and the level of detail applicable to audiences. For example, what is shared with someone in an Inform role is much less detailed than someone in a Responsible role who is actually doing the work. It can be applied at the project level or a business process level.

Following are typical definitions for each letter in the acronym, but I have seen them differ from client to client. Be sure to have a clear definition of what they mean to your project.

- **R = Responsible**. Person who completes or implements the work.
- **A = Accountable**. Person who must answer that the work was accomplished and has ultimate responsibility. This person may delegate some of the work (to someone who is "responsible") but cannot delegate accountability.
- **C = Consult**. Person who provides input to the work or decision.
- **I = Inform**. Person who is notified of the work or decision. Does not need to be consulted prior to the work being accomplished.

From the viewpoints of strictly hierarchical or time commitment to the project, ARCI is more appropriate. Accountable is the ultimate owner. Those Responsible have a bigger time commitment and answer to whoever is Accountable. Those in the Consult role, usually have a lesser time commitment. Those in the Inform role will have the least time commitment.

A variation on RACI adds an "S" (RASCI) for Supportive. If you use Supportive, be sure to describe what that means for your project (e.g., provide financial support, people resources, advocate, or play some other supporting role).

Template 4.10.1 can be used to identify roles related to the project. In the first column, list steps in a process, responsibilities related

Table 4.10.2 Stakeholder Analysis

What is a stakeholder?	What is their role?	How will they react?	What will be their primary concerns?	What do we need from them?	How should we work with them?
A stakeholder is any organization or person that: • Can influence the change • Is affected by the change Stakeholders can be: • Individuals • Senior leaders • Groups of employees such as IT or division managers • Committees • Customers • Government or other regulatory agencies • Brokers/ agents	Identify each stakeholder's role(s). Will this stakeholder: • Need to approve resources and/ or decide whether the change can proceed (thus acting as a sponsor or gatekeeper)? • Need to change as a result of the effort (a target)? • Need to implement changes or convince others to change (an agent)? • React to or judge the success of the effort? • Need to be an advocate of the effort (a champion)? • Perform work that can influence the success of the effort (a resource)?	How will the results of the effort be likely to impact the stakeholder? Will this stakeholder benefit or be adversely affected? Given the likely impact and prior behavior, how is this stakeholder likely to react? • Vocal, visible support? • Cooperative, quiet? • On the fence? • Say ok but be obstructive or complain behind the scenes? • Express concerns vocally?	What are the primary concerns of this stakeholder? • What do they need or expect from the change? • What might influence whether they are supportive of the change? • What will this stakeholder need to feel informed, involved, prepared, or validated during the change? • What are the "red flags" or hot buttons for this stakeholder?	What do we need from this stakeholder? • Approval/ resources • Visible support/ public endorsement • Access to them • Access to people on their team • Lack of interference with or blocking of the effort • Information • Task completion • Flexibility • Change in behavior	Given what we know, how should we work with this stakeholder? • How will we prepare them for the change? • How will we communicate with them? • How will we address their needs/ concerns? • Do we need to learn more about their needs, concerns, or likely reaction? • Should they be part of the change team directly or indirectly involved (be a representative on the team, solicit input, or provide regular feedback)?

Created by John Ladley and published in *Data Governance*. Second Edition (Elsevier, 2020). Stakeholder Analysis Table in Appendix 6. Used with permission.

to a specific process or the project as a whole. Add the name of the person, their title, and corresponding RACI role. Remember that one person can hold many RACI roles and a RACI role can be held by more than one person.

Communication and Engagement Plan

Use *Template 4.10.2* as a starting point for your communication and engagement plan. I added the word engagement into what might usually be called just a communication plan as a reminder that communication goes two-ways and you want to engage with people, not just talk at them. To build the plan,

begin with any of the topics in the template – write down specific audiences, messages, subjects needing input, or particular meetings where communications should be included. Organize and format the information in whatever way makes sense – often by date or audience. You can also include change management activities. Once the details are worked out, a summary of the communication plan can help track progress. If using a spreadsheet, the summary can be in the first worksheet, with additional worksheets in the same file used to document the details of each communication/engagement/change management event or activity.

Template 4.10.1 RACI Chart

Process Step or Project Responsibilities	Name	Title	RACI Roles			
			Accountable	Responsible	Consult	Inform

Template 4.10.2	Communication and Engagement Plan									
Audience	Message and Desired Action	Trigger	Communication Vehicle	Develop	Deliver	Preparation	Status	Target Date	Complete Date

Audience—Who needs to hear? Who will be affected? Consider organizations, teams, and individuals. Is there anyone specifically who should NOT receive the communication? Expect to have several audiences identified.

Message and desired action—What does the audience need to know? What is changing? What questions do you have for the audience? What action do you want them to take? How will the audience be impacted? How will they feel about what has transpired (e.g., resistant, neutral, supportive)? How do you want them to feel as a result of this communication and engagement? Think about how you will deal with various reactions.

Trigger—What initiates the communication? Is it timing or an event, such as the first week in the quarter, a monthly management meeting, when a phase of a project is completed?

Communication vehicle—What is the method of communication? Separately list communication vehicles that work well within your organization (e.g., 1-1 meeting, group workshop, internal website, newsletter, chat over lunch). Account for virtual and/or in-person. Select those appropriate for the audience and situation.

Develop—Who is responsible for developing and creating the communication? Who provides content and input?

Deliver—Who will present the communication? Often the person who develops content passes it on to someone else who delivers it.

Preparation—What action needs to be taken to prepare for and complete the communication?

Status—What is the status of the communication (e.g., Identified, In Progress, Complete)?

Target date—What is the planned date for the communication?

Complete date—What is the actual date when the communication was finished?

30-3-30-3 of Selling Data Quality

Table 4.10.3 outlines a technique to apply to communications when looking at the purpose, focus, message, etc. and the amount of time you might have.

Table 4.10.3	30-3-30-3 of Selling Data Quality			
	30 Seconds	3 Minutes	30 Minutes	3 Hours
Purpose of session	Generate curiosity (e.g., "elevator speech")	Describe status (e.g., status report)	Educate on value and answer questions (e.g., review session)	Collaboration (e.g., interactive workshop)
Focus of session	Future oriented and focus on the positive	Current status and value provided to business and technology users	Issues, concerns, success stories	Whole picture: cover all aspects of data quality; or deep dive into few aspects; leave no stone unturned …
What you want the audience to think	Your enthusiasm and passion for data quality	How much you have achieved with funding and resources available	Data quality is valuable but not easy	For example, data quality is integrated into all aspects of the project life cycle
Message	Simple and high-level; establish connections or relationships	Segmented into layers; simple and straightforward	Points of integration; how data quality impacts the business; ROI	Detailed definitions, examples of value, and stress on the importance of growth
Audience action desired	Request for additional information regarding data quality and your initiative	Support for data quality	Understand the value as well as the utility of data quality	Agreement and consensus
Are you prepared???				

Source: Adapted from R. Todd Stephens, PhD, Used with permission

Ten Steps in Action

Using the 30-3-30-3 Technique

Rodney Schackmann, Information Quality Program Manager for a global high-tech company, now retired, used the 30-3-30-3 technique to: 1) prepare targeted communications for audiences where information quality efforts might not be well understood or appreciated, and 2) create different versions of a story that needs to be told, particularly to various levels of management, where availability and attention spans vary dramatically. *Table 4.10.4* summarizes how he applied the technique. The "change" mentioned in the table refers to whatever you are sharing/requesting at the time (e.g., to start an information quality project to address a serious business need or implement specific recommendations based on a data quality assessment and root cause analysis).

He explained that a 30-second elevator pitch should lead to getting 3 minutes to create interest to get 30 minutes to create a degree of awareness. At each point you want to move to the next step with the people who need to:

- Understand the problem
- See the art of the possible along with the benefit
- Support the proposed solution

He shared an important insight in that each interaction is also an opportunity for *you* to listen, observe, and learn. In addition, the opportunity for these conversations or presentations occur more frequently than you might expect, so it is important to have appropriate levels of detail prepared and tunable for the specific audience. Remember, even if you have successfully launched an Information Quality Program, events such as personnel turnover, business priority shifts, and operational changes require quality efforts to be kept relevant, prioritized, and visible. This requires ongoing education and "selling." Having the right level of conversation ready is key for accomplishing that goal.

Table 4.10.4 Applying the 30-3-30-3 Technique

	30 Seconds	3 Minutes	30 Minutes	3 Hours
Purpose	Generate curiosity	Sell the concept, seek understanding for buying into the principles	Educate, sell the value, answer questions, seek operational buy-in	Provide context and skills training
Audience	Senior decision makers	Staff meeting for functional/operations owners	Operations managers and key operations people	All people directly doing the work
Strategy	Highlight a business problem that directly affects a focus area for that person(s). Ask if the problem could be improved by X amount, would there be interest? (Use real numbers if you can, otherwise use industry % ranges). Ask for the opportunity to illustrate and explore this with their key people.	Level set the problem and opportunity with the people who oversee change. Confirm whether narrow (hot-spot), or a broader approach is needed. Ask for buy-in and ask to meet with top people who can affect the change.	Communicate high-level problem and scope. Describe process to measure current state, improve quality, and glean value. Field questions.	Level set the problem and opportunities. Conduct high-level IQ assessment and establish an IQ Score. Gather input to inform the improvement process (Ten Steps)
Example format	Elevator speech	Staff presentation	Key stakeholder presentation	Workshop

Step 10 Summary

Working effectively with people and managing the project are not accomplished as a one-time effort. *Something* related to *Step 10* must be done in *every* other step. This step provided several ideas to help. Deciding when, how often, with whom, the message – are all up to you and are part of the art of data quality.

Communicate, Manage, and Engage

Suggestions for working effectively with people and managing the project in all steps:

- Consider the following related to working with people and managing a project. Use your best judgment to include in your project and apply appropriately throughout:
  - Communication and Engagement: awareness, out-reach, feedback, listening, education, training, documentation, negotiating, facilitating, writing, presentation skills, business storytelling, decision-making, internal consulting, networking, learning theory, and the list goes on
  - Change: management of change and associated impact, organizational change management, change control
  - Ethics: individual and societal good, justice, rights and freedoms, truthfulness, standards of conduct, avoiding harm, supporting well-being
  - Project management: managing teams (in person and virtually), holding effective meetings, status reports, basic skills related to the SDLC and project approach used (Agile, vendor SDLC, hybrid, etc.)

Checkpoint

Checkpoint Step 10

How can I tell if I am ready to move to the next step? Use the following guidelines to help incorporate *Step 10* into all the other steps and at the end of the project:

- For each step in your project:
    - Are results, learnings, recommendations, and completed actions documented, shared, feedback encouraged, and adjustments made as needed?
    - Is appropriate training provided to those who need it?
    - Are you getting necessary support, and if not, are you addressing it?
    - Are you soliciting help as needed from those with skills in the various aspects of communication, management, and engagement?
    - Generally, are you completing necessary activities to communicate with and engage people and manage the project?
    - Are you personally helping to create an atmosphere of cooperation and fun, where the project team is being productive and enjoying the journey?
    - Are you personally setting an example of and encouraging ethical behavior?
- At the end of the project:
    - Were project results documented and appropriately shared?
    - Was a project retrospective held, results shared and documented, and made available for future reference?
    - Were successes recognized and project sponsors, team members, other contributors and stakeholders thanked?
    - Have owners been identified, with support and resources committed, for ongoing processes, action items, and/or projects that resulted from the data quality project and are to be continued after it is concluded?

Chapter 4 Summary

Chapter 4 described the Ten Steps Process, with concrete instructions, sample output, templates, and just enough detail so you can execute your own data quality project. You have seen that thoughtful choices have to be made about what is relevant and what is the most useful level of detail when applying the steps, activities, and techniques. Guidelines were provided to help you make those choices. References were given to external resources and to other chapters when more detail was needed, such as concepts from the first three chapters and techniques in *Chapter 6* that could be used in more than one step. You were given real examples of how the Ten Steps have been applied in the *Sample Output* sections and the *Ten Steps in Action callout boxes*.

Step 1 emphasized the importance of selecting projects that will address high-priority business needs based on customers, products, services, strategies, goals, issues, and opportunities. *Chapter 5* supplemented Step 1 with guidance when structuring your project for the best chance of success.

Step 2 helped you analyze the information environment – the requirements and constraints, data and data specifications, processes, people/organizations, technology and the information life cycle within scope. What was learned provided input to ensure the data to be assessed for quality or business impact was the data actually associated with the business needs. It also provided background that will help you better understand and analyze assessment results.

Step 3 provided choices for assessing quality based on data quality dimensions – those aspects or features of information used for defining, measuring, and managing data. Suggestions for selecting the relevant

dimensions were given. The assessments showed the magnitude and type of data quality issues, overcoming opinions about the data and uncovering the facts.

Step 4 offered business impact techniques – qualitative and quantitative techniques for analyzing the impact of data quality issues. They were used anywhere in your project whenever there was a need to gain or sustain support for data quality efforts.

Step 5 provided techniques for root cause analysis so improvements in the next steps could address the true causes of the issues, not just the symptoms. Improvement plans were developed in *Step 6* and were based on everything learned in the prior steps.

Controls to help prevent data quality problems from reoccurring were actually implemented in *Step 7*. Current data quality errors found during the project were actually corrected in *Step 8*. Controls to be monitored on a regular basis were put into place in *Step 9*, so new issues could be seen and resolved quickly.

Because communications, engaging with people, and managing the project well were essential to any data quality project, you ensured that relevant activities from *Step 10* were done in every other step.

If you have finished your project – congratulations! I hope it was successful and that you put the Ten Steps Process to good use. You now have the experience to recognize aspects of data quality in the world around you and to apply the methodology to address any data quality situation. Keep this book close by and use it again and again, in different ways, to continue to provide value to your organization through high-quality data.

Please move on to *Chapter 7* for a few final words.

Structuring Your Project

Plan your work – work your plan.

— Norman Vincent Peale

*You don't have the luxury of choosing between building infrastructure
and producing results. You need both.*

— John Zachman, originator/creator of the Framework for Enterprise Architecture

In This Chapter

Introduction to Chapter 5

The three main parts of the Ten Steps methodology: Key Concepts, the Ten Steps Process, and Structuring Your Project were explained in *Chapter 2*. This chapter goes into more detail on the Structuring Your Project aspect. To successfully apply the Ten Steps methodology, it is essential those using it do a good job of organizing their work. Use the instructions in *Step 1.2 – Plan the Project* together with the information in this chapter to develop your project plan.

When managers are approached about addressing a data quality issue, the first questions are usually, "Why do you want to do this?" and "How will it help us?" Once those are answered, the next concerns relate to how much the effort will cost, how many resources are needed, and how it will be accomplished. Most people want something very specific: "If you have xyz problem, then you should do exactly these steps, at this level of detail, using this many resources, taking this long, and at this cost."

It is impossible for me to provide something that prescriptive since there are so many ways people and teams will apply the Ten Steps. However, the purpose of this chapter is to help you address those important concerns and guide your choices when setting up projects. Setting up your project well is crucial to managing your work throughout the project, which is vital to accomplishing what you set out to do.

Types of Data Quality Projects

As you know by now, this book uses projects as the vehicle for data quality work and how the methodology is applied. If you have a narrow view of the word "project," you will have to expand it to accommodate my definition and the many situations where the Ten Steps methodology can be applied. As described in *Chapter 3: Key Concepts*, generally, a project is a unit of work that is a one-time effort with specific business needs to be addressed and objectives to be achieved; here, the word project is used broadly to mean any structured effort that makes use of the Ten Steps methodology. In *Step 1.1*, situations with business needs and data quality issues were prioritized and the focus of the project was selected.

Next, activities that will address the project focus must be identified and organized. To do so, it is helpful to classify the project using the following categories, called project types, because how work is planned and coordinated differs between these project types.

- Focused Data Quality Improvement Project
- Data Quality Activities in Another Project
- Ad hoc Use of Data Quality Steps, Activities, or Techniques

These three types of projects were introduced in *Step 1.2* and are detailed further in this chapter. Classifying which of the three project *types* will be used sets the direction for the project *approach*. Remember the project approach is the means for organizing and carrying out your work, such as a favored SDLC (Agile, sequential, etc.). The project type and approach determine which project management activities are needed, such as a creating a project plan, charter, or features, user stories, etc. Project planning is where you decide how, specifically, to make the best use of the Ten Steps to address the problems using the chosen approach. You will use the steps within the Ten Steps Process in different combinations, at different levels of detail, with different type of projects and approaches to address the business needs and data quality issues in the situation that started it all.

The process just described, going from a situation to planning the project, can be summarized as:

Situation → Project focus → Type of project → Project approach → Project plan

The importance of being able to move from recognizing a problem situation to being able to take effective action to solve it cannot be underestimated. Hence, the reason for this chapter. Of course, you want to do this as quickly as possible. But if you do it well, the Ten Steps will be relevant and applicable no matter where you are on your data quality journey.

You must be able to identify the data quality aspects in real situations. As each of the three project types are discussed next, several examples are included to emphasize the variety of situations where the Ten Steps can be useful. Be aware that data quality is an aspect in many circumstances, even if it is not initially recognized as such.

Note that a few of the examples are listed under both a focused DQ improvement project and as DQ activities in another project. The situation is the same, but whether the data quality activities are managed as a standalone project or incorporated into another project depends on how the organization is managing the overall issue.

Project Type: Focused Data Quality Improvement Project

Description—A data quality improvement project concentrates on specific data quality issue(s) that are negatively impacting the organization. The goal is to support business needs by improving the quality of specific data where data quality issues are suspected or already known. This can be any set of data – internally created or externally acquired data.

This type of project selects the applicable steps from the Ten Steps Process to understand the information environment surrounding the data quality issue and business needs, assess the data quality, and show business value. For the most sustained results, the goal should be to identify root causes and improve the data by preventing the issues from arising again, such as by implementing new or enhancing existing processes to manage the data. Improving the data also includes correcting the current data errors. To sustain data quality, some of the improvements or controls may be candidates for on-going monitoring. Communicating, managing the project, and engaging with people are done throughout the project. The Ten Steps Process can provide the foundation for the project plan.

A variation of this type of project is to use the Ten Steps as the basis for creating a data quality improvement methodology customized to your particular organization.

Examples—Examples of situations that could be addressed by a focused data quality improvement project include the following. Note that some are similar to each other, but may be larger or smaller in scope:

- Poor-quality data needs to be improved to make it useful to the organization.
- Enhance the existing data lake ingestion process.
- Determine why reports for the same queries do not match and fix the causes.
- Data needs to be labeled, or needs higher quality labels, in order to get the best use from it.
- Your organization is trying to decide on a vendor from which to purchase data. It would be helpful to know more about the quality of the external data *before* signing a purchase agreement.
- Reduce the amount of time that data scientists spend wrangling data before they can use the data.
- Investigate complaints about poor data quality and establish a DQ baseline against which to monitor future improvements.
- Implement a dashboard to measure the on-going health of data and establish the process and owners to act on results.
- Determine root causes of known data quality problems, correct current errors and implement processes to prevent future data errors.
- A data quality issue continues to arise as part of an individual's daily responsibilities.
- Your organization has data quality problems and has decided the first step is to purchase a data profiling tool. You need a better approach which focuses more on business needs, processes, and outcomes than on just the tool.

Project approach and team—The Ten Steps Process works well as the foundation for building the project plan. The project team can be any size appropriate to the problem to be solved. It can be comprised of one person, a small team of 3-4 people with extended resources to turn to with occasional questions, or a large team.

You must have representation from those familiar with the business, the data, people/organizations, and the technology within scope of the project. For example, if improvements require technical changes to a system, the team would need to be augmented with IT expertise to implement these improvements. If systematically enforced controls are implemented, then IT will also be needed to implement those. If a business process is to be redesigned, then a business analyst or subject matter expert should be included.

As an individual, you may see an issue with data quality. Perhaps you are responsible on a daily, weekly, or monthly basis for receiving and loading files with data purchased from an external vendor. The data loads complete successfully for a time or two, then the load programs fail, data has to be backed out, analysis done, and the vendor is often required to resend the files. All this causes extra work and delays the data from being available to the users on a timely basis. In this case you can use the Ten Steps as the basis for a 4-week data quality improvement project. You spend a few hours formulating your project approach and objectives, present to your manager and get approval. The Ten Steps are applied in a quick, yet logical, fashion to determine root causes of the load failures and to implement better processes (perhaps including automated data profiling prior to loads to detect changes to file formats) that prevent the problem in the future. You communicate and engage appropriately with your manager and the vendor who sends the files.

The different types of projects represent different risks from a project management point of view. A focused data quality improvement project risks getting funding cut because, as Laura Sebastian-Coleman points out, "People don't like fixing things, they like building new things." You may have to continue to use business impact (from *Step 4*) and your best communication skills (from *Step 10*) at various points in your project to remind people of the benefits and ensure support until the end.

Timing—Estimating the timeline for this type of project is difficult. The reason is that until you assess the data, you don't know how large a problem you really have. What you find in *Step 3 – Assess Data Quality* will determine the time for the remaining steps. Do your best job at estimating and set expectations of stakeholders that these estimates will change and be updated once the data quality assessment results are in. Estimates may have to be updated again once the true root causes are found in *Step 5*, as these results will affect the prevention activities that should be put into place.

Timing guidelines—If conducting a data quality improvement project for the first time, try to scope it to 3-4 months with a project team of 2-4 people. Organizations lose interest if results take too long to deliver. In that time, it is reasonable to complete Steps 1-5, if assessing 1-2 data quality dimensions against one data source. Implementing improvements may take longer depending on assessment results and root cause analysis.

A quick data quality assessment could be done by one person, in one month, on a small set of data from one source. This project would be tightly scoped and timeboxed so the steps are completed in days, not weeks.

After the first project, you will be more familiar with the steps and how long they took to complete. You will be aware of the cultural and environmental aspects which impact how quickly or slowly work gets done in your organization. All this experience will help you better estimate subsequent improvement projects.

See the *Ten Steps in Action callout box* for how the Ten Steps Process was used for a focused data quality improvement project at a telecom in China. Note that the Ten Steps were also used for customized methodologies, training, and coaching.

Ten Steps in Action

Using the Ten Steps at a Telecom Company in China

Chen Liu, CEO of DGWorkshop (Beijing) Technology Consulting Co., Ltd., has designed customized methodologies based on the Ten Steps for his customers, along with providing training and coaching on the approach for both customers and colleagues. He shared the following project where the Ten Steps Process was used.

Customer—A provincial company of the largest telecom company in China, which has 950+ million mobile users overall. The provincial company has 12 branch subsidiaries, 1000+ channel partners and 30+ million users.

Background—The marketing group in the provincial telecom company received complaints from channel partners that sales commissions were late or miscalculated. This motivated the General Manager to emphasize the importance of data governance (DG) and assigned the big data team to implement data governance as one of the four key targets for the IT department. The team was under pressure to meet the business users and the General Manager's expectations.

Project—A project was launched and included involvement from executives, business, and IT. It was led by the big data team from the IT department, co-working with the marketing department. The following Ten Steps were used:

Step 1. Business Needs: Started with the business problem and project definition to determine what DG really meant for the company and the perceived value of the project. This led to defining the right scope for the business, organization, system, and data.

Step 2. Information Environment Analysis: Understood related business processes, systems, data and people responsibilities; drew data flow diagram and CRUD matrix to understand the whole environment; discovered possible conflicts or gaps in data processing by either systems or people.

Step 3. Quality Assessment: Used the data quality dimensions of completeness, consistency, timeliness, and metadata quality.

Step 4. Business Impact: Analyzed in terms of monetary impact and customer satisfaction, which led to focus on one essential problem, of five critical problems, out of 19 key findings after the first round of investigation.

Steps 5 – 9. Conducted root cause analysis; made corrections to business processes, business supporting systems, and data specifications; and enhanced data quality and governance capabilities from IT focus to business focus and corporate level.

Step 10. Communication. Paid attention to communication both in the project team and with business departments and executive leaders.

Benefits—Several benefits were seen as a result of this year-long project:

- The business case was made using analysis of the number of orders and monetary value related to poor-quality data. This impressed both the IT and business teams and was recognized by the vice president of the telecom company.
- Data problems were reduced and data quality improved, both of which were quantified.
- In addition to solving the original problem, they operationalized the achievements and made the program sustainable by defining the overall roles and responsibilities, policies, and processes covering data governance, quality, data life cycle, metadata management, etc.
- Provided direction for the next 1-3 years by designing roadmaps based on a data management maturity assessment.
- The project won the "Best Practice Award" in the 2nd China Data Standardization and Governance Awards in May 2018.

Project Type: Data Quality Activities in Another Project

Description—Address the quality of data by incorporating steps, techniques, or activities from the Ten Steps Process into other projects, methodologies, or SDLCs, where data is a component but often not the primary focus. Many projects include creating, capturing, enriching, enhancing, moving, integrating, or archiving data. Preparing the data to meet the business needs and addressing risks related to data will increase the overall success of such projects.

Data quality issues discovered early in these larger projects are much less expensive to correct than if they are addressed during final testing or just before going live with a new system. Including data quality-related tasks during the normal course of projects will prevent many problems from occurring once the work is in production. The quality of data can make the difference between a smooth transition and the ability of business to continue as usual and a rocky conversion and the inability to conduct even basic business activities (e.g., completing a timely financial close versus a late financial close; meeting manufacturing and shipping commitments versus needing expensive workarounds while issues are resolved).

An extension of this type of project is to incorporate data quality activities into the authorized project approach used by your organization, thereby enhancing the work done by multiple projects using the same methodology.

Examples—Generally, these projects develop solutions which include process improvements and/or purchasing or developing new applications. Migrating and integrating data from existing legacy sources is a large piece of many projects. Examples include implementing a new Human Resources system, building a new application and migrating data from legacy systems, or integrating multiple functional areas and data sources into an ERP (Enterprise Resource Planning system) which cannot succeed without an emphasis on data readiness. Do you recognize similar situations in your organization where including data quality would be important?

- Your organization is moving from an on-premises system to cloud-based and must ensure the transition for business processes, responsibilities, and data goes smoothly.
- Your global organization is overhauling its approach to managing human resources, with new processes being developed and a centralized application being installed.

- Your organization must comply with regulations such as the General Data Protection Regulation (GDPR) and a company-wide project has been initiated to ensure compliance.
- A major division of your company has been sold. Data related to this division must be uncoupled from the existing systems and passed to the new owner.
- Your organization is invested in machine learning, using data to train, validate, and tune models; the low quality and unknown quality of the data poses a risk to the veracity and usefulness of the output.
- Your agency is implementing a third-party vendor application that brings together data from legacy sources for the first time.
- A major system in your organization is being retired, and the team must ensure old data is archived and active data is moved to the current production system which replaced it.
- Your organization is developing a data lake. Including a focus on data quality will enhance the final product.
- Your organization has purchased a new company and must integrate their people, processes, and data.
- Your organization has an internally developed SDLC that is used for all projects. It will be more useful if the data aspect is enhanced with the right data quality activities.
- Your organization makes use of Six Sigma or Lean methodologies. Including the appropriate data quality steps, techniques, or activities will enhance the data aspect of the work.

Project Approach and Team—Relevant data quality activities from the Ten Steps can be incorporated into *any* SDLC that is the basis for the larger project (Agile, sequential, hybrid, etc.). Applicable Ten Steps techniques can also be combined with your organization's favored project management style or a third-party methodology being used in the project. For example, by including data profiling, you can improve the quality of, and decrease the time needed to complete, source-to-target mappings. Depending on the scope of the overall project, there may be one person or a team of people with specific data quality responsibilities working as part of the larger project.

When incorporating data quality work into another project, scheduling the data quality work is extremely important. Ensure data quality activities show up on the overall project plan, with clear responsibilities, deliverables, and due dates – just as any other tasks would appear. You might hear, "Oh yes, we think data quality is important. Why don't you go work on it (over there) and we'll continue our project? Be sure and talk to us when you're done." That is missing the essential piece – integrating the data quality work. Be sure those doing the data quality activities are acknowledged as core or extended team members or resources. Data quality work and people have to be visible, just as the other project work and people are visible.

Careful planning at the beginning of a project will guarantee that appropriate data quality activities are fully integrated into it. The earlier that data quality is incorporated into the project, the better. But even if you are engaging the project later in its timeline, adding in suitable data quality activities can still significantly contribute to its success. The output of this type of project can be new or modified operational processes where data quality activities or techniques are included.

Data should be profiled and assessed as early as possible in the project, so data quality problems can be uncovered while there is still time to address them. The risk of project delays will increase if those same issues are found late in the project or if they are ignored. If data quality problems are prioritized and resolved, it is less likely that the business will be disrupted after the move to production. It also decreases the likelihood that the warranty or stabilization period will have to be extended before moving support to the operational teams.

Quote to Remember

"Data profiling of production data is a required analysis activity that cannot be skipped from the life cycle of any data-oriented project and should be performed before requirements are completed. Tension frequently exists between the need to perform profiling as part of analysis and the need to keep production data private, but in choosing battles to fight in a data-centric project, this is not the battle to skip. Usually an acceptable compromise can be reached, or months should be added to the implementation schedule for redesign needed prior to system implementation."

– April Reeve, Managing Data in Motion (2013)

Warning

Ignoring data quality = risk! The alternative to directly addressing data means, by default, the project is making assumptions about the data. A classic attitude is often found in the following sentiment: "We, the application development team, are on a sexy new project. We cannot do anything about the quality of data from the source systems, so we will write our programs and develop our interfaces and release the new system, assuming the data will behave like we think or hope it should." A dangerous attitude indeed!

Project Type: Ad hoc Use of Data Quality Steps, Activities, or Techniques

Description—Make use of any portion of the Ten Steps Process to quickly address a business need or data quality issue, such as a support issue that arises in the course of your daily work, in an operational process, or to address an unusual or emergency situation. This is not a formal project in the usual terms, but does fit into the broad definition of project as used in this book.

For example, a critical business process has come to a stop and it is suspected that the quality of data is part of the problem. You could be working alone or with a small group of experts pulled together to address the problem. You remember *Step 1 – Determine Business Needs and Approach* and ask a few questions to ensure you understand the issue to be solved. You recall *Step 2 – Analyze Information Environment* and ensure you know just enough about the data, processes, people/organizations, and technology that surround where the problem appeared. You use life cycle thinking to trace back what was happening with those four key components. You find the root cause(s).

Do you remember the health analogy that started *Chapter 2*? Keeping the patient alive is the first priority during a heart attack. Keeping a critical business process going is an example of keeping the patient alive, so you quickly correct the data and implement short-term workarounds. Once the process is up and running, use the Ten Steps to address all root causes and prevent the issue from happening again. This may require you to start a separate focused data quality improvement project. It could mean incorporating data quality work into a larger project, if the scope of the larger project intersects with the support issue just addressed.

These examples show how the Ten Steps Process, once you are well-acquainted with it, can be applied to develop solutions to many situations you are likely to face. Whatever prompts the use of the Ten Steps, good decisions have to be made about which steps, techniques, or activities apply to the problem and how to organize your work. Everything in this book can help you use the Ten Steps Process in an ad hoc fashion or as an individual – it will just be implemented in a more abbreviated fashion than if you had a project team.

Examples—Become familiar with the Ten Steps so you can recognize which steps and techniques can help when special or unexpected situations arise.

- Some aspect of data management (governance, quality, modeling, etc.) is an important part – or the full focus – of your daily responsibilities.
- Managing data quality is NOT part of your daily responsibilities, but you recognize data quality problems are hampering your ability to do your job.
- A data quality issue comes to light and you need to quickly connect the issue with business needs to determine if spending time addressing the issue will be worthwhile.
- There is a need to better understand the origin of data that supports a key business process. Use selected steps from *Step 2 Analyze Information Environment* to research and document data lineage.
- There is a need to show the value of data-related activities such as data quality, data governance, business glossary, data modeling, etc.
- Within a data quality or governance program, there is a long list of data quality or governance activities under consideration for the upcoming year. There is a need to prioritize which activities will provide the most benefit and should be accounted for in the budget.

Project Approach and Team—Any of the Ten Steps can be used. You may find techniques that will become a standard part of your individual processes. For example, if you are responsible for loading data from external sources and have had issues with changing formats and content from the supplier, you may want to institute quick profiling of the data prior to the load. This prevents rework created when problems are found only when the load program fails. An even better prevention approach would be to institute regular communication with the data provider, conduct some root cause analysis, and improve the process.

The size and composition of the team will differ depending on the scope of the enquiry/analysis. With an ad hoc project, you may be a project team of one. Even so, consider the roles in the *Roles in Data Quality Projects* section below. Many roles can apply in a scaled-down way. Your manager may informally fulfill the role of project sponsor and you may not have an official team. Still, think through who would be interested in the work you are doing (potential stakeholders) and identify the subject matter experts with whom you may need to consult. Communication is not just for project teams. Ensure your manager is aware of and supports your work. Institute regular status reports and obtain feedback. Inform other staff in regular department meetings of your activities, progress, and results.

It is possible that an issue requires more formal attention. If so, you may institute your own short-term data quality focused project to complete in a few weeks. Carefully manage the scope and be sure to engage your manager and other stakeholders, as needed.

Why the Distinctions Between Project Types are Useful

Making distinctions between the three types of projects is useful when planning and executing your data quality project. Think of the project types on a continuum where ad hoc use is on the left. This indicates an ad hoc project is less time consuming, less complex, and usually less expensive than the other two. A focused DQ improvement project is in the middle (and can itself vary greatly depending on the scope). Including DQ activities in another project is on the right and will be more time consuming and more complex.

The following aspects impact the time and effort required for any project. They often differ between the three types of data quality projects and should be considered when planning the project: where the money comes from; who approves funding; the number of stakeholders; the scope and complexity of the project work itself; how long the work will take and when; the number of people and knowledge and skills needed; how decisions get made and who is involved; the scope of communication, engagement, and change management.

In addition, it can be challenging to actually measure the impacts of and benefits from projects. *Step 4* in the Ten Steps Process shares several techniques for assessing business impact which can be used in any type of data quality project. For all project types, make use of any formalized data governance that may already be in place to help identify and secure resources, get input, and make decisions throughout the project. If formalized data governance does not exist, plan on those activities taking longer.

Project Objectives

Following are examples of often-seen project objectives that can be articulated as part of a project plan in any of the three types of projects just described. Note that project objectives are NOT business needs, and they are NOT data quality issues. They are specific, measurable statements of work that, if completed during the project, will meet the business needs and address the data quality issues:

- Gain support for data quality
- Establish a data quality baseline
- Determine root causes of data quality issues
- Implement improvements (prevention, correction)
- Implement data quality metrics and other monitoring (detection)

These may not be the only project objectives, but they often apply to any type of data quality project. It is easy to see how establishing a data quality baseline makes sense for a focused data quality improvement project. But establishing a baseline for data also applies when incorporating data quality activities into application development and migration projects. Current data quality is assessed and compared to new system requirements, which reveals gaps between the two. Specific improvements to close the gaps, such as correcting data and fixing processes, then become additional objectives.

Figure 5.1 shows typical project objectives down the first column. Shaded cells highlight which of the Ten Steps would most likely be

Step # → Project Objective ↓	1 Determine Business Needs and Approach	2 Analyze Information Environment	3 Assess Data Quality	4 Assess Business Impact	5 Identify Root Causes	6 Develop Improvement Plans	7 Prevent Future Data Errors	8 Correct Current Data Errors	9 Monitor Controls	10 Communicate, Manage, and Engage People Throughout
Gain support for data quality										All objectives: apply Step 10 throughout
Establish a data quality baseline				All objectives: use Step 4 whenever needed						
Determine root causes of data quality issues	Make use of data quality baseline results, plus Step 5									
Implement improvements (prevention, correction)	Make use of DQ baseline results, root causes identified, plus Steps 6, 7, 8									
Implement data quality metrics and other monitoring (detection)	Make use of DQ baseline results, root causes identified, and improvements implemented, plus Step 9									

Figure 5.1 Data quality project objectives and the Ten Steps Process.

carried out to complete each of the stated objectives. You can see how some of the objectives build upon work done by previous objectives.

The figure does NOT indicate level of detail for each of the steps – that is a different choice. The figure also does NOT indicate time to complete, which is a function of level of detail and the project type and approach. *Chapter 4: The Ten Steps Process* provides details for carrying out each of the steps in the first-row column headings.

Comparing SDLCs

There are many different approaches to running a project. As noted, SDLC is a general term for solution/system/software development life cycle and is used in this book to refer to whichever approach is being used for the data quality project – be it waterfall, Agile, other,

or some combination. The SDLC defines the approach for developing solutions and the phases within the project. The SDLC provides the basis for the project plan and the tasks to be undertaken by the project team. The SDLC can be created by and used internally to your organization or be provided by a vendor. *Figure 5.2* shows the phases in a typical SDLC, compared to the phases used in four other SDLC variants.

While there are many useful SDLCs, many are missing key data quality (and governance) activities that would increase the chances of project success. For example, in almost every project there is some type of activity related to gathering requirements. You may call that phase by a different name; however, if you are gathering requirements, including a data quality perspective should be included during that phase of your project plan.

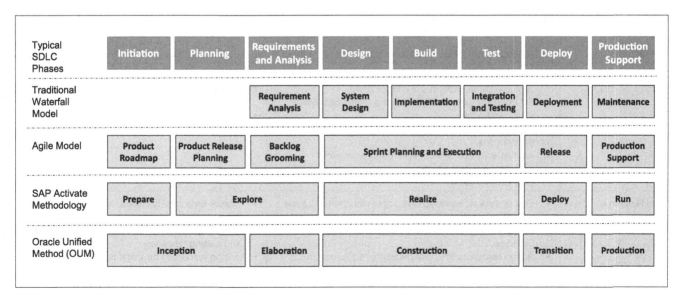

Figure 5.2 Solution Development Life Cycle (SDLC) comparison.

Data quality steps, techniques, and activities from this methodology can be integrated into *any* SDLC and project plan. Careful planning at the beginning of a project will guarantee that appropriate data quality activities are integrated into the overall project plan.

Data Quality and Governance in SDLCs

Including data quality and governance activities in any data-centric application development, data migration, or integration project is one of the best ways to prevent data quality problems. Quality pioneer W. Edwards Deming taught that quality is designed in, not inspected in. To drive this point home, he quoted Harold F. Dodge: "You cannot inspect quality into a product." Genichi Taguchi, famous for what was known as the Taguchi method, was another who emphasized improving product quality at the design stage by integrating quality control into product design. We would do well to learn from them and use the same philosophy by ensuring data quality is built into the design of information products and processes.

Tables 5.1 to 5.8 list some of the activities typically found within each of the SDLC phases just shown in the top row of *Figure 5.2*. Data governance and quality activities which could be carried out at the same time are included. *Table 5.9* maps activities for Scrum, a typical Agile approach, to the same SDLC phases. Each phase is briefly described below:

- **Initiation**. Articulate the problem or opportunity to be addressed; put the project into motion; authorize and define scope and goals; and initialize resource allocation
- **Planning**. Refine project scope and goals; develop a plan for managing, executing, and monitoring the project; identify project activities, dependencies, and constraints; and develop initial timeline
- **Requirements and analysis**. Research, evaluate, and identify detailed needs and objectives; establish priorities; and sequence activities and refine plans

- **Design**. Define solution options and select best option based on dependencies and constraints; determine how to meet the functional and quality requirements of the solution; and adjust plans and requirements as needed
- **Build**. Construct the solution
- **Test**. Determine if requirements have been met; adjust plans, requirements, and design as needed
- **Deploy**. Move the solution to production; deliver to users; stabilize the deployment; and transition to operations and support
- **Production support**. Maintain and enhance the solution; and support users in the operational environment

Within any particular SDLC, the phases will vary in name, organization, coordination, timing, and formality. Even so, you can map most to the eight phases here.

The first column in each table indicates the SDLC phase and typical activities that a project team would be engaged in during the phase. The next two columns list high-level data governance, stewardship, data quality and readiness activities during that team activity. Data governance and stewardship are grouped together because they are highly interdependent, nontechnical, and focus on decision making, whereas data quality and readiness activities focus more on the skills, techniques, and analysis that feed into solutions and decisions.

Use the information in the tables to enhance any SDLC and determine how these activities can be integrated into your project. The end goal is that resulting applications, processes, and data can be used to conduct business, and that any data that is passed on is of the quality so it can be used by others. This will reduce the negative impact of poor quality on the business and increase trust in the data by those dependent on them.

Many thanks to Masha Bykin for her expertise and input to this section. The tables were first published in McGilvray and Bykin, "Data Quality and Governance in Projects: Knowledge in Action,"

Table 5.1 SDLC Phase: Initiation – Data Governance and Quality Activities

Team Activity – Initiation Phase	Data Governance and Stewardship Activities	Data Quality and Readiness Activities
Define Business Problem and/or Opportunity	• Identify data subject areas required for scope and goals (e.g., customer, order history, products). • Set goals for data quality within the context of overall scope and goals. • Evaluate availability of definitions for data elements within the domains. • Articulate ways in which high-quality data and information support business goals and poor-quality data hinders them.	• Identify possible sources of data within scope. • Collect known data quality issues, existing quality metrics, and assess trust. • Identify potential risk and impact to the project of data quality issues found.
Initial Resource Allocation	• Ensure data stewardship and governance activities are accounted for when negotiating contracts, allocating human resources, approving budgets, and setting timelines. • Assign resources for initial planning, requirements analysis, and to support data quality assessments.	• Ensure data quality issues, activities, and tools are accounted for when negotiating contracts, allocating human resources, approving budgets, and setting timelines. • Assign resources for initial data quality assessments, and to support requirements analysis.

Table 5.2 SDLC Phase: Planning – Data Governance and Quality Activities

Team Activity – Planning Phase	Data Governance and Stewardship Activities	Data Quality and Readiness Activities
Determine How to Manage and Monitor the Project	• Determine how data governance and stewardship will engage with project team. • Plan for tracking and reporting status of data governance and stewardship activities. • Determine how the data knowledge network will interact with project and non-project resources for data readiness activities.	• Determine how data quality resources will engage with project team. • Plan for tracking and reporting status of data quality activities.
Research Activities That Will Support Goals	• Determine existence and completeness of glossary, data models, and other metadata for data sources, identify gaps, and necessary activities to close the gaps. • Identify the desired population of the data subject areas at a high level (e.g., all active customer records, order history from the past 10 years, all current and obsolete products from the past 5 years).	• Conduct quick, high-level data profiling of main data sources. Use to provide input to selection of data sources and initial insight into data quality issues that need to be accounted for during the project and in this planning phase. • Help to assess impact/risk to the project of data quality issues known at this time.
Identify High-Level Activities, Dependencies, Constraints	• Identify needed data governance and stewardship activities and incorporate into the project plan. Reference activities from the SDLC phases in this table. • Prioritize known data quality issues and work with data quality analysts to plan solutions. • Track progress of data readiness activities and manage as a dependency.	• Identify needed data quality and readiness activities and incorporate into the project plan (e.g., data profiling and other assessments, plan solutions to data quality issues). Reference activities from the SDLC phases in this table. • Identify dependencies and constraints that affect or hinder the ability to carry out data quality activities and may increase risk to the project if ignored. • Work with non-project teams to start data readiness based on known issues and current business needs (e.g., good housekeeping corrections, reduce data volume), not based on new requirements.
Develop Initial Timeline	• Estimate time and resources to perform stewardship to achieve goals. • Allocate time for analysis of data issues and decisions.	• Estimate time and resources to perform data quality activities to achieve goals, including known data quality issues.
Fine-Tune Resource Allocation	• Adjust resource allocations to account for the data governance and stewardship activities identified during planning.	• Adjust resource allocations to account for data quality issues and data readiness activities identified.

© 2013, 2020 Danette McGilvray and Masha Bykin

Table 5.3 SDLC Phase: Requirements and Analysis – Data Governance and Quality Activities

Team Activity – Requirements and Analysis Phase	Data Governance and Stewardship Activities	Data Quality and Readiness Activities
Create Use Cases	• Identify data elements within use cases. Ensure definitions are consistent across use cases and are captured in a glossary.	• Analyze the use cases to inform impact to the information/data life cycle (POSMAD – plan, obtain/create, store and share, maintain, apply, dispose).
Functional Requirements Analysis	• Include data stewards in functional requirements analysis (analysis sessions, process reviews, and artifact reviews). • Identify data elements associated with all the functional requirements. • Ensure business rules and data definitions and valid value sets are validated, aligned and documented. • Ensure alignment and updating of glossary and data definitions which will need to be used throughout the SDLC (design, build, etc.). • Ensure requirements are informed by data quality assessments and data readiness activities. Include recommended improvements based on root cause analysis. Ensure solutions consider both corrective and preventive measures (e.g., business process improvement, training, changes to roles/ responsibilities, automated business rules, data quality monitoring).	• Gather requirements for data quality dimensions such as integrity, completeness, timeliness, consistency, accuracy, de-duplication, etc. • Use business rule analysis to ensure requirements for data quality measures are understood and documented – for testing, initial loads, and on-going quality checks (to be done in production).

(Continued)

Table 5.3 SDLC Phase: Requirements and Analysis – Data Governance and Quality Activities *(Continued)*

Team Activity – Requirements and Analysis Phase	Data Governance and Stewardship Activities	Data Quality and Readiness Activities
Physical Data Analysis	• Follow-up on questions and issues uncovered by data quality activities. • Determine impact of data issues and readiness gaps to project. Prioritize and add resolutions to overall requirements artifacts, to ensure these are addressed during subsequent SDLC phases. • Update glossary based on findings from data quality activities (e.g., business rules, calculations, valid values). • Continue to work with non-project teams to address data readiness issues and dependencies.	• Perform in-depth data profiling and other applicable assessments (using full data sets) to identify gaps between the actual data and known requirements. Learnings will be used throughout the SDLC in design, build and test. • Finalize the data population of interest (i.e., the selection criteria) and how the data can be accessed. • Ensure findings from assessments are reflected in requirements and artifacts, to be handled during design, build, test. • Identify root causes of data quality issues. Use as input into both requirements and design.

© 2013, 2020 Danette McGilvray and Masha Bykin

Table 5.4 SDLC Phase: Design – Data Governance and Quality Activities

Team Activity – Design Phase	Data Governance and Stewardship Activities	Data Quality and Readiness Activities
Architecture	• Determine approaches to handling data based on requirements and identify gaps in existing architecture or tools (e.g., load using ETL tool or flat files).	• Consider appropriate handling of all categories of data in high level design (e.g., transactional, master, reference, configuration, purchased, metadata, etc.).
Issue Tracking and Resolution	• Determine status of data readiness dependencies previously identified. • Design workarounds for data quality issues that have not been resolved and that may need to be absorbed into the project. • Prioritize and make decisions about solution designs.	• Recommend solutions to close gaps between actual and required data quality, corrective (e.g., cleanse, correct, enhance, or create data) and preventive.
Data Model Design	• Participate in model creation. • Align data models and glossary definitions. • Identify inter-dependencies between subject areas and data elements.	• Use data profiling results to provide input into the creation of target models. Consider differences between existing data sources and new target models to facilitate integration.
User Interface Design	• Provide input into interface design to balance ease of use and timeliness of task execution with features that protect the quality of the data. • Identify data elements in screens. Ensure definitions are consistent across screens and are captured in a glossary. • Incorporate definitions into training and help content.	• Use profiling results to expose valid value sets, rules, and data quality issues that could be addressed in the user Interface.
Data Movement/ETL Designs	• Review and validate source-to-target mappings and transformation rules. • Look for opportunities to standardize valid value sets and hierarchies. • Ensure there is agreement on the overall flow of the data from sources to targets.	• Use profiling and other assessment results to identify data element contents so source-to-target mappings and transformations are based on the actual data, not column headings or opinions of content. • Help determine the optimal order in which to load data.
Test Planning	• Identify and prioritize key data elements, measures, and rules to be validated during testing. • Identify and prioritize key data elements, measures, and rules to be monitored on-going (i.e., after go-live).	• Identify sources for test data and profile to ensure contents are well known and comparisons will work (i.e., reduce time spent chasing issues during testing that are problems/deltas in the test data). • Plan for testing for all categories of data within scope (e.g., transactional, master, reference, configuration, purchased, created data, metadata, etc.). • Assist in designing test approaches for data quality. Consider reusability so tests can be repeated during test cycles and after go-live.
Deployment Planning	• Ensure data artifacts and documentation are available (e.g., business rules, glossary) for the production of help, training, and communication content.	• Document issues and solutions that involve manual processes and should be included in training and communication. • Include data readiness steps that cannot be automated and must be performed manually before the system is released to the users. • Include data quality checks in deployment plans (e.g., confirm correct data sources prior to load, data quality checks after).

© 2013, 2020 Danette McGilvray and Masha Bykin

Table 5.5 SDLC Phase: Build – Data Governance and Quality Activities

Team Activity – Build Phase	Data Governance and Stewardship Activities	Data Quality and Readiness Activities
Build Features	• Support developers and analysts in researching questions about meaning and correct use of data.	• Implement data readiness solutions and adjust based on requirements and design. • Create new data as part of data readiness if needed. • Implement business process improvements to prevent data quality problems after go-live.
Refinement of Requirements and Designs	• See *Tables 5.3 and 5.4* for activities as adjustments are made to requirements and designs.	• See *Tables 5.3 and 5.4* for activities as adjustments are made to requirements and designs.
Issue Tracking and Resolution	• Ensure recommended solutions for issues are handled consistently with definitions, rules, etc. and are not resolved in a way that could harm data quality. • Review issues for opportunities to resolve root causes (preferably in the current build cycle).	• Identify root causes of data quality issues and recommend solutions. • Record outcomes of issues, especially if resolutions result in residual impact to data quality or need to be included in training or communications.

© 2013, 2020 Danette McGilvray and Masha Bykin

Table 5.6 SDLC Phase: Test – Data Governance and Quality Activities

Team Activity – Test Phase	Data Governance and Stewardship Activities	Data Quality and Readiness Activities
Testing	• Align data elements in user interfaces and reports with glossary definitions and help content. • Ensure that usability testing verifies the features supporting data quality are working as designed and cannot be bypassed. • Support testers in researching questions about meaning and correct use of data.	• Profile and check data prior to, during, and after test loads. • Log any deltas between test results and specifications, including definitions and rules. • Create feedback loop between teams with dependencies on the data engaged in various types of testing. • Help analyze test results and provide feedback on solutions to issues found during testing.
Issue Tracking and Resolution	• Coordinate communication among stakeholders and provide input for issue prioritization.	• Ensure issues that are not fully resolved are documented and ready for follow-up by Production Support team (e.g., in backlog as defects alongside deferred requirements).

© 2013, 2020 Danette McGilvray and Masha Bykin

Table 5.7 SDLC Phase: Deploy – Data Governance and Quality Activities

Team Activity – Deploy Phase	Data Governance and Stewardship Activities	Data Quality and Readiness Activities
Release Changes to the Production Environment and Stabilize	• Help to communicate about and resolve data issues found during deployment. • Update data artifacts and documentation to reflect changes in the release.	• Participate per deployment plans. • Identify and research issues found during deployment and stabilization. • Help to implement on-going monitoring of data quality controls, making use of data quality assessments and testing done during the project. • Ensure training is completed for data quality activities incorporated into standard business processes.

© 2013, 2020 Danette McGilvray and Masha Bykin

Table 5.8 SDLC Phase: Production Support – Data Governance and Quality Activities

Team Activity – Production Support Phase	Data Governance and Stewardship Activities	Data Quality and Readiness Activities
Monitor System Heath, Support Users, Maintain and Enhance Iteratively	• Prioritize and make decisions about data quality checks as needed. Ensure accountability for taking action on results. • Repeat applicable SDLC activities from *Tables 5.2 to 5.7* to maintain and enhance data quality.	• Continue to find and recommend additional automated data quality checks as needed. • Perform routine data quality assessments. • Research, perform root cause analysis, and propose solutions for data quality issues identified. • Repeat applicable SDLC activities from *Tables 5.2 to 5.7* to maintain and enhance data quality.

© 2013, 2020 Danette McGilvray and Masha Bykin

Table 5.9 Agile and Data Governance and Quality Activities

Agile Scrum* Activity and Highlights	Same Activities as in related SDLC Phase Tables 5.1 – 5.8
Product Roadmap • Focus on product vision and high-value milestones, not end-to-end execution • Identify key roles, skills, resources; form small teams	Initiation (*Table 5.1*) Planning (*Table 5.2*)
Release Planning • Highest priority stories (based on roadmap) are selected from product backlog for upcoming releases • Focus on one or two upcoming releases, not whole roadmap	Planning (*Table 5.2*) Requirements and Analysis (*Table 5.3*) Design (*Table 5.4*)
Product Backlog Grooming • Done collaboratively by stakeholders and technical team • Starts during release planning, and continues through sprint planning and sprint execution (for upcoming sprints) • Stories are written, prioritized, sequenced, and sized into small increments • Iterative clarification of value, design approach, and acceptance criteria until story is ready for sprint	Requirements and Analysis (*Table 5.3*) Design (*Table 5.4*)
Sprint Planning • Small number of "ready" stories are sized in more detail and selected as sprint backlog • Sprint backlog decomposed into tasks	Planning (*Table 5.2*) Requirements and Analysis (*Table 5.3*) Design (*Table 5.4*)
Sprint Execution • Stories in sprint backlog are developed and packaged for release • Testing is part of construction, ideally integrated into build • Implementation exposes new requirements and design issues • Work that can't be completed goes back into product backlog, sometimes as debt • Retrospectives expose better processes	Requirements and Analysis (*Table 5.3*) Design (*Table 5.4*) Build (*Table 5.5*) Test (*Table 5.6*)
Release • One or more sets of sprint packages are moved to production • Issues and new requirements are managed iteratively through product backlog	Deploy (*Table 5.7*) Production Support (*Table 5.8*)
Production Support • Monitor operational processes and systems, including automated data quality checks • Provide input to sprint backlogs based on issues and impacts	Production Support (*Table 5.8*)

© 2013, 2020 Danette McGilvray and Masha Bykin
*Based on Kenneth S. Rubin, *Essential Scrum: A Practical Guide to the Most Popular Agile Process*. Addison-Wesley Professional, 2012.

The Data Insight & Social BI Executive Report, Vol. 13, No. 5. (2013, Cutter Consortium). A free download of the full Executive Report is available at https://www.cutter.com/offer/data-quality-and-governance-projects-knowledge-action-0. Please see this report for more details and insights.

Quote to Remember

"Organizations invest substantial resources in projects…. Clearly, the more effective the projects, the less cost to the company and the sooner the business can use those results to provide products, offer services, and increase revenue. Historically, many projects concentrated their efforts on people, process, and technology. In spite of this, many projects produce less than stellar results…A vast number of projects still fail to fully address the data and information aspects of their efforts. Many projects have failed due to this oversight, while others have left a wake of data quality issues that put long-term burdens on business processes and subsequent projects. We can increase the success of our project portfolios by making data quality and data governance activities an integral part of our project approach."

– Danette McGilvray and Masha Bykin, "Data Quality and Governance in Projects: Knowledge in Action," The Data Insight & Social BI Executive Report, (2013), p. 3.

Key Concept

The Developer's Role in Data Quality. Software is a primary source of data, and therefore, it is a primary source of data quality issues. Our software systems are designed and built by developers and engineers with technical education and skills. They are taught how to code and ensure that the application mechanically works correctly. They are often not educated about the fact that data is an important deliverable which must be handled properly. They usually have very little exposure to the impacts of poor data quality and may be unaware of the use of data downstream. It is easy to forget that the real purpose of business systems is to capture and make information available.

Many data quality issues are introduced in the course of development. Details must be worked out that are not covered by functional requirements, such as how to name entities and attributes, what data types to use, what sets of values to allow, how to implement business rules, etc. If developers are not aware of how they impact data quality, they may trade it in for short term delivery goals.

Developers should be trained and empowered in their role as technical data stewards, provided with detailed glossaries that document the expected meaning of data elements, and provided access to subject matters experts to answer questions. In the absence of these, time is spent dealing with the many ambiguities of how to handle the data. The burden is high, not feasible to fit into the tight timelines faced by the development team, and therefore much gets missed. When developers do get the right training and resources, it saves valuable time and they deliver a better system with much better data.

A holistic approach to data quality will enlist software developers as front-line stewards of data, will teach them the value of data, arm them with data tools, skills, and glossaries, and make data that meets quality standards part of software delivery goals.

– Masha Bykin, Senior Data Engineer

Roles in Data Quality Projects

To successfully complete a data quality project and sustain data quality requires knowledge and skills in business, data, and technology. It requires the ability to communicate at many levels within the organization and the capability to do detailed analysis. It requires the ability to see the big picture of organizational strategy and the ability to determine specific actions to improve data quality based on assessment results. It requires the ability to query data, understand constraints to the data, and interpret data models. It is unrealistic to expect that one person could have the ability to communicate well with everyone from the CEO to an individual data user, plus have the knowledge and skills to understand business needs and also write intricate program code. In other words, it takes a village to carry out data quality work.

When assembling a data quality project team, identify the skills, knowledge, and experience needed. They will vary depending on the project goals, scope, and timeline. Recognize where a person may not have all the skills needed but has the ability to learn. Consider where the personality of a person helps and where forcing certain personalities into some roles makes a bad fit, yet you can still take advantage of what they have to offer elsewhere in the project. Everyone brings their own knowledge, experience, and personality to their jobs. Good managers will mentor and coach those reporting to them, use their skills in the best way, and help them build additional skills where there is a gap.

Determine who will be core team members. Realize you will be reaching out to others for input and expertise from time to time. Some may be identified as extended team members who know they are part of the project but with less time commitment. Others will be contacted on an ad hoc basis.

Table 5.10 lists roles commonly needed for data quality projects, along with corresponding skills and knowledge. Job titles, roles, and responsibilities continue to evolve and the words used to describe them may differ across organizations. I have grouped some roles together that could be seen differently in your organization. Anything learned by doing a stakeholder analysis can also be helpful here (see *Step 10*).

For each role, find the people within your organization with the skills and knowledge. Of course, one person can fulfill many roles. And some roles require more than one person.

If you are working on a focused data quality improvement project, use the table when selecting the project team and extended team members. Extended team members are not part of the core team. They are resources with necessary knowledge and skills, who are familiar with the project, but who have a lesser time commitment than the core members. If incorporating data quality activities into another project, understand the roles and who is filling them in the overall project. Uncover and address any gaps between the existing roles and those needed to ensure the data quality work will be done. Having an intact data or data quality team that works with the other teams within the project can work well.

Add columns to the table to capture answers to the following questions as you consider each of the roles and how they apply to your project:

- Do you need this role for your project?
- What do you call the role or what title is used within your organization?
- Which skills and knowledge are needed for your project?
- Who, specifically, will fulfill the role for your project? Who manages them?
- Can you get the person (and his or her manager's) agreement and support to participate?
- Does this person want to be on the project? To the extent possible, take into account personal interests and motivation. Try to get those who have an interest in what the project is trying to accomplish. If they don't, realize you will need to account for additional time to get (and possibly keep) them motivated and engaged.

Managers, project managers, and program managers impact data quality work because they direct the individual contributors and practitioners actually doing the work. They assign resources, set priorities, and determine what gets funded. They ensure their people get training necessary to do their jobs. They open doors for obtaining additional help from other managers when the needs appear. These are also the people who can help a project go more smoothly because they prevent many roadblocks and handle the ones that do appear.

Table 5.10 Data Quality Project Roles

Roles	Responsibilities, Skills, Knowledge
Project sponsor	The person or group who provides the financial, human, and/or technical resources for the project. Should also show support for the project through words and actions.
Stakeholder	A person or group with an interest, involvement, or investment in or who will be impacted (positively or negatively) by the information and data quality work. Stakeholders may exert influence over the project and its deliverables. Stakeholders can be internal or external to the organization and can represent interests related to business, data, or technology. The list of stakeholders may be long or short depending on the project scope. This row is used to identify other stakeholders not included in the rows below (recognizing that every role in this table could generally be considered a stakeholder).
Project manager Scrum master Product owner	The person responsible for accomplishing the project objectives. Leads the project by initiating, planning, executing, monitoring, controlling, and closing the project, using the chosen project approach.

(Continued)

Table 5.10 Data Quality Project Roles *(Continued)*

Roles	Responsibilities, Skills, Knowledge
Business process owner Application owner Product manager	Those with accountability for the processes, applications, or products within scope of the project. Can be key stakeholders and influencers.
Data analyst Data engineer Data scientist Report developer/analyst	• Has knowledge of technology (systems/applications/databases) where data is used and stored. • Understands data structures, relationships, data/information models, and data requirements. • Has knowledge of data content within scope and related data specifications (e.g., metadata, data standards, and data requirements). • Understands industry standard languages (SQL, XML) and best practices for data store design (abstraction, normalization, etc.). • Has knowledge of data profiling and data catalogs. • Produces source-to-target mappings. • Understands or researches meaning.
Subject Matter Expert (SME) (for processes) Business analyst Business user Superuser/power user	• Understands business processes in-depth. • Has knowledge of the information that supports the processes. • Understands the business use and meaning of the data. • Understands the applications that work with the data being assessed. • Familiar with organizations, teams, roles, and responsibilities that impact the information throughout its life cycle. • Understands how data relates to processes. • Understands data definitions, including valid values and business rules.
Data stewards	In the second edition of his book, *Data Stewardship* (2020), David Plotkin outlines different types of data stewards – business data stewards and technical data stewards being the two primary types. Other variations of data stewards filling support roles are operational data stewards and project data stewards. See following lines summarizing his information for each of the types of data stewards.
Business data steward	Key representative for a specific business area or function and the data owned by that area. Responsible for quality, use, and meaning of that data in the organization. Typically knows the data, works closely with it, and knows who else to contact if there are questions.
Technical data steward	IT representatives with knowledge about how applications, data stores, and ETL (extract, transform, and load) processes work.
Operational data steward	Usually works directly with the data (e.g., inputting data), provides help and immediate feedback to the business data steward when issues with the data, including declining data quality, are found.
Project data steward	Represents data stewardship on projects, reporting back to the appropriate business data steward when data issues arise on the project or when new data must be governed.
Data modeler	• Responsible for creating and maintaining data models and data dictionary. • Has knowledge of related metadata.
Database administrator (DBA)	• Specifies, acquires, and maintains data management software. • Designs, validates, and ensures security of files or databases. • Performs day-to-day monitoring and care of the databases. • Works with the physical database design.
Developers (e.g., application, ETL, Web services, integration specialists)	• Develops programs and writes code. • Unit-tests programs and code. • Understands and develops ETL data processes to and from source systems, databases, data warehouses, data lakes, and other datastores. • Has knowledge of languages and technology related to your environment (e.g., XML, canonical models, integration programming, enterprise service bus).
Enterprise architect	• Ensures that an organization's strategic goals are optimized through enterprise data standards and technologies. • Understands architecture for the organization, business area, and/or applications within the scope of the project. • Ensures that quality and governance processes align with overall architecture for the organization.
Data architect	• Understands architecture for the organization, business area, and/or applications within the scope of the project. • Understands the nature of information management and how to effectively structure and apply data within his or her environment.
IT support	• Responsible for IT infrastructure, systems, software, network, system capacity, etc.

Project Timing, Communication, and Engagement

To close out this chapter, let's talk about timing, communication, and engagement generally, because they each have an impact when structuring any data quality project.

Data quality projects, as defined broadly in this book, are like other projects where timing is often difficult to estimate. The *assessment* aspect is what brings uncertainty into a data quality project plan. There are many opinions about the quality of the data. Only assessments show the magnitude and location of the actual data quality problems. What is learned from analyzing the information environment and assessing data quality and business impact will affect the rest of the project timeline and may change initial estimates.

Assessments often reveal more problems than those you set out to solve, and addressing root causes may involve more time or resources than you have available. Incorporating regular checkpoints throughout the project (to see results and then estimate next steps) will help you prioritize, make adjustments to the project based on what you learn, and keep your project on track.

Improvements recommended by the project will involve *change*. Change is not easy for people who have to take on new roles, learn new processes, or who now receive data that may be better but looks different. Therefore, every time changes are instituted during improvements, you should also provide a plan that includes communication, training, and documentation. These form a basis for good change management.

Most organizations have people familiar with project management, for whichever approach and SDLC are used. Fewer organizations are experienced in change management. Recruit knowledgeable people to advise you about the most effective approaches to managing the changes that will be introduced by your project. See *Step 10 – Communicate, Manage, and Engage People Throughout* for additional information.

Following are guidelines for engaging with others. Thanks to Rachel Haverstick for her assistance in describing these ideas:

Focus—Keep a tight focus on the business issue during meetings and activities. Appoint a meeting moderator who is known for his or her ability to keep the group on topic and can deflect tangential conversations with respect.

Early victories—As your first task, choose activities that have a good chance of success so that a team can report successes during the project's first few weeks.

Prepare the path—Discuss your team members' responsibilities with their individual managers. Give managers estimates of how much time you think members will spend on your project, and ask them to provide support when your team members need resources.

Spread the word—Make sure other working teams know about your project, its goals, and its status. Enable sharing of information across projects in order to foster collegiality as well as to prevent confusion and duplicated effort.

Divide and conquer—When facing a tight deadline, divide the project into several subtasks and assign them to small groups to accomplish simultaneously. Use your best judgment when dividing up the tasks—not every task in a project has to be completed at the same time. While Agile approaches do this well, this can be done with other project methodologies as well.

Celebrate—When your team has successfully completed a difficult set of tasks, give them a break and congratulate them. It will increase morale as well as help team members to perceive the project as manageable.

Chapter 5 Summary

In *Step 1.1*, you looked at the business needs and data quality issues to be addressed and finalized the project focus. The next step was to organize your work. Your starting point was *Step 1.2 – Plan the Project*. You used the instructions there along with the information here in *Chapter 5 – Structuring Your Project*.

The information in this chapter is crucial to the success of your project. You must be able to effectively identify, organize, and manage the people and activities needed to solve issues and to complete the work within your organization's environment and processes. If not done well, it is unlikely that you will be able to solve the business needs that triggered the project.

Guidance was given to help you best structure your project, as decisions are made regarding:

- Which project type applies to your data quality project. Is it a focused data quality improvement project? Are you incorporating data quality activities in another larger project? Or is this ad hoc use of a few selected data quality steps, activities, or techniques?
- Which project approach is the foundation for how the work will be carried out? Will you use a third-party or internal SDLC that is Agile, sequential, or a hybrid? Will the Ten Steps Process itself be the basis for the project plan?
- What are the project objectives and, specifically, which steps, activities, and techniques from the Ten Steps Process will be used to meet them? Pick and choose the steps that fit your situation. Any of the steps can be carried out at varying levels of detail. You make the choice as to which fits your needs.

To answer these questions and structure your project, supplement your own knowledge and experience with information from this chapter, *Chapter 2*, and *Step 1* and *Step 10* in *Chapter 4*. Make your best choices based on what you know now and make adjustments based on what is learned as the project proceeds. Structuring your project is part of the *art* of data quality. With practice you will get better and subsequent projects will go more smoothly. To keep moving forward, acquire a deeper understanding of key concepts in *Chapter 3* and execute your project using details in *Chapter 4*. The fun continues!

Other Techniques and Tools

Great things are not done by impulse,
but by a series of small things brought together.

— Vincent van Gogh

Executing Data Quality Projects. https://doi.org/10.1016/B978-0-12-818015-0.00003-7

Introduction to Chapter 6

Chapter 6 contains techniques and tools that can be applied many places in the Ten Steps Process. Return to this chapter throughout your project and as they are referenced in the book. Some of the techniques have their roots in manufacturing quality and project management and have been employed for many years in other quality efforts. Here their application to data quality is demonstrated. *Table 6.1* shows where the information in this chapter can be used as you apply the Ten Steps in *Chapter 4.*

Track Issues and Action Items

An important part of managing any project is the ability to track issues and action items. You may have a software application or other preferred method. If not, use *Template 6.1 – Action Items/Issue Tracking.* This works well in a spreadsheet format. You may have separate sheets for issues and for action items, or you can keep them together. Keep one sheet for open action items/issues and a closed sheet with the same format. Move closed items to the separate closed sheet. This will keep the open sheet clear of clutter,

Table 6.1 Where to Apply Chapter 6 Techniques	
Section in Chapter 6: Other Techniques and Tools	**Where the Information Can Be Applied in The Ten Steps**
Track Issues and Action Items	Start using in *Step 1 – Determine Business Needs and Approach.* Make it a standard practice to manage issues and action items *throughout your project*.
Analyze, Synthesize, Recommend, Document, and Act on Results	Start using in *Step 1 – Determine Business Needs and Approach.* Make it a standard practice *at the end of every step, assessment, technique, or activity* to understand the meaning of the work just completed, bring together with learnings from other activities, make initial recommendations based on what you know at that time, document properly, and act on the results when the time is right.
Design Data Capture and Assessment Plans	*Step 3 – Assess Data Quality* and *Step 4 – Assess Business Impact.* To plan the specifics of what, when, who, and how data will be captured and assessed for which data quality dimensions and which business impact techniques. This complements the instructions given in each of the substeps there.
Information Life Cycle Approaches	*Chapter 3: Key Concepts.* When learning about the concept of an Information Life Cycle and POSMAD.
	Step 1 – Determine Business Needs and Approach. Use a high-level Information Life Cycle to help determine project focus, and as input to the scope and project plan.
	Step 2 – Analyze Information Environment. To understand the Information Life Cycle in just enough detail to use in future steps.
	Step 3 – Assess Data Quality. To determine where data should be captured and assessed for quality.
	Step 4 – Assess Business Impact. To understand where in the Information Life Cycle work is happening that affects costs and revenue as input to a business impact assessment.
	Step 5 – Identify Root Causes. Use the Information Life Cycle as needed to track and trace the location of root causes.
	Step 6 – Develop Improvement Plans, Step 7 – Prevent Future Data Errors, and *Step 8 – Correct Current Data Errors.* As input to where along the life cycle preventive measure should be put into place and where data corrections should be made.
	Step 9 – Monitor Controls. To determine where in the Information Life Cycle controls should be put into place for on-going monitoring. Develop the Information Life Cycle for the on-going monitoring itself.
	Step 10 – Communicate, Manage, and Engage People Throughout. To understand where people are involved along the Information Life Cycle and the work they do as input to how to best communicate and engage with them.
Conduct a Survey	*Step 1 – Determine Business Needs and Approach*
	Step 3.1 – Perception of Relevance and Trust (as a Data Quality Dimension)
	Step 4.7 – Perception of Relevance and Trust (as a Business Impact Technique)
	Anywhere in the Ten Steps Process when gathering information in a formal way such as conducting interviews, facilitating workshops or focus groups, sending out large-scale surveys, etc.
Metrics	*Step 9 – Monitor Controls.* To implement on-going monitoring of data quality metrics.
Tools for Managing Data Quality	Reference *throughout the project.* To determine tools that can be used to augment your work.
The Ten Steps and Other Methodologies and Standards	Reference if your organization is using other methodologies (such as Six Sigma) or standards (such as ISO).

Template 6.1	Action Items/Issue Tracking							
Number	Description	Owner	Status*	Open Date	Due Date	Close Date	Comments/ Resolution
1							
2							
Etc.							

*Status Types that work well with a data quality project:
- O = Open. Item has been identified and logged, but work has not yet started.
- IP = In Progress. Item is being worked on.
- D = Done. Item has been resolved and completed.
- X = Cancelled. Item was closed without being resolved, e.g., no longer applicable.

while enabling you to have the closed items easily available to reference as needed. Add columns for other information important to you, such as priority. Of course, you must remember to use the spreadsheet. Ensure issues are being addressed and action items are being completed by regularly reviewing and updating the status.

Design Data Capture and Assessment Plans

Overview

Data capture and assessment planning are key activities for a data quality assessment where looking in-depth at the data itself, such as when profiling data in *Step 3.3 – Data Integrity Fundamentals*. For a business impact assessment, you might not need the detail outlined in a data *capture* plan, but you will still need an *assessment* plan.

Definition

Data Capture refers to how the data will be accessed or acquired for use, such as extracting data to a flat file and loading to a secure testing database or connecting directly to a reporting datastore. A **Data Capture Plan** details who will capture which data, from where, when, and by what method. This is also helpful any time a dataset needs to be captured for purposes such as a baseline/ad-hoc data quality assessment, migration, testing, reporting, or on-going data quality controls for metrics and a dashboard. A **Data Assessment Plan** is how you propose to evaluate the quality of the data and/or the business impact of the data.

Why data capture and assessment plans? Capturing the relevant data for an in-depth data quality assessment is usually more difficult than expected. Taking "just enough" time to think through how to capture and assess the data will save time, avoid rework, and prevent misunderstandings. Well thought out data capture and assessment plans can build confidence in those reviewing assessment results.

Develop your initial data capture and assessment plans at the beginning of *Step 3 – Assess Data Quality* or *Step 4 – Assess Business Impact* based on the data quality dimensions or business impact techniques within scope. Further refine and finalize your data capture and assessment plans as a first activity before assessing each dimension or using each technique. Use what you learned in

Step 2 – Analyze Information Environment. For example, knowing the information life cycle within scope helps you decide at what points to capture data for a data quality assessment. See the *Ten Steps in Action callout box* at the end of this section for an example.

Data Capture

Data capture refers to extracting, accessing, or acquiring data. Methods of data capture include extracting data to a flat file and loading to a secure testing database, connecting directly to a reporting datastore, or accessing data from a third-party vendor and loading to a secure landing area until ready for assessment. A data capture plan details how, when, where, and by whom the data will be acquired. It is helpful *any* time a set of data is needed for such purposes as:

- A first data quality assessment to set a baseline
- Any ad-hoc data quality assessment
- When monitoring data quality controls such as metrics and a dashboard
- When migrating data from a source to a target datastore
- When a particular dataset is needed for testing
- When a specific dataset is needed for reporting purposes
- To capture data to be corrected

Use *Template 6.2* when developing your data capture plan. The template provides a checklist for ensuring the data desired will be captured correctly for any of the reasons just listed. Capturing the data to be assessed for quality is often more problematic than expected. Adequate preparation will save time, prevent errors, and ensure that the data captured is actually the data you expected and is relevant to the business needs and project objectives. The time spent thoughtfully developing a data capture plan is minimal compared to the time it takes if you hastily extract data only to find the data was not what you wanted, requiring you to extract again and again. Communication comes into play if you have to go through a management chain to get permission to access the data.

Even if you have thoughtfully planned how to capture the data, be sure to document that plan! I learned this first-hand with one project. We had a meeting with the project team and technical resources to agree on the details for the data capture. However, we failed to document the process and decisions in an email. The first data extract did not contain what was expected, yet those who did it felt the data was captured according to their understanding.

Template 6.2 Data Capture Plan

Topic	Description	Describe for Your Project
Datastore	The datastore(s), application(s), or system(s) where the data of interest resides. Identify information below for each datastore, application, or system where data will be captured.	
Population Description	In plain language, define the population to be captured. This allows: 1) Non-technical people to discuss and understand the data to be assessed, and 2) Provides a basis for the selection criteria when capturing the data to be assessed. Consider the following: • Describe the type of records to be extracted in business language. For instance, assume the population to be assessed is "Active customers" or "Active Customers who have purchased products in the last year" or "Records for products currently available for sale today in France and Germany." • Include any time considerations such as when the record was created or last updated. For example, "The last 1000 records created by the customer support team, along with the date/time stamps" or "All records created in the last month."	
Selection Criteria	Consider the following for each specific datastore when selecting the population to be captured. • You may be particularly interested in CDEs, or critical data elements, that have been prioritized. Caution: When looking at CDEs for the first time include other fields in the same records that might be less important to you, but that should be seen because they provide context to help you understand the CDEs. This wider view will also help refine the selection criteria or confirm the criteria used the first time. • List exact table and field names (you may even include SQL statements). For example, determine how "Active Customers" are identified in the system. If the application has a flag designating that population, then the extract is relatively simple. Often the criteria are not so straightforward. The selection criteria may be more complex, such as "Active Customers" equals "All customer records where the central delete flag in ABC table = blank AND the reference server flag in SUB table = blank." • Consider the age of the records of interest by looking at insert, create, or update dates or history/journal/audit tables. • Consider the data model. How do the relationships affect the data to be extracted? For example, do you want site data and associated contacts or contacts with associated sites?	
Method of Data Capture	Include the data access method and output format, along with tools required. For example: • Use front-end application interface to select the data. • Extract from production database (and put into Access database). • Direct-connect to the reporting database (where data is the same as the production database, except for 12 hours delay). • Extract to a flat file (e.g., csv or xml format). • Extract to tables (e.g., to tables in secure staging area). • Direct-connect to a production database. (Warning! I don't recommend this because of impacts on production performance, but I have been told by a few people that this approach has been used successfully.) • Copy production data into the application test environment. (Also a caution since test environments by nature are always changing. It is better to put data into a controlled environment while completing the assessment.)	
Additional Data Elements or Tables	Identify additional data elements or tables to be captured that may not be tested for quality themselves but are needed for: • **Reference.** Code descriptions, associated reference tables • **Identification.** Unique record identifiers, cross-reference identifiers • **Analysis.** Last update date, grouped by certain codes • **Reporting.** By certain categories such as sales reps or geographic territories • **Root cause analysis.** Who created, updated, or deleted the record and when	
Sampling	The sampling method to be used, if and when sampling is needed. Important: Involve someone experienced in statistics to ensure your sampling methods are valid! Ensure there is no bias of any kind introduced when capturing the records.	

Template 6.2 Data Capture Plan *(Continued)*

Topic	Description	Describe for Your Project
Estimated Number of Tables and Records	Knowing the approximate number of tables and records can help provide an estimate for: 1) the space required to store the data during the assessment, and 2) the amount of work and time to assess the data.	
Timing	Identify when the data will be captured. Consider the following: • Any update schedules and production calendars. Time the data capture when it will have the least impact on a production system. • If capturing the same data in multiple systems, carefully coordinate the capture as the data moves through the information life cycle. • If receiving data from an external source, use the most recent possible. In one project an external file was sent quarterly. The next file was due in two weeks. We decided to delay the assessment until the next file came in so we could assess up-to-date data, not data that was over 2 months old. • You will be taking a snapshot in time when you capture the data. Plan to conduct your assessment as soon after the capture as possible.	
Responsibilities	Discuss, agree on, and document: • The specific data capture tasks. • Who will perform the tasks. • Any special knowledge, skills, experience, access authority, or logins to the data required. • When each task will be completed. • The sequence of activities to capture the data.	

Obviously, there was a miscommunication because the details had not been written down – we depended on the discussion in the planning meeting and each person's memory of it. Another meeting was held, details emailed, and then confirmed by each person. The next extract was completed successfully. But we lost more than a week in the process.

Verify the data capture specifications were met *after* capturing the data and *before* a full assessment, i.e., does the dataset reflect the desired population? Was the data captured at the right time, in the needed output format, and copied to the right location?

Sampling Method

In some cases, the entire population of interest can be assessed. Your entire population could be as small as the last 100 records created (where data is manually assessed). It could be as large as all active customers worldwide (where an automated data profiling tool is used to assess Data Integrity Fundamentals) and the entire population of records will be captured.

In other cases, a sample of the population has to be taken. Sampling is the use of a part of a set to determine the characteristics of an entire set. It is a technique in which representative members (e.g., records) of a population are selected for testing. Sampling is done when it is too expensive or time consuming to conduct an assessment on the total population of interest, such as when assessing accuracy by manually comparing to an authoritative source. The sampling method used must ensure the sample records to be assessed is a valid representation of the whole population of interest.

After capturing a valid sample, the assessment is completed against that sample. The results are then inferred to be representative of the population as a whole. That means for a data quality assessment, the results of the sampled records approximate

the data quality of the entire record population. There are two characteristics of a sample that determine how well it represents the population:

• **Size**. The minimum required number of records that need to be checked and completed in order to provide statistically valid results for the population.
• **Stability**. If a sample size produces a certain result, and then if the sample size is increased and the same results are produced, the sample has stability.

There are different sampling methods, but random sampling is very common. Random means that every member of the population (in this case every record) has an equal chance of being chosen to be part of the sample. Ensure both the target population and sampling method do not inadvertently reflect bias. That is, the target population and the subset obtained through the sample method do not leave out populations that should be accounted for.

 Warning

Ensure your sampling methods are valid! You may have access to a statistics team within your organization, a software quality assurance group with best practices for sampling, actuaries or data scientists who use statistics as part of their jobs. Ensure no bias is introduced where some members of the intended population are less likely to be included than others. You want the results of your survey to be valid and able to be generalized to the rest of the population.

Data Assessment Plan

For data quality, developing the data assessment plan assumes: 1) the data has been captured according to the data capture plan, and 2) the data to be assessed for quality is in a secure location available to the project team. For a data quality assessment, the data capture plan might be combined with the assessment plan. For a business impact assessment, often no detailed data is captured and so your focus would be on the assessment plan.

Definition

A **Data Assessment Plan** outlines how the quality of the data and/ or the business impact of the data will be evaluated.

See *Template 6.3 – Data Assessment Plan*. To identify the data assessment tasks, reference the instructions for the data quality dimensions or business impact techniques within scope of your project from *Steps 3* and *4* in *Chapter 4*. List the tasks in Column 1 and complete the remaining columns. Be sure to account for any tools that will be used in the assessments. See *Tools for Managing Data Quality* further in this chapter.

The division of responsibilities and people with the right skills and knowledge are important to the success of your assessment. Some assessment plans will be relatively simple with all the work being done by one or two people, while others will require coordination with several people. Either way, taking "just enough" time on an assessment plan is worthwhile. Develop the sequence of the assessment tasks, document, and ensure those involved are aware of and agree to their responsibilities. Don't forget the managers of those who will be doing the work. Your assessment will run much more effectively and efficiently than it would if planning was ignored.

Let's use an example of an assessment using *Step 3.3 – Data Integrity Fundamentals* where a data profiling tool is used that requires human intervention. Most tool vendors claim that their data profiling tool is easy enough to be used by anyone from the business. However, technical expertise is often needed to load the data into the profiling tool or point the tool to the desired dataset. Someone from the Information Technology group may have the passwords and access to capture the data. A project

team member with data experience may be able to run the tool, but who has the knowledge to analyze the results? How the specific tasks are delineated and assigned depends on the tool's ease-of-use, specific skills and knowledge of the individuals, and the time they have available. Consider the following sample tasks for a Data Integrity Fundamentals assessment using a data profiling tool:

- Capture the data to be assessed. This assumes the data has been acquired according to the data capture plan and is in a secure location available to the project team.
- Load data into tool or point the tool to the dataset.
- Run the tool.
- Review and analyze results. Possible options:
  - Data analyst (possibly with a technical expert) does preliminary analysis of results and facilitates a review session with the business expert, looking at the results from within the tool.
  - Data analyst prepares report with the results and facilitates a review session with the business expert.
  - Business experts review and analyze results themselves from within the tool.
  - Data and/or technical experts prepare report with the results and emails to the business expert asking for feedback. I do not recommend this approach, but it is an option. Good analysis requires context and discussion between someone on the project team and the subject matter experts to be most successful. If this option is chosen, the business expert must be fully informed about what is expected and why.
- Highlight issues found and capture questions and comments. This must be done for all options. Some tools have the functionality to document these within the tool.
- Synthesize results with results from other assessments.
- Make specific recommendations based on what you have learned.
- Document this step.
- Assign action items and determine next steps.
- See *Using Results – Analyze, Synthesize, Recommend, Document, and Act* in this chapter.

Template 6.3	Data Assessment Plan				
1	2	3	4	5	6
Data Assessment Task	Task Description	Who is Involved	Nature of Involvement (Accountable, Responsible, Consult, Inform)	Knowledge/ Skills/ Experience/ Access to the Data Needed	When the Task Will Be Performed

Ten Steps in Action

Data Capture and Assessment Plans – For Customer Master Data Quality Project

Business Need—One company had a database with customer master records that were used by marketing for planning, sales operations

for targeting, and product teams as a seed universe for new product releases, among other uses. There was concern about the quality of the data that supported these business uses. The core data quality project team consisted of Mehmet Orun, Wonna Mark, Sonja Bock, Dee Dee Lozier, Kathryn Chan, Margaret Capriles, and Danette McGilvray.

Ten Steps in Action *(Continued)*

Input to Plans—A context diagram was created in *Step 1 – Determine Business Needs and Approach.* It was further refined in *Step 2 – Analyze Information Environment.* The visual became the high-level information life cycle which was referenced throughout the project and used to develop the data capture and assessment plans. Two data quality dimensions were within scope: 1) Data Integrity Fundamentals, using the technique of data profiling, and 2) Consistency and Synchronization since data was profiled and compared in more than one datastore along the information life cycle path.

Benefits—Confidence in assessment results was helped in part because: 1) it was clear the actual data assessed was the data related to the business needs and project objectives, and 2) the assessments themselves were well planned and executed. Benefits from the project as a whole included focused data clean-up on known problems and process improvements as a way to prevent future issues.

Data Capture Plan—Three data sources (one internal and two external) were chosen to be within scope of the project. *Figure 6.1* shows the high-level information life cycle, with the datastores in each of the environments where the data flowed: Source to Stage 1 to Landing to Stage 2 to the Customer Master. The information life cycle is completed by listing current and potential future uses underneath the flow. These uses represent the Apply phase of POSMAD.

The data capture plan was carefully designed so data was extracted from all environments at the same time as the data flowed, with some to be assessed immediately and others to be set aside for later use. The data was then placed in separate, secure environments where the data would not change while the assessment was completed. Three of the environments (Source, Stage 1, and the Customer Master – indicated by dark arrows with a pattern) were profiled using a data profiling tool the company had recently purchased. Data in the Landing and Stage 2 environments was not assessed immediately; instead, it was saved in case it was needed later for root cause analysis.

Data Assessment Plan—Work was divided into "workstreams," which were logically grouped by data sources (A, B, C) or types of tables in the customer master environment (D, E). The workstreams are indicated by the small boxes with letters in *Figure 6.1*. They are also shown in *Figure 6.2*, which outlines the division of responsibilities for assessing the data within each workstream. Workstreams A, B, and C profiled their assigned data within the Source and Stage 1 environments and then compared results between the two. Within the Customer Master Environment, Workstreams D and E profiled their assigned tables, then compared between tables. The team determined the level of detail for profiling and analysis based on needs, resources, and time available. Analysis was done within each workstream before synthesizing results across all workstreams. This plan does not show the tools used.

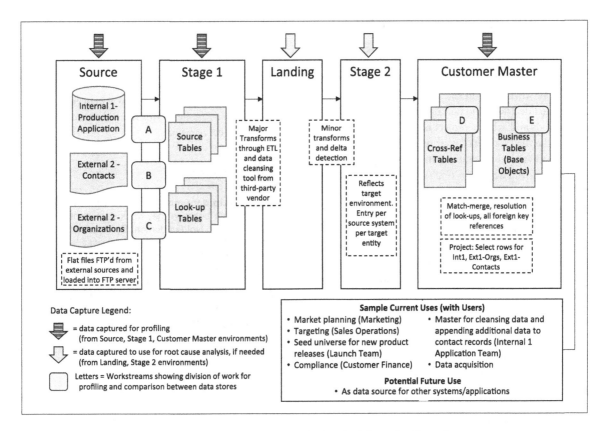

Figure 6.1 Example data capture and assessment plan visual using the information life cycle.

(Continued)

Ten Steps in Action (Continued)

Workstream	Responsible for:	Source Environment	Stage 1 Environment	Compare
A	Internal 1 Production Application	Profile Int1 App Table	Ext1 Org Table conduct: 1. Detailed column profiling 2. Single table structural profiling	Source to Stage 1: 3. Cross table analysis. Drill down only if differences
B	External 2 Contacts	Profile Ext2 Contact File	Ext2 Contact Table conduct: 1. Detailed column profiling 2. Single table structural profiling	Source to Stage 1: 3. Cross table analysis. Drill down only if differences
C	External 2 Organizations	Profile Ext2 Org File	Ext2 Org Table conduct: 1. Detailed column profiling 2. Single table structural profiling	Source to Stage 1: 3. Cross table analysis. Drill down only if differences

Workstream	Responsible for:	Customer Master Environment		Compare
D	Business Tables (Base Objects)	Business Tables (Base Objects): 1. Detailed column profiling 2. Single table structural profiling		Across Business Tables: 3. Cross table analysis.
E	Cross Reference Tables	Cross Reference Tables: 1. Detailed column profiling 2. Single table structural profiling		Across X-Ref Tables: 3. Cross table analysis.

Figure 6.2 Example data quality assessment plan.

Analyze, Synthesize, Recommend, Document, and Act on Results

Business Benefit and Context

Remember that all work done in the Ten Steps Process is to help you make informed decisions and take effective action – so you can meet business needs and achieve project objectives. This technique will help you make the best use of your work by providing a disciplined approach to analyzing, synthesizing, making recommendations, documenting, and acting on results. Start tracking results at the beginning of the project and continue with each step, assessment, technique, and activity.

Analyze means you evaluate and carefully examine the results of any one step, assessment, technique, or activity. **Synthesize** means to do the same thing looking at results from two or more of them. When analyzing, you look at a result and break it down into its constituent parts. When synthesizing, you bring together the multiple results and their parts to look for broader relationships, patterns, and connections to form better solutions. If multiple assessments are conducted at the same time, be sure to synthesize results by evaluating and interpreting them together. Without this broader view you run the risk of developing solutions that optimize one area while negatively impacting another – and you may not even know it. The best solutions will positively impact all parts and will have no negative impact, or at least they will minimize the negative impact if all cannot benefit from the solution. Remember that everything done in the project has some purpose and is leading you to make informed decisions and take effective action – about your data, about the project, about the business needs and project objectives.

Keep a running list of results (see *Template 6.4 – Analyze and Document Results*). Add to it anytime important observations are made. Make initial recommendations from what you know at each point in time. Modify those recommendations as you learn more. Document decisions and take action when the time is right. Bring this information to milestone meetings so you have the right input to make solid decisions. Document it all! Use these practices throughout your project, such as whenever you conduct a survey, complete an assessment, finish a milestone meeting, and make important project decisions.

 Warning

Do not skip documenting! Too many times people do not want to document because they think documentation is just a piece of paper or a file. No! Fundamentally, documentation is proof of work accomplished: what happened, what was learned, and what action was or will be taken. The output of your assessments, this visible proof of work, comes in the form of artifacts which themselves take many forms – issues/action item logs, mappings, tables, presentations, documents, spreadsheets, process flows, graphics, etc. The act of documenting – organizing and capturing your results – increases your understanding, and often leads to further analysis. Organize and store artifacts in a file structure that is logical and makes them easy to find again later. Documenting can also be as easy as capturing those "ah-ha" moments when the team is having a productive analysis session.

You will be questioned! Take a structured approach to analyzing, synthesizing, making recommendations, documenting, and acting on results. Being disciplined from the beginning saves time in every step of the project, avoids rework, ensures the right information is available when making decisions, and overall helps make the best use of your work. It prevents rework when the time comes to identify root causes and develop improvement plans. It also engenders confidence in your work because, when questioned, you can provide information that gives context for the recommendations made and actions taken. And you *will* be questioned or even challenged!

Template 6.4	Analyze and Document Results				
Step/ Assessment/ Technique/ Activity	Key Observations/ Lessons Learned/ Issues Uncovered/ Positive Discoveries	Known or Probable Impact (qualitative and/or quantitative; to revenue, costs, risks, business, people/org, technology, other data and information, etc.)	Potential Root Causes	Initial Recommendations	Action / Follow-up/ Open Questions

As needed, add separate worksheets with detail for line items above or indicate filenames where details can be found.				
Add a separate worksheet with list of final or almost-final recommendations, categorize and prioritize as needed.				
Number	Recommendation	Category	Notes	Priority
1				
2				
3				

Approach

Use the following approach to help analyze results after completing a step, data quality or business impact assessment, technique, or key activity.

1. Prepare for the analysis.

Be able to answer the following questions. This places the results to be analyzed in the appropriate context.

- What did we measure?
- How did we measure it? (include who measured it and when measurements were taken)
- Why did we measure it?
- What assumptions were used?

2. Format your results in a way that enhances understanding and is conducive to analysis.

Appropriate visualization of data is essential to understanding the data yourself and also communicating with others. How to create effective data visuals and communicate about data is outside the scope of this book, but several sources to help are readily available. See the section Visualization and Presentation further in this chapter.

- It is often easier to analyze results that are displayed visually, in graphs and charts, than it is to understand data presented in a large spreadsheet with many columns and rows.
- Be clear about what you are graphing – is it a fact (e.g., a city field has a completeness/fill rate of 99 percent) or an observation (e.g., by glancing through the records, you see what seems to be a high number of universities in the customer file).
- Keep visible any assumptions made while conducting the tests.

3. Conduct the analysis.

Carefully review and discuss the assessment results. You may be analyzing broadly across many datastores or deep within a focused data set. Consider the following ideas, which are adapted from and used with permission of AMACOM Books, Michael J. Spendolini, *The Benchmarking Book* (AMACOM, 1992), pp. 172–174.

Quote to Remember

"At their best, graphics are instruments for reasoning about quantitative information. Often the most effective way to describe, explore, and summarize a set of numbers – even a very large set – is to look at pictures of those numbers. Furthermore, of all methods for analyzing and communicating statistical information, well-designed data graphics are usually the simplest and at the same time the most powerful."

– *Edward R. Tufte, The Visual Display of Quantitative Information, Second edition, (2001)*

Identify patterns or trends—This is one of the most basic forms of analysis.

Check for misinformation—This is information that is incorrect because of factors such as misinterpretation, improper recording, purposeful misrepresentation, and errors. Look for the following clues:

- Does the information deviate significantly from what was expected or from other data that should be comparable?
- Are there conflicting data from multiple sources (e.g., information collected on the same subject by different members of the team)? Major discrepancies should be investigated.

Identify omissions or displacement—What is not present can often be as significant as what is. Omissions are missing data that should be available. Displacement involves significant changes in data trends without an explanation.

Check out-of-place information—Some information won't seem to "fit" with respect to other information, or it may deviate noticeably from the information you thought you would find.

Compare actual results to targets or requirements—Ask:

- Are there differences (either higher or lower)?
- Is there an explanation for the differences (e.g., targets were off due to unknowns at the time targets were set)?
- Are the differences in key data or less critical data?

Ask questions—Such as the following:

- Are there any immediately visible red flags or issues?
- Are there any possible causes and effects?
- What impact could these findings have on the business? It is always important to answer this question in as much detail as possible – even if the answers are qualitative, not quantitative.
- Is there a need for more information about business impact? If yes, see *Step 4 – Assess Business Impact*.
- Does additional information need to be gathered or do additional tests need to be conducted?
- Is this step considered complete for now?

Capture Reactions—Responses to the results:

- What are the team members' reactions to the results?
- What are reactions to the results from Subject Matter Experts, analysts, other users or individual contributors?
- What is management's reaction to the results?
- What results were expected?
- What results were surprises?

4. Repeat analysis as needed against other individual steps, assessments, techniques, or activities.

Recommendations resulting from individual assessments should be considered preliminary. Once all tests have been completed, they will be synthesized and finalized.

5. Synthesize the analysis and results from multiple steps, assessments, techniques, or activities.

Combine and analyze the results from all work done prior to this point. Use the same questions listed above when synthesizing results from more than one assessment. See *Template 6.4* and instructions in the *Sample Output and Templates* section below for additional questions. Look for correlations among them. For example, if you surveyed the users' perceptions of data quality, do those perceptions match the actual quality results from other dimensions assessed? Interpret the combined results and tie them into the original business needs.

Don't limit the synthesis to just other assessments in the project. Include other findings such as a report run by another team that includes pertinent information or a recent company announcement of a change in strategy that affects your project.

6. Complete any follow-up needed to understand the results.

Analysis and synthesis usually raise additional questions. You may want more detail about data already assessed, bring in related data not yet assessed, or talk with additional people.

7. Draw conclusions and make recommendations.

It can be a challenge to make logical comparisons and draw reasonable conclusions. Give yourself time to rest from the detail and then review again before finalizing the recommendations. Recommendations may include an action that should be taken immediately because something critical and unexpected was found. Recommendations can be a list of business rules or data quality

Best Practice

Avoid Scope Creep. You will learn many interesting things throughout your data quality project. You or the team can find yourselves spending much time following various leads to solve your data quality "crime." Some will be relevant to the project, some not. In one project, any team member at any time could ask the question, "Are we going down a rat hole?" This was the cue for the team to look at the additional details we were researching. We briefly revisited the project charter with the business needs and project objectives, then discussed the following questions:

- Will additional detail have a significant and demonstrable bearing on the business needs or project objectives?
- Will the detail provide evidence to prove or disprove a hypothesis about the quality or value of the data?

By doing so we prevented unwanted scope creep. When we *did* need to do additional work, it was a conscious decision made because we felt the extra time and effort would help the project.

Avoiding scope creep is an example of using your judgement and applying the "just enough" principle.

checks that should be considered for on-going monitoring of controls in a later step.

Recommendations may be considered preliminary until further information is known. Any investment in assessing data quality will yield valuable results, but the long-term benefit will only be realized when the root causes of the issues found during the assessment have been addressed. Include root cause analysis and preventive measures in your recommendations. Update existing recommendations and add new ones based on what else has been learned to that point.

8. Summarize and document output of the analysis and synthesis.

Use *Template 6.4* or something equivalent. Ensure that you have analyzed, made initial recommendations, and completed documentation whenever you conduct a survey, complete a step, assessment, technique or major activity, or meet a critical milestone in the project plan.

9. Take action when the time is right.

Take appropriate action on the recommendations when the time is right. Some recommendations should be implemented as quickly as possible and may be fairly easy to accomplish. If so, work them into your project plan now. Others should wait until all assessments and root cause analysis are done in order to get a more complete picture of the situation and ensure the improvements put into place are the right improvements. As at many places in the methodology, the timing of actions is about balance and good judgement. Don't drag your feet if it is clear something needs to be done now. On the other hand, do not fall into the "Ready, Fire, Aim" syndrome.

Sample Output and Templates

Reference *Template 6.4 – Analyze and Document Results*. Not only does it provide a format for documenting results, but answering these questions also further deepens your analysis and synthesis.

It can provide a checklist to see if you have thoroughly completed your step, assessment, technique, or activity. Discuss and document your answers to the following questions:

- Which step, assessment, technique, or activity was completed or is being discussed?
- What were your key observations?
- What lessons were learned?
- What issues were uncovered?
- What positive discoveries were made?
- What known or probable impacts were found? These can be qualitative and or quantitative impacts to revenue, costs, risk, the business, people/organizations (the organization as a whole, specific teams or individual people, suppliers, customers, business partners), processes, technology, quality of other data and information, etc.
- What potential root causes can you already see?
- Are there any initial recommendations you can formulate?
- What are your next steps? Is there follow-up needed? Any open questions? What needs to be done to address what you found during the analysis and synthesis and keep the project moving forward?

Be clear on specific action items, along with owners and due dates. Items in the last column can be entered into whatever method is being used to track issues and action items (such as *Template 6.1* earlier in this chapter) where details on owners, dues dates, etc. can be managed.

For any of the questions, it may be worthwhile to note which were expected and which were surprises. This is helpful when presenting results to management: "As expected, this issue was verified by the assessment. The resources to address this are known and available." or "This came as a surprise to the team. It is critical to address now and is something we did not anticipate. We recommend 4 additional resources will be needed for the next 2 weeks."

Additional details for each line item can be kept on a separate worksheet in the same file or list separate filenames where the detail can be found.

Add a separate worksheet with a list of final or almost-final recommendations. Categorize and prioritize as needed. For example, you may want to create a category for specific business rules or data quality checks that should be monitored on-going. Documenting these throughout the project will make it much easier to put into place when you get to *Step 9 – Monitor Controls*.

Figure 6.3 shows an example of how the template could be used when analyzing and documenting results. Note that information is known in some cases and not in others. As you continue through the project, you may uncover additional information to help you further understand earlier results.

Information Life Cycle Approaches

This section outlines four approaches for representing an information life cycle: Swim Lane, SIPOC, IP Map, and Table. It supplements the details in *Step 2.6 – Understand Relevant Information Life Cycle* in *Chapter 4: The Ten Steps Process*. For an introduction to the life cycle and POSMAD see *Chapter 3: Key Concepts*.

You may be familiar with data flow diagrams or business process flows. These can also show, or be used to document, an information life cycle. No matter how you choose to visualize it, remember the goal is to understand the interaction between the key components of data, processes, people/organizations, and technology throughout the life cycle of your data and information. Use "life cycle thinking" to: 1) recognize these key components in whatever graphics or documentation that already exist in your organization, 2) assess what is missing as it relates to the information life cycle, and 3) compile input to root cause analysis and improvements (prevention, correction, detection). Use available documentation and knowledge as you define the life cycle. Supplement what is already on hand with additional research.

The Swim Lane Approach

The information life cycle (or portions of it) are often illustrated using a flowchart, which is a graphical representation of a process. Flow charts can take different forms – horizontal, vertical, and at different levels of detail. Examples of flowcharts include process flows, process maps, flow diagrams, and data flow diagrams (graphical representations of information as it flows).

I particularly like using the swim lane method for visually representing the information life cycle. A swim lane is a type of process flow diagram that divides processes, tasks, workstreams, roles, etc., into lanes either horizontally or vertically. This method has held the test of time and was made popular in Geary Rummler and Alan Brache's 1990 book, *Improving Performance: How to Manage the White Space on the Organization Chart* (third edition, 2013). The swim lane approach can be used to show an at-a-glance view of the four key components (data, processes, people/organizations, and technology) as they appear throughout the life cycle phases. Remember POSMAD – Plan, Obtain, Store and Share, Maintain, Apply, and Dispose:

- **Data**. The subject of the graphic itself, e.g., life cycle for supplier master data
- **Processes**. Steps in the process are placed in the swim lanes using appropriate symbols with arrows between them indicating the flow of the process
- **People/Organizations.** Individual swim lanes indicate organizations, teams, or roles
- **Technology.** Can be shown in its own swim lane, often in the middle to show interactions between the process steps and the technology.

Decide which of the POSMAD phases and key components are within scope and the level of detail needed to move your project forward. If you are not sure what level of detail is needed, start at a high level and only go into more detail if you think the detail will give you important information needed at this point in time. *Template 6.5* shows a swim lane template with a horizontal orientation.

Swim lanes can also be vertical as illustrated in *Template 6.6*. This often works well at an organizational level, with each lane showing activities in the information life cycle under the control of a particular organizational unit and the relationship between them.

Step/Assessment/ Technique/Activity	Key Observations/ Lessons Learned/ Issues Uncovered/ Positive Discoveries	Known or Probable Impact	Potential Root Causes	Initial Recommendations	Action/Follow-up/Open Questions
From Step 2 – Analyze Information Environment					
Interactions between people/org, process, and data	Discovered Team A, thought to have read-only access to customer records, is actually creating customer records in Application 1.	Highly likely that the data being created by Team A will not be consistent with the same data being created by other teams. Credit team pulls data from both Applications 1 and 2. When data differs, does not know which data to use when deciding amount of credit to extend to customer.	Team A has had no training on data entry or standards. This appears to adversely affect the quality of the customer records.	Need to assess the organizational structure, roles, and responsibilities to understand data entry roles in Team A. If this team is duplicating data entry work done by other teams, determine if shift in people or responsibilities is needed. Either way, may need to train all data entry teams on how to enter data according to standards and why it is important. Data analyst will be able to use learnings from this step to create draft of data entry training.	When assessing data quality in Step 3, determine if quality of records created by Team A differs from those created by Team B. Originally planned to only profile customer data created by Team A in Application 1. Now also profile data created by Team B in Application 2 and compare. This adds data quality dimension of consistency and synchronization to project scope and will increase time. Data quality team lead to get agreement from Team B manager; obtain approval for increased scope from project sponsor.
Step 2.1 Understand Relevant Requirements and Constraints	Discovered that Legal has well-defined requirements for some of the data which will be assessed for quality.				Obtain agreement to have a subject matter expert (SME) from Legal review data quality assessment results. Have project team data analyst look at legal requirements and convert them into data rules that can be tested for compliance and included in data entry training.
Step 2.2 Understand Relevant Data and Data Specifications	Discovered that two teams are maintaining conflicting data models for the same entities.	The same data from the two applications will most likely not be consistent. This can cause confusion for users of the data.			Compare data from Application 1 and Application 2 to understand extent of the problem. Involve the data modelers from the two teams.
From Step 3 – Assess Data Quality					
Step 3.3 Data Integrity Fundamentals – completeness/ fill rate	The parent organization ID number has a lower fill rate than expected.	We think the fill rate is not low enough to be critical.			Is it really a low fill rate or are they stand-alone companies that don't have parent organization IDs? Have data analyst check with SME.
Step 3.3 Data Integrity Fundamentals – consistency	Inconsistencies between country code and country name were found in 30% of the records.	What is the impact to reports?			Understand the impact to reports before determining correction and prevention needed.

Figure 6.3 Example of analyzing and documenting results.

Template 6.5 Information Life Cycle Template – Swim Lane – Horizontal	
Title:	Data/Information:
Project:	Processes:
Created by:	People/Organizations:
Date:	Technology:
Role A	
Role B	
Technology	
Role C	
Role D	

Template 6.6 Information Life Cycle Template – Swim Lane – Vertical					
Title:			Data/Information:		
Project:			Processes:		
Created by:			People/Organizations:		
Date:			Technology:		
Business Unit 1	Business Unit 2	Business Unit 3	Business Unit 4	Business Unit 5	Business Unit 6

Figure 6.4 contains a list of symbols often used in flowcharts, along with their definitions. The symbols here are enough to get you started with almost any information life cycle.

Figure 6.5 shows a high-level information life cycle for a supplier master record using the swim lane approach. It begins with the initial request to create the master record, proceeds through several process steps, and ends with three main uses of the supplier master record: to order supplies, pay vendors, and reimburse employees for expenses.

Examination of the supplier master information life cycle uncovers things that don't make sense, such as the last swim lane where one of the uses is to reimburse employees. In order for employees to receive reimbursements for travel expenses, they had to be set up with a supplier master record. You might say "That is strange!" But it was the process at the time. Expect to find many things that seem unusual or cumbersome. Processes and technology evolve over time and workarounds are created in response to business changes. *Figure 6.5* is the current ("as-is") information life cycle. Seeing the current information life cycle can highlight duplicate effort and give clues to root causes of poor-quality data, which then informs improvements to those processes. Use the same swim lane approach to develop a more efficient future ("to-be") information life cycle.

SIPOC

A SIPOC diagram is often used in process management and improvement (such as Six Sigma and lean manufacturing) to show major activities in a business process. It is useful for a higher level, at-a-glance view of a process. It can also be used to visualize an information life cycle. SIPOC stands for Supplier-Input-Process-Output-Customer. Supplier indicates the people or organizations that provide information, material or other resources involved in the process. Inputs are the information or materials provided by the suppliers to the process. Process refers to the steps that transform, and hopefully add value, to the inputs. Outputs are what are used by the customer, such as a product, service, or information. Customer refers to people, organizations (internal or external), or other processes that receive the output from the process. Key requirements can also be added to this model. SIPOC can set the boundaries for more detailed process maps if they are needed. *Template 6.7* shows a template for the SIPOC technique.

Information Product Map (IP Map)

An Information Product Map (IP Map) is another approach to visualizing an information life cycle. According to Christopher Heien, CEO and Founder of IQOLab, a software and research consultancy, it represents data and processes throughout an Information

Flowchart Symbol	Description
Activity	Indicates an activity or a task in the process. This symbol can also be used when no other symbol is suitable. A brief title or short description of the activity is included in the rectangle.
Process Flow	Indicates the flow or direction of the process.
Decision Point	Indicates a point in the process where a decision is necessary. The outputs from the diamond are usually marked with options (e.g., Yes or No, True or False, or another required decision). The flow from the diamond proceeds in the direction of the option chosen (the decision). The resulting activities vary based on the decision.
Data	Indicates an electronic file.
Datastore	Indicates where the information is retrieved from or placed in a datastore, such as a database.
Document or Report / Multiple Documents	Indicates information captured as documentation or reports (e.g., hardcopy forms, written reports, computer printouts).
Terminator	Indicates the beginning and end points of a flowchart.
Con-nector	Used when there is a break or jump in the flowchart by placing a letter or number inside the circle to show where it is continued on the same page or a different page.
Inspection	Indicates an inspection activity where the process flow has stopped and the quality of the output is evaluated. The person who performed the previous activity does not normally perform the inspection. It can also designate when an approval signature is required.
Annotation	Used to note additional information about the symbol to which it is connected. A dotted line connects the open rectangle to the flowchart symbol so that it will not be confused with a solid line arrow that indicates the process flow.
I/O	Inputs to a process and outputs from a process.

Figure 6.4 Common flowchart symbols.

Manufacturing System (IMS) to manufacture Information Products (IP). The input is a Data Unit (DU), which is a conceptual grouping of data as it flows through the system. The IMS is the series of processes followed to create information from data. The IP is the final form of the data before it reaches a customer – meaning whoever uses or consumes the information. An IP can be a report, a transaction (such as a sales order, invoice, claim, service request), or it can take other forms (such as a PowerPoint presentation, audio file, graphic, or text). Still considered an emerging model, an IP Map is used to document IMSs and to simulate the flow of data while tracking DU cost, quality, and net value. It does not necessarily show a physical data flow (though it might), and it can represent a perceived understanding of the data flow. *Figure 6.6* shows a fundamental representation of an IMS as an IP Map, along with representations showing divisions by stakeholder roles or by SIPOC grouping.

As an example, an IP Map can be used to show what happens with data related to a delivery. IP Consumer 1 might be the delivery driver who needs information to deliver a package. The value of the Information Product to the delivery driver is that the delivery is completed successfully, and the driver will be paid. Consumer 2 might be the customer who gets information about the delivery date and time, with the value being customer satisfaction and increasing the chances of being a repeat customer. Consumer 3 could be an analyst in the Business Intelligence group who uses the delivery information to create a report and is trying to determine how to deliver packages faster. Each handoff of the Information Product to a Consumer has costs but also should bring value. Understanding

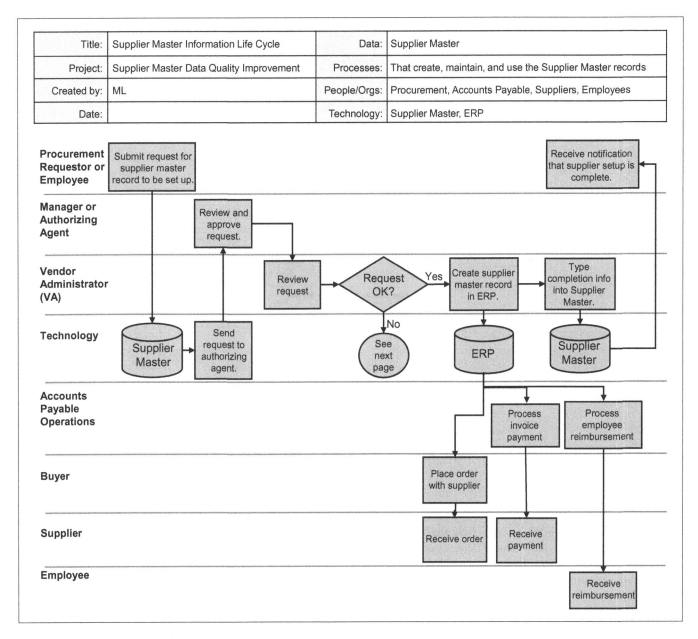

Title:	Supplier Master Information Life Cycle	Data:	Supplier Master
Project:	Supplier Master Data Quality Improvement	Processes:	That create, maintain, and use the Supplier Master records
Created by:	ML	People/Orgs:	Procurement, Accounts Payable, Suppliers, Employees
Date:		Technology:	Supplier Master, ERP

Figure 6.5 Information Life Cycle example using horizontal swim lane approach.

Template 6.7	Information Life Cycle Template – SIPOC				
Title:			Information/Data:		
Project:			Processes:		
Created by:			People/Organizations:		
Date:			Technology:		
Supplier	Input / Requirements	Process	Output / Requirements	Customer	Notes

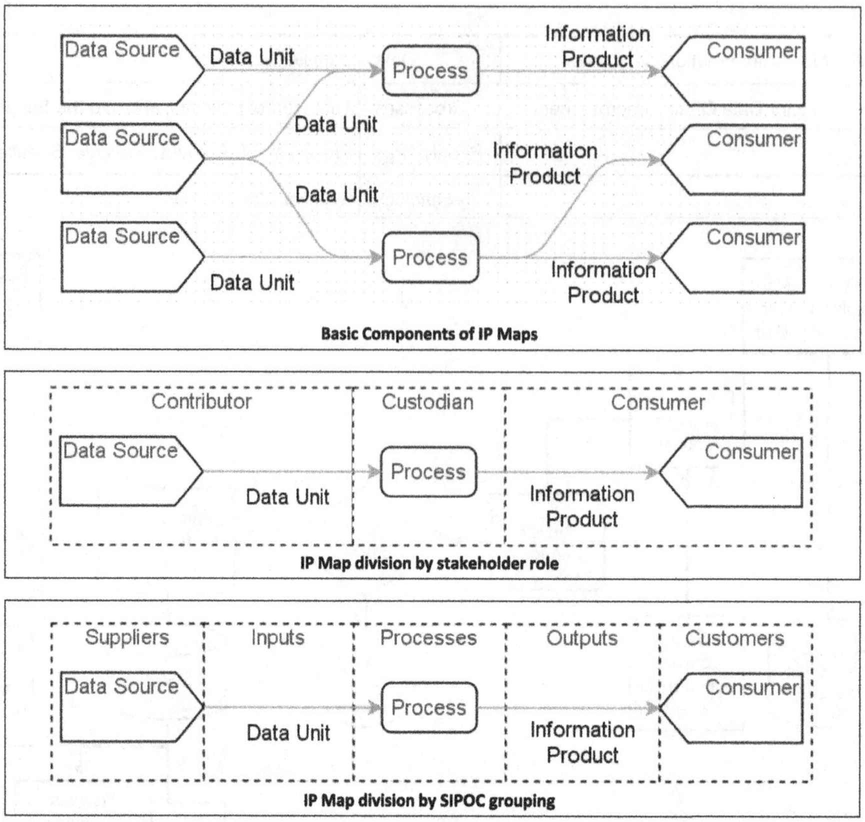

Basic Components of IP Maps

IP Map division by stakeholder role

IP Map division by SIPOC grouping

Source: Figures 1, 3, 4 in *Modeling and Analysis of Information Product Maps. Thesis (Ph.D.)*
By C.H. Heien. University of Arkansas at Little Rock, 2012.
Available at: https://library.ualr.edu/record=b1775281~S4. Used with permission.

Figure 6.6 Representations of IP Maps.

these interactions in the Information Manufacturing System allows one to understand the economic value of information products in a way that is similar to how a manufacturer might understand the economic value of a product line.

Definition

An **Information Product Map (IP Map)** is a "graphical model designed to help people to comprehend, evaluate, and describe how an information product such as an invoice, customer order, or prescription is assembled. The IP Map is aimed at creating a systematic representation for capturing the details associated with the manufacture of an information product that is routinely produced within an organization."

– Richard Y. Wang, Elizabeth M. Pierce, Stuart E. Madnick, and Craig W. Fisher (Eds.), Information Quality (2005), p. 10.

Thanks to Christopher Heien for his help and expertise in writing this section. For more information on IP Maps see: C. H. Heien, *Modeling and Analysis of Information Product Maps. Thesis (Ph.D.)* (2012); Heien, et al., "Methods and Models to Support Consistent Representation of Information Product Maps," (2014); and Lee, et al., "CEIP Maps: Context-embedded Information Product Maps," (2007).

The Table Approach

The table approach is a simple way of collecting information about a data life cycle. It involves creating a table to document and understand important attributes of a series of life cycle tasks or steps. The table approach is useful because the detail can easily show gaps or conflicts in tasks, roles, timing, and dependencies. You can also use this approach to develop new processes for your life cycle. *Table 6.2* shows an example of using the table approach and it can also be used as a template. Modify the column headings to reflect the information most important to capture for each of the activities or tasks in the rows below the summary information:

- **Table header information.** By now I hope you recognize the four key components that affect information quality: data, processes, people/organizations, and technology. If the key component applies to all of the tasks, keep in the header (e.g., the whole table applies to Financial Data). If any of the key components vary depending on the task, then you may want to add a column to capture those components.
- **No.** Number the tasks for ease of reference.
- **Activity.** Describe the activity or task in a verb-noun format.
- **Manual or automatic.** Indicate whether the task is completed by a person or automatically by a program.
- **Timing.** Describe when the activity takes place (e.g., daily, monthly, quarterly, annually). Be specific as needed, such as time of day (daily at 13:00 UTC), when in the month (workday 10),

Table 6.2 Information Life Cycle Example – Table Approach

Title:	Financial Data Archiving and Disposition of On Premises Tape Backups		Data:		Any financial Information		
Project:	Finance Data Archive Project		Processes:				
Created by:	JD		People/Orgs:		Finance, IT, Vaulting Vendor, Disposal Vendor		
Date:			Technology:		Tape backups and servers in Computer Center XYZ		

No.	Activity/Task	Manual or Automatic	Timing	Role	Employee/ Contractor/ Vendor	Notes
1	Identify records that need to be archived.	Manual	?	Legal? Finance?	Employee	Who determines when records should be archived? What are the criteria?
2	Tag associated media for archiving.					
3	Store tagged media in secure data center separate from all other media.					
4	Transfer tagged media to the vaulting vendor.					How are tagged media transferred to the vaulting vendor?
5	Store archived media until final disposition.					
6	Tag archived media for final destruction.			Offsite vaulting vendor		Who determines when records should be destroyed? What are the criteria?
7	Destroy media tagged for final destruction by shredding.			Disposal vendor		
8	Create certificate of destruction.					Where is the certificate kept?
9	Record destruction date, tape ID, who, location, etc.					Where is the destruction information recorded?

and dependencies on other processes (at completion of quarter-end financial close).

- **Role**. Title of the person or people who perform the task. You may want to add columns with specific names, team, and contact information.
- **Employee/contractor/vendor.** Is the person performing the task a company employee, a contractor, or a third-party vendor? This information is useful as communications and escalation of issues may differ depending on the designation.
- **Notes**. Additional information such as the output of this step, reference documents, open questions, or issues.

Table 6.2 shows how the table approach was used for a subset of the information life cycle, in this case archiving and destruction of on-premises tape backups for financial information, which is the Dispose phase. Note the many blank spaces, which indicate gaps in the understanding of the life cycle. Use the gaps as an opportunity to ask questions and fill in the missing pieces.

In this example, indicating if the task was done by an employee, contractor, or vendor helped to determine which different managers/teams/organizations to communicate with and where to escalate issues that could not be resolved by those working at the process level.

This approach can easily be used for representing a similar information life cycle using a cloud service provider for the archiving and destruction process. Ask questions of and work closely with your service provider to ensure your data will be archived and eventually completely destroyed or deleted when the time is right. Many people are under the false impression that they will no longer need to worry about these details because their data is "in the cloud." Don't be fooled. You are still responsible for your data.

Conduct a Survey

A survey is a formal data gathering method for assessing situations, conditions, or opinions. It is accomplished by collecting, analyzing, and interpreting the views of people from a target population. Your survey may be as simple as interviewing an individual in person or over the phone, or repeating the same interview separately with many individuals. It may be as complex as conducting a workshop or focus group with several people or collecting detailed responses online from hundreds of people.

Surveys can take the form of interviews, questionnaires, focus groups, or workshops. The steps below (from *Chapter 4: The Ten Steps Process*) often include surveys and can make use of the general information in this section. See the specific steps for instructions and examples of how surveys can be used.

- *Step 1.1 – Prioritize Business Needs and Select Project Focus*
  - Interview sponsors, stakeholders, and/or users to discover what is most important to the business right now and provide input to selecting the focus of the project.
  - Conduct a stakeholder analysis early in the project to understand stakeholders' roles in data quality work – either specific to the project or on the broader data quality program – and their perceptions of data quality and business needs.
- *Step 3.1 – Perception of Relevance and Trust* (a data quality dimension) and *Step 4.7 – Perception of Relevance and Trust* (a business impact technique)
  - Survey sponsors, stakeholders, and/or users to discover their perception of: 1) Relevance – indicates business value by understanding what is most important to them and the impact of poor-quality data on their job responsibilities, and 2) Trust – their opinion of the quality of the data.
  - Even though you might be more interested in either the data quality or business impact perspective, don't miss the opportunity when surveying to find out both.
  - Relevance results can be used to help build a business case for data quality efforts, provide input when prioritizing which data to include in a data quality project and assess for quality, or which data is important enough for on-going quality management.
  - Trust results can be used to compare *opinions* about the quality of the data to *actual* data quality based on other data quality assessment of data content. This allows you to address any gaps between perception and reality through communication.
- *Step 3.4 – Accuracy* (a data quality dimension)
  - Use a survey if you want to assess accuracy where the authoritative source of reference is a person. For example, a customer could be asked questions regarding the data about him/her in the organization's datastore to determine if it is correct or

not. This requires a carefully planned, standardized questionnaire and process to obtain valid results.
- *Step 4.4 – Five Whys for Business Impact*
  - If using this technique on more than one person about the same subject, create a questionnaire to ensure a standardized process and results which can be compared.
- *Any other steps, activities, or techniques* where information is gathered through surveys, interviews, questionnaires, workshops, focus groups, or other formal methods.

Approach

When developing and implementing your survey, adjust and apply the following steps as needed for the purpose, format, and the number of people involved. The process described below was developed based on input from Sarah Mae Sincero's, "Surveys and Questionnaires – Guide" (2012) (licensed under the Creative Commons-License Attribution 4.0 International, [CC BY 4.0]).

1. Clarify the purpose/business need of the survey and formulate survey goals.

Why are you doing the survey? What are the specific aims of the survey? What do you hope to learn from the survey? Depending on where you are in the project, work done on the business needs and the information environment in *Steps 1 and 2* may provide answers.

2. Identify the population to be surveyed, sample method, and survey method.

Target population—Determine the target population to be surveyed. Consider background, experience, skills, language, and geographic location. Possible populations to be surveyed as part of a data quality project include:

- Internal to your organization
  - All employees
  - All or selected employees within a team or business unit
  - All or selected employees that use the data in question as part of a business process or transaction, in a particular application, within a specific report, etc.
- External to your organization
  - Business partners who provide data to or use data from your organization
  - Customers who are the authoritative source of reference for an accuracy assessment of customer data
- By roles
  - Boards, executives, senior leaders
  - Managers, program and project managers
  - Individual contributors and practitioners who use the data of interest

Sampling method—If large numbers of people *need* to be surveyed but *cannot* be surveyed due to time and resource constraints, a subset of the population of interest, called a sample, must be selected using some type of sampling method. As with data sampling, the sampling method is the technique used to select representative members of a population for a survey, test, or assessment. Representative means that responses from the subset actually surveyed will approximate the responses of all those in the population, if everyone had been able to be surveyed. Random sampling is one method for selecting a subset of records for those people to be surveyed. After the survey is complete, results from the sample are inferred to be representative of the population as a whole. Ensure that neither the target population nor the sampling method, inadvertently reflects bias; that is, the target population and the subset obtained through the sample method should not leave out populations that should be accounted for and it should not over represent any segment of the population.

If surveying small numbers of people, an automated sampling method such as random sampling is not necessary. However, the *idea* of sampling should be considered when selecting those to survey. Carefully think through who, specifically, you want to survey. for example a few people from a large team or the three top sales agents, or the top ten customers from a region. In some cases, you simply want to select a few influential leaders or users to get their opinions, so sampling as described here is not an issue.

Survey method—A survey method is the technique used to gather the data. Determine the survey method that will best satisfy the purpose and survey goals, make the best use of resources, be completed within the available time, and obtain the desired response rate. A response rate, also known as completion rate or return rate, is the number of people who answered the survey divided by the number of people in the sample (that is, those who were provided the opportunity to participate in the survey) and is usually expressed as a percentage. Examples of survey methods include:

- **Online survey** (internet or intranet). With a url that links to survey where responses are entered online
- **Telephone survey**. Calling respondents and entering responses into a form
- **In-person or telephone interviews**. Ask questions of respondents and record answers
- **Email survey**. Send email with survey attached or with link to a url
- **Hardcopy questionnaire**. Completed manually by respondent, sent via mail or handed out in person
- **Focus group or workshop**. Questions are asked in a group setting with a facilitator

For some of the purposes in this book, one effective survey method is to interview people directly, either in-person or via video conferencing. Standardize some questions to be answered using a measurable scale. This helps you quantify responses when you analyze results. In addition, include open-ended questions that can encourage additional dialogue. This process often reveals important details which provide a more complete picture of the challenges people are facing. Surveys can also be conducted electronically, with follow-up phone calls, if needed, to clarify answers.

3. Verify resources.

Confirm you have the budget, people, and technology needed for the survey. The following people resources are needed in the survey.

- Those conducting the survey
  - Recruit those who will conduct the survey. There could be 1 or 2 people from the data quality team administering interviews, or you may have several people gathering responses.
  - Ensure that all have background on the survey and on why it is being conducted.

  - Provide training as needed so they will understand the questions, capture responses consistently, and encourage participation – all of which help ensure meaningful results.
- Those responding to the questionnaire
  - Ensure the survey respondents have the right knowledge and experience to answer the questions.
  - When conducting a survey of internal users of the data, it is helpful to notify their managers about the survey, so that they understand why it is being done and why their team has been asked to participate. A manager's support can help increase response rates.
  - If surveying business partners, be sure to inform the official liaison between your organization and the business partner about your plans.
- Those providing support for the survey
  - Depending on the survey method chosen, you might need technical support; for example, to set up a website, create a database to capture responses, or enable the creation of reports from the responses.
  - You may need management to encourage participation in the survey.

For anyone involved in the survey, gain their support and enthusiastic participation. Ensure they know the purpose of the survey and the role they play in ensuring the survey is a success.

4. Develop the questionnaire, supporting information, and the survey process.

Questionnaire and supporting information—The questionnaire is a survey instrument comprised of a set of questions to ask the participants in the survey. The questions are used to elicit ideas and behaviors, preferences, traits, attitudes, and facts. Supporting information refers to anything needed by the respondents to encourage their participation, provide context and background, and provide instructions for completing the survey. The following suggestions will help you present the information clearly.

- **Introduction**. Think of the survey from the respondent point of view. Explain why the survey is being conducted, and how the results will be used. Describe the benefit to the respondent and to the organization represented by the respondent. Call attention to the confidentiality of the survey (if that is true). Include a deadline for returning the survey and indicate who to call with questions. Capture pertinent information that will help you analyze survey results such as respondent name, title, function/team within the organization. When conducting the interview, document the date, time, location, respondents, those conducting the interview, and others listening in.
- **Body**. This is the question-and-response section. It should be comprehensive but concise. Responses should be in a format easy for the respondent to complete and easy for those collecting the data to capture, store, and document. Questions should draw out the information you need to support your goals.
- **Conclusion**. This should give the respondent the ability to provide additional information, insights, or feedback. End with a genuine thank you.

The questions can be:

- All qualitative and open-ended, with no response scale
- All quantitative, with a response scale for every question
- A combination of qualitative and quantitative

Response scale—A response scale provides a standardized way of answering questions and makes it easier to analyze responses. Response scales used in surveys vary depending on the type of question being asked. Responses can be as simple as a choice between "Yes" and "No" or as complex as choosing an answer among several response choices. See the *Best Practice callout box* for response scale options. Assigning a weight or number to each question and/or response option may help with calculations and analysis.

 Best Practice

Survey Response Scales—Options for responding to questions in a survey. Each response scale has advantages and disadvantages. The rule of thumb is that the best response scale to use is the one which can be easily understood by respondents and interpreted by the researcher.

Dichotomous Scales—A two-point scale which presents options that are absolute opposites of each other. This type of response scale does not give the respondent an opportunity to be neutral on the answer to the question. Examples:

- Yes/No
- True/False
- Fair/Unfair
- Agree/Disagree

Rating Scales—A rating scale provides more than two options. Three-point, five-point, and seven-point scales are all included under the term "rating scale." Examples:

1. Three-point Scales:
   - Good – Fair – Poor
   - Agree – Undecided – Disagree
   - Extremely – Moderately – Not at all
   - Too much – About right – Too little
2. Five-point Scales (e.g., Likert Scale):
   - Strongly Agree – Agree – Undecided/Neutral – Disagree – Strongly Disagree
   - Always – Often – Sometimes – Seldom – Never
   - Extremely – Very – Moderately – Slightly – Not at all
   - Excellent – Above Average – Average – Below Average – Very Poor
3. Seven-point Scales:
   - Exceptional – Excellent – Very Good – Good – Fair – Poor – Very Poor
   - Very satisfied – Moderately satisfied – Slightly satisfied – Neutral – Slight dissatisfied – Moderately dissatisfied – Very dissatisfied.

– Sarah Mae Sincero, "Survey Response Scales." (2012).

Survey process—The survey process outlines the details regarding how the survey will be administered, who is involved at each step, and the timeframe. Remember to include appropriate communications before, during, and after the survey. Use POSMAD, Information Life Cycle thinking, and the Framework for Information Quality as background when developing the survey process. The survey is just another set

of information with its own life cycle and it must result in high-quality information:

- **P**lan for the survey
- **O**btain the information of interest by conducting the survey
- **S**tore the results and have a method to **S**hare them by making them accessible to the project team
- **M**aintain/update responses if needed
- **A**pply the survey results by analyzing responses, making decisions, and taking action to further project goals. Communicate and engage with those who care about or are impacted by results.
- **D**ispose of the survey data when the time is right or archive for future reference. This data may include the respondent list, datastore with results, analysis, synthesis, recommendations, actions, and other documentation.

5. Test the questionnaire and survey process, revise as needed.

Test for clarity to ensure that respondents understand and can answer appropriately. Revise as needed to create a participant-friendly questionnaire. Test the user interface for entering the results into a survey tool, if one is being used. Test for ease of data entry and for the ability to analyze the survey results properly. Revise the survey as needed to create an effective data-gathering device.

6. Administer the questionnaire and complete the survey.

Create or extract the list of those to survey. Use the selected sampling method. Start the survey using the process designed. While the survey is being conducted:

- Collect results
- Monitor responses throughout the survey period to confirm that the survey is on track
- Stop the survey when the desired number of responses have been received or the time period has ended

7. Process and store response data.

After the survey has been completed, confirm that all responses have been captured and documented. Ensure the information is available for future reference.

8. Analyze and interpret the survey responses and make a conclusion.

See the section *Analyze, Synthesize, Recommend, Document, and Act on Results* in this chapter for additional details. Be sure to keep a copy of the survey itself, a list and number of those surveyed, a list of those who conducted the survey, the time period, process used, etc. Compare perceptions of quality with the actual quality results from other data quality assessments.

9. Share results and use to achieve project objectives.

Share survey results using communication methods appropriate for each audience who needs to hear them. Audiences may include sponsors and stakeholders of the project, those who conducted or supported the process in some way, and/or the respondents themselves and their managers. You may choose to hold a focus group meeting with respondents to discuss responses and perceptions. Emphasize decisions made (or needing to be made) and specific recommendations to put the results into action. See *Step 10* for ideas about communicating and engaging with people. You may share specific survey results, lessons learned, impact to the business, suggested root causes of data quality problems, and preliminary recommendations. An appendix may be included to provide background and additional details about the survey such as a copy of the survey, the respondents, the number of surveys sent vs. number of responses, those involved in planning and conducting the survey, and the survey process used.

Use the survey results to guide your decisions about the project so business needs will be addressed and project objectives achieved.

Metrics

Metrics are a type of control. See *Step 9 – Monitor Controls* to supplement what is found here. Metrics can be an important data quality control that provide business value by bringing visibility to data quality issues so you can act quickly upon them. This visibility allows you to address issues when they first appear, show progress when corrections are done, and highlight the success of preventive measures that have been adopted. However, metrics and a pretty dashboard are not the end in and of themselves. Metrics are useful for:

- Replacing opinions with facts
- Determining where to focus resources and efforts
- Identifying sources of problems
- Confirming the effectiveness of solutions
- Encouraging behavior that supports business needs through data and information
- Recognizing where things are going well and identifying where action is NOT needed

The last bullet is highly underrated. How many times does management wonder if issues are really being brought to light in a timely manner and if resources are being pointed at the right places? Metrics can help meet these needs. A metric that is green means you can rest easy, things are OK, no action needed. Red means this is critical, and we must take action now. It also means actions are being taken against those areas where they are most needed – assuming the metrics process has been thoughtfully created and people have agreed to and carry out their responsibilities.

When planning your metrics, be clear on the reason for them, their impact on the business, and why people should care. Implement just enough metrics to optimize those results. Never do metrics for the sake of metrics and because you want a cool dashboard. Make the information concise, easily visible, and understandable to those who use it.

Different Levels of Detail for Various Audiences and Uses

Consider three levels of detail for your metrics (as shown in *Figure 6.7*), with different audiences and uses for each. Think of the 3 Ds – dashboard, drilldown, and detail.

Dashboard—Summary-level metrics provide an at-a-glance view of the metrics. The reader can quickly interpret what was measured along with the status. Status indicates the condition of the metric in easy-to-understand terms. For example, you may use green to equal "results meet or exceed target"; yellow to equal "results fail target or unfavorable trend"; and red to equal "results well outside of tolerance limits or drastic unfavorable change."

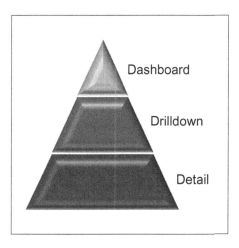

Figure 6.7 Levels of detail for metrics.

Drilldown—The drilldown is a mid-level view that provides additional information about the dashboard metrics. It shows more about the dashboard numbers – but not in excruciating detail. The drilldown level is often where trends and history over time are shown. It may show results of the data quality measurements, comparison to targets, and status for each of the measurements. The drilldown level is a good place to describe why these summarized metrics and/or individual tests are important. The primary audiences of the drilldown level are managers, data stewards, or other individual contributors who want more detail – but still a summarized view of the detail.

Detail—The detail often comes in the form of reports which are the output of the data quality tests and the actual records from which the drilldown and dashboard level metrics are summarized. Detailed reports are not normally viewed by management, but the output should be available if questions arise about the accuracy of the metrics themselves. They should be used to correct data identified as exceptions to the quality assessment by data quality, business, or IT teams – whoever has been identified as the most appropriate person to do the job. These reports can also be used as input to root cause analysis and continuous improvement. Be careful that only those people who are authorized to see this kind of detail have access to it.

Example and Terms

As an example, the dashboard level might show a summarized status of consistency of key product master attributes (description, unit of measure, etc.) across the four systems which use them. It may also include the level of compliance to the product enterprise data standards. The dashboard level includes a link to a drilldown page which concisely explains how item records are used in inventory, purchasing, order entry, engineering, bill of materials, material planning, and cost management. The dashboard level also illustrates how poor item data quality adds risk to all business areas.

The drilldown contains the status of the key attributes by system, along with links to the detail level page for each system. The detail level shows more information about tests in a red status, such as who is taking action (root cause investigation, prevention activities, and clean-up efforts) and the status of those actions. To control access to the files with the actual exception records, a notice is emailed to the person responsible for making the updates along with the link (instead of that link being on the online metrics page).

An important point: In this section, I use the word metrics to mean the on-going, overall effort of measuring and monitoring data quality. I use the word "test" to mean an individual data quality check or measurement. Within your organization, what do you call each measurement or test? Is it a metric? A business rule? A data quality check? Most of my clients have their own terms already in use. If your organization already uses a set of terms, be consistent with them. Otherwise, as a project team, define your terms and use them consistently.

General Guidelines for Metrics

Following are important points to keep in mind as you get started with metrics. Metrics should:

- **Relate to business needs** (customers, strategies, goals, issues, opportunities). Measure those things that make a difference.
- **Track and be a clear indicator of what needs to be improved**.
- **Promote desired behavior**. Define the desired behavior. Then determine the metrics needed to understand and encourage the desired behavior. Metrics can change behavior. Make sure they change the behavior you want. If you don't, you may get what you ask for, but it may not be what you want.
- **Be relatively easy to apply**. They should not complicate operations and create excessive overhead.
- **Be simple, straightforward, and meaningful**. Team members should be able to explain them to others.
- **Create or make use of an existing common language** among diverse team members and those using the metrics.
- **Be collected accurately, completely, and in a timely manner**. Data quality metrics must have high data quality themselves.
- **Be accurate in their representation and visualization**. *Step 3.10 – Presentation Quality* applies here, in that if our visualization of the metrics misrepresents or encourages misunderstanding, then our metrics themselves do not have high-quality data – even if the underlying numbers are correct.
- **Provide a balanced picture**. Focusing on any single piece of data can cause it to improve at the expense of others. You may want to track some general metrics to act as a check and balance.
- **Be reviewed**. Tap the experience of those closest to the data and the processes. Discuss your attempts to establish metrics, encourage everyone to find fault with them. As metrics are used, encourage everyone to report any questions or problems with them.

Warning

Metrics can change behavior! Make sure metrics change the behavior you want. If you don't, you may get what you ask for, but not really what you want. For example, I have seen those beginning their data quality metrics measure only completeness/fill rate. This makes sense because the first thing they want to know is if the data exists. The problem with stopping at completeness/fill rate is that it can encourage those entering the data to put anything in the field just to ensure their metrics are improving. When this happens, the completeness metrics are going up, but the quality of the data is actually going down. To offset this, always include some validity metrics in addition to completeness (x% of records have a value in the field, of that x% are valid).

Interpreting Results

Status Indicators—Numbers in and of themselves do not tell us what to do. We must provide context for test results so others can correctly interpret them. This helps them determine what action to take, if any. Status Indicators provide that context. Determine the scale and definitions that provide status for your metrics. See the two examples in *Figure 6.8*.

Status Selection Criteria—For any individual test result, you must determine exactly how to assign status (e.g., if data quality rule 1 is less than 100% is it green? At what point are results red, meaning action is required?) I refer to this as Status Selection Criteria. How to determine the Status Selection Criteria is, once again, all about context. See *Step 4.9 – Ranking and Prioritization* for a technique that provides needed context and can be used to determine status selection criteria for metrics. Study *Figure 6.9* for an example of how to capture results from a ranking and prioritization session as these apply to metrics.

Next use what has been learned from the ranking session to set the final Status Selection Criteria. In *Figure 6.9*, let's assume that the overall ranking for Patient Birthdate was High. Let's use that information as input to *Figure 6.10 – Example metrics status selection criteria*. Since Patient Birthdate was an important identifier, the status selection criteria for green was set at 100%. It was so important that anything less

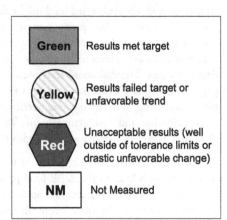

Figure 6.8 Two examples of status indicators.

Ranking and Prioritization Worksheet – Input to Metrics Status Selection Criteria				Registration	Hospital Adminis- tration	Nurses	Physicians	Overall Ranking (Highest ranking from any of the areas *)
Determine Perspective/Representation for Ranking: e.g. Line of Business, Departments, Key Business Processes, or Key Roles → Data Quality Rules/Tests								
Test #	Data Element	DQ Rule Type	DQ Rule Definition	In this row, for each column, list the name of who is representing each area for the ranking along with their role, e.g. enterprise data steward, subject matter expert, department head				
1A	Patient Birthdate	Completeness	Value exists in birthdate field.					e.g. High
1B	Patient Birthdate	Validity	Validity = Value is in format of YYYY-MM-DD					
2A	Diagnostic code	Completeness	Value exists in the Diagnostic Code field					
2B	Diagnostic code	Validity	Value matches a valid code in the Diagnostic Codes Reference Table					
Etc.								

If <Rule/Test> fails, what is the impact to <Line of Business, Department, Key Business Process, or Key Role?>:
 High (H) = complete failure of the process or unacceptable financial, compliance, legal, or other risk is highly likely
 Medium (M) = Process will be hampered and some economic consequences will result
 Low (L) = Minor economic consequences will result
 N/A = Data Quality Test not applicable to this area
E.g. if Patient Birthdate Completeness test fails (i.e. if Birthdate is missing), what would be the impact to Registration?"
You could also rank both tests for Patient Birthdate together, instead of separately.
* Whatever is the highest ranking from any area is the final ranking. Use this final ranking to help set the Status Selection Criteria. E.g. if the impact is High, then the criteria for green would be 100% or very close to that.

Figure 6.9 Ranking and prioritization as input to metrics status selection criteria.

Metrics Status Selection Criteria   Green   Yellow   Red

Data Quality Test #	Data Element	Test Type	Test Definition	Criteria for Green (Results met target)	Criteria for Yellow (Results failed target or unfavorable trend)	Criteria for Red (Unacceptable results. Immediate action needed)	Notes	This Month's Results
1A	Patient Birthdate	Completeness	Value exists in Birthdate field.	Target = 100% Completeness	N/A	99.9% or below		
1B	Patient Birthdate	Validity	Value is in format of YYYY-MM-DD	Target = 100% valid format	N/A	99.9% or below		
2A	Diagnostic Code	Completeness	Value exists in the Diagnostic Code field	Target = 95-100% valid diagnostic codes	94.9 – 85.0%	84.9% or below		
2B	Diagnostic Code	Validity	Value matches a valid code in the Diagnostic Codes Reference Table	Target = 100% valid diagnostic codes for those fields where there is a value.	Etc.			

Figure 6.10 Example metrics status selection criteria.

than 100% would move the status to red; therefore, a yellow status did not apply. You can see that there are two data quality rules for Patient Birthday that will be tested. If you ranked both Patient Birthdate tests together, the status selection criteria would be the same for both tests. Use the same line of thinking to work out the Status Selection Criteria for all the data quality tests.

Note that the data quality rule examples in *Figures 6.9* and *6.10* were all run using data profiling, the technique used in *Step 3.3 – Data Integrity Fundamentals*. Remember the data quality dimensions are categorized roughly by the approach used for assessing that dimension. That means when profiling the data, you will learn more about Patient Birthdate, Diagnostic Code, and other data fields than the two tests listed here (completeness and validity). You should decide which are the most important to monitor on-going. There is a cost to monitoring, so be thoughtful about what is worthwhile. *Step 4.9 – Ranking and Prioritization* helps here. In one project, the business initially prioritized a particular data field as very important. With the context provided during the ranking session, every line of business ranked it as low. You then must ask if the data field will provide enough value to continue monitoring it.

Visualization and Presentation

The spreadsheets shown so far are for working out the details. How you report out and visualize the results is a different question. Visualization and presentation refer to how results will be presented. You want people to learn something from the metrics and know what to do with them. The format, appearance, and display of the data and information should support their uses and is a data quality dimension covered in *Step 3.10 – Presentation Quality*.

Using the same example, you can decide – do I want to report out all tests by data element? Do I want to report out by data quality dimension or characteristic (e.g., by completeness and validity)? Do I want to report out all metrics of interest for a key business process or by line of business? Do I report results from the positive or negative aspect (e.g., do I say the completeness rate is 80% or that 20% of the records are missing data in that field)? Being consistent with reporting all from either the positive or negative can help avoid confusion for those looking at results. It is also good practice to display the last date/time the metrics were updated.

Many resources exist to help you learn about visualization and information graphics generally or designing dashboards.

Edward Tufte's *The Visual Display of Quantitative Information*, first published in 1983 and updated in 2001, is a classic. Stephen Few (2013), Wayne Eckerson (2011), Cole Kussbaumer Knaflic (2015), Stephanie D. H. Evergreen (2020), and Dona M. Wong (2010) are a few of my favorites. Incorporate graphics into your communication. One thing I learned early was to account for color blindness. Ensure that colors can be differentiated for those who are color blind, and if a color graphic is printed in grayscale or black and white. Using shapes and patterns to supplement color can help here.

All I can say in this limited amount of space is keep your audiences in mind: management (who want to quickly know status) or those who will act on the results, including their managers. Design, create a prototype, get feedback, adjust, and repeat. Your original design may not be possible depending on the visualization and reporting tool you have available. On the other hand, the tool may provide options for visualization that you had not considered. Once metrics are in production, continue to be open to feedback and build a mechanism into your process so those with questions and feedback can easily contact those responsible for the metrics. Ensure your process includes the ability to add/remove tests and to update/improve the process itself. Consider how to integrate your data quality metrics into other business dashboards, which demonstrates that data quality is equally important to management as the other items they track regularly. See the *Ten Steps in Action callout box* for one company's data quality metrics.

Communicate and Engage

Throughout this metrics section, I hope you have noticed that anything to do with metrics involves the need to communicate, gain support, prepare, listen to, and involve others. Recognize that engaging with people is as critical to the success of your metrics as running the data quality tests.

Quote to Remember

"Dashboards can be designed to tap into the tremendous power of visual perception to communicate rapidly and effectively, but only if we understand visual perception and apply design principles and practices that are aligned with the way people see and think."

– Stephen Few, Information Dashboard Design: Displaying data for at-a-glance monitoring, (Second edition, 2013). p. 1.

Ten Steps in Action

Metrics – State of Data Quality, Business Value of Data Quality, and Program Performance

Background—Thanks to Michele Koch, Barbara Deemer, and their teams for sharing their data quality metrics program with us. Navient is a US Fortune 500 company that provides education loan management and business processing solutions to education, healthcare, and government clients at the federal, state, and local levels. The Data Governance Program had been in place for three years when they established an enterprise Data Quality Program. This included the Data Quality Services Team organized under the umbrella of

the Data Governance Program, which is part of the Enterprise Data Management Strategy. The Data Quality Services team administers the Data Quality Program and provides services for data quality requests, project implementation, production support/data quality tool administration, on-going monitoring, data quality consulting, and training. They work closely with data stewards and others who are part of the Data Governance Program. Once the program was in place, the first project was to develop metrics. The metrics dashboard was put into production and is now on-going as an operational process. See *Figure 6.11* for a visual of their metrics dashboard and *Figure 6.12* for the metrics high level process flow.

Continued

Ten Steps in Action *(Continued)*

Metrics Explained—Three categories of metrics were developed and reported on:

- **State of Data Quality**. The data quality metrics (called business rules by Navient) are updated weekly and shown in the upper left quadrant of the dashboard. The process from *Step 3.3 – Data Integrity Fundamentals* was used to generate the initial baseline for data quality, utilizing a third-party data profiling tool. The same tool was also used for the metrics, taking advantage of its additional capabilities for monitoring, storing, and reporting results over time. A separate tool was used for visualizing the dashboard.
- **Business Value from Data Quality**. The business value metrics are updated monthly based on the results of the most recent run of the data quality business rules. To develop these metrics, three of the Business Impact Techniques were used: *Step 4.3 – Usage*, *Step 4.9 – Ranking and Prioritization*, and *Step 4.10 – Cost of Low-Quality Data*. They identified typical costs due to poor-quality data that applied to their company and mapped the costs to line items in the company's Operating Budget. The specific costs related to each business rule were then researched. The business value line items and results are mapped to and summarized in one of three categories: revenue generated, costs avoided, and intangible benefits. Summarized revenue and costs were quantified and are visible on the dashboard in the upper right quadrant. Intangible benefits were statements describing other value that was not easily quantified, yet important to highlight. These statements were available in the drilldown pages. For example, depending on the specific metric, the intangible benefits of managing data quality helped decrease the risk of: damage to reputation, organizational mistrust, lower employee morale, customer dissatisfaction, regulatory or compliance risk, lower ability to effectively compete, or impact to shareholder value.
- **Data Quality Program Performance.** These metrics are shown in the bottom two quadrants of the dashboard. They bring visibility to work done by the DQ Services team that is important and adds value, yet often goes unnoticed. There are two sections which are updated monthly: 1) Number of Data Quality Issues – with counts for Closed, Work in Progress, Monitoring, and Archived, and 2) Number of Data Quality Engagements – with counts for DQ Consulting, On-going Monitoring, and Project Support.

For each metrics category, a dashboard level status was summarized from detailed reports. There is the ability to click and drilldown within each section and select information based on business rules or line of business. Once in production, with experience, they continued to refine the operational processes for adding new metrics and working with the data stewards. The time from initial request for a metric to going into production was shortened dramatically.

To ensure the metrics are being acted upon, the Chief Data Steward and Data Governance Program Director track the activity of those involved in the process, recognize and thank those doing the work, and follow-up with managers, if needed, to encourage better participation.

Business Benefits—Over ten years the value shown from their metrics has funded other corporate initiatives and helped Navient increase revenue and decrease cost and complexity. It has given them confidence in their data and increased data literacy across the organization. Their Data Governance Program has won several industry awards over the years, with an important judging factor being the ability to demonstrate business value for the organization.

Data Quality (DQ) Dashboard — Note: With counts and $ amounts removed — Email Data Governance Office

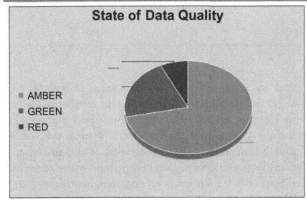

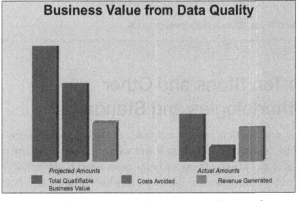

Business Rules Monitored:
Current Monitor Date:

Date as of:

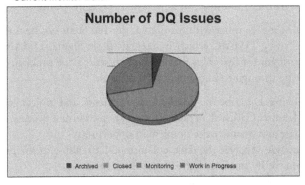

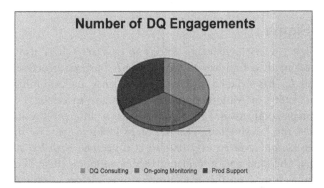

Copyright 2009-2019 Navient Solutions, Inc. All Rights Reserved Worldwide. Used with permission.

Figure 6.11 Example metrics dashboard.

Ten Steps in Action *(Continued)*

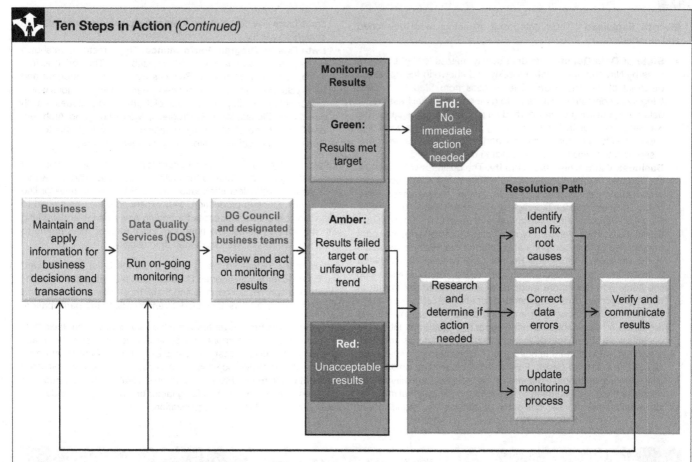

Figure 6.12 Metrics high-level process.

The Ten Steps and Other Methodologies and Standards

If your organization uses an external approach, methodology, or standard, become familiar with it and with the Ten Steps. Use the applicable steps, assessments, techniques, or activities from the Ten Steps to reinforce the data quality work which is being (or should be) addressed within those approaches. I will discuss only two here: Six Sigma and ISO 8000 Data Quality.

Six Sigma

Six Sigma refers to reducing defects to near zero. It is also a method used to improve an organization's business processes. Six Sigma has become well established since its beginnings in the 1980's at Motorola and has seen many successes. The Ten Steps complements Six Sigma but has a different starting point – the information. The Ten Steps looks to increase the success of whatever an organization is concerned with by improving the data and information which supports them. The Ten Steps brings together data, processes, people/organizations, technology, and the information life cycle in such a way that interactions between them are discovered and relationships are better understood. From this, new and better solutions can be devised and managed.

I asked one of my colleagues who was versed in both Six Sigma and the Ten Steps to describe how he saw the relationship between the two. He made two observations: 1) Six Sigma requires a hefty organizational commitment to implement, whereas the Ten Steps can be used immediately by an individual or any size team. Of course, any organization can gain benefit from wide-spread use of the Ten Steps. But if there is not yet organization-wide support, individuals and teams can still get value from applying the Ten Steps themselves. 2) Anyone who knows the Ten Steps will do a better job of the data and information aspects of a Six Sigma project.

For those familiar with Six Sigma, the Ten Steps can be understood using DMAIC which is integral to Six Sigma. DMAIC is an acronym for five steps that begin with stating the problem and working through to implementing a solution:

- **D**efine. Describe the problem, requirements, and project goals
- **M**easure. Gather data on key aspects of the current process, validate and quantify the problem or opportunity
- **A**nalyze. Analyze the data, enhance understanding of the problem, verify cause-and-effect, and find root cause
- **I**mprove. Implement solutions
- **C**ontrol. Measure and monitor results and take action as needed

Figure 6.13 shows a rough mapping of the Data Quality Improvement Cycle to DMAIC and then to the Ten Steps Process.

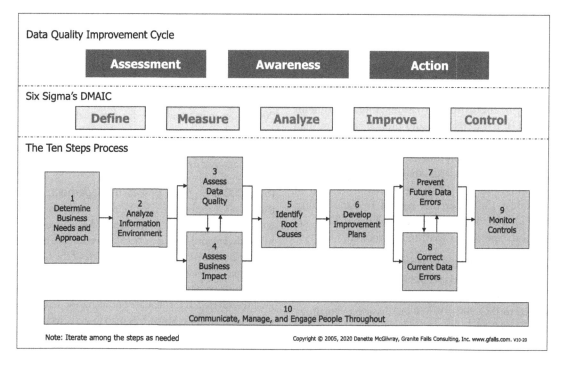

Figure 6.13 The Ten Steps and Six Sigma's DMAIC.

 Ten Steps in Action

Using Six Sigma and the Ten Steps Process to Improve Data Quality

Figure 6.14 shows how one company, which used Six Sigma as a standard for their projects, incorporated the use of the Ten Steps. They positioned Six Sigma as a quality process model for continued improvement that is systematic, scientific and fact-based, using Define, Measure, Analyze, Improve/Innovate and Control (DMAI2C). Together with the Ten Steps Process they created a data quality methodology with a foundation in Six Sigma.

A Six Sigma Green Belt Certified Project utilized the DMAI2C process and all of the Ten Steps to create process improvement and stronger data quality to support unit pricing. Other use cases, not pictured here, made use of various steps within the Ten Steps Process where applicable. For example, solutions were coordinated to prevent item records from being left in active status if there was no business activity for them.

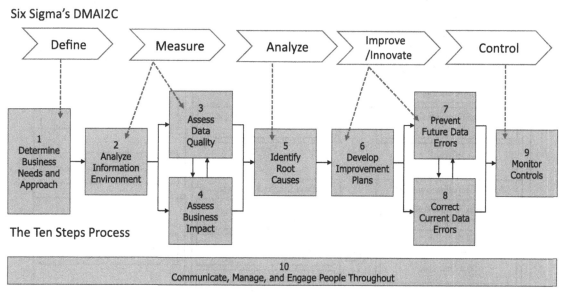

Figure 6.14 The Ten Steps and Six Sigma's DMAI2C applied to a project.

ISO 8000: The International Data Quality Standard

At the time of writing in 2020, the International Organization for Standardization (ISO), has developed and published more than 23,000 standards. The aim of ISO is to bring together experts to share knowledge and develop voluntary, consensus-based, market relevant International Standards that support innovation and provide solutions to global challenges. The remainder of this section introduces ISO standards related to data quality. Thanks to Peter Eales, an ISO recognized Industrial Data expert, for his help and expertise in writing this section.

ISO 9001 – *Quality management systems*—Readers may be familiar with the International Standard ISO 9001 – *Quality management systems*. A significant number of global organizations insist that their suppliers are certified to ISO 9001. When purchasing a centrifugal pump, for example, besides requiring that the supplier be certified to ISO 9001, an oil and gas organization will insist that the pump conforms to the standards API 610 – *Centrifugal pumps for petroleum, petrochemical and natural gas industries* or the identical ISO standard with the same title, ISO 13709. In this way by reference to the conformance clauses in the standard, the buyer can verify if the goods delivered meet the required standard and specification.

ISO 8000 – *Data quality*—The same general principles of quality management specified in ISO 9001 also apply to data quality management. However, there are unique quality management considerations that must be applied to data as a product, since it is intangible. The ISO 8000 – *Data quality* series does not establish a new management system. Rather, it extends or clarifies ISO 9001 for the case where data is the product and is the data quality series of standards. ISO 8000 adopts much (not all) of the vocabulary of the ISO 9000 series in its vocabulary for data quality. The ISO 8000 family is comprised of many individual parts. It is broken down into different subject areas pertaining to data quality, the main two subject areas being data quality management and master data quality.

ISO 8000-61 – *Data quality management: Process reference model*—Of the 60 series, ISO 8000-61 is the most relevant to the content of this book. It specifies the detailed structure required for data quality management [see *Figure 6.15*]. Overall data quality management is similar to what is called the Program side of the Data in Action Triangle in *Chapter 2: Data Quality in Action*. The program is the on-going foundation of managing data quality, an important piece for sustaining data quality, and details for that are outside of the scope of this book. Some of the individual ISO processes map to steps, techniques, or activities in the Ten Steps Process, where there is detail in how to carry them out. For example, the ISO process of "Data Quality Monitoring & Control" maps to *Step 9 – Monitor Controls*. In ISO 8000-61, each process is defined by purpose, outcomes, and activities that are to be applied for the assurance of data quality. The processes are used as reference to assess and improve process capability or organizational maturity for data quality management, and therefore provide a useful roadmap for any organization looking to improve in this area. ISO 8000-61 also contains fundamental principles of data quality management, the structure of data quality management processes, a description of each data quality management process, and covers the management of data quality for digital data sets. These data sets include not only structured data stored

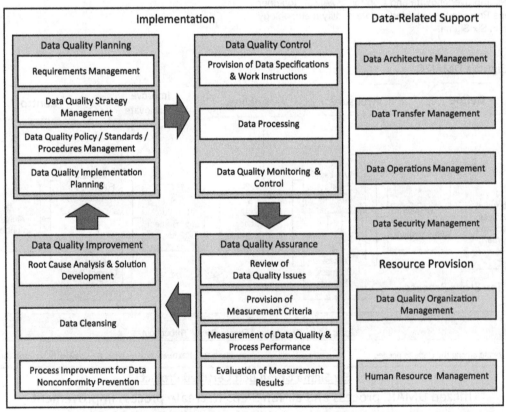

This figure is reproduced with permission from the International Organization for Standardization (ISO). It is published as Figure 2 in ISO 8000-61.

Figure 6.15 ISO 8000-61 – the detailed structure of data quality management.

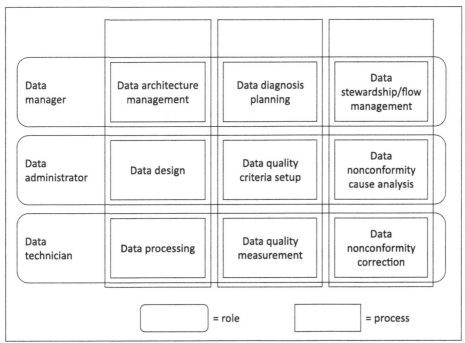

This figure is reproduced with permission from the International Organization for
Standardization (ISO). It is published as Figure B-1 in ISO 8000-150.

Figure 6.16 ISO 8000-150 Data quality management: Roles and responsibilities.

in databases but also less structured data such as image files, audio and video recordings, and electronic documents. For more detail on the ISO 8000-61 process model see *Managing Data Quality* (2020) by Tim King and Julian Schwarzenbach.

ISO 8000-150 – *Data quality management: Roles and responsibilities*—Used if an organization wants to understand the basics of roles and responsibilities. It provides an appendix which includes *Figure 6.16* and a clear explanation of the roles and responsibilities. If your organization is building a data quality program, Part 150 is a good place to start.

ISO 8000-100 – *Master data — Exchange of characteristic data: Overview*—The master data quality series addresses data quality from the bottom up, i.e., from the smallest meaningful element, the property value and the unit of measurement. More details are outlined in ISO 8000-110 – *Master data: Exchange of characteristic data: Syntax, semantic encoding, and conformance to data specification*.

ISO 8000 – *Data architecture*—The architecture that underpins ISO 8000 includes elements such as the data specifications, data dictionary, and an identification scheme. *Figure 6.17* is a modified version of Figure 1-Data architecture from ISO 8000-1. It shows how other ISO standards specify the particular elements in the architecture. These specifications indicate a standard for what constitutes high-quality data such as data type, representation (format), unit of measurement, qualifier of measurement (e.g., tolerance), and value hierarchy.

ISO Standards Related to Data Dictionaries—A common factor in organizations that suffer with poor-quality data is the absence of a data dictionary. *Figure 6.17* also shows that the data dictionary is a key element in the ISO 8000 data architecture. Data dictionaries as defined in ISO 29002 – *Industrial automation systems and integration – Exchange of characteristic data* and ISO 22745 – *Industrial automation systems and integration – Open technical dictionaries and their application to master data* are designed to link terms

and definitions with the same semantic content and to reference the original source of each term and definition. It should be noted that, these data dictionaries are not intended to duplicate existing standards, but to provide comprehensive collections of terminology used to describe individuals, organizations, locations, goods and services. Data dictionaries help to ensure that consistent terminology is used throughout an organization, and that terms can be understood by reference to their accompanying definitions.

Where a data dictionary uses identifiers from an identification scheme, this has the added benefit of enabling the data to be exchanged in a digital format, and this is vital in ensuring that the data is machine-readable, a key requirement in an organization's digital transformation journey.

ISO 25012 Standard Related to Data Quality—The ISO 25000 series of products, also known as SQuaRE (System and Software Quality Requirements and Evaluation), has the goal of creating a framework for the evaluation of software product quality. However, ISO/IEC 25012, defines a general data quality model for data retained in a structured format within a computer system, and further defines the following inherent data quality characteristics, or quality dimensions: accuracy; completeness; consistency; credibility; currentness; accessibility; compliance; confidentiality; efficiency; precision; traceability; and understandability. These characteristics or dimensions can be mapped to the Data Quality Dimensions as outlined in this book.

Benefits—By adopting standards such as ISO 8000, an organization does not have to reinvent what is included in data quality management. The adoption can be managed in stages to suit the maturity of the organization. In addition, standards can be referenced in contracts. Organizations already routinely specify standards in contracts. Many organizations required the ability to consume machine-readable data. If so, by adopting ISO 8000 they can add a suitable

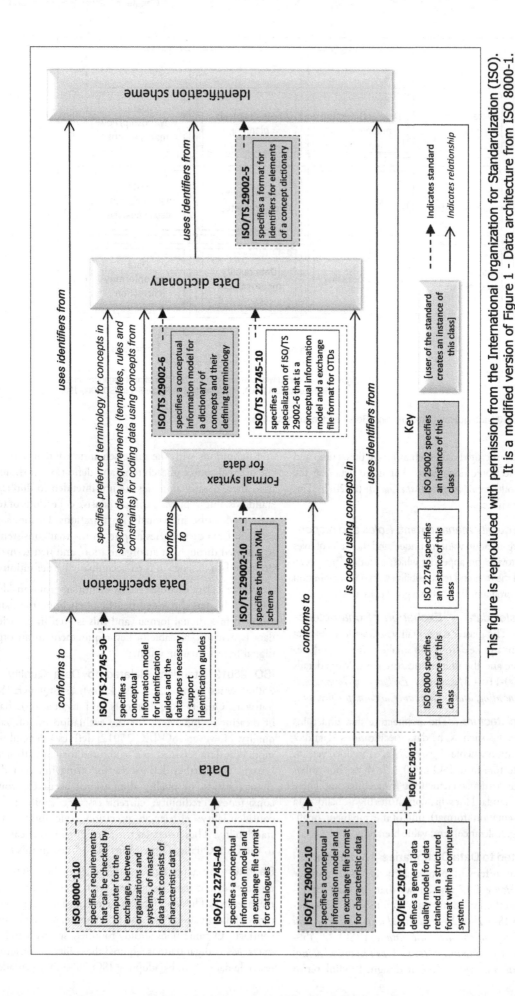

Figure 6.17 Data architecture with other ISO standards which specify elements within the architecture.

clause to contracts for any item or service being purchased. Asking for the product or service to be accompanied by the data record of that item or service can be achieved by quoting the relevant parts of ISO 8000 in the contract. This enables both parties to verify whether, or not, the deliverable satisfies the contract, as in the example below:

The contractor, sub-contractor or supplier shall, as and when requested to do so, supply technical data in electronic format on any of the items covered in this contract as follows:

The supplier shall supply technical data for the products or services they supply. Each item shall contain an ISO 8000-115* compliant identifier that is resolvable to an ISO 8000-110** compliant record with free decoding of unambiguous, internationally recognized identifiers.

*ISO 8000-115 – Master data – Exchange of quality identifiers: Syntactic, semantic and resolution requirements

**ISO 8000-110 – Master data – Exchange of characteristic data: Syntax, semantic encoding, and conformance to data specification

As you adopt International Standards, you will be able to draw the comparisons with the principals in this book and the standards. You will understand how this book and the standards both draw on commonly agreed principals. Importantly, this book demonstrates how to implement these principles and therefore the standards, in a practical way.

Tools for Managing Data Quality

The first question asked by many when starting their data quality work is, "What tool shall we buy?" Tools are tangible and vendors sales pitches are appealing. Data is so … well … intangible. I get it. But purchasing any tool to help manage data quality without knowing why, how, and when to use it will not give you high-quality data any more than buying a power saw will automatically give you custom-made cabinets. The right tools *can* make your job easier, but the tool in and of itself will not give you the quality of data to support business needs.

You also need people with the skills and knowledge who know how and when to make the best use of any tool. That is where the Ten Steps Process comes in. If you already have data quality tools but are not sure how to use them effectively, the Ten Steps can help. Think of the Ten Steps as a "wrapper" around a tool. The vendor should provide training on how to use a tool. Using the Ten Steps Process ensures you spend time on data that supports business needs, understand the information environment that created the data quality problems, decide what data should be assessed and why, and how to use results from a tool to improve the data – from both a correction and prevention standpoint. Value from tools will only be obtained if people with the appropriate knowledge of business needs, processes, and data work with those who have the skills to implement and use the technology.

Treat your technology experts as partners critical to your success – because they are. Imagine if we went back to the days of carbon paper and fax machines. What wonderful strides we have made in our organizations and as a society because of technology! As helpful as tools can be, they produce no miracles *on their own*. I emphasize this because often when resources are prioritized tools get funded, but no money goes toward the people, the processes, and the organizational structure needed for data quality management. Don't make the same mistake. Give emphasis to the data that is equal to that given to technology, processes, and people/organizations.

Be aware of the methods behind the functionality. Even the strides provided by artificial intelligence and machine learning to some of the functionality explained in the tables below do not guarantee high-quality data *on their own*. Some claim little or no human intervention is required. Test, look at results, modify algorithms. Ensure the tools produce what is needed before using their results for your initial data quality baseline or putting them into production. Work with your technology partners to determine what differences the underlying methods make to the functionality provided and the resources needed. Understand how the tool will be used within your environment.

Having highlighted my caution about taking only a tool-centric view, it is good to know there *are* tools available to help with many data quality tasks – and they are not always labeled as "data quality tools." Use tools judiciously.

The market for tools is constantly changing, so I won't mention specific tool names or vendors. Instead, I focus on functionality. Functionality that might be in a standalone version offered by a vendor one year may, by the next year, become one module of a larger toolset after the company is purchased by a competitor. Functionality may be provided by tools on-premises or in the cloud. Expect functionality and vendors to appear and disappear over time. How functionality is packaged, integrated, or separated will also change. Watch out for new functionality and new terms for old functionality. Terms used by data management may differ from terms used by data science, statistics, or software development for the same functionality (data cleansing vs. data wrangling or data munging vs. data editing). Keep your eyes open for "next generation" tools starting to appear that integrate and create functionality in ways not seen before.

Functionality Found in Tools

 Best Practice

Understand needs first, then find a tool. Michael Scofield, MBA, Assistant Professor, Loma Linda University, emphasizes the importance of understanding data quality needs first and then finding the tool to match. He lists three general data quality needs where tools can help:

- **Data understanding**. Being aware of and comprehending the meaning and behavior of data.
- **Data fixing**. Correcting or updating data, such as name and address updates and specialized find-and-replace functions.
- **Data monitoring**. Checking data as it flows or while at rest by applying tests that draw attention to new anomalies or highlight continuing problems you thought were solved.

Two tables on the following pages describe functionality found in tools. Any functionality or types of tools, if used properly, can enhance the quality of your data, create an environment and system design that enables higher quality data, or address some other quality issue. My thanks to Anthony J. Algmin for his expertise and assistance in preparing the information on functionality and tools.

- *Table 6.3* describes functionality often labeled as "data quality" or "data cleansing" functionality.
- *Table 6.4* lists functionality that can impact or support data quality, but that is not usually referred to as "data quality" functionality.

Table 6.3 Typical Functionality Found in Data Quality Tools

Data Quality Functionality	Definition and Notes
Data Discovery or Data Relationship Discovery	To manage data quality, you must first know what data you have. Discovery tools can look at multiple data sets, identify data available, and then find or validate relationships, transformations, and business rules hidden in the data.
	The use of automated data discovery tools can support data migrations, data modeling, business intelligence, and data quality and governance efforts, and may automate the source-to-target mapping process.
Data Profiling	The use of analytical techniques to discover the existence, validity, structure, content, and other basic characteristics of data. May also be known as domain analysis. Other tools may have an investigation or analysis functionality which is often similar to, but not as robust as, data profiling. Data profiling tools describe the data in detail and reveal associated metadata. Data profiling is used for analysis, but profiling tools usually do not change the data. In the big data world, there are similar tools optimized for larger sets of information.
	Data profiling can be carried out with a commercial tool (both paid and free open source options are available), or via other means such as the use of SQL to write queries, a report writer to create ad hoc reports, or a statistical analysis tool. See *Step 3.3 – Data Integrity Fundamentals* for more details on what you should expect to learn from data profiling.
Cleansing or Scrubbing	General terms used to indicate any updates to data such as preparing or correcting data. Techniques used include parsing, standardization, validation, augmentation, deduplication, and transforming. Keystroke emulation is another, though less used, method. The terms data wrangling or data munging, often used in the data science world, also refer to cleansing, transforming, enriching, or structuring raw data to make it more useable for analytics.
	Data cleansing functionality is often used to prepare data prior to matching since the better the quality of the fields themselves, the better the matching results. Cleansing tools can be used in batch mode for large scale updates or online in real time built into an application, which is useful for preventing data quality problems when data is first created.
Parsing	The ability to separate multi-valued fields into individual pieces, such as separating character strings or free form text fields into their component parts, meaningful patterns, or attributes, and moving the parts into clearly labeled and distinct fields. Having the data in distinct fields allows more flexible use of the data. Examples: separate a free-form text field for product description into height, weight, and other physical characteristics; divide a full name into first, middle, and last fields; separate an address into house number and street name
Standardization	General term used to indicate data being changed to adhere to rules and guidelines, such as similar format or approved values. Standardization often facilitates better parsing. In many tools, both standardization and parsing are used to facilitate better matching, linking, and deduplication. Examples: compare and update legacy code lists to approved valid values in a more recent reference data table, and update codes in associated active transactional records; standardize various formats for telephone numbers in source systems to one format used in a target system; update variations of a particular company name to the same version.
Enrichment or Augmentation or Enhancement	Terms that refer to adding new information to existing data. Examples: Add GPS coordinates to an existing physical location address record; add a Dun & Bradstreet DUNS number to improve matching and entity resolution
	There is a rich array of open data sets offered by public institutions that provide a tremendous amount of information for no cost. This external data gives additional context to expand the usefulness of your internal data. Examples: crime data used by local police departments to identify at-risk areas and determine where more regular patrols are needed; weather information used to know when to schedule workers to keep roads clear of snow and increase public safety; historical event information used by a transportation district to prepare for future events and avoid potential traffic disruptions
Validation and Verification	General terms used to indicate checking that the data entered into a computer is correct. (The software world has specific definitions for these two words. In the data world there is no consensus and they are sometimes used interchangeably.)
	Validation: A check that ensures entries into a production system adhere to standards and reasonableness. Note that validation does not tell if the entry was the correct entry for that record – which is accuracy – but does indicate if it is a valid value.
	Examples:
	• Compare and update a mailing address against a country's authorized postal service file. This can be done in batch mode or real-time as part of an application which checks when a new record is created.
	• Data entered into a screen is within a range of allowed values. If not, a popup box warns the data entry person who must change the value to a valid value before proceeding with the record.
	Verification: The process of ensuring data entered, or a copy made, exactly matches the original source.
	Examples:
	• Double entry where the data is entered twice, and the two copies are compared.
	• Proofreading data where a second person checks the data entered against the original source or document.
	• Backup software with built-in data verification functionality to ensure a copy of a disk is exactly the same as the original.

(Continued)

Table 6.3 Typical Functionality Found in Data Quality Tools *(Continued)*

Data Quality Functionality	Definition and Notes
Reconciliation	Reconciliation is a term often used when making processes consistent or compatible. Examples: • In finance, reconciliation of bank statements • In technology, reconciling the number of records from a data source vs. the number of records loaded to a target Many reconciliations do ensure the quality of data, but they are not usually referred to as such. Pay attention to reconciliations within the organization's standard processes that already support data quality. Look for opportunities to build in additional reconciliations to operational processes.
Transform or Transformation	General terms used to mean any changes to data. This includes resolving differences in the same data residing in various data stores in an ETL (Extract-Transform-Load) process. A Source-to-Target Mapping (STM) provides the necessary information to move data from a source to a destination along with needed transformation logic. Examples: • Parsing or standardizing data when moving it from a source to a target • Changing data to meet business or technology requirements when integrating multiple data sources
Uniqueness and Deduplication: Entity Resolution/ Record Matching/ Record Linking/ Record Deduplication	General terms related to the ability to determine if more than one reference to a real-world object (a person, place or thing) refers to the same object or to different objects and may include the process for merging records that represent the same real-world object. This is the main purpose of master data management. *Entity Resolution (ER)* – "is the process of determining whether two references to real-world objects are referring to the same object or to different objects. The term entity describes the real-world object, a person, place, or thing, and the term resolution is used because ER is fundamentally a decision process to answer (resolve) the question, 'Are the references to the same or to different entities?'" (Talburt, 2011, p. 1). *Record matching* – Identify records which have a high degree of similarity. For example, find duplicate name and address records, for customers, vendors, or employees; find duplicate product or item master records. *Record linking* – Process of assigning the same identifier to two or more records to indicate and preserve an important relationship, yet keeping individual records separate. Householding is a term used when linking all records associated with a particular household. For example, a young adult with a new checking account is linked to his or her parents, who may have many accounts with the bank. These terms are often used interchangeably, but technically are somewhat different. Entity resolution is the process of determining if two records are equivalent or not (i.e., duplicate records or not). While record matching is the most commonly used technique to accomplish entity resolution. See *Step 3.5 – Uniqueness and Deduplication* for more details. Note that these terms are not always used consistently. Confirm terms and definitions that are used by the tool vendor. Good resources for additional information: Herzog, Scheuren, and Winkler, *Data Quality and Record Linkage Techniques* (2007); Talburt, *Entity Resolution and Information Quality* (2011); and Talburt and Zhou, *Entity Information Life Cycle for Big Data* (2015).
Uniqueness and Deduplication: Survivorship/ Merge/ Consolidation/ Deduplication	Synonyms for the process of resolving duplicate records. Options: • One record can be chosen as the "master" with additional information being merged into it from the duplicate records • Build a new "best-of-breed" record by using the data from multiple sources and/or instances of the same entity • Non-merging (virtual merging) systems The merge process can be carried out automatically by the tool, or manually by a person reviewing a list of possible duplicates and completing the consolidation. *Match-Merge* or *Merge-Purge* – Commonly used phrases that include: 1) the identification of potential duplicate records, and 2) the consolidation or merging of the records.
Monitoring and Controls	The on-going ability to track adherence to data quality rules and other controls, providing alerts to potential problems. This is for proactively addressing issues, correcting data, and determining if preventive measures put into place have brought about the intended results.
Keystroke emulator	Used for updating data by automating use of the standard interface in an application through replication of keystrokes, as if done manually, similar to a macro in a spreadsheet. This can be helpful if there are too many records to be updated manually but the updates do not require the functionality of a data cleansing tool.
Screen scraping	A method of collecting and translating data from an on-screen display to another application.

Table 6.4 Functionality Found in Other Tools That Can Support Data Quality

Functionality	Definition
Data Governance	Many aspects of data management often fall under the "Data Governance" umbrella. You must look under the covers of any tool labeled data governance to understand specific functionality provided. These tools often include metadata management, data quality profiling and cleansing, workflow management, and monitoring.
Metadata Management	Any tools that capture and document metadata and make available for use. Types of metadata functionality: Metadata repository (datastore containing metadata), business glossary (business terms and definitions), data dictionary (detailed information about datastores, structure, tables, fields, relationships, format, usage, origin), labeling or tagging (classifying or categorizing data)
Data Catalog	We have always needed to inventory our data assets, just as we inventory products and know where our physical buildings are located. Data catalogs are a type of tool to help us know where our data assets are located and more about them. According to Bonnie O'Neil and Lowell Fryman in *The Data Catalog: Sherlock Holmes Data Sleuthing for Analytics* (2020), a data catalog is an "automated inventory of data assets… that enables users to discover and explore all the data sources available." They describe a data catalog as a reference for data and compare it to a card catalog for books or an online catalog for data shopping. A data catalog is often augmented or powered by machine learning. Data catalog tools include features such as data profiling capabilities, provide visibility to metadata, capture the information life cycle (using the word lineage), show related data assets, or may recommend other data assets based on your searches. Data catalogs come in different flavors, and the functions included will vary by vendor and tool. The origins of data catalogs were prompted by the need to facilitate ad hoc analytics and/or other data science activities against massive amounts of data.
Data Modeling	Data modeling is the ability to create diagrams (data models) that represent data, definitions, structure, and relationships. A data model is a way of visually representing the structure of an organization's data. It is also a specification of how data is to be represented in a database. The data model graphically reflects the way data is organized – and the more explicit the model the better as far as data quality is concerned.
Business Rules	Functionality that provides the ability to organize and store business rules so they can be used by other systems. A business rule is an authoritative principle or guideline that describes business interactions and establishes rules for actions. These interactions inform resulting data behavior which can be checked for quality. A business rule may also state the business process to which the rule is applied and why the rule is important to the organization. Various technologies such as a business rules repository, rules engine, or Business Rules Management System (BRMS) are available to coordinate between business logic and the technology required to manage and deploy decision logic within an organization.
Lineage	The ability to understand and visualize the movement of data and metadata over time and through the information life cycle. Data life cycle, data resource life cycle, provenance, data supply chain, and information value chain are other phrases associated with lineage.
Data Mapping Tools	A source-to-target mapping (STM) states the location of and information about a data source, where the data will be moved in the target datastore, and transformations that must happen to meet requirements of the target system. STMs can be managed manually in spreadsheets and used by developers to manually code transformations. Some tools transform requirements into mapping specifications that can be used by developers to generate code or used by data integration tools.
Extract-Transform-Load (ETL)	The Extract–Transform–Load process extracts data from a source datastore, transforms and aggregates data to meet target system requirements, and loads into a target datastore. ETL is both a development and operational process. Some ETL tools include functionality that performs data profiling. The careful use of ETL tools can have a positive impact on data quality.
Application Development Tools	Full-scale platforms or specialized development tools may contain developer tool kits or components that contribute to good data quality, that are already part of or available for the application: Examples: • A development component for easily verifying and standardizing addresses • Debug or testing tools that validate the results of data movement, such as inserting source data into target fields that are not long enough to hold the full value
Business Process Management (BPM) and Workflow Management	There is some confusion or disagreement as to the difference between BPM and workflow management. BPM coordinates processes across an entire organization as well as externally and includes continuous improvement of those processes. Workflow management can automate repetitive steps of a process with the ability to track multiple tasks and activities within a process; develop, organize, and route forms; and support specific roles that are part of the process. Workflow management is often included as part of BPM. These tools be used to integrate data quality tasks into business processes and to track data quality management processes, such as monitoring, assigning, escalating, and resolving data quality issues. They may also contain information about or be input to data specifications, particularly business rules.

(Continued)

Table 6.4 Functionality Found in Other Tools That Can Support Data Quality *(Continued)*

Functionality	Definition
Domain Specific Applications, such as Customer Relationship Management (CRM) and Enterprise Resource Planning (ERP)	Look for functionality built into applications focused on specific data subject areas that can enhance data quality or prevent data quality issues from appearing.
Search and Navigation	The ability to find information needed easily, reliably, quickly, and comprehensively. Search is about finding what is needed using the term itself, such as a Google search. Navigation is moving through a logical structure to find something, such as when clicking through a website.
OCR	Optical Character Recognition (OCR) is the process of converting images of text or hardcopy documents to digitized data. OCR is widely used, yet is a data gathering process that is especially susceptible to data errors and as a data creation method must be managed well to ensure high-quality data.
Voice Recognition	Voice recognition is the process of converting audio to digitized data. Like OCR, voice recognition is increasingly used, and is still a data gathering process that is especially susceptible to data errors.
Collaboration Tools	Collaboration tools help individuals and teams work together more productively. Examples include on-line calendars, video conferencing, instant messaging, and shared whiteboards. Ensuring high-quality data is a collaborative effort between people with skills and knowledge in business, data, and technology, in various levels within the organization, and usually in different geographical locations. Therefore, any tools that can help people better work together can support your data quality work.
Analytics, business intelligence, and data visualization	There are many tools available with this functionality which are used for decision making, both after-the-fact reporting and in real-time operations. These tools can help in the Ten Steps Process: • Often the output of these tools inadvertently uncovers data quality issues • Used in lieu of access to a true data profiling tool • Support analysis of data quality and business impact assessments • Show results of improvements (both correction and prevention) • Track and show results of monitoring data and implementing controls

How to Use the Tables

Make use of *Table 6.3* and *Table 6.4* in the following ways:

• Familiarize yourself with the functionality, definitions, and examples in the tables.
• Look for tools within your organization that have the functionality described, whether these are labeled as data quality tools or not. Make note of the tool and vendor names, versions in use, who to contact for more information, and how the functionality and tools can be used to support your data quality work.
• Use the information to interpret what vendors are telling you, whether at conferences, vendor shows, or when researching tools online. The specific capabilities and results derived from any tool will vary depending on the particular tool being used. Don't be afraid to ask questions! In some cases, open source tools can be helpful to experiment with before investing in a tool.
• Add synonyms, definitions, new functionality, and specific tools that apply to your needs as they are discovered.

• Many new and traditional tools have been enhanced with machine learning and artificial intelligence. You still need to understand the functionality provided.

Tools and the Ten Steps

It has already been stated that the Ten Steps Process is tool-independent, and that it will help you better use the tools you have. If you do need to buy a tool, remember to account for the selection process in your project activities, timeline, and budget. The selection process starts with developing a clear set of criteria to meet your business, technology, and data needs. Then identify tools with functionality that aligns with your selection criteria. Understand where the tool will be used and who will use it, along with the knowledge and experience required for those who will use the tool. Compare functionality, tools and vendors through research, interviews, demonstrations, and possibly a proof of concept. Make a final choice, negotiate, purchase, install the tools and obtain training. Apply the tools where needed within the construct of the Ten Steps Process.

Chapter 6 Summary

This chapter outlined techniques that can be applied in several places throughout the Ten Steps Process and detailing them here has helped avoid unnecessary repetition in *Chapter 4*. Return to *Table 6.1* at the beginning of the chapter for a reminder of where to use the information within the Ten Steps.

Techniques in this chapter include various approaches to visualizing an information life cycle, conducting surveys, developing data capture and assessment plans, and implementing metrics. The technique for tracking issues and action items helps with project management and another shows how the Ten Steps Process can be used with Six Sigma and ISO Standards. Every step, assessment and activity should make use of the technique *Analyze, Synthesize, Recommend, Document, and Act on Results.*

While the Ten Steps Process is not specific to any particular data quality tools, applying the right tools at the right time and place will help your data quality work. If you already have tools on-hand, the Ten Steps Process can be used to help implement them more effectively. If you are considering which tools could be applicable to your project, use the two tables that label and describe typical tool functionality (not specific tool names or vendors) in the last section, *Tools for Managing Data Quality.*

The more you use the techniques, along with the templates and examples, the better you will become at adjusting and applying them to fit your needs and circumstances.

Chapter 7

A Few Final Words

As you gain experience with the process,
many of the preparatory steps and technicalities become routine.
What's left is the process of discovery and learning,
of developing networks of interesting people,
of bringing new ideas into your own work and organization.
It can be a very rewarding experience
for people who are motivated to listen and learn.

— Michael Spendolini, *The Benchmarking Book (1994)*

Start where you are.
Use what you have.
Do what you can.

— Arthur Ashe

Executing Data Quality Projects. https://doi.org/10.1016/B978-0-12-818015-0.00010-4

Congratulations on making it this far! Whether you have completed your first, or tenth, project or have finished reading the book and are deciding where to begin – I hope you have found this book to be of value.

I am enthusiastic about the Ten Steps. The practical concepts, processes, and techniques presented here can be applied to any data or information that supports any part of any organization. They work no matter the language, culture, or country. I have seen it with my clients, and heard from those who used the first edition of the book or attended my training.

The Ten Steps methodology will work no matter your role or placement in your organization. It will work whether you are a beginner or more experienced. You might be a data quality pioneer – the first person to bring visibility to and tackle these issues. Even if many people are working on data quality now, there is something from the Ten Steps that can enhance their efforts. No matter your starting point, you can bring value to your organization.

The world continues to evolve. There will always be another buzzword and new technology. Internal reorganizations, mergers, acquisitions, and divestitures will change roles and responsibilities. Innovations or events beyond your control may turn the world upside down. All can affect business needs (customers, products, services, strategies, goals, issues, and opportunities). The good news is that the fundamentals outlined in the Ten Steps will guide you through these changes. No matter the circumstances, identify and prioritize business needs. Understand the information environment surrounding those needs – the related data, processes, people and organizations, and technology. Know what is happening throughout the information life cycle. Select those steps that will move you forward to effective solutions that will make a difference to your organization's success.

You will be most successful as you hone your people skills and increase your data skills. Reach out to others, offer to help, and take advantage of their expertise. With so many pieces and parts affecting data quality, it is impossible to do it all yourself. A fellow conference attendee once said, "I used to say that you cannot know everything. Now I say, there is so much to know, that you cannot even know all the important things about all the important things." So true!

Let me share a few last pieces of advice – critical success factors that will see ("C") you to success.

- **Commitment**. Don't give up.
- **Communication**. Make time for it.
- **Collaboration, Coordination, Cooperation**. Enough said.
- **Change**. Learn how to deal with change yourself. Change brings discomfort, so get comfortable with being uncomfortable. Help others deal with the changes that an emphasis on data quality will bring.
- **Courage**. We don't often talk about courage in the data quality world, but it does take courage to do something new, propose something different, and lead the way. It takes courage to move out of your comfort zone, stretch yourself, and innovate. It will take courage from the data quality team and from management who will have to defend and enforce change until successful results can speak for themselves.

While true sustainability of any data quality effort requires management support, don't be discouraged if you don't have the ear of the CEO right now. Of course, that would be nice, but don't let it stop you. Let me suggest the following dos and don'ts:

- You DON'T have to have the CEO's support to begin, but ... you DO have to have the appropriate level of management support to get started, while continuing to obtain additional support from as high up the chain as possible, with a goal of support from the top executives and the board.
- You DON'T have to have all the answers, but ... you DO need to do your homework and be willing to ask questions.
- You DON'T need to do everything all at once, but ... you DO need to have a plan of action and get started!

Get going or keep going, build on your experience, and continue to learn. Change the world with quality data and trusted information. Have fun and enjoy the journey!

Appendix: Quick References

Framework for Information Quality

The Framework for Information Quality (FIQ) can be easily understood by considering seven main sections. See *Figure A.1.*

1 – Business Needs – Customers, Products, Services, Strategies, Goals, Issues, Opportunities (Why)

An overarching phrase to indicate why we care about data quality – to support whatever is important to an organization and driven by customers, products, services, strategies, goals, issues, and opportunities.

2 – The Information Life Cycle (POSMAD)

Information should be properly managed throughout its life cycle in order to get the full use and benefit from it. Use the acronym POSMAD to remember the six phases in the Information Life Cycle. It may also be referred to as lineage, data life cycle, information value chain, information supply chain, information chain, or information resource life cycle.

Plan—Prepare for the information resource. Identify objectives, plan information architecture, develop standards and definitions. Many activities when modeling, designing, and developing applications, databases, processes, organizations, and the like could be considered part of the Plan phase for information.

Obtain—Acquire data and information. For example, create records (internally through an application or externally by customers entering information through a website), purchase data, or load external files.

Store and Share—Hold information and make it available for use through a distribution method. Data may be stored electronically (such as in databases or files) or as hardcopy (such as a paper application form kept in a file cabinet). Data is shared through such means as networks, an enterprise service bus, and email.

Maintain—Ensure the information continues to work properly. Update, change, transform, manipulate, parse, standardize, classify, curate, wrangle, munge, validate, verify, sort, classify, cleanse, or scrub data; enhance, enrich, or augment data; match or link records; deduplicate, merge, or consolidate records; and so forth.

Apply—Retrieve and use the information to support business needs. Make informed decisions and take effective action – whether by people or machines. This includes all uses such as completing transactions, writing reports, making decisions from reports, and running automated processes.

Dispose—Discard the information when it is no longer of use. Archive or delete data, records, files, or other sets of information.

3 – Key Components

Four main factors that affect information throughout its life cycle.

Data (What)—Known facts or items of interest. Here, data is distinct from information.

Processes (How)—Functions, activities, actions, procedures, or tasks that touch the data or information (business processes, data management processes, processes external to the company, etc.).

People and Organizations (Who)—Organizations, teams, roles, responsibilities, and individuals that affect or use the data or are involved with the processes.

Technology (How)—Forms, applications, databases, files, programs, code, and media that store, share, or manipulate the data, are involved with the processes, or are used by people and organizations. Technology includes both high-tech such as databases and low-tech such as paper copies.

4 – The Interaction Matrix

The **Interaction Matrix** shows relationships, connections, or interfaces between the Information Life Cycle phases and the Key Components of Data, Processes, People and Organizations, and Technology.

5 – Location (Where) and Time (When, How Often, and How Long)

Always account for where and when events, activities, and tasks take place, when information will be available, and how long it needs to be available.

Note that the top half of the FIQ, along with the first bar, answers the interrogatives of who, what, how, why, where, when, and how long.

6 – Broad-Impact Components

Additional factors that affect the quality of information. The categories below that make up those components create the acronym *RRISCCE* (pronounced "risky"). This is a reminder that it is risky to ignore the broad-impact components. The risk of poor-quality data will be lowered by ensuring the components have been addressed. If they are not addressed, the risk of poor-quality data increases.

Requirements and Constraints—Requirements are obligations that must be met. Data and information must support the ability of the organization to meet these obligations. Constraints are limitations or restrictions, that is, things that cannot or should not be done.

Responsibility—Responsibility refers to the fact that many people should answer for their part in ensuring high-quality data.

Improvement and Prevention—Continuous improvement is a reminder that having high-quality information is not accomplished through a one-time project or a single data clean-up activity. It includes identifying and preventing root causes of data quality issues.

Structure, Context, and Meaning—Information about the structure, context, and meaning of data is needed to make, build, produce, assess, use, and manage data and information.

Communication—Communication is a broad term that includes any activity that engages with people and addresses the human factor of data quality work. These activities are as essential to the success of any data quality effort as knowing how to conduct a data quality assessment.

Change—Two general aspects of managing change and its impacts: 1) Change control, which relates to technology and covers things such as version control and handling changes to a datastore, such as adding a data field, and resulting impacts on downstream screens or reports, and 2) Organizational change management (OCM), which includes managing transformations within organizations to ensure culture, motivations, rewards, and behaviors are aligned and encourage desired results.

Ethics—Ethics consider the implications of choices we make about the use of data on individuals, organizations, and society. Given the holistic approach to data quality in the Ten Steps methodology, these are also behaviors necessary for those who touch or use data in any way.

7 – Culture and Environment

Culture refers to an organization's attitudes, values, customs, practices, and social behavior. It includes both written (official policies, handbooks, etc.) and unwritten "ways of doing things," "how things get done," "how decisions get made," and so forth. **Environment** refers to conditions that surround people in your organization and affect the way they work and act. Culture and environment can also refer to broader aspects of society, country, language, and other external factors, such as politics, that impact the organization and may affect the quality of the data and information and how they are managed.

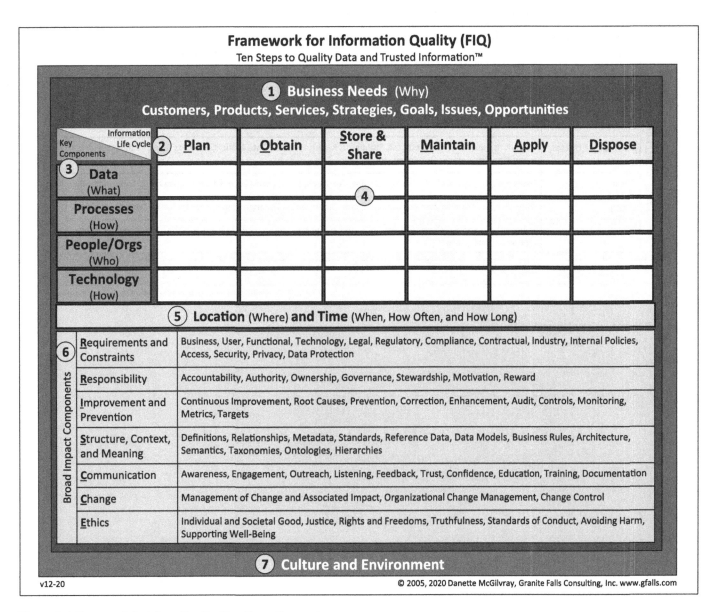

Figure A.1 Framework for Information Quality with section numbers.

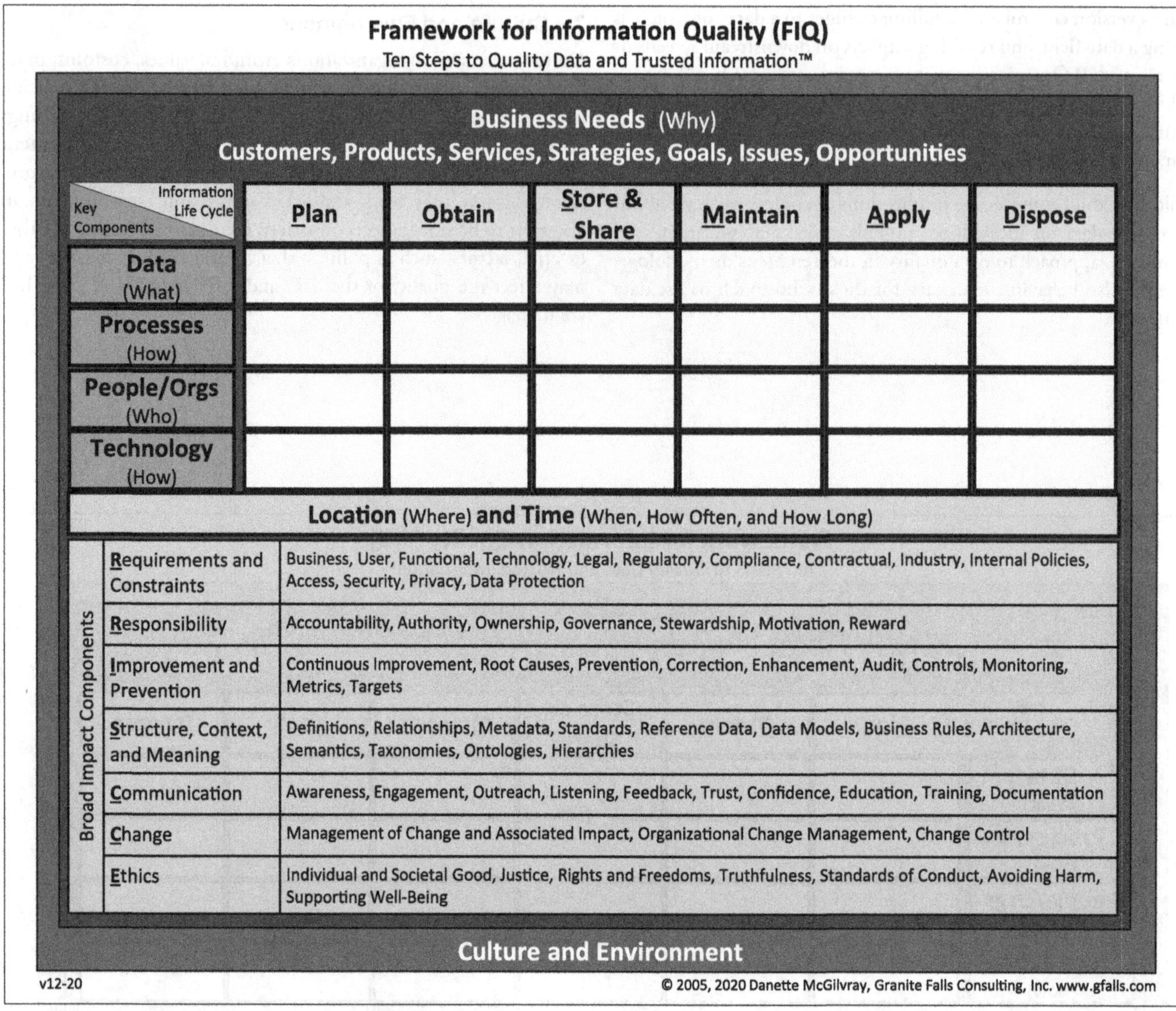
Framework for Information Quality (FIQ)
Ten Steps to Quality Data and Trusted Information™
Business Needs (Why)
Customers, Products, Services, Strategies, Goals, Issues, Opportunities
Information Life Cycle
Key Components
Plan
Obtain
Store & Share
Maintain
Apply
Dispose
Data (What)
Processes (How)
People/Orgs (Who)
Technology (How)
Location (Where) and Time (When, How Often, and How Long)
Broad Impact Components
Requirements and Constraints
Business, User, Functional, Technology, Legal, Regulatory, Compliance, Contractual, Industry, Internal Policies, Access, Security, Privacy, Data Protection
Responsibility
Accountability, Authority, Ownership, Governance, Stewardship, Motivation, Reward
Improvement and Prevention
Continuous Improvement, Root Causes, Prevention, Correction, Enhancement, Audit, Controls, Monitoring, Metrics, Targets
Structure, Context, and Meaning
Definitions, Relationships, Metadata, Standards, Reference Data, Data Models, Business Rules, Architecture, Semantics, Taxonomies, Ontologies, Hierarchies
Communication
Awareness, Engagement, Outreach, Listening, Feedback, Trust, Confidence, Education, Training, Documentation
Change
Management of Change and Associated Impact, Organizational Change Management, Change Control
Ethics
Individual and Societal Good, Justice, Rights and Freedoms, Truthfulness, Standards of Conduct, Avoiding Harm, Supporting Well-Being
Culture and Environment
v12-20
© 2005, 2020 Danette McGilvray, Granite Falls Consulting, Inc. www.gfalls.com

Figure A.2 Framework for Information Quality.

POSMAD Interaction Matrix Detail

The POSMAD Interaction Matrix is part of the Framework for Information Quality. *Figure A.3* contains sample questions in each cell of the matrix, which if answered, will help people to understand the relationships, connections, or interfaces between the Information Life Cycle phases and the key components of Data, Processes, People and Organizations, and Technology.

Interaction Matrix Detail with Sample Questions
From the Framework for Information Quality (FIQ)

Key Components \ Information Life Cycle	Plan	Obtain	Store & Share	Maintain	Apply	Dispose
Data (What)	What are the business needs and project objectives? Which data supports them? What are the applicable business rules, data standards, other data specifications?	Which data is acquired (internal and external)? Which data is entered into the system (individual data elements and/or new records)?	Which data is stored? Which data is shared? What is the key data to be backed up for rapid recovery after a disaster?	Which data is updated and changed? Which data will be transformed for sharing, migration, integration? Which data is calculated or aggregated?	What information is needed/available to support business needs, requirements, transactions, automated processes, analytics, decision making, metrics, etc.?	Which data needs to be archived? Which data needs to be deleted?
Processes (How)	What are the high-level processes? Detailed activities and tasks? What is the training and communication strategy?	How is data acquired from sources (internal and external)? How is data entered into the system? What are the triggers for creating new records?	What is the process for storing data? What is the process for sharing data?	How is data updated? Monitored to detect change? Assessed for impact? How are standards maintained? Triggers for updates?	How is the data used? Triggers for use? How is information accessed and secured? How is information made available for those using it?	How is data archived? How is data deleted? How are archive locations/processes managed? Triggers for archival? For final deletion?
People/Orgs (Who)	Who identifies/prioritizes business needs and project objectives? Who develops project plans? Who assigns resources? Who manages those involved in this phase?	Who acquires information from sources? Who enters new data/creates records? Who manages those involved in this phase?	Who develops and supports the storing technology? Who develops and supports the sharing technology? Who manages those involved in this phase?	Who decides what should be updated? Makes changes in system and ensures quality? Who needs to know about changes? Who manages those involved in this phase?	Who directly accesses the data? Who uses the information? Who manages those involved in this phase?	Who sets retention policy? Who can delete data? Who archives data? Who does final disposal? Who needs to know? Who manages those involved in this phase?
Technology (How)	What is the high-level architecture within scope of the project? What technology supports the business needs, processes, and people?	How is the technology used to load new records or create new data in the system?	What is the technology for storing the data? What is the technology for sharing the data?	How is data maintained and updated in the system?	What technology allows access to information? How are business rules applied in the application architecture?	What technology is used to delete data or records from system? What technology is used to archive data and how is it used?

v12-20

© 2005, 2020 Danette McGilvray, Granite Falls Consulting, Inc. www.gfalls.com

Figure A.3 POSMAD Interaction Matrix detail with sample questions.

Data Quality Dimensions

Table A.1 Data Quality Dimensions in the Ten Steps Process

Data Quality Dimension. A data quality dimension is a characteristic, aspect, or feature of data. Data quality dimensions provide a way to classify information and data quality needs. Dimensions are used to define, measure, improve, and manage the quality of data and information. Instructions for assessing data quality using the following dimensions are included in the Ten Steps Process in *Step 3 – Assess Data Quality*. See *Figure A.4*.

Substep	Data Quality Dimension Name and Definition
3.1	**Perception of Relevance and Trust.** The subjective opinion of those who use information and/or those who create, maintain, and dispose of data regarding: 1) Relevance – which data is of most value and importance to them, and 2) Trust – their confidence in the quality of the data to meet their needs.
3.2	**Data Specifications.** Data Specifications include any information and documentation that provide context, structure, and meaning to data. Data Specifications provide information needed to make, build, produce, assess, use, and manage data and information. Examples include metadata, data standards, reference data, data models, and business rules. Without the existence, completeness, and quality of data specifications it is difficult to produce high-quality data and harder to measure, understand, and manage the quality of data content.
3.3	**Data Integrity Fundamentals.** The existence (completeness/fill rate), validity, structure, content, and other basic characteristics of data.
3.4	**Accuracy.** The correctness of the content of the data as compared to an agreed-upon and accessible authoritative source of reference.
3.5	**Uniqueness and Deduplication.** The uniqueness (positive) or unwanted duplication (negative) of data (fields, records, or datasets) existing within or across systems or datastores.
3.6	**Consistency and Synchronization.** Equivalence of data stored or used in various datastores, applications, and systems.
3.7	**Timeliness.** Data and information are current and ready for use as specified and in the time frame in which they are expected.
3.8	**Access.** The ability to control how authorized users can view, modify, use, or otherwise process data and information.
3.9	**Security and Privacy. Security** is the ability to protect data and information assets from unauthorized access, use, disclosure, disruption, modification, or destruction. **Privacy** for an individual is the ability to have some control over how data about them as a person is collected and used. For an organization, it is the ability to comply with how people want their data to be collected, shared, and used.
3.10	**Presentation Quality.** The format, appearance, and display of data and information support their collection and uses.
3.11	**Data Coverage.** The comprehensiveness of data available compared to the total data universe or population of interest.
3.12	**Data Decay.** Rate of negative change to the data.
3.13	**Usability and Transactability.** Data produces the desired business transaction, outcome, or use for which it was intended.
3.14	**Other Relevant Data Quality Dimensions.** Other characteristics, aspects, or features of data and information that are deemed to be important for your organization to define, measure, improve, monitor, and manage.

Business Impact Techniques

Table A.2 Business Impact Techniques in the Ten Steps Process

Business Impact Techniques. A business impact technique is a qualitative and/or quantitative method for determining the effects of the quality of data on the organization. These effects can be good effects from high-quality data and/or adverse effects from poor-quality data. Instructions for assessing business impact using the following techniques are included in the Ten Steps Process in *Step 4 – Assess Business Impact*. See *Figure A.4*.

Substep	Business Impact Technique Name and Definition
4.1	**Anecdotes.** Collect examples of the negative impact of poor-quality data and/or the positive impact of good quality data.
4.2	**Connect the Dots.** Illustrate the connection between business needs and the data which supports them.
4.3	**Usage.** Inventory the current and/or future uses of the data.
4.4	**Five Whys for Business Impact.** Ask "Why?" five times to recognize the real effects of the quality of data on the business.
4.5	**Process Impact.** Illustrate the effects of data quality on business processes.
4.6	**Risk Analysis.** Identify possible adverse effects from poor quality data, evaluate the likelihood of them happening, severity if they do, and determine ways to mitigate the risks.
4.7	**Perception of Relevance and Trust.** The subjective opinion of those who use information and/or those who create, maintain, and dispose of data regarding: 1) Relevance – which data is of most value and importance to them, and 2) Trust – their confidence in the quality of the data to meet their needs.
4.8	**Benefit vs. Cost Matrix.** Rate and analyze the relationship between benefits and costs of issues, recommendations, or improvements.
4.9	**Ranking and Prioritization.** Rank the impact of missing and incorrect data on specific business processes.
4.10	**Cost of Low-Quality Data.** Quantify costs and the impact to revenue due to poor-quality data.
4.11	**Cost-Benefit Analysis and ROI.** Compare anticipated costs of investing in data quality to potential benefits through an in-depth evaluation, which may include calculating return on investment (ROI).
4.12	**Other Relevant Business Impact Techniques:** Other qualitative and/or quantitative methods for determining the effects of the quality of data on the business that are deemed important for your organization to understand.

The Ten Steps Process

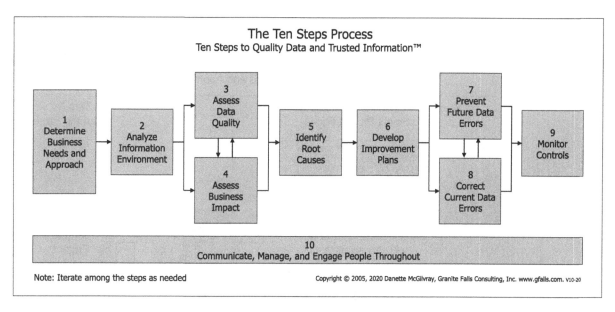

Figure A.4 The Ten Steps Process.

1. Determine Business Needs and Approach—Identify and agree on business needs (related to customers, products, services, strategies, goals, issues, and/or opportunities) and data quality issues to be within scope of the project. Reference them to guide work and keep at the forefront of all activities throughout the project. Plan the project and obtain resources.

2. Analyze Information Environment—Understand the environment surrounding the business needs and data quality issues: analyze relevant requirements and constraints, data and data specifications, processes, people and organizations, technology and the information life cycle, at the appropriate level of detail. All provide input for remaining steps, e.g., to ensure only pertinent data will be assessed for quality, as a basis for analyzing results, identifying root causes, and implementing what is needed to prevent future data errors, correct current data errors, and monitor controls.

3. Assess Data Quality—Select the data quality dimensions applicable to the business needs and data quality issues within scope of the project. Evaluate data quality for the chosen dimensions. Analyze individual assessments and synthesize with other results. Make initial recommendations, document, and take action as needed at the time. Results from the data quality assessment(s) guide where to focus efforts in the remaining steps.

4. Assess Business Impact—Determine the impact of poor-quality data on the business. A variety of qualitative and quantitative techniques are offered, with each placed on a continuum from, relatively speaking, taking less time and being less complex to assess, to taking more time and being more complex. This aids in selecting the best technique(s) to fit the purpose of the business impact and within the time and resources available.

Use any of the techniques at any time, in any step, whenever there is a need to gain support, establish the business case for data quality work, prioritize efforts, address resistance, and motivate others to participate in the project.

5. Identify Root Causes—Identify and prioritize the true causes of the data quality problems and develop specific recommendations for addressing them.

6. Develop Improvement Plans—Develop improvement plans, based on finalized recommendations, to prevent future data errors, correct current data errors, and monitor controls.

7. Prevent Future Data Errors—Implement improvement plans for solutions that address root causes of the data quality problems and will prevent data errors from reoccurring. Solutions may range from simple tasks to creating additional projects.

8. Correct Current Data Errors—Implement improvement plans that make appropriate corrections to the data. Ensure downstream systems can handle the changes. Validate and document changes. Ensure the data corrections do not introduce new errors.

9. Monitor Controls—Monitor and verify improvements that were implemented. Maintain improved results by standardizing, documenting, and continuously monitoring successful improvements.

10. Communicate, Manage, and Engage People Throughout—Communication, engaging with people, and managing the project throughout are essential to the success of any information and data quality project. These are so important that they should be included as part of every other step.

Process Flows for Steps 1-4

Figure A.5, Figure A.6, Figure A.7, and Figure A.8 show the process flows for Steps 1-4 in the Ten Steps Process shown in Figure A.4.

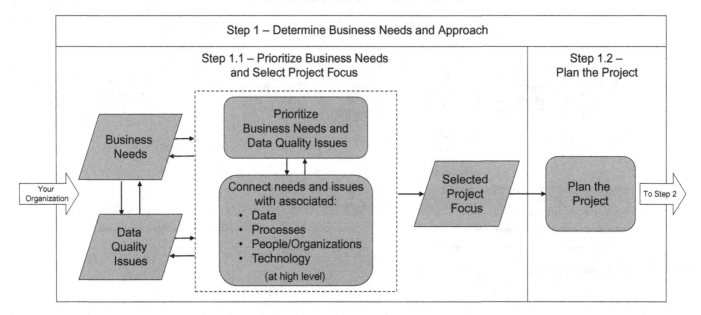

Figure A.5 Process flow for Step 1 – Determine Business Needs and Approach.

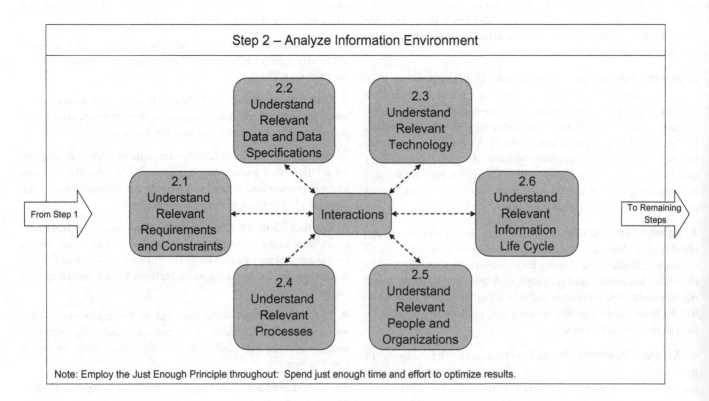

Figure A.6 Process flow for Step 2 – Analyze Information Environment.

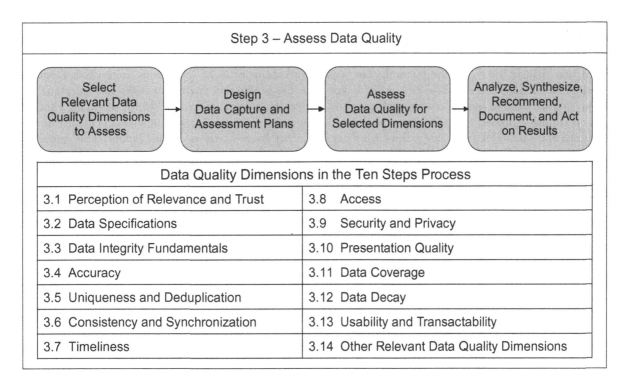

Figure A.7 Process flow for Step 3 – Assess Data Quality.

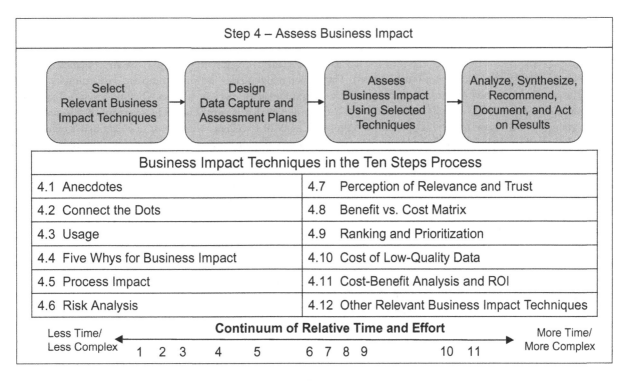

Figure A.8 Process flow for Step 4 – Assess Business Impact.

Data in Action Triangle

The Data in Action Triangle (see *Figure A.9*) places the Ten Steps methodology into the broader context of how data quality in general is put into practice to solve real issues – through programs, projects, and operational processes. The Ten Steps supports work done through each of them. When developing a data quality strategy (or any data strategy) account for each side of the triangle in the roadmap and execution plans. Work can start on any side of the triangle, with it being done in parallel, iteratively, or sequentially – whatever works best. But to sustain data quality in an organization, all sides must be addressed at some point.

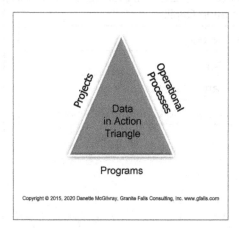

Figure A.9 Data in Action Triangle.

Projects

A **project** is a one-time effort that addresses a business need. The duration of the project is determined by the complexity of the desired results. Project deliverables often include implementing what then become ongoing production, or operational, processes. A project can be a structured effort to address an issue by one person, a large team, or it can include coordination across multiple teams. In the information technology (IT) world, projects could be somewhat synonymous with work done by an Application Development team in software development projects.

The project aspect of the Data in Action Triangle is covered by this book *Executing Data Quality Projects: Ten Steps to Quality Data and Trusted Information*, Second Edition. Projects are used as the vehicle for data quality work. The word itself is used broadly and includes three general types of projects: 1) Focused data quality improvement project, 2) Data quality activities in another project, such as application development, data migration or integration of any kind, and 3) Ad hoc use of data quality steps, activities, or techniques from the Ten Steps.

Operational Processes

Generally, **operational processes** are series of activities directed toward a specific aim taken within an operational environment (as opposed to a project environment). In the IT world, Operational Processes could be somewhat synonymous with work done by an IT Operations team which supports software in the production environment. From a data quality perspective, the operational process side of the triangle includes incorporating activities that will enhance data quality or prevent data quality issues in day-to-day operations, "run" processes, or production support work. For example, include awareness of data quality into new employee training, quickly apply Ten Steps thinking to an incident that arises in a supply chain process, or taking action on the results of data quality monitoring as a standard part of a person's role.

Programs

Generally, a **program** is an on-going initiative that manages related activities and/or projects in a coordinated way to obtain benefits that would not be available from managing them individually. A program avoids incurring duplicate time, effort, and costs from multiple business units developing their own services and data quality approaches. Having a program providing services that are used by many allows business units to spend their time adjusting those services to meet their own specific needs.

A data quality (DQ) program provides specialized data quality services that are utilized by projects or operational processes, such as training, managing DQ tools, and internal consulting using expert knowledge and skills to address data quality issues, conducting data quality health checks, raising awareness about data quality and gaining support for the work, adopting the Ten Steps as a standard or using it to develop your own data quality improvement methodology, etc.

A DQ program may be part of any organizational structure that makes sense for your company. For example, the DQ program may be part of a Data Quality Services Team, a separate program that is part of a Data Governance Office, a Data Quality Center of Excellence that is part of a data management function, a company-wide business function, or a branch of an enterprise data management team.

Having a data quality program is essential to sustaining the quality of data within an organization. Work on data quality can be started by implementing data quality projects, but projects eventually end. The program ensures the people with knowledge, skills, and experience with the data quality processes, methods, and tools used in the projects continue to be available to new projects and operational processes.

The Relationship

Programs, which are ongoing, provide services which can be used by both Projects and Operational Processes. Projects develop and implement operational processes that remain in place once the project goes into production. The project is then over, and the operational processes continue. In the course of business as usual (carrying out operational processes) business needs evolve, and issues or new requirements arise. A new project may be initiated to address these issues, which moves the work back to the project side of the triangle.

A Note about DevOps and DataOps

Figure A.10 shows the Data in Action Triangle applied to DevOps and DataOps, with the main high-level activities listed on each side of the triangle. While the words are different, the underlying ideas of the original Data in Action Triangle are the same. However, the cadence with DevOps and DataOps is more iterative than sequential.

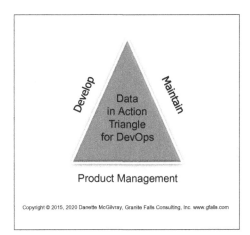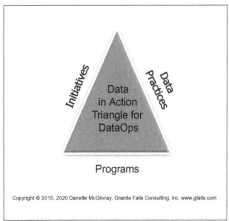

Figure A.10 Data in Action Triangle for DevOps and DataOps.

Glossary

I like good strong words that mean something.

— Louisa May Alcott, *Little Women*

So difficult it is to show the various meanings and imperfections of words when we have nothing else but words to do it with.

— John Locke

Words in *italics* are defined separately within the glossary.

5G In telecommunications, the fifth-generation technology standard for cellular networks which provides increased download speeds through greater bandwidth speeds and lowered *latency*.

Access A *data quality dimension*. The ability to control how authorized users can view, modify, use, or otherwise process data and information.

Accuracy A *data quality dimension*. The correctness of the content of the data as compared to an agreed-upon and accessible authoritative source of reference.

Action The third high-level step in the *Data Quality Improvement Cycle*. In this context, it refers to activities (resulting from *Assessment* and *Awareness*) such as preventing data quality problems, correcting current data errors, implementing controls, and verifying by periodic assessments.

Aggregate data Information that is collected from multiple records or sources and compiled into summaries. Often considered a *data category*.

Anecdotes A *business impact technique*. Examples of the negative impact of poor-quality data and/or the positive impact of good-quality data.

APPI From Japan, Act on the Protection of Personal Information (Act No. 57 of 2003).

Apply A *POSMAD information life cycle* phase. Retrieve and use the information to support *business needs*. Make informed decisions and take effective action—whether by people or machines. This includes all uses such as completing transactions, writing reports, making decisions from reports, and running automated processes.

Architecture Generally, components of a structure or system, how they are organized, and their relationship to each other. Many are familiar with architecture as it applies to the design of buildings, open areas, and their environments. Enterprise Architecture encompasses the domains of: "1) Business architecture, which establishes requirements for data, application and technology, 2) Data architecture, which manages data created and required by business architecture, 3) Application architecture, which acts on specified data according to business requirements, and 4) Technology architecture, which hosts and executes the application architecture." (DAMA International, 2017).

Artificial Intelligence (AI) "A collective term for computer systems that can sense their environment, think, learn, and take action in response to what they are sensing and their objectives." (PwC, 2020).

Assessment (1) The comparison of the actual environment and data to requirements and expectations. (2) The first high-level step in the *Data Quality Improvement Cycle*.

Audit trail metadata A specific type of *metadata*, typically stored in a log file and protected from alteration, which captures how, when, and by whom the data is created, accessed, updated, or deleted. Audit trail metadata is used for security, compliance, or forensic purposes. Although audit trail metadata is typically stored in a log file or similar type of record, *technical metadata* and *business metadata* are usually stored separately from the data they describe.

Awareness An understanding of the true state of data and information, impact to the business, and root causes. The second high-level step in the *Data Quality Improvement Cycle*.

Benefit vs. Cost Matrix A *business impact technique*. Rate and analyze the relationship between benefits and costs of issues, recommendations, or improvements.

Big Data Large amounts of data. Often described by "Vs," with the three most common being volume, velocity, and variety. Additional Vs include variability, veracity, vulnerability, volatility, visualization, and value.

Broad Impact Components A section in the *Framework for Information Quality*. Additional factors that affect the quality of information. The categories that make up those factors create the acronym *RRISCCE*.

Business Impact Technique A qualitative and/or quantitative method for determining the effects of the quality of data on the organization. These effects can be good effects from high-quality data and/or adverse effects from poor-quality data.

Business metadata *Metadata* that describes the nontechnical aspects of data and its usage.

Business needs An overarching phrase to indicate whatever is important to an *organization* and driven by customers, products, services, strategies, goals, issues, and opportunities. Said another way, business needs include whatever is required to provide products and services to customers; work with suppliers, employees, and business partners; and the strategies, goals, issues, and opportunities that must be addressed to do so. Also a section in the *Framework for Information Quality*.

Business rule An authoritative principle or guideline that describes business interactions and establishes rules for actions. It may also state the business process to which the rule is applied and why the rule is important to the organization. **Business action** refers to action that should be taken if the business rule is followed, in business terms. The behavior of the resulting data can be articulated as requirements or data quality rules and then checked for compliance. **Data quality rule specifications** explain, at the physical datastore level, how to check the quality of the data, which is an output of the adherence (or nonadherence) to the business rules and business actions.

Catalog metadata *Metadata* used to classify and organize collections of datasets.

Cause-and-Effect/Fishbone Diagram A *root cause analysis* technique. Identifies, explores, and arranges the causes of a data quality issue or error in which the relationships between causes are graphically displayed according to their level of importance or detail. It is a standard quality technique often used in manufacturing to uncover root causes of an event, problem, condition, or outcome, which also works well when applied to data and information quality.

CCPA From the State of California in the US, the California Consumer Privacy Act.

Change A *RRISCCE broad-impact component* in the *Framework for Information Quality*. Encompasses management of change and associated impact, organizational change management, and change control. If all kinds of change are not managed, it greatly increases the risk of NOT having improvements implemented and sustained. Two general aspects of managing change and its impacts: (1) change control, which relates to technology and covers things such as version control and handling changes to a datastore, such as adding a data field, and resulting impacts on downstream screens or reports, and (2) organizational change management (OCM), which includes managing transformations within organizations to ensure culture, motivations, rewards, and behaviors are aligned and encourage desired results.

Communication A broad term that includes any activity that engages with people and addresses the human factor of data quality work. These activities are as essential to the success of any data quality effort as knowing how to conduct a data quality assessment. Also a *RRISCCE broad-impact component* in the *Framework for Information Quality* that encompasses awareness, engagement, outreach, listening, feedback, trust, confidence, education, training, and documentation.

Completeness A characteristic of information quality that measures the degree to which there is a value in a field; synonymous with fill rate. Assessed in the *data quality dimension* of Data Integrity Fundamentals.

Connect the Dots A *business impact technique*. Illustrate the connection between *business needs* and the data which supports them.

Consistency and Synchronization A *data quality dimension*. *Equivalence* of data stored or used in various *datastores*, applications, and systems.

Constraints See *requirements and constraints*.

Control Used generally in this book to indicate various activities that check, detect, verify, constrain, reward, encourage, or direct work that will ensure high-quality data, prevent data quality issues or errors, or increase the chances of producing high-quality data. The controls can be one-time implementations or may continue to be monitored over time. More specifically, "A control is a form of feedback built into a system to keep it stable. A control has the ability to detect conditions that indicate a lack of stability (most often in the form of a measurement) and initiate action based on this observation." (Sebastian-Coleman, 2013).

Cost of Low-Quality Data A *business impact technique*. Quantify costs and the impact to revenue due to poor-quality data.

Cost-Benefit Analysis and ROI A *business impact technique*. Compare anticipated costs of investing in data quality to potential benefits through an in-depth evaluation, which may include calculating *return on investment* (ROI).

Coverage See *Data Coverage*.

Critical data elements (CDEs) The data *fields* tied to the most critical *business needs* and deemed to be most important to assess for quality and to manage on-going.

Culture and Environment A *RRISCCE broad-impact component* in the *Framework for Information Quality*. **Culture** refers to an organization's attitudes, values, customs, practices, and social behavior. **Environment** refers to the conditions that surround people in an *organization* and affect the way they work and act. Culture and environment can also refer to broader aspects of society, country, language, and other external factors, such as politics, that impact the organization and may affect the quality of the data and information and how they are managed.

Customer Those who make use of whatever products or services an *organization* provides. More broadly, within an organization, executives, managers, employees, suppliers, and business partners may be customers of the data and information provided. They then use the information to help provide products and services to the end customers.

Data Refers to known facts or items of interest. In the Ten Steps methodology, data is often used interchangeably with *information*, though there are a few places where the distinction between the two are important. Also, one of the four *key components* in the *Framework for Information Quality*.

Data-dependent Societies, families, individuals, and *organizations* (whether for-profit in any industry, nonprofit, government, education, healthcare, science, research, social services, medicine, etc.) all depend on information to succeed—whether they consciously recognize it or not.

Data-driven Specific efforts to help the organization deliberately make decisions based on data analysis or focused initiatives that work to change the culture and better use data to run a business more efficiently and effectively.

Data assessment plan How the quality of the data and/or the business impact of the data will be evaluated.

Data capture Method for accessing or acquiring data for assessment and other uses, such as extracting data to a flat file and loading to a secure testing database or connecting directly to a reporting *datastore*.

Data category A grouping of data with common characteristics or features. Data categories are useful for managing structured data because certain data may be treated differently based on their classification. The main data categories outlined in the Ten Steps are *master data*, *transactional data*, *reference data*, and *metadata*. These are common terms used by those who work with data. There are additional data categories that impact how systems and databases are designed and data is used, such as *aggregate data*, *historical data*, *reporting/dashboard data*, *sensitive data*, and *temporary data*. Understanding the relationship and dependency between the different categories can help direct data quality efforts.

Data Coverage A *data quality dimension*. The comprehensiveness of data available compared to the total data universe or population of interest.

Data Decay A *data quality dimension*. Rate of negative change to the data.

Data field See *field*.

Data governance The organization and implementation of policies, procedures, structure, roles, and responsibilities that outline and enforce rules of engagement, decision rights, and accountabilities for the effective management of information assets. (John Ladley, Danette McGilvray, Anne-Marie Smith, Gwen Thomas)

Data in Action Triangle A model showing that, in most organizations, work gets done through *projects*, *operational processes*, and *programs* and their relationships.

Data Integrity Fundamentals A *data quality dimension*. The existence (*completeness/fill rate*), *validity*, *structure*, content, and other basic characteristics of data.

Data lake A type of *datastore* that holds vast amounts of data. These large volumes of data are often referred to as *Big Data*.

Data model A visual representation, supported by text, of data structures in a specified domain. The data model may be either: (1) Business-oriented—representing what is important to an organization, visualizing the structure of an organization's data without regard to technology; (2) Technology-oriented—representing a specific collection of data in terms of a particular data management approach, showing where data will be held and how it will be organized (relational, object oriented, NoSQL, etc.). Data models are primary artifacts through which an organization represents its data to itself and through which it understands its data.

Data modeling The process of creating diagrams (*data models*) that represent data, definitions, structure, and relationships.

Data profiling The use of analytical techniques to discover the existence, validity, structure, content, and other basic characteristics of data. May also be known as domain analysis. The technique of data profiling is used to assess the *data quality dimension* of Data Integrity Fundamentals.

Data quality See *Information quality*.

Data Quality Dimension Characteristic, aspect, or feature of data. Data quality dimensions provide a way to classify information and data quality needs. Dimensions are used to define, measure, improve, sustain, and manage the quality of data and information.

Data Quality Improvement Cycle An illustration of the idea that managing data quality is a continuous process, done through three high-level steps: *Assessment*, *Awareness*, and *Action*. A modification of the familiar *Plan-Do-Check-Act (PDCA)* or *Plan-Do-Study-Act (PDSA)* techniques.

Data Specifications A *data quality dimension*. Any information and documentation that provide context, structure, and meaning to data. Data specifications provide information needed to make, build, produce, assess, use, and manage data and information. The phrase data specifications is also an overarching term used in the Ten Steps methodology to include any information and documentation that provide *context, structure, and meaning* to data and information. The Ten Steps emphasizes the data specifications of *metadata, data standards, reference data, data models,* and *business rules.*

Data standards Agreements, rules, or guidelines on how data is named, represented, formatted, defined, and/or managed. Data standards indicate a level of quality to which data should conform.

Data stewardship An approach to data governance that formalizes accountability for managing information resources on behalf of others and for the best interests of the organization. Formal roles associated with this approach are often, but not always, referred to as **data stewards**, with various types of data stewards such as enterprise data stewards, business data stewards, technical data stewards, domain data stewards, operational data stewards, and project data stewards.

DataOps Collaborative processes, use of tools, and partnerships between teams that might be separate (such as business users, data scientists, data engineers, analysts, and data management) to better manage data or deliver analytics.

Dataset A collection of data that is captured and used for assessment, analysis, correction, etc. and is often a subset of a full *datastore.*

Datastore Any collection of data that is created or obtained, held, and used, regardless of the technology involved.

Definition A statement of the meaning of a word or phrase. It is a general term used here as a reminder that a basic aspect of high-quality data is that the data is defined and the meaning is understood.

DevOps An approach that combines, or at a minimum encourages, collaboration and shared technologies between two historically separate Information Technology (IT) teams: one known as Application Development, which develops software and releases it; the other IT Operations, which deploys, maintains, and supports the software.

Disinformation "False information that is deliberately created to mislead, harm or manipulate a person, social group, organization or country." (Yakencheck, 2020)

Dispose A *POSMAD information life cycle* phase. Remove or discard the information when it is no longer of use. Activities within the dispose phase include archiving or deleting records, files, datasets or information.

Document as Discovered Capture insights and ideas whenever they come. They will be available to be used in the current step or later in the project. The insights and ideas won't be forgotten and rework later to re-discover will be avoided.

Duplication See *Uniqueness and Deduplication.*

DPA From the UK, Data Protection Act 2018.

Enterprise Resource Planning (ERP) Software that integrates processes and data often found in stand-alone systems, such as finance, human resources, manufacturing, distribution, sales, customer management, etc. The suite of applications within the ERP automates, manages, and supports administrative and operational business processes.

Equivalence The same data stored and used in various places should represent the same fact and be conceptually equal. It indicates that the data have equal values and meanings or are in essence the same. See *Consistency and Synchronization.*

Ethics A *RRISCCE broad-impact component* in the *Framework for Information Quality.* Ethics consider the implications of choices we make about the use of data on individuals, organizations, and society. Ideas which embody this broad-impact component of ethics include: individual and societal good, justice, rights and freedoms, truthfulness, standards of conduct, avoiding harm, and supporting well-being. Given the holistic approach to data quality in the Ten Steps methodology, these are also behaviors necessary for those who touch or use data in any way.

Event data Data that describes actions performed by things. Event data could be similar to *transactional data* or *measurement data.*

Extract-Transform-Load (ETL) A process where data is obtained (extracted) from a source system, changed (transformed) to be compatible with the target or destination system, and then put into the target system (load).

Field A location for storing a value. In relational databases, a field may also be called a column, a data element, or an attribute. Depending on the type of nonrelational database, a field may be a key, a value, a node, or a relationship. Also known as data field.

Fill rate See *Completeness.*

Fishbone Diagram See *Cause-and-Effect/Fishbone Diagram.*

Five Whys for Business Impact A *business impact technique.* Ask "Why?" five times to recognize the real effects of the quality of data on the business.

Five Whys for Root Causes A *root cause analysis* technique. Ask "Why?" five times to get to the real root causes of the data and information quality problem. It is a standard quality technique often used in manufacturing which also works well when applied to data and information quality.

Folksonomy Derived from "folk" and "*taxonomy*" and occurs primarily through tagging (adding metadata to content). It is also known as social tagging, collaborative tagging, social classification, and social bookmarking. The tags create an informal, unstructured taxonomy (as opposed to structured taxonomies) and are used to more easily locate content. Using the data in the tags gives improved content visibility, classification, and searchability. (Techopedia, 2014)

Framework for Information Quality (FIQ) A structure that visualizes and organizes the components necessary to ensure high-quality data. Using this framework helps make sense of the complex environments that create poor quality information and enables organized thinking to recognize which components are lacking or missing all together. This helps identify root causes and determine improvements needed to correct existing problems and prevent the problems from reappearing.

GDPR from the European Union, the General Data Protection Regulation.

Hierarchy A system of things ranked one above the other. It is a type of *taxonomy*. A parent-child relationship is a simple hierarchy. Other examples: an organizational chart, a chart of accounts in finance, or a product hierarchy. Some data relationships, and with them expectations for quality, can be understood through hierarchies.

HIPAA From the US, Health Insurance Portability and Accountability Act of 1996.

Historical data Significant facts, as of a certain point in time, which should not be altered except to correct an error. Often considered a *data category*.

Improvement and Prevention A *RRISCCE broad-impact component* in the *Framework for Information Quality*. A reminder that having high-quality data is not accomplished through a one-time project or a single data clean-up activity. Encompasses continuous improvement, root causes, correction, enhancement, audit, *controls, monitoring*, metrics, and targets.

Information *Data* (facts or elements of interest) within context. In the Ten Steps methodology, information is often used interchangeably with data, though there are a few places where the distinction between the two are important. Information is an asset that should be properly managed throughout its life cycle in order to get the full use and benefit from it.

Information environment The settings, conditions, and situations that surround, may have created or exacerbated information quality problems. These include *requirements and constraints, data* and *data specifications, processes, people and organizations, technology,* and the *information life cycle*.

Information Life Cycle The process of change and development throughout the life of data and information. *Data, processes, people and organizations,* and *technology* should be managed throughout the life of information in order to get the full use and benefit from it. The acronym *POSMAD* can be used to remember the six phases in the information life cycle. Also a section in the *Framework for Information Quality*. The information life cycle can be visualized using a variety of methods, such as *swim lane, SIPOC,* or *IP Map*.

Information Product Map (IP Map) "A graphical model designed to help people to comprehend, evaluate, and describe how an information product such as an invoice, customer order, or prescription is assembled. The IP Map is aimed at creating a systematic representation for capturing the details associated with the manufacture of an information product that is routinely produced within an organization." (Wang, et al, 2005). An approach to understanding and visualizing an *information life cycle*.

Information quality In The Ten Steps methodology, the degree to which *information* and *data* can be a trusted source for any and/or all required uses—the right set of correct information, at the right time, in the right place, for the right people to make decisions, run the business, serve customers, and achieve company goals. Also referred to as *data quality*.

Interaction Matrix A section in the *Framework for Information Quality*. Shows relationships, connections, or interfaces between the *information life cycle* phases and the *key components* of *data, processes, people and organizations*, and *technology*.

Internet of Things (IoT) System of connected interrelated "things" with sensors and unique identifiers (UIDs) which are able to transfer data over the internet without requiring human-to-human or human-to-computer interaction. These "things" can be computing devices, machines, objects, animals, or people. It is a sensor network of billions of smart devices that connect people, systems, and other applications to collect and share data and to communicate and interact with each other.

Just Enough Principle Spend "just enough" time and effort to optimize results—not a drop more, but not a drop less either! Just enough is not about being sloppy or cutting corners. It requires good critical thinking skills. Spend just enough time on the step, technique, or activity to optimize results—which might mean 2 minutes, 2 hours, 2 days, 2 weeks, or 2 months. Make decisions based on what is known and move on. Adjustments can be made later if additional information becomes known.

Key Components A section in the *Framework for Information Quality*. Four main areas that affect information throughout its life cycle: *data* (what), *processes* (how), *people and organizations* (who), and *technology* (how).

Knowledge worker A person who uses data or information to perform his or her work or to complete job responsibilities. Also known as information producer, information consumer, information customer, or *user*.

Label metadata *Metadata* used to annotate data or information sets, such as tags, and usually used with high volumes of data. While metadata for structured data is almost always stored separately from the data itself, with labeled data the metadata and content are stored together. See *labeled data*.

Labeled data Data that has been tagged or annotated. While *metadata* for structured data is almost always stored separately from the data itself, with labeled data the metadata and content are stored together in a way that computers and/or human analysts can interpret and act upon them; for example, for data used to train machine learning algorithms or models. Data labeling is a technique often used against large volumes of data held in nonrelational databases.

Latency The period or time delay between data as it travels from one node to another, the delay between stimulus or instruction and response.

Life cycle The process of change and development throughout the useful life of something. See *information life cycle* and *resource life cycle*.

Lineage The movement of data and metadata over time and through the *information life cycle*. Often used as a synonym for, or as a subset of, the information life cycle. Often used by tool vendors to describe functionality that provides the ability to document, visualize, and manage the information life cycle.

Location and Time A section in the *Framework for Information Quality*. Where and when events, activities, and tasks take place, where and when data and information will be available, and how long they need to be available.

Machine Learning (ML) A discipline within *artificial intelligence* which uses sophisticated algorithms to help computer software get better at making decisions.

Maintain A *POSMAD information life cycle* phase. Ensure the information continues to work properly. Activities within this phase include: update, change, transform, manipulate, parse, standardize, classify, curate, wrangle, munge, validate, verify, sort, classify, cleanse, or scrub data; enhance, enrich, or augment data; match or link records; deduplicate, merge, or consolidate records; and so forth.

Master data Describes the people, places, and things that are involved in an *organization*'s business. Examples include people (e.g., customer, employee, vendor, supplier, patient, physician, student), places (e.g., location, sales territory, office, geospatial coordinate, email address, url, IP address), and things (e.g., account, product, asset, device ID).

Master reference data (MRD) Combined *data categories* of *reference data* and *master data*.

Measurement data Data often captured in high volumes and at high velocity via meters, sensors, radio frequency identification (RFI) chips and other devices, and transmitted by machine-to-machine connections.

Media Various means of presenting information, whether electronic or hardcopy, which include (but are not limited to) reports, forms, user guides, surveys, posters, dashboards, application screens, and user interfaces.

Metadata Literally means "data about data." Describes, labels, or characterizes other data and makes it easier to filter, retrieve, interpret, or use information. Examples of metadata include *field* name descriptions, *definitions* of codes, *lineage*, domain values, context, quality, condition, characteristics, constraints, methods of change, and *rules*. Additional types of metadata include *technical metadata*, *business metadata*, *label metadata*, *catalog metadata*, and *audit trail metadata*.

Misinformation "Information that is false, but not created or shared with the intention of causing harm." (Yakencheck, 2020)

Monitoring The on-going ability to track adherence to data quality rules and other *controls*, providing alerts to potential problems.

Obtain A *POSMAD information life cycle* phase. Acquire the data or information. For example, create records (internally through an application or externally by customers entering information through a website), purchase data, or load external files.

Ontology From the world of philosophy, the science or study of being or the existence of things. From a data point of view, data should represent what exists. In this context, an ontology is a set of formal definitions for concepts, including how the concepts relate to one another. Data can be understood and cross-referenced through ontologies.

Operational processes Series of activities directed toward a specific aim taken within an operational or "business as usual" environment (as opposed to a project environment). One side of the *Data in Action Triangle*.

Organization An overarching word used to mean enterprises, institutions, agencies, establishments, and businesses of all sizes in any industry, such as for-profits, education, government, healthcare, nonprofits, charities, science, research, social services, etc. The Ten Steps applies to them all because every organization is in the "business" of providing some kind of product and/or service to customers and every organization depends on data and information to succeed.

Other Relevant Business Impact Techniques Other qualitative and/or quantitative methods for determining the effects of the quality of data on the business that are deemed important for your organization to understand.

Other Relevant Data Quality Dimensions Other characteristics, aspects, or features of data and information that are deemed to be important for your organization to define, measure, improve, monitor, and manage.

Other Relevant Root Cause Analysis Techniques Other applicable techniques that will help identify root causes.

Parsing The ability to separate multi-valued fields into individual pieces, such as separating character strings or free form text fields into their component parts, meaningful patterns, or attributes, and moving the parts into clearly labeled and distinct fields.

People and Organizations The structural elements of an *organization* (e.g., business unit, department), teams, roles, responsibilities, or individuals that affect the data, use the data, or are involved with processes in any of the phases of the *information life cycle*. Also, one of the four *key components* in the *Framework for Information Quality*.

Perception of Relevance and Trust A *data quality dimension* and a *business impact technique*. The subjective opinion of those who use information and/or those who create, maintain, and dispose of data regarding: (1) Relevance—which data is of most value and importance to them, and (2) Trust—their confidence in the quality of the data to meet their needs.

Plan A *POSMAD information life cycle* phase. Prepare for the information resource. Identify objectives, plan information *architecture*, and develop *standards* and *definitions*. Many activities when modeling, designing, and developing applications, databases, *processes, organizations,* and the like could be considered part of the Plan phase for information.

Plan-Do-Check-Act (PDCA) A basic quality technique for improving and controlling processes and products.

Plan-Do-Study-Act (PDSA) A variation on the *Plan-Do-Check-Act (PDCA)* technique where the Check step is replaced with Study.

POSMAD Acronym for the fundamental phases of the *information life cycle* (Plan, Obtain, Store and Share, Maintain, Apply, Dispose).

Presentation Quality A *data quality dimension*. The format, appearance, and display of data and information support their collection and uses.

Privacy See *Security and Privacy*.

Processes Functions, activities, actions, procedures, or tasks, that touch the data or information (business processes, processes external to company, data management processes, etc.). "Process" is the general term used to capture activities from high-level functions describing what is to be accomplished (such as "order management" or "territory assignments"), to more detailed actions describing how it is to be accomplished (such as "create purchase order" or "close purchase order") along with inputs, outputs, and timing. Also, one of the four *key components* in the *Framework for Information Quality*.

Process Impact A *business impact technique*. Illustrate the effects of data quality on business processes.

Profiling See *data profiling*.

Program An on-going initiative that manages related activities and/or projects in a coordinated way to obtain benefits that would not be available from managing them individually. One side of the *Data in Action Triangle*.

Project "A temporary endeavor undertaken to create a unique product, service, or result" (Project Management Institute, 2020). A unit of work that is a one-time effort with specific business needs to be addressed and objectives to be achieved. In this book, the word project is used broadly to mean any structured effort that makes use of the *Ten Steps methodology* to address *business needs*. See *project approach, project objectives*, and *project type*. Also one side of the *Data in Action Triangle*.

Project approach How solutions will be delivered and the framework or model used. It provides the basis for the project plan, tasks to be undertaken, resources needed, and structure of the project team. The model used can be the Ten Steps Process itself or any *SDLC* (Agile, sequential, etc.) that best fits the situation.

Project management "The application of knowledge, skills, tools, and techniques to project activities to meet the project requirements" (Project Management Institute, 2020). The need for project management applies to all *project approaches* and whichever *SDLC* is used, because all projects have to have a way of agreeing on objectives, getting work done, coordinating resources, tracking progress, communicating with each other, etc. However, the terminology may differ between approaches, for example, project charter vs. vision statement or sprints vs. phases. The *project type* and *project approach* determine which project management activities are needed and how work is planned and coordinated.

Project manager Person responsible for accomplishing the project objectives. Leads the project by initiating, planning, executing, monitoring, controlling, and closing the project, using the chosen *project approach*.

Project objectives Specific results to be met during the project, which should be aligned with the *business needs* and data quality issues to be addressed.

Project sponsor Person or group who provides the financial, human, and/or technical resources for the project. Should also show support for the project through words and actions.

Project type A classification of data quality projects into one of the following project types: (1) focused data quality improvement project, (2) data quality activities in another project, or (3) ad hoc use of data quality steps, activities, or techniques. The project type informs the *project approach* and how the project work will be organized, managed, and accomplished.

Ranking and Prioritization A *business impact technique*. Rank the impact of missing and incorrect data on specific business processes.

Record In a relational database, a record is a row and is made up of a number of fields or columns. In the nonrelational world, a record is not a consistently defined concept. "Record" may be heard in a nonrelational context and a definition of what specifically is meant by that word in that context should known by those working together. In this book, record is used generally to mean a group of *data fields*.

Reference data Sets of values or classification schemas that are referred to by systems, applications, *datastores*, *processes*, and reports, as well as by *transactional data* and *master data*. Examples include lists of valid values, code lists, status codes, territory or state abbreviations, demographic fields, flags, product types, gender, chart of accounts, product hierarchy, retail website shopping categories, and social media hashtags.

Relationship A general term for a connection or association, such as between data or between any of the four *key components*. Understanding relationships is essential for managing data quality, as many expectations about data may be expressed in terms of relationships. *Data models, taxonomies, ontologies*, and *hierarchies* all show relationships.

Reporting/dashboard data Data used in reports and dashboards, and seen as one of many uses of data, not as a separate *data category*. However, some may consider this its own data category.

Requirements and Constraints Requirements are obligations that must be met. Constraints are limitations or restrictions, that is, things that cannot or should not be done. Often looking from the point of view of "what I cannot do" uncovers additional considerations. The constraints then can often be stated in the positive to make a requirement. Sources of requirements and constraints can come from, or be based on, categories such as business, user, functional, technology, legal, regulatory, compliance, contractual, industry, internal policies, access, security, privacy, and data protection. Considering each of these will help uncover important items that must be met (requirements) or avoided (constraints) by the data itself or the project processes and outputs. A *RRISCCE broad-impact component* in the *Framework for Information Quality*.

Resource Life Cycle The processes required to manage any resource—people, money, facilities and equipment, materials and products, and information. Also known as the universal resource life cycle. See *information life cycle*.

Responsibility A *RRISCCE broad-impact component* in the *Framework for Information Quality*. Encompasses accountability, authority, ownership, governance, stewardship, motivation, and reward.

Return on Investment (ROI) (1) A measure of profit from an investment as a percentage of the amount invested. (2) Generally, any means of showing benefit from investing in data quality. See *Cost-Benefit Analysis and ROI*.

Risk Analysis A *business impact technique*. Identify possible adverse effects from poor-quality data, evaluate the likelihood of them happening, severity if they do, and determine ways to mitigate the risks.

ROI Return on investment. See *Cost-Benefit Analysis and ROI*.

Root Cause Analysis The study of all possible causes of a problem, issue, or condition to determine its actual cause(s).

RRISCCE (Pronounced "risky"). The acronym for the *broad-impact components* in the *Framework for Information Quality*: *Requirements and Constraints*; *Responsibility*; *Improvement and Prevention*; *Structure, Context and Meaning*; *Communication*; *Change, Ethics*. Used as a reminder that it is RRISCCE (risky) to ignore the broad-impact components. The risk of poor-quality data will be lowered by ensuring that components have been addressed. If they are not addressed, the risk of poor-quality data increases.

Rules See *business rules*.

SDLC A general term for solution/system/software development life cycle. Used in this book to refer to whichever *project approach* is being used for the data quality project (sequential, Agile, hybrid, etc.). The SDLC defines the approach for developing solutions and provides the basis for the project plan and the tasks to be undertaken by the project team. The SDLC used can be created internally by your organization or provided by a vendor.

Security and Privacy A *data quality dimension*. **Security** is the ability to protect data and information assets from unauthorized access, use, disclosure, disruption, modification, or destruction. **Privacy** for an individual is the ability to have some control over how data about them as a person is collected and used. For an organization, it is the ability to comply with how people want their data to be collected, shared, and used.

Semantics Generally, relates to the meaning of things, such as what a word, sign, or a sentence means, or is interpreted to mean. To manage the quality of data, what the data means and what people think it means must be known.

Sensitive data (or restricted data) Information that must be protected against unauthorized access. Sensitivity labels are assigned to information sets to aid in implementing *access*, *privacy*, and *security* controls. Sensitive data is associated with elevated risk, if it is viewed by those who are not authorized to see it. Most organizations implement security and/or privacy controls to add additional protection for sensitive data to protect it from unauthorized viewing. "Sensitive Data" can have specific meanings in particular regulatory contexts (e.g., data protection/privacy laws). Also, while data about people might be considered "sensitive" in an organization, some data (e.g., health related data or data about religious beliefs or political opinions) may be subject to a higher standard of "sensitivity". Can also be considered a *data category*.

SIPOC (Supplier-Input-Process-Output-Customer) A diagram often used in process management and improvement (such as Six Sigma and lean manufacturing) to show major activities in a business process. It can also be used to visualize an *information life cycle*.

Source-to-target mapping (STM) Provides information to move data from a source to a destination along with needed transformation logic. It states the location of and information about a data source, where the data will be moved in the target datastore, and transformations that must happen to meet requirements of the target system.

Stakeholder Person or group with an interest, involvement, or investment in or who will be impacted (positively or negatively) by the information and data quality work. Stakeholders may exert influence over the project and its deliverables. Stakeholders can be internal or external to the organization and represent interests related to business, data, or technology. The list of stakeholders may be long or short depending on the project scope.

Standard A general term for something that is recognized as authoritative and used as a basis of comparison or judgment. With data quality the focus is on *data standards*.

Store and Share A *POSMAD information life cycle* phase. Hold information and make it available for use through a distribution method. Data may be stored electronically (such as in databases or files) or as hardcopy (such as a paper application form kept in a file cabinet). Data is shared through such means as networks, an enterprise service bus, and email.

Structure, Context, and Meaning Generally, **structure** refers to the relationship and organization of parts and how they are arranged together. **Context** is the background, situation, or conditions surrounding something. **Meaning** refers to what something is or is intended to be, and can also include the purpose or significance of something. In order to manage the quality of data, there must be an understanding of how data is structured, how it relates to other data, the context in which it is used, and what it means. It is impossible to effectively manage anything that is not understood. A *RRISCCE broad-impact component* in the *Framework for Information Quality*, with topics that include *definitions*, *relationships*, *metadata*, *standards*, *reference data*, *data models*, *business rules*, *architecture*, *semantics*, *taxonomies*, *ontologies*, and *hierarchies*.

Subject Matter Expert (SME) Person who understands business processes in-depth, and has knowledge of the information that supports the processes. May also be called a super user or power user.

Survey A formal data gathering method for assessing situations, conditions, or opinions.

Synchronization See *Consistency and Synchronization*.

Swim Lane A type of process flow diagram that divides processes, tasks, workstreams, roles, etc. into lanes either horizontally or vertically. Can be used to show an at-a-glance view of the four *key components (data, processes, people/organizations, and technology)* as they appear throughout the *information life cycle* phases.

Taxonomy A system to classify things into ordered categories. For example, animals and plants are classified as kingdom, phylum, class, order, family, genus, and species. The Dewey Decimal system, used by libraries to classify books by divisions and subdivisions, is another taxonomy. These taxonomies must be understood in order to manage the data which supports them. Taxonomies are also created to better manage data itself, control vocabulary, build drill-down type interfaces, and to assist with navigation and search. See related term *folksonomy*.

Technical metadata *Metadata* used to describe technology and data structures.

Technology Forms, applications, databases, files, programs, code, or media that store, share, or manipulate the data, are involved in processes, or are used by people and organizations. Technology includes both high-tech such as databases and low-tech such as paper copies. Also, one of the four *key components* in the *Framework for Information Quality*.

Temporary data Data kept in memory to speed up processing. It is not viewed by humans and is used for technical purposes. May be considered a *data category*.

Ten Steps to Quality Data and Trusted Information™ A methodology for creating, assessing, improving, managing, and sustaining the quality of data and information. It is comprised of three main parts: Key Concepts—fundamental ideas crucial for the reader to understand in order to do data quality work well and integral components of the methodology; Structuring Your Project—guidance for organizing the work, not to replace other well-known project management practices, but to apply these principles to data quality projects; Ten Steps Process—instructions for putting the key concepts into action and the actual Ten Steps for which the overall methodology is named. For brevity "Ten Steps" refers to the full methodology. The "Ten Steps Process" refers to the steps themselves.

Timeliness A *data quality dimension*. Data and information are current and ready for use as specified and in the time frame in which they are expected.

Track and Trace A *root cause analysis* technique. Identifies the specific location of a problem by tracking the data through the *information life cycle*, comparing the data at entry and exit points of processing, and identifying where the problem first appears.

Transactability See *Usability and Transactability*.

Transactional data Data about internal or external events or transactions that take place as an organization conducts its business.

Trust Within the Ten Steps, confidence in the quality of data and information—by those who use data and information, that the data and information will meet their needs; by those who manage (plan, create, obtain, update, maintain, transform, store and share, dispose of, or archive) data and information, that the quality meets specifications and will meet the needs of *users* (people, processes, machines, etc.).

Uniqueness and Deduplication A *data quality dimension*. The uniqueness (positive) or unwanted duplication (negative) of data (*fields*, *records*, or *datasets*) existing within or across systems or *datastores*.

Usability and Transactability A *data quality dimension*. Data produces the desired business transaction, outcome, or use for which it was intended.

Usage A *business impact technique*. Inventory the current and/or future uses of the data.

User A general word to mean someone, in any role, who makes use of data and information. Synonyms for user include *knowledge worker*, information consumer, and information customer. A user can also be a machine or automated process.

Validation A check that ensures entries into a production system adhere to *standards* and reasonableness. Also see *verification*. While the software world has more specific definitions for validation and verification, in the data world there is no consensus and they are sometimes used interchangeably. Note that validation does not indicate if the entry is the correct entry, which is *accuracy*, but does indicate *validity*.

Validity Values in a data *field* conform to rules, guidelines, or *standards*. Indications of what is valid will vary from field to field. For example, is the value within a list of allowed values? Does the value fit a specified pattern or format? Does the value fall within a stated date range or other range with established maximum and minimum values? Does the value follow specific data entry standards? Assessed or measured as part of the *data quality dimension* of Data Integrity Fundamentals.

Verification The process of ensuring data entered, or a copy made, exactly matches the original source. Also see *validation*. While the software world has more specific definitions for validation and verification, in the data world there is no consensus and they are sometimes used interchangeably.

List of Figures, Tables, and Templates

Figures

Chapter 4: The Ten Steps Process

Introduction to Chapter 4

Step 1 – Determine Business Needs and Approach

Step 2 – Analyze Information Environment

Step 3 – Assess Data Quality

Step 4 – Assess Business Impact

Step 5 – Identify Root Causes

Step 6 – Develop Improvement Plans

Step 7 – Prevent Future Data Errors

Step 8 – Correct Current Data Errors

Step 9 – Monitor Controls

Step 10 – Communicate, Manage, and Engage People Throughout

Chapter 5: Structuring Your Project

Chapter 6: Other Techniques and Tools

Appendix: Quick References

Tables

Step 3 – Assess Data Quality

Step 4 – Assess Business Impact

Step 5 – Identify Root Causes

Step 6 – Develop Improvement Plans

Step 7 – Prevent Future Data Errors

Step 8 – Correct Current Data Errors

Step 9 – Monitor Controls

Step 10 – Communicate, Manage, and Engage People Throughout

Chapter 5: Structuring Your Project

Chapter 6: Other Techniques and Tools

Appendix: Quick References

Templates

Chapter 4: The Ten Steps Process

Step 1 – Determine Business Needs and Approach

Step 2 – Analyze Information Environment

Step 3 – Assess Data Quality

Step 4 – Assess Business Impact

Step 5 – Identify Root Causes

Step 8 – Correct Current Data Errors

Step 9 – Monitor Controls

Step 10 – Communicate, Manage, and Engage People Throughout

Chapter 6: Other Techniques and Tools

Bibliography

Adelman, S., Abai, M. and Moss, L. (2005). *Data Strategy*. Upper Saddle River: Addison-Wesley.

Algmin, Anthony. (2019). *Data Leadership: Stop Talking About Data and Start Making an Impact!* Studio City: DATAVERSITY Press.

Al-Hakim, L. (ed.). (2007). *Challenges of Managing Information Quality in Service Organizations*. Idea Group, Inc.

Allemang, D. and Hendler, J. (2011). *Semantic Web for the Working Ontologist: Effective Modeling in RDFS and OWL*. Waltham: Morgan Kaufmann.

Allyn, B. (2020). '"The Computer Got It Wrong": How Facial Recognition Led to False Arrest of Black Man'. NPR.org. <www.npr.org/2020/06/24/882683463/the-computer-got-it-wrong-how-facial-recognition-led-to-a-false-arrest-in-michig> Accessed 25 June 2020.

Altarade, M. (n.d.). 'The Definitive Guide to NoSQL Databases'. <https://www.toptal.com/database/the-definitive-guide-to-nosql-databases> Accessed 5 June 2020.

Anand, S. (2011). 'Oracle Unified Method (OUM)'. OracleApps Epicenter. <http://www.oracleappshub.com/methodology/oracle-unified-method-oum/> Accessed 8 May 2020.

Barker, R. (1989). *Case*Method: Entity Relationship Modelling*. Boston: Addison-Wesley.

Batini, C. and Scannapieco, M. (2006). *Data Quality: Concepts, Methodologies, and Techniques*. Berlin: Springer.

Beattie, A. (2020). 'A Guide to Calculating Return on Investment (ROI)'. Investopedia.com. <https://www.investopedia.com/articles/basics/10/guide-to-calculating-roi.asp> Accessed 29 May 2020.

Beckhard, R. and Harris, R.T. (1987). *Organizational Transitions: Managing Complex Change*. Boston: Addison-Wesley.

Biere, M. (2018). *Business Intelligence for the Enterprise*. IBM Press/Pearson.

Booch, G., Rumbaugh, J. and Jacobson, I. (2017). *The Unified Modeling Language User Guide*. 2nd ed. Boston: Addison-Wesley.

Borek, A., Parlikad, A., Webb, J., and Woodall, P. (2014). *Total Information Risk Management: Maximizing the Value of Data and Information Assets*. Waltham: Morgan Kaufmann.

Brackett, M. (2000). *Data Resource Quality*. Boston: Addison-Wesley.

Brassard, M. and Ritter, D. (2018). *The Memory Jogger II: A Pocket Guide of Tools for Continuous Improvement & Effective Planning*. 2nd ed. Methuen: GOAL/QPC. (Original publication, 1994).

Bridges, W. with Bridges, S. (2016). *Managing Transitions: Making the Most of Change*. Boston: Da Capo Press.

British Library. (n.d.) 'Business and management Genichi Taguchi'. <https://www.bl.uk/people/genichi-taguchi> Accessed 11 June 2020.

Brue, G. and Launsby, R. (2003). *Design for Six Sigma*. New York: McGraw-Hill.

Cavoukian, A. (2011). 'Privacy by Design: The 7 Foundational Principles'. (PDF). <https://iapp.org/resources/article/privacy-by-design-the-7-foundational-principles/> Accessed 31 Aug 2020.

Championing Science. (2019). 'In honor of Albert Einstein's birthday – Everything should be made as simple as possible, but no simpler'. <https://championingscience.com/2019/03/15/everything-should-be-made-as-simple-as-possible-but-no-simpler/> Accessed 24 Jan 2020.

Chang, R.Y. and Morgan, M.W. (2010). *Performance Scorecards: Measuring the Right Things in the Real World*. San Francisco: Jossey-Bass.

Chapin, D. (2008). 'MDA Foundational Model Applied to Both the Organization and Business Application Software'. *Object Management Group (OMG) Working Paper*. March.

Cloudflare. (n.d.). 'What Is a Public Cloud? | Public vs. Private Cloud'. <https://www.cloudflare.com/learning/cloud/what-is-a-public-cloud/> Accessed 6 June 2020.

CNBC. (2020). 'About $1.4 billion in stimulus checks sent to deceased Americans'. <https://www.cnbc.com/2020/06/25/1point4-billion-in-stimulus-checks-sent-to-deceased-individuals.html> Accessed 30 June 2020.

Codd, E.F. (1970). 'A Relational Model of Data for Large Shared Data Banks'. *Communications of the ACM*, 13, No. 6 (June). <https://www.seas.upenn.edu/~zives/03f/cis550/codd.pdf> Accessed 29 July 2020.

Cole, A. (2018). 'The Crucial Link Between AI and Good Data Management'. Techopedia.com. <https://www.techopedia.com/the-crucial-link-between-ai-and-good-data-management/2/33477> Accessed 26 June 2020.

Conley, C. (2007). *PEAK: How Great Companies Get Their Mojo from Maslow*. San Francisco: Jossey-Bass.

Cooks Info. (Modified 2018). 'Soft-ball Stage'. <https://www.cooksinfo.com/soft-ball-stage> Accessed 19 March 2020.

Covey, S. (2004). *Seven Habits of Highly Effective People.* New York: Free Press, a Division of Simon & Schuster, Inc.

Crosby, P. (1996). *Philip Crosby's Reflections on Quality.* McGraw-Hill.

Cuzzort, R. and Vrettos, J. (1996). *The Elementary Forms of Statistical Reason.* New York: St. Martin's Press.

DAMA International. <www.dama.org> Accessed 25 March 2020.

DAMA International. (2020). 'Certified Data Management Professionals'. <https://cdmp.info/> Accessed 24 July 2020.

DAMA International (2017). *DAMA-DMBOK: Data Management Body of Knowledge.* 2nd ed. Henderson, D., Early, S., Sebastian-Coleman, L. (eds.). Basking Ridge: Technics Publications.

Dannemiller, K. D. and Jacobs, R. W. (1992). 'Changing the Way Organizations Change: A Revolution of Common Sense'. *The Journal of Applied Behavioral Science*, December. Revised Gleicher change equation from Beckhard & Harris (1987).

Dean, W. (2020). 'Using artificial intelligence, agricultural robots are on the rise'. *The Economist.* <https://www.economist.com/science-and-technology/2020/02/06/using-artificial-intelligence-agricultural-robots-are-on-the-rise> Accessed 15 Feb 2020.

Deming, W. E. (2000). *Out of the Crisis.* Cambridge: MIT Press. Pgs. 29, 227.

Dennedy, M., Fox, J. and Finneran, T.R. (2014). *The Privacy Engineer's Manifesto: Getting from Policy to Code to QA to Value.* Berkeley, CA: Apress Media.

Dietz, K. and Silverman, L. (2013). *Business Storytelling for Dummies.* Hoboken: John Wiley & Sons.

Doherty-Nicolau, K., Hovasha, J., O'Keefe, K. and O Brien, D. (2020). 'Guidance on Temperature Scans in the Workplace'. Castlebridge. <https://castlebridge.ie/product/guidance-on-temperature-scans-in-the-workplace/> Accessed 4 Sep 2020.

Dontha, Ramesh. (2017). 'Who came up with the name Big Data?' Tech Target: Data Science Central. Blog. <https://www.datasciencecentral.com/profiles/blogs/who-came-up-with-the-name-big-data> Accessed Aug 31, 2020.

Doran, G. (1981). 'There's a S.M.A.R.T. way to write management's goals and objectives'. *Management Review*, 70 (11): 35–36.

Earley, S. (ed.). (2011). *The DAMA Dictionary of Data Management.* 2nd ed. DAMA International. Basking Ridge: Technics Publications.

Eckerson, W. W. (2011). *Performance Dashboards: Measuring, Monitoring, and Managing Your Business.* Hoboken: Wiley.

Edvinsson, H. (2019). 'Data Diplomacy: Data Design with Lasting Peace'. Conference Session. DATAVERSITY: DG Vision. (December).

English, L. (1999). *Improving Data Warehouse and Business Information Quality.* John Wiley & Sons.

English, L. (2009). *Information Quality Applied.* Indianapolis: Wiley Publishing, Inc.

Encyclopædia Britannica. (2017). 'William of Ockham,' Vignaux, P. contributor. <https://www.britannica.com/biography/William-of-Ockham> Accessed 24 Jan 2020.

Eppler, M. J. (2003). *Managing Information Quality: Increasing the Value of Information in Knowledge-intensive Products and Processes.* Berlin: Springer.

Evans, N. and Price, J. (2012). 'Barriers to the Effective Deployment of Information Assets: An Executive Management Perspective'. *Interdisciplinary Journal of Information, Knowledge, and Management* Volume 7. <http://www.ijikm.org/Volume7/IJIKMv7p177-199Evans0650.pdf> Accessed 6 Feb 2020.

Everest, G.C. (1976). 'Basic Data Structure Models Explained with a Common Example'. Computing Systems 1976, *Proceedings Fifth Texas Conference on Computing Systems*, Austin, TX, 1976 October 18-19, pp. 39-46. (Long Beach, CA: IEEE Computer Society Publications Office). <https://www.researchgate.net/publication/291448084_BASIC_DATA_STRUCTURE_MODELS_EXPLAINED_WITH_A_COMMON_EXAMPLE> Accessed 24 Jan 2020.

Evergreen, S.D. (2020) *The Data Visualization Sketch Book.* Thousand Oaks: SAGE Publications.

Few, S. (2013), *Information Dashboard Design: Displaying data for at-a-glance monitoring.* 2nd ed. El Dorado Hills: Analytics Press.

Firican, G. (2017). 'The 10 Vs of Big Data'. TDWI.org. <https://tdwi.org/articles/2017/02/08/10-vs-of-big-data.aspx> Accessed 27 Jan 2020.

Foote, K. D. (2017). 'A Brief History of Big Data'. DATAVERSITY.net. <https://www.dataversity.net/brief-history-big-data/> Accessed 10 Jan 2020.

Forsey, C. (n.d.). 'What is Semi-Structured Data?' Hubspot. <https://blog.hubspot.com/marketing/semi-structured-data> Accessed 5 June 2020.

Fournies, F. (2000). *Coaching for Improved Work Performance.* New York: McGraw-Hill.

FreeCountryMaps.com. (n.d.). 'Free Country Maps'. <https://www.freecountrymaps.com/map/country/france-map-fr/> Accessed 13 May 2020.

Gonick, L. and Smith, W. (1993). *The Cartoon Guide to Statistics.* HarperCollins.

Gordon, K. (2013) *Principles of Data Management: Facilitating Information Sharing.* 2nd ed. Swindon: BCS Learning and Development Ltd.

Gorman, A. (2009). 'Many refugees celebrate assigned birthdays on Jan. 1'. *Seattle Times.* <https://www.seattletimes.com/nation-world/many-refugees-celebrate-assigned-birthdays-on-jan-1/> Accessed 10 Jan 2020.

Grady, R. B. (1992). *Practical Software Metrics for Project Management and Process Improvement*. Englewood Cliffs: Prentice-Hall.

Grady, R. B. and Caswell, D. L. (1987). *Software Metrics: Establishing a Company-Wide Program*. Englewood Cliffs: Prentice-Hall.

Greenberg, P. (2018). 'Evolution of data platforms: Using the right data for the right outcomes'. Social CRM: The Conversation. ZDNet.com. <https://www.zdnet.com/article/evolution-of-data-platforms-using-the-right-data-for-the-right-outcomes/> Accessed 24 July 2020.

Greenberg, P. (2018). 'What to do with the data? The evolution of data platforms in a post big data world.' Social CRM: The Conversation. ZDNet.com. <https://www.zdnet.com/article/evolution-of-data-platforms-post-big-data/> Accessed 25 June 2020.

Guaspari, J. (1991). *I Know It When I See It: A Modern Fable About Quality*. 1st ed. New York: AMACOM.

Halpin, T. (2015). *Object-Role Modeling Fundamentals: A Practical Guide to Data Modeling with ORM*. Basking Ridge: Technics Publications.

Harvard Graduate School of Business Administration. (2002). *Finance for Managers*. Boston: Harvard Business School Press.

Hay, D.C. (1996). *Data Model Patterns: Conventions of Thought*. New York: Dorset House, p. 254.

Hay, D. (2006). *Data Model Patterns*. Burlington: Elsevier.

Hay, D. (2011). *Enterprise Model Patterns: Describing the World*. Basking Ridge: Technics Publications.

Hay, D. (2018). *Achieving Buzzword Compliance: Data Architecture Language and Vocabulary*. Basking Ridge: Technics Publications.

Hay, D. and Von Halle, B. (2003). *Requirements Analysis*. Upper Saddle River: Prentice Hall PTR.

Heien, C.H., (2012). '*Modeling and Analysis of Information Product Maps*'. PhD Thesis. University of Arkansas at Little Rock. <https://library.ualr.edu/record=b1775281~S4> Accessed 20 March 2020.

Heien, C., Wu, N., and Talburt, J. (2014). '*Methods and Models to Support Consistent Representation of Information Product Maps*'. Proceedings of the 19th International Conference on Information Quality (ICIQ), Xi'an, China, August. <https://drive.google.com/file/d/0B81NXHLVoIS3aHltLWtyOG9GVms/view?usp=sharing> Accessed 20 March 2020.

Herzog, T.N., Scheuren, F.J., and Winkler, W.E. (2007). *Data Quality and Record Linkage Techniques*. New York: Springer.

Hirsi, I. (2017). 'Why so many Somali-Americans celebrate their birthday on Jan. 1'. *MinnPost*. <https://www.minnpost.com/new-americans/2017/01/why-so-many-somali-americans-celebrate-their-birthday-jan-1/> Accessed 10 Jan 2020.

Hoberman, S. (2015). *Data Model Scorecard: Applying the Industry Standard on Data Modeling Quality*. Basking Ridge: Technics Publications.

Hoberman, S. (2016). *Data Modeling Made Simple: A Practical Guide for Business and IT Professionals*. 2nd ed. Basking Ridge: Technics Publications.

Hoberman, S. (2020). *The Rosedata Stone: Achieving a Common Business Language*. Basking Ridge: Technics Publications.

Hoff, R. (1992). *"I Can See You Naked": A Fearless Guide to Making Great Presentations*. Andrews and McMeel.

Huang, K., Lee, Y. W., and Wang, R. Y. (1999). *Quality Information and Knowledge*. Prentice Hall PTR.

IBM. (n.d.). 'Relational Database'. <https://www.ibm.com/ibm/history/ibm100/us/en/icons/reldb/> Accessed 6 June 2020.

Idexcel Technologies. (2019). 'The Differences Between Cloud and On-Premises Computing'. idexcel.com. <https://www.idexcel.com/blog/the-differences-between-cloud-and-on-premises-computing/> Accessed 6 June 2020.

Imai, M. (1997). *Gemba Kaizen: A Commonsense, Low-Cost Approach to Management*. McGraw-Hill.

Inmon, B. (2016). *Data Lake Architecture: Designing the Data Lake and Avoiding the Garbage Dump*. Basking Ridge: Technics Publications.

Inmon, W.H. (2005). *Building the Data Warehouse*. 4th ed. Indianapolis: Wiley Publishing. Inc.

Inmon, W.H., O'Neil, B., and Fryman, L. (2008). *Business Metadata: Capturing Enterprise Knowledge*. Morgan Kaufmann.

International Organization for Standardization (ISO). (2008) *ISO/IEC 25012:2008 Software engineering – Software product Quality Requirements and Evaluation (SQuaRE) – Data quality model*.

International Organization for Standardization (ISO). (2010) *ISO/TS 22745-10:2010 Industrial automation systems and integration – Open technical dictionaries and their application to master data – Part 10: Dictionary representation*.

International Organization for Standardization (ISO). (2010) *ISO/TS 29002-6:2010 Industrial automation systems and integration – Exchange of characteristic data – Part 6: Concept dictionary terminology reference model*.

International Organization for Standardization (ISO). (2011a) *ISO/TS 8000-1:2011 Data quality – Part 1: Overview*. Figure 1: Data architecture.

International Organization for Standardization (ISO). (2011b) *ISO/TS 8000-150:2011 Data quality – Part 150: Master data: Quality management framework*. Figure B-1: Data quality management: Roles and responsibilities.

International Organization for Standardization (ISO). (2015) *ISO 9001:2015 Quality management systems – Requirements*.

International Organization for Standardization (ISO). (2016a) *ISO 8000-61:2016 Data quality – Part 61: Data quality management: Process reference model.* Figure 2: The detailed structure of data quality management.

International Organization for Standardization (ISO). (2016b) *ISO 8000-100:2016 Data quality – Part 100: Master data: Exchange of characteristic data: Overview.*

IQ International. (n.d.). 'IQ Performance Domains'. <https://www.iqint.org/certification/exam/iq-performance-domains/> Accessed 25 March 2020.

IQ International. (n.d.). 'Code of Ethics and Professional Conduct'. <https://www.iqint.org/about/code-of-ethics-and-professional-conduct/> Accessed 11 June 2020.

Jacobs, R.W. (1997). *Real-Time Strategic Change.* Berrett-Koehler Publishers.

Jugulum, R. (2014). *Competing with High Quality Data: Concepts, Tools, and Techniques for Building a Successful Approach to Data Quality.* Wiley.

Juran, J. M. (1988). *Juran's Quality Control Handbook.* 4th ed. McGraw-Hill.

Juran, J. M. (1995). *Managerial Breakthrough: The Classic Book on Improving Management Performance.* McGraw-Hill.

Kaplan, S. and Garrick, B.J. (1981). 'On the Quantitative Definition of Risk'. *Risk Analysis*, Vol. 1, No. 1. <https://www.nrc.gov/docs/ML1216/ML12167A133.pdf> Accessed 22 Feb 2020.

Kau, M. (2019). 'Top 10 real-life examples of Machine Learning'. Bigdata-Madesimple.com. <https://bigdata-madesimple.com/top-10-real-life-examples-of-machine-learning/> Accessed 26 June 2020.

Kimball, R. and Ross, M. (2005). *The Data Warehouse Toolkit.* 3rd. ed. Indianapolis: John Wiley and Sons, Inc.

King, T. and Schwarzenbach, J. (2020). *Managing Data Quality.* BCS Learning & Development Ltd.

Knaflic, C.N. (2015). *Storytelling with data: a data visualization guide for business professionals.* Hoboken: John Wiley & Sons.

Knight, M. (2021). 'What is DataOps?' DATAVERSITY.net <https://www.dataversity.net/what-is-dataops/> Accessed 9 March 2021.

Kotter, J. P. (2012). *Leading Change.* Harvard Business Review Press.

Ladley, J. (2017) 'Why Data Debt is a Powerful Metric for Proving Data Management and Governance'. Blog. <https://www.firstsanfranciscopartners.com/blog/data-debt-data-management-metric/> Accessed 29 July 2020.

Ladley, J. (2020a). 'A Bit More on Data Debt'. Blog. <https://johnladley.com/a-bit-more-on-data-debt/> Accessed 17 Aug 2020.

Ladley, J. (2020b). *Data Governance: How to Design, Deploy, and Sustain an Effective Data Governance Program.* 2nd ed. Elsevier Academic Press.

Ladley, J., McGilvray, D., Price, J., Redman, T. (2017). 'The Leader's Data Manifesto'. <www.dataleaders.org> Accessed 6 May 2020.

Laney, D. (2018). *Infonomics: How to Monetize, Manage, and Measure Information as an Asset for Competitive Advantage.* New York: Bibliomotion, Inc.

Lee, Y., Fisher, J., McDowell, D., Simons, J., Chase, S., Leinung, A., Paradiso, M., and Yarsawich, C. (2007). *'CEIP Maps: Context-embedded Information Product Maps'.* Proceedings of the Thirteenth Americas Conference on Information Systems. Key Stone, Colorado, August 2007. <http://mitiq.mit.edu/Documents/Publications/Papers/2007/Lee%20et%20al%20CEIP%20Maps%20AMCIS%202007.pdf> Accessed 20 March 2020.

Lee, Y.W., Pipino, L.L., Funk, J.D., and Wang, R.Y. (2006). *Journey to Data Quality.* MIT Press.

Lindstedt, D. and Olschimke, M. (2016). *Building a Scalable Data Warehouse with Data Vault 2.0.* Waltham: Morgan Kaufmann.

Lombardi, E. (2019). 'Quotes About the Importance of Words.' ThoughtCo.com. <https://www.thoughtco.com/quotes-about-words-738759> Accessed 20 April 2020.

Loshin, D. (2001). *Enterprise Knowledge Management: The Data Quality Approach.* San Diego: Morgan Kaufmann, pp. 83-93, 389–391.

Loshin, D. (2003). *Business Intelligence: The Savvy Manager's Guide.* Morgan Kaufmann.

Loshin, D. (2006). 'The Data Quality Business Case: Projecting Return on Investment'. Informatica White Paper.

Mansfield, S. (2019). *How to Write A Business Plan (Your Guide to Starting a Business)*, Kindle ed. <https://www.amazon.com/Write-Business-Plan-Guide-Starting-ebook/dp/B07Q3N5BBR/> Accessed 28 Feb 2020.

Marr, B. (2019). 'What's the Difference Between Structured, Semi-Structured and Unstructured Data?'. Forbes.com. <https://www.forbes.com/sites/bernardmarr/2019/10/18/whats-the-difference-between-structured-semi-structured-and-unstructured-data/#45acc04b2b4d> Accessed 5 June 2020.

Maydanchik, A. (2007). *Data Quality Assessment.* Bradley Beach: Technics Publications, p. 7.

McComb, D. (2004). *Semantics in Business Systems: The Savvy Manager's Guide.* Morgan Kaufmann.

McGilvray, D. (2013). 'Data Quality Projects and Programs' In: Sadiq S. (ed.) *Handbook of Data Quality: Research and Practice.* Berlin: Springer. pp. 41-73.

McGilvray, D. and Bykin, M. (2013). 'Data Quality and Governance in Projects: Knowledge in Action'. *The Data Insight & Social BI Executive Report*, Vol. 13, No. 5. Cutter Consortium, p. 1. <https://www.cutter.com/offer/data-quality-and-governance-projects-knowledge-action-0> Accessed 26 June 2020

McGilvray, D. and Redman, T. (2012). '"My Life is a Data Quality Battle": Is This How Your Customers Talk About

Your Company?' IQ International. <https://www.iqint.org/publication/life-data-quality-battle-customers-talk-company/> Accessed 19 Feb 2020.

McGilvray, D., Price, J., and Redman, T. (2016) 'Barriers that slow/hinder/prevent companies from managing their information as a business asset'. Diagram. Dataleaders.org. <https://dataleaders.org/tools/root-cause-analysis/> Accessed 28 July 2020.

Mezak, S. (2018). 'The Origins of DevOps: What's in a Name?' DevOps.com. <https://devops.com/the-origins-of-devops-whats-in-a-name/> Accessed 25 June 2020.

Moen, R.D. and Norman, C.L. (2010) 'Circling Back: Clearing up the myths about the Deming cycle and seeing how it keeps evolving'. QP. November, pgs. 22-28. <http://www.apiweb.org/circling-back.pdf> Accessed 30 July 2020.

MongoDB. (n.d.). 'NOSQL Explained'. <https://www.mongodb.com/nosql-explained> Accessed 19 Sept 2019.

Myers, D. (2018) '"Know Thy Self" IQCP Assessment'. <http://dqmatters.com/silver_package> Accessed 28 July 2020.

Myers, D. (n.d.). 'Research on the Dimensions of Data Quality'. <http://dimensionsofdataquality.com/research> Accessed 17 Aug 2020.

Nagle, T., Redman, T. and Sammon, D. (2017). 'Only 3% of Companies' Data Meets Basic Quality Standards'. *Harvard Business Review.* <https://hbr.org/2017/09/only-3-of-companies-data-meets-basic-quality-standards> Accessed 13 June 2020.

NAICS Association. (n.d.). 'Frequently Asked Questions'. <https://www.naics.com/frequently-asked-questions/#NAICSfaq> Accessed 3 April 2020.

O'Keefe, K. and O Brien, D. (2018). *Ethical Data and Information Management: Concepts, Tools, and Methods.* London: Kogan Page.

Olson, J.E. (2003). *Data Quality: The Accuracy Dimension.* San Francisco: Morgan Kaufmann.

O'Neil, B. and Fryman, L. (2020). *The Data Catalog: Sherlock Holmes Data Sleuthing for Analytics.* Kindle ed. Basking Ridge: Technics Publications.

O'Rourke, C., Fishman, N., and Selkow, W. (2003). *Enterprise Architecture: Using the Zachman Framework.* Thomson Course Technology.

Pande, P.S., and Holpp, L. (2002). *What Is Six Sigma?* McGraw-Hill.

Pande, P.S., Neuman, R.P., and Cavanagh, R.R. (2000). *The Six Sigma Way.* McGraw-Hill.

Pande, P.S., Neuman, R.P., and Cavanagh, R.R. (2002). *The Six Sigma Way: Team Fieldbook.* McGraw-Hill.

Parker, M.M., Benson, R.J., and Trainor, H.E. (1988). *Information Economics: Linking Business Performance to Information Technology.* Prentice Hall.

Peale, N.V. (1992). *Norman Vincent Peale: Three Complete Books: The Power Of Positive Thinking; The Positive Principle Today; Enthusiasm Makes The Difference.* New York: Wings Books.

Plotkin, D. (2012). 'Designing in Data Quality with the User Interface'. DATAVERSITY.net. <https://www.dataversity.net/designing-in-data-quality-with-the-user-interface/> Accessed 11 June 2020.

Plotkin, D. (2014). *Data Stewardship: An Actionable Guide to Effective Data Management and Data Governance.* 1st ed. Waltham: Morgan Kaufmann.

Plotkin, D. (2020). *Data Stewardship: An Actionable Guide to Effective Data Management and Data Governance.* 2nd ed. Elsevier Academic Press.

Project Management Institute. (2020). 'What is Project Management?'. <https://www.pmi.org/about/learn-about-pmi/what-is-project-management> Accessed 27 July 2020.

PwC. (2020). 'Sizing the prize: What's the real value of AI for your business and how can you capitalize?' <https://www.pwc.com/gx/en/issues/analytics/assets/pwc-ai-analysis-sizing-the-prize-report.pdf> pp. 1-2. Accessed 26 June 2020.

Ranger, S. (2020). 'What is the IoT? Everything you need to know about the Internet of Things'. ZDNet.com. <https://www.zdnet.com/article/what-is-the-internet-of-things-everything-you-need-to-know-about-the-iot-right-now/> Accessed 22 June 2020.

Redman, T.C. (1992). *Data Quality: Management and Technology.* Bantam.

Redman, T.C. (1996). *Data Quality for the Information Age.* Boston: Artech House, pp. 155-183.

Redman, T.C. (2001). *Data Quality: The Field Guide.* Woburn: Digital Press, p. 66, 227.

Redman, T.C. (2008). *Data Driven: Profiting from Your Most Important Business Asset.* Boston: Harvard Business Press.

Redman, T.C. (2013). 'Data's Credibility Problem'. *Harvard Business Review.* <https://hbr.org/2013/12/datas-credibility-problem> Accessed 21 March 2020.

Redman, T.C. (2016a). 'Assess Whether You Have a Data Quality Problem'. *Harvard Business Review.* <https://hbr.org/2016/07/assess-whether-you-have-a-data-quality-problem> Accessed 9 Aug 2019.

Redman, T.C. (2016b). *Getting in Front on Data: Who Does What.* Basking Ridge: Technics Publications.

Redman, T.C. (2017a). 'Seizing Opportunity in Data Quality'. *MIT Sloane Management Review.* <https://sloanreview.mit.edu/article/seizing-opportunity-in-data-quality/> Accessed 13 June 2020.

Redman, T. (2017b). 'The Data Manifesto: A TDAN.com Interview'. Interviewed by Robert Seiner for TDAN.com, May 17. <http://tdan.com/the-data-manifesto-a-tdan-com-interview/21432> Accessed 20 May 2017.

Redman, T.C. (2018). 'If Your Data Is Bad, Your Machine Learning Tools Are Useless'. *Harvard Business Review*. <https://hbr.org/2018/04/if-your-data-is-bad-your-machine-learning-tools-are-useless> Accessed 10 October 2019.

Redman, T. C. and Kushner, T. (2019). 'Data Quality and Machine Learning Readiness Test'. <https://dataleaders.org/wp-content/uploads/2019/12/DQ-MLReadinessTest_final.pdf> Accessed 19 June 2020.

Reeve, A. (2013). *Managing Data in Motion: Data Integration Best Practice Techniques and Technologies*. Waltham: Morgan Kaufmann.

'risk, n.'. OED Online. (2020). Oxford University Press. <https://oed.com/view/Entry/166306?rskey=c4JYpg&result=1> Accessed 24 Feb 2020.

Ross, R.G. (2013). *Business Rule Concepts: Getting to the Point of Knowledge*. 4th ed. Business Rule Solutions, LLC., p. 25, 38, 84.

Rouse, M. (2005). 'Injectable ID chip (biochip transponder)'. WhatIs.com. <https://internetofthingsagenda.techtarget.com/definition/injectable-ID-chip-biochip-transponder?vgnextfmt=print> Accessed 10 Jan 2020.

Rouse, M. (n.d.). 'Change Management'. Brunskill, V. and Pratt, M., contributors. WhatIs.com. <https://searchcio.techtarget.com/definition/change-management> Accessed 22 May 2020.

Rouse, M. (n.d.). 'Organizational Change Management (OCM)'. WhatIs.com. <https://searchcio.techtarget.com/definition/organizational-change-management-OCM> Accessed 22 May 2020.

Rubin, K.S. (2012). *Essential Scrum: A Practical Guide to the Most Popular Agile Process*. Boston: Addison-Wesley Signature Series, Pearson Education, Inc.

Rummler, G.A. and Brache, A.P. (1990). *Improving Performance: How to Manage the White Space on the Organization Chart*. San Francisco: Jossey-Bass.

Rummler, G.A. and Brache, A.P. (2013). *Improving Performance: How to Manage the White Space on the Organization Chart*. 3rd ed. San Francisco: Jossey-Bass.

Schneider, W.E. (1999). *The Reengineering Alternative: A Plan for Making Your Current Culture Work*. New York: McGraw-Hill.

Schneider, W.E. (2017). *Lead Right for Your Company's Type: How to Connect Your Culture with Your Customer Promise*. New York: AMACOM.

Scofield, M. (2008). 'Fundamentals of Data Quality'. NoCOUG Journal, February.

Seattle Public Utilities. (2020). <http://www.seattle.gov/utilities> Accessed 28 July 2020.

Sebastian-Coleman, L. (2013). *Measuring Data Quality for Ongoing Improvement: A Data Quality Assessment Framework*. Waltham: Morgan Kaufmann, p. 52.

Sebastian-Coleman, L. (2018). *Navigating the Labyrinth: An Executive Guide to Data Management*. DAMA International. Basking Ridge: Technics Publications.

Seiner, R. (2014). *Non-Invasive Data Governance*. Basking Ridge: Technics Publications.

Sessions, R. (1950). 'How a "Difficult" Composer Gets That Way'. *New York Times*. 8 January, p. 89. <https://timesmachine.nytimes.com/timesmachine/1950/01/08/90480390.pdf> Accessed 28 Jan 2020.

Sharma, S. (2017). ' "Activate" is new SAP Implementation methodology'. Practical Project Insights. <https://www.projectmanagement.com/blog-post/26378/Activate--is-new-SAP-Implementation-methodology> Accessed 8 May 2020.

Shiba, S., Graham, A., and Walden, D. (1993). *A New American TQM: Four Practical Revolutions in Management*. Productivity Press and Center for Quality Management.

Shillito, M.L., and De Marle, D.J. (1992). *Value: Its Measurement, Design & Management*. John Wiley & Sons.

Silverman, L. (2006). *Wake Me Up When the Data Is Over: How Organizations Use Stories to Drive Results*. Jossey-Bass.

Silverman, L. (2020). 'Making SMARTER™ Decisions with Data—Creating a Data-Informed Enterprise ("Level Up With Lori" Ep. 10).' <https://www.youtube.com/playlist?list=PLifX31Xz9ggX9yUE6f6Z5dpbEMTyn8doe> Accessed 30 April 2020.

Silverston, L. (2001a). *The Data Model Resource Book* (Revised ed.) *Volume 1: A Library of Universal Data Models for All Enterprises*. John Wiley & Sons.

Silverston, L. (2001b). *The Data Model Resource Book* (Revised ed.) *Volume 2: A Library of Universal Data Models for All Enterprises*. John Wiley & Sons.

Silverston, L. and Agnew, P. (2009). *The Data Model Resource Book: Volume 3: Universal Patterns for Data Modeling*. Indianapolis: Wiley Publishing, Inc.

Simsion, G.C. and Witt, G.C. (2005). *Data Modeling Essentials*. 3rd ed. San Francisco: Morgan Kaufman Publishers, p. xxiii, p. 17.

Sincero, S.M. (2012a). 'Surveys and Questionnaires – Guide.' Explorable.com. (Jul 10, 2012) <https://explorable.com/surveys-and-questionnaires> Accessed 22 Aug 2019. The text in this article is licensed under the Creative Commons-License Attribution 4.0 International (CC BY 4.0).

Sincero, S.M. (2012b). 'Survey Response Scales'. Explorable.com. (June 6, 2012). <https://explorable.com/survey-response-scales> Accessed 22 Aug 2019. The text in this article is licensed under the Creative Commons-License Attribution 4.0 International (CC BY 4.0).

Spendolini, M. J. (1992). *The Benchmarking Book*. New York: AMACOM, pp. 172-174.

Spewak, S.H., and Hill, S.C. (1992). *Enterprise Architecture Planning: Developing a Blueprint for Data, Applications and*

Technology. New York: John Wiley & Sons, Inc., pp. xix–xx. Winchester Mystery House story.

Steenbeek, I. (2019). *The Data Management Toolkit.* Data Crossroads, p. 147.

Stephens, R.T. (2003). 'Marketing and Selling Data Management'. Conference session, DAMA International Symposium/Wilshire Meta-Data Conference, Orlando.

Sterbenze, C. (2013). '12 Famous Quotes That Always Get Misattributed'. Business Insider. <https://www.businessinsider.com/misattributed-quotes-2013-10> Accessed 10 Jan 2020.

Sullivan, D. (2015). *NoSQL for Mere Mortals.* Hoboken: Addison Wesley.

Swanson, R.C. (1995). *The Quality Improvement Handbook: Team Guide to Tools and Techniques.* St. Lucie Press.

Talburt, J.R. (2011). *Entity Resolution and Information Quality.* San Francisco: Morgan Kaufmann.

Talburt, J.R. and Zhou, Y. (2015). *Entity Information Life Cycle for Big Data: Master Data Management and Information Integration.* Waltham: Morgan Kaufmann.

Techopedia. (2014). 'Folksonomy'. <https://www.techopedia.com/definition/30196/folksonomy> Accessed 28 Apr 2020.

Thamm, A., Gramlich, M. and Borek, A. (2020). *The Ultimate Data and AI Guide.* Munich: Data AI Press.

Thomas, G. (2008). Poem. <http://datagovernance.com/dh3_song_parodies.html> Accessed 1 March 2008.

Tufte, E.R. (1983). *The Visual Display of Quantitative Information.* Cheshire: Graphics Press.

Tufte, E.R. (2001). *The Visual Display of Quantitative Information.* 2nd ed. Cheshire: Graphics Press.

tutorialspoint. (2020). 'SDLC – Waterfall Model'. <https://www.tutorialspoint.com/sdlc/sdlc_waterfall_model.htm> Accessed 8 May 2020.

Two-Bit History. (2017). 'The Most Important Database You've Never Heard of'. <https://twobithistory.org/2017/10/07/the-most-important-database.html> Accessed 18 Sept 2019.

University of Arkansas at Little Rock. (n.d.). 'Information Quality Program.' <https://ualr.edu/informationquality/> Accessed 20 May 2020.

US Bureau of Labor Statistics. (2020). 'Table 16. Annual total separations rates by industry and region, not seasonally adjusted'. <https://www.bls.gov/news.release/jolts.t16.htm> Accessed 13 April 2020.

US Department of Agriculture. (2020). 'My Plate'. <https://www.myplate.gov/> Accessed 29 Dec 2020.

US Department of Commerce, National Institute of Standards and Technology. (n.d.). 'Information Security'. <https://csrc.nist.gov/glossary/term/information_security> Accessed 4 Jan 2020.

US Food & Drug Administration. (2018). 'Facts About the Current Good Manufacturing Practices (CGMPs)'. <https://www.fda.gov/drugs/pharmaceutical-quality-resources/facts-about-current-good-manufacturing-practices-cgmps>. Accessed 16 May 2020.

Wacker, M. B., and Silverman, L. L. (2003). *Stories Trainers Tell: 55 Ready-to-Use Stories to Make Training Stick.* Jossey-Bass/Pfeiffer.

Walmsley, P. (2002). *Definitive XML Schema.* Upper Saddle River: Prentice Hall PTR.

Wang, R.Y., Pierce, E.M., Madnick, S.E., and Fisher, C.W. (eds.) (2005). *Information Quality.* Armonk: M.E. Sharpe. p. 10.

West, M. (2011). *Developing High Quality Data Models.* Burlington: Morgan Kaufmann.

Wiefling, K. (2007). *Scrappy Project Management™: The 12 Predictable and Avoidable Pitfalls Every Project Faces.* Silicon Valley: Scrappy About™.

Witt, G. (2012). *Writing Effective Business Rules: A Practical Method.* Waltham: Morgan Kaufmann.

Wikipedia. (2020). '5G'. <https://en.wikipedia.org/wiki/5G> Accessed 22 June 2020.

Wikipedia. (2020). 'SMART criteria'. <https://en.wikipedia.org/wiki/SMART_criteria#cite_note-Doran-1981-1> Accessed 4 May 2020.

Wong, D. M. (2010). *The Wall Street Journal Guide to Information Graphics: The Dos & Don'ts of Presenting Data, Facts, and Figures.* New York: W. W. Norton & Company.

Yakencheck, J. (2020). 'Combating disinformation campaigns ahead of 2020 election' <https://searchsecurity.techtarget.com/post/Combating-disinformation-campaigns-ahead-of-2020-election> Accessed 10 Dec 2020.

Zachman, J. (2016). 'The Framework for Enterprise Architecture: Background, Description and Utility'. Zachman International Enterprise Architecture. Zachman.com. <https://www.zachman.com/resources/ea-articles-reference/327-the-framework-for-enterprise-architecture-background-description-and-utility-by-john-a-zachman> Accessed 1 Dec 2019.

Index

Note: Page numbers followed by *f* indicate figures, *t* indicate tables, and *b* indicate boxes.

About the Author

Danette McGilvray has devoted more than 25 years to helping people around the world enhance the value of the information assets on which their organizations depend. Focusing on bottom-line results, she helps them manage the quality of their most important data, so the resulting information can be trusted and used with confidence—a necessity in today's data-dependent world.

Danette and her company, Granite Falls Consulting, excel in bridging the gap between an organization's strategies, goals, issues, and opportunities and the practical steps necessary to ensure the "right-level" quality of the data and information needed to provide products and services to their customers. Communication, change management, and human factors are also emphasized because they affect the trust in and use of data and information.

Granite Falls' "teach-a-person-how-to-fish" approach helps organizations meet their business objectives while enhancing skills and knowledge that can be used to benefit the organization for years to come. Client needs are met through a combination of consulting, training, one-on-one mentoring, and executive workshops, tailored to fit any situation where data is a component.

Danette first shared her extensive experience in her 2008 book, *Executing Data Quality Projects: Ten Steps to Quality Data and Trusted Information*™ (Morgan Kaufmann), which has become a classic in the data quality field. Her Ten Steps™ methodology is a structured yet flexible approach to creating, assessing, improving, and sustaining data quality. It can be applied to any type of organization (for profit, government, education, healthcare, nonprofit, etc.), and regardless of country, culture, or language. Her book is used as a textbook in university graduate programs. The Chinese translation was the first data quality book available in that language.

Danette's 2021 second edition (Elsevier/Academic Press) updates how-to details, examples, and templates, while keeping the basic Ten Steps, which have held the test of time. With her holistic view of data and information quality, she truly believes that data quality can save the world. She hopes that this edition can help a new generation of data professionals, in addition to inspiring those who already care about or have been responsible for data and information over the years.

Danette can be reached at danette@gfalls.com. Connect with her on LinkedIn and follow her on Twitter at Danette_McG. To see how Granite Falls can help on your journey to quality data and trusted information, and for free downloads of key ideas and templates from the book, see www.gfalls.com.

Printed in the United States
by Baker & Taylor Publisher Services